S0-AZW-984

SMALL BUSINESS FUNDAMENTALS

THOMAS W. ZIMMERER
Clemson University

NORMAN M. SCARBOROUGH
Presbyterian College

MERRILL PUBLISHING COMPANY
A Bell & Howell Information Company
Columbus • Toronto • London • Melbourne

Cover Photos: Merrill, William Tyler (tops) and
Larry Hamill

Published by Merrill Publishing Company
A Bell & Howell Information Company
Columbus, Ohio 43216

This book was set in Garamond

Administrative Editor: Paul Lee
Production Editor: Pamela Hedrick-Bennett
Art Coordinator: Patrick Welch
Cover Designer: Cathy Watterson
Text Designer: Connie Young

Copyright © 1988, by Merrill Publishing Company.
All rights reserved. No part of this book may be
reproduced in any form, electronic or mechanical,
including photocopy, recording, or any information
storage and retrieval system, without permission in
writing from the publisher. "Merrill Publishing
Company" and "Merrill" are registered trademarks of
Merrill Publishing Company.

Library of Congress Catalog Card Number: 87-73203
International Standard Book Number: 0–675–20786-X
Printed in the United States of America
1 2 3 4 5 6 7 8 9—92 91 90 89 88

This book is humbly dedicated to our wives, whose love, support, and encouragement have shaped our lives.

For Patricia Ricks Zimmerer

T.W.Z.

For Cindy Easler Scarborough

N.M.S.

PREFACE

The true cost of small business failures will never be totally known. When a business fails, more than a financial investment is lost. The authors have no illusion that this text will stop every new business from failing or make every existing small business succeed. We hope that the readers of this text will avoid the pitfalls as they develop and manage their businesses. The authors hold in high regard those who accept the challenge of beginning a business. Entrepreneurs are the lifeblood of our economic system.

Capitalism is built upon risk-taking entrepreneurs. Its products and services support our daily existence. However, the spirit and motivation that drives entrepreneurs will not guarantee success in today's competitive world. Entrepreneurs must be equipped with the knowledge and skill to operate a small business successfully. This book contains the tools that will, with skillful application, convert the novice entrepreneur into an effective small business executive.

Small Business Fundamentals focuses on the practical aspects of successfully launching and managing a small enterprise. We have provided comprehensive coverage of relevant topics in a direct, easy-to-understand fashion. This text can be used by students in the classroom or it can serve as a general guide to an actual business start-up.

This text has several unique features:

- The chapters are laid out in the order that potential new business owners would make decisions.
- It contains complete coverage of material on financial matters. The accounting and financial section provides readers with the skills and tools required to analyze a business and improve its management.
- Special emphasis has been placed on the strategic management process for the small business. The development and use of a business plan is stressed throughout the text.
- The text includes comprehensive coverage of location, layout and physical facilities, computers in small business, purchasing and inventory control, as well as a three chapter sequence on marketing.
- Comprehensive coverage of topics affecting the creation and operation of a small business.
- Small Business Reports bring the reader the most current happenings in the world of small business.

v

These reports are drawn from *Inc., Venture, The Wall Street Journal, Changing Times, Nation's Business,* and a wide variety of business journals.

■ Student Involvement Projects place the student in the world of small business. The authors believe that students need experience beyond the classroom, and these projects encourage the students to analyze actual business situations and interaction with small business owners.

Small Business Fundamentals is supplemented by an extensive *instructor's manual,* containing lesson plans, solutions to questions and cases, film lists, suggested readings, overhead transparency masters, as well as the largest *test bank* of any text in the field. The questions in the test bank have been tested in the classroom. Another ancillary, the *student study guide,* presents chapter outlines, identifies key terms and concepts, and offers sample test questions. The complete package will facilitate the teaching and the learning of entrepreneurial skills so vital to this nation's economy.

Small Business Fundamentals also offers a manual called *Building a Business Plan with Lotus 1-2-3* and a *Lotus 1-2-3 template diskette* to instruct students in using the most popular business software package to develop a business plan. Computer-based supplements are fast becoming an integral part of teaching students to manage a small business successfully.

It is the authors' hope that students who use this text will accept the challenge of economic independence through entrepreneurship. Our goal is to provide them with the tools to make their dreams come true.

ACKNOWLEDGMENTS

We would like to give special recognition to Betty Woodall, whose dedication to this project made our jobs much easier. She worked endless hours at her word processor and never failed to amaze us with her professional skills. She transformed our rough prose into the textbook you are about to enjoy.

We also would like to thank the academic administrators of our schools, who supported our work. Dr. Ken Orr, President of Presbyterian College; Dr. William Moncrief, Vice-President for Academic Affairs at Presbyterian College; Dr. Fred Chapman, Chairman of the Department of Economics and Business Administration at Presbyterian College; and Dr. Ryan C. Amacher, Dean of the College of Commerce and Industry at Clemson University. Special thanks also must go to Mrs. Ann Martin, whose organizational and administrative skills helped bring this text to life.

Many of our fellow faculty members volunteered their ideas, suggestions, and time. Without their help, this book would not have the depth we have been able to give it. We are grateful to Carl Arnold, Foard Tarbert, Sam Howell, Dick Pilsbury, Meredith Holder, Tony Czajkowski, and George Van Clouse.

We further gratefully acknowledge those who reviewed our manuscript and made many valued constructive suggestions for improvement: Nancy Bowman, Baylor University; Michael Broida, Miami (Ohio) University; John deYoung, Cumberland Community College; Art Elkins, University of Massachusetts; W. Bruce Erikson, University of Minnesota; Nick Sapantakes, Austin (Texas) Community College; and Gregory Worosz, Schoolcraft College, Michigan.

It is difficult to recall with total accuracy the many people who labored to assist us with the thousands of small details that go into the writing and production of our manuscript, but these people deserve our applause: Beth Hudson, Andrea Pruitt, Ruthie Beale, Connie Cline, Julie Walker, Elizabeth Van Buren, Jodi Grieve, Teresa Powell, Briggs Patterson, Martie Martin, Addie Wilkes, Myra Templeton. Our thanks also go to the Merrill staff who made the production of this book possible: Paul Lee, Administrative Editor; Pam Hedrick-Bennett, Production Editor, and Pat Welch, Art Coordinator.

CONTENTS

SECTION FIVE
Controlling the Small Business: Techniques for Enhancing Profitability   275

SECTION SIX
Managing People: The Most Valuable Resource   339

SECTION SEVEN
Marketing for the Small Business: Building a Competitive Edge   367

APPENDICES

SECTION ONE

ENTREPRENEURSHIP AND SMALL BUSINESS: THE CHALLENGE OF INDEPENDENCE

Entrepreneurs: The Driving Force Behind Small Business

I don't believe in taking foolish chances, but nothing can be accomplished without taking any chance at all.

Charles Augustus Lindbergh

For me, small business is the heart and soul of our free enterprise system.
Ronald Reagan

About the only thing that can be achieved without much effort is failure.
Wes Izzard

Upon completion of this chapter, you will be able to:

- Define the role of the entrepreneur in American business.

- Explain how learning management skills can help prevent small business failures.

- Explain the high achievement needs of the typical entrepreneur.

- Evaluate your potential as an entrepreneur.

- Outline the benefits and opportunities of owning a small business.

- Outline the potential drawbacks of owning a small business.

- Understand the importance of small business ownership to women and minorities.

- Describe why small businesses fail.

- Explain the problems faced by small business managers and how these cause business failure.

- Analyze the major pitfalls involved in managing a small business and introduce basic methods to help the small business owner avoid them.

This is the age of the entrepreneur. Never before have so many people pursued The Great American Dream of owning and operating an independent business. New business incorporations registered a record 702,101 in 1986, and preliminary figures show 1987 start-ups running 4 percent ahead of 1986 numbers (see figure 1–1). This resurgence of the entrepreneurial spirit is the most significant economic development of this decade. These new entrepreneurs are rekindling an intensely competitive business environment that had all but disappeared for nearly three decades. Their businesses are creating innovative products and services, pushing back technological frontiers, creating jobs, and, in the process, waking up a sluggish economy.

Small business plays a key role in moving our nation toward certain basic economic objectives—more employment opportunities, new technical innovations, economic growth, and a higher standard of living—as well as supplying goods and services to our people. It gives anyone willing to take the chance the opportunity for economic expression. After traveling across the United States interviewing hun-

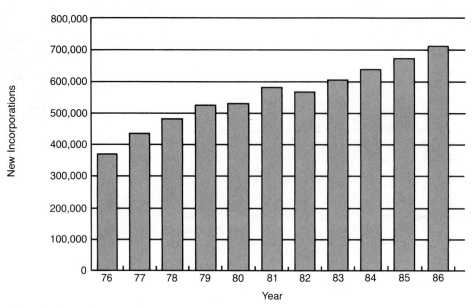

FIGURE 1–1   New business incorporations.

Source: Data from "Current Economic Indicators," #86M12, Dun & Bradstreet Corporation, New York, N.Y., 1986.

dreds of entrepreneurs, Curtis Hartman concludes:

> America is filled with entrepreneurs ..., men and women helping to build the future. They are the new pioneers, immigrants and children of immigrants, rebels and refugees, dreamers of every age and color .... They are the builders. But they create more than just new companies; more, even, than new products and new jobs. They also create new human connections, new ways of joining people together to meet our common needs. That is how America has always been built, by pioneers, coming together to push back the frontiers.[1]

Who are these entrepreneurs and what drives them to work so hard with no guarantee of success? What is it that makes them risk so much and work so hard in an attempt to achieve an ideal? This chapter

Source: From *The Wall Street Journal,* June 16, 1982, p. 27. Reprinted with permission of *The Wall Street Journal* © Dow Jones & Company, Inc., 1982. All rights reserved.

[1] Curtis Hartman, "The Spirit of Independence—Part Five: Frontiers," *Inc.,* July 1985, p. 85.

Entrepreneurship 101

In 1982, Dan Bienenfeld borrowed $2,000 from his father to produce a calendar featuring photographs of handsome male "hunks." The venture grossed $10,000. A year later, Bienenfeld and two partners published a more polished calendar called *California Dreaming* and sold it nationwide. Calendar sales reached $200,000 in 1984. This year, College Look Inc., as the company now is known, expects sales of $3 million from its product line of calendars and gift and novelty items.

But, Bienenfeld's business history is more than just another success story; he accomplished all of this while still in college. The college campus has become a training ground for small business management for a few students who see opportunities to "earn as they learn." A couple of other examples will show how a little ingenuity and hard work can pay off for college students.

Richard Gilbertson created Fast Breaks to deliver "midnight snacks" from the local McDonald's and Taco Bell to students in Indiana University's dormitories. A detailed market study of 400 students showed that they would be willing to pay for fast food delivery during the prime snack hours of between 10 P.M. and 2 A.M. Gilbertson and his partners won't release specific figures, but they do say they are earning a profit. They expect to recoup their original $10,000 investment within six months. But, says Mr. Gilbertson, "setting up a business like this isn't as easy as it looks."

Steve Schaffer earns a nice profit selling flowers to his classmates for "that special date." Because he keeps his overhead costs low, Schaffer can beat the prices of the local flower shops. Business is brisk before big dances and on football weekends.

Entrepreneurship on the campus has become so popular that there is an Association of Collegiate Entrepreneurs with more than 170 member colleges. Verne Hornish, national director of the Association, claims, "It's become fashionable on campus to be 19 and say 'I have my own company.'"

Sources: Adapted from Karen Blumenthal, "On Campuses, Making Dean's List Comes Second to Making a Profit," *The Wall Street Journal,* April 4, 1985; Robert Johnson, "Students Make Mark Ferrying Fast Foods," *The Wall Street Journal,* December 7, 1984, with permission of *The Wall Street Journal,* © Dow Jones & Company, Inc. All rights reserved.

---

will explore the entrepreneurs—a driving force behind the American economy.

I. CHARACTERISTICS OF ENTREPRENEURS

In his classic book, *The Achieving Society,* David McClelland reports his research on the personality characteristics of entrepreneurs. Dr. McClelland describes the entrepreneur as having a dominant psychological drive to achieve. The following is a brief summary of the entrepreneurial personality.[2]

1. *Desire for responsibility.* Entrepreneurs feel a personal responsibility for the outcome of ventures in which they are associated. They prefer to be in control of their resources, and use those resources to achieve self-determined goals.

2. *Preference for moderate risk.* Entrepreneurs are not wild risk-takers, but are instead calculating risk-takers. Unlike professional gamblers, they rarely "gamble." The entrepreneur looks at the project or venture in terms of some personal level of risk. The goal may be high in terms of other's perceptions, but he has usually thought through the situation and believes that the goal is reasonable and attainable.

3. *Confidence in personal success.* Entrepreneurs believe in themselves and support this belief by

[2]David McClelland, *The Achieving Society* (Princeton, N.J.: D. Van Nostrand Co., Inc., 1961), p. 16.

getting the facts before making decisions. Entrepreneurs believe they have the capabilities necessary for success. This explains why some of the most successful entrepreneurs failed several times before finally succeeding.

4. *Desire for immediate feedback.*   Entrepreneurs like to know how they are doing and are constantly looking for reinforcement. Tricia Fox, founder of Fox Day Schools, Inc., claims, "I like being independent and successful. Nothing gives you feedback like your own business."[3]

5. *High level of energy.*   Entrepreneurs are more energetic than the average person.

6. *Future orientation.*   Entrepreneurs have a well-defined sense of searching for opportunities. They look ahead and are less concerned with what was done yesterday than what might be done tomorrow.

7. *Skilled in organization.*   Entrepreneurs know how to put the right people together to accomplish the task. The effective combination of people and jobs will inevitably lead to the accomplishment of objectives.

8. *Money, although a great way to keep score, is not as important as achievement.*   One of the most common misconceptions about entrepreneurs is that they are driven wholly by the desire to make money. Money is very important because it is a symbol of achievement, which is the *real* driving force behind the typical entrepreneur. Possessing money, and the things money can buy, is evidence of their success and justification for the long hours worked to attain that success.

II. THE BENEFITS AND OPPORTUNITIES OF SMALL BUSINESS OWNERSHIP

A survey by Heller Small Business Institute of chief executives of small companies found that 73 percent thought they worked harder, 72 percent thought they earned more money, and 91 percent thought they were happier than if they worked for a big firm.[4] When asked who should be an entrepreneur, one small business founder echoed these statements, "(an entrepreneur is) anyone who wants to experience the deep, dark canyons of uncertainty and ambiguity and wants to walk the breathtaking highlands of success. But I caution: Do not plan to walk the latter until you have experienced the former."[5]

Before launching any business venture, every potential entrepreneur should consider the benefits and opportunities of small business ownership.

The opportunity to gain control over your own destiny. While this may not be the reason most often given for wanting to own a business, it is likely to be the reason most consistent with the personality profile of entrepreneurs. Business ownership provides independence and the opportunity to achieve what is important to the individual. Entrepreneurs want to "call the shots" in their own lives, and they use the business as an extension of this spirit. The business is a passport to personal freedom.

The rewards of ownership come in the freedom to make decisions and take risks; to challenge your competitor; and to reap the intrinsic rewards of knowing you were the driving force behind the business. One frustrated employee-turned-entrepreneur says, "Your mistakes are your own. Your successes are yours. There is a sense of controlling your own destiny."[6]

The opportunity to reach your full potential. Too often, people find their work unchallenging. The small business, therefore, becomes an instrument for self-expression and self-actualization. In the business, all of your skills and abilities will likely be challenged. The only barriers to success are those which your creativity and determination cannot overcome, not things artificially created by the organization

---

[3] Sabin Russell, "Being Your Own Boss in America," *Venture,* May 1984, p. 40.

[4] "News & Trends at a Glance," *Inc.,* January 1981, p.27.
[5] Jeffry A. Timmons, "An Obsession with Opportunity," *Nation's Business,* March 1985, p. 68.
[6] Russell, op. cit. p. 52.

which employs you. Of course, success is not guaranteed. In fact, you are likely to find the going tough even with adequate preparation. But you will get your chance. Entrepreneurs continually reach out to achieve what they believe is possible. Buoyed by self-confidence and a hope to be all they can be, they start businesses despite economic conditions.

The opportunity to reap unlimited profits. Although money is not the primary force driving most entrepreneurs, their ability to keep the money their businesses earn certainly is a critical factor in their decisions to launch companies. There are dozens of "rags-to-riches" stories of businesses which flourished due to their founders' creativity and ingenuity.

Without question, men and women who apply their knowledge to produce valuable goods and services and to solve problems in our society often are rewarded bountifully. But, owning your own business is *not* an automatic goldmine. Pitfalls and risks abound along the path to business success. Facts regarding the profit potential of a business are important in curbing an entrepreneur's unwarranted expectations.

Profit and income can have different meanings to each potential entrepreneur. Some expect immediate returns, and they will seek to start businesses which derive income from seizing opportunities which might be temporary. Such entrepreneurs may

---

Her Own "Little Company"

SMALL
BUSINESS
REPORT
1–2

In 1973, Sandra Kurtzig launched her computer software company with $2,000 and a healthy dollop of hope. She ran the business from a room in her home and kept all the firm's cash in a shoebox.

Today, Kurtzig is still president of that same computer software company, ASK Computer Systems. However, sales of the "little company" have grown to $22 million a year, and the firm has 200 employees and a reputation as a leader in developing computer software. Recalling her first days in business, Mrs. Kurtzig says, "I had no management experience. My long-range plans were figuring out where to go for lunch."

ASK's first product allowed newspapers to keep track of their carriers. The package sold well and soon Kurtzig hired several bright computer specialists to develop programs for specific business applications. The team developed ten software packages, testing and debugging them at night at nearby Hewlett-Packard. A highly successful inventory control program soon followed.

Over the years, Mrs. Kurtzig has learned her management lessons well. A Hewlett-Packard executive explains, "She didn't try to become all things to all people." Indeed, part of ASK's success has come about because Kurtzig decided to develop specialized computer software for manufacturers and to focus on sales and customer service. And, as in most Silicon Valley businesses, Mrs. Kurtzig keeps employee relations informal and fun. She chuckles and explains, "You have to be able to drink at the company's Friday beer blast."

Source: Adapted from Earl C. Gottschalk, Jr., "Distaff Owners: More Women Start Up Their Own Businesses, with Major Successes," *The Wall Street Journal,* May 17, 1983, with permission of *The Wall Street Journal,* © Dow Jones and Company, Inc., 1983. All Rights Reserved.

Racing the Clock . . . for Profit

Does it absolutely, positively have to be there overnight? Fred Smith was betting that it did when he started Federal Express in 1973. The story of Smith's company, which created the $4 billion industry that delivers time-sensitive packages overnight, has become a legend in American business. Smith first formulated his idea in a paper he wrote for a college economics course at Yale in 1966. The idea of routing packages from all across the country into a central hub and then transporting them to the appropriate destinations earned Smith a "C." After all, how efficient could it be to send a package from Albany, New York, to Freeport, Maine, by way of Memphis, Tennessee?

After serving two distinguished tours of duty in Vietnam, Smith decided it was time to go into business. Although he was fortunate enough to have $8.5 million of family money to invest, Smith knew that the capital intensive business he proposed required a much larger cash infusion to survive. To attract investors, Smith paid for elaborate market studies. "We purchased the credibility we needed to entice capital sources," he says.

Still, Federal Express hung on the verge of bankruptcy for several years. Operating a fleet of airplanes, delivery trucks, satellite offices, and a complex distribution system with thousands of employees consumed massive amounts of capital. In the early days, pilots used their own credit cards to purchase fuel for their planes and helped with the sorting, which was all done by hand. (On its first night, Federal Express sorted 18 packages.) Smith once met part of a payroll with $27,000 he had won playing blackjack.

Through clever marketing, sheer perseverance, and good fortune, Federal Express survived and prospered. The company earned its first profit, $3.6 million, in 1976. Today, Federal Express hustles over 67 million packages a year through its Memphis hub, where 2,000 workers unload, sort, and reload every kind of package imaginable (once, even a human eyeball for a transplant) in a frenzy of activity.

More than 26,000 employees, a fleet of 61 purple, orange, and white jets, 20 miles of high-speed conveyor belts, and outstanding customer service have helped Federal Express maintain its leadership in the industry. When asked if they would do it again, one of Smith's cofounders says, "If I can make something else happen that's grand, I'll work like hell to make it happen."

Sources: Adapted from Eugene Linden, "Frederick W. Smith of Federal Express: He Didn't Get There Overnight," *Inc.,* April 1984, p. 89; Cindy Skrzycki, "An Industry That Keeps Promises—Overnight," *U.S. News and World Report,* October 22, 1984, pp. 53–54, with permission of the publishers.

start dozens of businesses in their lifetimes. Others may see profits as a long-term reward for building a stable and reliable business deeply rooted in the community. They may plan to bring the children, and later the grandchildren, into the business. These entrepreneurs measure income by a different standard.

The opportunity to make a contribution to society and receive recognition for your efforts. Entrepreneurs are generally proud of the role they play in society. We are no longer a people who can depend solely on our own skills to provide for our needs. Entrepreneurs provide the rest of us with the goods and services we need, but they are often taken for granted.

While entrepreneurs work to satisfy personal needs, they also play necessary roles in the economy. Small business managers enjoy the recognition they receive from customers who they have served faithfully over the years. Business deals based on trust and mutual respect are the hallmark of many established businesses. Being a part of the business system and knowing that his work has a direct bearing on how our economy functions is another reward for a small business manager.

III. THE POTENTIAL DRAWBACKS OF ENTREPRENEURSHIP

While entrepreneurship has many benefits and provides many opportunities, anyone planning to enter the small business world should be aware of its potential drawbacks.

Can You Teach Entrepreneurship?

Courses in entrepreneurship are popping up at colleges and universities all across the country, and enrollments are booming. Recent surveys estimate that 240 institutions offer at least one course in entrepreneurial studies, a dramatic increase from 36 in 1971. Most courses involve visiting professors, venture capitalists, and entrepreneurs who have launched businesses. Sometimes, students are required to prepare business plans and problems. Some advanced courses teach the finer points of obtaining venture capital and marketing small business' goods and services.

Some graduates practice what their professors preach. After taking entrepreneurial classes at Baylor University, Dee Crowe developed a business plan for turning around his father's catfish farm. He developed a model that allowed him to forecast his annual harvest, a major cause of the business' unpredictability. Crowe claims that the income from his business "has paid for half the time I spent there—in my first year of business."

Alfred Osborne, director of UCLA's MBA program, explains the popularity of entrepreneurial studies, "We're seeing more and more students who are concerned with starting their own companies. But it's not the family business or a small business they want to run. It's their own growing corporation . . . and they expect to learn how to do that now in business school." Jeffry Timmons, professor at Babson College, says, "Students have recognized that being an entrepreneur is the only real way to achieve financial independence and true flexibility in their lives."

But, can anyone transform a student into an entrepreneur? Most professors don't think so. Says one, "Either they have it or they don't. But we can teach them to analyze . . . (the) risks, to be analytical about their choices, and to learn from mistakes made in the past."

Sources: Adapted from Kevin Farrell, "Why B-Schools Embrace Entrepreneurs," *Venture,* February 1984, pp. 60–63; Stephen Robinett, "What Schools Can Teach Entrepreneurs," *Venture,* February 1985, pp. 50–58, with permission of the publishers.

SMALL BUSINESS REPORT 1–4

Uncertainty of income. Opening and running a business provides no guarantees that an entrepreneur will earn enough money to survive. Some small businesses barely earn enough to provide the owner-manager with an adequate income. In the early days of a business, the owner often has trouble meeting financial obligations and may have to live on savings. The regularity of income that comes with working for someone else is absent. The owner is always the last one to be paid.

Risk of losing your entire invested capital. Small business survival rate is low. Eighty percent of all new businesses fail in the first year and 92 percent have failed by the end of five years. Some of these entrepreneurs will have lost their personal savings. To many of them the loss is more than just financial. They are hurt personally and psychologically since business failure implies personal failure. Often, other investors in the small business lose their money, increasing the entrepreneur's personal burden. Many entrepreneurs rebound quickly from failure to begin again, but some are scarred long into the future.

Before reaching for the golden ring, entrepreneurs should ask themselves if they can cope psychologically with the consequences of failure. The risk-reward trade-off should be calculated and considered before personal savings and health are placed in jeopardy.

Lower quality of life until the business gets established. Who will open the business every morning and close it at night? Entrepreneurs might as well forget the eight-hour day! For the first few years, they may put in 12 to 16 hours per day; in some businesses, six and seven days a week with no paid vacations are the norm. When the business closes, the revenue stops coming in and the customers go elsewhere. However, the toll of long hours on energy and health can be considerable. If you have a family, ask yourself what the effects are likely to be on them. Do they really want you to be away from them so long? If you plan to have them work in the business, will this cause a strain on the relationship? It is not easy to spend 10 hours or more a day in the business and then go home to spend more time with the same people. It does not take long for the benefits of togetherness to wear thin. Marriage and friendship are too often casualties of a small business.

Complete responsibility. It's great to be the boss, but many entrepreneurs find that they must make decisions on issues about which they are not really knowledgeable. When there is no one to ask, the pressure can build quickly. The realization that the decisions they make are the cause of success or failure of the business has a devastating effect on some people. Small business owners realize quickly that they *are* the business.

IV. WOMEN AND MINORITIES AS ENTREPRENEURS

Despite years of legislative efforts, women and minorities still face discrimination in the work force. However, small business has been a leader in offering women and minorities the opportunity for economic expression through employment and entrepreneurship. Women are opening businesses of their own in record numbers (see figure 1–2). In fact, women are launching companies at a rate five times faster than that of men. By 1984, over 3 million women were employed, a 33.4 percent increase from 1977.[7] Today, women create about a third of all new businesses which account for over $40 billion in annual revenues. Carolyn Doppelt Gray of the U.S. Small Business Administration says, "The 1970s was the decade of women entering management, and the 1980s is turning out to be the decade of the woman entrepreneur."[8]

---

[7] Gail Gregg, "Women Entrepreneurs: The Second Generation," *Across the Board,* January 1985, p. 10.

[8] Earl C. Gottschalk, Jr., "More Women Start up Their Own Businesses, with Major Successes," *The Wall Street Journal,* May 17, 1984, pp. 1, 22.

Tiny 94 on Your FM Dial

A recent Federal Communications Commission decision reducing the minimum distance between FM broadcasting stations has added more than 500 new stations—primarily in the South and the Midwest—to radio dials. The majority of the stations are small Class A bases that broadcast no more than 15 miles. The FCC's strategy is to fill in the rural gaps between large urban stations.

The decision has created business opportunities for many entrepreneurs, including Peter and Carol Hunn. The couple owns and operates WHRC–FM, one of the nation's smallest radio stations, and serves Port Henry, New York (population 5,000). Their small house is the broadcast station, and a corner of the living room serves as the studio. The Hunns play a broad spectrum of music (soft rock, classical music, and hymns) since their audience is quite diverse—ranging from college students to farmers.

A staff of two means long hours for the disk jockeys. Peter's broadcast day begins at 6 A.M.; his live radio show runs until 1 P.M. Carol takes over the afternoon shift while Peter sells advertising time to local merchants. Sign-off is 10 P.M.

The work is hard, and the hours are long, but, the Hunns are earning a profit from their station. And, most importantly, they are taking charge of their own destinies. Still, there are drawbacks. Peter jokes, "We'll never have any kids this way."

Source: Adapted from Leslie M. Schultz, "Backyard Broadcasting," *Inc.,* April 1984, pp. 51–53, with permission of the publishers.

Observers point to a number of reasons for the growing trend in entrepreneurship among women. Currently, women comprise 44 percent of the U.S. labor force, and not all of them can fit into the executive suite. As women find the door to the executive domain closed, more of them are choosing to strike out on their own. Frustration created by discrimination in the corporate ranks pushes some women to start their own companies. The climbing age and education levels of the work force also contribute to the trend. In addition, more fathers are willing to turn the family business over to their daughters. Further, women also find that owning a business allows them to satisfy personal needs (family involvement or childrearing) more easily than working for a large company.

Women entrepreneurs have significant barriers to overcome. Although 22 percent of all sole proprietorships belong to women, these firms account for only 8 percent of proprietors' income.[9] Women entrepreneurs' income may be limited for a number of reasons. For instance, social pressures, like child-rearing and family unity, often cause women to devote less than full time to their businesses. Recent research also suggests that female entrepreneurs suffer from a "confidence gap" in developing their businesses, primarily because of a lack of successful role models after which to pattern themselves.[10] Many women business owners find that the rest of the business world views them with skepticism. Kristin Wilson, owner of a small residential remodeling firm, jokes about how paint and lumber salesmen used to laugh at her. Her firm now grosses over $500,000 a year and, she says, "They don't do that

---

[9] Sharon Nelton, "A Business of Her Own," *Nation's Business,* November 1984, p. 70.

[10] Gregg, op. cit. p. 12.

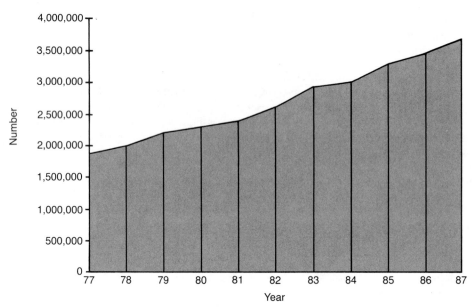

FIGURE 1–2   Number of women entrepreneurs.

Source: The Internal Revenue Service.

Entrepreneurs are risk takers. Not all of them are successful. (Photo courtesy of John Scarborough.)

anymore."[11] Probably the biggest obstacle facing women entrepreneurs, however, is access to capital. Some women complain of discrimination by bank loan officers, and this restricts the number of start-ups as well as the growth of existing businesses. However, as these barriers are broken down, more women are going into business for themselves. Most women entrepreneurs choose the traditional areas of retail trade and services, but a few are launching into manufacturing, finance, wholesale, and real estate businesses.

Like women, minorities also are choosing the path of entrepreneurship more often than ever before. From 1972 to 1982, the number of minority self-employed workers increased by 43 percent. Of the basic minority groups, Asians, Hispanics, and blacks,

[11] Nelton, op. cit. p. 72.

She Sells Ice to the Eskimos

Where can you find nomadic polar bears, temperatures as low as 99 degrees below zero, nights that last three months, and authentic Mexican food all in the same place? At Pepe's North of the Border, of course. Pepe's is the most out-of-place Mexican restaurant in the world. Located in Barrow, Alaska, the official northernmost tip of the U.S., Pepe's is the only place to get "tacos on the tundra."

Owner Fran Tate took a chance that Eskimos would dine on Mexican fare in addition to their normal diets of muktuk (raw whale skin), caribou roasts, and polar bear steaks when she located Pepe's 500 miles from anywhere in the Arctic Circle. Eleven banks thought the venture was too risky and turned down Mrs. Tate's loan request. A twelfth bank loaned—involuntarily—Tate the money to purchase kitchen equipment when she overdrew her checking account by $11,000. "I just thought the spicy food in this climate might just go over big," she says.

That was in 1978. Mrs. Tate jokes, "Luckily we got busy real fast and I was able to cover the checks." Since then, Pepe's has expanded, but the restaurant has kept its authentic Mexican atmosphere. A cheery oasis in the frozen isolation of the Arctic tundra, Pepe's decor could match that of any south-of-the-border restaurant. The sound system plays marachi music, and hand-painted murals of bullfights and posters of matadors decorate the walls. The menu is comprehensive, and the service is impeccable.

All of the staff as well as the food is imported from Mexico. To entice workers to come to Barrow, Mrs. Tate pays them well. Cooks, for example, start at $9.15 an hour, not quite double the rate in the lower 48 states. "It took me a while to explain where Barrow was and what it was like," she says. Then, "Word got around that this was a pretty neat place to work."

Most of Pepe's customers are the local Eskimos, who comprise about 80 percent of Barrow's 2,800 residents, although a few tourists dine there on occasion. "But the tourists are usually pretty cheap," says Mrs. Tate. Cheap, maybe. But paying $15 for a burrito plate (a gallon of milk sells for $6 and a gallon of gas goes for $3.50 in Barrow) often sends tourists into shock. Natives, however, don't even flinch at the high prices that reflect the cost of transporting goods into the middle of nowhere.

Mrs. Tate's future plans include opening the Arctic's first ice cream parlor. "Why not?" she beams, "It just might work." Several years ago, she gambled that Eskimos, who were surrounded by thousands of miles of ice, wanted something other than sea ice to put in their drinks. So, she started selling ice—to the Eskimos—at $3 a bag. "Sometimes, I can't keep up with the demand," Mrs. Tate says.

Source: Adapted from Ken Wells, "Hot Stuff in Arctic: Mexican Restaurant Is Far-North Success," *The Wall Street Journal,* February 7, 1984, with permission of *The Wall Street Journal,* © Dow Jones & Company, Inc. 1984. All rights reserved.

respectively, are most likely to become entrepreneurs. Minorities own 2 percent of all U.S. businesses, most of which are concentrated in the traditional areas of services, retail trade, and construction.

Discrimination along the corporate ladder has motivated many minority entrepreneurs to strike out on their own. Advises one black executive-turned-entrepreneur, "If you show results, you'll get promoted at first, but sooner or later you'll hit a bottleneck and know that's as far as any black is going to go

Small businesses exist in every type of industry. (Photos, from right to left, courtesy of M.S. Bailey and Sons, John Scarborough, and Mark King.)

in the company. Then you've got to decide whether to keep banging on the door to go higher, or to go it alone."[12]

Three significant factors affect the creation and the survival of minority-owned businesses: education level; relevant business experience and training; and access to adequate capital and credit.

Educational attainment is important because it often determines one's ability to earn and save a pool

of funds to feed a small company's start-up and growth. Studies show that one of the entrepreneur's common sources of start-up capital is personal savings and the savings of relatives and friends. Traditionally, minority members' educational levels and incomes have been lower than those of whites. This creates a significant barrier to entrepreneurship for many minorities, who often find it difficult to raise capital and attract customers because of racial discrimination.

However, the future does look bright for minority entrepreneurs. Gradual improvements in edu-

<hr />

[12.] Carol Hymowitz, "Many Blacks Jump off the Corporate Ladder to be Entrepreneurs," *The Wall Street Journal,* August 2, 1984, p. 1.

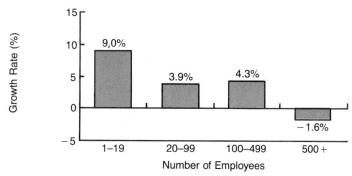

FIGURE 1–3 Job growth by company size.

Source: Data from U.S. Small Business Administration. Office of Advocacy, Small Business Data Base.

cational attainment mean more experience and greater access to capital. The average age of minority entrepreneurs is dropping. These younger, better educated risk-takers are opening businesses in previously untested areas like finance, real estate, and high tech.

V. WHAT IS A "SMALL" BUSINESS?

Of the 17.3 million businesses in the United States today, approximately 16.95 million, or 98 percent, can be considered small. Their contributions to the economy are as numerous as the businesses themselves. For example, small companies employ one-half of the nation's private sector work force, even though they possess less than one-fourth of total business assets. And, because they are primarily labor intensive, small businesses actually create more jobs than do big businesses (see figure 1–3). Between 1980 and 1982, small companies with fewer than 20 employees created all of the 984,000 jobs added to the U.S. economy. Small businesses also produce 38 percent of the country's Gross National Product (GNP) and account for 42 percent of business sales. Overall, small firms provide directly or indirectly the livelihoods of over 100 million Americans. Research conducted for the National Science

Foundation concluded that small firms create four times more innovations per research and development (R&D) dollar than medium-sized firms and 24 times as many as large companies.[13] Many important inventions trace their roots to an entrepreneur. For example, the zipper, FM radio, air conditioning, the escalator, the light bulb, and the automatic transmission all originated in small businesses!

In the business world, defining a *small* business is not merely academic because unless a firm meets certain requirements it is not eligible for financial, educational, and advisory services from the Small Business Administration (SBA). On a broader basis, administrators and legislators must understand what small business is so that the proper economic policies can be enacted to encourage its growth. Presently, there is no universal definition of a small business, and many qualitative, as well as quantitative, definitions have been applied over the years. However, the SBA's standards are most popular.

The Small Business Administration Act of 1953 defines a small business as "one which is independently owned and operated and not dominant in its field of operation." The act also empowers the SBA to identify standards of size for number of employ-

---

[13]."How Startups Create New Jobs," *Venture,* June 1980, pp. 58–60.

ees and sales volume. In 1984, the SBA updated its sales volume standards to reflect the impact of inflation; therefore, some 46,000 firms that did not meet the definition of the small business under the old criteria now qualify. The size requirements vary by Standard Industrial Classification (SIC) code, as illustrated in the following list. The SBA also recognizes that certain special circumstances may justify variations from these guidelines.

■ *Wholesale Trade.* Annual receipts not exceeding $9.5 to $22 million, depending on the specific industry.
■ *General Construction.* Annual receipts not exceeding $17 million.

■ *Special Trade Construction.* Annual receipts not exceeding $7 million.
■ *Services.* Annual receipts not exceeding $2.5 million to $14.5 million, depending on the specific industry.
■ *Retail Trade.* Annual receipts not exceeding $3.5 million to $13.5 million, depending on the specific industry.
■ *Agricultural Production.* Annual receipts not exceeding $100,000 to $3.5 million, depending on the specific industry.
■ *Mining.* Maximum number of employees is 500.
■ *Manufacturing.* Maximum number of employees is either 500, 750, 1000, or 1500, depending on the specific industry.

SMALL BUSINESS REPORT 1–7

How Small is "Small"?

The SBA's size standards are *extremely* important to many business owners, especially those who compete for federal contracts. Under its "set aside" program, the federal government reserves a portion of its purchases of goods and services for small businesses. The philosophy is to allow small firms in various industries to bid on federal contracts without having to compete against industry giants. Only those companies meeting the SBA's criteria of "small" are eligible for the set-aside program.

Gibralter Industries, Inc. understands the importance of maintaining its status as a small business. The company makes clothing for the Defense Department under "set-aside" contracts, which account for nearly 100 percent of its revenue. Every time Gibralter wins a government contract under the program, any losing bidder can— and usually does—challenge its "small business" status. Recently, Gibralter lost a protest because of its affiliation with a subcontractor, Edcar. The SBA's Size Appeals Board ruled that Gibralter had significant control over Edcar and that the two firms' rolls exceeded the 500 employee limit. But, Gibralter appealed to the New York regional SBA office and earned recertification as a small business.

Chairman Wallace Forman expects the stream of protests from Gibralter's competitors to continue. "It's been endless. It is very grueling and very expensive," he says.

Source: Adapted from Sanford L. Jacobs, "How The SBA Defines 'Small' Upsets Some Contract Bidders," *The Wall Street Journal,* March 25, 1985, p. 31; Sanford L. Jacobs, "Concern Continues to Survive Challenges to 'Small' Status," *The Wall Street Journal,* August 8, 1983, p. 19. With permission of *The Wall Street Journal* © Dow Jones & Company, Inc. 1985, 1983. All rights reserved.

Source: From *The New Yorker,* 62, no. 49, January 25, 1982, p. 27. Drawing by Levin,
© 1982, *The New Yorker Magazine, Inc.*

VI. THE BUSINESS FAILURE RECORD: CAN YOU BEAT THE ODDS?

Because of their limited resources and a lack of financial stability, small businesses suffer a mortality rate significantly higher than larger established businesses. Figure 1–4 shows the business failure rate per 10,000 listed concerns since 1926. Exploring the circumstances surrounding failure may help you avoid it.

Factors Influencing Business Failure or Success

Five general factors influence the ability of any small business to survive in a given year: business cycles, inflation, interest rates, access to capital, and government regulation.

Business Cycles.   History shows that the American economy is characterized by extended periods of growth interrupted by different degrees of business declines (recessions or depressions). Small businesses are strongly affected by these economic ups and downs. Recessions and business slowdowns always cause quantum leaps in the rate of small business failures! Since small businesses are more susceptible to swings in the economy, they are more likely to fail during recessions.

Inflation.   Inflation causes serious problems for small business owners because it tends to compound all of their other operational problems. For example, inflation boosts the costs of the small retailer's inventory, as well as all operating costs, pushing up working capital requirements. Many small businesses cannot cope with high levels of inflation for extended periods. Most of them are in keenly competitive markets with very little control over the prices they can charge, and they usually cannot quickly and effectively establish cost controls. The result is that small businesses are particularly vulnerable to inflationary price movements.

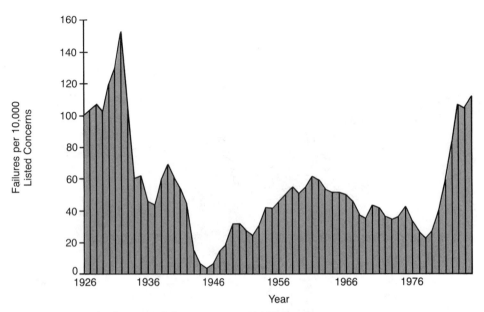

FIGURE 1–4 The business failure rate per 10,000 listed concerns.

Source: Data from *The Dun and Bradstreet Business Failure Record* (New York: Dun and Bradstreet, 1982), p. 2, © Dun and Bradstreet, Inc. 1982. Used with permission.

Interest Rates. By the early 1980s, high (and rising) interest rates had replaced inflation as the most important problem facing small business owners. Small firms are especially vulnerable to the periods of high interest rates because they rely heavily on financial institutions for seasonal borrowing needs.

Approximately 80 percent of small businesses obtain financing from depository institutions; therefore, rising interest rates, which reflect the scarcity of loanable funds, tend to affect small firms more severely than large firms. In particular, high interest rates tend to intensify cash flow problems, which quite often spell disaster for a small business. One reason for this is that many small businesses are undercapitalized but are faced with heavy capital requirements for expansion. For most small operators, the cost of capital is a substantial cost of production, and rising interest rates boost the overall costs of operation to intolerable levels. Climbing interest rates also tend to reduce a small firm's net worth (or equity), as debt comprises a large portion of its capi-

talization. The resulting interest burden often threatens the company's survival when an economic slowdown occurs.

Recent surveys by the National Federation of Independent Businesses (NFIB) report that "interest rates and financing" now rank second to taxes as small business owners' most important problem. Its slip in the ranking has paralleled the decline in interest rates.[14]

Access to Capital. Normally, small businesses are at a disadvantage in the competition for capital required for growth and expansion. Small firms are simply "crowded out" of available working funds as banks choose to meet the larger loans demanded by big firms. A recent study of the financial structure of small businesses found that small firms rely heavily on internal sources of funds to meet their capital re-

[14]*NFB Quarterly Economic Report for Small Business,* National Federation of Independent Businesses, Report #47, April 1985, p. 30.

quirements—only 39 percent of their capital originated outside the business and its owners.[15]

Economies of scale virtually prohibit small
firms from using other sources of capital such as
public stock issues. Intense regulation of public
stock offerings makes this option impractical for
small firms because they cannot spread the cost of
the issue over a large number of shares. Many large
banks and insurance companies do not consider it
sound banking policy to give loans to more vulnerable small businesses. The result is that small firms
must depend on small local banks to meet their capital requirements.

Another factor contributing to this inaccessibility of capital is the smaller pool of funds available to
business in general. Inflation and high marginal tax
rates, which result in "bracket creep" for most tax-
payers, have reduced the incentive to earn and save
larger amounts of money. Add to this the unbridled
deficit spending by the federal government (which
makes the government a heavy borrower and
"crowds out" money for businesses), and it is little
wonder that the pool of "seed money" has dwindled
in recent years.

Government Regulation. Government intervention
into the operations of businesses has expanded rapidly. Although these regulations are well-intentioned
and their benefits without question, their costs have
been high. Government regulation costs businesses
billions of dollars each year. Of course, the consumer ultimately bears the cost of such regulation in
the form of higher prices. Government regulation
has also been accused of distorting the operation of
the free market system by impeding competition.

Many of the regulations require the same level
of compliance for small businesses as for large enterprises. But, the burden of regulation is much heavier
for small businesses because they lack the broad financial bases and the larger volumes of output of
their large counterparts. Research by the Battelle
Human Affairs Research Center indicates that regula-

tory costs are exponentially higher per unit of sales
for firms with fewer than 50 employees than for
larger firms.[16] Several SBA studies have concluded
that this disproportionate regulatory burden on the
small business sector has been a key factor in its declining influence on the U.S. economy.

Specific Reasons for Business Failures

In addition to the general causes of business failure,
the prospective small business owner should be
aware of several more controllable factors causing
business failure. In most small businesses, management inexperience or poor decision-making ability
is the chief problem of the failing enterprise. This
section will explore several factors that potential
small business managers should be aware of if they
are to avoid failure.

Management Incompetence. Dun & Bradstreet statistics show that 50 percent of the business failures
are attributed to the incompetence of the owner/
manager.[17] Sometimes the manager of the small
business does not have the capacity to operate it successfully. The owner lacks the leadership ability and
knowledge necessary to make the business work.
Many managers simply do not have what it takes to
run a small enterprise. For example, a welder, tired
of unsteady employment caused by economic fluctuations, wanted to manufacture custom-made
woodstoves and fireplace insets. During an interview
with a consultant, he quickly discovered how little he
knew about financial statements, accounting systems,
marketing plans, layout and design, and other essen-
tials. When faced with the challenge of operating a
business on his own and armed with little skill and
no experience, the welder wisely decided against
going into business for himself. Anyone considering

---

[15]Transmittal to Congress, *The State of Small Business: A Report to
the President,* 98th Congress, 2nd Session, March 1982, p. 189.

[16]"Complying with Government Requirements, The Costs to
Small and Large Businesses," (Batelle Human Affairs Research
Center, Report completed under SBA grant #SA–1A–0004–01–0,
September 1951).

[17]*The Dun and Bradstreet Business Failure Record,* (New York:
Dun and Bradstreet, 1986), 12–13.

Some businesses do not survive. (Photo courtesy of Jill R. Johnson.)

starting a business should first consider his knowledge of basic business practice.

Lack of Experience.   Small business managers need to have experience in the field they want to enter. For example, if a person wants to open a retail clothing business, he should first work in a retail clothing store. This will give him practical experience as well as help him learn the nature of the business. This type of experience can spell the difference between failure and success.

Often an entrepreneur has been successful in a field and then expands into another "related field" which he knows little or nothing about. For example, the owner of an exclusive art gallery was quite successful until she decided to sell antiques. She discovered that buying and selling antiques required special knowledge and experience that she did not have. Fortunately, she dropped the line of antiques before her entire business collapsed.

In other instances, the small business manager is without the managerial experience required to build and operate a functional organization. The classic example is the "crackerjack salesperson" who

starts his own company. He knows how to sell the goods, but he dislikes the office work required and ignores it. He views his job as that of "head salesperson" and neglects his duties as "head manager." Without competent leadership to make managerial decisions, the business is doomed.

Finally, the manager may have unbalanced experience which creates problems for the business. Ideally, the prospective entrepreneur should have adequate technical ability (a working knowledge of the physical operations of the business; sufficient conceptual ability); the power to visualize, coordinate, and integrate the various operations of the business into a synergistic whole; and the skill to manage the people in the organization and motivate them to higher levels of performance. A survey of business owners conducted by Dun & Bradstreet suggested that the successful owner needs "balanced experience" in purchasing, production and products, attracting customers, and handling finances.[18]

The former production manager turned entre-

[18] *The Pitfalls of Managing a Small Business* (New York: Dun and Bradstreet, 1977), p. 3.

preneur who focuses on the production aspect of the operation to the exclusion of the selling function is guilty of unbalanced management. It shows up in the business as miserable sales revenues and alienated customers.

The poor management resulting from incompetence and lack of experience causes over 90 percent of all business failures in any given year!

Poor Financial Control. Sound management is the key to a small company's success, and effective managers realize that any successful business venture requires proper financial control. The margin for error in managing finances is especially small for most small businesses. Three pitfalls affecting small business' financial health are common: undercapitalization, lax customer credit policies, and overinvesting in fixed assets.

Lack of Capital. Many small business owners make the mistake of beginning their businesses on a "shoestring," which is the fatal error leading to business failure. Entrepreneurs tend to be overly optimistic, and, as a result, often misjudge the requirements of going into business. As one entrepreneur testifies:

> The first pitfall I encountered was that of simply not having enough money. For the first several years, I was forced to borrow money from banks and friends, with a resulting loss of profits through interest rates. I progressed from borrowed funds to special terms with my suppliers, but still sacrificed profits through loss of discount.[19]

Another entrepreneur's experience shows that hard work can overcome undercapitalization on rare occasions:

> When my partner and I started the business five years ago, we actually started in the hole. Both of us borrowed $20,000 for our initial investment and, as a consequence, we were $40,000 in debt from our first day of operations. We soon found out we could not be executives in that position.

> We had no employees and had to run the machines ourselves. During those first few months there were times when we went forty-eight hours without getting home. One of us would run the machine during the day while the other went out and made sales. Then the two of us would work during the night to produce the materials sold. We managed, in time, to work ourselves out of this hole.[20]

Lax Customer Credit. The pressure for a small business to sell on credit is intense. The manager may believe that she can gain a competitive edge by granting credit, or she may feel forced to keep up with competitors who already sell on credit. Whatever the case, the small business owner must control credit sales carefully as failure to do so can devastate a small company's financial health. Poor credit practices are common to many small business bankruptcies.

Before creating a policy of credit sales, the small business manager should ask herself two questions: Do I have enough capital to support credit sales? and Do I know how to collect?

Because of the lag between the sale of an item and the actual collection of the proceeds, a credit policy requires additional capital. Usually, if credit terms are 30 days, an additional capital investment equal to 45 days' sales is required. So, if your store sells $16,000 per month in cash, the implementation of credit sales may require an additional $24,000 in capital to continue operations. Further, credit collecting can be an extremely difficult task requiring a great deal of skill and persistence. Some people are simply not good collectors, and this results in uncollected accounts and therefore lower net profits.[21]

Overinvesting in Fixed Assets. Many small business managers invest in an inordinate amount of capital in land, buildings, equipment, and other fixed assets. This money normally comes from working capital or borrowing, so when expansion is needed most, no funds exist to finance it. For example, the owner of a

---

[19] Ibid.

[20] Ibid.
[21] Ibid.

Credit Policies

Sign in local gas station: "In God we trust. All others pay cash."

Credit policy of a rental partnership: "If you don't pay, you don't stay."

Credit policy of a small town gas station: "We don't give credit, and 'I'll pay you Saturday' is the same thing."

---

small shoe store insisted on owning his building. The capital requirements for the building alone practically used up his borrowing capacity. When he needed a seasonal inventory loan, all the banks considered him "borrowed up."

Also, the manager may spend money to enhance his personal image, rather than using funds to increase productivity, attract customers, or generate profits. One Florida company leased a Learjet, purchased Lincoln Continental town cars, and bought an assortment of personal luxury items for both of the owners, which certainly enhanced their personal esteem but added nothing to the value of the company. Within six months from its inception, the firm showed a $300,000 profit from operations but was in bankruptcy.

Failure to Plan. So many small business owners do not realize the importance of proper planning to their firm's success. Failing to plan the company's future at the outset will have a devastating effect on its existence. This failure to plan that weakens the entire company often manifests itself in two ways: lack of a strategic plan and unplanned expansion.

Lack of a Strategic Plan. A strategic plan plots the overall direction of the company and identifies methods for maximizing its strengths and overcoming its weaknesses. It addresses questions such as:

- What business am I in?
- What are my strengths and weaknesses?
- Who are my customers?
- What are they buying?

- Who are my competitors?
- What are their strengths and weaknesses?

Chapter 2 is devoted entirely to the strategic planning process.

Unplanned Expansion. Growth is a natural, healthy, and desirable part of any business enterprise, but it must be planned carefully. Ideally, expansion should be financed by retained earnings or by capital contributions from the owner, but most businesses wind up borrowing at least a portion of the capital investment.

Expansion usually requires major changes in organizational structure, business practices such as inventory and financial control procedures, personnel assignments, and perhaps other areas. But the most important change occurs in managerial expertise. As the business increases in size and complexity, problems tend to increase in proportion, and the manager must learn to deal with this. Sometimes entrepreneurs encourage rapid growth, and the business outstrips their ability to manage. For example, WAT and Associates, an architectural and engineering firm, grew at a rate of 2,950 percent over a two-year period. At first, the firm generated glowing results in productivity and profit. Then, as managing the firm's projects became more difficult, the organizational structure broke down and productivity and profitability plunged. Says David Wolfberg, one of the founders and remaining partners, "We started spending like drunken sailors. Then, one day there was no money . . . . We began noticing the big office syndrome taking hold. We were losing our ability to respond."[22]

Inappropriate Location. For any business, choosing the right location is partly an act and partly a science. Too often, business locations are selected without proper study, investigation, and planning. Some beginning owners choose a particular location just because they noticed a vacant building. But the location question is much too critical to leave to chance. Es-

---

[22.]Curtis Hartman, "You'd Be Surprised How Easy it is to Succeed," *Inc.,* November 1984, pp. 119–20.

pecially for retailers, the lifeblood of the business—sales—is influenced heavily by choice of location. One small merchandiser located in a rural area was heavily dependent on the customers of a nearby restaurant for her clientele. Because of the inconvenience of this location, sales suffered and the business failed.

Another factor to consider in selecting location is the amount of rent to be paid. Although it is prudent not to pay an excessive amount for rent, business people should weigh the cost against the location's effect on sales volume. If a poor but inexpensive location is chosen, sales may be lost and profits lower than if the more expensive location had been selected. One experienced small business owner said this about location:

> I've been associated with some businesses where we rented stores at very low rates. Volume was poor. Almost always a low-rent location is a poor bargain. The additional rent needed at a more active location is more than paid for by the increased volume.[23]

So, location has two important features: what it costs and what it generates in sales volume.

Lack of Inventory Control. Normally, the largest investment the small business manager must make is in inventory; yet, inventory control is one of the most neglected of all the managerial responsibilities. Insufficient inventory levels result in shortages and stockouts causing customers to become disillusioned and not return. A more common situation is that the manager not only has too much inventory but also too much of the *wrong type* of inventory. Many small firms have an excessive amount of working capital tied up in an accumulation of needless inventory. When one small department store owner began reorganizing her storage room, she found a huge quantity of outdated slacks, shirts, and ties that were virtually unsalable. This kind of waste through spoilage or obsolescence of the merchandise represents huge actual costs and opportunity costs to the

small firm. Not only is it expensive to carry excess merchandise for an extended period of time, but the money invested in it could be put to more productive uses.

Another inventory management problem encountered by small businesses is improper pricing. Most small businesses tend to underprice their goods and services, resulting in lower revenues and profits. Small businesses often provide faster, more personalized service or unique products, but they fail to charge enough for them.

Improper Attitudes. A number of obstacles to success may arise from the attitude of the small business manager. First, he must be prepared to work hard and make sacrifices. If he thinks small business management is easy he should not go into business for himself. Success requires hard work—and a lot of it.

Second, he must avoid the fatal mistake of saying, "I'm the boss and I can take off whenever I please." Without enthusiasm and guidance, the business is likely to fail. A South Carolina sporting goods store owner assumed this attitude after two years in business, and while he was fishing, the business was dying.

Third, he must not overextend himself. While having outside interests and activities is healthy for both the owner and his business, overcommitting himself is dangerous. He cannot expect to simultaneously head the local school board, the United Way campaign, the Ducks Unlimited chapter, and run a business competently.

Finally, he must practice ethical behavior. Small business owners who practice deceit may profit in the short run, but, in the long run, they usually lose.

How to Avoid the Pitfalls

We have seen the most common reasons behind many small business failures. Now we must examine the ways to avoid becoming another failure statistic and gain insight into what makes a successful business. The suggestions for success follow naturally from the causes of business failures.

---

[23]*The Pitfalls of Managing a Small Business*, p. 8.

Murphy Was an Optimist . . . .

When you become an entrepreneur you can go up awfully fast but you can go down just as fast.

Adam Osborne

Adam Osborne has seen the top and the bottom of entrepreneurship. His idea was to market a portable computer, including a package of useful software, and sell it for a relatively low price. In July of 1981, the company shipped the first Osborne, a 26-pound portable with a five-inch screen priced at $1,795. It caught on quickly, and sales rocketed. Says one competitor, "He was a screaming success." Osborne began planning his company's first public offering to raise capital. Osborne was walking atop the rapidly growing computer industry, the envy of many competitors.

Then, the bottom fell out.

Everything that could go wrong did. The company outgrew its organization and control structure. Its rapid growth outstripped financial and inventory controls. A former employee claims, "Everybody was trying to buy anything they wanted. Managers didn't know how much inventory they had. They didn't know how much they were spending."

The timing of Osborne's introduction of its "second generation" portable computer was off. And, according to one former executive, "Everything is timing in this business." In an attempt to introduce the new machine with appropriate fanfare, Osborne allowed news about it to leak out well before expected shipping dates. "We wanted this big roar of publicity," says Osborne. Instead, what he got was a flurry of order cancellations for the Osborne I from dealers eagerly awaiting the arrival of the new machine. Production delays compounded the problem. Osborne claims, "We had an April with no income." Production costs on the new machine were climbing and the result was a severe cash crisis. The company hired professional managers.

Know Your Business in Depth. The need for the right type of experience in the field has already been emphasized. In addition to this, the small business owner must be able to recognize personal limitations as well as those of the business. No small business manager can be an expert in every function of the business and must accept this fact. Every business, no matter how large or small, also has limitations. One small manufacturer of electrical components received a major order after the third month of operation. The owner knew the order could not be completed by the required deadline, and so turned it down. Even though the business was needed, the manufacturer recognized the risk of gaining a poor reputation among potential customers when the order was not completed on time. Once limitations are recognized, they can be reduced.

Plan. Planning is critical to the success of any business. Without a sound business plan, a firm merely drifts along without any real direction.

The small business manager should begin by writing down the answer to the very basic question, "What business am I in?" This may sound elementary, but answering this question with thought and consideration will help the entrepreneur focus on the major purpose of the business, which leads to establishing goals and objectives. In turn, these serve as aids in creating strategies, policies, and procedures. Every small business should have policies concerning credit, customers, product lines, image, prices, advertising, everything. It is important to plan in *writing;* otherwise, the planning function either is ignored altogether or is conducted too informally.

Planning allows the manager to replace "I

One former employee says, "They found that Osborne was not in the financial condition they thought it was."

Osborne's biggest error was his miscalculation of IBM's impact on the computer market. As soon as it was introduced, IBM's PC became the industry standard. But, Osborne's early machines were not compatible with the IBM PC. "Osborne didn't realize how fast he had to move to change course," says one employee.

Sales continued to slip, and in an even more damaging development, Osborne lost its status as the only producer of portable computers. It no longer had a distinctive competence. Osborne scrapped his plan for the public offering, and, finally, filed for protection from credits under Chapter 11 of the federal bankruptcy laws, $45 million in debt.

After reorganizing, Osborne emerged from bankruptcy proceedings with a plan to market a $1,295 portable computer in the U.S. and Europe. The corporate staff is now 35, down from 1,000 in previous years, and the firm will use only 120 dealers instead of the 1,000-plus it used during its hey-day to sell its computers. Says Osborne, whose company now has positive cash flows, "our strategy is to find the niches." Despite his company's problems, failure, and scaled-down recovery, Osborne maintains a positive attitude, "You've got to fail some of the time or you aren't trying hard enough."

Sources: Adapted from Erik Larson, "Snags in Introducing New Computer Sidetrack Osborne's Stock Offering," *The Wall Street Journal,* July 13, 1983, p. 33; Erik Larson and Ken Wells, "Shaken Osborne Computer Seeking Suitor in the Face of Possible Failure," *The Wall Street Journal,* September 12, 1983, p. 35; Erik Larson, "Osborne Takes Little of the Blame for Fall of His Computer Company," *The Wall Street Journal,* October 13, 1983, p. 31; Deborah Wise, "Osborne: Counting On Loyal Customers," *Business Week,* March 4, 1985, pp. 112–13; Robert A. Mamis, "Face to Face: Adam Osborne," *Inc.,* November 1983, pp. 21–22.

think" with "I know." In many cases, businesses are built on faulty assumptions like "I think there are enough customers in town to support a health food shop." The experienced entrepreneur investigates these assumptions and replaces them with facts *before* he makes the decision to go into business.

Understand Your Financial Statements. Every business owner must depend on records and financial statements to know the condition of the business. All too often, these records are used only for tax purposes and are not employed as vital control devices. To truly understand what is going on in the business, the small business manager must have at least a basic understanding of accounting and finance.

When analyzed and interpreted properly, these financial statements are reliable indicators of a small firm's health. They can be quite helpful in raising "red flags" to alert the owner to potential problems. For example, declining sales, slipping profits, rising debt, and deteriorating working capital are all symptoms of potentially lethal problems that require immediate attention. Other symptoms, including increased absenteeism and tardiness among employees, more customer complaints, and an increase in faulty products, may also point to critical problems in the business enterprise.

Manage Financial Resources. The best defense against financial problems is developing a practical information system and then *using* this information to make business decisions. A manager cannot maintain control over a business unless he is able to judge its financial health.

Seek Professional Assistance.   A small business manager cannot have expert ability in every area of business operation. As a result, the owner on occasion must rely on the experience and advice of attorneys, accountants, bankers, and others. The small business owner should establish a solid relationship with a banker early on since this is a primary source of a crucial raw material—money. Attorneys, accountants, and consultants may be hired on a temporary basis or employed through retainers.

Keep in Tune with Yourself.   One of the most vulnerable spots in the management of a small business is the owner's health. The success of the small business usually depends on the constant presence and attention of the owner, so it is critical to monitor his health closely. Stress is a primary problem, especially if it is not kept in check. Employees may also be affected by health problems. In an attempt to counter dwindling morale and productivity, some small businesses have found it cost effective to create company-sponsored fitness programs.

VII. SUMMARY

Capitalistic societies depend on entrepreneurs to provide the drive and risk-taking necessary for the system to supply people with the goods and services they need. Entrepreneurs have some common characteristics, including independence; willingness to take risks; self-confidence; eagerness to see results; energy; and good organization. In a phrase, they are high achievers. Driven by these personal characteristics, entrepreneurs establish and manage small businesses in order to gain control over their lives, become self-fulfilled, reap unlimited profits, and gain recognition from society.

Small business ownership has some potential drawbacks. There are no guarantees that the business will make a profit or even survive. The time and energy required to manage a new business may have dire effects on the owner and family members.

The failure rate for small businesses is higher than that for big businesses, and profits fluctuate with general economic conditions. The age of the business is also relevant; half of the small businesses started fail in the first five years. Some general factors related to small business failures are business cycles, inflation, interest rates, access to capital, and government regulation. There are more controllable factors that cause small business failure, and the chief problem is the firm's management. While over 90 percent of small business failures are caused by the manager's incompetence and lack of experience, other reasons include lack of capital, inappropriate location, lack of inventory control, overinvesting in fixed assets, poor credit practices, unplanned expansion, and improper managerial attitudes.

There are several general tactics the small business owner can employ to avoid these pitfalls. The entrepreneur should know the business in depth, avoid assumptions through proper planning, understand financial statements, seek professional assistance when necessary, and try to stay healthy.

STUDENT INVOLVEMENT PROJECTS

Are You Entrepreneurial Material?

Are you an "entrepreneur-in-the-rough"? The following quiz will help you discover how closely you fit the entrepreneurial profile.

1. You are: **A.** female   **B.** male
If female, answer question 2A; if male, answer question 2B.

2A. Your height is:
   A. 5' or under
   B. 5'1" to 5'5"
   C. 5'6" or over
2B. Your height is:
   A. 5'6" or under
   B. 5'7" to 5'11"
   C. 6' or over
3. Your age is:
   A. under 30
   B. 31–40
   C. 41–50
   D. 51 or over
4. You are:
   A. married
   B. single
   C. divorced
5. You are:
   A. the first born
   B. the middle child
   C. the youngest child
   D. an only child
   E. other
6. Are your parents immigrants?
   A. yes
   B. no
7. Were either of your parents self-employed?
   A. yes, both were.
   B. yes, one parent was.
   C. no, neither was.
8. How would you characterize your early childhood?
   A. destitute
   B. struggled to make ends meet
   C. very comfortable
   D. "silver spoon"
9. What is your highest level of educational attainment?
   A. high school diploma
   B. some college courses
   C. bachelor's degree
   D. master's degree
   E. Ph.D.

10. What portion of your college expenses did you earn?
   A. 50 percent or more
   B. less than 50 percent
   C. none
11. In college, your academic performance was:
   A. above average
   B. average
   C. below average
12. How many companies have you worked for in your career?
   A. 4 or more
   B. 3
   C. 2
   D. only 1
13. You got your first job:
   A. before age 15
   B. between ages 15 and 18
   C. between ages 19 and 21
   D. after age 21
14. Did you operate any businesses before age 21?
   A. yes
   B. no
15. What is your basic reason for opening a business?
   A. I want to make money.
   B. I want to control my own destiny.
   C. I hate the frustration of working for someone else.
16. Which phrase best describes your attitude toward work?
   A. I can keep going as long as I need to; I don't mind working for something I want.
   B. I can work hard for a while, but when I've had enough, I quit.
   C. Hard work really doesn't get you anywhere.
17. How would you rate your organizing skills?
   A. superorganized
   B. above average
   C. average
   D. I do well to find half the things I look for.
18. You are primarily a(n):
   A. optimist

B. pessimist

C. neither

19. You are faced with a challenging problem. As you work, you realize you are stuck. You will most likely:

A. give up

B. ask for help

C. keep plugging; you'll figure it out

20. You are playing a game with a group of friends. You are most interested in:

A. winning

B. playing well

C. making sure that everyone has a good time

D. cheating as much as possible

21. How would you describe your feelings toward failure?

A. Fear of failure paralyzes me.

B. Failure can be a good learning experience.

C. Knowing that I might fail motivates me to work even harder.

D. "Damn the torpedoes! Full speed ahead."

22. Which phrase best describes you?

A. I need constant encouragement to get anything done.

B. If someone gets me started, I can keep going.

C. I am energetic and hardworking—a self-starter

23. Which bet would you most likely accept?

A. a wager on a dog race

B. a wager on a racquetball game in which you play an opponent

C. neither. I never make wagers.

24. At the Kentucky Derby, you would bet on:

A. the 100-to-1 long shot

B. the odds-on favorite

C. the 3-to-1 shot

D. none of the above

Scoring

1. A. 10 **B.** 8   Although most entrepreneurs are men, there is a growing trend among women

entrepreneurs. U.S. Department of Labor statistics show that women are opening businesses at a rate five times faster than men. Over 2.7 million women were self-employed in 1983, a 72 percent increase from 1973. Many of these women entrepreneurs are "baby-boomers," frustrated with the discrimination and the barriers of corporate cultures.

2A and 2B. A. 10 **B.** 5 **C.** 0   Entrepreneurs—both men and women—tend to be shorter than average. In the U.S., the average woman stands 5 feet 3.5 inches tall and the average man 5 feet 9 inches.

3. A. 8 **B.** 10 **C.** 2 **D.** 0   The average age of entrepreneurs has declined steadily over the last two decades. Most launch their businesses when they reach their 30s, after gaining enough capital and experience to step out on their own. But, a recent study by the National Federation of Independent Businesses (NFIB) found that its members found that one-third of all new businesses were started by people 30 years old or younger!

4. A. 10 **B.** 3 **C.** 2   Most studies have found that about 75 percent of all entrepreneurs are married. Some researchers conclude that successful entrepreneurs have very supportive spouses.

5. A. 10 **B.** 0 **C.** 0 **D.** 5 **E.** 0   Studies show that entrepreneurs are most often the oldest children in their families. Only children also rank high in entrepreneurial potential.

6. A. 5 **B.** 2   Survey results support the stereotype of the immigrant entrepreneur who has come to "the land of opportunity" to build a business. Often, immigrants believe they do not "fit in" with American culture, and business ownership can help bridge the cultural gap.

7. A. 10 **B.** 6 **C.** 2   Entrepreneurs learn by example. Children whose parents (or at least one parent) are self-employed are much more likely to create businesses of their own. In the "nature vs. nurture" argument in entrepreneurship, "nurture" wins hands down.

8. A. 2 **B.** 10 **C.** 4 **D.** 0   Entrepreneurs most often come from backgrounds where the family "struggled to make ends meet." Perhaps this is how many entrepreneurs acquired the ability to gain maximum benefits from limited resources. It appears that these meager beginnings are a source of motivation for many.

9. **A.** 2 **B.** 4 **C.** 10 **D.** 8 **E.** 4 Most entrepreneurs complete four years of college. Although the stereotype of the high school dropout who builds a business empire is popular, it simply is not true in most cases. In fact, a growing number of entrepreneurs have earned master's degrees. Entrepreneurs appear to recognize the value of an education in helping them launch their businesses.

10. **A.** 10 **B.** 5 **C.** 0 Most entrepreneurs work while in school, earning at least one-half of their college expenses. Not only do they work while attending school, many head their own business ventures. Campus entrepreneurship has become so popular that students have formed a national Association of Collegiate Entrepreneurs, and its ranks are swelling.

11. **A.** 10 **B.** 6 **C.** 2 Despite their busy work schedules in school, entrepreneurs manage to keep their grades up. One recent survey found that only 38 percent were average or below-average academic performers.

12. **A.** 10 **B.** 8 **C.** 2 **D.** 0 Entrepreneurs tend to be restless, and this is evident in their careers. They are likely to be job-hoppers who do not fit neatly into the corporate environment.

13. **A.** 10 **B.** 8 **C.** 4 **D.** 0 Entrepreneurs start working early in life, most starting by age 15.

14. **A.** 10 **B.** 2 Youngsters with paper routes, lawn care businesses, or delivery services find their appetites for "calling the shots" whetted in later life. An ample dose of entrepreneurship at an early age typically leads to a career highlighted by independence and self-employment.

15. **A.** 2 **B.** 8 **C.** 10 **D.** 0 It is a myth that the primary motivating force behind most entrepreneurs is profit. Of course, earning a profit is necessary for business survival, but it is *not* the driving force. Today, entrepreneurs are most likely to cite dissatisfaction with working for someone else or with lacking control over their lives as key reasons for starting businesses.

16. **A.** 10 **B.** 2 **C.** 0 Entrepreneurs are not afraid of hard work. They are willing to do whatever it takes to get the job done. Further, entrepreneurs do not separate work and play. Their work is a source of fun and excitement.

17. **A.** 10 **B.** 6 **C.** 4 **D.** 0 Entrepreneurs usually are good organizers. Building a business from scratch requires valuable organizing skills. Putting together the pieces of a business puzzle—employees, financing, inventory, etc.—requires someone with the ability to visualize the proper way to organize them.

18. **A.** 10 **B.** 0 **C.** 2 No doubt about it, entrepreneurs are optimistic. Sometimes, however, their excessive optimism gets them into trouble.

19. **A.** 0 **B.** 0 **C.** 10 Entrepreneurs are fiercely independent. They are extremely reluctant to ask for outside help, whether from a consultant or an attorney. When faced with a difficult problem, most entrepreneurs simply roll up their sleeves and get to work. And, they don't quit until the problem has been solved.

20. **A.** 10 **B.** 8 **C.** 0 **D.** 0 Entrepreneurs are intense competitors, and losing is *not* an acceptable outcome. Many embrace the feeling expressed by Vince Lombardi who said, "Winning isn't everything; it's the only thing." Of course, entrepreneurs don't always win. But, when they fail, they tend to view it as a learning experience. Many owners of successful businesses failed at least once before establishing a foothold. The threat of failure seems to motivate many entrepreneurs to do everything in their power to avoid it.

21. **A.** 0 **B.** 8 **C.** 10 **D.** 2 Entrepreneurs are risk-takers, and they recognize that failure is a possibility (although most believe a small one).

22. **A.** 0 **B.** 2 **C.** 10 Entrepreneurs definitely are "self-starters." They are much more energetic and enthusiastic than average, especially where their work is concerned.

23. **A.** 2 **B.** 10 **C.** 0 Entrepreneurs have a

need to be in control of a situation. They are much more likely to take a chance on events they can influence themselves rather than on some externally imposed situation. Bold self-confidence allows an entrepreneur to believe that she can turn the odds in her favor if given the opportunity.

24. A. 0 **B.** 2 **C.** 10 **D.** 0   Despite widely held beliefs to the contrary, entrepreneurs are not *extreme* risk-takers. Studies show that they set reasonable, attainable goals and take calculated risks to reach them. They "gamble" only when they believe the odds of winning are in their favor.

Total Score _____

195–235	Entrepreneur Extraordinaire
165–194	Budding Entrepreneur
140–164	Potential Entrepreneur
125–139	Entrepreneur-in-the-Rough
Below 125	Journeyman

This entrepreneurial test can help you compare your personality to the "entrepreneurial profile." But, a high score on *any* entrepreneurial test does not guarantee success as a business owner; similarly, a low score does not mean you will fail as an entrepreneur. These tests, however, can encourage you to take a more objective look at yourself before you decide whether to launch a business venture.

DISCUSSION QUESTIONS

1. What factors cause individuals to need greater personal control over their lives?
2. What are the characteristics of entrepreneurs identified by McClelland?
3. What are the major benefits of business ownership?
4. Which of the potential drawbacks to business ownership are most critical in your opinion?
5. How realistic are most individuals when they assess their reasons for going into business?
6. Outline the general causes of small business failures. Does the entrepreneur have any control over these factors?
7. List and briefly describe the specific causes of most small business failures. Which problems underlie the majority of failures?
8. How can the small business owner avoid the common pitfalls which often lead to business failure?
9. Why is it important to study the small business failure rate and its causes?

ENDNOTES

Karen Blumenthal, "On Campuses, Making Dean's List Comes Second to Making a Profit," *The Wall Street Journal,* April 4, 1985, p. 33.

Ellen Graham, "The Entrepreneurial Mystique," A Special Report: Small Business, *The Wall Street Journal,* May 20, 1985, pp. 1C, 4C, 7C, and 8C.

Andrew Feinberg, "Inside the Entrepreneur," *Venture,* May 1984, pp. 80–86.

Joseph Mancuso, "The Entrepreneur in You," *Across the Board,* July/August, 1984, pp. 1–4, 43–47.

Sharon Nelton, "The People Who Take the Plunge," *Nation's Business,* June 1984, pp. 22–26.

Sabin Russell, "Being Your Own Boss in America," *Venture,* May 1984, pp. 40–52.

Lewis Beale, "Young Entrepreneurs," *Venture,* October 1983, pp. 40–48.

Patricia M. Scherschel, "The Comeback of Risk Takers: They're Reshaping Business," *U.S. News and World Report,* September 24, 1984, pp. 60–62.

Gordon Bock, "Capitalists Prosper on College Campuses," *U.S. News and World Report,* May 28, 1984, pp. 77–78.

SECTION TWO

BUILDING A BUSINESS PLAN: BEGINNING CONSIDERATIONS

Strategic Planning for the Small Business

2

Failing to plan is planning to fail.

Robert M. Fulmer

It does not do to leave a live dragon out of your calculations, if you live near him.
J.R.R. Tolkien

Ready! Fire! Aim!

Anonymous

Upon completion of this chapter, you will be able to:

- Understand the importance of strategic management and planning for the small business.

- Demonstrate a working knowledge of the concept of the business mission.

- Understand how to assess a firm's competitive situation.

- Develop a strategic plan for a business.

- Recognize the need to develop objectives.

- Recognize that a firm's strategies are its game plan to achieve its objectives.

- Understand the role of policies and procedures in the business.

- Recognize that operational plans are the day-to-day extensions of the firm's strategic plans.

- Understand that the application of the firm's plans requires decision making and problem-solving.

- Understand the importance of controls in the planning process.

There is no substitute for strategic planning. Before an entrepreneur launches a business, she must address some basic questions that will launch her into the strategic thinking process. This process forces the entrepreneur to evaluate the clear realities of the business world. Some great ideas pale when the prospective owner views them in terms of where she wants them to lead and how they will fare in the competitive environment.

I. THE IMPORTANCE OF STRATEGIC PLANNING

Many empirical studies have concluded that the presence of strategic planning is a key determinant of the ultimate survival of small companies. Successful small businesses exhibit greater evidence of advanced planning and an ability to evaluate alternative courses of action. Other studies show that among small companies, lack of planning and systematic decision making are key reasons for failure. According to one small business researcher, "'Planning,' it turns out, is really no more—and no less—than another word for good management. And maybe you can *start* a company without knowing how to plan—but if you don't learn, sooner or later you'll pay an enormous price."[1]

Developing a strategic plan also is critical to the creation of a small company's "competitive edge"—the aggregation of factors that sets the small business apart from its competitors. The small firm must establish a plan for creating a unique image in the minds of its potential customers. Such a plan defines the type of enterprise the business will be. For example, successful restaurants project specific images, aim their menus at particular market segments, and match their prices and their atmospheres to create the desired ambiences. One exclusive steak house located in a stylish old mansion offers high-quality meals at above-average prices and aims its menu at high-income customers in its trading area. One key to this restaurant's success is the owner's conscious decision years ago to develop an exclusive image for his business. Everything about the restaurant, including the authentic antiques, the highly trained, professional staff, and the owner's penchant for every detail of the meal, contributes to this image.

No business can be everything to everyone. Developing a strategic plan prevents the small business from stumbling into the pitfall of failing to differentiate itself from its competitors. In fact, operating a small business without a strategic plan is senseless, especially since small companies have a natural advantage over their larger competitors. The typical small business has narrower product lines, a better defined customer base, and a specific geographic market area. Consequently, small businesses will find that strategic planning may come more naturally to them than to larger companies. Usually, the small business owner is in very close contact with his market, giving him valuable knowledge on how to best serve the customer's needs. It is logical for an entrepreneur to incorporate a marketing approach into the process of strategic planning for a small business.

It is a mistake to attempt to apply "big business strategic development techniques" to a small business because "a small business is not a little big business." Because of their size and their particular characteristics—resource poverty, a flexible managerial style, an informal organization structure, and adaptability to change—small businesses need a different approach to strategic planning.

The planning process can increase a small firm's effectiveness, but what owners first need is a procedure designed to meet their needs and their business' special characteristics. The strategic planning procedure for a small business should have the following characteristics.

- The planning horizon should be relatively short—two years or less for most small companies.
- The process should be informal and not overly structured; a "shirt-sleeve" approach would be ideal.
- The procedure should encourage the participation of outside parties to improve the reliability and the creativity of the resulting plan.
- The process should *not* begin with setting objectives. Extensive objective setting early on may interfere with creating a successful plan.

II. THE STRATEGIC PLANNING PROCESS FOR SMALL BUSINESSES

Successful entrepreneurs have one common characteristic: an idea for a product or service that is valuable to society and has potential to produce profits. Very few of these are "big ideas" destined to be recorded in the business history books. Instead, virtually all of them are "little big ideas"; they affect a specific area of the entrepreneur's business interest. For example, when Fred Smith started Federal Express, he had a "little idea" about a distribution network that would deliver packages overnight. He had

---

[1] Bruce G. Posner, "Real Entrepreneurs Don't Plan," *Inc.,* November 1985, p. 129.

no intention of launching a $3.3 billion industry of-
fering fast, reliable delivery of time-sensitive packages. Steven Jobs and Steve Wozniak built their first
computer from a kit in a garage. From such humble
beginnings was born Apple Computers, a company
which pioneered the surge into the microcomputer
industry.

Fred Smith and Steven Jobs, like all successful
entrepreneurs, had ideas about the future. They
were "little ideas" that eventually had a big impact on
society. Their visionary foresight stimulated important innovations for the economy. But, was their success the result of mere chance—being in the right
place at the right time? Hardly! Luck plays a role in
any business venture, but these little ideas could not
have come to fruition without the guiding hand of a
strategic plan. Peter Drucker writes, "The future cannot be known . . . [it is] as yet unborn, uninformed,
undetermined. It can be shaped by purposeful
action."[2] Linking the "purposeful action" of strategic
planning to an entrepreneur's "little ideas" can produce results that will shape the future. In fact, strategic planning is nothing more than a comprehensive
procedure designed to help the firm anticipate the
future and prepare for it logically.

III. THE EIGHT STEPS IN STRATEGIC PLANNING

Step 1:   Develop a Clear Mission Statement

It is essential to answer the "first question" of any
venture: "What business am I in?" Establishing the
purpose of the business in writing must come first to
give the company a sense of direction. Without a concise, meaningful mission statement, the small business will wander aimlessly in the marketplace. The
business owner without a clear mission statement

has no idea of where he wants to go or how he
should go about getting there.

Answering the "What business am I in?" question seems a simple matter at first glance. "Oh, that's
easy," said one entrepreneur, "I'm in the restaurant
business." The answer is *not* that simple! Such a
statement is useless for planning purposes. What
kind of restaurant is it? Who are its customers? What
image will it portray in the marketplace? What customer needs will the business satisfy? What methods
will be used to satisfy these needs?

Again, quoting Peter Drucker:

Only a clear definition of the mission and purpose of the business makes possible clear and
realistic strategies, plans, and work assignments. It
is the starting point for the design of managerial
jobs and, above all, for the design of managerial
structure.[3]

A business' existence is determined, above all
else, by whether it can create a body of customers to
support that business because *without customers
there is no business.*

A functional mission statement should locate
the firm's present position in the marketplace as well
as suggest its future direction. The mission statement's focus should be on creating a competitive
advantage for the firm by identifying a new, better, or
different way to satisfy customer needs. This
"bottom-up" approach for defining the scope of the
business operation should include identifying segments of the market to target as customer bases as
well as positioning the company (and its goods and
services) to reach these market segments most effectively.

Market segmentation is important because few
businesses succeed by trying to be "everything to
everyone." Segmenting a market involves carving up
the mass market into smaller, more homogeneous
units and then attacking each segment with a specific
marketing strategy designed to appeal to its mem-

---

[2] Peter Drucker, "The Big Power of Little Ideas," *The Harvard
Business Review,* May–June 1964, p. 6.

[3] Peter Drucker, *An Introductory View of Management* (New York:
Harper College Press, 1977), p. 66.

bers. This requires *information*—knowing who the firm's customers are and what they are like. Table 2–1 presents a customer-base analysis form for evaluating a small company's clientele.

To segment a market successfully, the small business owner must first identify the characteristics of two or more groups of customers with similar needs or wants. The owner must develop a basis for segmenting the market—benefits sought, product usage, brand preference, purchase patterns, etc.— and then must use this basis to identify the various submarkets to enter. Then the owner must verify that the segments are large enough and have enough purchasing power to generate a profit for the firm, because segmentation is useless if the firm cannot earn a profit serving its segments. Finally, he must reach the market. To be profitable, a segment must be accessible. Typical market segments might include college students, retired people, young singles, ethnic groups, or high-income individuals.

Positioning the company in the market involves influencing customer perceptions to create the de-

TABLE 2–1   Analysis of the customer base.

To analyze your customer base, answer the following questions:

1. Who are the customers for your product or service?
2. What are your customers' characteristics (e.g., age, income, buying habits, location, etc.)?
3. Why do they buy your goods or use your service?
4. How loyal are they to their present supplier?
5. What factors cause them to increase or decrease purchases?
6. Are there major customers in the market? If so, who are they?
7. What portion of total sales do they represent? From whom do they currently buy and why?

sired image for the business and its goods and services. Most often, a business attempts to position its products by differentiating them from those of competitors using some characteristic important to the

---

SMALL BUSINESS REPORT 2–1

Know Thy Business

"What business am I in?" When George Patterson, cofounder of City Gardens, Inc., asked this question, he discovered that his answer was "I'm not sure." After nearly 15 years of growth, the company's original focus—selling and maintaining plants for offices—had become muddled. City Gardens had diversified and expanded into new businesses and new markets without a plan. Patterson confesses, "We lost a lot of money and we were going nowhere."

Patterson and his partner finally decided that their business should be interior landscaping. "Our edge was knowledge of the local market," he says.

Everett Jewell, founder of Jewell Building Systems, Inc., built his company's competitive edge on price. The manufacturer of prefabricated steel buildings had established a profitable niche selling small prefab structures at low prices. Then, Jewell discovered that customers valued reliable, on-time deliveries more than bargain prices. "We're at a point where we don't just sell *buildings*. We sell solutions to *problems*," he says. Jewell is now focusing on selling larger, more expensive buildings and on providing high quality and reliable service.

Source: Adapted from Bruce G. Posner, "Real Entrepreneurs Don't Plan," *Inc.,* November 1985, p. 132, with permission of the publisher.

customer such as price, quality, service, or perform-ance. For example, Dannon has stressed the health and diet features of its yogurt and has convinced a segment of the market that its higher-priced product is different from (and better than) those of its com-petitors.

Proper positioning provides the small business with a source for developing a competitive edge—some way of setting itself apart from the competition. Lower prices are a common method of establishing a competitive edge, but this can be especially danger-ous for small businesses which cannot rely on the economies of scale that larger businesses can. A smarter tactic for the small business owner is to rely

A "Simple" Competitive Edge

Ryan's Family Steak Houses, Inc. is a leader in its segment of the hotly contested fast-food market. The innovative company has become an industry leader by pursuing a strategy contrary to accepted industry patterns and by understanding what its cus-tomers really want. Founder Alvin McCall, Jr.'s philosophy is amazingly simple: good food with good service at a good price. For example, Ryan's does not rely on dis-count coupons, giveaways, or flashy ads to win customers. "We put that money in the food budget, where it belongs," McCall claims. He brags about his company having "the highest food cost in the industry," while most competitors strive to cut costs to meet close margins. Individual restaurants buy their produce from local suppliers to ensure freshness.

Ryan's focus on quality does not mean that the company is careless about cost control, however. The company centrally purchases meat and supplies so that all units have the same costs on these items. All wasted food is collected and weighed. Says Ryan's director of training, "By studying the waste, we get to see where purchas-ing mistakes were made."

Chief operating officer Mark McCall, the founder's son, devised one of the company's most successful product innovations—its "mega" food bar. One step be-yond the traditional salad bar, the mega food bar offers a wide range of hot food items and desserts—from barbecued ribs and meat loaf to banana pudding and chocolate mousse. Ryan's, with General Mills' help, also introduced its own proprie-tary bread recipe to distinguish its dinner rolls from those of the competition. "Most companies figure suppliers are a nuisance. Ryan's uses them as a resource," says a General Mills spokesperson.

McCall has helped Ryan's isolate the key success factors in a highly competitive business. By focusing on these forces, McCall has built an industry-leading company feared by its competitors. According to McCall:

> There's nobody can touch us for dollar value. They're just not going to do it. Yet it's so simple. They don't think like we do. They don't think quality. They think about cutting cost—down, down, down—but that's where they're wrong. Nobody thinks like we do. Thank goodness they don't—that's why we're able to put twice as much on the bottom line as our nearest competitors.

Source: Adapted from Robert A. Mamis, "Meat and Potatoes," *Inc.,* July 1986, pp. 53–63, with permission of the publisher.

on a "natural advantage" e.g., the small firm's flexibility in reaching the market, a wider variety of customer services, or special knowledge of the good or service—to gain a competitive edge. For example, small independently owned drugstores cannot offer lower prices than the chain drugstores that can take advantage of high volume purchases to get quantity discounts. However, local drugstores can develop a competitive edge by offering "extras" such as more convenient hours, customer credit, delivery services, or some special feature like an old-fashioned soda fountain. These features set independent drugstores apart from their larger competitors in the customers' eyes.

Creating a sound mission statement requires information about the market and the business itself. Locating and interpreting relevant information is crucial to the development of a strategic plan. Faulty or misinterpreted information results in a deficient plan.

What are the sources of this information? The source depends on the type of information needed, which, in turn, depends on the owner's desired use of it. There are three categories of information needs confronting the manager: the firm itself, the industry and the market, and competitors.

Step 2: Assess the Firm's Strengths and Weaknesses

The best place to begin collecting strategic information—the ammunition for the strategic planning weapon—is within the firm itself. The owner must understand his business as it exists. One very effective technique for taking this "strategic inventory" is to prepare a "balance sheet" of company strengths and weaknesses. Strengths are positive internal factors that contribute to the accomplishment of objectives; weaknesses are negative internal factors that inhibit the accomplishment of objectives.

Table 2–2 presents a form to assist the owner in itemizing his firm's strengths and weaknesses. The positive side should reflect important skills, knowl-

TABLE 2–2   Strengths and weaknesses of the firm (internal).

Strengths (+)	Weaknesses (−)
Specific skills of the firm	What the firm is lacking in skills
Unique knowledge	What we do not know about our business or its customers
Special resources of the firm	Resources the firm is lacking

edge, or resources that contribute to the firm's success. The negative side should record honestly key limitations that detract from the company's ability to compete. This balance sheet should analyze all key performance areas of the business—personnel, finance, production, marketing, product development, organization, and others. This analysis should give the owner a more realistic perspective of his business. It will point out foundations on which he can build future strengths and obstacles which he must remove for business progress. This is an important bridge in moving from one's present position to future actions.

Step 3: Conduct a Thorough Market Segment Analysis

The market segment analysis should perform a dual function—to identify any opportunities and threats in the environment that might have a significant impact on the business, and to isolate the key factors required for success in that specific market segment.

Opportunities and Threats. Opportunities are positive external options the firm could employ to accomplish its objectives. The number of potential opportunities is limitless, so the manager must restrict his analysis to only factors significant to the business (probably two or three at most). For example, the owner of a small restaurant concluded that

he faced two realistic opportunities: opening a second shop across town or buying a franchised outlet
from a national company. When identifying opportunities, the owner must pay close attention to new
potential markets. Are competitors overlooking a
niche in the market you could fill profitably? One
fast-food franchisee noted the dramatic increase in
the number of health-conscious diners who ques-
tioned the nutritional value of their fast-food fare.
Acting on a primary opportunity, he developed the
idea for his own fast-food restaurant that specializes
in a "lite," nutritional menu. He sold his franchise
and opened his own store catering to customers who
wanted the convenience of fast food but still wanted
nutritious meals.

Threats are negative external forces that inhibit
the firm's ability to achieve its objectives. Threats to
the business can take a variety of forms, such as new
competitors entering the local market, a government
mandate regulating a business activity, an economic
recession, rising interest rates, and technological
advances making a company's product obsolete. The
owner must prepare a plan for shielding his business
from the adverse impact of such threats. Table 2–3
presents a "balance sheet" to help the small business
owner evaluate relevant opportunities and threats in
the competitive environment.

Key Factors for Success.   This stage of the analysis
also should identify the key factors required for success in the business. Every business is characterized
by a set of controllable variables that determines the
relative success (or lack of success) of market participants. Identifying these variables and manipulating
them is how a small business gains a competitive
advantage. Such factors lead to what are often dramatic differences in performance levels within the
same business.

Sources of competitive advantage come in a
variety of different patterns depending on the industry involved. Simply stated, they are relationships
between a controllable variable (e.g., plant size, size
of sales force, advertising expenditures, product

TABLE 2–3   Opportunities and threats facing the firm
(external).

Opportunities (+)	Threats (−)
(Consider 2 or 3 factors significant to the business, paying close attention to potential markets)	(New competitors, government regulation, economic recession, interest rates, obsolescence)

packaging, etc.) and a critical factor influencing the
firm's ability to compete in the market. Many of these
sources of competitive advantages are based on cost
factors—manufacturing cost per unit, distribution
cost per unit, development cost per unit. Some are
less tangible and less obvious, but are just as important—product quality, services offered, store location, customer credit.

The owner must use the information gathered
to analyze his business, its competitors, and the industry to isolate these sources of competitive advantage and then to evaluate how well his business
meets these criteria for successfully competing in the
market. Highly successful companies know and understand these relationships, while marginal competitors are mystified by which factors determine success in that particular business. For example, a small
manufacturer of cosmetics may discover that shelf
space, broad exposure, efficient distribution, and
long production runs are crucial to business success.
On the other hand, a small retail chain owner may
find that broad product lines, customer credit, personalized service, capable store management, and
low distribution costs determine success in his business.

Locating all of this information might appear to

be impractical due to cost considerations. However, much of the needed information is available at no cost or for a minimal charge. In-house records on production, sales, finance, and marketing could provide useful data. Managers and employees from the various functional areas of the business usually have extensive knowledge of their specialties and are eager to share it. Publications are another source of valuable information. Business periodicals and newspapers like *Business Week, Forbes, Fortune, Inc., Venture,* or *The Wall Street Journal* publish articles pertaining to specific businesses. Governments at all levels—federal, state, and local—are veritable storehouses of knowledge. They offer everything from census data and industry financial statements to economic forecasts and management assistance programs. The wise manager should familiarize himself with the inventory of government publications and utilize those relevant to his business. Customers and competitors are another prime source of useful information in conducting an environmental scan.

One source of information deserves special attention. A professional advisory board, comprised of competent individuals whose experience is strongest in areas where the owner's is weakest, can provide an objective viewpoint in the planning process. This board should be able to criticize managerial decisions, offer advice, and provide a larger pool of knowledge from which to draw. Other outside planners might include consultants from SBA programs such as the Small Business Development Centers (SBDC), Small Business Institute (SBI), Active Corps of Executives (ACE), or Service Corps of Retired Executives (SCORE).

Step 4:   Analyze Competitors

Potential small business owners should know their competitors and their potential behavior almost as well as they know themselves. Strategies formulated within any organization must be implemented in a world full of aggressive competitors who are not likely to set back passively while others capture their market share. However, the rules which govern the actions of competitors are often ignored or unknown.

In his book, *Competitive Strategy,* Michael Porter outlines some barriers for competitor analysis.[4] How competitors are likely to behave is determined by an assessment of various areas: what the competitors are presently doing and what they have the potential of doing, as well as what drives the competitors to behave in the manner they do. Like your business, competitors have both strengths and weaknesses; they have assumptions about how the market operates and what competitive actions are likely to be most beneficial to them. Competitors have goals and objectives which they would like to accomplish. These goals can be assessed by observing their behavior toward risk, as well as the values they hold. Some business managers pride themselves as being leaders in the market; others may be extremely quality or service conscious. What a competitor values determines, to a large degree, the actions she is likely to take.

The small business executive is most interested in determining how each competitor is likely to react to his own strategic moves. If competitors do not view his actions as harmful to their position, they are not as likely to retaliate. If, on the other hand, competitors are more powerful and tend to be sensitive about the actions they are contemplating, a reassessment of the strategy may be necessary. It is generally unwise to pick a fight with a competitor who has the economic power to seriously injure the business.

What actions do the competitors normally take in certain situations? Some competitors respond to situations with a well-defined pattern. Knowing these patterns can allow the business executive to take actions to either counter the negative influences of their actions or defeat their strategies with her own strategic actions.

Are there competitors who are vulnerable to your strategic actions? Small businesses do not need to always behave in a defensive fashion. If the owner

---

[4]Michael E. Porter, *Competitive Strategy* (New York: The Free Press, 1980), pp. 47–74.

identifies the vulnerability of competitors, the next step is to determine if his business has the resources to take advantage of that vulnerability. If the firm has the resources to mount an attack on a competitor's market, what is likely to be the short-term and long-term effects of such strategic actions? If there are no significant negative effects, then an aggressive strategic initiative can begin. Potential retaliation by competitors must always be assessed. No one wishes to begin a "war" in the market where he eventually loses or creates a great deal of long-term turbulence and instability.

How successful are your competitors and what factors have led to their success? Truly successful competitors should be studied to determine what makes them successful and the marginal firms should be studied to determine what causes them to fail. Sometimes marginal competitors may enact strategies which seem irrational but are a product of their fear of failure. These strategies may be last ditch efforts to save themselves from going under. They are typically associated with deep price cutting to convert costly inventories into cash. Inventories may be sold below cost because the cash is needed to keep the business afloat. Such actions can produce significant turbulence in the market. So don't ignore a competitor just because he is not successful; he may be desperate, causing more conflict than those who are most successful.

We can learn what works from successful competitors. What distinctive competences have they developed? How do customers or clients view the leading competitors in the market? How do the customers describe their products or services; their way of doing business; the additional services they might supply? Then we must ask ourselves the critical question "Can our business match or exceed the competitors on the behavior or performance of those high profitability competitors?"

Sizing up the competition gives the manager a more realistic view of the market and his position in it. Who are your major competitors? How do their cost structures compare to yours? Are new competitors entering the business? Can you identify key strategies of your major competitors? What are their strengths and weaknesses? Table 2–4 presents a summary form to assist in this analysis.

This assessment should produce the beginnings of a strategic plan. By this stage, the owner has begun to compare his firm's strengths to those of his competitors and to formulate ways of magnifying his strengths and exploiting their weaknesses. In other words, the owner is looking toward the future and is planning for it. The strategic planning process is beginning to work.

Step 5:   Create Company Goals and Objectives

Before the small business manager can build a comprehensive set of strategies, he must first establish business goals and objectives. Goals and objectives give the owner targets to aim for and provide a basis for evaluating company performance. Without them,

TABLE 2–4   Analysis of the market and competitors.

Describe the specific market(s) you plan to compete in:			
Major Competitor	Strengths	Weaknesses	Market Share
1.			
2.			
3.			
4.			
5.			

the manager cannot know where the business is going or how well it is performing. The following conversation between Alice and the Cheshire Cat taken from Lewis Carroll's *Alice in Wonderland* illustrates the point:[5]

> "Would you tell me please, which way I ought to go from here?" asked Alice.
> "That depends a good deal on where you want to get to," said the Cat.
> "I don't much care where . . . ," said Alice.
> "Then it doesn't matter which way you go," said the Cat.

A small business that doesn't "much care where" it wants to go will find that "it really doesn't matter which way" it chooses to go! Creating goals and objectives is an essential part of the strategic management process.

Goals are the broad, long-range attributes the business seeks to accomplish; they tend to be general and sometimes abstract. Goals are not intended to be specific enough for a manager to act on, but simply state the general level of accomplishment the manager seeks. Do you want to boost your market share? Does your cash balance need strengthening? Would you like to enter a new market or increase sales in a current one? What return on your investment do you seek? Addressing these broad issues will help the manager focus on the next phase—developing specific, realistic objectives.

Common types of objectives deal with profitability, productivity, growth, efficiency, markets, financial resources, physical facilities, organizational structure, employee welfare, and social responsibility. Clearly, some of these objectives might conflict with one another; thus, the manager must establish priorities. Which objectives are most important? Which are least important? Arranging objectives in a hierarchy according to their priority can help the small business manager resolve conflicts when they

arise. Well-written objectives have the following characteristics.

- They are *specific.* Objectives should be quantifiable and precise. For example, "to achieve a healthy growth in sales" is *not* a meaningful objective; "to increase retail sales by 12 percent and wholesale by 10 percent in the next fiscal year" is precise and spells out exactly what management wants to accomplish.

- They are *measurable.* Managers should be able to plot the organization's progress toward its objectives; this requires a well-defined reference point from which to start and a "scale" for measuring progress.

- They are *attainable.* To motivate managers and employees effectively, objectives must be attainable; otherwise, people see only futility in achieving objectives and stop striving for them. This does not mean, however, that objectives should be easy to accomplish.

- They are *realistic and challenging.* Objectives must be within the reach of the organization or motivation dwindles. However, managerial expectations must remain high! In other words, the more challenging an objective (within realistic parameters), the higher the performance. Set objectives that will challenge your business and its employees.

- They are *timely.* Objectives not only must specify *what* is to be accomplished but also *when* it is to be accomplished. A time frame for achievement is important.

- They are *written.* This writing process does not have to be complex; in fact, the manager should make the number of objectives relatively small—from five to fifteen.

The strategic planning process works best when subordinate managers and employees are actively involved in setting objectives. Developing a plan is top management's responsibility, but encouraging managers and employees to participate broadens the plan's perspective and increases motivation

---

[5]Lewis Carroll, *Alice in Wonderland,* (Mount Vernon: Peter Pauper Press), pp. 78–79.

to make the plan work. In addition, these individuals possess a great deal of knowledge about the organization and usually are willing to share it. A Management by Objectives (MBO) program, in which subordinates and managers establish objectives jointly, may improve the quality of the small firm's strategic plan. Under MBO, objective setting begins at the top of the organization and "trickles down" as managers and subordinates establish objectives by mutual agreement. Participation at lower levels is important since this is where the plans for achieving objectives will be implemented.

Step 6: Formulate Strategic Options and Select the Appropriate Strategies

By now, the small business owner should have a clear picture of what his business does best and what its competitive advantages are. Similarly, he should know what the firm's weaknesses and limitations are as well as those of its competitors. The next step is to evaluate strategic options and then prepare a "game plan" designed to accomplish the business' objectives.

A strategy is a set of actions the manager plans to take to achieve the firm's defined objectives. It is the master plan that covers all of the major parts of the organization and ties them together into a unified whole. The plan must be action-oriented—that is, it should breathe life into the entire planning process. The manager must build a sound strategy from the preceding five steps in the planning process. It should focus on the key areas the manager has outlined in analyzing his business.

A successful strategy is comprehensive and well-integrated. It must focus on establishing the key success factors that the manager identified in Step 3. For instance, if maximum shelf space is a key success factor for a small manufacturer's product, the strat-

"All Together Now: Plan!"

SMALL BUSINESS REPORT 2–3

Before he attended a planning seminar, John Sandford, president of a Memphis advertising agency, had not done much strategic planning. What little planning Sandford did, he did alone.

Today, his company has an 11-member executive planning committee that is preparing the company's first strategic plan. Top managers and department heads serve on the committee, and each manager is responsible for coordinating plans for a specific function. The planning process has proved to be extremely valuable. Sandford claims, "What [the planning] has done among this group of people is amazing; it's more profitable than the document itself will ever be. Our people are now working together toward the achievement of common goals and shared values."

James Tyler, president of a small plastic-card manufacturing company, agrees that participative strategic planning is best. Involving subordinates in the planning process requires time and hard work, but the effort pays off. Tyler claims, "It's *their* goals they are meeting, not yours. It gives them a truer sense of the company's future."

Source: Adapted from Roberta Shell, "The Team Approach," *Inc.*, November 1985, p. 162, with permission of the publisher.

egy must identify techniques for gaining more shelf space (e.g., offering higher margins to distributors and brokers than competitors, assisting retailers with in-store displays, or redesigning a wider, more attractive package).

The strategies of the "microbreweries" across the U.S. provide a good illustration of this strategic planning process in action.[6] These small, regional beer brewers have intentionally limited the scope of their operations and have focused their strategies on reaching a particular segment of the beer-drinking populace—sophisticated beer drinkers who loathe domestic beers and seek more freshness from imported brews. These small breweries have gained a competitive advantage through product differentiation; they offer a variety of "boutique" brews like ales, porters, stouts, and pilsners, all quite different from the lagers major U.S. brewers produce. Their pricing strategies reflect the unique image they portray and are aimed at distinctive drinkers who are able (and willing) to pay premium prices. The boutiques' advertising campaigns stress the unique attributes of their beer and contribute to the mystique of drinking it. These microbreweries do not attempt to compete with the major brewers on a head-to-head basis; instead, they pursue "niche" strategies, focusing on a small segment of the market in a limited geographical region.

However, plotting strategy is not without risk and danger. Many microbreweries, for example, must struggle to capture a large enough share of a small market to be profitable—sales of microbreweries account for less than 1 percent of domestic beer sales. None of the 30 microbrewers produce more than 30,000 gallons per year, while Anheuser-Busch sells nearly 2 billion gallons each year! There is also the danger of the larger U.S. brewers eroding the boutiques' profitable niches. Several

large beermakers have developed beers to compete with many microbreweries' products.

An effective strategic plan will identify a complete set of success factors—financial, operating, marketing—that, taken together, yield a competitive advantage for the small business. The resulting action plan will distinguish the firm from its competitors by exploiting its competitive advantage. The focal point of this entire strategic plan is the *customer* (from Step 1). The customer is the nucleus of the business, so developing a competitive strategy will succeed if it is aimed at serving its customers better than the competitor does.

So, the strategic plan draws out the competitive advantage in a small company by building on its strengths; its focal point is the hub of the entire business—the *customer*. It also designates methods for overcoming the firm's weaknesses, and it identifies opportunities and threats from the external environment that demand action.

Step 7: Translate Strategic Plans into Action Plans

No strategic plan is complete until it is put into action. The small business manager must convert strategic plans into operating plans that guide the company on a daily basis. Operating plans must be consistent with the comprehensive strategic plan, and must become a visible, active part of the business. The small business does not benefit from a strategic plan sitting on a shelf collecting dust.

To help translate strategic plans into operating plans, the manager should develop policies, procedures, and budgets that reflect the plans' intentions. This will permit the owner to delegate more authority to subordinates in the strategic planning process. These are the plans that will affect them most, and they have an interest in helping shape them. The MBO process mentioned earlier will improve the quality of the operating plans and will increase subordinates' acceptance of them.

---

[6] Liz Roman Gallege, "New Little Breweries Cause Some Ferment in the Beer Business," *The Wall Street Journal,* March 15, 1983, p. 1.

Step 8: Establish Accurate Controls

So far, the planning process has created company objectives and developed a strategy for reaching them. Rarely, if ever, will the company's actual performance match stated objectives. The manager quickly realizes the need to control actual results that deviate from plans.

Planning without control is of little operational value. A sound planning program requires a practical control process. In fact, the two functions are closely linked. The plans created in this process become the standards against which actual performance is measured. It is important for *everyone* in the organization to understand—and to be involved in—the planning process.

Operating data from normal business activity are the guideposts for detecting deviations from standards. Accounting, production, sales, inventory, and other operating records are key sources of data the manager can use for controlling activities. As conditions change, the manager must make corrections in performances, policies, strategies, and objectives to get performance back on track. A practical control system is also economical to operate. Most small businesses have no need for a sophisticated, expensive control system. The system should be so practical that it becomes a natural part of the management process.

IV. WHY STRATEGIC PLANNING FAILS IN SMALL BUSINESSES

If strategic planning is so critical to business success and is naturally suited to small operations, why, then, do small business managers ignore it? When ques-

---

Coping Effectively with a Load of Negative Forces

It's not a good sign when your traditional market is shrinking in size and foreign competitors are storming the gates with less expensive products. That is exactly what Arnold Hiatt faced as president and chief executive officer of Stride-Rite Corporation. Stride-Rite had a reputation for top quality children's shoes for over 50 years. But the declining birthrate of the 1970s made it clear to Mr. Hiatt that a shift in strategy was necessary. Imported shoes now account for approximately 60 percent of the U.S. shoe market and seem to be growing every year. Since 1970 more than 350 U.S. shoe manufacturers have gone out of business.

To fight the imported shoe threat and declining market for children's shoes, the Stride-Rite people launched a strategy of building brand identification and loyalty. They have made themselves the top marketing firm in the shoe industry. They have chosen products that meet the demands of new customer groups. Products were targeted at growth markets. Stride-Rite's main lines include Herman Boots, Keds sneakers, Grasshoppers women's casuals, and Sperry Top-Sider boat shoes.

Despite negative forces that have crippled competitors, Arnold Hiatt's action at Stride-Rite is an example of how strong, aggressive strategies win markets.

Source: Adapted from Johnnie L. Roberts, "By Concentrating on Marketing, Stride-Rite Does Well Despite Slump for Shoe Makers," *The Wall Street Journal,* February 23, 1983, with permission of *The Wall Street Journal,* © Dow Jones & Company, Inc., 1983. All rights reserved.

SMALL
BUSINESS
REPORT
2–5

Four Strategies to Fight the Giants

1. Don't Play by Big League Rules

If you can't afford to play the low cost-big promotion game, be sure you have other qualities that the customer is willing to pay for. In 1982, Vlasic pickles, a part of the Campbell Soup Company, launched a market share attack against a small, but strong, local Seattle, Washington, product, Farman's Pickles. Vlasic pulled out all the stops . . . it cut price, offered retailers substantial discounts, and conducted a major television campaign. Farman's stood its ground. It could not match the discounts and price reductions of Vlasic. Farman had to depend on a strong customer loyalty based on an established reputation for quality. The Farman strategy seems to be working; it has a 60% market share in its Seattle market.

2. Hit 'Em Where They Ain't

This expression is taken from the baseball old-timer "Wee-Willie" Keller. In today's competitive world it suggests that *small businesses take advantage of the opportunities given them by large competitors.* Alpha Microsystems is an excellent example of how to succeed in a market dominated by the giants through the use of a highly focused strategy. The Alpha Micro (which competes with the IBM microcomputers) is designed to sell to highly specialized markets. Working closely with a software firm, they have tailored their system for municipalities, dentists, doctors, hospital administrators, and even funeral directors. The result has been a 184% increase in net income between 1982 and 1984.

3. Innovate—Then Innovate Again

Responding faster to changing customer needs and wants is an advantage that small business must master. New products or services can become an effective tool at fighting off big competitors. Robert Lynch, president of Harmony Foods Inc., credits has Santa Cruz, California, company's survival on new product introductions. "America's taste in foods is changing . . . small companies should be able to take advantage of this trend as long as they innovate."

4. Build a Better Mousetrap

Small but better can often work. DEP Corporation competes against some formidable established firms in the hair styling market. In order to keep up, Bob Berglass brought out a new hair mousse which is in a nonaerosol dispenser and contains no alcohol. Alcohol dries hair out. DEP hopes that there are customers who are knowledgeable about their product's superiority and willing to choose it above competitors.

Source: Adapted from Joel Kotkin, "The Revenge of the Fortune 500," *Inc.,* August 1985, p. 41, with permission of the publisher.

---

tioned, most small business owners extol the virtues of planning the launching and managing of a successful venture. Yet, when asked, "Do you use strategic planning in your business?" a surprisingly large proportion would reason: "No, but. . . ." In fact, it is very unlikely that the typical small business manager engages in much strategic planning at all (see figure 2–1)! Exploring the reasons for this failure to plan will help develop a more practical approach for the typical small business manager.

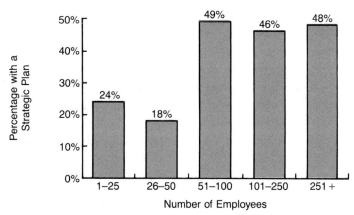

FIGURE 2–1   Do small firms really plan?

Lack of expertise. Sound planning is a skill that, like any other, must be learned. Frequently, the small business owner has a broad background of practical experience, making him a "generalist." As a result, the owner may lack the specific skills required to be an effective planner. Few small business owners are trained in the nuances of strategic planning.

Inability to get started. Usually, the most difficult step in the planning process is the first one—getting started. Some business owners see the need to plan but "stall out" when they face the question, "Where do I begin?" Few entrepreneurs have been exposed to the planning process and many of the variables in a plan are difficult to grasp.

Uncontrollable, often intangible, variables. A major complicating factor in the development of any plan is the large number of uncontrollable (and often intangible) variables involved and the novice planner can be overwhelmed quickly. Many small business owners are quite uncomfortable about creating plans that focus on an uncertain future. Frequently, when the owner does plan he attempts to derive a "most probable scenario" (a best guess) of the future environment and then develops a plan to respond to that scenario. Unfortunately, so many uncontrollable variables are involved that the fore-casted environment never materializes, and the

owner quickly loses faith in the strategic planning process.

Resource poverty. Most small businesses suffer from a condition called "resource poverty": they often lack adequate capital, managerial experience, outside advice, management specialists, and other key assets. Managing for business survival under such conditions requires a significant proportion of the owner's time and energy that otherwise could be devoted to planning.

Focus on daily operations. The daily struggle to keep the small business alive in a competitive environment forces strategic planning out of the owner's schedule. The owner is so concerned with "putting out fires" and dealing with daily emergencies that he has no time and energy left for planning. A vicious cycle develops as the failure to plan leads to more daily emergencies.

Failure to realize the importance of strategic planning. Too often, owners do not recognize the necessity of strategic planning for business success. They see it as a useful "fringe" to be performed if time permits. An owner can rationalize his failure to plan easily: "My business is so small and the system so simple that I really wouldn't benefit from it." However, studies on the value of strategic planning suggest otherwise.

V. CONCLUSION

The strategic planning process does not end with the steps outlined here; it is an ongoing procedure that the small business owner will repeat over and over. With each round, he gains experience, and the steps become much easier. The planning process outlined here is designed to be as simple as possible. No small business should be burdened with an elaborate, detailed formal planning process that it cannot use effectively. Such programs require excessive amounts of time to operate, and they generate a sea of paperwork. The small business manager needs neither.

What does this process lead to? It teaches the small business owner a degree of discipline that is important to business survival. It assists him in learning about his business, his competitors, and, most importantly, about his customers. Although strategic planning cannot guarantee success, it does increase drastically the small firm's chances of survival in a hostile business environment.

VI. SUMMARY

Strategic planning, often ignored by small companies, is a crucial ingredient in business success. The planning process forces the potential entrepreneur to subject his "great idea" to an objective evaluation in the competitive market.

Empirical studies have concluded that the presence of strategic planning is a key determinant of the ultimate survival of small companies. Developing a plan also gives the firm a way to create a "competitive edge"—the set of factors that sets the small business apart from its competitors.

Small businesses need a strategic planning process designed to suit their particular needs. It should be relatively short, be informal and not structured, encourage the participation of outside parties, and *not* begin with extensive objective setting. Linking the "purposeful action" of strategic planning to an entrepreneur's "little ideas" can produce results that will shape the future.

The strategic planning process should follow a "bottom-up" approach, placing special emphasis on the customer and following these steps:

Step 1. Develop a clear mission statement. The firm's mission statement answers the "first question" of any venture: "What business am I in?" The bottom-up approach for defining the firm's mission should identify target market segments and outline how to position the firm in those markets. The owner must identify some way to differentiate her business from competitors.

Step 2. Assess the firm's strengths and weaknesses. Developing a sound mission statement requires quality information. There are three information needs facing the small business manager: the firm itself, the industry and the market, and the competitors.

Step 3. Conduct a thorough market segment analysis. The owner must identify his firm's strengths and weaknesses (as well as those of competitors), its opportunities and threats, and the key success factors in the business. These key success factors are the source of the firm's competitive edge.

Step 4. Analyze competitors. Know them as well as you know yourself.

Step 5. Create company goals and objectives. Goals are the broad, long-range attributes the firm seeks to accomplish. Objectives are quantifiable and more precise; they should be specific, measurable, attainable, realistic, timely, and written. The process works best when subordinate managers and employees are actively involved.

Step 6. Formulate strategic options and select the appropriate strategies. A strategy is the "game plan" the firm plans to use to accomplish its objectives and its mission. It must focus on establishing for the firm the key success factors identified in Step 2.

Step 7. Translate strategic plans into action plans. No strategic plan is complete until the owner puts it into action.

Step 8. Establish accurate controls. Actual performance rarely, if ever, matches plans exactly. Operating data from the business serves as the guidepost for detecting deviations from plans. Such information is helpful in plotting future strategies.

The strategic planning process does not end with these eight steps; it is an ongoing process the owner will repeat over and over.

STUDENT INVOLVEMENT PROJECT

Interview several small business owners in the local community. Does the owner engage in strategic planning? Does he have a written statement of the firm's mission, objectives, policies, and procedures? What portion of the manager's planning is spent on short-range planning and long-range planning?

DISCUSSION QUESTIONS

1. What are the stages in the strategic management process?
2. What are strengths, weaknesses, opportunities, and threats? Give an example of each.
3. Explain the characteristics of effective objectives. Why is setting objectives important?
4. What are business strategies?
5. What functions do policies and procedures serve?
6. What are the advantages of involving operative employees in the planning process?
7. How is the controlling process related to the planning process?

Forms of Ownership

First law of bridge: It's always the partner's fault.

Anonymous

Acting on a good idea is better than just having a good idea.

Robert Half

Upon completion of this chapter, you will be able to:

- Assess the factors in deciding which form of ownership is best suited for a potential business.

- Outline the advantages and disadvantages of a sole proprietorship.

- Define what a partnership is and explain the nature of the partnership agreement.

- Explain the Uniform Partnership Act.

- Describe the types of partners.

- Outline the advantages and disadvantages of a partnership.

- Describe how a partnership can be terminated or dissolved.

- Explain the corporate form of ownership and describe how a business is incorporated.

- Outline advantages and disadvantages of the corporate form of ownership.

- Become familiar with such "hybrid" forms of ownership as the limited partnership, the joint venture, and the S Corporation.

When the prospective small business owner decides to go into business, he must quickly decide on the legal form of ownership he will establish. This chapter presents the fundamental considerations in choosing a form of ownership.

Each form of ownership has both advantages and disadvantages. The entrepreneur must base his choice on a careful analysis of the pros and cons of each form of ownership. Specifically, he should consider the following questions. The prospective business owner's answers will determine the "ideal" form of ownership for his particular set of circumstances.

1. How much money will I need to get the business started? Where do I plan to obtain the money?
2. What is a realistic net profit projection from this business for each of the first five years?
3. What specific skills do I have and how will they contribute to the success of the business? Are there skills which I lack, or areas of the business in which I have no experience?
4. How big does this business have potential of becoming, and will I be able to manage it?

5. How much control do I wish to have in the decisions of the company? Am I willing to share my idea and its potential profits with others who can help me build a successful business?

6. Are tax considerations of importance to my decision? Do I have other sources of income, and do I wish to shelter some of my income?

7. In case of failure, to what extent am I willing to be personally responsible for debts created by the business?

8. Is it important that the business continue in case of my incapacity or death?

9. Do I wish to be the sole or major benefactor of my business success? Am I the type of person who doesn't mind taking all the risks but expects to reap all the benefits if successful?

10. Am I willing to put up with the time-consuming bureaucratic red tape associated with more complicated forms of ownership? What is my emotional reaction to government regulations and their accompanying paperwork requirements?

We will explore each of these questions in our discussion of the common forms of business ownership. The potential small business owner must assess which factors are most critical in his personal decision. While there is no one best form of ownership, there may well be one best form of ownership for each person's circumstances. Therefore, one should never simply follow the leader and choose the form of ownership everyone else is using without seriously relating the choice to the responses to the 10 questions listed above. Figure 3–1 reveals the relative importance of each of the major forms of business ownership.

I. SOLE PROPRIETORSHIP

The sole proprietorship, a business owned and managed by one individual, is by far the most popular form of business ownership. Approximately 74 percent of all businesses in the United States are proprietorships.

Advantages of a Proprietorship

Simplicity in Creation.   One of the most attractive features of a proprietorship is how fast and simple it is to begin operations. If you wish to operate the business under your own name (e.g., Rick's Lumber), you simply obtain the necessary local licenses and begin operation. In a proprietorship, you are the business. For a simple business, it would not be impossible to start a proprietorship in a single day.

Least Costly Form of Ownership to Begin.   In addition to being easy and simple to begin, the proprietorship is generally the least expensive form of ownership to establish. You do not need to file legal papers as is recommended for a partnership and required for a corporation. You will normally go to your local government and state the nature of the business in which you wish to engage. The government will then assess the appropriate fees and license cost. Once paid, you are then able to do business in that jurisdiction.

If you plan to conduct business under a trade name (e.g., Ace Auto Parts), you will need to acquire a Certificate of Doing Business Under an Assumed Name from the state in which the business will operate. The fee for the certificate is usually very nominal. The reason for such a certificate is to ensure that the name you have chosen for your business is not already being used and to notify the state whom the actual owner of the business is.

One major advantage to the proprietorship is that after all debts are settled, the owner receives all the profits (less tax liability). For individuals with a high need for personal achievement, profits represent an excellent way of keeping score of success.

The Owner Has Total Decision-Making Authority. Since the sole proprietor is in total control of operations, he can respond quickly to changes, which is an asset in a rapidly shifting market. The freedom to set the course of action is a major motivational force. For the individual who thrives on the enjoyment of seeking new opportunities and then modifying the busi-

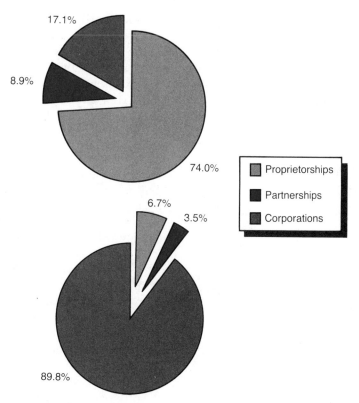

FIGURE 3–1   Forms of ownership by (a) percent of businesses and (b) percent of business receipts.

Source: Statistical Abstract of the United States 1985, U.S. Department of Commerce, Bureau of Census, Washington, D.C., p. 516.

ness to satisfy these new market opportunities, the freedom from impediments to the decision process is vital.

There Are No Special Legal Restrictions.   The proprietorship is the least regulated form of business ownership. In a time when government requests for information seem never-ending, this feature has much merit.

Easy to Discontinue.   If the owner cannot continue operations, he can terminate the business quickly. The owner will still be liable for all outstanding

debts and obligations, but in a short time he can cease all operations and discontinue the business.

Disadvantages of a Proprietorship

Unlimited Personal Liability.   Unlimited personal liability means that the sole proprietor is personally liable for all debts of the business. The owner owns all the assets of the business and, if the business fails, these assets can be sold to cover debts. If, after the sale of the business assets there are still unpaid debts, the owner's personal assets can be sold to cover the remaining debt. Failure of the business can ruin the owner financially. Because the law views the proprietor and the business as the same, the business' debts *are* the owner's debts. Most states have laws that protect an individual's assets to a degree. If he has substantial personal assets, the proprietorship could create unwarranted risk.

Limited Skills and Capabilities. The sole owner may not have the wide range of skills a successful business requires. Each of us has areas in which our education, training, and work experience have taught us a great deal. However, in the majority of cases failure is caused by our lack of knowledge in other areas. Often sole owners might have been successful if they had some knowledge of potential problems and had obtained good advice. As the business grows, there is an increasing tendency toward expanding into areas where the owner has no skills or abilities. When there is no one to ask, it is easy to feel confused and frustrated. The problems for which there are no answers are often pushed aside in favor of ones that can be solved. The problems set aside seldom solve themselves.

Some proprietors are too proud to ask for help, even when the problems become obvious. They believe their independence has taken them this far and it will see them through. However, sole owners need to recognize their shortcomings and then find help in becoming proficient in those areas. Successful small business managers are always seeking to keep abreast of the changes in a variety of areas.

Limited Access to Capital. For a business to grow and expand, a sole proprietor generally needs additional financial resources. However, many proprietors have already put all they have in the business, and often used their personal assets as collateral on existing loans. In short, proprietors, unless they have great personal wealth, find it difficult to raise additional money while maintaining sole ownership. In the case of a recession in the economy, the proprietor often cannot obtain the credit needed to weather the financial storm. The business may be sound in the long run, but the short-term cash flow difficulties can create financial turmoil. Most banks and other lending institutions have well-defined formulas for borrowers' eligibility. The proprietor often may find that the assets of the business are tied up in inventory and accounts receivable. In a recession, these assets may be extremely difficult to convert into needed dollars to pay debts, and may be significantly discounted by the bank in its valuation.

Lack of Continuity of the Business. Lack of continuity is inherent in the sole proprietorship. Since people look for employment where there is security and an opportunity for advancement, proprietorships, being small, often have trouble recruiting and retaining good employees.

Also, if the owner becomes ill or disabled and a family member or employee cannot effectively take over, the entire business can be in jeopardy. If the proprietor dies, the business is automatically dissolved. If no one is trained to run the business, creditors can petition the courts to liquidate the assets of the dissolved business to pay outstanding debts.

Because of the disadvantages or limitations of the proprietorship, it is common to find that, in time, partnerships are formed to replace the sole ownership. When one individual lacks specific managerial skills or has insufficient access to needed capital, the solution is often to form a partnership.

II. PARTNERSHIP

A partnership is an association of two or more persons who engage in business as co-owners for the purpose of making a profit. In a partnership, the co-owners (partners) share the assets and the liabilities of the business, and the profits, if any, according to the terms of a partnership agreement entered into prior to going into business.

The law does not require a partnership agreement, or articles of partnership, but it is wise to work with an attorney to develop one that spells out the exact status and responsibility of each member in the partnership. All too often the parties think they know what they are agreeing to, only to find later that no real meeting of the minds took place. The partnership agreement states in writing all of the terms of the partnership.

When a partnership agreement does not exist, the courts will be forced to assume that the value of each partner's contribution is equal and that each is entitled to an equal share of the profits or assets if the business is dissolved. The creation of a partnership agreement is not costly. In most cases, the partners can discuss in advance each of the provisions and, when all sections have been agreed to, have an attorney commit these provisions to a formal document. Banks often will want to see a copy of the partnership agreement before lending the business money. Probably the most important feature of the partnership agreement is that it resolves potential sources of conflict which, if not covered in the agreement, could later result in the dissolution of an ongoing business.

It is not feasible to include here all of the variations of partnership agreements, but we can list the most typical provisions. The standard partnership agreement will likely include the following:

1. The *name* of the partnership (name of the business).
2. The *purpose* of the business. What is the reason the business was brought into being (e.g., to operate a construction company to build homes)?
3. The *domicile* of the business. Where the principal business will be located (e.g., 1200 South Kings Highway, St. Louis, Mo.).
4. The *duration* of the partnership. How long will the partners operate this business as a partnership? You may plan to operate the business on a continuing basis, or the partnership may be formed to do only a single job or operate for a specific period of time.
5. Who the *partners* are and what their *legal addresses* are.

6. *Contributions* of each partner to the business, both at the creation of the partnership and later. This would include the investment of each partner in the business. (One partner may contribute a building, a second the needed tools, and a third the cash required to start the business.) In some situations a partner may have assets that are not likely to appear on a balance sheet. Experience, sales contacts, or a good reputation in the community may be reasons for asking a person to join in partnership.
7. An agreement on *how the profits (or losses) will be distributed.* Will each partner share equally? If not, be sure that the percentage going to each partner is clearly spelled out.
8. An agreement on *salaries or drawing rights* against profits for each partner. Will some partners be paid a salary because of their activity in the operations of the business? Will some partners be paid commissions on sales? If so, how much and under what conditions? How will business expenses be handled? Can some partners be reimbursed for business expenses while others are not? These are the items which strain a partnership. It is always best to include them in the agreement in a clear fashion to reduce later confusion.
9. Procedure for *expansion through the addition of a new partner,* if desired. Must every partner agree? Many a partnership has "hit the rocks" over the proposed addition of new partners. The partnership agreement can set procedures by which new partners are added. This procedure may not resolve your interpersonal problem with your partner, but it may prevent you from having your income reduced by an unneeded and unwanted partner.
10. If the *partners voluntarily dissolve the partnership, how will the assets of the partnership be distributed*? It is not unusual to find that this formula for the distribution of assets is quite different from that for the distribution of profits from the ongoing business. Let us assume that

one partner has $1 million in cash and the other has a patent, the value of which is difficult to assess. It may be fair and equitable to split the profits equally if the patent results in a product that produces a substantial return on investment. However, in the absence of a separate formula for the distribution of profits, the owner of the patent would be entitled to half of the tangible assets (half of $1 million) while relinquishing half of a patent of questionable value.

11. *Sale of partnership interest.* The articles of partnership should include a written agreement on how a partner can sell his interest in the business. Generally, this section will include a provision for veto of the sale to outsiders by any one of the remaining partners. This prevents a partner wishing to sell his interest in the business from burdening the remaining partners with an unacceptable replacement. In some cases, the partner wishing to sell his interest must offer it first to the remaining partners. When this is the requirement, there must also be a clearly defined procedure for evaluating the partner's interest. Such a procedure will reduce later conflict concerning what a partner's share is worth.

12. *Absence or disability* of one of the partners. If

SMALL BUSINESS REPORT 3–1

A Lasting Partnership

In 1837, William Procter, a British candlemaker, and James Gamble, an Irish soap-maker, formed a partnership at the suggestion of their father-in-law. (The two had married sisters.) Since the major component in both candles and soap was animal fat, Cincinnati, nicknamed "Porkopolis" from its butchering industry, was an ideal location for the new business.

The partners complemented each other well, and they divided managerial responsibilities according to their skills. Procter managed the office, while Gamble supervised the factory. The two met in Procter's parlor every Saturday night to review the past week's business and coordinate the next week's activities. By the end of the Civil War in 1865, Procter & Gamble was the largest business in Cincinnati. By this time, the firm had developed a logo—the man in the moon and 13 stars—that is still used on all P&G products today.

Until 1930, descendants of the original founders managed the business. In fact, Procter's son, Harley, was the original marketing genius for P&G. While competitors produced large chunks of soap for retailers, who then carved out "bars" for customers, Harley Procter decided to market his new white soap as individually wrapped cakes. The name for this new product struck him on Sunday in 1879 as he listened to the 45th Psalm: "All thy garments smell of myrrh, and aloes, and cassia, out of the ivory palaces whereby they have made thee glad." Thus, Ivory soap, "99 44/100% pure," was named.

Today, P&G still maintains its reputation as one of the most successful marketers in the world. The company spends more money on advertising than any other company in the country, and sales prove it. Many of P&G's brands, such as Ivory Soap, Crest toothpaste, Pampers disposable diapers, Charmin tissue, Bounty paper towels, and Tide laundry detergent rank first in sales.

Because of its effective production and marketing strategy, Procter & Gamble is a well-respected and feared competitor. Not a bad reputation for a company that began as a small partnership in "Porkopolis" before the Civil War.

"·A·BUSY·DAY·"

An 1896 advertisement for Procter & Gamble's Ivory Soap. (Photo courtesy of Procter & Gamble.)

Source: Adapted from Milton Moskowitz, Michael Katz, and Robert Levering, eds., *Everybody's Business: An Almanac* (New York: Harper & Row, 1980), pp. 355–361, with permission of publisher.

one of the partners is absent or disabled for an extended period of time, should the partnership continue? Will the absent or disabled partner receive the same share in the distribution of profits as she did prior to her absence or disability? Should the absent or disabled partner be held responsible for debts incurred while unable to participate? Although disability is an event we hope never occurs, provisions should be made to clearly protect all parties to the business.

13. *Alterations or modification of the partnership agreement.* No document is written to last forever. Partnership agreements should contain provisions for alterations or modifications.

Uniform Partnership Act

The Uniform Partnership Act codifies the body of law dealing with partnerships in the United States. It was first passed in 1914 by Pennsylvania, and since then all states except Georgia, Louisiana, and Mississippi have adopted it to replace the common law relating to partnerships.

The UPA defines a partnership as "an association of two or more persons to carry on as co-owners a business for profit." The three key elements of any partnership are common ownership interest in a business, sharing the profits and losses of the business, and the right to participate in managing the operations of the partnership. Under the act each partner has the *right* to:

1. share in the management and operation of the business.
2. share in any profits the business might earn from operations.
3. receive interest on additional advances made to the business.
4. be compensated for expenses incurred in the name of the partnership.
5. have access to the business' books and records.
6. receive a formal accounting of the business affairs of the partnership.

The UPA also sets forth the general obligations of the partners. Each partner is obligated to:

1. share in any losses sustained by the business.
2. work for the partnership without salary.
3. submit to majority vote or arbitration differences that may arise in the conduct of the business.
4. give the other partners complete information about all business affairs.
5. give a formal accounting of the business affairs of the partnership.

Beyond what the law prescribes, a partnership is based above all else on mutual trust and respect. Any partnership missing these elements will quickly fail.

Types of Partners

Not all partners are necessarily equal owners of the business. When partners share in the ownership and management of the business, they are *general partners.* All partnerships must have at least one general partner. Each general partner has unlimited personal liability and is expected to take an active role in the management of the business. *Limited partners* have limited financial liability. They can lose only what they have invested in the business. There may be any number of limited partners. They cannot take an active role in the management of the firm. If they do, they will be treated as general partners and will lose their limited liability protection. Among limited partners there are both silent and dormant partners. Silent partners are not active in the operation of the business but are generally known to be members of the partnership. Dormant partners are neither active in the partnership nor generally known to be associated with the business.

Two other terms sometimes are used in discussing limited partnership—secret partners and honorary or nominal partners. However, neither is a limited partner. A secret partner is not known to the public, but does take an active role in the management of the business. Because they do take an active role, secret partners are considered general partners in the eyes of the law. The honorary or nominal partner is not an owner, and does not take an active part in the firms' management, but does lend his name to the business. The honorary partner is generally paid for the publicity or public relations value of his name.

Advantages of the Partnership

Easy to Establish. Like the proprietorship, the partnership is easy and inexpensive to establish. The owners must obtain the necessary business licenses, but beyond that the law requires only a minimal number of forms. In most states, partners must file a Certificate for Conducting Business as Partners if the business is run under a trade name. As was mentioned previously, it is very important, although generally not legally required, to develop a partnership agreement or articles of partnership.

Division of Profits. There are no restrictions on how profits must be distributed as long as they are consistent with the partnership agreement and do not violate the rights of any partner. The partnership agreement can articulate the nature of each partner's contribution and his proportional share of the profits.

Larger Pool of Capital. The partnership form of ownership can significantly broaden the pool of capital available to the business. Each partner's asset base improves the ability of the business to borrow needed funds. Therefore, a double impact occurs: each individual has more to contribute in equity capital, and together their personal assets will support a larger borrowing capacity. We saw in chapter 2 that lack of sufficient capital (undercapitalization) was a major cause of small business failure.

Ability to Attract Limited Partners. There can be any number of limited partners as long as there is at least one general partner. A partnership can attract investors who, with limited liability, still retain the potential of realizing a substantial return on their investment if the business is successful. There are a great many individuals who find it very profitable to invest in high-potential small businesses as limited partners.

Little Governmental Regulation. Like the proprietorship, the partnership form of operation is not burdened with red tape.

Flexibility. Although not as flexible as sole ownership, the partnership can generally react quickly to changing market conditions since no giant organization stifles quick and creative responses to new opportunities.

Taxation. The partnership itself is not subject to federal taxation; its net income is distributed directly to the partners as personal income, and the partners pay income tax on their distributive shares. The partnership, like the proprietorship, avoids the double taxation applicable to the corporate form of ownership.

Disadvantages of Partnerships

Unlimited Liability of at Least One Partner. At least one member of every partnership must be a general partner. The general partner has unlimited personal liability, even though he often is the partner with the least personal resources.

Capital Accumulation. Although the partnership form of ownership is superior to the proprietorship in its ability to attract capital, it is generally not as effective in that respect as the corporate form of ownership.

Difficulty in Disposing of Partnership Interest without Dissolving the Partnership. Most partnership agreements restrict how a partner can dispose of his share of the business. It is common to find that a partner is required to sell his interest to the remaining partners. But even if the original agreement contains such a requirement and clearly delineates how the value of each partner's ownership will be determined, there is no guarantee that the other partner(s) will have the financial resources to buy the seller's interest. When the money is not available to purchase a partner's interest, the other partner(s) may be forced to either accept a new partner to purchase a partner's interest; accept a new partner; or dissolve the partnership, distribute the remaining assets, and begin again. When a partner withdraws from the partnership, the partnership ceases to exist unless there are specific provisions in the partnership agreement for a smooth transition. When a general partner dies, becomes incompetent, or withdraws from the business, the partnership automatically dissolves, although it may not terminate. Even when there are numerous partners, if one wishes to disassociate his name from the business,

the remaining partners will probably form a new partnership.

Lack of Continuity.   If one partner dies, complications arise. Partnership interest is often nontransferable through inheritance because the remaining partner(s) may not wish to be in partnership with the person who inherits the deceased partner's interest. Partners can make provisions in the partnership agreement to avoid dissolution due to death if all parties agree to accept as partners those who inherit the deceased's interest.

Potential for Personality and Authority Conflicts. Friction between people is inevitable and difficult to control. Disagreements over what should be done or what was done have led many a partnership into dis-

---

SMALL BUSINESS REPORT 3–2

Keeping the Peace in Partnerships

Partnerships usually start with the best intentions. Each partner is willing to do his part to make the business a success. Each partner has his perception of what the other partners expect of him and what he expects from them. However, it doesn't take long for friction to begin, so for a lasting partnership it is best for the partners to mutually agree on some important ground rules prior to forming the business.

1. Who will be responsible for which specific activities and decisions?
2. If a disagreement arises, how will it be settled? Often, a person or persons can be designated as an arbitrator.
3. Is the partnership drawing on the best talents of each partner? The most successful partnerships are built on the unique strengths of each participant.
4. Do you know your partners well? Do you know their personal behaviors and can you tolerate and accept the personal quirks of each partner? Working with a partner day in and day out can cause friction. This can become intolerable if the partner has personal behavior which is irritating to others. If this is likely to be a problem, state your concern up front and reach an agreement on the behavior.
5. Will your spouse support you? If married, inform your spouse about the entire arrangement prior to the partnership. Support from a spouse is critical to success. He needs to share the dream of the business as well as recognize your responsibilities to the business.

Put it all into the partnership agreement. Spell it out. Talk it out. Put it down in writing.

solution. Much of the conflict can be avoided by stating clearly in the partnership agreement who has authority in what areas. This can resolve many of the functional problems but not necessarily the overall policy issues (e.g., Should we expand?). Despite this gloomy assessment of potential personality clashes and disputes over authority, many partnerships survive decades without major conflict.

Partners Are Bound by the Law of Agency.   A partner is like a wife or husband in that decisions made by one, in the name of the partnership, bind all. Each partner is an agent for the business and can legally bind the other partners to a business agreement. Because of this agency power, all partners must exercise good faith and reasonable care in the performance of their responsibilities.

Termination and Dissolution of Partnerships

Termination of a partnership is the final act of winding up the business. Dissolution results from a change in the partnership relationship caused by any one general partner ceasing to be associated with the business. Dissolution is not the same as termination of the partnership. Termination occurs after the partners express their intent to cease operations and all affairs of the partnership are concluded. Dissolution is caused by one or more of the following:

1. Expiration of a time period or completion of the project undertaken as delineated in the partnership agreement.
2. Expressed wish of any general partner to cease operation.
3. Expulsion of a partner under the provisions of the agreement.
4. Withdrawal, retirement, or death of a partner (except when the partnership agreement provides for a method of continuation).
5. Bankruptcy of the partnership or any general partner.
6. Admission of a new partner resulting in the dis-

solution of the old partnership and establishment of a new partnership.
7. Any event which makes it unlawful for the partnership to continue operations or for any general partner to participate in the partnership.
8. A judicial decree that a general partner is insane or permanently incapacitated, making performance of responsibility under the partnership agreement impossible.
9. Mounting losses that make it impractical for the business to continue.
10. Impropriety of any general partner, or improper behavior which reflects negatively on the business.

In most states, certain property belonging to a bankrupt proprietor or general partner is exempt from attachment by creditors of the business. The most common exemption is the homestead exemption which allows the debtor's home to be sold to satisfy the debt, but stipulates that a certain dollar amount be reserved to allow the debtor to find other shelter. Some states require that the debtor have a family before the homestead exemption is allowed. Also, state laws normally exempt certain personal property items from attachment by creditors. For example, household furniture (up to a specified amount), clothing and personal possessions, and pensions and bonuses from the government or military are protected and cannot be taken to satisfy an outstanding debt of the business.

III.   CORPORATIONS

The corporation is the most complex of the three major forms of business ownership. It is a separate entity apart from its owners and may engage in business, make contracts, sue and be sued, and pay taxes. The Supreme Court has defined the corporation as "an artificial being, invisible, intangible, and existing only in contemplation of the law." The life of the corporation is independent of the owners' lives. Because the owners, called shareholders, are legally separate from the corporation, they can sell their interests in the business without affecting the continuation of the business.

When a corporation is founded, it accepts the regulations and restrictions placed on it by the state in which it is incorporated and any other state in which it chooses to do business. Generally, the corporation must report its financial operations to the state's attorney general annually. These financial reports become public record. If the stock of the corporation is sold in more than one state, the corporation must comply with federal regulations governing the sale of corporate securities. In addition to these requirements, there are substantially more reporting requirements for a corporation than for the other forms of ownership.

SMALL BUSINESS REPORT 3–3

Keeping the Partnership Together

Partnerships are often compared to marriages—a comparison that contains more than a grain of truth. A partnership requires a great deal of energy and effort to stay afloat, but many partners dissolve their business dealings each year. One attorney says, "splitting up a partnership is just like a divorce without the kids." In many cases, a partnership dissolution can be as emotion-wrenching as a divorce. Stephen Davis, an ex-partner of an environmental consulting firm, learned this the hard way and offers three rules to help partners stay partners.

Share and share alike. Make sure that all partners know of the hard work involved in making a small business work and are prepared to make certain sacrifices for the benefit of the business, especially in the beginning. Clarify beforehand the roles and the expectations of each partner involved. If equitable assignments and responsibilities cannot be agreed upon at this stage, the partnership is doomed. The philosophy that "some of us are more equal than others" does not make for a lasting partnership.

Get it in writing. Once duties, responsibilities, roles, vacations, contributions, etc., have been settled, write them down so that all the partners know exactly what is being agreed upon. This allows for proper planning, record keeping, and protection of the partners.

The next step is to translate these key policy matters into an organized plan to give the business guidance and direction. To be effective, the plan must be flexible and be used in the operation of the business. Plans that are never used are worthless.

Don't lie. Resist the temptation to protect the other partners from any bad news "that would only upset them." News, good and bad, provides useful feedback to company managers who must adjust the business' course to changing environmental conditions.

Partnerships can be extremely effective since each partner's strengths may compensate for the others' weaknesses; but they require attention and effort to make them successful.

Source: Adapted from Stephen Davis, "Why Partnerships Break Up," *Inc.* 3, No. 7, July 1981, pp. 67-70, with permission of publisher.

How to Incorporate

Once the owners decide to form a corporation, they must choose the state in which to incorporate. If the business will operate within a single state, it is probably most logical to incorporate in that state. There are differences in the requirements each state places on the corporations it charters, and how it treats a corporation chartered in another state (called a *foreign* corporation). States differ in the tax rate imposed on corporations, the restrictions placed on their activities, the capital required to incorporate, and the fee or organization tax charged to incorporate. It may not be profitable to incorporate in a state with a low corporate income tax if you must have your annual meeting in that state and have to travel a thousand miles to conduct it. You may find that the state in which you plan to operate does not treat foreign corporations in a favorable fashion. Look at the total cost of doing business before deciding where to incorporate the company.

Every state requires a Certificate of Incorporation or charter which is filed with the state's attorney general. The following information is generally required to be in the Certificate of Incorporation.

The name of the corporation. The corporation must choose a name that is not so similar to that of another firm that it causes confusion or lends itself to deception.

Statement of the purpose of the corporation. In this section, the incorporators must state in general terms the intended nature of the business. The purpose must, of course, be lawful. An illustration might be "to engage in the sale of office furniture and fixtures." The purpose should be broad enough to allow for some expansion in the activities of the business as it develops.

Time horizon of the corporation. In most cases, corporations are formed with no specific termination date; they are formed for "perpetuity." However, it is possible to incorporate for a specific duration.

Names and addresses of the incorporators. The incorporators must be identified in the articles of incorporation and are liable under the law to attest that all information in the articles of incorporation is factual and correct. In some states, one or more of the incorporators must reside in the state in which the corporation is being incorporated.

Place of business. The post office address of the principal office of the corporation must be listed. This is the address to which all official correspondence will be sent. This address, for a domestic corporation, must be in the state in which incorporation takes place.

Capital stock authorization. The articles of incorporation must include the amount and class (or type) of capital stock the corporation wishes authorization to issue. This is not the amount of stock that the corporation *must* issue. They may issue any amount not in excess of that authorized. This section also must define the different classifications of stock and any special rights, preferences, or limits each class might have.

Capital required at the time of incorporation. It should be determined whether the state in which you are incorporating requires that a specific percentage of the par value of the capital stock be paid in cash and deposited in a bank prior to incorporation.

Provisions for preemptive rights, if any, that are granted to stockholders.

Restrictions on transferring shares. Many closely held corporations—those owned by a small number of persons, often family members—might require shareholders to offer their stock to the corporation first. This is often called "a right of first refusal" and allows the corporation better control of its ownership.

Names and addresses of the persons who will serve as the *initial officers and directors* of the corporation.

The bylaws under which the corporation will operate. Bylaws are the rules and regulations established by the corporation for its internal management and operations.

Once the attorney general of the state in which

you have chosen to incorporate has approved your request for incorporation and the corporation pays its fees, the approved articles of incorporation become its charter. With the charter in hand, the next order of business is to hold an organizational meeting for the stockholders to formally elect directors who, in turn, will appoint the corporate officers.

Advantages of Corporations

Limited Liability of the Stockholders. The corporation allows investors to limit their liability to the total amount of their investment. This legal protection of personal assets beyond the business is of critical concern to many potential investors. The separate legal status of the corporation creates the limited liability protection. Creditors of the corporation cannot attach stockholders' personal assets to satisfy business debts.

Ability to Attract Capital. Based on the protection of limited liability, corporations have proved to be the most effective form of ownership in accumulating large amounts of capital. Limited only by the number of shares authorized in its charter (which can be amended), the corporation can raise money to begin business and expand as opportunity dictates.

Ability of the Corporation to Have "Perpetual Life." Unless limited in its charter, the corporation as a separate legal entity theoretically can continue indefinitely. The existence of the corporation does not depend on the fate of any single individual. Unlike a proprietorship or partnership, where death of a founder ends the business, the corporation lives beyond the lives of those who gave it life. This feature of "perpetual life" gives rise to the next major advantage—transferable ownership.

Transferable Ownership. If an owner of stock in a corporation is displeased with the progress of the business, he can sell his shares to another individual. Stocks can be transferred through inheritance to a new generation of owners. This feature has allowed a large percentage of our population to be part owners of businesses. Either directly, or indirectly through pension funds and other investments, individuals have learned to take part in the capitalistic system. Millions of shares of stock are traded daily. If any person wishes to own some shares in a firm, and there is someone who would like to sell his interest in that firm, an exchange is possible. During all this change of ownership, business continues.

Larger Pool of Skills, Expertise, and Knowledge. Unlike the proprietor who is often the only active member of management, the corporation can draw on the skills, expertise, and knowledge of its officers and board of directors. Even small corporations can attract persons to their boards of directors whose knowledge and experience can be used to shape the direction of the firm. In many cases, the board members act as advisors, giving the stockholders the advantage of years of experience applied to the problems of the business.

Disadvantages of Corporations

Cost and Time Involved in the Incorporation Process. There is no such thing as the "instant" creation of a corporation. Corporations are costly to establish. The owners are giving birth to an artificial legal entity—and the gestation period can be prolonged. In most states, an attorney must handle an incorporation. There are a variety of fees associated with incorporation that are not applicable to proprietorships or partnerships.

Taxation. Because the corporation is a separate legal entity, the income of the corporation is taxed by the federal government, by most state governments, and by some local governments. Before the owners receive a penny of the income as dividends, the corporation must pay these taxes. Then, corporate stockholders must pay taxes on the dividend share they receive from these same profits. This "double taxation" is a distinct disadvantage of the corporate form of ownership. Many governmental units have been quicker to tax "the big corporations" than individuals because they assume that these taxes will likely find their way back into the prices we pay for the goods and services produced.

Potential for Diminished Managerial Incentives. When the original founders realize that they are not receiving all of the rewards from their entrepreneurship, some become resentful of the other stockholders. They will feel that those who invested "only" money have gotten a free ride on the founders' labor and ingenuity. The incentive to make the business all it can become is often lost. Although this is not necessarily logical, it does happen. When the business becomes adequately financed, the difficulties faced before the infusion of capital often are forgotten. Each of us sees our own contribution as primary in the success of the business.

Legal Restrictions and Regulatory Red Tape. Corporations are required to file what seems to be an endless stream of reports with government agencies. These burdensome reports produce no profit and become a source of irritation to the small business manager.

Potential Loss of Control by the Founder(s) of the Corporation. When you sell stock in the corporation, you relinquish some control. If your business needs a great amount of capital, you may need to relinquish a very significant amount of control. It is common in these situations for the founder not to be the majority stockholder. When large blocks of stock are sold to outside interests to raise necessary capital, the founder should understand that his ownership in the company will be diluted. He surrenders the right to select the board of directors and officers and to set the policies of the business unilaterally.

IV. "HYBRID" FORMS OF OWNERSHIP

Limited Partnership

A limited partnership, which is a modification of a general partnership, comprises at least one general partner and at least one limited partner. In a limited partnership the general partner is treated, under the law, exactly as he would be treated in a general partnership. The limited partner(s) is treated more as an investor in the business venture; limited partners have limited liability. That is, they are liable only to the extent of their investment. The limited partnership lies somewhere between a general partnership and a corporation.

Most states have ratified the Revised Limited Partnership Act. The formation of a limited partnership requires its founder to file a Certificate of Limited Partnership with the proper state office in which the limited partnership plans to conduct business. The Certificate of Limited Partnership should include the following information:

1. The name of the limited partnership.
2. The general character of its business.
3. The address of the office of the firm's agent authorized to receive summonses or other legal notices.
4. The name and business address of each partner, specifying which ones are general partners and which are limited partners.
5. The amount of cash contributions actually made, and agreed to be made in the future, by each partner.
6. A description and statement of value of noncash contributions made or to be made by each partner.
7. The times at which additional contributions are to be made by any of the partners.
8. Whether and under what conditions a limited partner has the right to grant limited partner status to an assignee of his or her interest in the partnership.
9. If agreed upon, the time or the circumstances when a partner may withdraw from the firm.
10. If agreed upon, the amount of, or the method for determining, the funds to be received by a withdrawing partner.
11. Any right of a partner to receive distributions of cash or other property from the firm, and the times and circumstances for such distributions.

12. The time or circumstances when the limited partnership is to be dissolved.
13. The rights of the remaining general partners to continue the business after withdrawal of a general partner.
14. Any other matters the partners wish to include.

The general partner has basically the same rights and duties as he would under a general partnership. He has the right to make decisions for the business, to act as an agent for the partnership, to use the property of the partnership for normal business, and to share in the profits of the business. The limited partner does not have the right to manage the business in any way. He has the right to inspect the business and make a copy of business records. The limited partner is, of course, entitled to a share of the business profits as agreed upon and specified in the Certificate of Limited Partnership.

S Corporation

In 1954, the Internal Revenue Service Code created the Subchapter S Corporation. In recent years, the IRS has changed the title to S Corporation along with a few modifications in its qualifications. An S Corporation is only a distinction which is made for federal income tax purposes. The S Corporation is, in terms of legal characteristics, no different from any other corporation. An S Corporation must meet the following criteria.

1. It must be a domestic corporation.
2. It cannot have a nonresident alien as a shareholder.
3. It can issue only one class of stock, although voting and nonvoting common stock can be issued.
4. It must limit its shareholders to individuals, estates, and certain trusts.
5. It cannot have more than 35 shareholders.

If a corporation satisfies the definition for an S Corporation, the owners must actually elect to be treated as one. The election is made by filing IRS Form 2553, and *all* shareholders must consent to have the corporation treated as an S Corporation. To be treated as an S Corporation, the election must be filed in the previous year.

The Advantages of an S Corporation. The S Corporation retains all of the advantages of a regular corporation, such as continuity of existence, transferability of ownership, and limited liability. The most notable provision of the S Corporation is that it avoids the corporate income tax and enables the business to pass through operating profits or losses to the shareholders. In effect, the tax status of an S Corporation is dramatically similar to that of a proprietorship or partnership. The S Corporation is the IRS' attempt to achieve a measure of tax neutrality among small business corporations, proprietorships, and partnerships.

Joint Ventures

A joint venture is very much like a partnership, except that it is formed for a specific, limited purpose. To illustrate how this form of ownership can be used, let's assume you have a 500-acre tract of land 60 miles from Chicago. This land has been cleared and is normally used in agricultural production. You have a friend who has solid contacts among major musical groups and would like to put on a concert. You expect prices for your agricultural products to be low this summer, so you and your friend form a joint venture for the specific purpose of staging a three-day concert. Your contribution will be the exclusive use of the land for one month, while your friend will provide all the performers as well as technicians, facilities, and equipment. All costs will be paid out of receipts and the net profits will be split, with you receiving 20 percent for the use of your land. When the concert is over, the facilities removed, and the accounting for all costs completed, the profits will be split 20-80 and the joint venture is terminated.

In any endeavor where neither party can effectively achieve the purpose alone, but together they can, a joint venture becomes a common form of ownership. A new joint venture is established each time a new project is undertaken. The income derived from a joint venture is taxed as if it arose from a partnership.

V. SUMMARY

Each form of business ownership has its specific advantages and disadvantages, as outlined in table 3–1. Every partnership should draw up a partnership agreement prior to beginning business. Review the items suggested in the chapter that should be included in a partnership agreement. Further, become familiar with the rights and obligations of partners as specified in the Uniform Partnership Act.

Corporations all require a Certificate of Incorporation or charter. Become familiar with the items that must be included in filing for incorporation.

Review the special forms of ownership—the joint venture and limited partnership and S Corporation—to determine if your situation would lend itself to consideration of each.

Before you make any choice regarding the form of ownership best suited to your business, consult an attorney and accountant.

TABLE 3–1   Advantages and disadvantages of forms of business ownership.

Proprietorship	Partnership	Corporation
ADVANTAGES		
1. Simplicity in creation	1. Ease of establishment	1. Limited liability of stockholders
2. Low cost to establish	2. Division of profits based on partnership agreement	2. Ability to attract larger amounts of capital
3. Owner receives all profits	3. Larger pool of capital than proprietorship	3. Ability to have "perpetual life"
4. Owner retains all decision-making authority	4. Larger pool of talent	4. Ease of transfer of ownership
5. No special legal restrictions	5. Ability to attract limited partners	5. Larger pool of skill, talent, and knowledge
	6. Little governmental regulation	6. Potential for economies of scale in operations
	7. Flexibility	
	8. Business income taxed as individual income	
DISADVANTAGES		
1. Unlimited personal liability	1. Unlimited liability of general partners	1. Cost and time involved in incorporation process
2. Limited skills and capabilities	2. Limited capability for capital accumulation	2. Subject to corporate taxes
3. Limited access to capital	3. Difficulty in disposing of partnership interest without dissolving partnership	3. Potential for diminished managerial incentives
4. Lack of continuity of the business	4. Lack of continuity	4. Legal restrictions and regulatory red tape
	5. Potential for personal and authority conflicts	5. Potential loss of control by founder(s) of corporation
	6. Partners are bound by law of agency	

STUDENT INVOLVEMENT PROJECTS

1. Call or visit the office of an investment firm and ask for a copy of a limited partnership agreement. Study the major terms of the agreement and determine the specific duties and responsibilities of the general partners and the rights of the limited partners. Report your findings to the class.
2. Write the attorney general of your state and ask for a copy of the forms for incorporation. Also, write the Internal Revenue Service and ask for a copy of the forms corporations must typically file. Read through these forms and develop a brief explanation of how a potential new small business owner can fill out and file such forms.

DISCUSSION QUESTIONS

1. Why are sole proprietorships so popular in our economy?
2. How does personal conflict affect partnerships? How can co-owners avoid becoming sparring partners?
3. What issues should the Articles of Partnership address? Why are the articles important to a successful partnership?
4. Can one partner commit another to a business deal without the other's consent? Why or why not?
5. Without a partnership agreement, how are profits and assets distributed in a dispute?
6. Can there be such a thing as a limited secret partner? Why or why not?
7. What issues should the Certificate of Incorporation cover?
8. How does an S Corporation differ from a regular corporation?
9. How does a joint venture differ from a partnership?
10. Briefly outline the advantages and the disadvantages of the major forms of ownership.

Franchises: Are They Right for You?

4

Make preparation in advance. You never have trouble if you are prepared for it.

Theodore Roosevelt

The man walking down the street holding a cat by the tail is getting forty times the experience in cat-carrying as the man watching him.

Mark Twain

Upon completion of this chapter, you will be able to:

- Demonstrate the importance of franchising in the U.S. economy.
- Define the concept of franchising and show how it operates.
- Describe the benefits and limitations of franchising for both the franchisor and the franchisee.
- Illustrate clues helpful in detecting dishonest franchisors.
- Use a checklist to assist you in evaluating franchise agreements.
- Understand the provisions of the FTC's Trade Regulation Rule.
- Describe the franchise contract and some of its usual provisions.
- Understand the trends in franchising and forecast the future of franchising.

Franchising is one of the growth fields of the decade. Much of its popularity arises from its ability to offer those who lack business experience the chance to own and operate a business with a high probability of success. Franchising's growth in recent years truly has been phenomenal, carrying the concept far beyond the traditional auto dealerships and fast-food outlets. Through franchised businesses, consumers can buy nearly every good or service imaginable— from singing telegrams and suntans to maid service and real estate. Over 2,000 franchisors operate about 481,234 franchise outlets throughout the world, and the growth rate still remains above that for the economy as a whole. A McDonald's restaurant opens every 17 hours, a Diet Center franchise every other day, and a Software City store every 10 days.[1] Franchises account for 34 percent of all retail sales, totaling $529.3 billion (see figure 4–1)! This represents a 58 percent increase in sales since the beginning of the decade. By the year 2000, franchise sales will account for 50 percent of total retail sales.[2] Franchises

---

[1] Meg Whittenmore and Carol Steinberg, "Venture's Guide to Franchising," *Venture,* July 1985, p. 75.

[2] "Sixth Annual Franchise 500," *Entrepreneur,* January 1985, p. 82.

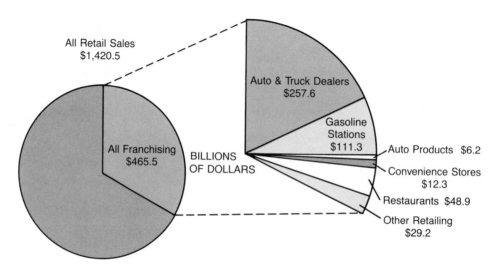

FIGURE 4–1 Franchising encompasses 33% of retail sales.

Source: U.S. Department of Commerce, *Franchising in the Economy,* Washington, D.C., 1986, p. 11.

also employ more than 5.5 million people.[3] This chapter will examine franchising and its benefits and disadvantages for a potential business owner.

I. WHAT IS FRANCHISING?

The concept of franchising can be traced to Civil War times when the Singer Sewing Machine Company began franchising retail outlets to sell its products. From this meager beginning as a distribution system, franchising has become a substantial force in the U.S. economy. James Threthewey, president of the International Franchise Association (IFA), says, "Franchising has become more than simply a way of doing business. It has become a way of life."[4]

Early in this century, franchises were confined primarily to automobile dealerships, gasoline stations, and soft drink bottlers. Although these three businesses continue to make up the largest volume of franchises with over 73 percent of all franchising

sales dollars, franchises have expanded into a broad range of retail and service businesses. Retail outlets dominate franchising, totalling 87 percent of all franchise sales. However, increasing demand for consumer and business services is producing a boom among service-oriented franchises.[5]

In franchising, a company (the franchisor) grants others (the franchisees) the right and license (the franchise) to sell a product or service and possibly to use the business system developed by the company. The International Franchise Association defines franchising as "a continuing relationship in which the franchisor provides a licensed privilege to do business, plus assistance in organizing, training, merchandising, and management in return for a consideration from the franchisee."[6] In essence, franchising is a method of doing business based on a continuing relationship between the franchisor and the franchisee. It involves a system of distribution in which a series of individually owned businesses op-

---

[3]*Franchising in the Economy 1983–1985,* U.S. Department of Commerce, Washington, D.C., 1985, p. 1.

[4]Whittenmore and Steinberg, op. cit p. 75.

[5]*Franchising in the Economy 1983–1985,* p. 14.

[6]*Franchise Opportunities Handbook,* U.S. Department of Commerce, Washington, D.C., 1984, p. xxvii.

erate as if part of a large "chain." Often the franchisee is granted an exclusive right or license to distribute the franchisor's goods or services in a specific geographic region. But the franchisor normally directs the distribution methods used and establishes standards of performance and quality that the franchisee must meet. As a result, the franchisor maintains substantial control over the business.

Franchising works like this: Mortimer develops an idea for a new computerized personnel selection system aimed at the banking industry. Lacking sufficient capital to expand the business himself, Mortimer licenses the idea and a comprehensive business package, including a brand name, to other entrepreneurs who in turn use their own capital to expand the business. Mortimer charges an initial franchise fee for licensing the brand name and the business package. He then collects a continuing fee based on a percentage of sales as a "royalty" and frequently imposes an additional fee to support a national advertising campaign. Mortimer achieves the desired expansion of his business, and the entrepreneurs have an opportunity to own and operate their own businesses for a specified investment, usually with a high probability of success.

II. TYPES OF FRANCHISING

There are three basic types of franchising: tradename franchising, product distribution franchising, and pure franchising. *Tradename franchising* involves a brand name such as True Value Hardware or Western Auto. Here, the franchisee purchases the right to become identified with the franchisor's trade name without distributing particular products exclusively under the manufacturer's name. *Product distribution* franchising involves licensing the franchisee to sell specific products under the manufacturer's brand name and trademark through a selective, limited distribution network. This system is commonly used to

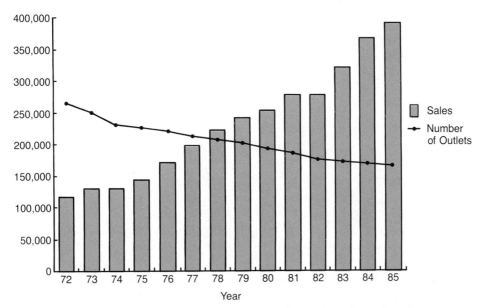

FIGURE 4–2 Product and tradename franchising, sales and number of outlets.

Source: U.S. Department of Commerce, *Franchising in the Economy,* Washington, D.C., 1986, p. 3.

A Different Song and Dance

What do Ronald Reagan, Burt Reynolds, Charlton Heston, and the Bee Gee's have in common? For one thing, each has been the recipient of an Eastern Onion singing telegram. Founded in 1976 with $700 by Mary Flatt, Eastern Onion is the nation's largest and fastest growing singing telegram service.

Although "big business" tends to dominate franchising, small businesses like Eastern Onion are discovering that franchises are a relatively fast, efficient method of expansion. Eastern Onion began franchising in 1978 and since then has sold about 40 franchises across the country at prices ranging from $15,000 to $50,000, depending on location. Future plans call for more franchises to be added to the chain. The franchise package includes a complete business system—songs, costumes, acts, accounting methods, advertising plans, and talent-scouting advice.

More than 400 messengers deliver telegrams selected from over 100 different tunes with original lyrics to celebrate any occasion—or no occasion at all. Since 1976, Eastern Onion has sent over 750,000 singing telegrams. Each delivery begins with the messenger blowing a special whistle imported from England and starting a battery-powered monkey who bangs cymbals together. Eastern Onion messengers themselves are unique—over 45 costumed characters ranging from belly dancers to Fairy Onions to French maids designed to offer vibrant messages to unsuspecting recipients.

The cost of an Eastern Onion telegram ranges from $25 for a traditional tuxedoed messenger to $150 for a three-member harem. As a remembrance of the occasion, the firm also offers special keepsake gifts.

Eastern Onion advertises its singing telegram as "a gift, an expression of love, a tongue-in-cheek salute to some special occasion." As Ms. Flatt says of her prospering business, "The premise of Eastern Onion is simple. We turn a memorable occasion into something even more memorable, with a song and messenger for any situation you can think of. Eastern Onion telegrams are not just songs—they're live entertainment acts, and it's obvious that people love to send them."

---

market automobiles (Chevrolet, Oldsmobile, Chrysler), gasoline products (Exxon, Sunoco, Texaco), soft drinks (Pepsi Cola, Coca-Cola), bicycles (Schwinn), appliances, cosmetics, and other products.

These two distribution systems allow franchisees to acquire some of the parent company's identity. Franchisees concentrate on the franchisors product line, although not necessarily exclusively. Since 1972, the number of product and tradename franchises has declined rapidly due to intense competition and general economic conditions. But, sales of these two franchising systems have climbed steadily since 1972 (see figure 4–2).

The third type of franchising, called *pure* (or *comprehensive* or *business format* franchising), involves providing the franchisee with a complete business format, including a license for a tradename, the products or services to be sold, the physical plant, the methods of operation, a marketing strategy plan, a quality control process, a two-way communications system, and the necessary business services. The franchisee purchases the right to use all the elements of a fully integrated business operation. Pure franchising is growing most rapidly of all types of franchising and is common among fast food restaurants, lodging establishments, business service firms, car rental agencies, educational institutions, beauty

Eastern Onion's French Maid and Fairy Onion. (Photo courtesy of Eastern Onion Singing Telegrams.)

Source: Adapted from the Eastern Onion Franchise Prospectus.

aid retailers, and other promising growth industries. Figure 4–3 shows that both the number and sales volume of pure franchisees have increased continuously since 1972. Typically, large franchisors have dominated business format franchising. Figure 4–4 shows the relative proportion of product/tradename and pure francising sales since 1972.

III. THE BENEFITS AND DRAWBACKS OF FRANCHISING

The 1980s have been described as "the golden age of the merger." Because of this trend toward consolidation it is likely that in the future there will be fewer businesses, but they will be larger. Some experts see franchising as the last hope for independent firms in an age of vertical integration. By providing improved chances of survival and a recognized name and product, franchising enables small businesses to compete with industry leviathans.

Franchising's popularity stems from several underlying trends. The rekindling of the entrepreneurial "spirit" in America is encouraging more individuals to launch businesses, and for many, franchising is the ideal path. Says Earle Swensen, founder of Swensen's Ice Cream Company, "There has always been a strong desire on the part of [the individual] to realize that great American Dream of owning his

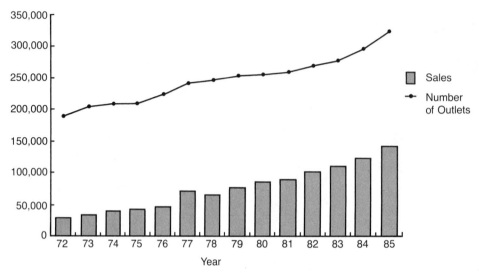

FIGURE 4–3   Pure franchising, sales and number of outlets.

Source: U.S. Department of Commerce, *Franchising in the Economy,* Washington, D.C., 1986, p. 4.

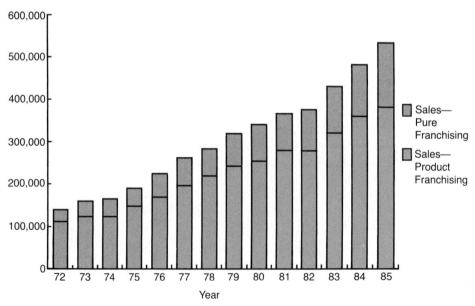

FIGURE 4–4   Franchising sales, pure versus product franchising.

Source: U.S. Department of Commerce, *Franchising in the Economy,* Washington, D.C., 1986, p. 3–4.

Getting It Right the First Time

SMALL
BUSINESS
REPORT
4–2

To launch a franchise successfully, entrepreneurs are learning that they must develop an efficient, smooth-running prototype. By getting the system into place and working the bugs out early, potential franchisors find it much easier to raise the capital to finance growth and to sell the business to franchisees. But, building a successful prototype business is not easy. It may take years and millions of dollars to make mistakes, learn from them, and build a better system. Advises one national franchisor, "I would counsel anyone who wants to go into franchising to devote a great deal of time and effort to making absolutely sure the prototype is as efficient as possible before launching into franchised sales."

James Edgette and Steven Heller spent three years and $1.6 million designing and redesigning a model for their retail computer business, Entre Computers. Edgette says, "A prototype will enable you to do a tremendously refined job of opening a center." In addition to boosting sales and paving the way for financing, a prototype also can serve as a model and a training ground for franchisees. Edgette claims, "A prototype should be something that proves the system works."

But, Heller and Edgette learned that a standardized operation won't always work. Says Edgette, "We learned that you can't cookie-cutter the sales process in our industry; it must be tailored for the individual center. Selling a (computer) system to a farmer in Iowa is different from selling to a government consulting firm in suburban Washington." The hard work the two put into developing their prototype of Entre Computers paid off. Just one year after beginning franchise sales, Entre had sold over 200 outlets and was selling new franchises at a rate of 10 per month. Today, it remains one of the fastest growing computer franchises in the country.

Entre has discovered the benefits of doing something right the first time.

Source: Adapted from Kevin Farrell, "Franchise Prototypes," *Venture,* January 1984, pp. 38–43 with permission of the publisher.

---

own business and being a success in his own right. I think franchising has made that possible for a great number of people."[7]

Demographic factors and shifting lifestyles, such as the rise of the "baby boomers" and the proliferation of the dual career couple, have put a premium on convenience and service—two of franchising's specialties. For example, Capt. Crab's Take-Away, a fast seafood service franchise in Miami, is building its system on these trends. According to Jeffry Prince, director of the National Restaurant Association, Capt. Crab's and other restaurant chains are aiming at diners who "were weaned on fast foods,"

but who now are "more sophisticated and want better, fresher food in a nicer atmosphere."[8]

Perhaps the most important reason franchising has been so successful is the mutual benefits it offers franchisors and franchisees. In a franchising relationship each party depends on the other for support, so what benefits one benefits the other. As Earle Swensen of Swensen's Ice Cream Company emphasizes, " . . . we are seeking to ensure . . . (the) franchisee's success. After all, his success is our success, too."[9]

---

[7] J. A. Dunnigan, "Two Veterans Discuss the Evolution of Franchising," *Entrepreneur,* January 1985, p. 48.

[8] Lee Kravitz, "Fast Food's Fast Movers," *Venture,* November 1984, p. 43.
[9] Dunnigan, op. cit. p. 52.

Benefits for the Franchisor

For the franchisor, franchising offers a relatively quick way to expand a distribution system with minimum capital. The franchisor sells the rights to her goods or service and the accompanying business system to prospective entrepreneurs, who provide the majority of the capital for expansion. Thus, franchising is still viewed as one of the best ways to enlarge a business within the constraints of a limited supply of investment funds.

Another attraction of franchising for the franchisor is the ability to grow without the cost and inconvenience of locating and developing key managers. Of course, the franchisor must screen out those potential entrepreneurs who are unqualified, but the task generally is much simpler than the personnel functions involved in internal expansion. For example, the chairman of a newly developed franchise operation selling computer software, The Program Store, states: "Franchising is the best way to find entrepreneurs who are willing to run stores while we concentrate on organization and expansion."[10]

Franchisors also receive income from franchises through franchise fees and ongoing royalties. For example, in only its second year of operation, Entre Computers collected not only a $30,000 franchise fee from each store it licensed, but also 8 percent of each store's sales for a whopping $3.8 million total![11]

Through franchising, a franchisor gains the opportunity to grab a share of a regional or national market relatively quickly without having to invest huge amounts of her own money, and gets paid while she does it.

Benefits for the Franchisee

A franchising arrangement offers the franchisee a host of benefits. Generally, a franchisee gets the opportunity to own a small business relatively quickly. And, because of the identification with an established product and brand name, the franchise often reaches the break-even point faster than if a traditional form of ownership had been chosen. Franchisees also benefit from the franchisor's business experience. Many entrepreneurs go into business by themselves and make many costly mistakes because they lack experience. Since the margin for error is small in a new business venture, the owner cannot afford to make many mistakes. In a franchising arrangement, the franchisor already has worked out the kinks in the system by trial-and-error. Mike Bloom, founder of Orange Julius of America, says:

> . . . when an individual buys a franchise, he is buying a proven trademark, an established reputation, and customer recognition, all in one. He's buying the expertise of that particular franchisor, and . . . all the mistakes that someone *could* make in that business have been made long before that franchisee even buys his franchise. He can thereby avoid all those pitfalls simply by following the franchisor's instructions.[12]

With this in mind, let us investigate the specific advantages of franchising to the franchisee.

The Advantages of Franchising. Before jumping at a franchise opportunity, the entrepreneur should consider carefully the question "What can a franchise do for me that I cannot do for myself?" The answer to the question will depend on the particular situation, and is not as important as the systematic evaluation of the franchise opportunity. After careful deliberation, the franchisee may conclude that the franchise offers nothing that could not be done independently; on the other hand, it may turn out that the franchise is the key to success as an entrepreneur. Some advantages franchising might offer are discussed next.

Management Training and Counseling. In chapter 2, we saw that over 90 percent of all business failures

---

[10]Kevin Farrell, "Franchising Hits a Snag," *Venture,* February 1982, p. 69.

[11]Kevin Farrell, "Franchise Prototypes," *Venture,* January 1984, p. 43.

[12]Dunnigan, op. cit. pp. 52–53.

are caused by incompetent management. Franchisors are well aware of this, and, in an attempt to reduce the number of franchise casualties, may offer managerial training programs to franchisees prior to opening a new outlet. Many franchisors, especially the well-established ones, also provide follow-up training and counseling services. This service is vital, especially since most franchisors do not require a franchisee to have experience in the business.

Training programs vary in degree of formality and comprehensiveness. Some franchisors rely almost exclusively on manuals and booklets with very little personal interaction or instruction. Other franchisors provide extensive programs at a company location using classroom training, discussion groups, simulations, and other techniques to familiarize the franchisee with the basic operation of the business. Before beginning operations, McDonald's franchisees spend 14 days in Illinois at Hamburger University where they learn everything from how to scrape the grill correctly to how to handle the accounting system. Burger King sponsors Burger King University, which offers franchisees classroom and in-restaurant training. H & R Block trains its franchisees to unravel the mysteries of tax preparation, while Dunkin Donuts trains a franchisee for as long as five weeks in everything from accounting to dough making.

The range of topics covered in training programs is quite varied. Standard subjects include store layout and design; equipment purchasing and operation; insurance needs; inventory control; advertising techniques; accounting methods; employee selection and training; and store management. For example, Earle Swensen says that his ice cream franchise offers "training schools which train everyone how to make ice cream, how to prepare food, how to clean the equipment, and even how to keep required company records."[13]

To ensure a franchisee's success, some franchisors supplement the start-up training with continuous guidance and instruction. Some programs feature "refresher" courses, manuals and audio-visual aids, and traveling consultants. For example, Kentucky Fried Chicken provides continuing assistance to franchisees in customer service, general restaurant management, quality control, and employee training. Franchisors offer these training programs because they realize that their ultimate success depends on the franchisee's success.

Despite the positive features of training, inherent dangers exist in the trainer/trainee relationship. Every would-be franchisee should be aware that, in some cases, the assistance of the franchisor tends to drift into control over the franchisee's business. Also, some franchisors charge fees for their training services so the franchisee should know *exactly* what he is agreeing to, and what it costs.

Brand Name Appeal. A licensed franchisee purchases the right to use a nationally known and advertised brand name for a product or service. Thus, the franchisee has the advantage of identifying his business with a widely recognized name, and this usually provides a great deal of drawing power. Customers recognize the identifying trademark, the standard symbols, the store design, and the products of an established franchise. For example, nearly everyone is familiar with the golden arches of McDonald's or the orange roof of Howard Johnson's and the standard products and quality offered at each. A customer is confident that the quality and content of a meal at McDonald's in Fort Lauderdale will be consistent with a meal at a San Francisco McDonald's. As a McDonald's affiliate, a franchisee buys a "total package" that customers instantly recognize. Says a McDonald's spokesman, "You get the golden arches behind you."[14]

Standardized Quality of Goods/Services. A franchisee purchases a license to sell the franchisor's product or service and the privilege of using the associated brand name. So, the quality of the goods or

[13]Ibid. p. 52.

[14]Whittenmore and Steinberg, op. cit. p. 75.

service sold by the franchisee determines the franchisor's reputation. Building a sound reputation in business is not achieved quickly, but destroying a good reputation takes no time at all. If some franchisees were allowed to operate at substandard levels, the image of the entire chain would suffer irreparable damage. So, franchisors are normally very stringent in demanding compliance with uniform standards of quality and service throughout the entire chain. In many cases, the franchisor conducts periodic inspections of local facilities to assist in maintaining acceptable levels of performance. Maintaining quality is so important that most franchisors retain the right to terminate the franchise contract and to repurchase the outlet if the franchisee fails to comply with established standards. The individual franchisee's business is enhanced by the franchisor's focus on assuring consistent, quality establishments. Also, franchisees benefit from ongoing product research and development that the franchisor conducts to develop new and better products and methods.

National Advertising Programs. An effective advertising program is essential to the success of virtually all franchise operations. Marketing a brand name product or service over a wide geographic area requires a far-reaching advertising campaign. A regional or national advertising program benefits all franchisees.

Normally, such an advertising campaign is organized and controlled by the franchisor. It is financed by each franchisee's contribution of a percentage of monthly sales, usually in the range of 1 to 5 percent, or a flat monthly fee. For example, Wendy's International, Inc., the cook-to-order hamburger chain, requires that a franchise owner contribute at least 1 percent of gross sales to Wendy's national advertising program. Kentucky Fried Chicken franchisees must pay 1.5 percent of gross revenues to the KFC national advertising program. Funds from franchisee contributions are pooled and used for a "cooperative" advertising program, which offers the entire franchise synergistic benefits.

In addition to contributing to a national advertising fund, many franchisors require franchisees to spend a minimum amount on local advertising. To supplement their national advertising efforts, both Wendy's and Burger King require franchisees to spend at least 3 percent of gross sales for local advertising. Some franchisors assist each franchisee in designing and producing its local ads. Many companies help franchisees create promotional plans and provide press releases and advertisements for grand openings. By requiring franchisee contributions for national and local advertising campaigns, franchisors ensure adequate public exposure of the product or service and the associated brand name.

Financial Assistance. One of the primary advantages some franchise packages offer is a capital requirement lower than would be required to start a similar independent business. As a result, most franchisors do not provide any extensive financial help for their franchisees. Usually, they do not make loans to enable the franchisee to pay the initial franchise fee. To do so would conflict with the basic premise of franchising: franchisors employ their franchisees' resources and capital to expand their businesses.

However, once a franchisor locates a suitable prospective franchisee, he may offer the qualified candidate limited financial assistance in specific areas. In fact, nearly half of the International Franchise Association's members indicate that they offer some type of financial assistance to potential franchisees. Some franchisors may finance a portion of the capital required to purchase equipment or inventory. For example, International Dairy Queen offers qualified franchisees financing for restaurant equipment for up to five years. A few franchisors offer qualified franchisees financing for a portion of the initial capital requirement, including the franchise fee. For example, Dunhill Personnel Systems will finance the initial $15,000 franchise fee over four years.

In most instances, financial assistance takes some form other than direct loans, leases, or short-term credit. Franchisors usually are willing to assist the qualified franchisee in establishing relationships with banks, private investors, and other sources of funds. They are willing to offer guidance and advice in obtaining financing from lending institutions. Their managerial support may enhance the franchisee's credit standing since lenders recognize the lower incidence of failure among franchisees. The nature of the financial assistance franchisors provide varies tremendously, and the franchisee must investigate and completely understand the help, if any, to be received. Some franchisors offer no financial assistance; many will help the franchisee prepare a loan package to present to lending institutions; others will make sales of inventory and equipment on credit, while still others may co-sign notes or make direct loans to qualified candidates to meet capital requirements. Generally, the larger and more established franchisors are less likely to offer direct financial assistance to franchisees than are smaller, upstart franchisors.

Proven Products and Business Formats. A franchise owner does not have to "build the business from scratch." Instead of being forced to rely solely on personal ability to establish a business and attract a clientele, the franchisee can depend on the methods and techniques of an established business. These standardized procedures and operations greatly enhance the franchisee's chances of success and avoid the most inefficient type of learning—trial and error.

The franchisor also offers a proven product or service that is widely known and accepted. A franchisee does not have to struggle for recognition in the local marketplace as much as an independent owner might. Wayne Boggs, who converted his 35-year-old independent security and protection shop into a Security Alliance franchise, learned these benefits firsthand. He became interested in the franchising concept when he noticed that "we weren't growing as fast as the market was expanding." With the franchisor's help in recruiting and training an effective sales force and in establishing a standardized sys-

tem, Bogg's sales surged 20 percent. For him, franchising proved to be a key factor in the expansion and survival of his business venture.

Centralized Buying Power. A significant advantage a franchisee has over the independent small business owner is participation in the franchisor's centralized buying power. Because the franchisors purchase standardized items in large volume, franchisees are able to take advantage of economies of scale and buy materials and equipment at lower prices. In many cases, the franchisor passes on the cost savings from quantity discounts to the franchisee. For example, it is unlikely that a small, independent ice cream parlor could match the buying power of Baskin-Robbins with its 3,000 retail ice cream stores. In many instances, economies of scale simply preclude the independent owner from competing head-to-head with a franchise operation.

Territorial Protection. A proper location is critical to the success of any small business, and franchises are no exception. In fact, franchise experts consider the three most important factors in franchising to be *location, location, and location.* Many franchisors will make an extensive location analysis for each new outlet, including studies of traffic patterns, zoning ordinances, accessibility, and population density, to help the franchise find the most suitable site.

Location is probably the biggest obstacle facing the entire franchising industry today. Most of the traditional, high volume locations are already taken, a fact that will slow the franchising growth rate in the future. To get prime locations, some franchises have bought and converted existing franchise outlets.

In addition to assisting in site selection, franchisors may offer a franchisee territorial protection, which gives the franchisee the right to exclusive distribution of brand name goods or services within a particular geographic area. The size of a franchisee's territory varies from industry to industry. For example, Hardee's, a fast food restaurant, agrees not to license another Hardee's franchisee within a mile and a half of existing locations. But, one soft serve ice cream franchisor defines its franchisees' territories on the basis of ZIP code designations. The purpose of such protection is to prevent an invasion of the existing franchisee's territory and the accompanying dilution of sales.

Greater Chance for Success. Investing in a franchise is *not* risk-free. In fact, the typical franchise does not reach the break-even point until 18 to 36 months after its inception, and the owner must be prepared to withstand the losses incurred during this time. For example, Wanda Stauffer quit her job and invested nearly all of her family's life savings in a Pop'Ins Inc. maid service franchise. After nine months of losses, her business finally began to earn a profit. "There were times when I wondered whether I would make it," Mrs. Stauffer says.[15]

Some franchises do not survive. But, available statistics indicate that franchising is less risky than building a business from the ground up. According to SBA statistics, 33 percent of new businesses fail in the first two years and 65 percent fail within five years. The Commerce Department estimates that only 4 to 6 percent of all franchises fail in any given year. This impressive success rate for franchises is attributed to the broad range of services, assistance, and guidelines the franchisor provides. These statistics must be interpreted carefully, however, because when a franchise is in danger of failing, the franchisor often repurchases or relocates the outlet and does not report it as a failure. As a result, some franchisors boast of never experiencing a failure.

The risk of purchasing a franchise is two-pronged; success—or failure—depends on the entrepreneur's managerial skills and on the franchisor's business experience and system. Many owners are convinced that franchising has been a crucial part of their success. Says one franchisor, "It's the opportunity to be in business for yourself but not by yourself."[16]

Drawbacks of Franchising

Obviously, the benefits of franchising can mean the difference between success and failure for a small business. Many entrepreneurs have fulfilled their dreams of owning a small business through a franchising arrangement. However, the potential franchisee must recognize that some freedom of action and decision making inherent in independent business must be sacrificed. As a franchisee, the owner relinquishes some personal independence and control to the franchisor and sometimes plays the role of "employee." Other limitations of franchising should be explored before the prospective franchisee decides to undertake this form of ownership.

Franchise Fees and Profit Sharing. Virtually all franchisors impose some type of fees and demand a share of the franchisee's sales revenues in return for the use of the franchise's name, products or services, and business system. The fees and the initial capital requirements vary among the different franchisors. The Commerce Department reports that total investments for franchises range from $1,000 for business services up to $10 million for hotel and motel franchises.[17] For example, H & R Block requires a capital investment of $2,000 to $3,000; I Can't Believe It's Yogurt requires $55,000 to $60,000 in equity capital; and McDonald's requires an investment of $325,000 to $350,000 (but McDonald's owns the land and the building).

Start-up costs for franchises often include numerous additional fees. Most franchises impose a franchise fee up front for the right to use the company name. Wendy's International, for example, charges a $20,000 "technical assistance fee" for each restaurant a franchisee opens. Other additional start-up costs might include site purchase and preparation, construction, signs, fixtures, equipment, management assistance, and training. Some franchise fees include these costs, while others do not. Before signing any contract, a prospective franchisee should determine the *total* cost of a franchise. For example,

[15]William Cellis, III, "Franchises Can Be Profitable, But Which One?" *The Wall Street Journal*, April 10, 1985, p. 31.
[16]Whittenmore and Steinberg, op. cit., p. 75.

[17]Ibid p. 84.

R. David Thomas, founder of Wendy's International, states that a franchisee must "have about $700,000 in credit and $150,000 in liquid assets" to launch a Wendy's restaurant.[18] Holiday Inns, Inc. provides prospective franchisees with the following estimates of start-up costs for a 100-room, two-story hotel:[19]

Initial franchise application fee		$ 30,000
Building	$2,200,000–	2,275,000
Furniture, fixtures, and equipment	250,000–	350,000
Opening inventory	100,000–	175,000
Working capital	75,000–	200,000
Great sign	29,000–	36,000
Training expenses	1,750–	3,000
Holidex terminal	5,850–	8,300
Total	$2,691,600–	$3,527,300

+ Real estate cost (3.5 to 5 acres)

In addition to the start-up costs, franchisors impose continuing royalty fees as profit-sharing devices. The royalty usually involves a percentage of gross sales with some required minimum, or a flat fee levied on the franchise. Royalty fees typically range from 1 percent to 11 percent and can increase the franchisee's overhead expenses significantly. Variable royalty fees that rise as sales increase are popular among some franchises. According to one franchise attorney, "A basic problem is that the royalties a franchisor exacts are often about what the normal profit margin is for a franchise . . . ."[20]

Wendy's and Kentucky Fried Chicken each receive a 4 percent royalty on gross sales. Some franchisors impose other types of continuing fees, such as those for advertising, rent, advisory services, and "technical assistance." A franchisee must find out what fees are required (some are merely "recommended") and then determine what services and benefits the fees cover. One of the best ways to do this is to itemize what you are getting for your money, and then determine whether the cost corresponds to the benefits provided.

Strict Adherence to Standardized Operations. Although the franchisee owns the business, she does not have the autonomy of an independent owner. To protect its public image, the franchisor requires that the franchisee maintain certain operating standards. If a franchise constantly fails to meet the minimum standards established for the business, its license may be terminated. Determining compliance with standards is usually accomplished by periodic inspections.

At times, strict adherence to franchise standards may become a burden to the franchisee. The owner may believe that the written reports the franchisor demands require an excessive amount of time. In other instances, the owner may be required to enforce specific rules even though she believes they are inappropriate or unfair.

Restrictions on Purchasing. Often, in the interest of maintaining quality standards, the franchisee is required to purchase products or special equipment from the franchisor, and perhaps other items from an "approved" supplier. For example, Kentucky Fried Chicken requires that franchisees use only seasonings blended by a particular company. A poor image could result from the use of inferior products to cut costs. Under some conditions, such purchase arrangements may be challenged in court as a violation of antitrust laws, but generally the franchisor has a legal right to see that franchisees maintain acceptable quality standards. A franchisor may set the prices paid for such products but may not establish the retail prices to be charged on products sold by the franchisee. A franchisor legally can suggest retail prices, but cannot force the franchisee to abide by them.

Limited Product Line. In most cases, the franchise agreement stipulates that the franchise can sell only those products approved by the franchisor. Unless

---

[18]"Where's the Beef in Franchising?" *Money,* March 1985, p. 149.
[19]Holiday Inn Franchising Package, Memphis, Tennessee, Holiday Inns, Inc., 1984.
[20]"Franchising: The Strings Attached to Being Your Own Boss," *Changing Times,* September 1984, p. 70.

The King of Franchising

McDonald's didn't invent franchising, but it certainly has earned its reputation as the king of franchising. Nearly everyone recognizes the chain's golden arches and its "Mc-spokesperson," Ronald McDonald. Ronald (who originally was portrayed by zany weatherman Willard Scott from NBC's *Today* Show) is so widely known that he rivals Santa in popularity.

The fast-food restaurant chain has grown rapidly since Ray Kroc met Mac and Dick McDonald in their tiny drive-in hamburger stand in San Bernadino, California, in 1954. Kroc had acquired the rights to a machine that would mix six milkshakes simultaneously, and he was selling them "door-to-door." The McDonald's hamburger stand caught Kroc's attention when the brothers ordered eight of his milkshake machines. Kroc said, "I was amazed. This little drive-in having people standing in line. The volume was incredible." The McDonald brothers had already franchised six stores in California, but Kroc offered them a franchise deal that involved less trouble—and fewer headaches. Kroc struggled in the early days even though the franchises sold well. Sometimes he didn't have enough cash to pay his secretary's salary, so she accepted McDonald's stock in lieu of her paycheck. When she retired from the company, she owned an estimated one million shares of stock!

By 1966, Kroc had bought out the McDonald brothers and built the chain up to 100 stores with annual sales of $200 million. McDonald's, now with more than 7,500 franchises, has sold over 45 *billion* hamburgers since it began. More than 11 million customers each day visit the golden arches to feast on Big Macs, McDLT's, Egg McMuffins, Quarter Pounders, and other "Mc-treats."

Much of McDonald's success comes from the assembly line techniques it brought to hamburger production. While the hamburger patties are grilling, a production worker toasts the buns and then dresses them with premeasured dollops of

willing to risk license cancellation, a franchisee must avoid selling any unapproved products through the franchise. For example, the local Popeye's Famous Fried Chicken franchisee could not offer a fish sandwich unless the franchisor approved it. Probably the most common restraints among franchisors concern the product line and its quality. Claims a franchisee of The Original Great American Chocolate Chip Cookie Company, "They (the franchisor) use the McDonald's theory. Everyone sells the same thing so when a customer walks in, he knows what he's getting."[21]

It is possible that a franchise may be required to carry an unpopular product or be prevented from introducing a desirable one by the franchise agreement. In this way, the freedom to adapt a product line to local market conditions is restricted. But, some franchisors solicit product suggestions from their franchisees. In fact, McDonald's franchisees came up with the highly successful "Big Mac" and "Egg McMuffin."

Unsatisfactory Training Programs. Every would-be franchisee must be wary of the unscrupulous franchisors who promise extensive services, advice, and assistance, but deliver nothing. For example, one owner relied on the franchisor to provide what had been described as an "extensive, rigorous training program" after paying a handsome "technical assistance fee." The "program" was nothing but a set of pamphlets and do-it-yourself study guides. Other

---

[21]Whittenmore and Steinberg, op. cit. p. 78.

mayonnaise, mustard, and ketchup. Electronically controlled vats cook french fries to golden-brown perfection and then signal that they are done. French-fry scoops ensure that standard quantities of fries go into each package. Electronic soft drink dispensers minimize wasteful overflows. The system demands that all franchisees conform to the McDonald's motto of "quality, service, cleanliness, and value." For example, burgers can remain in the warming bin no longer than 10 minutes and french fries no more than 7 minutes before they must be "wasted." The goal of this hamburger assembly line is to provide customers with the same quality product whether they buy it in Tokyo, Japan, or in Moncks Corner, South Carolina. Says one customer as he gobbles down a Quarter Pounder, "You know what you're getting when you come to McDonald's." Speed is also important. Every fast-food crew strives to serve a customer within 60 seconds of placing an order.

The system works well for both franchisor and franchisees. McDonald's collects 11.5 percent of franchisees' annual sales in return for a variety of services it provides them. The typical restaurant's profit ranges from 5 to 15 percent of sales.

McDonald's is changing to keep up with the shifts in the fast-food industry. Changes in public tastes have led McDonald's to introduce new products like Chicken McNuggets. But not all new products are successes; McDonald's withdrew the McRib barbecue sandwich after disappointing sales. The company also is moving into more unusual locations like hospitals, airports, zoos, and military bases. Still, McDonald's maintains its image as a family restaurant.

The king of franchises is not likely to abdicate its position. Says one long-time franchisee, "I knew all along we would be successful, but I never dreamed it would be this good."

Source: Adapted from Lawrence D. Maloney, "Recipe for Success in the Fast-Food Game," *U.S. News & World Report,* November 21, 1983, pp. 58–59; "Horatio Hamburger & the Golden Arches," *Business Week,* April 12, 1976, with permission of the publishers.

examples include those impatient entrepreneurs who paid initial franchise fees without investigating the business and never heard from the "franchisor" again. The point is that although disclosure rules have reduced the severity of the problem, dishonest, "shady" characters still thrive on unprepared prospective franchisees.

Less Freedom. When a franchisee signs a contract, he agrees to sell the franchisor's product or service by following its prescribed formula. Franchisors want to ensure success, and most monitor their franchisees' performances closely. So, entrepreneurs who want to "be their own bosses" may be disappointed with a franchise. Explains one franchise attorney, "The basic tension between franchisor and franchisee is that the franchisor usually wants a lot of control to protect what he has built up and the franchisee wants to be an independent businessperson."[22] Highly autonomous entrepreneurs probably should not choose franchising. Advises IFA president Stanley Bresler, "Franchising is not for everyone. If you are the go-my-own-way type, the autonomous posture is probably the better route to take."[23]

IV. WHAT DO FRANCHISORS LOOK FOR IN A FRANCHISEE?

What kind of person does the typical franchisor look for?

[22]"Franchising: The Strings Attached to Being Your Own Boss," p. 70.
[23]"Sixth Annual Franchise 500," p. 89.

SMALL
BUSINESS
REPORT
4–4

Trouble at the Top

Mark Weiss developed an idea for a fast-food restaurant aimed at "baby-boomers" wanting a variety of fresh, nutritious foods and serviced by a unique support system. He called it Fresher Cooker. Franchisees are required to build a central kitchen that prepares all of the food for 20 to 30 nearby restaurants. Weiss' strategy was to keep costs down by eliminating duplicate kitchen facilities in each restaurant. Says marketing director Brian Guilliom, "It keeps equipment, investment, and utility costs low, about 60 percent of the industry's average." The plan works; Fresher Cooker's average check size is just under $3, a rarity among the new fast-food chains.

The company's menu, designed with its target market in mind, is another key feature. The menu is flexible; 80 percent of it is standard and the remaining 20 percent is tailored to the tastes of each particular market. Says Guilliom, "We're the first fresh people, and . . . we've designed our system so that we can pull items on and off the menu at will."

Fresher Cooker had a head start on many of its fast-food competitors aiming at health-conscious consumers. Then, five months after the company went public, Weiss, the driving force behind Fresher Cooker, had a heart attack and could no longer work. The chain began to lose money, and a major franchisee folded six restaurants and absorbed a $3 million loss. Says one investor, "There were other people with restaurant experience at the company, but they didn't have the leadership Weiss had."

Fresher Cooker is counting on a $4 million private placement to help it regain its position. Until then, new president Frank Dwyer will be playing "catch-up."

Source: Adapted from Lee Kravitz, "Fast Food's Fast Movers," *Venture,* November 1984, pp. 42–52; Gail Collins, "When the Key Man Is Struck Down," *Venture,* July 1985, pp. 118–120, with permission of the publishers.

Experienced? Not necessarily. In fact, "no experience necessary" is a key selling point of franchising. Most franchisors do not require franchisees to have experience since they have "worked the bugs" out of their franchise system. Most franchisees find, however, that a certain level of business know-how and "savvy" is crucial to a successful franchise operation. A basic understanding of business law and finance is useful since franchisees must make decisions and solve problems pertaining to both areas.

Hard Working? Definitely. Most franchisees work long hours. There are no more 8-hour days five days per week. A franchisee must be willing to do any job that needs to be done—preparing paperwork, reconciling the bank statement, sweeping the floor, and selling merchandise. Earle Swensen of Swensen's Ice Cream explains, "We look for someone who won't look at the clock but instead puts in the time necessary to do the job."[24] A franchisee cannot be allergic to hard work because that is what is required to get the business established.

Leadership and Management Skills? No doubt. Managing people is a significant part of every successful business operation. A franchisee must be able to lead, motivate, and work with other people. Nick and Mayo Boddie, franchisors of over 200 Hardee's restaurants, credit much of their success to " . . . the corporate equivalent of the Golden Rule—demanding that others produce and perform as you would like them to, and rewarding them in kind."[25]

---

[24]Dunnigan, op. cit. p. 50.
[25]Craig R. Waters, "Franchise Capital of America," *Inc.,* September 1984, p. 104.

Franchisees must realize that they are in "the people business" and that their work force often is unskilled and transitory. So, successful franchisees must be able to train and coach subordinates to perform their jobs properly.

Risk Averse? Definitely not. Although franchises have a much lower failure rate than do independent businesses, they are not without risks. There is no guarantee of success included in a franchise package. One study found that 56 franchisors operating 2,165 outlets failed. An additional 63 companies decided to discontinue franchising as a way of doing business.[26]

Educated? Yes. A franchisee does not have to have an MBA and a Ph.D. in management to run a franchise successfully, however. Mike Bloom of Orange Julius says his company prefers someone who "has a good basic education, either scholastically or experientially."[27]

Financially stable? Certainly. Some franchises have breathtakingly high capital requirements; others, especially the new growth-oriented service franchises, are much more affordable. Still, every franchisor requires each applicant to submit a personal financial statement proving that he is financially sound. Earle Swensen states, "Our preference is to see franchisees get into their operation without having to borrow too much money . . . . " Mike Bloom continues, "We scrutinize every financial statement a potential franchisee submits to us because we don't want to give someone a franchise and then see that person get into trouble."[28] And franchisors *do* screen applicants. Out of the 3,000 applications that Wendy's International receives each year, it franchises only about 30 of them![29]

A Desire to Succeed? Absolutely. A burning desire to succeed and a healthy dose of enthusiasm can carry a franchisee through may difficult situations that, at times, seem hopeless.

V. DETECTING DISHONEST FRANCHISORS

The best defenses a prospective entrepreneur has against unscrupulous franchisors are preparation, common sense, and patience. By investigating thoroughly before investing in a franchise, a potential franchisee eliminates the risk of being "hoodwinked" into a nonexistent business. If he asks the right questions and does not rush into an investment decision, the entrepreneur will be able to verify the franchisor's reliability. The president of a franchise consulting firm estimates that 5 to 10 percent of franchisors are dishonest—"the rogue elephants of franchising."[30] Potential franchisees must beware. Says one franchise attorney, "There's an enormous amount of fly-by-nighters coming into this business."[31]

Dishonest franchisors tend to follow certain patterns. The following clues might arouse the suspicion of an entrepreneur about to invest in a franchise:

- Attempts to discourage you from allowing an attorney to evaluate the franchise contract before you sign it.
- No written documentation to support claims and promises.
- A "high pressure" sale—sign the contract now or lose the opportunity.
- Claiming to be exempt from federal laws requiring complete disclosure of franchise details.
- "Get-rich-quick schemes," promises of huge profits with only minimum effort.
- Reluctance to provide a list of present franchisees for you to interview.
- Evasive, vague answers to your questions about the franchise and its operation.

---

[26]*Franchising in the Economy, 1983–1985*, p. 12.
[27]Dunnigan, op. cit. p. 50.
[28]Ibid.
[29]"Where's the Beef in Franchising?" p. 151.

[30]"Franchising: The Strings Attached to Being Your Own Boss," p. 70.
[31]Sabin Russell, "A Formula That Works," *Venture*, September 1985, p. 38.

Often, abuses do not occur until the franchise contract is in effect. For example:

- A franchisor misdirected a portion of his franchisees' advertising funds into its own operating funds.
- A franchisor sold used equipment to franchisees at new equipment prices.
- A franchisor issued discount coupons that franchisees were obligated to honor. The discount eliminated the franchisees' profit margin, and they had to pay royalties on higher sales revenues.[32]

One of the best ways to evaluate the reputation of a franchisor is to interview several franchise owners who have been in business at least one year concerning the positive and the negative features of the agreement, and whether the franchisor delivers what was promised. In some cases, the franchisees for a particular company have formed an association which might provide information. The National Franchise Association Coalition in Chicago can help locate franchise assistance. Remember, if the deal sounds too good to be true, it probably is.

VI. FRANCHISE EVALUATION CHECKLIST

The key to determining whether a franchise opportunity is a wise investment is investigation. Be patient, do your "homework," and, above all, ask plenty of questions. In addition to interviewing franchisees, prospective franchise owners can protect their interests by exploring specific areas of the agreement. The following checklist illustrates some of the questions that should be asked before entering into any franchise agreement.

The Franchisor and the Franchise

1. Is the potential market for the product or service adequate to support your franchise? Will the prices you charge be in line with the market?
2. Is the market's population growing, remaining static, or shrinking? Is the demand for your product or service growing, remaining static, or shrinking?
3. Is the product or service safe and reputable?
4. What will the competition, direct or indirect, be in your sales territory? Do any other franchisees operate in this general area?
5. Is the franchise international, national, regional, or local in scope? Does it involve full- or part-time involvement?
6. How many years has the franchisor been in operation? Does it have a sound reputation for honest dealings with franchisees?
7. How many franchise outlets now exist? How many will there be a year from now? How many outlets are company-owned?
8. How many franchises have failed? Why?
9. What service and assistance will the franchisor provide? Training programs? Continuous in nature?
10. Will the firm perform a location analysis to help you find a suitable site?
11. Will the franchisor offer you exclusive distribution rights for the length of the agreement, or may it sell to other franchises in this area?
12. What facilities and equipment are required for the franchise? Who pays for construction? Is there a lease agreement?
13. What is the total cost of the franchise? What are the initial capital requirements? Will the franchisor provide financial assistance? Of what nature? What is the interest rate? Is the franchisor financially sound enough to fulfill all its promises?
14. How much is the franchise fee? *Exactly* what does it cover? Are there any continuing fees? What additional fees are there?
15. Does the franchisor provide an estimate of expenses and income? Are they reasonable for your particular area? Are they sufficiently documented?

---

[32]"Franchising: The Strings Attached to Being Your Own Boss," p. 70.

16. How risky is the franchise opportunity? Is the return on the investment consistent with the risks?

17. Does the franchisor offer a written contract which covers all the details of the agreement? Have your attorney and your accountant studied its terms and approved it? Do *you* understand the implications of the contract?

18. What is the length of the franchise agreement? Under what circumstances can it be terminated? If you terminate the contract, what are the costs to you? What are the terms and costs of renewal?

19. Are you allowed to sell the franchise to a third party? If so, will you receive the proceeds?

20. Is there a national advertising program? How is it financed? What media are used? What help is provided for local advertising?

The Franchisee

21. Are you qualified to operate a franchise successfully? Do you have adequate drive, skills, experience, education, patience, and financial capacity? Are you prepared to work hard?

22. Are you willing to sacrifice some autonomy in operating a business to own a franchise?

23. Can you tolerate the financial risk?

24. Are you genuinely interested in the product or service you will be selling?

25. Has the franchisor investigated your background thoroughly enough to decide if you are qualified to operate the franchise?

26. What can this franchisor do for you for that you cannot do for yourself?

VII. FRANCHISING AND THE LAW

The franchising boom spearheaded by McDonald's in the late 1950s brought with it many prime investment opportunities. The explosion of legitimate franchises also ushered in with it several "fly-by-night" franchisors who defrauded their franchisees. In response to these specific incidents and to the poten-tial for deception inherent in a franchise relationship, the Federal Trade Commission (FTC) enacted the Trade Regulation Rule in October 1979 to require all franchisors to disclose detailed information on their operations at the first personal meeting or at least 10 days before a franchise contract is signed, or before any money is paid. The purpose of the regulation is to assist the potential franchisee's investigation of the franchise deal and to introduce consistency into the franchisor's disclosure statements. The philosophy of the FTC is not so much to prosecute abusers as to provide information to prospective franchisees and help them make intelligent decisions. Although the FTC requires each franchisor to provide a potential franchise with this information, it does not verify its accuracy. So, the wise entrepreneur should use such data only as a starting point for the investigation. The Trade Regulation Rule requires a franchisor to include 20 major topics in its disclosure statement:

1. Information identifying the franchisor and its affiliates, and describing their business experience.

2. Information identifying and describing the business experience of each of the franchisor's officers, directors, and management personnel responsible for the franchise program.

3. A description of the lawsuits in which the franchisor and its officers, directors, and managers have been involved.

4. Information about any bankruptcies in which the franchisor and its officers, directors, and managers have been involved.

5. Information about the initial franchise fee and other payments required to obtain the franchise.

6. A description of the continuing payments franchisees are required to make after start-up.

7. Information about quality restrictions on goods and services used in the franchise and where they may be purchased, including restricted purchases from the franchises.

8. A description of any financial assistance available

from the franchisor in the purchase of the franchise.

9. A description of any restrictions on the goods or services franchises are permitted to sell.

10. A description of any restrictions on the customers with whom franchisees may deal.

11. A description of any territorial protection that will be granted to the franchise.

12. A description of the conditions under which the franchise may be repurchased or refused renewal by the franchisor, transferred to a third party by the franchisee, and terminated or modified by either party.

13. A description of the training programs provided to franchisees.

14. A description of the involvement of celebrities and public figures in the franchise.

15. A description of any franchisor assistance in selecting a site for the franchise.

16. Statistical information about the present number of franchises; the number of franchises projected for the future; the number of franchises terminated; the number the franchisor has not renewed; and the number repurchased in the past.

17. The financial statements of the franchisors.

18. A description of the extent to which franchisees must participate personally in the operation of the franchise.

19. A complete statement of the basis for any earnings claims made to the franchisee, including the percentage of existing franchises that have actually achieved the results that are claimed.

20. A list of the names and addresses of other franchises.

In addition to the protection offered potential franchisees through the Trade Regulation Rule, 15 states have enacted the Uniform Franchise Offering Code, developed by the Midwest Securities Commission in 1976. Some proponents say it is more comprehensive than the FTC rule. The UFOC has been approved by the FTC, so prospective franchisees in these 15 states should expect franchisors' disclosure statements to conform to this code (see figure 4–5).

Of course, disclosure of information does not fully protect the potential franchisee from deception, nor does it guarantee success. It does, however, provide enough information to begin a thorough investigation of the franchisor and the franchise deal.

VIII. FRANCHISE CONTRACTS

The amount of franchisor-franchisee litigation has risen steadily over the past several years, and the total number of franchise-related lawsuits is substantial. A common source of much of this litigation is the interpretation of the franchise contract's terms. Most often, difficulties arise *after* the agreement is in operation. Typically, because the franchisor's attorney prepares franchise contracts, the provisions favor the franchisor. The courts have relatively little statutory law and few precedents on which to base decisions, resulting in minimal protection for franchisees. The problem results from the tremendous growth of franchising, which has outstripped the growth of franchise law.

Every potential franchisee should verify that the formal contract incorporates *all* the terms of the franchise agreement. The contract summarizes the details that will govern the franchisor-franchisee relationship over its life. It outlines *exactly* the rights and the obligations of each party and sets the guidelines which govern the franchise relationship. To protect potential franchisees from having to rush into a contract without clearly understanding its terms and their implications, the Federal Trade Commission requires that the franchisee receive the completed contract with all revisions at least five business days before it is signed.

Every potential franchisee should have an attorney evaluate the franchise contract and review it with the investor *before* he signs anything. Claims one attorney, "Sometimes the best advice a lawyer can give a client is to stay away from a particular franchisor."[33]

---

[33]"Teri Agins, "Owning Franchises Has Pluses, but Wealth Isn't Guaranteed," *The Wall Street Journal,* October 22, 1984, p. 34.

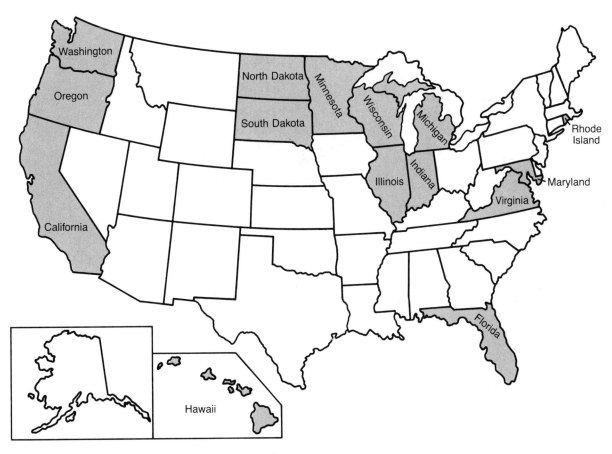

FIGURE 4–5 States that have adopted the Uniform Franchise Offering Code.

Usually the franchise contract is long term, although some franchisors offer a period, such as one year, in which to decide whether the two parties will conduct business together. As figure 4–6 shows, contract terms range from one year to perpetual, but 51 percent are for 15 years or more. For example, Holiday Inns, Inc., franchise contracts run for 20 years. Sometimes, other contractual agreements affect the length of the franchise arrangement. For example, a Dunkin' Donuts franchise has a 20-year term, but the contract terminates earlier if the store's lease is shorter.

It is crucial that the potential franchisee understand the terms of a franchise contract *before* he signs it. *Do not blindly accept a contract* as "the standard agreement." Too many franchisees have discovered unfavorable terms in their contracts only to find that they must abide by them. The typical franchise contract covers many topics, including the following:

- initial fees
- continuing fees
- payment schedules
- lease arrangements
- approved suppliers
- territorial protection
- training programs
- quality standards
- breach of contract and others

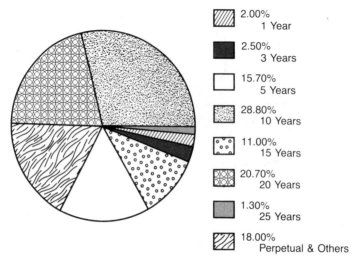

2.00%
1 Year

2.50%
3 Years

15.70%
5 Years

28.80%
10 Years

11.00%
15 Years

20.70%
20 Years

1.30%
25 Years

18.00%
Perpetual & Others

FIGURE 4–6   Length of franchise contracts.

Source: U.S. Department of Commerce, *Franchising in the Economy,* Washington, D.C. p. 4.

Termination.   Probably the most litigated subject of a franchise agreement is the termination of the contract by either party, but laws controlling contract terminations have been slow to develop. A recent study of 6,906 franchise contract terminations found that franchisors terminated 2,577[*]; franchisees terminated 3,867; and both parties mutually consented to terminate 462 contracts.[34] As one attorney who represents franchisors in termination suits, says, "A franchise contract is written by and for the franchisor to do whatever it wants to do and to make sure there are serious penalties on a franchisee who deviates from the agreement."[35]

Under most agreements, termination must be for "just cause," but a franchisee must understand clearly the particular terms of the termination clause. When and under what conditions can the franchisee terminate the contract? When and under what condi-

tions can the franchisor terminate the contract? For example, one franchisor permits the franchisee to end the contract only in the early stages of franchise formation. Other agreements require the terminating party to give 30 to 60 days' notice.

Generally, the franchisor has the right to cancel a contract if a franchisee declares bankruptcy, fails to make required payments on time, or fails to maintain quality standards.[36] For example, one franchisor reserves the right to terminate within 30 days of a franchisee's bankruptcy, within 7 days of default on the continuing franchise royalties, or "if the franchise owner fails to comply with any of the requirements imposed . . . by the franchise agreement." Note that the breadth and scope of this last clause leaves room for interpretation.

Terminations usually are costly to both parties and are seldom surrounded by a sense of goodwill. For instance, one franchise contract states that there is "no provision for compensating the franchise owner for his interest, if any, in the franchised busi-

---

[*]Of contracts terminated by the franchisor, 1,458 were for nonpayment of royalties or other obligations, 220 were for quality control problems, and 899 were for other reasons.

[34]*Franchising in the Economy, 1983-1985,* p. 13.

[35]"Terminating a Contract," *Venture,* January 1982, p. 20.

[36]*Small Business Reporter: Buying a Franchise,* Bank of America, San Francisco, California, 1981, p. 7.

ness upon termination or failure to renew . . . the agreement." Frequently, contracts specify that upon termination, the franchisee must pay the total amount owed the franchisor—often in a lump sum. The franchisee must cease using the franchisor's tradename and sometimes must give the franchisor the right to purchase any physical assets he owns.

Most attorneys encourage franchisees to avoid conditions for termination or to use alternative routes like formal complaints through franchise associations, arbitration, or ultimately selling the franchise. If a franchisee believes he was deceived in an agreement, he can contact the FTC for assistance although it may not be swift; presently, its staff consists of four full-time investigators.

Renewal. Franchisors usually retain the right to renew or refuse to renew franchisees' contracts. A recent study of 11,584 franchise contracts up for renewal found that 90 percent were renewed. Of the 1,147 contracts not renewed, 451 ended because of objections by the franchisor, 380 because of hesitation by the franchisee, and 316 by mutual agreement.[37]

If a franchisee fails to make payments on schedule or does not maintain quality standards, the franchisor has the right to refuse renewal. For instance, one franchise contract states that if the franchisee's "quality rating" is below average, the franchisor will not renew. In some cases, the franchisor has no obligation to offer contract renewal to the franchisee.

If the franchisor grants renewal, the two parties must draw up a new contract. Frequently, the franchisee must pay a "renewal fee" and may be required to "cure" any deficiencies of the outlet or to modernize and upgrade it. The FTC's Trade Regulation Rule requires the franchisor to disclose these terms before any contracts are signed.

Transfer and Buybacks. Under most franchise contracts, the franchisor retains the right to repurchase an outlet upon termination or failure to renew. Typically, the franchisee cannot sell the franchise to a

third party or will it to a relative without the franchisor's approval. In most instances, franchisors do approve a franchisee's request to sell an outlet to another person. One study of 3,634 franchisees who applied for permission to sell their franchises to third parties found that franchisors approved 97 percent of the transfers.[38] Still, most franchisors retain "the right of first refusal" in franchise transfers. In other words, the franchisee wishing to sell out must offer the franchise to the franchisor first. For example, McDonald's Corporation recently repurchased 13 restaurants under its "first refusal" clause from a franchisee wanting to retire.[39] If the franchisor refuses to buy the outlet, the franchise may sell the outlet to a third party, as long as he meets the franchisor's approval.

The option to sell the franchise back to the franchisor can be an important advantage for the franchisee. Some contracts specify a formula for computing the business' value. Often, contracts call for a buyback price that includes only the book value of the assets. That is, the franchisee receives no goodwill value in the purchase price since the franchisor's business system is the source of goodwill.

IX. TRENDS IN FRANCHISING

The franchise boom of the past two decades has slowed significantly in the 1980s although a record number of businesses use franchising to expand into larger markets. Long-term growth for franchising should remain very strong, however, as retailing and services continue to increase their shares of franchising sales.

The slowest growth is expected to occur among the older, more established franchises. Many of these franchisors will experience difficulty achieving their growth targets because of excessively high capital requirements and a lack of prime locations. Traditional fast foods, automotive replacement parts,

---

[37]*Franchising in the Economy,* 1983-1985, p. 13.

[38]Ibid.

[39]Fred Monk, "McDonald's Franchise Changes Hands," *The State,* March 1, 1985, Section C, p. 1.

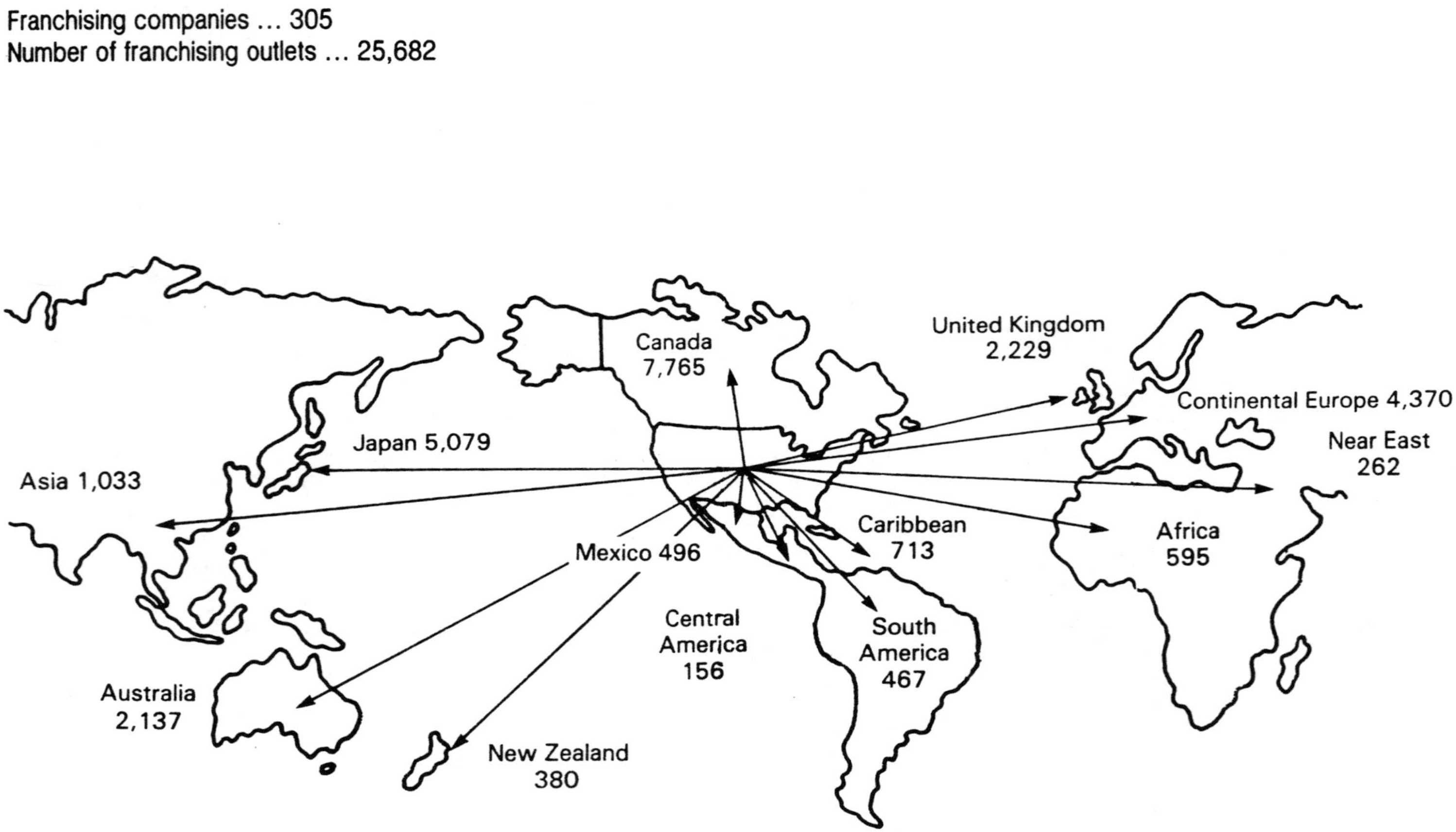

Franchising companies ... 305
Number of franchising outlets ... 25,682

FIGURE 4–7 International franchising, number of foreign outlets.

Source: U.S. Department of Commerce, *Franchising in the Economy*, Washington, D.C., 1986.

hotels and motels, printing and copying, and rental services will find it more difficult to expand due to these factors. Some of these industries have grown so rapidly in the past that the market has reached the "saturation point" from so many competitors.

The real growth in the franchising industry will come from innovative, nontraditional franchisors with fresh approaches to the market and lower capital requirements. These companies feature start-up costs in the $2,000 to $250,000 range. Franchised restaurants will continue to be the industry leader although the growth will not come from traditional fast food chains, where the 14 largest franchisors account for nearly 60 percent of all sales.[40] Instead, the most promising candidates are the innovative restaurateurs who cater to the "baby-boomers" and develop unique location and expansion strategies. For example, Papa Aldo's sells take-out pizzas that customers bake at home. Founder John Gundle ran a full service pizza franchise and noticed that take-out customers always complained of cold pizzas. "So," he reasoned, "how about giving them fresh, ready-to-bake pizza—pizza they can bake at home and experience at the moment of perfection . . . ."[41] Other retail businesses—ice cream, yogurt, popcorn, home furnishings, security systems, and video equipment— also should grow rapidly in the near future.

Franchised service businesses will thrive, too. Business and personnel services will be among the leaders in this sector. Other personal services also should boom: maid service, home repair and remodeling, auto repair, travel agency services, health care, and various maintenance and cleaning services. According to IFA president Stanley Bresler, "Changing American lifestyles and rising incomes have contributed to the creation of service-oriented businesses. Young, affluent Americans are a brand-new market, and franchising is making its mark on businesses catering to these more specialized and sophisticated tastes."[42]

More women and minorities will become franchise owners in the future. Lack of capital and managerial experience are the primary barriers to business ownership for these two groups, and franchising offers a way to overcome them. Although minority ownership of franchises is small—only 1.53 percent of all outlets—it is growing.

The recent trend toward conversion franchising, where owners of independent businesses become franchisees to gain the advantage of name recognition, will continue. The biggest force in conversion franchising has been Century 21, the real estate sales company. But other businesses, including instant photo finishing labs and home repair services, are choosing growth strategies based on conversion franchising.

Franchising also will continue its push into the international arena. Many U.S. franchisors are attracted to international markets to boost their sales and their profits. As figure 4–7 shows, Canada leads the way as a prime market for U.S. franchisors, with Japan and Continental Europe following.

So, franchising has proved its viability in the U.S. economy as a practical way for businesses— large and small—to achieve growth and expansion on limited capital. It is an important concept to the small business sector since it offers many would-be entrepreneurs the opportunity to own and operate a business with above-average chances for success. Despite its inherent drawbacks, franchising will continue to be a dominant force in the U.S. economy for a long time.

X. SUMMARY

Franchising is not a new method of conducting business. Despite the fact that automobile dealerships and gasoline stations account for over three-fourths of all franchise sales, virtually every type of product and service is sold through franchises.

Franchising is a method of doing business involving a continuous relationship between a franchisor and a franchisee. The franchisor retains possession of the distribution system, while the

[40]Kravitz, op. cit. p. 42.
[41]Ibid. p. 43
[42]"Sixth Annual Franchise 500," p. 83.

The Colonel in Japan

Japan is the second largest consumer market in the world, and Kentucky Fried Chicken wants a piece of the action. Japanese consumers spend about $90 billion each year dining out, and the fast-food business has expanded 400 percent in the last decade.

KFC opened its first store in Japan in 1970; today, it has nearly 500, most of which are franchises. The company's key to success has been its ability to adapt. Loy Weston, chairman of KFC, Japan, has boosted the company's performance in this highly protected economy by tuning into the Japanese culture quickly and by delegating authority to his Japanese staff. For instance, KFC has changed the nature of its training program since companies in Japanese subscribe to the lifetime employment concept. Training is quite rigorous and expensive. In Basic Operating Training (BOT), which lasts nine days, employees learn everything from company philosophy (quality, service, and cleanliness) to behind-the-counter techniques. Then, the employees must go through on-the-job training.

Another example of KFC's ability to adapt concerns its stores. The first three stores the company built were exact replicas of those in the U.S. Claims one Japanese KFC executive, "It's like bringing in a full-size Cadillac and trying to drive around the narrow streets of Tokyo." So, the managers began to design stores more appropriate to space-conscious Japan. They would find a suitable location and shrink equipment and maximize space requirements to fit the space. These much smaller stores still manage to average the same volume of business as their full-sized American counterparts.

KFC also found it necessary to adapt its menu to suit local tastes. The chicken the Japanese stores sell is identical to the chicken sold in the U.S., but the foreign outlets also sell smoked chicken, yogurt, and fish and chips. In addition, says Weston, "The Japanese aren't thrilled about mashed potatoes and gravy . . . so we substituted french fries. Management remedied cole slaw that the Japanese considered too sweet by cutting the sugar in half. "Another no-brainer," claims Weston.

KFC also found that its advertising theme must take a different slant from those in the Western world. The company's Japanese ads stress its product's authenticity, its American heritage, and its "aristocratic elegance." One ad even features "My Old Kentucky Home" sung in Japanese.

Before opening a new restaurant, the manager and the supervisor must make a courtesy tour of all the businesses in the neighborhood (including

franchisee assumes all of the normal daily operating functions of the business. There are three types of franchising: tradename franchising, where the franchisee purchases only the right to use a brand name; product distribution franchising, which involves a license to sell specific products under a brand name; and pure franchising, which provides a franchisee with a complete business system. The last type is growing most rapidly.

Franchising has been a successful business format, in part, because of the mutual benefits provided. The franchisor has the benefits of expanding his business on limited capital and growing without developing key managers internally. The franchisee also receives many key benefits: management training and counseling; customer appeal of a brand name; standardized quality of goods and services; national advertising programs; financial assistance;

(Photo courtesy of Kentucky Fried Chicken Corporation.)

competitors) with gifts of smoked chicken and discount coupons. For over 300 years, Japanese merchants have opened businesses with this public relations ritual to solicit good wishes for their new ventures. Every new store also must be christened through a special Shinto opening ceremony that uses century-old prayers and rituals so that the business will prosper.

Kentucky Fried Chicken faces stiff competition from native restaurants as well as from Western eating establishments. But its success in this foreign market arises from its ability to adapt its marketing program to the needs and expectations of the Japanese consumer and its capacity to adopt a long-range view of its business.

Source: Adapted from "The Colonel Comes to Japan," *Enterprise* Television Series, 1984, with permission.

proven products and business formats; centralized buying power; territorial protection; and greater chances for success. Before deciding on any franchise, the entrepreneur should be aware of the disadvantages involved: franchise fees and profit sharing, strict adherence to standardized operations; restrictions on purchasing; limited product lines; possible ineffective training programs; and less freedom.

Before investing in a franchise, an entrepreneur must ask a probing question: What can a franchise do for me that I cannot do for myself? The franchisee must also take steps to recognize and avoid unscrupulous franchisors.

The FTC's Trade Regulation Rule is designed to help the franchisee evaluate a franchising package. It requires each franchisor to disclose information covering 20 topics at least 10 days before accepting payment from a potential franchisee.

A common source of litigation in franchising is the contract, particularly the termination provisions. Since the franchise contract is prepared by the franchisor's attorney, it tends to favor the franchisor. Potential investors should also pay close attention to the contracts renewal, transfer, and buy-back provisions.

The growth which occurred during the franchise boom of the 1960s and 1970s has slowed considerably during this decade, especially among the more traditional franchise industries, because of high start-up costs and lack of prime sites. As a result, innovative, less costly franchises have grown more rapidly. International franchising is another growth field; there are 25,682 U.S.-based franchise outlets in foreign countries, with Canada the largest market. Generally, franchising will continue to be an important segment in the U.S. economy.

STUDENT INVOLVEMENT PROJECTS

1. Visit a local franchise operation. Is it a tradename, product distribution, or pure franchise? To what extent did the franchisee investigate before investing? What assistance does the franchisor provide?

2. Consult a copy of the U.S. Department of Commerce publication *Franchise Opportunities Handbook* (the library should have a copy). Write several franchisors in a particular business category and ask for their franchise packages. Write a report comparing their treatment of the topics covered by the Trade Regulation Rule.

3. Ask a local franchisee to approach his regional franchise representative about leading a class discussion on franchising.

DISCUSSION QUESTIONS

1. What is franchising?
2. Describe the three types of franchising and give an example of each.
3. How does franchising benefit the franchisor?
4. Discuss the advantages and the limitations of franchising for the franchisee.
5. How beneficial to the franchisee is a quality training program? Why?
6. Compare the failure rates for franchises with those of independent businesses.
7. Why might an independent entrepreneur be dissatisfied with a franchising arrangement?
8. What do franchisors look for in a franchisee?
9. What are the clues in detecting an unreliable franchisor?
10. Should a prospective franchisee investigate before investing in a franchise? If so, how and in what areas?
11. What is the function of the FTC's Trade Regulation Rule?
12. Outline the rights given all prospective franchisees by the Trade Regulation Rule.
13. What is the source of most franchisor-franchisee litigation? Whom does the standard franchise contract favor?
14. Describe the current growth rate of franchises. Why have the "traditional franchisors" experienced difficulty in meeting their growth targets?
15. What areas of franchising offer the greatest growth potential in the near future? Why?

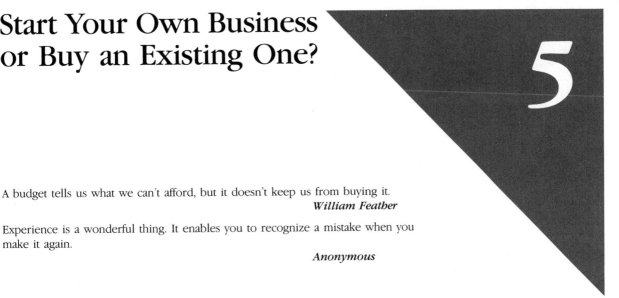

Start Your Own Business or Buy an Existing One?

A budget tells us what we can't afford, but it doesn't keep us from buying it.
William Feather

Experience is a wonderful thing. It enables you to recognize a mistake when you make it again.

Anonymous

Upon completion of this chapter, you will be able to:

- Understand the advantages and disadvantages of starting a business from scratch.
- Understand the advantages and disadvantages of buying an existing business.
- Evaluate an existing business that is offered for sale.
- Outline the various ways of determining the value of a business.
- Highlight the process of negotiating the lowest price and best terms in the purchase of an existing business.

After the entrepreneur decides to accept the risks and pursue the rewards of small business ownership, she must decide whether to start a new business or buy an existing one. Just as in choosing the best form of ownership, the decision to start or buy a business depends on the particular circumstances facing the entrepreneur, and she must know how to evaluate the alternatives facing her.

I. STARTING YOUR OWN BUSINESS

Advantages of Starting Your Own Business

It's All Mine and I'll Set It Up the Way I Want It. Many entrepreneurs believe that the best way to go into business is to "start from scratch." This allows them to construct the business just as they perceived it in their dreams and plans. Confidence in the decision to go into business is reinforced as owners watch their dreams take shape. Indeed, the experience of shaping a business from the original idea until it opens for business is quite rewarding and satisfying. The owner knows that what she has is what she designed. It is hers—financially and emotionally.

You Do Not Inherit Ill Will. Not all businesses up for sale have a reputation that will support a claim of good will. In some cases, the reputation of the store or its owner was such that "ill will" was created.

Starting a business avoids the problem of guilt by location.

New Ideas Deserve a Fresh Start. When an entrepreneur has an idea that truly is unique, existing businesses may not meet her needs. The nature of the new business may be such that it is impractical to convert an existing business into the desired project.

Disadvantages of Starting Your Own Business

Can the Market Support a New Competitor? Often a new competitor enters a market without an accompanying influx of new customers. This problem may not be meaningful in a large city, but it is a real problem in small and medium-sized cities. For example, a small town had an "explosion" of jewelry stores. The population supported two stores adequately, but after two more were added sales revenues and income profits were too thin. Thus, all the jewelers were unable to show a profit.

Existing competitors are not likely to welcome new businesses with open arms. They will see new businesses as threats and will increase competitive pressure to retain their own customers. Experienced small business managers are familiar with the approximate number of customers in the local market and recognize that their share of sales is best protected by keeping the number of competitors at a minimum. In some markets, keeping out new competitors is a group effort.

Cost of New Equipment. When an entrepreneur decides to begin a new business as opposed to buying a new one, she will normally incur higher costs due to the price of equipment. Sometimes used equipment is available, but the new manager must know where to look. Even if she finds used equipment, the cost may exceed that of similar equipment obtained when purchasing an existing business. In the existing business, equipment will be depreciated over the years since its purchase, so these assets carry a much lower book value.

Who Can You Go to for Advice? When an entrepreneur starts her own business, she quickly has questions to which she has no answers. Who are the most reputable and reliable vendors? How much business can she expect to have during certain seasons of the year? Usually, the previous owner is best qualified to answer these questions. When this is her first venture in a particular type of business or market, advice from a previous owner can save a great deal of money. When starting a business "from scratch," there may be few reliable sources of such information available.

Name Recognition. Overcoming consumer inertia is a major barrier for many new businesses. There is a great deal of value in a name that customers have confidence in. Some customers are hesitant to try new unfamiliar businesses. If the costs of your products or services is high, you have a greater probability of a delayed response. Such delays can crimp sales revenue and make the firm a small business fatality before it has a chance to prove itself.

II. BUYING AN EXISTING BUSINESS

Advantages of Buying an Existing Business

A Successful Existing Business May Continue to be Successful. Assuming that an entrepreneur can purchase an existing business at an acceptable price, the ongoing business with a record of success increases the likelihood of success. The previous management already has established a customer base, built supplier relationships, and set up a business system. The new owner's objective should be to make modifications that will attract new customers while at the same time retaining the firm's existing customers. Maintaining the proper balance of old and new is not an easy task.

However, the new owner should not tinker too much with the established business. Too many new owners have destroyed successful businesses in an attempt to build an even more successful business. The customer base that you inherit through purchasing an established business can carry you while you study how the business has become successful and why customers buy from you. Time spent learning about the business and its customers before introducing changes will increase the probability that the changes you do introduce will be successful.

An Existing Business May Already Have the Best Location.   When the location of the business is critical to its success, it may be wise to purchase a business which is already in the right place. Opening in a second-choice location, hoping to draw customers, may prove fruitless. The existing business' biggest asset may be its location. If this advantage cannot be matched by other locations, an entrepreneur may have little choice but to buy instead of build.

Employees and Suppliers Are Established.   The existing business already has experienced employees, so there are fewer problems associated with the "shakedown" phase of getting started. Often, experienced employees can help the company earn money while the new owner learns the business. In addition, an existing business has an established set of suppliers with a history of business dealings. Those vendors can continue to supply the business while the new owner investigates the products and services of other suppliers. Thus, the new owner is not pressured to choose a supplier quickly without thorough investigation.

Equipment Is Installed and Productive Capacity Is Known.   Acquiring and installing new equipment exerts a tremendous strain on a fledgling company's financial resources. In an existing business, a potential buyer can determine the condition of the plant and equipment and know its capacity before he buys. The previous owner may have established an efficient production operation through trial-and-error, although the new owner may need to make modifications to improve it. In many cases, the entrepre-

neur can purchase physical facilities and equipment at prices significantly below replacement costs.

Inventories Are in Place and Trade Credit Has Been Established.   The proper amount of inventory is essential to both cost control and sales volume. If the business has too little inventory, it will not have the quantity and variety of products to satisfy customer demand. If the business has too much inventory, too much capital is tied up, increasing costs and reducing profitability. Many successful established businesses have learned a balance between these extremes. Previous owners have established trade credit relationships of which the new owner can take advantage. The proven track record of the business provides the new owner with leverage in negotiating for trade credit concessions. No vendor wants to lose a good client.

The Business "Hits the Ground Running."   The entrepreneur who purchases an existing business saves the time, costs, and energy required to plan and launch a new business. The day he takes over the ongoing business is the day his revenues begin. In this way, he "earns while he learns."

The New Owner Can Use the Experience of the Previous Owner.   Even if the previous owner is not around after the sale, the new owner has access to all of the business' records. These records can guide the new owner until he becomes acclimated to the business and the local market. He can trace the impact on costs and revenues of the major decisions the previous owner made and can learn from his mistakes and profit from his achievements. In many cases, the previous owner will spend time in an "orientation period" with the new owner. This gives the new manager the opportunity to question him about the policies and procedures he developed and the reasons for them. Previous owners also can be extremely helpful in unmasking the unwritten rules of business in the area—what types of behavior are acceptable, whom to trust or not to trust, and other important "intangibles." After all, most business owners who sell out want to see the buyer succeed in carrying on the business.

It's a Bargain. Some existing businesses may be real bargains. The present owner may wish to sell on short notice, which may lead to him selling the business at a low price. The more specialized the business, the greater the likelihood that a bargain might be found. If special skills or training are required to operate the business, the number of potential buyers is significantly reduced. If the owner wants a substantial down payment or the entire selling price in cash, few buyers may qualify; however, those who do may be able to negotiate a good deal.

Disadvantages of Buying an Existing Business

It's a "Dog." A business may be for sale because it has never been profitable. Such a situation may be disguised; owners can employ various "creative accounting techniques" that make the firm's financial picture much brighter than it really is. The actual reason the business is for sale will seldom be stated honestly as "It's losing money." If there is an area of business where the maxim "let the buyer beware" still prevails, it is in the sale of a business. Any buyer unprepared to do a complete and thorough analysis of the business may be stuck with a real "dog."

Ill Will May Have Been Created by the Previous Owner. Just as proper business dealings create good will over the years, some managers create ill will by improper business behavior. The business may look great on the surface, but customers, suppliers, creditors, or employees may have extremely negative feelings about it. Gradually deteriorating relations may have begun with their long-term effects not yet reflected in the business' financial statements. Ill will can continue with a business for years.

Employees Inherited with the Business May Not Be Suitable. If the new owner plans to make changes in the business, present employees may not suit her needs. Previous managers may have kept marginal

employees because they were close friends or because they "started off with the company." The new owner may have to make some very unpopular termination decisions. Often, employees do not welcome the new owner because they feel a threat to their job stability. Further, employees who may have wanted to buy the business themselves but who could not afford it are likely to see the new owner as the person who stole their opportunity. Bitter employees are not likely to be productive workers.

The Business Location May Have Become Unsatisfactory. What was once or is presently an ideal location may become obsolete as market and demographic trends change. Large shopping malls, new competitors, or highway reroutings could spell disaster for a small retail shop. New owners should always evaluate the existing business' surrounding area as well as its potential for expansion.

Equipment and Facilities May Be Obsolete or Inefficient. Potential buyers sometimes neglect to have an expert evaluate a firm's facilities and equipment prior to purchase. Later, they discover that the equipment is not cost efficient. Thus excessive production costs result, and the business may suffer losses. Equipment may have been well suited to the business you purchased, but not to the business you want to build. Modernizing equipment and facilities is seldom inexpensive!

Change and Innovation Are Difficult to Implement. It is easier to plan for change than it is to implement it. Methods previously used in a business may have precedents that are hard to modify. For example, if the previous owner allowed a 15 percent discount to customers purchasing 100 units or more in a single order, it may be almost impossible to eliminate the discount practice without losing some of those customers. The previous owner's policies, even if proven unwise, still affect the changes you can make. It is just as difficult to reverse a downward trend in sales. Implementing changes to bring in new business and convince former clients to return can be an expensive and laborious process.

Corporate Orphans Offer Entrepreneurial Opportunities

The 1960s was the age of corporate growth through acquisition. But, in the 1980s, many large companies are re-evaluating the businesses they acquired and are shedding units in unrelated fields. When these companies sell units to refocus on their primary businesses, they create unique opportunities for entrepreneurs.

Michael Cinquanti is one entrepreneur who took advantage of General Electric's decision to sell his Research and Development unit. Cinquanti remembers, "My manager at General Electric called me into his office and said, "Research and development wants to get rid of your unit. First, they'll attempt to find a GE group to take it over. If that doesn't work, they'll have to decide whether to sell you or dissolve you." Within 10 minutes, Cinquanti decided to buy the unit from GE. "Something went boom in my head and I knew what I wanted—to own my own business. It shook me awake," he says. Cinquanti and three members of his staff bought the unit from GE in a leveraged buyout (LBO), and GE even financed the entire purchase price over three years for the entrepreneurs.

Indeed, many parent companies that sell units are willing to help finance the deals, especially if managers are the buyers. They cite satisfying long-time customers and keeping employees working as key benefits of bankrolling LBOs by managers. For example, when vice-president Nathaniel Howe bought out his machine tools group from Litton, Inc., the company accepted a "significant" portion of the purchase price in promissory notes when the buyers came up with a 40 percent down payment. Outside lenders and even employees are potential sources of funds for buyouts. One manager-turned-entrepreneur raised $15 million for an LBO when he sold stock in the company to employees.

Most often, companies sell to the highest bidder, whether it is an "insider" or an "outsider." But, an insider frequently is the top bidder. Current managers, confident that they can earn higher profits, are willing to pay premium prices to outbid outsiders. Says one merger and acquisition expert, "The parent often gets better than market price and the new owner gets both a piece of the action and, because of the leverage, a good return on investment."

But, paying a premium price for a company can strain its cash flow to the breaking point. Excessive debt weighs the company down. One buyout expert explains, "The problem with a lot of LBOs is that the price is too high for what is essentially an average-growth business."

As more corporate conglomerates choose to divest unrelated units, a growing number of managers are finding their entrepreneurial spirits ignited. A corporate "misfit" in the hands of a motivated entrepreneur has almost unlimited potential.

Source: Adapted from Margaret Mahar, "Corporate Cast-Offs," *Venture*, May 1985, pp. 78–84, with permission of the publisher.

Inventory May Be Outdated or Obsolete. Inventory is valuable only if it is salable, or can be converted into salable products. Never trust the firm's balance sheet valuation of inventory. Some of it may actually appreciate in value in periods of rapid inflation, but more likely it has depreciated. Inventory should be judged on the basis of its *market* value, not its book value. A potential owner should check the age of the inventory to see if it is outdated. He should make sure it is still salable and, if so, at what price.

Accounts Receivable May Be Worth Less than Face Value. Like inventory, accounts receivable rarely are worth their face value. The prospective buyer should age the accounts receivable to determine their collectibility. The older the receivables, the less likely they are to be collected, and, consequently, the lower their value. Small Business Report 5–2 shows a simple but effective method of evaluating accounts receivable once they have been "aged."

The Business May Be Overpriced. Each year, many people purchase businesses at prices far in excess of their value. However, if accounts receivable, inventories, and other assets had been correctly valued, the new owners might have been able to negotiate a price that would have allowed the business to be profitable. Making payments on a business that was overpriced is a millstone around the neck of the new owner. It is difficult to carry this excess weight and keep the business afloat.

Five Critical Areas for Analysis When Evaluating an Existing Business

Why Does the Owner Wish to Sell? Every prospective business owner should investigate the *real* reason the business owner wants to sell. A recent study by the Geneva Corporation found that the most common reasons owners of small and medium-sized businesses gave for selling were boredom and burn out. Others sell because they are violating the rule that says a prudent man should have no more than 20 percent of his net worth tied up in any one asset.[1] Still others decide to cash in their business investments and diversify into other types of assets.

Some other less obvious reasons a business owner might have for selling his venture include intense competition, highway rerouting, expiring lease agreements, cash flow problems, a declining customer base, or any other calamity. Every prospective

[1] Richard M. Rodnick, "Getting the Right Price for Your Firm," *Nation's Business*, March 1984, p. 70.

buyer should study carefully the business he is considering and should explore local economic conditions to determine whether they are forcing the present owner to sell. The buyer should investigate thoroughly any reason the seller gives for selling the business.

Businesses do not last forever, and most owners know when the time has come to sell. Some owners consider their behavior ethical only if they do not make false or misleading statements. However, they may not disclose the "whole story." In most business sales, the buyer bears the responsibility of determining whether the business is a good value. Visiting local business owners may reveal general patterns about the area and its overall vitality. The local Chamber of Commerce also may have useful information. Suppliers and competitors may be able to shed light on why the business is up for sale. By combining this information with an analysis of the company's financial records, the potential buyer will be able to develop a clearer picture of the business and its real value.

> The following ad appeared in a Colorado newspaper:
>
> "Health Foods Business for Sale! In Wray, Colorado. Must sell because of ill health."

What Is the Physical Condition of the Business? A prospective buyer should evaluate the business' assets—both tangible and intangible—to determine whether they are transferable. Are they reasonably priced? Are they obsolete? Will they need to be replaced soon? Do they operate efficiently? The potential buyer should check the condition of the equipment of the building. It may be necessary to hire a professional to evaluate the major components of the building—its structure, plumbing, electrical, and heating and cooling systems. Renovations are rarely inexpensive or simple. One couple located a suitable building for their restaurant, but found that transforming it would cost $100,000! Unexpected renova-

Valuing Accounts Receivable

A prospective buyer asked the present owner of a business about the value of the firm's accounts receivable. The owner's records showed $80,000 in receivables. But, when the prospective buyer "aged" them and then multiplied them by his estimated collection probability, he discovered their *real* value, as follows.

Age of Accounts	Amount	Collection Probability	Value
0–30 days	$40,000	90%	$36,000
31–90 days	20,000	80%	16,000
91–120 days	10,000	60%	6,000
121–180 days	5,000	40%	2,000
Greater than 180 days	5,000	10%	500
	$80,000		$60,500

Had he blindly accepted the owner's value, this prospective buyer would have overpaid nearly $20,000 just for accounts receivable!

---

tion expenses can punch a big hole in a buyer's financial plan.

How fresh and salable is the firm's inventory? Is it consistent with the image the new owner wants to project? How much of it would the buyer have to sell at a loss? A potential buyer may need to get an independent appraisal to determine the value of the firm's inventory and other assets, since the present owner may have priced them far above their actual value. These items typically comprise the largest portion of a business' value, and a potential buyer should not accept the seller's asking price blindly. "Book value" is not the same as "market value." Usually, a buyer can purchase equipment and fixtures at substantially lower prices than "book value." Value is determined in the market, not on a balance sheet.

Other important factors the potential buyer should investigate include:

■ *Accounts Receivable.* If the sale includes accounts receivable, the buyer should check their quality before purchasing them. How creditworthy are the accounts? What portion of them are past due? By "aging" the accounts receivable, the buyer can judge their quality and determine their value.

■ *Lease Arrangements.* Is the lease included in the sale? When does it expire? What restrictions does it have on renovation or expansion? The buyer should determine *beforehand* what restrictions the landlord has placed on the lease and negotiate any change then.

■ *Business Records.* Well-kept business records can be a valuable source of information and can tell a prospective buyer a lot about the company's pattern of success (or lack of it). Does the owner have customer or mailing lists? These can be a valuable marketing tool for a new business owner.

■ *Intangible Assets.* Does the sale include any intangible assets like trademarks, patents, copyrights, or good will? Determining the value of such intangibles is much more difficult than computing the value of the tangible assets. (This will be covered later in the chapter.)

■ *Location and Appearance.* The location and the overall appearance of the building are important factors for a prospective buyer to consider. What had been an outstanding location in the past may be totally unacceptable today. Even if the building and equipment are in good condition and are fairly priced, the business may be located in a declining area. What kind of businesses are in the area? Very few people would patronize an ice cream shop located in a neighborhood housing pornographic theaters and adult book stores. Every buyer should consider the location's suitability several years into the future.

The potential buyer should also check local zoning laws to ensure that any changes he wants to make are legal. In some areas, zoning laws are very difficult to change and, as a result, can restrict the business' growth.

What Is the Potential for the Company's Products or Services? No one wants to buy a business with a dying market. A thorough market analysis will lead to a more accurate and more realistic sales forecast. This study should tell a buyer whether he should consider a particular business any further, and help define the *trend* in the business' sales and customer base.

Customer Characteristics and Composition. Before purchasing an existing business, a potential business owner should analyze both his existing and potential customers. He should ask questions such as:

- Who are my customers in terms of race, age, sex, and income level?
- What do the customers want the business to do for them?
- How often do customers buy? Do they buy in seasonal patterns?
- How loyal are my present customers?
- Is it practical or even possible to attract new customers? If so, are the new customers significantly different from my existing customers?
- Does the business have a customer base? Do customers come from a large geographical area or do they all live near the business?

Analyzing these questions can help the potential owner implement a marketing plan. Most likely he will try to keep the business attractive to existing customers, but also change some features of its advertising plan to attract new customers.

Competitor Analysis. A potential buyer must identify the company's direct competition—those businesses in the immediate area that sell similar products or services. The potential profitability and survival of the business will depend partially on the behavior of these competitors. In addition to analyzing direct competitors, the buyer should identify businesses that compete indirectly. For example, supermarkets and chain drugstores often carry a basic product line of automobile supplies (oil, spark plugs, and tune-up kits), competing with full-line auto parts stores. These chains often purchase bulk quantities at significant price reductions and do not incur the expense of carrying a full line of parts and supplies. As a result, these large chains may be able to sell such basic products at lower prices. Even though these chains are not direct competitors, they may have a significant impact on local auto parts stores.

Frequently, indirect competitors aim their limited product lines at the most profitable segments of the market. By concentrating on high volume or high profit items, they can pose a serious threat to other businesses.

A potential buyer should also evaluate the trend in the competition. How many similar businesses have closed in the past five years? What caused these failures? Perhaps the market cannot support the similar existing businesses. Also, how many similar businesses have entered the market in the past five years? Being a late comer in an already saturated market is not the path to long-term success.

In evaluating the competitive environment, the prospective buyer should answer other questions:

- Which competitors have survived and what characteristics have led to their success?
- How do competitors' sales volumes compare to that of the business the entrepreneur is considering?
- What unique services do competitors offer?
- How well organized and coordinated are the marketing efforts of competitors?

- What are the competitors' reputations?
- What are the strengths and weaknesses of the firm's competitors?
- What competitive edge does each competitor have?

What Legal Aspects Should Be Considered? Typically, the key legal issue involved in the sale of any asset is the proper transfer of good title from seller to buyer. However, since most business sales involve a collection of assorted assets, the transfer of good title is more complex. Some business assets may have liens against them. Unless these liens are satisfied before the sale, the buyer assumes them and becomes financially responsible for them. A clause in the sales contract stating that any liabilities not shown on the balance sheet on the transfer date are the responsibility of the seller would protect the buyer. A prospective buyer should have an attorney thoroughly investigate all of the assets for sale and their lien status *before* purchasing anything.

To protect against surprise claims from the seller's creditors after purchasing a business, the buyer should meet the requirements of a bulk transfer under Section 6 of the Uniform Commercial Code. Suppose that an owner owing many creditors sells his business to a buyer. The seller does not use the proceeds of the sale to pay his debts to business creditors. Without the protection of a bulk transfer, those creditors could make claim to the assets the buyer purchased to satisfy those debts (within 6 months).

To be effective, a bulk transfer must meet the following criteria:

- The seller must give the buyer a sworn list of existing creditors.
- The buyer and the seller must prepare a list of the property included in the sale.
- The buyer must keep the list of creditors and the list of property for six months.
- The buyer must give notice of the sale to each creditor at least 10 days before he takes possession of the goods or pays for them (whichever is first).

By meeting these criteria, a buyer acquires free and clear title to the assets purchased.

The buyer must investigate the rights and the obligations he would assume under existing contracts with suppliers, customers, employees, lessors, and others. To continue the smooth operation of the business, the buyer must assume the rights of the seller under existing contracts. For example, the present owner may have four years left on a ten-year lease and will need to assign this contract to the buyer. Generally, the seller can assign any contractual right, unless the contract specifically prohibits the assignment or the contract is personal in nature. For instance, loan contracts sometimes prohibit assignments with due-on-sale clauses. These clauses require the buyer to pay the full amount of the remaining loan balance or to finance the balance at prevailing interest rates. Thus, the buyer cannot "assume" the seller's loan (at a lower interest rate). Also, a seller usually cannot assign his credit arrangements with suppliers to the buyer because they are based on the seller's business reputation and are personal in nature. If such contacts are crucial to the business operation and cannot be assigned, the buyer must renegotiate new contracts.

The prospective buyer also should evaluate the terms of any other contracts the seller has, including:

- patent, trademark, or copyright registrations
- exclusive agent or distributor contracts
- real estate leases
- financing and loan arrangements
- union contracts

One of the most important and most often overlooked legal considerations for a prospective buyer is negotiating a covenant not to compete (or restrictive covenant) with the seller. Under a restrictive covenant, the seller agrees not to open a new competing store within a specific time period and geographic area of the existing one. However, the covenant must be part of a business sale and must be reasonable in scope to be enforceable. Without such protection, a buyer may find his new business eroding beneath his feet. For example, Bob Mabry purchases a tire business from Alex Brady whose reputation in town for selling tires is unequaled. If Bob fails to negotiate a restrictive covenant, nothing can stop Alex from opening a new shop next to his old one and keeping all of "his" customers, driving Bob out of business. A reasonable covenant in this case may restrict Alex from opening a tire store within a three-mile radius for three years. Every business buyer should negotiate a covenant not to compete with the seller.

Is the Business Financially Sound?   The prospective buyer must analyze the financial records of the business to determine its health. He shouldn't be afraid to ask an accountant for help. Accounting systems and methods vary tremendously from one type of business to another and can be quite confusing to a novice. Current profits can be inflated by changes in the accounting procedure or in the method for recording sales.

A buyer must remember that he is purchasing the future profit potential of an existing business. To evaluate the firm's potential, a buyer should review past sales, operating expenses, and profits as well as the assets used to generate those profits. He must compare current balance sheets and income statements to previous ones and then develop projected statements for the next two to three years. Sales tax records, income tax returns, and financial statements are valuable sources of information.

Are profits consistent over the years, or are they erratic? Is this pattern typical in the industry, or is it a result of unique circumstances or poor management? Can the business survive with such a serious fluctuation in revenues, costs, and profits? If these fluctuations are caused by poor management, can a new manager turn the business around?

A potential buyer must look for suspicious deviations from average (in either direction) for sales, expenses, profits, assets, and liabilities. Have sales been increasing or decreasing? Is the equipment really as valuable as it is listed on the balance sheet?

Is advertising expense unusually high? How is depreciation reflected in the financial statements?

This financial information provides the buyer with the opportunity to verify the seller's claims about the business' performance. However, sometimes an owner will take short-term actions that produce a healthy financial statement but weaken the firm's long-term health and profit potential. For example, a seller might lower costs by gradually eliminating equipment maintenance or boost sales by selling to marginal businesses that will never pay their bills. Such techniques can artificially inflate assets and profits, but a well-prepared buyer can see through them.

Finally, a potential buyer should always reconsider purchasing a business if the present owner refuses to disclose financial records.

Determining the Value of a Business

Perhaps the most difficult stage in a buyout is determining an acceptable price for the business. Computing the value of the company's tangible assets usually poses no major problem, but assigning a price to the intangibles, such as goodwill, almost always creates controversy. The seller expects goodwill to reflect the hard work and long hours invested in building the business. The buyer, however, is willing to pay extra only for those intangible assets that produce exceptional income.

So, how can the buyer and the seller arrive at a fair price? There are few universal rules in establishing the value of a business, but both parties should observe the following guidelines:

- There is no single "best" method for determining a business' worth since each business sale is unique. The wisest approach is to compute a company's value using several techniques and then choose the one that makes the most sense.
- The deal must be financially feasible for both parties. The seller must be satisfied with the price he receives for the business. Claims one valuation

specialist, "Frequently, the entrepreneur feels like he is selling his baby. So, he doesn't want to leave a dime on the table."[2] But, the buyer cannot pay an excessively high price that would require heavy borrowing and would strain cash flows from the outset.

■ The buyer and the seller should have access to business records. Valuations should be based on facts, not fiction.

■ No surprise is the best surprise. Both parties should deal with one another honestly and in good faith.[3]

The primary reason buyers purchase existing businesses is to get their future earning potential. The second most common reason is to get an established asset base. It is much easier to buy assets than to build them.[4] Evaluation methods should take these characteristics into consideration. This section will describe three techniques and several variations for determining the value of a hypothetical business, Lewis Electronics.

Balance Sheet Technique. The balance sheet technique is one of the most commonly used methods of evaluating a business, although it is not highly recommended because it oversimplifies the valuation process. This method computes the company's net worth or owner's equity (net worth = assets − liabilities) and uses this figure as the value. The first step is to determine which assets are included in the sale. In most cases, the owner has some personal assets he does not want to sell. Professional business brokers can help the buyer and the seller arrive at a reasonable value for the collection of assets included in the deal. Remember that net worth on a financial statement will likely differ significantly from actual net worth in the market. For Lewis Electronics, net worth is $241,000 − $90,000 = $151,000.

Variation: Adjusted Balance Sheet Technique. A more realistic method for determining a company's value is to adjust the book value of net worth to reflect actual market value. Typical assets in a business sale include notes and accounts receivable, inventories, supplies, and fixtures. If a buyer purchases notes and accounts receivable, he should estimate the likelihood of their collection and adjust their value accordingly (refer to Small Business Report 5–2).

In manufacturing, wholesale, and retail businesses, inventory usually is the largest single asset involved in the sale. Taking a physical inventory count is the best way to determine accurately the quantity of goods to be transferred. The sale may include three types of inventory, each having its own method of valuation: raw materials, work-in-process, and finished goods. The buyer and the seller must arrive at a method for evaluating the inventory. First-in–first-out (FIFO), last-in–first-out (LIFO), and average costing are three frequently used techniques, but the most common methods use the cost of last purchase and the replacement value of the inventory.

Before accepting any inventory value, the buyer should evaluate the condition of the goods. One young couple purchased a lumber yard without examining the inventory completely. After completing the sale, they discovered that most of the lumber in a warehouse they had neglected to inspect was warped and was of little value as building material. The "bargain price" they paid for the business turned out not to be the good deal they had expected. To avoid such problems, some buyers insist on having a knowledgeable representative on an "inventory team," which counts the inventory and checks its condition. Nearly every sale involves merchandise which cannot be sold; but, by taking this precaution, a buyer minimizes the chance of being "stuck" with worthless inventory.

Fixed assets transferred in a sale might include land, buildings, equipment, and fixtures. Business owners frequently carry real estate and buildings at prices well below their actual market value. Equip-

---

[2]Sanford L. Jacobs, "Small Business," *The Wall Street Journal*, September 20, 1982, p. 33.

[3]Rodnick, op. cit pp. 70–71.

[4]Ibid. p. 71.

ment and fixtures, depending on their condition and usefulness, may increase or decrease the true value of the business. Appraisals of these assets on insurance policies are helpful guidelines for establishing market value. Also, business brokers can be useful in determining the current value of fixed assets. For Lewis Electronics, adjusted net worth is $160,000, indicating that some of its assets were undervalued on its books.

Business evaluations based on balance sheet methods suffer one major drawback: they do not consider the future earning potential of the business. These techniques value assets at current prices and do not consider them as tools for creating future profits. The next method for computing the value of a business is based on its expected future earnings.

Earnings Approach. The buyer of an existing business is essentially purchasing its future income. The earnings approach is more refined since it considers the future income potential of the business. We will explore three versions of the earnings approach.

Variation 1: Excess Earnings Method. This method combines both the value of the firm's existing assets (over its liabilities) and an estimate of its future earnings potential to determine a business' selling price. One advantage of this technique is that it offers an estimate of goodwill. Goodwill is an intangible asset that often creates problems in a business sale. In fact, the most common method of valuing a business is to compute its tangible net worth and then to add an often arbitrary adjustment for goodwill. In essence, goodwill is the difference between an established, successful business and one which has yet to prove itself. It is based on the company's reputation and its ability to attract customers. A buyer should not accept blindly the seller's arbitrary adjustment for goodwill since it is likely to be inflated.

The excess earnings method provides a more consistent and realistic approach for determining the value of goodwill. It assumes that the owner is entitled to a reasonable return on the firm's adjusted tangible net worth.

Step 1: Compute adjusted tangible net worth. Using the previous method of valuation, the buyer should compute the firm's adjusted tangible net worth. Total tangible assets (adjusted for market value) minus total liabilities yields adjusted tangible net worth. In the Lewis Electronics example, adjusted tangible net worth is $250,000 − $90,000 = $160,000.

Step 2: Calculate the opportunity costs of investing in the business. Opportunity costs represent the cost of forgoing a choice. If the buyer chooses to purchase the assets of a business, he cannot invest his money elsewhere. So, the opportunity cost of the purchase would be the amount the buyer could earn by investing the same amount *in a similar risk investment*. A "normal risk" business typically indicates a 25 percent rate of return. In the Lewis Electronics example, the opportunity cost of the investment is $160,000 × 25% = $40,000.

The second part of the buyer's opportunity cost is the salary he could earn working for someone else. For the Lewis Electronics example, if the buyer purchases the business, he must forgo the $25,000 he could earn working elsewhere. Adding these amounts together yields a total opportunity cost of $65,000.

Step 3: Project net earnings. The buyer must estimate the company's net earnings for the upcoming year *before* subtracting the owner's salary. Averages can be misleading, so the buyer must be sure to investigate the trend of net earnings. Have they risen steadily over the past five years; dropped significantly; remained relatively constant; or fluctuated wildly? Past income statements provide useful guidelines for estimating earnings. In the Lewis Electronics example, the buyer projects net earnings to be $74,000.

Step 4: Compute extra earning power. A company's extra earning power is the difference between forecasted earnings (Step 3) and total opportunity costs (Step 2). Most small businesses that are for sale do not have "extra earning power" (i.e., excess earnings), however. They show marginal or no profits.

The extra earning power of Lewis Electronics is
$74,000 − $65,000 = $9,000.

Step 5: Estimate the value of intangibles. The
owner can use the extra earning power of the business to estimate the value of its intangible assets—
that is, goodwill. Multiplying the extra earning power
by a "years of profit" figure yields an estimate of the
intangible assets' value. The years of profit figure for
a normal risk business ranges from three to four. A
very high-risk business may have a years of profit
figure of 1, while a well established firm might use a
figure of 5. For Lewis Electronics, the value of intangibles (assuming "normal risk") would be $9,000 ×
3 = $27,000.

Step 6: Determine the value of the business.
To determine the value of the business, the buyer
simply adds the adjusted tangible net worth (Step 1)
and the value of the intangibles (Step 5). Using this
method, the value of Lewis Electronics would be
$160,000 + $27,000 = $187,000.

Both the buyer and seller should consider the
tax implications of transferring goodwill. The
amount the seller receives for goodwill is taxed as
ordinary income. The buyer cannot count this
amount as a deduction since goodwill is a capital
asset that cannot be depreciated or amortized for tax
purposes.[5]

The success of this approach depends on the
accuracy of the buyer's estimates of net earnings. But,
it does offer a systematic method for assigning a
value to goodwill. Says one business appraiser,
"What it really does is recognize tomorrow's success
by adding to today's value."[6]

Variation 2: Capitalized Earnings Approach.
Another earnings approach capitalizes on expected
net profits to determine the value of a business. The
buyer should prepare his own pro forma income
statement and should ask the seller to prepare one

also. Many appraisers use a five-year weighted average of past sales to estimate sales for the upcoming
year.

Once again, the buyer must evaluate the risk
involved in purchasing the business to determine the
appropriate rate of return on the investment. The
greater the risk involved, the higher the return the
buyer requires. Risk determination is always somewhat subjective, but it is necessary for proper evaluation.

The capitalized earnings approach divides estimated net earnings (after subtracting the owner's
reasonable salary) by the rate of return that reflects
the risk level. For Lewis Electronics, the capitalized
value (assuming a reasonable salary of $25,000)
would be:

$$\frac{\text{net earnings (after deducting}}{\text{owner's salary)}}{\text{rate of return}} = \frac{\$74,000 - \$25,000}{25\%}$$

$$= \$196,000$$

Clearly, firms with lower risk factors are more
valuable (a 10 percent rate of return would yield a
value of $499,000) than those with higher risk factors
(a 50 percent rate of return would yield a value of
$99,800). Most normal risk businesses use a rate of
return factor ranging from 25 percent to 33 percent.
The lowest risk factor most buyers would accept for
any business is 20 percent.

**Variation 3: Discounted Future Earnings Ap-
proach.** This variation of the earnings approach assumes that a dollar earned in the future is worth less
than that same dollar today. Therefore, using this
approach, the buyer estimates the company's net income for several years into the future and then discounts these future earnings back to their present
value. The resulting present value is an estimate of
the company's worth.

The reduced value of future dollars has nothing to do with inflation. Instead, present value represents the "cost" of the buyer giving up the opportunity to earn a reasonable rate of return by receiving

---

[5]"Small Business Reporter: How to Buy or Sell a Business," Bank
of America, 1982, p. 8.
[6]William Meyers, "Determining a Value," *Venture*, January 1985, p.
35.

income in the future instead of today. To illustrate the importance of the time value of money, consider two $1 million sweepstake winners. Rob wins $1 million in a sweepstakes, but he receives it in $50,000 installments over 20 years. If Rob invested every installment at 15 percent interest, he would have accumulated $5,890,505.98 at the end of 20 years. Lisa wins $1 million in another sweepstakes, but she collects her winnings in a lump sum. If Lisa invested her $1 million today at 15 percent, she would have accumulated $16,366,537.39 at the end of 20 years. The difference in their wealth is the result of the time value of money.

The discounted future earnings approach involves five steps:[7]

Step 1: Project future earnings for five years into the future. One way is to assume that earnings will grow by a constant amount over the next five years. Perhaps a better method is to develop *three* forecasts—an optimistic, a pessimistic, and a most likely—for each year and then find a weighted average using the formula:

$$\text{Forecasted earnings for year } i = \frac{\begin{array}{c}\text{Optimistic}\\\text{earnings}\\\text{for year } i\end{array} + 4 \times \begin{array}{c}\text{Most likely}\\\text{forecast}\\\text{for year } i\end{array} + \begin{array}{c}\text{Pessimistic}\\\text{forecast}\\\text{for year } i\end{array}}{6}$$

For Lewis Electronics, the buyer's forecasts might be:

Year	Pessimistic	Most Likely	Optimistic	Weighted Average
19X1	$65,000	$ 74,000	$ 92,000	$ 75,500
19X2	74,000	90,000	101,000	89,167
19X3	82,000	100,000	112,000	99,000
19X4	88,000	109,000	120,000	107,333
19X5	88,000	115,000	122,000	111,667

The buyer must remember that the farther into the

[7]"Selling Your Business," Special Report No. 4, *The Business Owner*, p. 8.

future he forecasts, the less reliable are his estimates.

Step 2: Discount these future earnings at the appropriate present value rate. The rate the buyer selects should reflect the rate he could earn on a similar risk investment. Since Lewis Electronics is a normal risk business, the buyer chooses 25 percent.

Year	Forecasted income	× Present value factor (at 25%)*	= Net present value
19X1	$ 75,500	0.8000	$ 60,400
19X2	89,167	0.6400	57,067
19X3	99,000	0.5120	50,688
19X4	107,333	0.4096	43,964
19X5	111,667	0.3277	36,593
Total			$248,712

*The appropriate present value factor can be found by looking in published present value tables, by using modern calculators or computers, or by solving the formula:

$$\text{Present value factor} \times \frac{1}{(1 + k)^t}$$

where k = rate of return
  t = year (t = 1,2,3, . . . ,n).

Step 3: Estimate the income stream beyond five years. One technique suggests multiplying the fifth year income by 1/rate of return. For Lewis Electronics, the estimate would be:

$$\text{Income beyond 1993} = \$111,667 \times \frac{1}{25\%} = \$446,668$$

Step 4: Discount the income estimate beyond five years using the present value factor for the sixth year. For Lewis Electronics,

$$\frac{\text{Present value of}}{\text{income beyond 1993}} = \$446,668 \times 0.2622 = \$117,116$$

Step 5: Compute the total value.

Total value = $248,712 + $117,116 = $365,828

The primary advantage of this technique is that it values a business solely on the basis of its future earning potential, but its key disadvantage is the uncertainty of forecasting future earnings.

Market Approach.   The market (or price/earnings) approach uses the price/earnings ratios of similar businesses to establish the value of a company. The buyer must use businesses whose stocks are publicly traded to get a meaningful comparison. A company's price/earnings ratio (or P/E ratio) is the price of one share of its common stock in the market divided by its earnings per share (after deducting preferred stock dividends). To get a representative P/E ratio, the buyer should average the P/E's of as many similar businesses as possible.

To compute the company's value, the buyer multiplies the price/earnings ratio by the company's estimated earnings. Using a P/E ratio of 4 for Lewis Electronics yields a value of $296,000 (4 × $74,000).

The biggest advantage of the market approach is its simplicity. But, this method suffers form several disadvantages, including:[8]

- Necessary comparisons between publicly traded and privately owned companies. The stock of privately owned companies is illiquid, and, therefore, the P/E ratio used is often subjective and lower than that of publicly held companies.
- Unrepresentative earnings estimates. The private company's net earnings may not realistically reflect its true earning potential. To minimize taxes, owners usually attempt to keep profits low and rely on "fringe benefits" to make up the difference.
- Finding similar companies for comparison. Often, it is extremely difficult for a buyer to find comparable publicly held companies when estimating the appropriate P/E ratio.

Despite its drawbacks, the market approach is useful as a general guideline to establishing a company's value.

Which of these methods is best for determining the value of a small business? Simply stated, there is no single "best" method (see table 5–1). Valuing a business is partly an art and partly a science. Using these techniques, a range of values will emerge. The buyer should look for values that might cluster together and then use his best judgment to determine his offering price.

Negotiating for the Business

Even though the buyer has determined the value of the business, there is no guarantee that he can buy it at that price. Of course, the final price should not be far out of line with the value, but the buyer must realize that the final price he pays is influenced by his skills as a negotiator. The buyer must not confuse "price" with "value." Value is what the business is worth; price is what the buyer and the seller finally agree upon. Buying a business involves a certain amount of "horse trading." The better bargainer usually comes out on top. What the seller wants is:

- to get the highest possible price for his business.
- to get his money from you as agreed in the sale contract.
- to sever liability ties.
- to avoid unreasonable contract terms that might limit future opportunities.

The buyer normally seeks to:

- obtain the business at the lowest possible price.
- negotiate terms of payment favorable to him.
- know that statements he receives from the seller are true and honest.

Factors Affecting the Negotiation Process.   Before beginning negotiations, the buyer should consider some basic issues. How strong is the owner's desire to sell? Will the seller finance part of the price? What are the terms? What is the time factor surrounding the deal? Is it urgent that the seller close the deal quickly? What is the impact of economic conditions on the price of the business? Business prices tend to follow overall economic conditions. Sellers tend to have the upper hand during prosperous conditions, and buyers are favored during economic recessions.

---

[8]Ibid. p. 7.

TABLE 5–1 What's it worth?

This section has covered several methods for determining the value of a small business. The following summarizes the results of these methods for Lewis Electronics:

Balance Sheet Technique

$$\text{Book value of net worth} = \text{assets} - \text{liabilities}$$
$$= \$241,000 - \$90,000$$
$$= \$151,000$$

Variation: *Adjusted balance sheet technique*

$$\text{Adjusted net worth} = \$250,000 - \$90,000$$
$$= \$160,000$$

Earnings Approach

Variation 1: *Excess earnings method*

Step 1   Adjusted tangible net worth = $\$250,000 - \$90,000 = \$160,000$

Step 2   Opportunity costs = $\$160,000 \times 25\% + \$25,000 = \$65,000$

Step 3   Estimated net earnings = $\$74,000$

Step 4   Extra earning power = estimated net earnings − opportunity costs
$$= \$74,000 - \$65,000 = \$9,000$$

Step 5   Value of intangibles = extra earnings power × years of profit figure
$$= \$9,000 \times 3 = \$27,000$$

Step 6   Value of business = tangible net worth + value of intangibles
$$= \$160,000 + \$27,000$$
$$= \$187,000$$

Variation 2: *Capitalized earnings approach*

$$\text{Value} = \frac{\text{net earnings (after deducting owner's salary)}}{\text{rate of return}}$$
$$= \frac{\$74,000 - \$25,000}{25\%}$$
$$= \$196,000$$

Variation 3: *Discounted future earnings approach*

Step 1   Projected future earnings approach

The Negotiation Process.   The process of negotiation is simple, but will be unique to the two parties involved. Both parties want optimum fulfillment of their needs and wants, but realize the transaction must finally be completed if they are to achieve anything. If an agreement is not reached, the negotiation process was unsuccessful. Recognizing that no one benefits without an agreement, both parties must work to achieve their goals while making concessions to keep the negotiations alive. Figure 5–1 is an illustration of two individuals prepared to negotiate for the purchase and sale of a business. The buyer

TABLE 5–1 *Continued*

Year	Pessimistic	Most Likely	Optimistic	Weighted* Average
19X1	$65,000	$ 74,000	$ 94,000	$ 75,500
19X2	74,000	90,000	101,000	89,167
19X3	82,000	100,000	112,000	99,000
19X4	88,000	109,000	120,000	107,333
19X5	88,000	115,000	122,000	111,667

$$*\frac{p + 4ml + o}{6}$$

Step 2   Discount future earnings at the appropriate present value factor

Year	Forecasted Earnings	× Present Value Factor =	Net Present Value
19X1	$ 75,500	0.8000	$ 64,400
19X2	89,167	0.6400	57,067
19X3	99,000	0.5120	50,688
19X4	107,333	0.4096	43,964
19X5	111,667	0.3277	36,593
Total			$248,712

Step 3   Estimate income stream beyond 5 years

$$\frac{Income}{stream} = \frac{Fifth\ year}{income} \times \frac{1}{Rate\ of\ return}$$

$$= \$111,667 \times \frac{1}{25\%}$$

$$= \$446,668$$

Step 4   Discount income stream beyond five years (using sixth year present value factor)

$$\frac{Present\ value}{of\ income\ stream} = \$446,668 \times 0.2622 = \$117,116$$

Step 5   Compute the total value

$$Total\ value = \$248,712 + \$117,116 = \$365,828$$

Market Approach

$$Value = estimated\ earnings \times representative\ price\text{-}earnings\ ratio$$
$$= \$74,000 \times 4 = \$296,000$$

Which value is correct? Remember, there is no best method of valuing a business. These techniques provide only *estimates* of a company's worth. The particular method used depends on the unique qualities of the business and the special circumstances surrounding the sale.

and seller both have high and low bargaining points in this example. The buyer would like to purchase the business for $90,000, but would not pay more than $130,000. The seller would like to get $150,000 for the business, but would not take less than $100,000. If the seller insists on getting $150,000, the business will not be sold to this buyer. Likewise, if the buyer stands firm on an offer of $90,000, there will be no deal. The bargaining process will eventually lead both parties into the bargaining zone. The bargaining zone is the area within which an agreement can be reached. It extends from above the lowest price the seller is willing to take to below the maximum price the buyer is willing to pay.

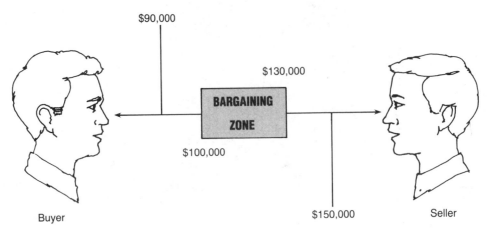

FIGURE 5–1 The negotiating process.

The dynamics of this negotiation process and the needs of each party ultimately will determine whether the buyer and seller can reach an agreement, and at what price.

III. SUMMARY

The potential small business manager has two alternatives: to start her own business from scratch or purchase an existing business. If the business is started fresh, the advantages are:

1. The business is not a made-over version of someone else's place, but it is formed the way she thinks it should be.
2. She does not run the risk of inheriting a business with a poor reputation.
3. If the concept she has for the business is so unusual, this is her only alternative.

The creation of a new business also has some substantial drawbacks, including:

1. Too small a market for the product or service.
2. High cost of new equipment.
3. Lack of a source of advice on how things are done and who can be trusted.
4. Lack of name recognition. It may take a long time to persuade customers to give the business a try.

Buying an existing business also has advantages and disadvantages. The major advantages are:

1. A successful business may provide the buyer with an immediate source of income.
2. An existing business may already be the best location.
3. An existing business already has employees who are trained and suppliers who have established ties to the business.
4. Equipment is already installed and the productive capacity of the business is known.
5. Inventories are in place, and suppliers have extended trade credit which can be continued.
6. There is no loss of momentum. The business is already operating.
7. The buyer has the opportunity to obtain advice and counsel from the previous owner.
8. Often a buyer can purchase the business at a price much lower than the cost of starting the same business from scratch.

Purchasing an existing business can have some drawbacks, including:

1. The buyer can be misled and end up with a business that is a "dog."
2. The business could have been so poorly managed

Anatomy of a Sale

When it comes to selling a business, well-planned, creative deals can benefit both the buyer and seller. Such sales can maximize the seller's compensation without overburdening the buyer. A recent deal negotiated by an acquisition specialist between the owner of a manufacturing company (the seller) and a public company (the buyer) illustrates these trends.

The buyer refused to pay any more than the $3.2 million book value for the business, and the seller did not want to receive the total amount up front because income tax would devour his receipts. The deal that emerged involved three separate payments to the owner: one for the assets; one for the owner's consulting services; and one for a covenant not to compete. At the closing, the owner received "the magic number," $1 million, and the right to collect lump sum and annual payments for twenty years. His total receipts over the twenty-year period is $8 million.

But, the buyer pays out only $3.2 million. The company purchased a $1.4 million annuity that pays the seller $200,000 annually and $800,000 worth of zero-coupon bonds that provide the lump-sum payments. The $200,000 annual payments are treated as "compensation" for the seller, and the buyer can deduct the bonds as a business expense.

The corporate buyer wanted to avoid buying "goodwill" because it offers no tax advantages; an intangible asset like goodwill cannot be depreciated. Sellers, however, prefer goodwill sales because the amount is taxed at lower capital gain rates. Frequently, sellers pay buyers more than the book value of their businesses without using goodwill. The deal instead includes royalty payments to the owner. "Royalties are a good way to cover goodwill," says one acquisitions specialist. Sellers pay the lower capital gains tax on them, and buyers can deduct them as business expenses.

The lesson is clear: planning a business sale carefully can benefit both the buyer and the seller.

Source: Adapted from Sanford L. Jacobs, "Selling Out: Top Dollar Comes From Well-Structured Deals," *The Wall Street Journal*, February 11, 1985, with permission of *The Wall Street Journal*, © Dow Jones & Company, Inc. 1985. All rights reserved.

---

by the previous owner that the buyer inherits a great deal of ill will.

3. A poorly managed business may have employees who are unsuited to the business or poorly trained.

4. The location of the business may have become, or is becoming, unsuitable.

5. The equipment may have been poorly maintained or even be obsolete.

6. Change can be difficult to introduce in an established business.

7. Inventory may be out of date, damaged, or obsolete.

8. The buyer can pay too much for the business.

To avoid buying a business that cannot be made profitable, investigate six critical areas:

1. Why does the owner wish to sell? Look for the *real* reason.

2. Determine the physical condition of the business. Consider the building and its location.

3. Conduct a thorough analysis of the market for your products or services. Who are the present and potential customers? Conduct an equally thorough analysis of competitors, both direct and indirect. How do they operate and why do customers prefer them?

4. Consider all of the legal factors which might con-

strain the expansion and growth of the business. Become familiar with zoning restrictions.

5. Identify the actual owner of the business and all liens that might exist.

6. Analyze the financial condition of the business.

One of the most difficult steps in buying an existing business is determining its value. There are three basic techniques (with several variations): the Balance Sheet Technique (Adjusted Balance Sheet Technique); the Earnings Approach (Excess Earnings Method, Capitalized Earnings Approach, and Discounted Future Savings Approach); and the Market Approach. There is no single "best" method for determining a business' value.

The final price of the business depends on the process of negotiation. For a deal to be struck, there must be a "bargaining zone" between the buyer and the seller.

STUDENT INVOLVEMENT PROJECTS

1. Visit a business broker and ask him how he brings a buyer and seller together. What does he do to facilitate the sale? What methods does he use to determine the value of a business?

2. Ask several new owners who purchased existing businesses the following questions:

   a. How did you determine the value of the business?

   b. How close was the price paid for the business to the value assessed prior to purchase?

   c. What percentage of the accounts receivable was collectible?

   d. How accurate have their projections been concerning customers (sales volume and number of customers, especially)?

DISCUSSION QUESTIONS

1. How would you go about determining the value of the assets of a business if you were unfamiliar with them?

2. How should goodwill be valued?

3. Is it fair to ask the seller of a travel agency located in a small town to sign a noncompetitive agreement for one year covering a 20-square-mile area?

4. How much negative information can you expect the seller to give you about the business?

5. What are some examples from your city of too many businesses of a certain type?

6. Which method of valuing a business is best? Why?

SECTION
THREE

BUILDING A BUSINESS PLAN: ACCOUNTING AND FINANCIAL CONSIDERATIONS

Financial Recordkeeping

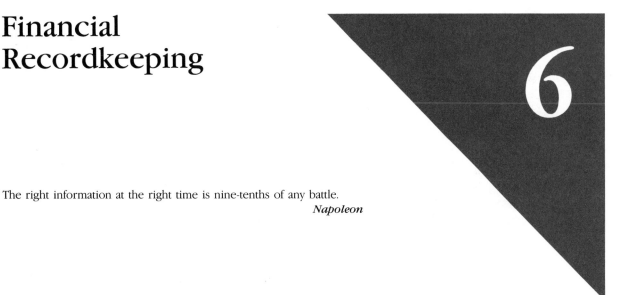

6

The right information at the right time is nine-tenths of any battle.
Napoleon

Upon completion of this chapter, you will be able to:

■ Explain the importance of establishing a reliable recordkeeping system and identify the characteristics of such a system.

■ Distinguish between the accrual method and cash method of accounting.

■ Explain the accounting equation and differentiate between single-entry and double-entry bookkeeping.

■ Understand a typical system for properly recording daily transactions in the business.

■ Explain the use of the various accounting journals and ledgers in a typical small business.

■ Understand the elements of each of the basic financial reports—the balance sheet, the income statement, and the statement of sources and uses of funds.

■ Understand other basic records which might improve the manager's control over the business.

To match the present pace of change in the business world and maintain a competitive edge, the small business owner must know her business' daily financial position. Yet, many managers are unaware of their business' financial status and are unable to make sound decisions because of inadequate recordkeeping or failure to keep records up-to-date. Also, because many small business managers do not understand the functions of financial management, they often neglect this aspect of the business. For instance, the owner of a small repair shop began to encounter cash flow problems and requested the help of Small Business Development Center consultants. During the initial interview, the owner produced a stack of financial reports and told the consultants, "Here they are, but I don't know what's in them or what they mean. My accountant handles all of that financial stuff." Clearly, this business owner lacked the tools and the ability to manage the financial affairs of the business. Table 6–1 shows the percentage of failures for four major business categories that resulted from the manager's inability to avoid

TABLE 6–1   Causes of business failures—percentage of industry precipitated by inadequate records.

Cause of Failure	Percentage of Failures[a]			
	Manufacturing	Wholesaling	Retailing	Services
Inadequate sales volume	73.5	76.4	78.3	79.4
Heavy operating expenses	35.5	30.7	24.7	23.6
Receivables difficulty	10.0	10.6	2.3	4.6
Inventory difficulty	1.1	2.7	3.2	0.5
Excessive fixed assets	5.3	1.1	2.2	4.1

[a]Because some failures were attributed to a combination of causes, totals may exceed 100 percent.

Source: Business Failure Record (New York: Dun & Bradstreet, 1985), p. 15.

certain problems which adequate records would have detected in time for early correction.

An adequate, reliable recordkeeping system can be simple as long as it provides the small business manager with the needed information. However, she should not spend her precious time and money compiling information that will never be used. Further, reliable business records are critical to managing a firm successfully; however, the owner must not be so preoccupied with keeping records that she neglects the primary purpose of the business. The owner of one retail store spent so much time generating records and reports that she ignored the principal function of the business—selling.

The small business owner may design her own accounting and recordkeeping system either alone or with the help of an accountant; or she may rely on a standardized package, such as the popular Dome System available at most office supply stores. These packages are relatively simple to operate and quite inexpensive; however, they lack flexibility and may not suit the owner's specific recordkeeping needs. But, for many small businesses, these packages provide sufficient detail for maintaining adequate records. The proliferation of microcomputers for business applications has produced a growing number of computerized accounting packages, which often are designed for a specific operation for a particular type of business. For example, the owner of a small hardware store can purchase standard packages for accounts receivable, accounts payable, inventory control, payroll, and many other recordkeeping functions. These packages are much less expensive than custom-designed programs, but they may not suit the owner's needs exactly.

Whatever recordkeeping system the small business owner chooses, it should have the following characteristics:[1]

1. It must be *simple to use*. Unless a recordkeeping system is simple to use, the owner, who usually is pressed for time, probably will disregard it.
2. It must be *easy to understand*. The system must be so clear that everyone who uses it knows how it operates.
3. It must be *reliable*. The recordkeeping system must perform the functions it is designed to perform and measure the aspects of the business it is intended to measure.
4. It must be *accurate*. Financial management can be only as accurate as the records and reports used. Faulty information leads to faulty managerial decisions.
5. It must be *consistent*. The system must parallel the

[1]U.S. Small Business Administration, *Keeping Records in Small Business*, Small Marketers Aid No. 155, Washington, 1979, p. 2.

operation of the business and should reflect the firm's financial status consistently over time.

6. It must be *designed to provide timely information.* To make sound day-to-day managerial and financial decisions, the manager requires up-to-date information.

I. SETTING UP BUSINESS RECORDS

One of the first decisions the manager must make in establishing a workable recordkeeping and accounting system is which tax year to use—a calendar year (12 months ending December 31) or a fiscal year (either 12 months ending on the last day of any month except December, or a 52/53-week year). If the owner currently reports income using a calendar year (either as an individual or as a business), he cannot switch to another type of year without IRS approval.

Next, the manager must select the particular accounting method he will use to determine when and how to record business income and expenses. Two primary accounting methods are available—the cash method and the accrual method—but a hybrid method is allowed if certain requirements are met. Under the cash method, the owner records income when it is actually (or constructively) received and expenses when they are actually paid. In other words, the business must record all monetary transactions as they occur. The cash method is easiest in

terms of keeping accounting records, and most individuals and small businesses with no inventories use it. But in some cases, the cash method distorts the true financial picture of the business over an extended period of time.

Using the accrual method, the firm records income and expenses at the time they are earned or incurred regardless of when the actual monetary transaction takes place. In other words, this accounting system records transactions on the basis of the *right* to receive income or the *obligation* to pay debts instead of on the actual receipt or payment of money. If inventories are an important source of income for a small business, the IRS requires that the accrual method be used to present an accurate financial picture of operations.

The difference between the two methods can be illustrated by a simple example. Suppose that The Pipe Dream, Inc., has credit sales of $84 on December 22 and collects payment on January 15. If the firm reports on the cash method, the sale will not be recorded until January 15; but, under the accrual method, it will be recorded on December 22 (see figure 6–1).

Under certain circumstances, the business may use a combination of these two accounting methods as long as it reports income and expenses accurately. The IRS places some restrictions on the use of this hybrid method. If the firm uses the accrual method for purchases and sales, it may use the cash method for recording all other income and expense items.

FIGURE 6–1 Cash versus accrual accounting.

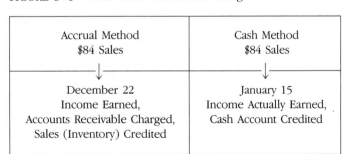

Accrual Method $84 Sales	Cash Method $84 Sales
↓	↓
December 22 Income Earned, Accounts Receivable Charged, Sales (Inventory) Credited	January 15 Income Actually Earned, Cash Account Credited

But if it uses the cash method for determining gross income, it must use the cash method for reporting business expenses. If it employs the accrual method for reporting business expenses, it must use the accrual method for determining gross income.

The small business must employ the same accounting method from year to year and generally must determine its taxable income under the same method. Whatever method the owner chooses, it must clearly reflect business income.

II. THE ACCOUNTING EQUATION

The basis for any accounting system is the accounting equation, which includes three elements: assets, liabilities, and capital (or owner's equity). An asset is anything the business owns which has value. Typical assets include cash, land, buildings, inventory, supplies, and accounts receivable. Current assets are typically not for resale; instead, they are employed in the long-term operation of the business. Assets also may be intangible. Many owners recognize goodwill, the value of the firm's reputation in the community and among its customers.

A liability is anything that the business owes; in other words, liabilities represent the creditors' claims against business assets. They are the debts the business owes (except those owed to the owners). Common liabilities include accounts payable, notes payable, accrued wages, interest payable, and taxes payable. Current liabilities are those that must be paid within one year, while long-term liabilities are not due for a year or longer.

Owner's equity (or capital) represents the difference between what the business owns and what it owes—its assets less its liabilities. Equity is the investment of the owner(s) plus any profits the business retains (or minus any losses incurred). Table 6–2 shows the determination of capital for each type of business.

The accounting equation expresses the relationship among the business' assets, liabilities, and capital and is the foundation for building the firm's financial records. The total assets of the business will always equal its total liabilities plus capital:

$$assets = liabilities + capital$$

Any change in the firm's asset accounts must be offset by an equal change in either the liability or the capital accounts. For example, suppose that Ayer's Pharmacy receives an invoice for $125 from one of its suppliers and pays the bill by check. One of its asset accounts—cash—decreases by $125, but one of its liability accounts—accounts payable—also decreases by $125. The accounting equation remains in balance.

III. SINGLE-ENTRY VS. DOUBLE-ENTRY BOOKKEEPING

Before establishing a recordkeeping system, the owner must decide whether to use the single-entry

TABLE 6–2   Capital: The value of the business to its owners.

For proprietorships or partnerships:

$$capital = \frac{\text{all owner}}{\text{investment}} + \frac{\text{all profit ever}}{\text{made by the firm}} - \frac{\text{all withdrawals}}{\text{ever made}}$$

For corporations:

$$capital = \frac{\text{par value of all stock (plus any earned surplus)}}{} + \frac{\text{all profit}}{\text{ever made}} - \frac{\text{all dividends}}{\text{ever paid}}$$

or double-entry method. The single-entry method of bookkeeping is easier to operate and is very useful for small firms just beginning in business. This system records the flow of income and expenses through the business with a daily and monthly summary of cash receipts, and a monthly summary of cash disbursements. Despite its simplicity, the single-entry method has a major disadvantage in that it is not self-balancing.

The example just presented illustrating the effect of transactions on the accounting equation had a double effect on the business books. A transaction is simply an exchange of one item for another, and the double-entry bookkeeping system reflects this by recording each entry twice—as a debit to one account and as a credit to another. Table 6–3 shows the five classes of accounts, what type of entry increases or decreases each account, and the normal balance maintained in each account.

The double-entry bookkeeping system relies on journals and ledgers to record business transactions. All transactions are first entered in a daily journal as debits and credits, and then totals of these amounts are posted to the appropriate ledger accounts periodically (usually monthly). Typically, income and expense accounts are closed at the end of the firm's accounting year, but asset, liability, and capital (net worth) accounts remain open permanently.

The primary advantage of the double-entry system is that it is self-balancing; in other words, the total amount entered as debits must equal the total amount entered as credits. Once the journal entries are entered in the proper ledger accounts, the manager should prepare a trial balance (usually at the end of each month). If the sum of the debit entries equals the sum of the credit entries, the accounts are in balance and no errors exist. Thus, the trial balance detects any errors made in posting journal entries to the various ledger accounts before they are buried too deeply in the accounting system.

IV. SETTING UP THE BOOKS

Daily Summary of Sales and Cash Receipts

Every small business depends on sales of its goods or services for survival, and the owner must establish proper records to account for these daily transactions. At the end of each business day, the manager must reconcile the actual amount of cash on hand in the register with the total amount of the receipts recorded for the day by using the Daily Summary of Sales and Cash Receipts. Figure 6–2 shows a sample Daily Summary for a typical small business' daily transactions.

Cash Receipts. The cash receipts section of the Daily Summary reports all the cash the small business receives from any source during the day. Of course, in the typical small firm, most cash receipts originate from cash sales, so the amount is obtained from the cash register tape. The business may collect cash from customers as payment for previous sales made on account. Usually, these payments are rung on the cash register, but the owner also should record payments separately and provide each customer with a receipt. The owner should verify that the total of the individual receipts equals the total of the collections shown on the cash register tape; this amount then is recorded on the daily summary sheet.

TABLE 6–3 Double-entry bookkeeping: debits and credits.

Type of Account	To increase the account	To decrease the account	Normal balance
Asset	Debit	Credit	Debit
Liability	Credit	Debit	Credit
Capital	Credit	Debit	Credit
Income	Credit	Debit	Credit
Expense	Debit	Credit	Debit

FIGURE 6–2   Daily summary of sales and cash receipts for March 15, 198X.

Cash Receipts			
1.	Cash sales		$1,865.57
2.	Collections on account		240.35
3.	Miscellaneous receipts		0.00
4.	Total receipts to be accounted for		$2,105.92
Cash on Hand			
5.	Cash in register:		
	Coins	51.53	
	Bills	860.00	
	Checks	1,287.97	
	Total cash in register		$2,199.50
6.	Petty cash slips		12.42
7.	Total cash accounted for		$2,211.92
8.	Less change/petty cash fund:		
	Petty cash slips	12.42	
	Coins and bills	87.58	
	Change & petty cash fund (Fixed)		100.00
9.	Total cash deposit		$2,111.92
10.	Cash short (if Item 4 > Item 9)		—
11.	Cash over (if Item 9 < Item 4)		6.00
Total Sales			
12.	Cash sales		$1,865.57
13.	Credit sales		520.25
14.	Total sales		$2,385.82

Miscellaneous receipts include those cash receipts other than for sales and credit collections. For example, the firm may take in cash from rebates, rent collections, or refunds. The owner should file a memorandum for each miscellaneous cash receipt, and each such item should be recorded on the back of the Daily Summary. The sum of cash sales, collections on account, and miscellaneous receipts gives the total amount of cash receipts to be accounted for.

Cash on Hand.   The second section of the Daily Summary reports the total amount of cash on hand so that this total may be reconciled with the total of section one, cash receipts. At the end of each business day, the manager must count the money in the cash register to prepare the bank deposit. Totals for coins, bills, and checks are recorded separately on the daily summary.

During a typical day, the small business owner

will need to make purchases of items in amounts too small to justify writing a check. To make such small purchases, the owner creates a petty cash fund, a fixed amount of money set aside in the cash register or some other safe place. Whenever the owner makes a withdrawal from this fund, he must complete a petty cash slip documenting the amount and the reason for the purchase (see figure 6–3) and file it with the petty cash fund.

At any time, the sum of the petty cash slips and the remaining cash in the petty cash fund should equal the fixed amount in the fund. As the petty cash fund is drawn down toward zero, the owner should make out a check to "Petty Cash" for the amount of the slips, bringing the fund back to the original fixed amount. At the end of the day, the total amount of the slips is recorded on the Daily Summary. The petty cash slips must be canceled to prevent their reuse and abuse.

Most small businesses require a certain amount of cash-on- hand in various denominations to make change for daily business transactions. Although the amount of money needed to make change varies with the size of the business and the day of the week, the simplest approach is to establish a fixed amount large enough to cover the firm's normal volume of trade. At the end of each business day, the owner must take out of the day's receipts the bills and coins totaling the fixed amount of the change fund to use

in the next day's business. In some cases, the petty cash fund and the change fund are combined into a single total. For example, if the manager needs $75 for change and $25 for petty cash, a single fund of $100 can be set aside. Since this amount is on hand at the beginning of each business day, it must be subtracted from the total cash to be accounted for to determine the amount of the day's cash deposit. If the amount of the total cash deposit does not equal the total receipts to be accounted for, the owner must verify that all calculations on the Daily Summary are correct. If no mathematical errors were made, the difference must be recorded as either "cash short" or "cash over" (see Small Business Report 6–1).

Total Sales. The final section of the Daily Summary summarizes the day's sales by dividing them into two categories: cash sales and credit sales. Some retail operators may wish to break down these subtotals even further (e.g., by departments, salespersons, or divisions).

So, the Daily Summary of Sales and Cash Receipts can provide the manager with complete, detailed operating data for each business day. As soon as the Daily Summary is completed, the cash deposit should be prepared and placed in the bank *immediately*. Cash should not be left in the register overnight, and most banks provide night deposit boxes

FIGURE 6–3   Petty cash slip.

No. 36	Date 10/7/8X

PETTY CASH PAYMENT

Amount $1.28

For Postage on special delivery package

Approved BGJ   Signed K. Danzig

SMALL
BUSINESS
REPORT
6–1

Possible Errors in Case of a Cash Shortage or Overage

If the amount to be deposited is *more* than the total receipts recorded for the day, the overage could be caused by:

- neglecting to record or ring up a transaction
- recording or ringing up a transaction for less than the proper amount
- giving a customer too little change

If the amount to be deposited is *less* than the total receipts recorded for the day, the shortage could be caused by:

- recording or ringing up more than the proper amount for a transaction
- giving a customer too much change
- taking money from the cash register or till without recording it

Source: Adapted from U.S. Small Business Administration, *Financial Record Keeping for Small Stores*, Small Business Management Series No. 32, Washington, 1976, p. 18.

for the convenience of those business owners who close their shops after banking hours. To protect against bank errors, the manager should file a duplicate copy of the bank deposit slip with each Daily Summary.

V. RECONCILING THE BANK STATEMENT

All deposits made and all checks written on the business account (including those to petty cash) are recorded in the business checkbook. The easiest type of checkbook to use for maintaining business records is the desk style with three checks per page and check stubs allowing a complete description of each check. For security reasons, all checks should be pre-numbered. If a check is invalid for any reason, the owner should write "VOID" across it and remove the signature portion of the check to prevent abuse.

The manager should keep on file the proper supporting documents for each check written. To avoid paying a bill twice, when paying each invoice the owner should mark it paid and record the check number and date on it (see figure 6–4). Once the check is written and the invoice is marked with PAID, the owner should file the invoice and supporting

papers in a paid bill file arranged alphabetically according to payee.

The bank normally will return the canceled checks and a statement of the account monthly to allow the owner to reconcile the business' records with the bank's records. Reconciling the checking account monthly is a vital link in maintaining accurate records.

In practice, the reconciliation process is not very complex; in fact, most banks provide a form for reconciliation on the reverse side of the bank statement. To begin the reconciliation, the owner must have the preceding month's reconciliation, the canceled checks, checkbook stubs, and the bank statement. First, he arranges all the canceled checks in numerical order and records the balance shown on the bank statement on the first line of the reconciliation. Then he adds any outstanding deposits—those listed in his checkbook, but not credited to his account by the bank—in the second section of the reconciliation. Typically, only one or two deposits made at the end of the month will be listed here. Next, he must check off on each stub all canceled checks returned with the bank statement. The owner will disregard any checks written after the closing date of the statement. Then he must subtract any outstanding

126

FIGURE 6–4 Paid invoice.

Invoice #	10608		Date	3/15/8X

Midland Electronic Supply Co.
3825 West 25th Street
Chicago, Illinois

Terms ____ net 30
F.O.B. ____ Tempe

Sold to: South Western Electric Cooperative
1165 San Pedro Blvd.
Tempe, Arizona

Ship to: Same

Quantity	Description	Unit Price	Total
20	325X Switchgear	$1,960.00	$39,200.00
3	Single phase transformers	150.00	450.00
100 yds.	Wire—copper	1.00/yd.	100.00
4	Pads	30.00	120.00
Total			$39,870.00

PAID
Check #424
4/12/8X
BgT

checks—those deducted in the business checkbook but not yet deducted from his account by the bank—in the third section. There will usually be some canceled checks that were outstanding from the previous month's reconciliation; but some checks from the previous month may still be outstanding. The result is the adjusted balance of the bank statement.

Then the owner records the balance shown in his checkbook on the closing date of the statement. If any errors were uncovered in the preceding steps (e.g., transposed numbers on checks and deposits) they must be listed and either added or subtracted from this balance. For example, if check number 561 for $76.43 was entered as $74.63, then $1.80 ($76.43

– $74.63) must be subtracted from the checkbook balance to correct the error. Finally, any service charges imposed by the bank must be deducted to yield the adjusted checkbook balance, which should equal the adjusted bank statement balance.

VI. ACCOUNTING JOURNALS AND LEDGERS

In the typical small business double-entry recordkeeping system, daily transactions are entered chronologically as debits and credits in a journal. Then summary totals of these amounts are posted to the appropriate accounts in the general ledger. Figure

SMALL
BUSINESS
REPORT
6–2

Bank Errors

Banks, like other enterprises, are not perfect. Errors committed by the bank usually affect the small business' checking account. For example, the bank may:

- post another person's check or deposit to the small business' account
- post the small business' check or deposit to another's account
- post a check or deposit incorrectly
- add or subtract deposits and checks incorrectly

The manager must report such errors to the bank immediately and make the proper adjustments in the bank reconciliation.

Source: Adapted from U.S. Small Business Administration, *Financial Record Keeping for Small Stores,* Small Business Management Series No. 32, Washington, 1976, p. 39.

6–5 summarizes the process of recording daily transactions and posting them to the proper ledger account.

Journals

A small business can employ different types of journals to record daily business transactions, but the one generally used is the two-column format shown in figure 6–6. Journalizing a business transaction is a simple procedure. The manager records the date of the transaction, the name of the account to be debited, the name of the account to be credited, the amount of the transaction, and a brief explanation of the entry. In the journal shown in figure 6–6, notice that the entries maintain the equilibrium of the accounting equation.

All business transactions are recorded in the journal as debits and credits to specific accounts. The firm can set up as many accounts as needed depending on the type of business, its volume, and the need

for detailed records. Figure 6–7 illustrates a chart of accounts for a typical small business. Each account is assigned a number. The first digit corresponds to the type of account (refer to figure 6–7)—1 for assets, 2 for liabilities, 3 for capital, 4 for income, and 5 for expenses. The second digit defines the specific account within each general category. Using this method, the manager is able to add accounts in each category as needed.

Obviously, recording a large number of transactions in a two-column journal soon becomes impractical due to the time and cost involved. Although the two-column journal is still widely used, the increasing availability of computers has enabled many businesses, even small ones, to replace traditional journals with computer-generated reports. Another alternative is for the small business to utilize a multi-column journal, which includes a column for transactions in each specific account. For example, there is a special column for recording debits to accounts receivable and a column for recording credits to ac-

FIGURE 6–5 Recording business transactions.

| Transactions occur daily (cash sales, cash disbursements, credit sales, etc.) | → | Proper supporting documents are prepared (sales tickets, check stubs, etc.) | → | Debits & credits are recorded in the journal | → | Summary totals are posted to the ledger |

FIGURE 6–6   General journal, Sam's Appliance Shop.

Date	Account Titles & Explanations	P.R.	Debit	Credit
10/5	Advertising Expense	57	75.00	
	Cash	11		75.00
	Advertisement in The Chronicle			
10/5	Cash	11	2030.00	
	Sales	41		2030.00
	Cash sales for the day			
10/6	Rent Expense	52	275.00	
	Cash	11		275.00
	Rent for building			
10/6	Telephone Expense	58	62.00	
	Cash	11		62.00
	Telephone bill			
10/6	Cash	11	1960.00	
	Sales	41		1960.00
	Cash sales for the day			
10/7	Store Equipment	16	83.00	
	Accounts Payable	21		83.00
	Purchased equipment on account			
10/9	Purchases	55	650.00	
	Accounts Payable	21		650.00
	Purchased inventory on account			

counts receivable. Clearly, having too many columns in a multi-column journal is impractical and leads to errors.

If an all-purpose multi-column journal is not adequate to handle the business transactions, the owner may use certain special journals to record frequently occurring transactions. Special journals are used most often to record sales, cash receipts, cash disbursements, and purchases.

Sales Journal.   The sales journal is used to record only credit sales of merchandise. All cash sales are recorded in the cash receipts journal. Figure 6–8 shows the sales journal of Sam's Appliance Shop for a portion of October. Invoice number 1017 reports the sale of merchandise on credit to E.M. Thornley for $1,178.00, the amount debited to accounts receivable (increase) and credited to sales (increase).

Cash Receipts Journal.   Any transaction which brings cash into the business is recorded in the cash receipts journal. The most common sources of cash in the typical small business are cash sales and collections on credit sales, but the owner should establish as many special columns as needed. Figure 6–9 shows the cash receipts journal for Sam's Appliance Shop for part of October. The first entry records the payment of $100 E.M. Thornley made on his account

FIGURE 6–7   Chart of accounts, Sam's Appliance Shop.

1.	Assets		4.	Income
11	Cash		41	Sales
12	Petty cash		42	Miscellaneous income
13	Accounts receivable			
14	Merchandise inventory		5.	Expenses
15	Supplies		51	Salary expense
16	Store equipment		52	Rent expense
19	Accumulated depreciation		53	Supplies expense
			54	Interest expense
2.	Liabilities		55	Purchases expense
21	Accounts payable		56	Depreciation expense
22	Salaries payable		57	Advertising expense
23	Taxes payable		58	Telephone expense
24	Mortgages payable		59	Miscellaneous expense
25	Notes payable			
3.	Capital			
	Sam Lewis, Capital			
	Sam Lewis, Drawing			
	Daily Summary of Sales/Cash Receipts			

on October 3. The second October 7 entry reports the cash sales for the day.

Cash Disbursements Journal. The cash disbursements journal records all cash expenditures other than those for purchase of inventory the small business makes. The number of columns included in this journal depends on the nature and the frequency of the cash expenditures the business incurs. Figure 6–10 illustrates the cash disbursements journal for Sam's Appliance Shop for part of October. The check number for each expenditure provides a cross-refer-

FIGURE 6–8   Sales journal, Sam's Appliance Shop.

Date	Account Debited	Invoice Number	P.R.	Amount
10/10	E. M. Thornley	1017	✔	1178.00
10/15	C. S. Easler	1018	✔	46.00
10/17	M. K. Blackmon	1019	✔	57.00
10/19	W. S. Kodama	1020	✔	73.00

FIGURE 6–9   Cash receipts journal, Sam's Appliance Shop

Date	Account Credited	Explanation	P.R.	Other Accounts Credit	Accounts Receivable Credit	Sales Credit	Sales Discounts Debit	Cash Debit
10/3	E. M. Thornley	Collection on account	✔		100.00			100.00
10/5	Notes Receivable	Collection on note	✔	800.00				800.00
10/6	Sales	Cash sales for the day	✔			2350.00		2350.00
10/7	Truax, Inc.	Collection on account	✔		715.00			715.00
10/7	Sales	Cash sales for the day	✔			2100.00		2100.00

ence for each disbursement. The first entry records the tuition payment to Tri-County Technical County for a short course in "Accounting for Small Business."

Purchases Journal. The purchases journal should be set up to record all credit purchases of inventory items, business supplies, and equipment. Each entry shows the amount debited to purchases (increase) and credited to accounts payable (decrease) for each purchase. (If office supplies and store supplies are purchased only occasionally, these two columns may be omitted from the journal and replaced with a "Miscellaneous Debit" column.) Figure 6–11 shows the purchases journal for Sam's Appliance Shop for part of October.

Ledgers

Periodically, summary totals from the four types of journals (or from the all-purpose multi-column journal) must be recorded in the ledger. Most small businesses post summary totals to the ledger at the end of each month. If there are many accounts with a common characteristic, they may be combined into a separate subsidiary ledger. For example, a small firm

FIGURE 6–10   Cash disbursements journal, Sam's Appliance Shop.

Date	No.	Payee	Account Debited	P.R.	Other Accounts Debit	Accounts Payable Credit	Purchases Discounts Credit	Cash Credit
10/3	471	Tri-County Tech. College	Miscellaneous expense	✔	230.00			230.00
10/5	472	Mars & Associates	Advertising expense	✔		500.00		500.00
10/5	473	Joe Arnold	Sales salaries expense	✔	212.00			212.00
10/5	474	Lewis Chapman	Sales salaries expense	✔	175.00			175.00
10/7	475	State Tax Comm.	Sales tax expense	✔	78.00			78.00
10/7	476	Easler Supply Co.	Accounts payable	✔		635.00		635.00
10/7	477	VOID						
10/9	478	Bowen Distributors	Accounts payable	✔		200.00		200.00

FIGURE 6–11   Purchases journal, Sam's Appliance Shop.

Date	Account Credited	Date of Invoice	Terms	P.R.	Accounts Payable Credit	Purchases Debit	Store Supplies Debit	Office Supplies Debit
10/3	Easler Supply Co.	9/5/8X	Net 30	✔	2780.00	2780.00		
10/5	Appliance Wholesale, Inc.	9/6/8X	Net 30	✔	5820.00	5820.00		
10/7	Elgin Electric Co.	9/6/8X	Net 30	✔	110.00	110.00		
10/7	Bowen Distributors	9/28/8X	2/10, Net 30	✔	5865.00	5865.00		

might use a separate subsidiary ledger to post accounts payable (a creditor's ledger) and accounts receivable (a customer's ledger). Each subsidiary ledger is summarized by an account in the general ledger called a controlling account. Of course, the total of the accounts in each subsidiary ledger must equal the balance of its controlling account in the general ledger.

Today many accounting systems rely on computerized systems to perform the tedious process of posting journal entries to the ledger. Still, many small businesses must post journal entries to ledger accounts manually. Posting is performed according to the following procedure:[2]

- Record the date and amount of the journal entry in the appropriate ledger account.
- Record the page number of the journal in the Posting Reference column of the ledger.
- Record the ledger account number in the Posting Reference column of the journal.

Figure 6–12 illustrates a page of the general ledger from Sam's Appliance Shop. The entries posted are the journal entries shown in figure 6–6. In practice, each account would be on a separate page of the general ledger.

[2]Phillip E. Fess and Carl S. Warren, *Accounting Principles*, 14th ed. (Cincinnati: South-Western, 1984), pp. 46–47.

Owner Withdrawals

In most businesses, the owners withdraw normal salaries on a regular basis; but these withdrawals are not subject to the same employment taxes and withholdings as employees' wages, so they are not treated in the same manner. All withdrawals made by the owner are recorded in journals and ledgers as "Proprietor's Drawings" or "Partner's Drawings."

In many instances, the owner withdraws merchandise from the store for personal use. Frequently the owner is tempted to take the items out of stock without recording them in the business records since they "belong to me anyway." These unreported withdrawals reduce the firm's profits and its income taxes and are frowned upon by the IRS. But recording these withdrawals as regular sales is not proper either. This would artificially inflate the firm's profits and its income tax unnecessarily. So, to report merchandise withdrawals properly, the items should be recorded at cost in the proprietor's drawing account.

VII. BASIC FINANCIAL REPORTS

Managing the financial assets of the small business is one of the most challenging and most difficult tasks facing the owner. Establishing the basic records of the firm (discussed in the last section) requires a sound understanding of accounting principles, a skill that owners often lack. To manage a small business

FIGURE 6-12 General ledger, Sam's Appliance Shop.

Date	Explanation	P.R.	Debit	Credit	Balance
	CASH				Acct. No. 11
10/1	Balance	✔	2600.00		2600.00
10/5	Advertisement in The Chronicle	23		75.00	2525.00
10/5	Sales for the day	23	2030.00		4555.00
10/6	Rent for building	23		275.00	4280.00
10/6	Telephone bill	23		62.00	4218.00
10/6	Sales for the day	23	1960.00		6178.00
	STORE EQUIPMENT				Acct. No. 16
10/1	Balance	✔	855.00		855.00
10/7	Store equipment	23	83.00		938.00
	ACCOUNTS PAYABLE				Acct. No. 21
10/1	Balance	✔		435.00	435.00
10/7	Purchased equipment on account	23		83.00	518.00
10/9	Purchased inventory on account	23		650.00	1168.00
	SALES				Acct. No. 41
10/5	Sales for the day	23		2030.00	2030.00
10/6	Sales for the day	23		1960.00	3990.00
	RENT EXPENSE				Acct. No. 52
10/1	Balance	✔	500.00		500.00
10/6	Rent on building	23	275.00		775.00
	PURCHASES				Acct. No. 55
10/1	Balance	✔	750.00		750.00
10/9	Purchases	23	650.00		1400.00
	ADVERTISING EXPENSE				Acct. No. 57
10/1	Balance	✔	200.00		200.00
10/5	Advertisement in The Chronicle	23	75.00		275.00
	TELEPHONE EXPENSE				Acct. No. 58
10/1	Balance	✔	45.00		45.00
10/6	Telephone bill	23	62.00		107.00

successfully, it is important to understand the basic tools of financial management. To be a successful financial manager requires well-organized accounting records (journals, ledgers), regular financial reports (balance sheet, income statement), and techniques for analyzing these reports (ratios, comparative statements). The last section described the necessary accounting records, and this section focuses on the basic financial reports. Chapter 8 covers specific techniques for analyzing these financial reports and for incorporating them into the decision-making process.

These tools provide a financial map for the small business and enable the manager to diagnose problems early and take corrective actions before they develop into more serious threats. Three common reports provide the manager with the financial information needed to maintain the firm's health: the balance sheet, the income statement, and the sources and uses of funds statement.

The Balance Sheet

The balance sheet provides the owner with an estimate of the firm's worth on a given date. Its two major sections show what assets the business owns and what claims creditors and owners have against those assets. The balance sheet is usually prepared on the last day of the month. Figure 6–13 shows the balance sheet for Sam's Appliance Shop for December 31, 198X.

The balance sheet is built upon the fundamental accounting equation: Assets = Liabilities + Owner's Equity. Any increase or decrease on one side of the equation must be offset by an equal increase or decrease on the other side; hence, the name "balance sheet." The first section of the balance sheet lists the firm's assets and shows the total value of everything the business owns. Current assets consist of cash and items to be converted into cash within one year, such as accounts receivable and inventory, while fixed assets are those acquired for long-term use in the business. Intangible assets include items

which, while valuable, do not have tangible value, such as goodwill, copyrights, and patents.

The second section shows the business' liabilities the creditors' claims against the firm's assets. Current liabilities are those debts that must be paid within one year, and long-term liabilities are those that come due after one year. This section of the balance sheet also shows the owner's equity, the value of the owner's investment in the business.

The Income Statement

The income statement (or profit and loss statement) compares expenses against revenue over a certain period of time to show the firm's net profit or loss. The income statement is a "moving picture" of the firm's profitability over time. The annual P&L statement reports the "bottom line" of the business over the fiscal/calendar year. Figure 6–14 shows the income statement for Sam's Appliance Shop for the year ended December 31, 198X.

Source: From *The New Yorker* 40, November 1981, p. 47. Drawing by D. Reilly. © 1981 by *The New Yorker* Magazine, Inc.

FIGURE 6–13   Balance sheet, Sam's Appliance Shop.

ASSETS

Current Assets:

Cash		$ 49,855.00
Accounts Receivable	$179,225.00	
Less Allowance for Doubtful Accounts	6,000.00	173,225.00
Inventory		455,455.00
Prepaid Expenses		8,450.00
TOTAL CURRENT ASSETS		$686,985.00

Fixed Assets:

Land		$ 59,150.00
Buildings	$ 74,650.00	
Less Allowance for Depreciation	7,050.00	67,600.00
Equipment	22,375.00	
Less Allowance for Depreciation	1,250.00	21,125.00
Furniture and Fixtures	10,295.00	
Less Allowance for Depreciation	1,000.00	9,295.00
TOTAL FIXED ASSETS		$157,170.00

INTANGIBLES		3,500.00
TOTAL ASSETS		$847,655.00

LIABILITIES

Current Liabilities:

Accounts Payable	$152,580.00
Notes Payable	83,920.00
Accrued Wages/Salaries Payable	38,150.00
Accrued Interest Payable	42,380.00
Accrued Taxes Payable	50,820.00
TOTAL CURRENT LIABILITIES	$367,850.00

Long-Term Liabilities:

Mortgage	$127,150.00
Note	85,000.00
TOTAL LONG-TERM LIABILITIES	$212,150.00

OWNER'S EQUITY

Sam Lloyd, Capital	$267,655.00
TOTAL LIABILITIES AND STOCKHOLDER'S EQUITY	$847,655.00

FIGURE 6–14 Income statement, Sam's Appliance Shop.

SALES REVENUE		$1,870,841.00
Cost of Goods Sold:		
Beginning Inventory 1/1/8X	$ 67,280.00	
Purchases	1,281,177.00	
Goods Available for Sale	1,348,457.00	
Less Ending Inventory 12/31/8X	58,340.00	
COST OF GOODS SOLD	1,290,117.00	
GROSS MARGIN		$ 580,724.00
Operating Expenses:		
Advertising	$ 149,670.00	
Insurance	56,125.00	
Depreciation		
Building	18,700.00	
Equipment	9,000.00	
Salaries	224,500.00	
Travel	4,000.00	
Entertainment	2,500.00	
TOTAL OPERATING EXPENSES		$ 464,495.00
General Expenses		
Utilities	$ 5,300.00	
Telephone	2,500.00	
Postage	1,200.00	
Payroll Taxes	25,000.00	
TOTAL GENERAL EXPENSES		$ 34,000.00
Other Expenses		
Interest	$ 19,850.00	
Bad Check Expense	1,750.00	
TOTAL OTHER EXPENSES		$ 21,600.00
TOTAL EXPENSES		$ 520,095.00
NET INCOME		$ 60,629.00

To calculate net profit or loss, the owner records sales revenues for the year, which includes all income that flows into the business from sales of goods and services. Income from other sources (rent, investments, interest) also must be included in the revenue section of the income statement. Cost of goods sold represents the total price, including shipping costs, of the merchandise sold during the year. Most wholesalers and retailers calculate cost of goods sold by adding purchases to beginning inventory and subtracting ending inventory. Service companies typically have no cost of goods sold. Operating expenses include those costs that contribute directly to the manufacture and distribution of goods. General expenses are indirect costs incurred in operating the business. "Other expenses" is a catchall category covering all other expenses not fitting into the other two categories. Total revenue minus total expenses gives the net profit (or loss) for the year.

The Statement of Sources and Uses of Funds

The statement of sources and uses of funds (or the Statement of Changes in Financial Position) shows the change in the firm's working capital since the beginning of the year by listing the sources of funds and the uses of these funds. Many small businesses never need to prepare such a statement, but in some cases creditors, investors, new owners, or the IRS may require this information.

To prepare the statement, the balance sheets and the income statements summarizing the present year's operations must be assembled. Then the sources of funds—net income, borrowed funds, owner contributions, depreciation, and any others—are listed. Depreciation is listed as a source of funds because it is a non-cash expense that is deducted as a cost of doing business. But since the owner has already paid for the item being depreciated, its depreciation is a source of funds. Next the uses of these funds are listed—plant and equipment purchases,

dividends to owners, repayment of debt, and so on. The difference between the total sources and the total uses is the increase or decrease in working capital. By investigating the changes in the firm's working capital and the reasons for them, the owner can create a more practical financial plan of action for the future of the enterprise.

These statements are more than just complex documents used only by accountants and financial officers. When used in conjunction with the analytical tools described in the next chapter, they can help the small business manager map the firm's financial future and actively plan for profit. Mere preparation of these statements is *not* enough; the owner must *understand and use* the information contained in them. These data are critical to the success and the ultimate survival of the business.

VIII. OTHER BASIC RECORDS

In addition to the transactions recorded in the various journals and ledgers and the information summarized on the three financial statements, the owner may require additional records to control the business properly. These records might include the following:

- *Insurance.* The manager should maintain an insurance register, recording types and amounts of insurance, policy numbers, premiums, and payment dates.
- *Maintenance.* Maintenance records should include the date, nature, and costs associated with maintenance of plant and equipment.
- *Accounts Receivable.* Periodically, the manager should "age" the firm's accounts receivable. Aging the receivables shows which credit customers are slow in paying and allows the manager to make informed decisions on credit-granting policy and collection procedures. Small Business Report 6–3 shows the effects of failing to collect accounts receivable.
- *Quality.* A manufacturer must maintain statistical

Failure to Collect Accounts Receivable

Some business owners feel obligated to grant credit to their customers in order either to stay a step ahead of the competition or to meet competitors' selling terms. But many managers who choose to sell on credit are poorly qualified to collect their accounts. Failure to collect is tremendously costly, as the following table shows.

			Net Profit Margin (Net Profit ÷ Net Sales)					
1%	2%	3%	4%	6%	8%	10%		
Additional Sales Needed							To offset a loss of:	
$ 1,000	500	333	250	167	125	100	$	10
5,000	2,500	1,666	1,250	833	625	500		50
10,000	5,000	3,333	2,500	1,666	1,250	1,000		100
20,000	10,000	6,667	5,000	3,333	2,500	2,000		200
30,000	15,000	10,000	7,500	5,000	3,750	3,000		300
40,000	20,000	13,333	10,000	6,666	5,000	4,000		400
50,000	25,000	16,666	12,500	8,300	6,250	5,000		500
100,000	50,000	33,333	25,000	16,667	12,500	10,000		1,000
500,000	250,000	166,667	125,000	83,333	62,500	50,000		5,000
1,000,000	500,000	333,333	250,000	166,667	125,000	100,000		10,000

So, only the owner who is a good collector can afford to sell goods and services on credit!

records detailing the quality of the products produced.

- *Office Records.* The owner should retain records of business correspondence, mailing lists, contracts, and other important papers in a safe place (preferably a fireproof cabinet or safe).
- *Inventory Records.* The manager must keep an accurate record of the firm's inventories.

To "age" the accounts, the manager should prepare a statement like the one shown in figure 6–15. The total amount outstanding on each customer's account is listed in the first column. Then, depending on the firm's credit terms, the owner determines what portion of the account is current, 30–60 days late, 60–90 days late, and so on. Each column is totaled and the percentage of total accounts for each column is calculated. This allows the small business manager to identify his "slow-paying customers" and helps him avoid writing off many accounts as costly bad debt expenses.

IX. IMPORTANCE OF RECORDKEEPING

Adequate, accurate financial recordkeeping is crucial to the successful operation of any small business. The owner must maintain the records that provide the information needed to manage and control the business' finances. Without the information provided by such records, the manager cannot expect to make the sound business decisions required in today's competitive environment. The following financial

FIGURE 6–15 Aging accounts receivable.

Customer	Total Amount	Current	30–60 Days	60–90 Days	90–180 Days	180–270 Days	270–350 Days	Over 1 yr.
T. Dikes	87.88	55.30	32.58					
M. Martin	68.00			68.00				
F. Edgefield	32.00					32.00		
D. Sexton	100.52	50.52	25.00		25.00			
. . .								
Total	xxxxxx	xxxxx	xxxxx	xxxxx	xxxxx	xxxxx	xxxxx	xxxxx
Percent	100	78	14	1	3	2	1	1

checklist summarizes the financial information every business manager should have at hand.

Daily

1. Amount of cash on hand.
2. Bank balance (keep business and personal funds separate).
3. Daily Summary of Sales and Cash Receipts
4. Corrections of all errors in recording collections on accounts.
5. A record of all monies paid out, by cash or check.

Weekly

1. Accounts receivable status (take action on slow payers).
2. Accounts payable status (take advantage of discounts).
3. Payroll status (records should include name and address of employee, social security number, number of exemptions, date pay period ends, hours worked, rate of pay, total wages, deductions, net pay, check number).
4. Status of taxes and reports to state and federal government (sales, withholding, social security, and perhaps others).

Monthly

1. Journal entries classified according to like elements (these should be generally accepted and standardized for both income and expense) and posted to the general ledger.
2. A profit and loss statement for the month, available within a reasonable time (usually 10 to 15 days after the close of the month). This shows the income of the business for the month, the expense incurred in obtaining the income, and the profit or loss resulting. From this, take action to eliminate loss (adjust mark-up? reduce overhead expense? pilferage? incorrect tax reporting? incorrect buying procedures? failure to take advantage of cash discounts?).
3. A balance sheet to accompany the profit and loss statement.
4. The reconciled bank statement.
5. The balanced Petty Cash Account.
6. Records that show all federal tax deposits for withheld income and FICA taxes (Form 50) are made, and state taxes paid.
7. Aged accounts receivable (follow up all bad and slow accounts).
8. Records that show inventory control is "worked" to remove dead stock and order new stock. (What

moves slowly? Reduce. What moves fast? Increase.)[3]

Avoiding Information Overload

The goal of a records management program is to identify those items which provide critical information to the owner and protect them during their useful lives. The focus is on maintaining efficient records, not merely keeping every bit of information produced. The program applies to computerized data as well as to paper records. In addition to improving control over valuable information, this program can produce tangible labor and material savings in maintaining records by eliminating useless, outdated, and duplicate information.

One records manager suggests the following procedure for improving records management:[4]

Step 1. Analyze all of the records currently kept in the business. This can be a lengthy process, but it brings the problem into focus. Look for:

- the types of records kept.
- the location of the records. the existence of duplicate records.
- the existence of non-record materials.
- the percentage of active versus nonactive records.
- dangerous practices such as storing records in dry areas with a high risk of fire.
- misuse of expensive storage equipment.
- types of storage equipment used.
- the number of people involved in maintaining records.

Step 2. Resolve high priority record problems first. High priority items involve protecting the records that the firm *must* have to conduct business. The so-

lution may be as simple as off-site storage or duplicate copies in several locations. Usually, only a small percentage of the company's records are vital.

Step 3. Conduct a more detailed analysis of the small company's records needs. After resolving the record "emergencies," the owner should take an inventory of the remaining records to determine their usefulness and life spans. Ask questions such as:

- What kind of records are they—purchase orders, travel vouchers, etc.?
- Why should the records be maintained?
- Who uses the records?
- How are they used (reference material, document transactions)? How often are they used?
- What is the format of the records—paper, microfiche, microfilm, computer disk?
- How large is the record series and how fast does it grow?
- Are the records duplicated elsewhere?
- Where are the records presently located?

Step 4. Prepare a schedule showing how long and in what form each record series should be retained. This "record retention schedule" reflects a record series' value in four categories:

- Historical.   A record has historical value if it documents some significant event in the growth and development of the company.
- Administrative.   A record has administrative value if it is used in day-to-day operation.
- Legal.   A record has legal value if federal, state, or local laws require the company to keep it.
- Fiscal.   Fiscal records (such as tax returns) usually have low activity levels, but are valuable to the company.

The manager must determine each record's value by estimating the number of years it retains value in each of these four categories. Then, the owner simply keeps the record for the time corresponding to its highest value. For example:

---

[3]*Keeping Records in Small Business*, p. 8.
[4]Louis E. Washington, "Reaping the Rewards of Sound Records Management," *SAM Advanced Management Journal*, Summer 1983, pp. 45–51.

Series#	Historical	Administrative	Legal	Fiscal
100	0	2	3	5
110	0	2	5	7
115	1	1	2	3

The owner would keep record series #100 for 5 years, #110 for 7 years, and #115 for 3 years. Finally, given the retention schedule and the nature of the records, the owner must determine the most efficient format for maintaining them. For instance, one retail shop owner kept her seasonal inventory records in an index card file and her permanent inventory records on specially designed sheets in a notebook.

X. SUMMARY

Proper financial records are essential in operating a successful small business. Many studies have shown the link between inadequate records and small business failures. A good recordkeeping system does not have to be complex; in fact, it should be simple to use, easy to understand, reliable, accurate, consistent, and designed to provide information on a timely basis.

To establish a sound recordkeeping system, the manager first must choose a tax year and then select an accounting method which accurately reflects business income and expenses. The cash method records all income and expenses at the time they are received or paid. The accrual method reports transactions on the basis of the right to receive income or the obligation to pay debts. In certain situations, the IRS allows the small business to use a combination of these two methods.

The foundation for any accounting system is the accounting equation: Assets = Liabilities + Capital. Assets are anything the business owns that has value. Liabilities represent creditors' claims against

Who Should Keep the Books?

Once a bookkeeping system has been established for the small business, the owner must decide who will maintain it. There are four possibilities to choose from:

The public accountant. The Certified Public Accountant offers a wide range of accounting services to the small business. He may help establish the appropriate accounting system, maintain the books, audit them, offer tax advice, prepare financial statements, and perform other functions. Many firms employ CPAs to perform the bookkeeping function. One chief disadvantage of this option is the cost of retaining the CPA. Another drawback is that it may keep the owner from being closely attuned to the firm's financial position.

The small business owner. Another option is for the owner to personally maintain the books. Clearly, this takes time and motivation, and because of the intense time pressures on the owner that is not always practical.

The freelance bookkeeper. The owner may choose to hire a professional bookkeeper—a freelancer who hires his services out to several firms. Still, the owner should have the books audited annually.

An employee. Many firms hire an extra person to maintain the books. Often, a part-time employee can keep the books adequately.

the firm's assets. Capital is the difference between what the business owns and what it owes.

The owner must select either a single-entry or double-entry bookkeeping system. A single-entry system uses daily and monthly summaries of cash receipts and cash disbursements. This method is simple to use, but it is not self-balancing. The double-entry bookkeeping system records each business transaction twice—first as a debit to one account and then as a credit to another. This system uses journals and ledgers to report business transactions and is self-balancing. To reconcile the actual amount of cash on hand at the end of the day with the total receipts and disbursements recorded, the owner using the single-entry system should prepare a Daily Summary of Sales and Cash Receipts. This report summarizes all cash receipts for the day and compares this amount to the actual cash on hand at day's end. Based on the information gained from the Daily Summary, the manager must prepare his daily bank deposit.

The business checkbook is one of the most important records since all deposits and checks are recorded there. The manager should keep a file of all supporting documents for each check and should mark each invoice "PAID" to prevent duplicate payment. Periodically, the bank will return the canceled checks with a statement showing the account balance. The owner must reconcile this statement at least monthly and apprise the bank of any errors discovered.

If a double-entry bookkeeping system is used,

the manager must record all daily transactions in chronological order as debits and credits in journals. If the number of daily transactions is not too large, the owner may use a two-column journal; but recording a large number of entries in a two-column journal is impractical. In this situation, the owner may rely on EDP-generated reports or may use a multi-column journal, with separate columns for each account. Another option is to use special journals, each designed for a specific type of transaction.

Summary totals of the accounts from the journals are posted to ledgers periodically. The general ledger contains the controlling accounts for each entry in the journals.

At regular intervals the firm must prepare financial reports to help manage and control its assets. Three financial statements are commonly prepared—the balance sheet, income statement, and Statement of Sources and Uses of Funds. The balance sheet is a "still picture" of the business' value as of a particular day, showing the firm's assets, liabilities, and capital. The income statement compares costs and expenses with revenue to determine the net profit or loss. The statement of sources and uses of funds shows the change in the firm's working capital over the year. Some managers may need to keep additional records, such as insurance registers, maintenance records, office records, and perhaps others.

Unless the manager establishes an accurate, reliable recordkeeping system, the information needed to map the financial plan for the small business will not be available.

STUDENT INVOLVEMENT PROJECTS

1. Ask a local certified public accountant to address your class on recordkeeping for the small business.
2. Contact several local small business owners. How

do they keep their business records? Who "keeps the books?" Do most operate on a calendar year or a fiscal year? Does the owner use the cash, accrual, or hybrid method? Why?

DISCUSSION QUESTIONS

1. Why must a small business keep adequate financial records?
2. Outline the characteristics of a good recordkeeping system.
3. Describe the difference between the cash method and the accrual method of accounting.
4. What is the accounting equation? List and describe the elements of the equation.
5. Describe the differences between single-entry and double-entry bookkeeping.
6. Briefly outline the bank statement reconciliation process.
7. Outline the process of recording daily transactions for a small business. How are journals used? Describe the four types of special journals used.
8. How are ledgers used? Describe the procedure for recording ledger entries.
9. Outline and briefly describe the three major financial statements. What information can be obtained from each of these reports?
10. Outline the steps included in developing an efficient records management system. What are the benefits of such a system?

Cash Flow Management

7

Though my bottom line is black, I am flat upon my back;
My cash flows out and customers pay slow.
The growth of my receivables is almost unbelievable;
The result is certain—unremitting woe!
And I hear the banker utter an ominous low mutter,
"Watch cash flow."

Herbert S. Bailey, Jr.

Upon completion of this chapter, you will be able to:

- Understand the importance of cash management to the success of the small business.

- Differentiate between cash and profits.

- Demonstrate the steps in creating a cash budget.

- Describe fundamental principles involved in managing receivables and payables.

- Outline the steps involved in developing an assertive credit collection program.

- Demonstrate the value of negotiating favorable credit terms and investing surplus cash.

Cash—a four-letter word that has become a curse for many small businesses. Lack of this valuable asset has driven countless small companies into bankruptcy. Unfortunately, many more firms will become failure statistics because their owners have neglected the principles of cash management—principles that can spell the difference between success and failure for a small business.

I. CASH MANAGEMENT

It is often said that cash is the most important yet least productive asset that a small business owns. The business must have enough cash to meet its obligations or it can be declared bankrupt. Creditors, employees, and lenders expect to be paid on time, and cash is the required medium of exchange. But some firms retain an excessive amount of cash to meet any unexpected circumstances that might arise. These dormant dollars have an income-earning potential that the owners are ignoring, and this restricts the firm's growth and lowers its profitability. Proper cash management permits the owner to adequately meet the cash demands of the business, to avoid retaining unnecessarily large cash balances, and to stretch the profit-generating power of each dollar the business owns.

A recent study by three universities discovered that small business owners cited cash management as their chief problem more frequently (61 percent) than any other area, including pricing strategies (53 percent), or cost reduction (47 percent).[1] Managing cash flows is an acute problem especially for rapidly growing businesses. In fact, "fast-track" companies are most likely to suffer cash shortages. Many "successful, growing, and profitable" businesses fail because they become insolvent; they do not have adequate cash to meet the needs of a growing business with a booming sales volume. If a company's sales are up, the owner also must hire more employees, expand plant capacity, increase the sales force, build inventory, and incur other drains on the firm's cash supply. The resulting cash crisis may force the owner to lose equity control of the business or, ultimately, declare bankruptcy and close.

The uneven cash flows that virtually every small business encounters also create financial problems. Nearly every product—from glass cleaner and clothing to water skis and Christmas trees—follows seasonal sales patterns which produce oscillating cash receipts. Similarly, cash disbursements often fluctuate drastically from one month to another; tax prepayments, employee bonuses, inventory payments, and other significant expenditures wreak havoc on the small company's cash balance. Slow-paying or non-paying customers only complicate the problem. Only the small business owner who uses cash management techniques can foresee these problems and plan for them.

In analyzing cash flow, a small business manager must understand that cash and profits are *not* the same. Profit is the net increase in capital cycled through the business over a period of time. It indicates how effectively the firm is being managed.[2] It is the difference between total revenue and total expenses, and can be "tied up" in many forms, such as inventory, computers, or machinery. Creditors, employees, and lenders cannot be paid in profits, but only in cash. Cash is the money that flows through

business in a continuous cycle without being tied up in any other asset. It represents liquidity since it is available to spend.

Figure 7–1 shows the flow of cash through a typical small business. Cash flow is the volume of cash that comes into and goes out of the business during an accounting period.[3] Decreases in cash occur when the business purchases, on credit or for cash, goods for inventory or materials for use in production. The resulting inventory is sold either for cash or on credit. When cash is taken in or when accounts receivable are collected, the firm's cash balance increases. Notice that purchases for inventory and production lead sales; that is, these bills typically must be paid before sales are generated. But, collection of accounts receivable lags behind sales; that is, customers who purchase goods on credit may not pay until next month.

II. THE CASH BUDGET

Every small business manager should track the flow of cash through her business so she can project the cash balance at specific intervals during the year. Many managers operate their businesses without knowing the pattern of their cash flows, feeling that the process is too complex or time consuming. In reality, the small business manager simply cannot afford to disregard the process of cash management. The owner must ensure that an adequate, but not excessive, supply of cash is on hand to meet her operating needs.

How much cash is enough? What is suitable for one business may be totally inadequate for another, depending on each firm's size, nature, and particular situation. The small business manager should prepare a cash budget, which is nothing more than a "cash plan," showing the amount and timing of the cash receipts and the cash disbursements day-by-day, week-by-week, or month-by-month. It is used to pre-

---

[1] William G. Shepherd, Jr., "Internal Financial Strategies," *Venture*, September 1985, p. 66.

[2] "Cash Flow/Cash Management," *Small Business Reporter* 3, No. 9, 1982, p. 1.

[3] U.S. Small Business Administration, *Cash Flow in a Small Plant*, Small Management Aid No. 229, Washington, D.C., 1982, p. 3.

Fast Growth Requires "Fast" Cash

After a decade of hard work and modest profits, Joseph Turek was ready to reap the rewards of owning his own business. Since 1975 he had struggled to sell his line of intrusion-detection devices for buildings and plowed any profits back into the company. At last, the sacrifices paid off; sales jumped 40 percent to $1.2 million in just one year. The company, American Industries, Inc., had built a substantial clientele, and orders were coming in at a rate of $175,000 per month.

But, something happened. Turek's company ran out of cash.

American Industries' growth simply outstripped its supply of cash. The cash shortage was so severe that Turek could not invest in research and development, marketing his products, or building inventories of raw materials. American Industries then had to order components almost daily, rather than monthly, in an attempt to shorten the gap between accounts payable and accounts receivable. On such a slim delivery schedule, late shipments would set back the entire production process. Turek also had to suspend advertising in trade magazines, and he was forced to dismiss four newly hired technicians and a sales manager.

American Industries' biggest setback came when its bank cut its line of credit from $650,000 to $150,000 because of the company's reliance on a single supplier. Turek had to drop his plans to promote and expand his product line just as competitors began to move in. Turek says, "If they come in, we won't be able to compete. We'll keep our customers, but we'll never grow."

Even though American Industries is down, the company certainly is not out. But, owner Turek has learned the hard way that fast growth requires "fast" cash.

Source: Adapted from Edmund L. Andrews, "Running Out of Money," *Venture,* January 1986, pp. 32–35, with permission of the publisher.

dict the amount of cash the firm will need to operate smoothly over a specific period of time.

III. PREPARING THE CASH BUDGET

Typically, a small business should prepare a projected monthly cash budget for at least one year into the future and a quarterly estimate several years in advance. It must cover all seasonal sales fluctuations. The more variable the firm's sales pattern, the shorter its planning horizon should be. For example, a firm whose sales fluctuate widely over a relatively short time frame might require a weekly cash budget. However, regardless of the time frame selected, the cash budget must be written down for the

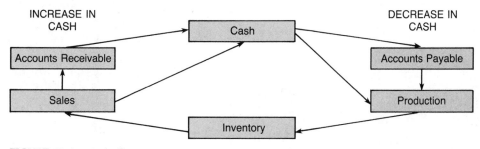

FIGURE 7–1   Cash flow.

TABLE 7–1   Cash budget for small department store.

Assumptions:

Cash balance on December 31 = $12,000
Minimum cash balance desired = $10,000
Sales are 75% credit and 25% cash.

Credit sales are collected in the following manner:

- 60% collected in the first month after the sale
- 30% collected in the second month after the sale
- 5% collected in the third month after the sale
- 5% are never collected

Sales forecasts are as follows:	Pessimistic	Most Likely	Optimistic
October (actual)		$300,000	
November (actual)		350,000	
December (actual)		400,000	
January	$120,000	150,000	$175,000
February	160,000	200,000	250,000
March	160,000	200,000	250,000
April	250,000	300,000	340,000
May	190,000	250,000	310,000

The store pays 70% of sales price for merchandise purchased, and pays for each month's anticipated sales in the preceding month.

Rent is $2,000 per month.

An interest payment of $7,500 is due in March.

A tax prepayment of $50,000 must be made in March.

A capital addition payment of $130,000 is due in February.

Utilities expenses amount to $850 per month.

Miscellaneous expenses are $70 per month.

Interest income of $200 will be received in February.

Wages and salaries are estimated to be:

January–$30,000
February–$40,000
March–$45,000
April–$50,000

Cash Budget
Pessimistic Sales Forecast

	Oct.	Nov.	Dec.	Jan.	Feb.	Mar.	Apr.	May
Cash Receipts:								
Sales	$300,000	$350,000	$400,000	$120,000	$160,000	$160,000	$250,000	$190,000
Credit Sales	225,000	262,500	300,000	90,000	120,000	120,000	187,500	142,500
Collections:								
60%—1st month after sale				180,000	54,000	72,000	72,000	112,500
30%—2nd month after sale				78,750	90,000	27,000	36,000	36,000
5%—3rd month after sale				11,250	13,125	15,000	4,500	6,000
Cash Sales				30,000	40,000	40,000	62,500	47,500
Interest				0	200	0	0	0
Total Cash Receipts				$300,000	$197,325	$154,000	$175,000	$202,000
Cash Disbursements:								
Purchases				$112,000	$112,000	$175,000	$133,000	—
Rent				2,000	2,000	2,000	2,000	
Utilities				850	850	850	850	
Interest				0	0	7,500	0	
Tax Prepayment				0	0	50,000	0	
Capital Addition				0	130,000	0	0	
Miscellaneous				70	70	70	70	
Wages/Salaries				30,000	40,000	45,000	50,000	
Total Cash Disbursements				$144,920	$284,920	$280,420	$185,920	
End of Month Balance:								
Cash (Beginning of month)				$ 12,000	$167,080	$ 79,485	$ 10,000	
+ Cash Receipts				300,000	197,325	154,000	175,000	
− Cash Disbursements				144,920	284,920	280,420	185,920	
Cash (End of month)				167,080	79,485	(46,935)	(920)	
Borrowing				0	0	56,935	10,920	
Cash (End of month [After borrowing])				$167,080	$ 79,485	$ 10,000	$ 10,000	

TABLE 7–1 *Continued*

		Cash Budget Most Likely Sales Forecast						
	Oct.	*Nov.*	*Dec.*	*Jan.*	*Feb.*	*Mar.*	*Apr.*	*May*
Cash Receipts:								
Sales	$300,000	$350,000	$400,000	$150,000	$200,000	$200,000	$300,000	$250,000
Credit Sales	225,000	262,500	300,000	112,000	150,000	150,000	225,000	187,500
Collections:								
60%—1st month after sale				$180,000	$ 67,500	$ 90,000	$ 90,000	$135,000
30%—2nd month after sale				78,750	90,000	33,750	45,000	45,000
5%—3rd month after sale				11,250	13,125	15,000	5,625	7,500
Cash Sales				37,500	50,000	50,000	75,000	62,500
Interest				0	200	0	0	0
Total Cash Receipts				$307,500	$220,825	$188,750	$215,625	$250,000
Cash Disbursements:								
Purchases				$140,000	$140,000	$210,000	$175,000	—
Rent				2,000	2,000	2,000	2,000	
Utilities				850	850	850	850	
Interest				0	0	7,500	0	
Tax Prepayment				0	0	50,000	0	
Capital Addition				0	130,000	0	0	
Miscellaneous				70	70	70	70	
Wages/Salaries				30,000	40,000	45,000	50,000	
Total Cash Disbursements				$172,920	$312,920	$315,420	$227,920	
End of Month Balance:								
Cash (Beginning of month)				$ 12,000	$146,580	$ 54,485	$ 10,000	
+ Cash Receipts				307,500	220,825	188,750	215,625	
− Cash Disbursements				172,920	312,920	315,420	227,920	
Cash (End of month)				146,580	54,485	(72,185)	(2,295)	
Borrowing				0	0	82,185	12,295	
Cash (End of month [After borrowing])				$146,580	$ 54,485	$ 10,000	$ 10,000	

Cash Budget
Optimistic Sales Forecast

	Oct.	Nov.	Dec.	Jan.	Feb.	Mar.	Apr.	May
Cash Receipts:								
Sales	$300,000	$350,000	$400,000	$175,000	$250,000	$250,000	$340,000	$310,000
Credit Sales	225,000	262,500	300,000	131,250	187,500	187,500	255,000	232,500
Collections:								
60%—1st month after sale				180,000	78,750	112,500	112,500	153,000
30%—2nd month after sale				78,750	90,000	39,375	56,250	56,250
5%—3rd month after sale				11,250	13,125	15,000	6,563	9,375
Cash Sales				43,750	62,500	62,500	85,000	77,500
Interest				0	200	0	0	0
Total Cash Receipts				$313,750	$244,575	$229,375	$260,313	$296,125
Cash Disbursements:								
Purchases				$175,000	$175,000	$238,000	$217,000	—
Rent				2,000	2,000	2,000	2,000	
Utilities				850	850	850	850	
Interest				0	0	7,500	0	
Tax Prepayment				0	0	50,000	0	
Capital Addition				0	130,000	0	0	
Miscellaneous				70	70	70	70	
Wages/Salaries				30,000	40,000	45,000	50,000	
Total Cash Disbursements				$207,920	$347,920	$343,420	$269,920	
End of Month Balance:								
Cash (Beginning of month)				$ 12,000	$117,830	$ 14,485	$ 10,000	
+ Cash Receipts				313,750	244,575	229,375	296,125	
– Cash Disbursements				207,920	347,920	343,420	269,920	
Cash (End of month)				117,830	14,485	(99,560)	36,205	
Borrowing				0	0	109,560	0	
Cash (End of month [After borrowing])				$117,830	$ 14,485	$ 10,000	$ 32,205	

small business manager to properly visualize the firm's cash position. Creating a written cash plan is not an excessively time-consuming task, and can help the owner avoid unexpected cash shortages, a situation that bankers and other potential lenders frown upon. The cash budget also lets the owner know if he is keeping excessively high amounts of cash on hand.

The cash budget is based on the cash method of accounting, which means that cash receipts and cash disbursements are recorded in the forecast only when the cash transaction is expected to take place. For example, credit sales to customers are not reported until the cash from them is expected to be received. Similarly, purchases made on credit are not recorded until the invoices are expected to be paid. Since depreciation, bad debt expense, and other non-cash items involve no cash transfers, they are omitted from the cash budget.

The cash budget is nothing more than a forecast of the firm's cash inflows and outflows for a specific time period, and it will never be completely accurate. But, it does give the small business manager a clear picture of the firm's estimated cash balance for the period, pointing out where external cash infusions may be required or where surplus cash balances may be available for investment. Also, by comparing actual cash flows with projections, the owner can revise his forecast so that future cash budgets will be more accurate.

Formats used to prepare a cash budget vary depending on the pattern of the particular firm's cash flow. Table 7–1 shows a monthly cash budget for a small department store over a four-month period. Each monthly column should be divided into two sections—estimated and actual (not shown)—so that each succeeding six-month forecast can be updated according to actual cash transactions. There are five basic elements in completing a cash budget:

- determining an adequate cash balance
- forecasting sales
- forecasting cash receipts
- forecasting cash disbursement
- determining the end-of-month cash balance

Determining an Adequate Cash Balance

What is considered an excessive cash balance for one small business may be inadequate for another, even though the two firms are in the same trade. Some suggest that a firm's cash balance should equal at least one-fourth of its current debts,[4] but this clearly will not work for all small businesses. The most reliable method of deciding cash balance is based on past experience. Past operating records should indicate the proper cash "cushion" needed to cover any unexpected expenses after all normal cash outlays are deducted from the month's cash receipts. For example, past records may indicate that it is desirable to maintain a cash balance equal to five days' sales. Seasonal fluctuations may cause the firm's minimum cash balance to change. For example, the desired cash balance for a retailer in December may be greater than in June.

Forecasting Sales

The heart of the cash budget is the sales forecast. It is the central factor in creating an accurate picture of the firm's cash position, since sales ultimately are transformed into cash receipts and cash disbursements (see figure 7–2). For most businesses, sales constitute the major source of the cash flowing into the business. Similarly, sales of merchandise require that cash be used to replenish inventory. As a result, the cash budget is only as accurate as the sales forecast from which it is derived.

For the established business, the sales forecast can be based on past sales, but the owner must be careful not to be excessively optimistic in projecting sales. Clearly, economic swings, increased competition, fluctuations in demand, and other factors can drastically alter sales patterns.

Several quantitative techniques, which are beyond the scope of this text (linear regression, multiple regression, time series analysis, exponential

---

[4] "Cash Flow/Cash Management," p. 1.

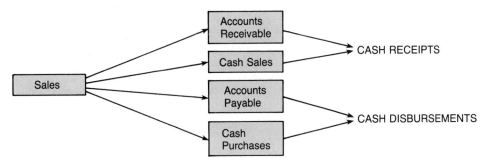

FIGURE 7–2   Sales forecast.

smoothing) are available to the owner of an existing business with an established sales pattern for forecasting sales. These methods enable the small business owner to extrapolate past and present sales trends to arrive at a fairly accurate sales forecast.

The task of forecasting sales for the new firm is more difficult, but not impossible. For example, the new owner might conduct research on similar firms and their sales patterns in the first year of operation to come up with a forecast. The local Chamber of Commerce and trade associations in the various industries also may assist in providing such information. Marketing research is another method that may be used to estimate annual sales for the fledgling firm. Other potential sources which may help predict sales include: census reports; newspapers; radio and television customer profiles; polls and surveys; and local government statistics. Small Business Report 7–2 gives an example of how an entrepreneur may use such marketing information to derive a sales forecast for the first year of operation.

No matter what techniques the small business manager employs, he must recognize even the best sales estimate will be wrong. So, many financial analysts suggest that the owner create three estimates— an optimistic, a pessimistic, and a most likely sales estimate—and then make a separate cash budget for each forecast. This dynamic forecast enables the owner to determine the range within which his sales will likely be as the year progresses.

Forecasting Cash Receipts

As noted earlier, sales constitute the major source of cash receipts. When a firm sells goods and services on credit, the cash budget must account for the delay between the sale and the actual collection of the proceeds. For instance, proceeds for an appliance sold in February might not be collected until March or April, and so the cash budget must reflect this delay. To project accurately the firm's cash receipts, the owner must analyze the accounts receivable to determine the collection pattern. For example, past records may indicate that 20 percent of sales will be for cash, 50 percent will be paid in the month following the sale, 20 percent will be paid two months after the sale, 5 percent after three months, and 5 percent will never be collected. In addition to cash and credit sales, the small business may receive cash in a number of forms—interest income, rental income, dividends, and others. Small Business Report 7–3 illustrates the importance of controlling accounts receivable.

Forecasting Cash Disbursements

Most owners of established businesses have a clear picture of the firm's pattern of cash disbursements. In fact, many cash payments, such as rent, loan repayments, and interest, are fixed amounts due on specified dates. The key factor in forecasting disbursements for a cash budget is to record them in the

Sales Forecasting

Robert Adler wants to open a repair shop for imported autos. The trade association for automotive garages estimates that the owner of an imported car spends an average of $415 per year on repairs and maintenance. The typical garage attracts its clientele from a trading zone (the area from which a business draws its customers) with a 20-mile radius. Census reports show that the families within a 20-mile radius of Robert's proposed location own 84,000 cars, of which 24 percent are imports. Based on a local consultant's opinion, Robert believes he can capture 11 percent of the market this year. Robert's estimate of his first year's sales is:

Number of autos in trading zone	84,000 autos
× Percent of imports	× 24%
Number of imports in trading zone	20,160 imports
Number of imports	20,160
× Average expenditure on repairs/ maintenance	× $415
Total import repair sales potential	$8,366,400
Import repair sales potential	$8,366,400
× Estimated share of market	× 11%
Estimated Sales	$ 920,304

So, Robert Adler can take this annual sales estimate of $920,304 and convert it into monthly sales estimates for use in his firm's cash budget.

---

month in which they will be paid, not when the obligation is incurred. Of course, the number of cash disbursements varies with each particular business, but the following disbursement categories are standard: purchase of inventory or raw materials; wages and salaries; rent, taxes, loans and interest; selling expenses; overhead expenses; and miscellaneous expenses.

Often, the small business manager underestimates cash disbursements, resulting in a cash crisis. To prevent this, the wise owner will cushion each cash disbursement account assuming it will be higher than expected. This is particularly true of entrepreneurs opening new businesses. In fact, some financial analysts recommend that a new owner estimate cash disbursements as best he can and then add on another from 25 to 50 percent of the total. What-

ever forecasting technique is used, the small business manager must avoid underestimating cash disbursements, which may lead to severe cash shortages and possibly bankruptcy.

Estimating the End-of-Month Cash Balance

To estimate the firm's cash balance for each month, the small business manager first must determine the cash balance at the beginning of each month. The beginning cash balance includes cash-on-hand as well as cash in checking and savings accounts. As development of the cash budget progresses, the cash balance at the end of a month becomes the beginning balance for the succeeding month. Next, the owner simply adds total cash receipts and subtracts

SMALL
BUSINESS
REPORT
7–3

Managing Your Accounts Receivable

Are your customers who purchase on credit paying late? If so, these outstanding accounts receivable probably represent a significant leak in your company's profits. Regaining control of these late payers will likely improve the firm's profits and cash flow.

Slow-paying credit customers, in effect, are borrowing money from your business interest free! They are using your money without penalty while you forgo opportunities to place it in interest-earning investments. Exactly how much is poor credit control costing you? The answer may surprise you!

The first step is to compute the company's average collection period rate (see the "operating ratios" section in this chapter). The second step is to "age" the firm's accounts receivable (see figure 6–15) to determine how many accounts are current and how many are overdue. The following example shows how to use these facts to compute the cost of the past due accounts:

Average collection period	65 days
Less: selling items	−30 days
Excess in accounts receivable	35 days
Average daily sales of $21,500[a] × 35 days	$752,500
Normal rate of return on investments	× 12%
Annual cost of excess	$ 90,300

If your business is highly seasonal, quarterly or monthly figures may be more meaningful than annual ones.

Source: Adapted from "Financial Control," *Inc.* reprint, with permission of the publisher.

---

total cash disbursements to obtain the end-of-month balance before any borrowing takes place. A positive amount indicates that the firm has a cash surplus for the month while a negative amount shows a cash shortage will occur unless the manager is able to collect or borrow additional funds.

Normally, a firm's cash balance fluctuates from month to month, reflecting seasonal sales patterns. Such fluctuations are normal, but the small business owner must watch closely any increases and decreases in the cash balance over time. A trend of increases indicates that the small firm has ample cash that could be placed in some income-earning investment. On the other hand, a pattern of cash decreases should alert the owner that the business is approaching a cash crisis.

Clearly, the cash budget not only illustrates the flow of cash into and out of the small business, but it also allows the owner to anticipate cash shortages and cash surpluses. "Then," explains a small business consultant, "you can go to the bank and get a 'seasonal' line of credit for six months instead of twelve. Right there you can cut your borrowing costs in half."[5] By planning cash needs ahead of time, the small business is able to:

- take advantage of money-saving opportunities, such as economic order quantities and cash discounts.
- make the most efficient use of cash.
- finance seasonal business needs.
- develop a sound borrowing program.

---

[5]Shepherd, op. cit. p. 67.

- develop a workable program of debt repayment.
- provide funds for expansion.
- plan for the investment of surplus cash.[6]

Clearly, the small business manager simply cannot afford to lose the benefits that come from cash planning.

IV.   AVOIDING THE CASH CRUNCH

Nearly every small business has the potential to improve its cash position with little or no investment. The key is to make an objective evaluation of the company's financial policies, searching for inefficiency in its cash flow. Young firms cannot afford to waste resources, especially one as vital as cash. By focusing control efforts on the following areas, the small business manager can get maximum benefit from the company's pool of cash.

Managing Receivables and Payables

A firm should always try to accelerate a firm's receivables and to stretch out its payables. As one company's chief financial officer stated, the idea is to "get the cash in the door as fast as you can, cut costs, and pay people as late as possible."[7]

Receivables.   Small business owners quickly discover that customers will postpone their payments as long as possible. Efficient cash management requires the prompt collection of every sales dollar. While some firms can require customers to pay in advance, most small businesses grant some type of credit. It is estimated that 90 percent of industrial and wholesale sales are on credit and that 40 percent of retail sales are on account.[8] An assertive collection program is

essential in managing the company's cash balance.

The first step is to screen customers carefully *before* granting credit. The savings from lower bad debt expenses can more than offset the cost of using a credit research service. One retailer of large appliances advertised, "Good credit, bad credit, no credit at all! Come see us!" His sales volume was high, but his extremely low collection rate forced him out of business.

The next step involves establishing a firm written credit policy and letting every customer know in advance the company's credit terms. When will you invoice? How soon is payment due—immediately, 30 days, 60 days? Will you add a late charge? If so, how much? The credit policies should be as "tight"as possible and within federal and state credit laws. The owner must send invoices promptly since customers rarely pay *before* they receive their bills.

The small business owner must take immediate action once an account becomes overdue. The longer an account is past due, the lower the probability of collection. Once again, the owner must establish a timetable for following up with past due notices, telephone calls, and personal calls.

Small business owners can rely on a variety of techniques for speeding cash inflows. Depositing customer checks and credit card receipts *daily* improves the firm's cash balance. Some banks allow owners to deposit receipts directly into interest-bearing accounts. Most banks also offer lockbox collection services, where customers send payments to a post office box the bank maintains. The bank collects the payments several times each day and deposits them immediately into the company's account. The procedure sharply reduces processing and clearing times, especially if the lockboxes are located close to the firm's biggest customers' business addresses. The system can be expensive to operate and is most economical for companies with a high volume of large checks.

Payables.   The timing of payables is just as crucial to proper cash management as the timing of receiva-

---

[6]*A Handbook of Small Business Finance*, Small Business Management Series No. 15, U.S. Small Business Administration, pp. 33–34.

[7]George Anders, "Truckers Trials: How One Firm Fights to Save Every Penny as Its Profits Plummet," *The Wall Street Journal*, April 13, 1982, pp. 1, 22.

[8]"Cash Flow/Cash Management," p. 5.

bles, but the objective is exactly the opposite! The small business manager should strive to stretch out his payables as long as possible *without damaging the company's credit rating*. Otherwise, suppliers may begin demanding prepayment or C.O.D. terms, which severely impairs the company's cash flow. It is entirely reasonable for a small business owner to regulate payments to his company's advantage. Efficient cash managers set up a payment calendar each month that allows them to pay their bills on time and to take advantage of cash discounts for early payment.

Generally, it is a good idea for the owner to take advantage of cash discounts vendors offer. A cash discount (e.g., "2/10, net 30"—take a 2 percent discount if you pay the invoice within 10 days; otherwise, total payment is due in 30 days) offers a price reduction if the owner pays an invoice early.

A clever cash manager also will negotiate the best possible credit terms with his suppliers. Almost all vendors grant their customers "trade credit," and the small business owner should take advantage of it. However, because trade credit is so easy to get, the owner must be careful not to abuse it, putting the business in a precarious financial position.

Favorable credit terms can make a tremendous difference in a firm's cash flow. Table 7–2 shows the same "most-likely" cash budget (from table 7–1) with one exception: instead of purchasing on C.O.D. terms (table 7–1), the owner has negotiated "net 30" payment terms (table 7–2). Notice the drastic improvement in the company's cash flow resulting from improved credit terms.

Some small business owners do not seek trade credit from vendors because they are embarrassed. One entrepreneur says, "I was always afraid people would think I was going out of business—that I was failing."[9] Such an attitude only increases the pressure on a firm's cash balance.

If an owner does find himself financially strapped when payment to a vendor is due, he should avoid making empty promises that "the check is in the mail." Instead, he should discuss openly the situation with the vendor. Most vendors will work out payment terms for extended credit. One small business owner who was experiencing a cash crisis claims:

> One day things got so bad I just called up a supplier and said, "I need your stuff, but I'm going through a tough period and simply can't pay you right now." They said they wanted to keep me as a customer, and they asked if it was okay to bill me in three months. I was dumbfounded: *They didn't even charge me interest.*[10]

The small business owner also can improve the firm's cash flow by scheduling "controllable" cash disbursements so that they do not come due at the same time. For example, paying employees every two weeks (or every month) rather than every week reduces administrative costs and gives the business more time to use its cash. Owners of fledgling businesses may be able to conserve cash by hiring part-time employees or by using freelance workers rather than full-time, permanent workers. Scheduling insurance premiums monthly or quarterly rather than annually also improves cash flows.

Wise use of business credit cards is another way to stretch the firm's cash balance. However, the owner should avoid cards that charge transaction fees. Credit cards differ in their interest-charging policies; most begin charging interest from the date of purchase, but some charge interest only from the invoice date.

Inventory

Inventory is a significant investment for many small businesses and can create a severe strain on cash flow. Surplus inventory yields a zero rate of return and unnecessarily ties up the firm's cash. Marking down items that don't sell will keep inventory lean and allow it to turn over frequently. Even though

[9]Shepherd, op. cit. p. 68.

[10]Ibid.

TABLE 7—2   Cash budget,* most likely sales forecast.

	Jan.	Feb.	Mar.	Apr.
Cash Receipts:				
Sales	$150,000	$200,000	$200,000	$300,000
Credit Sales	112,500	150,000	150,000	225,000
Collections:				
60%—1st month after sale	$180,000	$ 67,500	$ 90,000	$ 90,000
30%—2nd month after sale	78,750	90,000	33,750	45,000
5%—3rd month after sale	11,250	13,125	15,000	5,625
Cash Sales	37,500	50,000	50,000	75,000
Interest	0	200	0	0
Total Cash Receipts	$307,500	$220,825	$188,750	$215,625
Cash Disbursements:				
*Purchases	$105,000	$140,000	$140,000	$210,000
Rent	2,000	2,000	2,000	2,000
Utilities	850	850	850	850
Interest	0	0	7,500	0
Tax Prepayment	0	0	50,000	0
Capital Addition	0	130,000	3	0
Miscellaneous	70	70	70	70
Wages/Salaries	30,000	40,000	45,000	50,000
*Total Cash Disbursements	$137,920	$312,920	$245,420	$262,920
End of Month Balance:				
*Cash (Beginning of month)	$ 12,000	$181,580	$ 89,485	$ 32,815
*+ Cash Receipts	307,500	220,825	188,750	215,625
*− Cash Disbursements	137,920	312,920	245,420	262,920
*Cash (End of month)	181,580	89,485	32,815	(14,480)
*Borrowing	0	0	0	24,480
*Cash (End of month [After borrowing])	$181,580	$ 89,485	$ 32,815	$ 10,000

*After negotiating "net 30" trade credit terms.

volume discounts lower inventory costs, large purchases may tie up the company's valuable cash. In fact, only 20 percent of a typical business' inventory turns over quickly, so the owner must watch constantly for "stale" items.[11] Finally, scheduling inventory deliveries at the latest possible date will prevent premature payment of invoices.

Bartering

Bartering, the exchange of goods and services for other goods and services, is an effective way to conserve cash. An ancient concept, bartering began to regain popularity during recent recessions. In the last decade, more than 500 barter exchanges have cropped up, catering primarily to small and medium-sized businesses. Small firms reap other benefits from bartering, such as:

■ uncovering markets for overstocked inventory items
■ collecting what otherwise would be uncollectible debts
  maintaining contact with potential cash customers
■ discovering new advertising possibilities[12]

The owner of the country's largest bartering firm says, "Bartering is as expansive and exciting and rewarding as your own creativity."[13] For example, one restaurateur traded meals for repair work on company vans, a roll of carpet, and pest control services. Trading goods for sale allows the small business owner to maintain the firm's profitability even when cash is scarce.

Investing Surplus Cash

Because of the uneven flow of receipts and disbursements, a company will often temporarily have more cash than it needs—for a week, month, quarter, or longer. When this happens, most small business owners simply ignore the surplus since they are not sure how soon they will need it. They feel that relatively small amounts of cash sitting around for just a few days or weeks are not worth investing. However, this is not always the case. The small business manager who puts surplus cash to work *immediately* rather than allowing it to sit idle soon discovers that the yield adds up to a significant amount over time. This "found money" can help ease the daily cash crunch during business troughs.

However, when investing surplus cash, the owner's primary objective should *not* be to earn the maximum yield (which usually carries with it maximum risk); instead, the focus should be on the safety and the liquidity of the investments. Small Business Report 7–4 shows the negative aspect of investing cash. The need to minimize risk and to have ready access to the cash restricts the small business owner's investment options to just a few.

A very popular tool for investing short-term cash is a money market account (MMA) offered by most banks and investment companies. These accounts maximize liquidity, professional management, and diversification. In fact, managers of MMAs typically invest in Treasury bills, Treasury bonds, Treasury notes, Certificates of Deposits, bankers' acceptances, repurchase agreements, and high-quality commercial paper. Most accounts have minimum investments of $5,000, although some will permit smaller sums.

Money market mutual funds (MMMFs) invest in the same instruments as MMAs. Small business owners who buy shares in MMMFs may get preferential tax treatment. Under current tax law, corporations (except S Corporations) can exclude 85 percent of any dividend income received from the preferred stock of certain types of companies. Says one money manager, "We take operating income taxed at 46 percent and replace it with intercorporate dividends which are taxed at a maximum of 6.9 percent."[14] Some owners invest directly in financial instruments.

[11]Ibid.
[12]"Asset Management," *Venture*, June 1984, p. 100.
[13]Henry Eason, "Barter Boom," *Nation's Business*, March 1985, p. 18.

[14]"Asset Management," p. 100.

SMALL
BUSINESS
REPORT
7–4

High Returns . . . or High Risks?

A basic rule for investing a small company's surplus cash is to stick to financial instruments offering security and liquidity. Richard Russell, vice-president and treasurer for Davis Industries Corporation, learned this lesson the hard way. He invested a sizable portion of the family-owned company's idle cash in Mead Money Management's Corporate Cash Management Fund, a mutual fund with over $200 million in assets. Soon afterwards, the fund's share price plummeted.

Russell had set gain and loss limits on the returns from the fund. When the price reached the lower limit, Russell sold Davis' shares. The company lost $20,000 of its principal amount. Today, when Russell invests Davis' surplus cash, he looks for security and liquidity *first* and high after-tax yields second.

The investments a small business owner chooses depend on several factors. A company with $5 million to invest has more options than one with $5,000. The length of time the company will invest the money also is important. Money-market mutual funds are best suited to intermediate and long-term investments; savings accounts, CDs, and money-market accounts are better short-term investments. The company's tax position also influences its investment choice. Corporations paying the maximum tax rate must consider carefully the tax implications of its investments. Finally, executives must evaluate the amount of time they have to spend managing the company's investments. Advises one executive, "Your job is not to be a financial wizard. It's to make widgets or whatever else it is you are in business to do."

Source: Adapted from Donna Sammons Carpenter, "Play Money," *Inc.*, December 1984, pp. 220–24, with permission of the publisher.

Minimum purchase prices, however, can be quite high, ranging from $10,000 to $500,000.

Trimming Overhead Costs

High overhead expenses can strain a small firm's cash supply to the breaking point. Frugal small business owners can trim their overhead in a number of ways.

When practical, lease instead of buying. By leasing automobiles, computers, equipment, and other assets, the entrepreneur avoids large capital outlays frequently required as "down payment."

Avoid nonessential outlays. By forgoing costly ego indulgences like ostentatious office equipment and flashy company cars, an owner can make efficient use of the company's cash.

Control employee advances and loans. A manager should grant only those advances and loans that are necessary and he should keep accurate records on payments and balances.

Establish an internal security and control system. Too many owners encourage employee theft by failing to establish a system of controls.

Conclusion

Successful owners run their businesses "lean and mean." Trimming wasteful expenditures, investing surplus funds, and carefully planning and managing the company's cash flow enables them to compete effectively in a hostile market. The simple, but effective, techniques covered in this chapter can improve every small company's cash position.

V. SUMMARY

Cash is the most important but least productive asset the small business has. The manager must maintain enough cash to meet the firm's normal requirements (plus a reserve for emergencies) without retaining excessively large, unproductive cash balances. Cash and profits are not the same. More businesses fail for lack of cash than for lack of profits. The cash budgeting procedure outlined in this chapter tracks the flow of cash through the business and enables the owner to project cash surpluses and cash deficits at specific intervals. The cash budget takes relatively little time to prepare, and it shows the owner when he may need a cash infusion and when he may have excess idle funds that might be invested to earn income.

To avoid a cash crunch, the small business owner must establish a functional policy for handling receivables and payables. The principal idea is to accelerate the firm's receivables and to stretch out its payables (without damaging its credit rating). This gives the owner maximum use of his money's earning power.

Inventory frequently causes cash headaches for the small business manager. Excess inventory earns a zero rate of return and ties up the firm's cash unnecessarily. Owners must constantly watch for stale merchandise. Bartering, exchanging goods and services for other goods and services, is an ideal way to preserve cash. It also can uncover new potential markets and allows collection of what otherwise would be uncollectible accounts.

Investing surplus cash maximizes the firm's earning power and eases the pressure on its cash balance. However, the owner should not be distracted by promises of high yields. The primary criteria for investing this cash are security and liquidity.

Finally, trimming overhead costs by leasing assets, avoiding nonessential outlays, and implementing a security and control system boosts the firm's cash position.

STUDENT INVOLVEMENT PROJECT

Ask several local small business owners about their cash management policies. Do they know how much cash their businesses have during the month? How do they track their cash flows? Do they use some type of cash budget? If not, ask if you can help the owner develop one. Does the owner invest surplus cash?

DISCUSSION QUESTIONS

1. Why must the small business concentrate on cash management?
2. Explain the difference between cash and profit.
3. Outline the steps involved in developing a cash budget. What information does a cash budget provide?
4. How can an entrepreneur launching a new business forecast sales?
5. Outline the basic principles of managing a small firm's receivables and payables.
6. How can bartering improve a company's cash position?
7. What should be a small business owner's primary concern when investing surplus cash?

Planning for Profit

8

Businesses exert the tightest controls over the easiest things to control, rather than the most critical.

Kenneth B. Collins

It is better to solve problems than crises.

John Guinther

Upon completion of this chapter, you will be able to:

- Understand the importance of *planning* for profit.

- Understand how to prepare financial statements and use them to manage the small business.

- Understand the basic financial statements through ratio analysis.

- Explain how to interpret financial ratios.

- Create pro forma financial statements.

The very survival of the small business depends on its ability to make a profit. But making a profit normally does not happen by accident; it requires careful planning, a lot of sound management and control techniques, and a bit of good fortune. To reach profit objectives, the small business manager must be aware of the firm's overall financial position and must be aware of changes in financial status that occur over time.

This chapter focuses on some very practical tools that will keep the small business manager aware of her financial position and enable her to actively plan for profit. Instead of waiting for events in the environment to change the firm's financial standing and then reacting to them, she can use these tools to help her anticipate changes and plot an appropriate profit strategy to meet them head on. These profit planning techniques are *not* difficult to master, nor are they overly time consuming. These tools can be computerized quite easily, and they provide the owner with timely information about the firm's fiscal health. In many cases, these tools could detect financial difficulties before they become business-threatening crises.

In chapter 6 we saw that the balance sheet presents a picture of what the firm owns and what it owes at a particular time, while the income statement reflects the success or failure of the firm's operations over a period of time. While these figures are important *gauges* of financial health, they are not the *solution* to financial well-being. It is not enough simply to gather financial data and organize them into concise records. The small business manager must analyze these financial statements and use them in operating the firm.

I. RATIO ANALYSIS

Ratio analysis, a method of expressing the relationships between any two accounting elements, provides a convenient technique for performing financial analysis. These comparisons allow the small business manager to determine if the firm is carrying excessive inventory, experiencing heavy operating expenses, overextending credit, managing to pay its debts on time, and answer other questions relating to the efficient operation of the firm. But how many ratios should the small business manager monitor to maintain adequate financial control over the firm? The number of ratios that could be calculated is limited only by the number of accounts recorded on the firm's financial statements. However, a study conducted by the American Society of Accounting Executives concluded that, "Ratios may lose their significance and accuracy when they become excessively detailed . . . . "[1]

Ten Key Ratios

We will describe 10 key ratios that will enable the owner to monitor the firm's financial position without becoming "bogged down" in financial details. This chapter presents explanations of these ratios and examples based on the balance sheet and the income statement for Sam's Appliance Shop shown in figures 6–13 and 6–14.

Liquidity Ratios.   Liquidity ratios tell whether the small business will be able to meet its maturing obligations as they come due. They include both current and quick ratios.

Current Ratio.   The current ratio measures the small firm's solvency by indicating its ability to pay

[1] U. S. Small Business Administration, *Ratio Analysis for Small Business*, Small Business Management Series No. 20, Washington, 1977, p. 8.

current debts from current assets. It is calculated in the following manner:

$$\text{current ratio} = \frac{\text{current assets}}{\text{current liabilities}}$$
$$= \frac{686,985}{367,850}$$
$$= 1.87$$

Current assets are those which the manager expects to convert into cash in the ordinary business cycle, and normally include cash, notes/accounts receivable, inventory, and any other short-term marketable securities. Current liabilities are those short-term obligations that come due within one year, and include notes/accounts payable, taxes payable, and accruals.

The current ratio is sometimes called the working capital ratio and is the most commonly used measure of short-term solvency. Typically, financial analysts suggest that a small business maintain a current ratio of at least 2:1 (i.e., two dollars of current assets for every one dollar of current liabilities) to maintain a comfortable cushion of working capital. Generally, the higher the firm's current ratio, the stronger its financial position; but a high current ratio does not guarantee that the firm's assets are being used in the most profitable manner. For example, the business may be maintaining excessive balances of idle cash or may be overinvesting in inventory.

With its current ratio of 1.87, Sam's Appliance Shop could liquidate its current assets at 53.5% (1 ÷ 1.87 = 0.535) of book value and still manage to pay its current creditors in full.

Quick Ratio.   The quick ratio (or the "acid test" ratio) is a more conservative measure of a firm's liquidity since it shows the extent to which its most liquid assets cover its current liabilities. It is calculated as follows:

$$\text{quick ratio} = \frac{\text{quick assets}}{\text{current liabilities}}$$
$$= \frac{686,985 - 455,455}{367,850}$$
$$= 0.63$$

Quick assets include cash as well as assets which can be converted into cash immediately if needed, such as cash, readily marketable securities, and notes/accounts receivable. Most small firms determine quick assets by subtracting inventory from current assets, since inventory cannot be converted into cash quickly. Also, inventories are the assets on which losses are most likely to occur in case of liquidation.

The quick ratio is a more specific measure of a firm's ability to meet its short-term obligations and is a more rigorous test of its liquidity. It expresses capacity to pay current debts if all sales income ceased immediately. Generally, a quick ratio of 1:1 is considered satisfactory. A ratio of less than 1:1 indicates that the small firm is overly dependent on inventory and on future sales to satisfy short-term debt. A quick ratio of more than 1:1 indicates a greater degree of financial security.

Leverage Ratios. Leverage ratios measure the financing supplied by the firm's owners against that supplied by its creditors. Generally, small businesses with low leverage ratios are less affected by economic downturns, but the returns for these firms are lower during economic booms. Conversely, small firms with high leverage ratios are more vulnerable to economic slides, but they have greater potential for large profits.

Debt Ratio. The small firm's debt ratio measures the percentage of total funds in the business provided by its creditors. The debt ratio is calculated as follows:

$$\text{debt ratio} = \frac{\text{total debt (or liabilities)}}{\text{total assets}}$$
$$= \frac{367,850 + 212,150}{847,655}$$
$$= 0.68$$

Total debt includes all current liabilities and any outstanding long-term notes and bonds. Total assets represent the sum of the firm's current assets, fixed assets, and intangible assets. Clearly, a high debt ratio means that creditors provide a large percentage of the firm's total financing. Owners generally prefer a high leverage ratio; otherwise, business funds must come either from the owners' personal assets or from taking on new owners, which means giving up more control over the business. Also, with a greater portion of the firm's assets financed by creditors, the owner is able to generate profits with a smaller personal investment. On the other hand, creditors typically prefer moderate debt ratios since a lower debt ratio indicates a small chance of creditor losses in case of liquidation.

Debt-to-Net Worth Ratio. The small firm's debt-to-net worth ratio also expresses the relationship between the capital contributions from creditors and those from owners. This ratio compares what the business owes to what it owns. It is a measure of the small firm's ability to meet both its creditor and owner obligations in case of liquidation. The debt-to-net worth ratio is calculated as follows:

$$\frac{\text{debt-to-net}}{\text{worth ratio}} = \frac{\text{total debt (or liabilities)}}{\text{tangible net worth}}$$
$$= \frac{367,850 + 212,150}{267,655 - 3,500}$$
$$= 2.20$$

Total debt is the sum of current liabilities and long-term liabilities, while tangible net worth represents the owners' investment in the business (capital + capital stock + earned surplus + retained earnings) less any intangible assets (e.g., goodwill) the firm owns.

The higher this ratio, the lower the degree of protection afforded creditors if the business should fail. Also, a higher debt-to-net worth ratio means that the firm has less capacity to borrow; lenders and creditors see the firm as being "borrowed up." Conversely, a low ratio typically is associated with a higher level of financial security, giving the business greater borrowing potential.

As the firm's debt-to-net worth ratio approaches 1:1, the creditors' interest in the business approaches that of the owners'. If the ratio is greater than 1:1, the creditors' claims exceed those of the owners', and the business may be undercapitalized. In other words, the owner has not supplied an adequate amount of capital, forcing the business to be overextended in terms of debt.

Operating Ratios.   Operating ratios help the owner evaluate the small firm's performance and indicate how effectively the business employs its resources. They are designed to help the owner operate his enterprise as efficiently as possible.

Average Inventory Turnover.   The small firm's average inventory turnover ratio measures the number of times its average inventory is sold out, or turned over, during the year. This ratio tells the owner whether the firm's inventory is being managed properly. It apprises the owner of whether the business

inventory is understocked, overstocked, or obsolete. The average inventory turnover ratio is calculated as follows:

$$\begin{aligned} \frac{\text{average inventory}}{\text{turnover ratio}} &= \frac{\text{cost of goods sold}}{\text{average inventory}} \\ &= \frac{1{,}290{,}117}{(805{,}745 + 455{,}455) \div 2} \\ &= 2.05 \text{ times/year} \end{aligned}$$

Some businesses compute inventory turnover using sales instead of cost of goods sold as the numerator, but most firms carry inventories at cost. Therefore, it is more appropriate to use cost of goods sold to compute inventory turnover. Average inventory is found by adding the firm's inventory at the beginning of the accounting period to the ending inventory and dividing the result by 2.

This ratio tells the owner how fast the merchandise is moving through the business. To determine the average number of days units remain in inventory, divide the average inventory turnover ratio into the number of days in the accounting period (e.g., 365 ÷ average inventory turnover ratio). The result is called days' inventory. A high inventory turnover indicates that the small business has a healthy, salable, and liquid inventory and a supply of quality merchandise supported by sound pricing policies. A low inventory turnover suggests an illiquid inventory characterized by obsolescence, overstocking, and stale merchandise.

The inventory turnover ratio can be misleading, however. For example, a high ratio could mean the firm has a shortage of inventory and is experiencing stockouts. Similarly, a low ratio could be the result of planned inventory stockpiling to meet seasonal peak demand. Another problem is that the ratio is based on an inventory balance calculated from two days out of the entire accounting period. Thus, inventory fluctuations due to seasonal demand patterns are ignored, which may bias the resulting ratio. There is no universal, ideal inventory turnover ratio. Financial analysts suggest that a favorable turnover ratio depends on the type of business, its size,

"Nice try, Henderson, but the stockholders
will see right through it."

Source: From *The Wall Street Journal,* August 24, 1984, p. 15. Used with permission of *The Wall Street Journal,* © Dow Jones & Company, Inc., 1984. All rights reserved.

its profitability, its method of inventory valuation, and other relevant factors.

Average Collection Period. The small firm's average collection period ratio tells the average number of days it takes to collect accounts receivable. To compute the average collection period ratio, we must first calculate the firm's receivables turnover. If Sam's credit sales for the year were $1,309,589, then the receivables turnover ratio would be:

$$\frac{\text{receivables}}{\text{turnover}} = \frac{\text{credit sales (or net sales)}}{\text{accounts receivable}}$$
$$= \frac{1,309,589}{179,225}$$
$$= 7.31 \text{ times/year}$$

This ratio measures the number of times the firm's accounts and notes receivable "turn over" during the accounting period. Sam's Appliance Shop turns over its receivables 7.31 times per year. The higher the firm's receivables turnover ratio, the shorter the time lag between the sale and the cash collection.

To calculate the firm's average collection period ratio:

$$\frac{\text{average collection}}{\text{period ratio}} = \frac{\text{days in accounting period}}{\text{receivables turnover}}$$
$$= \frac{365 \text{ days}}{7.31}$$
$$= 49.95 \text{ days}$$

So, Sam's Appliance Shop's accounts and notes receivable are outstanding for an average of 50 days. Typically, the higher the firm's average collection period ratio, the greater the chance of bad debt losses.

One of the most useful applications of the collection period ratio is to compare it to the industry average and to the firm's credit terms. Such a comparison will indicate the degree of the small company's control over its credit sales and collection techniques. Some financial analysts consider a firm's collection procedures inadequate if its average collection period ratio is 10 to 15 days longer than its credit selling terms. For example, if Sam's selling terms are net 30, his collection period ratio of 50

days indicates that his collection techniques are unsatisfactory. Another rule of thumb suggests that the firm's average collection period ratio should be no more than one-third greater than its credit terms. For example, if a small company's credit terms are net 45, its average collection period ratio should be no more than 60 days. A ratio greater than 60 days would indicate poor collection procedures.

Net Sales to Total Assets. The small company's net sales-to-total assets ratio (also called the total assets turnover ratio) is a general measure of its ability to generate sales in relation to its assets. It describes how productively the firm employs its assets to produce sales revenue. The total assets turnover ratio is calculated as follows:

$$\frac{\text{total assets}}{\text{turnover ratio}} = \frac{\text{net sales}}{\text{net total assets}}$$
$$= \frac{1,870,841}{847,655}$$
$$= 2.21$$

The denominator of this ratio, net total assets, is the sum of all of the firm's assets (cash, inventory, land, buildings, equipment, tools, everything owned) less depreciation. This ratio is meaningful only when compared to that of similar firms in the same industry category. A total assets turnover ratio below the industry average may indicate that the small firm is not generating an adequate sales volume for its asset size.

Net Sales to Working Capital. The net sales-to-working capital ratio measures how many dollars in sales the business makes for every dollar of working capital (working capital = current assets − current liabilities). Also called the turnover of working capital ratio, this proportion tells the owner how efficiently working capital is being used to generate sales. It is calculated as follows:

$$\frac{\text{net sales to working}}{\text{capital ratio}} = \frac{\text{net sales}}{\text{current assets} - \text{current liabilities}}$$
$$= \frac{1,870,841}{686,985 - 367,850}$$
$$= 5.86$$

An excessively low net sales-to-working capital ratio indicates that the small firm is not employing its working capital efficiently or profitably. On the other hand, an extremely high ratio points to an inadequate level of working capital to maintain a suitable level of sales, which puts creditors in a more vulnerable position. This ratio is very helpful in maintaining sufficient working capital as the small business grows. It is critical for the small firm to keep a satisfactory level of working capital to nourish its expansion, and the net sales-to-working capital ratio helps define the level of working capital required to support higher sales volume.

Profitability Ratios.   Profitability ratios indicate how effectively and efficiently the small firm is being managed. They provide the owner with information about the company's "bottom line"—in other words, they describe how successfully the firm is conducting business.

Net Profit on Sales.   The net profit on sales ratio (also called the profit margin on sales) measures the firm's profit per dollar of sales. The computed percentage shows the number of cents of each sales dollar remaining after deducting all expenses and income taxes. The profit margin on sales is calculated as follows:

$$\text{net profit on sales ratio} = \frac{\text{net profit}}{\text{net sales}}$$
$$= \frac{60,629}{1,870,841}$$
$$= 3.24\%$$

Most small business owners believe that a high profit margin on sales is necessary for a successful business operation, but this is a myth. To evaluate this ratio properly, the owner must consider the firm's asset value, its inventory and receivables turnover ratios, and its total capitalization. For example, the typical small supermarket earns an average net profit of only one cent on each dollar of sales, but its inventory may turn over as many as 20 times a year. If the firm's profit margin on sales is below the indus-

try average, it may be a sign that its prices are relatively low, or that its costs are excessively high, or both.

Net Profit to Equity.   The profit-to-equity ratio (or the return on net worth ratio) measures the owners' rate of return on investment. Since it reports the percentage of the owners' investment in the business that is being returned through profits annually, it is one of the most important indicators of the firm's profitability of a management's efficiency. The net profit to equity ratio is computed as follows:

$$\text{net profit to equity} = \frac{\text{net profit}}{\text{owners' equity (or net worth)}}$$
$$= \frac{60,629}{267,655}$$
$$= 22.65\%$$

This ratio compares profits earned during the accounting period with the amount the owner has invested in the business during that time. If this interest rate on the owners' investment is excessively low, some of this capital might be better employed elsewhere.

Interpreting Business Ratios

Ratios are useful yardsticks in measuring the small firm's performance and can point out potential problems before they develop into serious crises. But calculating the various ratios is not enough to insure proper financial control. In addition to knowing how to calculate these ratios, the owner must understand how to interpret them and apply them to the operation of the firm.

One valuable way to utilize these ratios is to compare them with those of similar businesses in the same industry. By comparing the company's financial statistics to industry averages, the owner is able to locate problem areas and maintain adequate financial controls.

Several organizations regularly compile and publish operating statistics, including key ratios, summarizing the financial performance of many businesses across a wide range of industries. Some of these reports are available free and others for a fee. The local library should subscribe to most of these publications. The following organizations publish composite financial data that the small business owner can use in financial planning.

- *Dun & Bradstreet, Inc.* Since 1932, Dun & Bradstreet has published "Key Business Ratios" which covers 22 retail, 32 wholesale, and 71 industrial business categories. Dun & Bradstreet also publishes "Cost of Doing Business," a series of operating ratios compiled from the IRS's "Statistics of Income."
- *Robert Morris Associates.* Established in 1914, Robert Morris Associates publishes *Annual Statement Studies*, showing ratios and other financial data for over 350 different industrial, wholesale, and retail categories.
- *Bank of America.* Periodically, the Bank of America publishes many documents relating to small business management, including the *Small Business Reporter* which details costs-of-doing-business ratios.
- *Trade Associations.* Virtually every type of business is represented by a national trade association, which publishes detailed financial data compiled from its membership. For example, the owner of a small supermarket could contact the National Association of Retail Grocers for assistance in gathering financial statistics relevant to his operation.
- *Government Agencies.* Several government agencies (the Federal Trade Commission, Interstate Commerce Commission, Department of Commerce, Department of Agriculture, and Securities and Exchange Commission) offer a great deal of financial operating data on a variety of industries, although the categories are more general. In addition, the IRS annually publishes "Statistics of Income," which includes income statement and balance sheet statistics compiled from income tax returns. The IRS also publishes the "Census of Business" which gives a limited amount of ratio information.
- *Other Sources.* In addition to the sources of financial information already listed, management consulting firms, universities, and a number of companies (e.g., Eli Lilly, Eastman Kodak, NCR Corporation) provide useful statistics.

When comparing ratios for their individual businesses to published statistics, small business owners must remember that the comparison is made against averages. The owner must strive to achieve ratios that are at least as good as these average figures. In other words, these published statistics serve as a floor below which the owner's business ratios should not remain for very long. As an owner, your goal should be to manage your business so that its financial performance is above average.

As the owner compares financial performance to those covered in the published statistics, he inevitably will discern differences between them. Those items which are substantially out of line from the

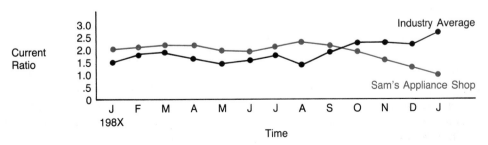

FIGURE 8–1 Trend analysis of ratios.

Comparing Ratios to Industry Averages

Ratios, by themselves, tell little about the small company's health. But, when compared to typical ratios for businesses of comparable size in the same industry, they come alive and offer a great deal of information. For example, comparing the ratios already computed from the operating data for Sam's Appliance Shop to those taken from Robert Morris Associate's *Annual Statement Summaries* we find the following:

	Sam's Appliance Shop	**Industry Median***
1.	Current Ratio = 1.87	1.5
	Sam's Appliance Shop does not measure up to the rule of thumb of 2:1; but since its ratio is above the industry median, the firm should be able to pay its short-term obligations.	
2.	Quick Ratio = 0.63	0.5
	Again, Sam's is below the rule of thumb of 1:1; but the company passes this test of liquidity when measured against industry figures. This indicates that Sam's Appliance Shop tends to rely on inventory to help satisfy short-term debt.	
3.	Debt Ratio = 0.68	1.75
	Sam's does not rely on creditors to provide an excessive amount of financing. Unlike many firms in this industry, Sam's is not top heavy with debt.	
4.	Debt-to-Net Worth Ratio = 2.20	1.9
	With a relatively high debt-to-net worth ratio, creditors and lenders will see Sam's as being "borrowed up." The firm's borrowing	

*The ratio falling exactly in the middle when sample elements are arranged in ascending or descending order.

---

industry average should be noted. However, a ratio which varies from the average does not *necessarily* mean that the small business is in financial jeopardy. Instead of making drastic changes in financial policy, the owner must explore *why* the figures are out of line. There may be a perfectly valid reason for the discrepancy. For example, a small company's inventory turnover ratio may be excessively low because the owner is building up the inventory to meet peak demand. In other cases, the discrepancy may point to a financial problem requiring immediate attention.

In addition to comparing ratios to industry averages, the owner should analyze the firm's financial ratios over time. By themselves, these ratios are "snapshots" of the firm's finances at a single instant; but by examining these trends over time, the owner can detect gradual shifts that otherwise might go unnoticed (see figure 8–1).

Ratio analysis is *not* a substitute for sound financial judgment; it will not provide a miracle cure for an ailing business. Ratios are convenient devices for measuring financial performance and help the small business owner establish financial policy and pinpoint problem areas in the operation.

capacity is limited since creditors' claims against the business are more than double those of the owner. Sam's investment in his business appears to be low.

5. Average Inventory Turnover Ratio = 2.05
   Merchandise is moving through Sam's business at a relatively slow pace. He should check his inventory for obsolete or stale merchandise.

   3.8
   times/year

6. Average Collection Period Ratio = 34.96
   Sam's average collection period is more than twice as long as that of the typical firm in the industry. If credit terms are comparable, he should concentrate on improving his collection procedures.

   22.26
   days

7. Net Sales-to-Total Assets Ratio = 2.21
   Sam's is not generating enough sales revenue relative to its asset size. This also could be a sign of improper inventory, poor sales personnel, or bad location.

   2.7

8. Net Sales-to-Working Capital Ratio = 5.86
   Sam's working capital simply is not generating enough sales revenue. If the business is growing rapidly, it will probably experience a shortage of working capital soon. Sam's *must* increase sales revenue.

   10.7

9. Net Profit on Sales Ratio = 3.24%
   After deducting all expenses, 3.24¢ of each dollar of sales remains as profit for Sam's (well below the industry average). Since the firm's inventory turnover is low, this probably indicates that Sam's costs are excessive.

   7.6%

10. Net Profit-to-Equity Ratio = 22.65%
    Sam is earning 22.65 percent on the money he has invested in the business. This yield is well above the industry median and is probably more a result of his low investment in the business than of the firm's profitability.

    12.8%

II. CREATING PROJECTED FINANCIAL STATEMENTS

Many small business failures result from neglecting to plan for the financial needs of the firm. No entrepreneur should launch an enterprise without first creating a sound financial plan for the business and then obtaining enough capital to operate it. A key element in creating such a plan is the budget, an important managerial tool which focuses on future profits and on future capital requirements. Creating projected financial statements via the budgeting process helps the small business owner transform business goals into reality. Once developed, the budget will answer such questions as: What profit can the business be expected to obtain? If the owner's profit objective is x dollars, what sales level must be achieved? What expenses, fixed and variable, must be incurred to reach this level of sales? The answers to these and other questions are critical in formulating a successful financial plan for the small business; still, many owners operate their enterprises without using the budgeting process and the related projected financial statements.

Budgeting for Profit

A budget is simply a written financial plan for the future. It serves as a blueprint for the small company's operating future. The key elements of any budget are establishing financial objectives and comparing actual results with predetermined goals. The feedback from analyzing variances from budgeted figures is an important financial control tool which enables the owner to take early corrective action.

The entire budgeting process normally begins with a sales budget, or sales revenue target. The firm's cost of goods sold typically is estimated on the basis of past experience. For example, Lenox Wholesale Jewelry Company finds that its cost of goods sold is normally 70 percent of net sales.

Instead of detailing operating expenses, general expenses, and other expenses, a budget forecasts fixed and variable expenses. Fixed expenses are those which, regardless of sales volume, stay the same. Fixed expenses might include rent, certain salaries, depreciation expense, interest payments, and taxes. Variable expenses are those costs that vary with the level of sales. For example, wages, raw material costs, commissions, and utility costs are likely to fluctuate with business activity.

Once these components of the budget are assembled, the manager is ready to test her budget. After deducting variable expenses from expected gross margin, will there be enough left to cover fixed costs and yield a reasonable profit? If not, what adjustments to the business operation can she make? The owner may have to prepare several different budgets, each illustrating a different strategy, to decide which course the business should follow.

Budgets are useful control tools. Normally, the manager should prepare an annual budget broken down into quarters. A quarterly plan enables the owner to detect and to correct problems on a more timely basis, preventing them from developing into crises.

This section will focus on creating projected income statements and balance sheets for the small business. These projected (or pro forma) statements estimate the profitability and the overall financial condition of the business for future months. Because these statements project the firm's financial position through the end of the forecasted period, they help the owner plan the route to improved financial strength and healthy business growth. Generally, the small business manager should prepare these projected statements quarterly unless the company is in a precarious financial position, in which case they must be prepared monthly.

Since the established business has a history of operating data from which to construct pro forma financial statements, the task is not nearly as difficult as it is for the beginning business. Small Business Report 8–2 outlines the budgeting process for an established small business.

Lenox Wholesale Jewelry Company
Budget for 198X

Estimated Sales Revenue		$875,000
Estimated Cost of Goods Sold		612,500
Estimated Gross Margin		$262,500
Variable Expenses:		
Utilities	$10,800	
Office Supplies	700	
Wages	42,000	
Sales Commissions	20,000	
Travel	11,800	
Miscellaneous	1,200	
TOTAL VARIABLE EXPENSES		$ 77,500
Margin for Fixed Expenses and Net Income		$185,000
Fixed Expenses:		
Depreciation		
Fixtures	$ 1,600	
Truck	1,000	
Equipment	900	
Insurance	9,500	
Advertising	20,000	
Salaries	40,000	
Taxes	8,000	
Interest	5,800	
Rent	18,000	
TOTAL FIXED EXPENSES		$104,800
ESTIMATED NET INCOME		
(Before Federal Income Taxes`		$ 80,200

Pro Forma Statements for the New Small Business

One of the most important tasks confronting the entrepreneur launching a new enterprise is to determine the funds needed to begin operation as well as those required to keep going through the initial growth period. Clearly, the amount of money needed to begin a business depends on the type of operation; its location, inventory requirements, sales volume; and other factors. But every new firm must have enough capital to cover all start-up costs, including funds to rent or buy plant, equipment, and tools and supplies, as well as pay for advertising, licenses, utilities, and other expenses. In addition, the owner must maintain a reserve of capital to carry the company until it begins to make a profit. Too often the entrepreneur is overly optimistic in his financial plan and fails to recognize that expenses initially exceed income for most small firms. This period of net losses is normal and may last from just a few months to well over a year. The owner must be able to meet payrolls, maintain adequate inventory, take advantage of cash discounts, grant customer credit, and meet personal obligations during this time.

The Pro Forma Income Statement.   In creating a projected income statement, the owner has two options: to develop a sales forecast and work down, or set a profit target and work up. Most businesses employ the latter method—the owner targets a profit figure and then determines what sales level he must achieve to reach it. Then he can prepare an outline of the expenses the business will incur in securing those sales. In any small business, the annual profit must be large enough to yield the owners a return for time spent operating the business, plus a return on their investment in the business.

Any entrepreneur who begins a small business that earns less than he could earn working for someone else has made a poor decision. Why be exposed to all of the risks, sacrifices, and hard work of beginning and operating a small business if the rewards are less than those of remaining in the secure employment of another? So the firm's net profit after taxes should be at least as much as the owner could earn by working for someone else.

An adequate profit must also include a reasonable return on the owner's total investment in the business. The owner's total investment is the amount contributed to the company at its inception plus any retained earnings (profits from previous years funneled back into the operation). If a would-be owner has $70,000 to invest, and can invest it in securities and earn 12 percent, she should not consider investing it in a small business that would yield only 3 percent.

So the owner's target income is the sum of a reasonable salary for the time spent running the business and a normal return on the amount invested in the firm. Determining how much this should be is the first step in creating the pro forma income statement.

The owner then must translate this target profit into a net sales figure for the forecasted period. To calculate net sales from a target profit, the owner must have the published statistics for this type of business. Suppose an entrepreneur wants to launch a small retail bookstore and has determined that his target income is $29,000 annually. Statistics gathered from Robert Morris Associates' *Annual Statement Studies* show that the typical bookstore's net profit margin (net profit ÷ net sales) is 9.3 percent. Using this information, he can compute the sales level required to produce a net profit of $29,000:

$$\text{net profit margin} = \frac{\text{net profit}}{\text{net sales (annual)}}$$

$$9.3\% = \frac{29,000}{\text{net sales (annual)}}$$

$$\text{net sales} = \frac{29,000}{0.093}$$

$$= \$311,828$$

Now the entrepreneur knows that to make a net profit of $29,000 (before taxes), he must achieve annual sales of $311,828. To complete the projected income statement, the owner simply applies the appropriate statistics from *Annual Statement Studies* to the annual sales figure. Since the statistics for each income statement item are expressed as percentages of net sales, he merely multiplies the proper statistic by the annual sales figure to obtain the desired value. For example, cost of goods sold usually comprises 61.4 percent of net sales for the typical small bookstore. So the owner of this new bookstore expects his cost of goods sold to be:

$$\text{cost of goods sold} = \$311,828 \times 0.614$$
$$= \$191,462$$

The bookstore's complete projected income statement is shown as follows:

Net sales	(100%)	$311,828
Cost of goods sold	(61.4%)	191,462
Gross profit margin	(38.6%)	$120,366
Operating expenses	(29.3%)	91,366
Net profit (before taxes)	(9.3%)	$ 29,000

At this point, the business appears to be a lucrative venture. But the entrepreneur must remember that this income statement represents a goal that may not be attainable. The next step is to determine whether this required sales volume can be met or exceeded. One useful technique is to break down the required annual sales volume into daily sales figures. Assuming the store will be open six days per week for 50 weeks, (300 days), then

$$\text{average daily sales} = \frac{\$311,828}{300 \text{ days}}$$
$$= \$1,039/\text{day}$$

This calculation gives the owner a better perspective of the sales required to yield an annual profit of $29,000.

To determine whether the profit expected from the business will meet or exceed the entrepreneur's target income, the prospective owner should create an income statement based on a realistic sales estimate. The previous analysis showed the owner what sales level is needed to reach his desired profit. But what happens if sales are lower? It is obvious that the entrepreneur requires a reliable sales forecast, but how can he obtain it? Earlier in this chapter we outlined several procedures for arriving at a sales forecast. The prospective bookstore operator should choose the method that best suits his needs. For example, he could hire a professional market research company to conduct a survey if he lacks the time or the inclination to do the research himself. Suppose the market research firm projects the proposed bookstore's annual sales to be only $250,000. The owner must then take this expected sales figure and develop a pro forma income statement as follows:

Net sales	(100%)	$250,000
− Cost of goods sold	(61.4%)	153,500
Gross profit margin	(38.6%)	96,500
− Operating expenses	(29.3%)	73,250
Net profit (before taxes)	(9.3%)	$ 23,250

Thus, based on a realistic sales estimate of $250,000, the entrepreneur should expect a net profit (before taxes) of $23,250. If this amount is acceptable as a return on the investment of time and money, he should proceed with his planning.

At this stage in developing the financial plan, the owner should create a more detailed picture of the firm's expected operating expenses. One common method is to use the operating statistics data found in Dun & Bradstreet's "Cost of Doing Business" reports. These booklets document typical selected operating expenses (expressed as a percentage of net sales) for 190 different lines of businesses.

To ensure that no business expenses have been overlooked in the preparation of the business plan, the entrepreneur should list all of the initial expenses he will incur and have an accountant review the list. Figures 8–2 and 8–3 show two useful forms designed to help assign dollar values to anticipated expenses. Totals derived from this list of expenses should approximate the total expense figures calculated from published statistics. Naturally, an entrepreneur should be more confident of the total from his own list of expenses since this reflects his particular set of circumstances.

Developing a projected income statement is an important part of any financial plan. This process forces the entrepreneur to examine the firm's future profitability and serves as an early screening device in making the decision to open the business. Also, the pro forma income statement is required by potential lenders.

The Pro Forma Balance Sheet. In addition to projecting the small firm's net profit or loss, the entrepreneur must develop a pro forma balance sheet outlining the fledgling firm's assets and liabilities. The owner naturally is concerned about the firm's profitability, but the importance of the business assets is less obvious. In many cases, the small company begins its life in a weak financial position because the owner fails to determine the firm's total asset requirements. To prevent this major oversight, the owner should prepare a projected balance sheet listing every asset the business will need and all the claims against these assets.

Worksheet No. 2

Estimated Monthly Expenses Item	Your estimate of monthly expenses based on sales of $ _____. per year	Your estimate of how much cash you need to start your business (See column 3.)	What to put in column 2 (These figures are typical for one kind of business. You will have to decide how many months to allow for in your business.)
	Column 1	Column 2	Column 3
Salary of owner-manager	$	$	2 times column 1
All other salaries and wages			3 times column 1
Rent			3 times column 1
Advertising			3 times column 1
Delivery expense			3 times column 1
Supplies			3 times column 1
Telephone and telegraph			3 times column 1
Other utilities			3 times column 1
Insurance			Payment required by insurance company
Taxes, including Social Security			4 times column 1
Interest			3 times column 1
Maintenance			3 times column 1
Legal and other professional fees			3 times column 1
Miscellaneous			3 times column 1
Starting Costs You Have to Pay Only Once			Leave column 2 blank
Fixtures and equipment			Fill in worksheet 3 and put the total here
Decorating and remodeling			Talk it over with a contractor
Installation of fixtures and equipment			Talk to suppliers from who you buy these
Starting inventory			Suppliers will probably help you estimate this
Deposits with public utilities			Find out from utilities companies
Legal and other professional fees			Lawyer, accountant, and so on
Licenses and permits			Find out from city offices what you have to have
Advertising and promotion for opening			Estimate what you'll use
Accounts receivable			What you need to buy more stock until credit customers pay
Cash			For unexpected expenses or losses, special purchases, etc.
Other			Make a separate list and enter total
Total Estimated Cash You Need To Start		$	Add up all the numbers in column 2

FIGURE 8–2 Anticipated expenses.

Source: U.S. Small Business Administration, *Checklist for Going into Business*, Small Marketers Aid No. 71, Washington D.C., 1982, pp. 6–7.

Worksheet No. 3
List of Furniture, Fixtures and Equipment

Leave out or add items to suit your business. Use separate sheets to list exactly what you need for each of the items below.	If you plan to pay cash in full, enter the full amount below and in the last column.	If you are going to pay by installments, fill out the columns below. Enter in the last column your downpayment plus at least one installment.			Estimate of the cash you need for furniture, fixtures and equipment
		Price	Downpayment	Amount of each installment	
Counters	$	$	$	$	$
Storage shelves, cabinets					
Display stands, shelves, tables					
Cash register					
Safe					
Window display fixtures					
Special lighting					
Outside sign					
Delivery equipment if needed					
Total Furniture, Fixtures, and Equipment (Enter this figure also in worksheet 2 under "Starting Cost You Have To Pay Only Once.")					$

FIGURE 8–3 Anticipated expenditures for fixtures and equipment.

Source: U.S. Small Business Administration, *Checklist for Going into Business,* Small Marketers Aid No. 71, Washington, D.C., 1982, p. 12.

The Pro Forma Statement of Assets. Cash is one of the most useful assets the business owns; it is highly liquid and can quickly be converted into other tangible assets. But how much cash should a small business have at its inception? Obviously, there is no single dollar figure that fits the needs of every small firm. One practical rule of thumb, however, suggests that the company's cash balance should cover its operating expenses (less depreciation, a non-cash expense) for one inventory turnover period. The cash balance for the small bookstore is calculated as follows:

Operating expenses = $73,250 (from projected income statement)

Less: depreciation (0.9% of annual sales[2]) of $2,250
Equals: cash expenses (annual) = $71,000

$$\text{Cash requirement} = \frac{\text{cash expenses}}{\text{average inventory turnover}}$$
$$= \frac{71,000}{3.5}$$
$$= \$20,286$$

Notice the inverse relationship between the small firm's average inventory turnover ratio and its cash requirements.

Another decision facing the entrepreneur is

[2]*Annual Statement Studies* (New York: Robert Morris Associates, 1986), p. 245.

FIGURE 8–4   Projected balance sheet for a small bookstore.

Assets		Liabilities	
Current Assets:		**Current Liabilities:**	
Cash	$20,286	Accounts Payable	$21,929
Inventory	43,857	Notes Payable	3,750
Miscellaneous	1,800		
TOTAL CURRENT ASSETS	$65,943	TOTAL CURRENT LIABILITIES	$25,679
Fixed Assets:		**Long-Term Liabilities:**	
Fixtures	$ 7,500	Notes Payable	$20,000
Office Equipment	1,100	Owners' Equity	$30,364
Cash Register	1,200		
Signs	300		
TOTAL FIXED ASSETS	$10,100		
		TOTAL LIABILITIES AND	
TOTAL ASSETS	$76,043	OWNER'S EQUITY	$76,043

how much inventory the business should carry. A rough estimate of the inventory requirement can be calculated from the information found on the projected income statement and from published statistics:

Cost of goods sold = $153,500 (from projected income statement)

$$\text{Average inventory turnover} = \frac{\text{cost of goods sold}}{\text{inventory level}}$$
$$= 3.5 \text{ times/year}[3]$$

Substituting

$$3.5 \text{ times/year} = \frac{\$153,500}{\text{inventory level}}$$

Solving algebraically,

$$\text{Inventory level} = \$43,857$$

The owner can use the planning forms shown in figures 8–2 and 8–3 to estimate fixed assets (land, building, equipment, and fixtures). Suppose the estimate of fixed assets is:

Fixtures	$ 7,500
Office equipment	1,100
Cash register	1,200
Signs	300
Total	$10,100

To complete the projected balance sheet, the owner must record all of the small firm's liabilities—the claims against the assets. The bookstore owner was able to finance 50 percent of the inventory and fixtures through suppliers. The only other major claim against the firm's assets is a note payable to the entrepreneur's father-in-law for $20,000.

The final step is to compile all of these items into a projected balance sheet, as shown in figure 8–4.

The entrepreneur must remember that these

[3]Ibid.

Are You a Financial Illiterate?

One of the first tasks most small business owners delegate is managing the company's financial affairs. Unfortunately, too many executives lose contact with the firm's financial position completely. One executive remembers, "I used to think I didn't have to worry about financial problems as long as we were making money. Now I realize its crazy to think I've got any control over our operations if I'm a financial illiterate."

To have a firm grasp of his firm's financial position and an understanding of its future, the small business owner should be able to answer the following thirteen questions:

1. How much does each of my products cost? To understand this issue, the owner must know material costs, direct labor costs, indirect costs, capital expenses and start-up costs.
2. How much does each product contribute to profits? Knowing each product's contribution margin tells the owner which ones are most valuable to the company's "bottom line."
3. What's the monthly "net"? In other words, what are the firm's fixed costs—those basic operating expenses that must be paid even if the company had no sales at all.
4. What's my breakeven point? Separating costs into their fixed and variable components allows the owner to compute his breakeven point.
5. How do I measure the performance of marketing and sales departments? Total sales by department are important, but even more important to long-term success is gross margin on sales.
6. How much inventory do I really have? Balance sheet figures are merely estimates. A cycle count system for high dollar-value items improves inventory control.
7. How long should it take to close the books each month? A well-organized accounting system should provide up-to-date information, especially if it is computerized.
8. What are the key points to watch in summary financial statements? This depends on the particular company, but items affecting future profitability and liquidity are prime candidates. Comparing these items to the budget and to the industry average gives a valuable frame of reference.
9. What are the right categories to use for analyzing costs? Historical records are worthless if they are broken down into meaningless categories.
10. Who should make sure that cash is being managed aggressively? Unless someone has specific responsibility, it is likely that the company's surplus cash is sitting idle rather than being invested.
11. What's a short-term cash flow forecast? This often is a financial manager's most important tool, and it can be computerized easily, allowing him to perform sensitivity analysis.
12. How do I find out what expenses we'll have in the next three or four months? This poses unique problems for fast-growing businesses. A dynamic budgeting process and a purchase order system can help the manager anticipate expenses.
13. How often should sales and cost forecasts be revised? Dynamic forecasts are the key here. Pessimistic, most likely, and optimistic forecasts give the manager a relevant range of sales and costs.

Source: Adapted from Michael Gonnerman, "What's Your Financial I.Q.?" *S.A.M. Advanced Management Journal,* Winter 1984, pp. 4–9, with permission of the publisher.

pro forma financial statements can be constructed in a number of ways, depending on what information is available and how accurate it is. Also, these statements are built on estimates and provide only a rough idea of the company's financial performance. Still, the information gleaned from them is invaluable to the owner in planning for the firm's financial future.

III. SUMMARY

To survive, a small business must make a profit. Reaching one's profit objectives does not happen by chance; it requires planning, hard work, and good fortune. This chapter focuses on two profit-planning techniques: ratio analysis and projected financial statements.

Ratio analysis is a tool designed to help the owner interpret the firm's financial statements to learn how efficiently the organization is being managed. The ten key ratios described in this chapter are divided into four major categories: liquidity ratios, which show the small firm's ability to meet its cur-

rent obligations; leverage ratios, which tell how much the company's financing is provided by owners and how much by creditors; operating ratios, which show how effectively the firm uses its resources; and profitability ratios, which disclose the company's profitability. To benefit from ratio analysis, the small company should compare its ratios to those of other companies in the same line of business. Many agencies and organizations regularly publish such statistics. If there is a discrepancy between the small firm's ratios and those of the typical business, the owner should investigate the reason for the difference. A below average ratio does not necessarily mean that the business is in trouble.

Projected financial statements are a basic component of a sound financial plan. They help the manager plot the company's financial future by setting operating objectives and by analyzing the reasons for variations from targeted results. Also, the small business in search of start-up funds will need these pro forma statements to present to prospective lenders and investors. They also assist in determining the amount of cash, inventory, fixtures, and other assets the business will need to begin operation.

STUDENT INVOLVEMENT PROJECT

Ask the owner of a small business to provide your class with copies of the firm's financial statements (current or past).

1. Using these statements, compute the 10 key ratios described in this chapter.

2. Compare the firm's ratios with those of the typical firm in this line of business.
3. Interpret the ratios and make suggestions for operating improvements.

DISCUSSION QUESTIONS

1. How should a small business manager use the ratios discussed in this chapter?
2. Outline the key points of the 10 ratios discussed in this chapter. What signals do each give the manager?

3. Describe the method for building a projected income statement and a projected balance sheet for a beginning business.
4. Why are pro forma financial statements important to the financial planning process?

Building the Business Plan

9

Success is the old ABC's—Ability, Breaks, and Courage.

Charles Luckman

Nothing is ever as simple as it seems.

Murphy's Law

Upon completion on this chapter, you will be able to:

- Explain the importance of preparing a well-developed loan and investment package.
- Understand the use of break-even analysis in a loan and investment package.
- Calculate the break-even point in dollars and in units.
- Illustrate the preparation of a break-even chart.
- Outline the 5 C's of credit.

To establish a solid financial base when starting a business, most entrepreneurs must look for lenders and investors as external sources of funds. However, it is not always easy to convince people to invest their money in another's business. The entrepreneur first must convince potential lenders and investors that her business idea is promising, the market accessible, the firm's management capable, and the return on investment attractive. To accomplish these objectives, the entrepreneur should develop an attractive business plan. Often, the presence or absence of such a plan is *the* critical factor in a lender's or investor's decision to invest or not to invest in a small business. This chapter will focus on preparing and using this vital business document.

I. BREAK-EVEN ANALYSIS

The small firm's break-even point is the level of operation (sales dollars or production quantity) at which it neither earns a profit nor incurs a loss. At this level of activity, sales revenue equals expenses—that is, the firm "breaks even." By analyzing costs and expenses, the owner can calculate the minimum level of activity required to keep the firm in operation. These techniques can then be refined to project the sales needed to generate the desired profit. Most potential lenders and investors will require the potential owner to prepare a basic break-even analysis to assist them in evaluating the earning potential of the new business. And, in addition to it being a simple, useful screening device for financial institutions, break-even analysis can also serve as a planning device for the small business owner. It occasionally will show a poorly prepared entrepreneur just how unprofitable a proposed business venture is likely to be.

Calculating the Break-Even Point

The small business owner can calculate the firm's break-even point by using a simple mathematical formula. To begin the analysis, the owner must determine fixed costs and variable costs. As described in chapter 8 (see Small Business Report 8–2) fixed expenses are those that do not vary with changes in the volume of sales or production (e.g., rent, depreciation expense, interest payments). Variable expenses, on the other hand, vary directly with changes in the volume of sales or production (e.g., raw material costs, sales commissions).

Some expenses cannot be neatly categorized as fixed or variable because they contain elements of both. These "semi-variable" expenses change, although not proportionately, with changes in the level of sales or production (electricity would be one example). These costs remain constant up to a particular production or sales volume, and then climb as that volume is exceeded. To calculate the break-even point, the owner must separate these expenses into their fixed and variable components. A number of techniques can be used (which are beyond the scope of this text), but a good cost accounting system can provide the desired results.

We will illustrate the steps the owner must take to compute the break-even point using an example of a typical small business, the Magic Shop. The owner of the Magic Shop would complete the following steps.

1. Determine the expenses the business can expect to incur. Using the budgeting process described in chapter 8, develop estimates of sales revenue, cost of goods sold, and expenses for the upcoming accounting period. The Magic Shop expects net sales of $950,000 in the upcoming year, with a cost of goods sold of $646,000 and total expenses of $236,500.

2. Categorize the expenses estimated in step 1 into fixed expenses and variable expenses. Separate semi-variable expenses into their component parts. From the budget, the owner anticipates variable expenses (including the cost of goods sold) of $705,125 and fixed expenses of $177,375.

3. Calculate the ratio of variable expenses to net sales. For the Magic Shop, this percentage is $705,125 \div \$950,000 = 74$ percent. So the Magic Shop uses $0.74 out of every sales dollar to cover variable expenses, leaving $0.26 as a "contribution margin" for covering fixed costs and making a profit.

4. Compute the break-even point by inserting this information into the following formula:

$$\frac{\text{break-even}}{\text{sales (\$)}} = \frac{\text{total fixed costs}}{\text{contribution margin expressed as a percentage of sales}}$$

The same break-even point will result from solving the following equation algebraically:

$$\frac{\text{break-even}}{\text{sales}} = \text{fixed expense} + \frac{\text{variable expenses}}{\text{expressed as a percentage of sales}}$$

$$= \$ \quad 177,375 + 0.74S$$
$$100S = 17,737,500 + 74S$$
$$26S = 17,737,500$$

$$\overline{S = \$682,212}$$

$$\text{break-even sales} = \frac{\$177,375}{0.26}$$

$$\overline{\text{break-even sales} = \$682,212}$$

Thus, the Magic Shop will break even with sales of $682,212. At this point, sales revenue generated will just cover total fixed and variable expense. The Magic Shop will earn no profit and will incur no loss. To verify this:

Sales at break-even point	$682,212
Variable expenses (74% of sales)	−504,837
Contribution margin	177,375
Fixed expenses	−177,375
Net profit (or net loss)	$ 0

Adding in a Profit. But what if the Magic Shop's owner wants to do *better* than just break even? His analysis can be adjusted to consider such a possibility. Suppose the owner expects a reasonable profit (before taxes) of $80,000. What level of sales must the Magic Shop achieve to generate this? He can calculate this by treating the desired profit as if it were a fixed cost. In other words, he modifies the formula to include the desired net income:

$$\text{sales (\$)} = \frac{\text{total fixed expenses} + \text{desired net income}}{\text{contribution margin expressed as a percentage of sales}}$$

$$= \frac{177,375 + 80,000}{0.26}$$

$$\underline{\text{Sales (\$)} = \$989,904}$$

So to achieve a net profit of $80,000 (before taxes), the Magic Shop must generate net sales of $989,904.

Break-Even Point in Units

Some small businesses may prefer to express the break-even point in units produced or sold instead of in dollars. Manufacturers often find this approach particularly useful. The following formula computes the break-even point in units:

$$\frac{\text{break-even}}{\text{volume}} = \frac{\text{total fixed costs}}{\frac{\text{sales price}}{\text{per unit}} - \frac{\text{variable cost}}{\text{per unit}}}$$

For example, suppose that Trilex Manufacturing Company estimates its fixed costs for producing its line of small appliances at $390,000. The variable costs (including materials, direct labor, and factor overhead) amount to $12.10 per unit, and the selling price per unit is $17.50. So Trilex computes its contribution margin this way:

$$\frac{\text{contribution}}{\text{margin}} = \text{price per unit} - \text{variable cost per unit}$$

$$= 17.50 - 12.10$$

$$= \$5.40$$

So, Trilex's break-even volume is:

$$\frac{\text{break-even volume}}{\text{(units)}} = \frac{\text{total fixed costs}}{\text{per unit contribution margin}}$$

$$= \frac{390,000}{\$5.40}$$

$$= 72,222 \text{ units}$$

To convert this number of units to break-even sales dollars, Trilex simply multiplies it by the selling price per unit:

$$\text{break-even sales} = 72,222 \text{ units} \times \$17.50$$

$$= \$1,263,889$$

Trilex could compute the sales required to produce a desired profit by treating the profit as if it were a fixed cost:

$$\text{sales (units)} = \frac{\text{total fixed costs} + \text{desired net income}}{\text{per unit contribution margin}}$$

For example, if Trilex wanted to earn a $60,000 profit, its required sales would be:

$$\frac{390,000 + 60,000}{5.40} = 83,333 \text{ units}$$

Constructing a Break-Even Chart

It is possible to construct a graph that visually portrays the firm's break-even point (that point where revenues equal expenses). The break-even chart is useful for financial planning since every small business owner should know the firm's anticipated break-even point *before* opening for business. The following outlines the procedure for constructing a break-even chart.

1. On the horizontal axis, mark a scale measuring sales volume in dollars (or in units sold or some other measure of volume). The break-even chart for the Magic Shop shown in figure 9–1 uses sales volume in dollars because it applies to all types of businesses, departments, and products.
2. On the vertical axis, mark a scale measuring income and expenses in dollars.
3. Draw a fixed expense line intersecting the vertical axis at the proper dollar level parallel to the hori-

zontal axis. The area between this line and the horizontal axis represents the firm's fixed expenses. On the break-even chart for the Magic Shop shown in figure 9–1, the fixed expense line is drawn horizontally beginning at $177,375 (point A). Since this line is parallel to the horizontal axis, it indicates that fixed expenses remain constant at all levels of activity.

4. Draw a total expense line that slopes upward beginning at the point where the fixed cost line intersects the vertical axis. The precise location of the total expense line is determined by plotting the total cost incurred at a particular sales volume. The total cost for a given sales level is found by the following formula:

$$\text{total expenses} = \text{fixed expenses} + \left(\begin{array}{c} \text{variable expenses} \\ \text{expressed as a} \\ \text{percentage of sales} \end{array} \times \begin{array}{c} \text{sales} \\ \text{level} \end{array} \right)$$

Arbitrarily choosing a sales level of $950,000, the Magic Shop's total costs would be:

$$\begin{aligned} \text{total expenses} &= \$177,375 + (0.74 \times \$950,000) \\ &= \$880,375 \end{aligned}$$

Thus, the Magic Shop's total cost is $880,375 at a net sales level of $950,000 (point B). The variable cost line is drawn by connecting points A and B. The area between the total cost line and the fixed cost line represents the total variable expenses at different sales volumes. The area between the total cost line and the horizontal axis measures the total costs the Magic Shop incurs at various levels of sales. For example, if the Magic Shop's sales are $850,000, its total costs will be $806,375.

5. Beginning at the graph's origin, draw a 45-degree revenue line showing where total sales volume equals total income. For the Magic Shop, point C shows that sales = income = $950,000.

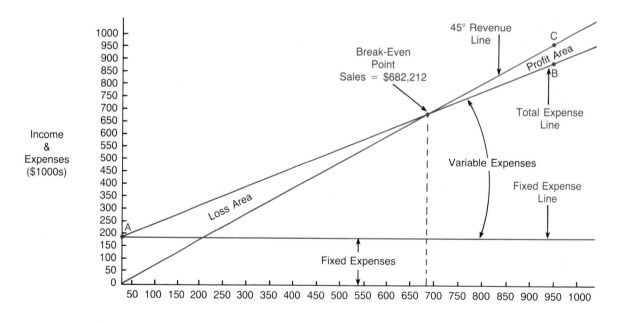

FIGURE 9–1   Break-even chart, The Magic Shop.

6. Locate the break-even point by finding the intersection of the total expense line and the revenue line. If the Magic Shop operates at a sales volume to the left of the break-even point, it will incur a loss, since the expense line is higher than the revenue line over this range. This is shown by the triangular section labeled "Loss Area." On the other hand, if the firm operates at a sales volume to the right of the break-even point, it will earn a profit, since the revenue line lies above the expense line over this range. This is shown by the triangular section labeled "Profit Area."

Employing Break-Even Analysis

Break-even analysis is a useful planning tool for the potential small business owner, especially when approaching potential lenders and investors for funds. It provides an opportunity for integrated analysis of sales volume, expenses, income, and other relevant factors. Break-even analysis is a simple, preliminary screening device for the entrepreneur faced with the business start-up decision. It is easy to understand and use. With just a few calculations, the small business owner can determine the effects of various financial strategies on the business operation.

But break-even analysis does have certain limitations. It is too simple to use as a final screening device because it ignores the importance of cash flows. Also, the accuracy of the analysis depends on the accuracy of the revenue and expense estimates. Finally, the assumptions pertaining to break-even analysis may not be realistic for some businesses. Break-even calculations assume the following: fixed expenses remain constant for all levels of sales volume; variable expenses change in direct proportion to changes in sales volume; and changes in sales volume have no effect on unit sales price. Relaxing these assumptions does not render this tool useless, however. For example, the owner could employ nonlinear break-even analysis using a graphical approach.

II. DETERMINING FINANCIAL NEEDS

Before approaching any potential lender or investor, the small business manager must decide exactly how large a cash infusion he needs and how the funds will be used. Will the entrepreneur use the cash to start a new business, or will he purchase an existing company? Does the small business owner need money to build inventory for approaching seasonal peaks, or does he need to increase the company's working capital? Will the owner use the funds to purchase new equipment and facilities or to finance expansion into new markets? Once the owner determines the purpose of the funds, he can calculate more accurately the exact amount required. The planning techniques and forms described in chapter 8 can assist the owner in pinpointing the amount of cash needed to maintain the firm's financial health.

The importance of planning ahead for financial needs cannot be overemphasized. Too often small business owners approach potential lenders and investors unprepared to plead their cases for additional funds. Simply scribbling rough figures on a note pad to support a loan application is not enough. Applying for loans or attempting to attract investors without financial planning rarely produces desired results. Small Business Report 9–1 illustrates the importance of developing a functional business plan to the success of a fledgling small business.

III. THE BUSINESS PLAN

One of the best ways for the entrepreneur to avoid being rejected by potential lenders and investors is to prepare a sound business plan. The business plan is a written summary of the proposed venture, its operational and financial details, and its managers' skills and abilities. The entrepreneur must develop it with great attention to detail since it is a key factor in her "sales presentation" to potential lenders and investors. In most cases, the quality of the firm's business plan will weigh heavily in the decision to lend

Fashioning Success From a Business Plan

Danny and Annette Noble knew a great deal about designing women's clothes when they launched their company, Danny Noble Ltd. But, they didn't know anything about the financial aspects of running a company. In just a few short years, though, sales have topped $5 million and the industry's biggest names recognize and buy the couple's designs.

Vaulting to the top quickly is not uncommon in the fashion industry, but neither is plummeting to the bottom. Frequently, problems occur because designers concentrate on "doing fabulous clothes" while ignoring production, cash flow, and financing.

The Nobles were determined to avoid this trap. Before launching their firm, they hired a local accountant to help them prepare a business plan to attract capital. With only $900 in equity, the Nobles, armed with their business plan, convinced a private investor to put up $150,000 for a one-third interest in the business.

The loan got the company off the ground. Their spring line of clothing scored a big hit, but as fall neared, the designers discovered first-hand the meaning of a "cash crisis." Lacking cash to pay for their fabric in advance, they could not obtain $30,000 worth of material to meet fall orders. Says one fashion director, "Most young designers are so strapped for cash that they can't purchase the kind of materials they need to get their clothes into the store."

Because their equity was almost nonexistent, the Nobles could not get any trade credit from suppliers. But, with the help of their accountant, a local bank agreed to lend the cash-strapped company $50,000.

As their reputations grew, the Nobles found credit easier to obtain. They negotiated a $75,000 term loan and a $250,000 line of credit with a local bank. Owner's equity now totals $300,000.

The Nobles still follow their accountant's advice to run "lean and mean." Their headquarters is in budget-minded Philadelphia rather than in New York City. Mr. Noble prefers to use materials that are in stock at fabric houses and buys only enough to cover orders, which lowers inventory carrying costs. The company still subcontracts all production to other firms, avoiding huge equipment investments.

By sticking to the ideas laid out in their business plan, the Nobles hope to achieve success in a highly competitive industry.

Source: Adapted from Alix M. Freedman, "An Eye on the Bottom Line Aids Fashion Designers' Rise," *The Wall Street Journal*, January 28, 1985, p. 33, with permission of *The Wall Street Journal,* © Dow Jones and Company, Inc. 1985. All rights reserved.

---

or to invest funds. The quality of the business plan determines the first impression the potential lenders and investors have of the company and its managers. Therefore, the finished product should be highly polished and professional in both form and content.

A plan is a reflection of its creator. It should demonstrate that the entrepreneur has thought seriously about the venture and what will make it suc-

ceed. It forces the entrepreneur to consider both the positive and the negative aspects of the business. Explains one venture capital manager, "The first thing venture capitalists react to is the business plan because it shows that the individuals have done the necessary spade work to show that they are serious. I want to see that management has had the discipline to put the plan down on paper which means that they have a half-way decent chance of building a business. If they don't do this exercise, they probably won't have the discipline to build a business."[1]

The business plan's primary purpose is to swing the potential investor's or lender's decision in favor of the small business owner. As one bank senior vice-president states, "If an'applicant does not have a business plan, he starts off six feet deep in a hole."[2] The typical business plan summarizes the small firm's past and current operations, and projects how the loan or investment would contribute to achieving business objectives.

This section will outline the primary components of a solid business plan, but every small business owner must recognize that such a plan should be tailor-made, emphasizing the company's strengths. Many small business managers employ the professional assistance of attorneys and accountants in preparing their business plans. For those owners who are unfamiliar or uncomfortable with business planning, hiring such professionals to organize and polish the plan may be wise. But, the proliferation of standardized planning formats has resulted in a trend toward "mass-produced" business plans that fail to produce results. The entrepreneur should beware of this "cookie cutter"[3] approach because it neglects to sell the unique strengths of a proposed business venture.

The entrepreneur cannot allow others to prepare the business plan *for* him. Because he will have to make the presentation to potential lenders and investors, the owner must understand the details of the entire business plan. If the entrepreneur lacks a *complete* understanding of the plan, he will receive a negative evaluation. In most cases, the result will be rejection by the financial institution or investor. The

owner of one small manufacturing operation recalls, "I blew it. I went into my bank for a loan with five years of good financial statements, and suddenly I couldn't answer half the questions my banker was asking me . . . I really felt like a jerk."[4]

Careful, thoughtful preparation can make the difference between success and failure when shopping the capital market. As one successful applicant who used professional assistance stated, "I had never borrowed a lot of money before, but I felt comfortable talking with bankers because I had a proposition I believed in and had the necessary information."[5]

Although each company's business plan should emphasize the unique "personality" of the venture, every plan should follow certain guidelines. This section highlights the major elements of an effective business plan.

Parts of the Business Plan

The Cover Letter. To introduce the presentation to each potential financial institution or investor, the entrepreneur should develop an individual cover letter. It should be concise—a maximum of two pages—and should summarize all of the relevant points of the proposed deal. The letter should explain the purpose of the financial request, the dollar amount requested, how the funds will be used, and how any loans will be repaid. A well-developed, coherent cover letter introducing the financial proposal will establish a favorable "first impression" of the owners and the business, and can go a long way toward obtaining financing.

Officers'/Owners' Resumes. The most important factor in the success of a business venture is its management. Financial officers and investors weigh heavily the ability and experience of the firm's managers in financing decisions. Explains one venture capital-

[1]Susan Schoch, "The Rarefied Path of a Successful Business Plan," *Venture*, June 1985, p. 78.

[2]Ronald Tanner, "Hidden Costs of Bank Loans," *Venture*, October 1982, pp. 24–25.

[3]Stanley R. Rich and David E. Gumpert, "Business Plans that Win $$$: Lessons from the MIT Enterprise Forum," *Venture*, June 1985, p. 62.

[4]Michael Gonnerman, What's Your Financial I.Q.?" *S.A.M. Advanced Management Journal*, Winter 1984, p. 4.

[5]"Raising the Cash to Go Into Business," *Changing Times*, January 1981, p. 56.

The Rich-Gumpert Evaluation System

Stanley Rich and David Gumpert, relying on their experience and their skills in critiquing business plans, have developed a system for evaluating fledgling enterprises. The system relies on a matrix to make an evaluation of a venture's product/service status and its management status (see figure below).

Each axis has four "levels." A company with Level 4 management status has a fully staffed, experienced management team, while a Level 1 venture relies on a single would-be entrepreneur. Level 4 on the product/service status axis indicates that the company has a fully developed product or service in an established market with many satisfied users. At the other extreme, a Level 1 venture has only a product or service idea (not even a prototype) and only a "hypothesized" market.

The various combinations of the 16 cells in the matrix indicate how likely a business venture is to acquire funds. A "4/4" business, with a first-class management team and an established product, is most desirable and is most likely to win investment funds at the lowest cost for the money. On the other hand, a "1/1" venture, with a single entrepreneur and an unproved idea, barely has a chance to attract capital unless the founder has a spectacular track record.

This system can help an entrepreneur anticipate his business plan's strengths and weaknesses *before* submitting it to potential lenders and investors. For example, two entrepreneurs had a plan for a venture that would produce recorded cassette tapes of information for senior executives. They had the idea for the tapes' format and content but had never produced a single tape. The entrepreneurs had marketing and financial experience, but they lacked experience in developing their proposed product. Therefore, their rating on the Rich-Gumpert system was a rather poor 1/2. Realizing that their venture was not likely to attract the needed capital, the entrepreneurs set out to make it more attractive. They found an experienced editor to help develop a prototype tape and join the company as an employee once the funding materialized. Then, they produced a prototype tape that could be produced in quantity. These actions boosted the venture's rating to 3/3, and, based on a new business plan, the entrepreneurs quickly attracted interest from potential investors.

---

ist, "When it comes down to it, when you put your hard-earned cash into a venture, you are betting on the people. You can take 'B' people and an 'A' plan and they won't build a business. You can have 'A' people and a 'B' plan and you still have a chance for a super business."[6] The plan should include the resumes of business officers, key directors, and any person with at least 20 percent ownership in the company. *Remember: lenders and investors prefer experienced managers.* A venture capitalist claims,

"Question No. 1 for investors is, 'Have you ever started up a company and made money for anyone else?'"[7] This section should emphasize how team members' skills complement one another.

A resume should summarize the individual's education, work history (emphasizing managerial responsibilities and duties), and relevant business experience. When compiling a personal profile, the owner should review the primary reasons for small business failure (see chapter 1) and show how the

---

[6]Schoch, op. cit. p. 81.

[7]Ibid.

The Rich-Gumpert Evaluation System

	Most Desirable →			
Level 4 Product/service fully developed. Many satisfied users. Markets established.	4/1	4/2	4/3	4/4
Level 3 Product/service fully developed. Few (or no) users as yet. Market assumed.	3/1	3/2	3/3	3/4
Level 2 Product/service pilot operable. Not yet developed for production. Market assumed.	2/1	2/2	2/3	2/4
Level 1 A product or service idea, but not yet operable. Market assumed.	1/1	1/2	1/3	1/4
	Level 1 A single would-be founder-entrepreneur.	**Level 2** Two founders. Additional slots. Personnel not identified.	**Level 3** Partly staffed management team. Absent members identified, to join when firm is funded.	**Level 4** Fully staffed. Experienced management team.

PRODUCT/SERVICE STATUS (vertical axis label)

MOST DESIRABLE (vertical axis label)

— Management Status —

Source: Adapted from Stanley R. Rich and David E. Gumpert, "Business Plans that Win $$$: Lessons from the MIT Enterprise Forum." Copyright © 1985 by Stanley R. Rich and David E. Gumpert. Reprinted by permission of Harper & Row, Publishers, Inc.

---

team will use its skills and experience to avoid them. (Key owners in the business should include a list of credit references, a current personal financial statement, and individual income tax returns for the past two or three years.) *Remember: financial officers investigate the owners' credit ratings as well as the company's.*

Company History. The manager of an existing small business should prepare a brief history of the operation, highlighting the significant financial and operational events in the company's life. This section should focus on the successful accomplishment of past objectives and should indicate the firm's image.

General Business Description. To familiarize lenders and investors with the nature of the business, the owner should incorporate into the business plan a general description of its operation. This section should begin with a statement of the company's general business goals and a narrower definition of its immediate objectives. Goals are long-range, broad statements of what the company plans to accomplish in the distant future. They are aspirations which

189

guide the overall direction of the company and express the company's *raison d'etre*. In other words, they answer the question, "Why am I in business?"

The owner of a small chain of baby products stores has clearly defined his company's mission:

> To serve best the needs of customers who are buying for babies and children under seven in retail stores offering an incomparable combination of selection, quality, and service at competitive prices.[8]

Objectives, on the other hand, are short-term, specific targets which are attainable, measurable, and controllable. Every objective should reflect some general business goal and include a technique for measuring progress toward its accomplishment. Also, to be meaningful, an objective must have a time frame for achievement.

In summarizing the small company's background, the owner should describe the present "state of the art" in the industry and identify the key factors needed for success in the industry. He should describe the current applications of the product/service in the market and include projections for future applications. For example, a manufacturer of silicon chips could discuss the key role his product plays in computer technology and could project increased demand by robot manufacturers. In addition, the owner should incorporate into the plan general long-term growth trends for the entire industry, including stability for product demand and emerging trends affecting demand.

This section also should describe the influence of government regulation and legislation in the business operation.

Business Strategy.   An even more important part of the business plan is the owner's view of the strategy needed to meet the competition. It should comment on how the owner plans to achieve business objectives in the face of competition and government regulation. One investment advisor states, "Many business plans give fancy, impressive financial projections, but don't sufficiently tell you how the company is going to reach these projections."[9] The manager also must describe the firm's desired "character"—the image the business will try to project. For example, a clothing store could project several images—a high quality, classic merchandise shop; a trendy, high fashion store; or an economy-oriented discount outlet. This segment of the business plan should outline the methods the company can use to meet the key requirements for success identified earlier. If, for example, a strong, well-trained sales force is considered a critical element for success, the owner must develop a plan of action for assembling one.

Description of Firm's Product/Service.   The business owner should supply lenders and investors with a general description of the company's overall product line, giving an overview of how the goods/services are used. Drawings, diagrams, and illustrations may be required if the product is highly technical. A statement of the goods' position in the product life cycle might also be helpful. The manager should include a summary of any patents or copyrights protecting the product or service from infringement by competitors. Finally, the owner should provide an honest comparison of the company's product or service with those of competitors, citing specific advantages or improvements which make his goods or services unique and indicating plans for developing "next generation" goods and services evolving from the present product line.

Manufacturers should provide a description of the production process employed, strategic raw materials required, and sources of supply used. In addition, they should summarize the method of production and illustrate the plant layout.

Marketing Strategy.   One of the most crucial concerns of potential lenders and investors is whether there is a real market for the proposed good or serv-

---

[8]"Operations Manual," Carolina Baby Inc.

[9]Schoch, op. cit. p. 82.

ice. Every small business owner seeking funds must incorporate into the business plan a description of the company's target market and its characteristics. For example, the owner of a small chain of baby products stores identified his firm's typical customer as an expectant mother 18 to 34 years old (an average of 26.3 years) in the fifth to eighth month of pregnancy. One venture capitalist claims that the investor "needs to believe that the company has targeted an attractive market and has developed a plan to capture an unfair share of it."[10]

Proving that a profitable market exists involves two steps:[11]

1. *Showing marketplace interest.* The entrepreneur must be able to prove that customers in the marketplace have a need for the good or service and are willing to pay for it. This phase is relatively straightforward for a company with an existing product or service, but can be quite difficult for one with only an idea or a prototype. In this case, the entrepreneur might offer the prototype to several potential customers to get written testimonials and evaluations to show investors. Or, the owner could sell the product to several customers at a significant discount. This would prove that there are potential customers for the product and would allow demonstrations of the product in operation.

2. *Documenting market claims.* Too many business plans rely on vague generalizations like, "This market is so huge that if we get just 1 percent of it, we will break even in eight months." Such statements are not backed by facts and may not be realistic. Says one venture specialist, "I'm really not interested in having a 2-percent market share of an $8-billion business because I know that you can't get that kind of market share with a new venture."[12]

Claims of market size and growth rates should be supported by facts. Results of market surveys, customer questionnaires, and demographic studies lend credibility to an entrepreneur's frequently optimistic sales projections. Quantitative market data are important since they form the basis for all of the company's financial projections in the business plan.

The entrepreneur also should describe the competition the company faces in the market. Failure to provide a realistic assessment of competitors makes the owner appear to be poorly prepared or dishonest. Gathering information on competitors' market shares, products, and strategies usually is not difficult. Trade associations, customers, industry journals, marketing representatives, and sales literature are valuable sources of data. The focus of this section should be to demonstrate how the entrepreneur's company has an advantage over its competitors. According to one financial expert, "The most successful small companies are those that begin with a marketing approach which determines what the market wants and then invents it."[13]

This portion of the plan also should describe the channel of distribution the small business will employ (mail, in-house sales force, sales agents, retailers). Also, the owner should summarize the firm's overall pricing policies as well as its promotion policies, including the advertising budget, media used, and publicity efforts. The company's warranties and guarantees for its products and services should be addressed.

Plan of Operation. To complete the description of the business, the owner must construct a functional organizational chart which identifies key positions and the personnel occupying them. Assembling a management team with "the right stuff" is difficult, but keeping it together until the company gets established may be harder. Thus, the entrepreneur should describe briefly the steps taken to encourage key officers to remain with the company. Employment con-

[10]Ibid. p. 81.
[11]Rich and Gumpert, op. cit. p. 64.
[12]Schoch, op. cit. p. 82.
[13]Ibid. p. 81.

tracts, shares of ownership, and perks are commonly used to keep and motivate key employees.

Finally, a description of the form of ownership (partnership, joint venture, S Corporation) and of any leases, contracts, and other relevant agreements pertaining to the operation is also helpful.

Financial Data.   One of the most important sections in the business plan is a detailed outline of the loan or investment package—the "dollars and cents" of the proposed deal. Financial officers use past financial statements to judge the health of the small company and its ability to repay loans or generate adequate returns. The owner should supply copies of the firm's major financial statements from the past three years. These statements should be audited by a certified public accountant, since financial institutions prefer that extra reliability. However, a financial review of the statements by an accountant may satisfy some requirements.

The manager must carefully prepare monthly projected (or pro forma) financial statements for the operation for the next two years (and possibly for two more years by quarters) using past operating data, published statistics, and judgment to derive *two sets* of forecasts (see chapter 8) of the income statement, balance sheet, cash budget, and schedule of planned capital expenditures. One set of forecasts should be based on expected results *without* the requested loan or investment, and the other on the assumption that the cash infusion will be obtained. It is critical that both sets of projections be realistic. Financial officers will compare these projections against published industry standards and will detect unreasonable forecasts. In fact, some venture capitalists automatically discount an entrepreneur's financial projections by as much as 50 percent. Once the forecasts are completed, the owner can perform break-even and ratio analyses on the projected figures.

The Loan Proposal.   This section of the business plan should tell the financial officer the purpose of

the loan, the amount requested, and the plans for repayment. When describing the purpose of the loan, the owner must remember to be specific in explaining the planned use of the funds. General requests for funds using terms such as for "modernization," "working capital," or "expansion," are unlikely to win the officer's approval. Instead, descriptions such as "to modernize production facilities by purchasing five new, more efficient looms which will boost productivity by 12 percent" or "to rebuild merchandise inventory for fall sales peak, beginning in early summer" should be used. The entrepreneur also must specify the precise amount requested and include relevant backup data, such as vendor estimates of costs or past production levels. The owner should not hesitate to request the amount of money needed, but should not inflate the amount anticipating the financial officer to "talk him down." Financial officers are familiar with industry cost structures.

Another key element of the loan or investment proposal is the repayment schedule. A banker's primary consideration in granting a loan is the reassurance that the applicant will repay, while an investor's major concern is earning a satisfactory rate of return. Financial projections must reflect the firm's ability to repay loans and produce adequate yields. Without this proof, a request for additional funds stands little chance of being accepted. It is critical for the owner to produce tangible evidence showing the ability to repay or to generate attractive returns.

Finally, the owner must include a timetable for implementing the proposed plan. He should present a schedule showing the estimated start-up date for the project and noting any significant milestones along the way.

Preparing a sound business plan to present to prospective investors and lenders clearly requires time and effort, but the benefits gained greatly exceed the costs of developing a plan. Financial officers are favorably impressed by small business owners who are *informed* and *prepared* when making a loan or investment request. Failure to collect, to interpret, and to present relevant financial and operational data with a request for debt or equity funds often leads to rejection. Honesty is also a critical factor in preparing a business plan. It is not wise to try to fool a financial officer by "adjusting" figures to portray the business more favorably. They know their business and frown on fraudulent attempts to obtain financing.

Small Business Report 9–3 describes what venture capitalists like—and don't like—to see in a business plan. Appendix A at the end of the text contains a sample business plan.

What Does a Loan Officer Look For?

Banks are a common source of debt capital for small businesses. Existing small businesses may need periodic cash infusions, for which they rely on lines of credit from their bankers. To improve the chance of obtaining such loans, the entrepreneur should know what a loan officer looks for in a "bankable" small business loan. Most bankers consider a loan acceptable if it conforms to the "five Cs" of credit: capital, capacity, collateral, character, and conditions.

Capital. A small business must have a stable capital base before a bank will grant a loan. Otherwise the bank, in effect, would be making a capital investment in the business. Most banks refuse to make loans that are capital investments because the potential for return on the investment is limited strictly to the interest on the loan, and the potential loss would probably exceed the reward. A recent study of 150 large and regional U.S. banks found that one-third of the respondents cited "undercapitalization or too much debt" as a major reason for rejecting small business loan applications.[14] The bank expects the small business to have an equity base of investment by the owner(s) that will help support the venture during times of financial strain.

Capacity. A synonym for capacity is "cash flow." The

bank must be convinced of the firm's ability to meet its regular financial obligations and to repay the bank loan. In chapter 7 we saw that more small businesses fail from lack of cash than from lack of profit. It is possible for a company to be showing a profit and still have no cash—that is, to be technically bankrupt. Bankers expect the small business loan applicant to pass the test of liquidity, especially for short-term loans. The bank will study closely the small company's cash flow position to decide whether it meets the capacity required.

Collateral. Collateral includes any assets the owner pledges to the bank as security for repayment of the loan. If the company defaults on the loan, the bank has the right to sell the collateral and use the proceeds to satisfy the loan. Typically, banks make very few unsecured loans (those not backed by collateral) to small businesses. Bankers view the owner's willingness to pledge collateral (personal or business assets) as an indication of the small business owner's dedication to making the venture a success.

Character. Before approving a loan to a small business, the banker must be satisfied with the owner's character. The evaluation of "character" frequently is based on intangible factors like honesty, competence, "polish," determination, intelligence, and ability. Although the qualities judged are abstract, this evaluation plays a critical role in the banker's decision. One financier explains, "The most exciting thing to the venture capitalist is talking to management one-on-one. To invest, you have to get caught up in the high-energy level, enthusiasm of people and their ability to impress you that they know their business."[15]

Loan officers know that most small businesses fail because of incompetent management, and they try to avoid extending loans to "high risk" managers. The business plan described earlier in this chapter and a polished presentation by the entrepreneur can go far in convincing the banker of the owner's capa-

---

[14]Doran Howitt, "Step to the Head of the Line," *Inc.*, November 1981, pp. 39–56.

[15]Schoch, op. cit. p. 83.

SMALL
BUSINESS
REPORT
9–3

Overcoming the Hurdles

In a typical year, a large venture capital firm receives from 500 to 1,500 business plans. Most of them are read, but only about 1 percent are ever funded. One entrepreneur explains, "Most venture capitalists are so inundated with business plans that they are looking for something in the plan that will let them say no, and quickly." While there are no set rules for constructing a plan, the key is to avoid the obvious turn-offs for venture capitalists.

Realizing that a business plan is a serious summary of company strategy and not a flashy sales gimmick is the first step. Brevity also is of prime importance since venture capitalists are extremely pressed for time. One venture capitalist recalls one 12-volume plan that arrived in two cardboard boxes. "We knew we weren't going to read them," he says. Ideally, a plan should be no more than 40 pages—roughly 1/4 to 1/2 inches thick—and bound in a clear plastic cover.

Projected financial statements are an integral part of every business plan, but some entrepreneurs go overboard with computer-generated financial scenarios. Claims one venture capitalist, "One thing VisiCalc has done for the world is make business plans 50 percent larger. We want to know if somebody really sat and thought about those numbers, or if they just punched them in."

Venture capitalists describe the ideal business plan as "crisp." It should show the new company's market and its strategy to reach it; the amount of money needed; sales, cash and profit forecasts; and the composition of the management team. To boost his plan's chances, the entrepreneur also should arrange an introductory call from a well-connected attorney, accountant, or business owner who has already been

---

bility. As one successful loan candidate who painstakingly prepared a business plan and perfected a presentation technique says, "Many applicants shuffle in with their hands in their pockets and their eyes on their shoes. They don't quite know how to make a presentation."[16]

Conditions. The conditions surrounding a loan request also affect the owner's chance of receiving funds. Banks will consider factors relating to the business operation such as potential growth in the market, competition, location, form of ownership, and loan purpose. Again, the owner should provide this relevant information in an organized format in the business plan. Another important condition influencing the banker's decision is the shape of the overall economy, including interest rate levels, inflation rate, and demand for money.

The higher a small business scores on these "five Cs," the greater its chance of receiving a loan. The wise entrepreneur will keep this in mind when preparing a business plan and presentation.

IV. SUMMARY

Attracting capital to launch a new business or to boost an existing one is not an easy task. The entrepreneur must prove to potential lenders that the business is a good credit risk and must show potential investors that an investment in the business offers the potential for an attractive return. To improve the chance of attracting debt or equity capital, the entrepreneur must prepare a well-organized business plan. This document gives lenders and investors an opportunity to evaluate the firm's strengths. Developing a sound business plan also provides the entre-

---

[16]"Raising the Cash to Go into Business," pp. 54–58.

funded by the firm. Advises one capitalist, "You have to gain access through an intermediary whom the venture capitalist or financial institution knows and respects." Plans that arrive "cold" simply don't get the attention that those which have been introduced do.

The surest path to rejection is sending a business plan to a venture capitalist who doesn't fund that particular type of business. Relying on research and contacts should uncover the kinds of business venture capitalists focus on. An accountant says, "We know that certain venture capital firms are interested in certain kinds of products. Since firms do change their selection criteria, we usually know on a timely basis their investment preferences."

A business plan should be neatly typed and free of poor grammar and spelling errors, but an excessively polished plan raises eyebrows, too. One venture capitalist says, "It shouldn't read like a sales brochure with a lot of flowery non-essentials. It should get to the point." Most venture capitalists warn against hiring outside professionals to write business plans. Says one, "A professionally prepared business plan is a turn-off if the entrepreneur is not the guiding force behind it." Another adds, "If it's not really (an entrepreneur's) business plan, venture capitalists see through it very quickly.

Although a business plan is a necessary tool to obtain financing from lenders and investors, it is only the first step. One venture capitalist explains, "The value of a business plan is in the process. The important part is the thinking that goes on to come up with it."

Sources: Adapted from Sabin Russell, "What Investors Hate Most About Business Plans," *Venture*, June 1984, pp. 52-53; Susan Schoch, "The Rarefied Path of a Successful Business Plan," *Venture*, June 1985, pp. 78–83, with permission of the publisher.

preneur with the foundation for preparing a coherent presentation to lenders and investors. Without these preparations, the small business owner greatly reduces the chances of obtaining financing.

Every business plan should contain a simple break-even analysis, which shows the level of operations at which total revenues equal total costs. Although just a simple screening device, break-even analysis is a useful planning tool for the entrepreneur, and it allows lenders and investors to evaluate the potential success of a small business.

Too often, entrepreneurs approach potential lenders and investors poorly prepared to prove their need for financing and the worth of their businesses. The result is almost always refusal of the loan request. To avoid being rejected, the well-prepared owner will develop a business plan summarizing the relevant operational detail of the proposed venture. Most financial officers weigh heavily the quality of the owner's business plan and its presentation in making a lending or investing decision. The following should be included in a typical business plan: the cover letter; the owners' and officers' resumes; the company history; the general business summary, defining the organization's primary mission, as well as its goals and its objectives; the business strategy; the description of the product or service; the marketing strategy; the plan of operation; the financial plan; and the loan proposal.

Banks are an important source of small business financing. The small business owner seeking additional funds must be aware of the "five Cs" of credit—capital, capacity, collateral, character, and conditions—and their importance to bankers.

By preparing a thoughtful, coherent business plan and by making a smooth, polished loan request presentation, the entrepreneur can greatly improve the chances of attracting debt and equity funds.

STUDENT INVOLVEMENT PROJECTS

1. Interview a local banker who has experience in giving loans to small businesses. Ask him the following questions.
   a. How important is a well-prepared business plan?
   b. How important is a smooth presentation?
   c. How does the banker evaluate the owner's character?
   d. How heavily does the bank weigh the "five Cs" of credit?
   e. What percentage of small business owners are well prepared to request a bank loan?
   f. What are the major reasons for the bank's rejection of small business loan applications?

2. Interview a small business owner who has requested a bank loan or an equity investment from external sources. Ask her these questions.
   a. Did you prepare a written business plan before approaching the financial officer?
   b. (If she answers "yes" to part A) Did you have outside or professional help in preparing it?
   c. How many times have your requests for additional funds been rejected? What reasons were given for the rejection?
   d. How does the business score on the Rich-Gumpert Evaluation System?

DISCUSSION QUESTIONS

1. Define the break-even point. How can the small business owner use break-even analysis?
2. Outline the steps used in calculating the break-even point in sales dollars and in units. How is a desired profit treated in the analysis?
3. How do fixed expenses, variable expenses, and semi-variable expenses differ? Give examples of each.
4. How are semi-variable expenses treated in a break-even analysis?
5. Outline the steps in calculating a break-even chart.
6. What are the limitations of break-even analysis?
7. Why should an entrepreneur develop a business plan?
8. Briefly describe the 10 major components of a business plan.
9. Distinguish between goals and objectives.
10. What are the "five Cs" of credit? How does the banker use them in evaluating loan requests?

Potential Sources of Funds

Don't ever borrow a little bit of money because when you borrow a little bit of money, you have a serious creditor if you run short. And, if you borrow a lot of money, you have a partner when you get into trouble.

Fred Smith

Nothing ever gets built on schedule or within budget.

Anonymous

Everything takes more time and money.

Annie DeCaprio

Upon completion of this chapter, you will be able to:

■ Understand the problems involved in raising the capital to launch or expand a business.

■ Define the three types of capital required by small business: fixed, working, and growth.

■ Explain the difference between equity financing and debt financing. Describe the various sources of equity capital and the advantages and disadvantages of each.

■ Identify the ownership and control implications of equity capital.

■ Describe the various sources of debt capital and the advantages and disadvantages of each.

■ Illustrate the sources of government financial assistance and the loan programs offered.

■ Identify valuable methods of financing growth and expansion internally.

Raising the money to go into business is often an insurmountable barrier for many would-be entrepreneurs. In some cases, the prospective small business owner has the creativity and skills required to start and manage an enterprise, but lacks the knowledge and the ability to "sell" himself and his idea to potential lenders and investors. Without adequate financing, the small business "never gets off the ground." The entrepreneur is often trapped in a vicious cycle: undercapitalization is a contributing factor to many business failures, but, because of the high mortality rate of new small businesses, financial institutions are unwilling to lend or invest in these new ventures. This inaccessibility to start-up capital leaves the new business on a weak financial foundation, vulnerable to the causes of business failure.

The money an entrepreneur needs to begin a business is called "seed money," "adventure capital," or "injection capital." Where to find this seed money depends, in part, on the nature of the proposed business, on the amount of money required, and on the purpose for which it is to be used. For example, the originator of a computer software firm would have different capital requirements than the initiator of a coal mining operation. Although both entrepreneurs would probably approach some of the same types of lenders and investors, each would likely be more successful among a few particular sources of funds suited to each industry's characteristics and needs. Thus, it is important to understand the nature of the capital requirement to determine the appropriate sources of capital.

In searching for funds to operate or expand an existing small firm, the owner faces most of the same questions as the prospective entrepreneur. However, some of the sources and types of funds are different. This chapter will explore the different types of capital, as well as some of the many sources of business capital for the entrepreneur.

I. CAPITAL

Basically, capital is any form of wealth employed to produce more wealth for the firm. It exists in many forms in a typical business, including cash, inventory, plant, and equipment. For example, a textile manufacturer employs its plant and equipment to create an inventory used to fill customer orders. The revenue generated from the sales is used to purchase more raw materials and possibly to expand the plant or buy more equipment. This cycle continues, increasing the capacity (and, hopefully, the profitability) of the firm until the point of diminishing marginal returns is reached. Thus, the manufacturer's original capital has helped create more wealth for the business and for society in general.

Financial managers commonly identify three basic types of capital required by businesses: fixed capital; working capital; and growth capital.

Fixed Capital

Fixed capital is needed to purchase the business' permanent or fixed assets. These assets are used in the production of goods and services and are not for sale. Buildings, land, computers, and equipment are not converted into cash during normal business operations, so money invested in these fixed assets tends to be "frozen" since it cannot be used for any

other purpose. Typically, huge sums of money are involved in purchasing fixed assets, and credit terms are frequently lengthy. Lenders of fixed capital funds will expect the assets purchased to increase the efficiency and, thus, the profitability of the business, and to create improved cash flows to ensure repayment over the years.

Working Capital

Working capital represents the business' temporary funds; it is the capital used to support the business' normal short-term operation. Accountants define working capital as current assets less current liabilities. The need for working capital is created by the uneven flow of cash into and out of the business due to normal seasonal fluctuations. Just as an individual's income does not exactly match expenditures, a company's revenue does not match its cash outflow. Obviously, credit sales, predictable seasonal sales patterns, or unforeseeable changes in demand will create fluctuations in any small company's cash flow. For example, Molly's Bait & Tackle Shop's busiest season begins in early spring and runs through the summer; however, Molly must begin building a healthy inventory in mid-winter, just when her supply of cash is likely to be lowest. Firms subject to such fluctuations usually need working capital infusions at the start of their production or sales cycles and are able to repay the loans when they convert inventory and receivables into cash.

Working capital normally is used to buy inventory, pay bills, finance credit sales, pay wages and salaries, and take care of any unexpected emergencies. Lenders of working capital expect it to produce higher cash flows to ensure repayment at the end of the production/sales cycle.

Growth Capital

Growth capital, unlike working capital, is not related to the seasonal fluctuations of a small business. Instead, growth capital requirements surface when an existing business is expanding or changing its primary direction. For example, a small manufacturer of silicon microchips for computers saw his business skyrocket in a short time period. With orders for chips rushing in, the growing business needed a sizable cash infusion to increase plant size, expand its sales and production work force, and buy more equipment. During times of such rapid expansion, the growing company's capital requirements are similar to those of the fledgling business. Like lenders of fixed capital, growth capital lenders expect the funds to be employed so that the profitability and the cash flow position of the business are improved, thus ensuring repayment.

The entrepreneur must keep the three types of capital requirements—fixed, working, and growth—separate during financial planning. Although the three are interdependent, each has certain sources, characteristics, and effects on the business and its long-term growth.

II. TYPES AND SOURCES OF EQUITY FINANCING

Once the new owner identifies the type of capital she needs to get the business going, she must begin to shop the financial market for the funds. As the entrepreneur surveys the various sources of funds, she will find numerous alternatives that fall into two categories: equity financing and debt financing. These two major types of funding are discussed at length in this chapter and are listed in detail in table 10–1.

Equity Financing

Equity financing represents the personal investment of the owner (or owners) in the business, and is sometimes called "risk capital" because these investors assume the primary risk of losing their funds if the business fails. However, if the venture succeeds, they also share in the benefits, which can be quite substantial. The founders of Federal Express, Intel, and Compaq Computers gained multi-millionaire status when their equity investments finally paid off.

Small Business Report 10–1 demonstrates how some owners put to work the equity in their small companies.

Common Sources of Equity Capital

The primary advantage of equity capital is that it does not have to be repaid like a loan does. The investor simply is guaranteed a voice in the operation of the business and a percentage of any future earnings. Some common sources are discussed in this section.

Personal Savings. The most common source of equity funds used to start a small business is the entrepreneur's pool of personal savings. If a single owner capitalizes the venture with only her savings and assets (and her borrowing capacity), a proprietorship is created. As chapter 3 illustrated, this form of ownership allows the owner to retain maximum control over the business, but it offers the least ability to accumulate capital. No matter what form of business ownership the entrepreneur selects, she must invest some of her own money. As a general rule, the entrepreneur should expect to provide at least half of the start-up funds in the form of equity capital. If the entrepreneur is not willing to risk her money, other potential investors are not likely to risk their money in the business either. Further, if the owner contributes any less than half of the initial capital requirement, an excessive level of borrowing is required to fund the business properly, and the high repayment schedule puts intense pressure on cash flows.

Friends, Relatives, "Angels." If the entrepreneur lacks sufficient equity capital to begin the business, there are still several options available for raising the start-up funds. The business owner should first turn to wealthy friends and relatives who might be willing to invest in the venture. She must be careful, however, to honestly present the investment opportunity and its inherent risks to avoid alienating family members and friends if the venture fails. Treating all loans and investments in a business-like manner, no matter

TABLE 10–1   Small business financing guide.

Use of Funds	Type of Money	Source	Financing Vehicle
Business Start-Up	Equity	Nonprofessional investor	Partnership formation
			Stock issue
		Venture capitalist	Stock issue
		SBIC-MESBIC	Convertible debentures
			Debt with warrants
	Long-term debt	Bank	Term loan (limited)
			Unsecured term loan
			Equipment loan
			Equipment leasing
			Real estate loan
		SBIC-MESBIC	Term loan (limited)
			Unsecured term loan
			Equipment loan
			Equipment leasing
		Commercial finance company	Equipment loan
			Equipment leasing
			Real estate loan
		Life insurance company	Policy loan
			Real estate loan
		Savings and loan association	Real estate loan
		Leasing company	Equipment leasing
		Consumer finance company	Personal property term loan
		Small Business Administration	Term loan guarantee
		Economic Development Administration	Direct term loan (limited)
		Local development company	Facilities/equipment financing
		Farmers Home Administration	Term loan guarantee
Working Capital	Long-term debt	Bank	Unsecured term loan
			Equipment loan
			Real estate loan
		Commercial finance company	Equipment loan
			Real estate loan
		Life insurance company	Policy loan
			Real estate loan
			Unsecured term loan (limited)
		Savings and loan association	Real estate loan
		Consumer finance company	Personal property loan
		Small Business Administration	Term loan guarantee
		Economic Development Administration	Direct term loan (limited)
		SBIC-MESBIC	
		Farmers Home Administration	Term loan guarantee

TABLE 10–1 (*continued*)

Use of Funds	Type of Money	Source	Financing Vehicle
Seasonal Peak	Short-term debt and Line of credit	Supplier	Trade credit
		Bank	Commercial loan
			Accounts receivable financing
			Inventory financing
			Flooring
			Indirect collection financing
			Unsecured line of credit
		Commercial finance company	Accounts receivable financing
			Inventory financing
			Factoring
		Factor	Factoring
		Life insurance company	Policy loan
		Consumer finance company	Personal property loan
		Small Business Administration	Line of credit guarantee (limited)
Equipment or Facilities Acquisition	Long-term debt	SBIC-MESBIC	Term loan
		Bank	Equipment loan
		Commercial finance company	Equipment leasing
			Real estate loan
		Life insurance company	Policy loan
			Unsecured loan (limited)
			Real estate loan
		Savings and loan association	Real estate loan
		Consumer finance company	Personal property term loan
		Leasing company	Equipment leasing
		Small Business Administration	Term loan guarantee
		Economic Development Administration	Direct term loan (limited)
		Local development company	Facilities/equipment financing
		Farmers Home Administration	Term loan guarantee
Sharp, Sustained Growth	Equity	Nonprofessional investor	Partnership formation
			Stock issue
		Venture capitalist	Stock issue
		SBIC-MESBIC	Convertible debentures
			Debt with warrants
	Long-term debt	SBIC-MESBIC	Term loan
		Bank	Unsecured term loan
			Equipment loan
			Equipment leasing
			Real estate loan
		Commercial finance company	Equipment leasing
			Real estate loan

TABLE 10–1   (*continued*)

Use of Funds	Type of Money	Source	Financing Vehicle
		Life insurance company	Unsecured term loan
			Policy loan
			Real estate loan
		Savings and loan association	Real estate loan
		Consumer finance company	Personal property loan
		Leasing company	Equipment leasing
		Small Business Administration	Term loan guarantee
		Economic Development Administration	Direct term loan (limited)
		Local development company	Facilities/equipment financing
		Farmers Home Administration	Term loan guarantee
	Line of credit	Supplier	Trade credit
		Bank	Unsecured line of credit
			Accounts receivable financing
			Inventory financing
			Flooring
			Indirect collection financing
		Commercial finance company	Accounts receivable financing
			Inventory financing
			Factoring
		Factor	Factoring
		Small Business Administration	Line of credit guarantee (limited)

Source: Reprinted with permission of Bank of America, NT&SA, "Financing Small Business," *Small Business Reporter,* vol. 14, no. 10, pp. 30–31, Copyright 1980.

how close the friendship or family relationship, can avoid many problems down the line.

Another group of promising investors are known as "angels"—outsiders in search of tax shelters who are willing to invest money in potentially profitable ventures. Professionals in high tax brackets (doctors, attorneys, dentists, accountants) are good candidates. In some cases, a creative entrepreneur is able to invest as little as 10 percent of the initial capital requirement. The important point is that an entrepreneur should not surrender all hope of going into business just because he is unable to provide half of the starting funds.

Partners.   Of course, an entrepreneur can choose to take on a partner to expand the capital foundation of the proposed business. As described in chapter 3, there are two basic types of partners: general partners, who are personally responsible for the debts of the business; and limited partners, whose limited liability protects their personal assets from the claims of the firm's creditors. Before entering into a partnership arrangement, however, the owner must consider the impact of giving up some personal control over operation and of sharing the profits with one or more partners.

Public Stock Sale.   The owner could elect to incorporate and "go public" by selling stock. This is an effective method of raising needed capital, but it can

Hitching onto the Equity Star

At one time, ownership in a small business meant nothing to anyone except the founder. These days, however, everyone from customers and suppliers to venture capitalists and bankers wants a piece of the entrepreneurial pie. One furniture distributor, who has sold his products to start-up firms in exchange for shares of ownership, explains the trend of hitching onto what may become the next small business store, "I've watch these people get so wealthy overnight, and I guess I got tired of watching."

Owners of start-ups are discovering that they can put the equity in their businesses to work. They can now "buy" needed goods and services and pay for them with stock and stock options instead of cash. This can be the difference between success and failure for some cash-hungry new businesses. One young computer company couldn't afford to pay for the legal services it needed, so the owner traded 5 percent of the company for an attorney's help. (When the company went public two years later, the attorney's shares were worth $400,000.) Another gets a price reduction on computer casings and print jobs by giving stock to suppliers. One medical equipment manufacturer offers stock options as incentives to sell its new product.

Equity deals can be risky since many start-ups fail, but some pay off. Wayne Gionotti, the furniture distributor, traded furnishings for stock at $1 per share that he later sold at $6.90 per share. "We ended up making about $300,000," he says. But, another deal flopped. Gionotti sold office furniture in exchange for equity to a start-up that later filed for Chapter 11 bankruptcy. "The furniture becomes part of the assets of the corporation, so we really took it in the back pocket," he laments.

Some companies are putting their equity to work as a competitive weapon. Using stock ownership and stock option programs, they are recruiting top performers away from larger competitors and motivating them to higher levels of performance. The owner of Microwave Filter Company knew that he could not compete directly for talent with giants like GE, where an engineer could earn 50 percent more in salary. So, he began to offer stock options to key people and to allow every employee to buy stock at 20 percent below the market price. Some owners believe so strongly in the motivational power of company ownership that they require every employee to buy stock in the business. Others use equity as a reward. One owner says, "How do you reward a young guy for loyalty? I hear them calling their wives at 9 o'clock to say they're missing dinner. They're giving their leisure time . . . . How do you say thanks to people like that?"

While stock ownership is not *the* answer to all the problems a start-up company faces, "equity kickers" can help entrepreneurs unleash the true potential of their businesses.

Sources: Adapted from Lynn Asinoff, "Equity Swaps Gain as Form of Payment," *Wall Street Journal*, July 17, 1984, p. 33; Bruce G. Posner, "In Search of Equity," *Inc.*, April 1985, pp. 51–60.

be an expensive and time-consuming process filled with regulatory nightmares. Before choosing to take a company public, the entrepreneur should consider carefully both the advantages and the disadvantages of making a public offering. The advantages include the following.[1]

Ability to Raise Large Amounts of Capital. The biggest benefit of a public offering is the capital infusion the company receives. After going public, the corporation has the cash to fund R&D projects, expand plant and facilities, repay debt, or boost working capital balances. Additionally, the company avoids the interest cost and the obligation to repay associated with debt financing.

Improved Access for Future Financing. Going public typically boosts a company's net worth and broadens its equity base. Its improved financial strength makes it easier for the firm to attract more capital—both debt and equity.

Improved Corporate Image. All of the media attention a company receives during the registration process makes it more visible. Plus, becoming a public company in some industries improves its "prestige" and enhances its competitive position.

Once a market emerges for a public firm's stock, it can attract and retain quality employees more easily. Employee stock ownership plans (ESOPs) and stock purchase plans are popular recruiting and motivational tools in many small corporations. Says the CEO of a small manufacturing company which offers its employees an incentive stock ownership program, "My goal is to have them watch out for the company's assets the way I do."[2]

Listing on a Stock Exchange. Being listed on an organized stock exchange, even a small regional one, improves the marketability of a company's shares and enhances its image.

The disadvantages of going public include the following.

Dilution of Founder's Ownership. Whenever an entrepreneur sells stock to the public, he automatically dilutes his ownership in the business. Most owners retain a majority interest in the business, but they may still run the risk of unfriendly takeovers years later after selling more stock.

Loss of Privacy. Taking a company public can be a big ego boost for an owner, but he must realize that it is no longer solely "his" company. Information that was once private must now be available for public scrutiny. The initial prospectus and the continuous reports filed with the Securities & Exchange Commission (SEC) disclose a variety of information about the company and its operators—from sales and profits to legal matters and patents.

Reporting to the SEC. Publicly held companies must file periodic reports with the SEC, which often requires a more powerful accounting system, a larger accounting staff, and greater use of attorneys and other professionals. The SEC is not concerned with judging the quality of public offerings (nor with eliminating those companies that appear to be "bad investments"); instead, its goal is to protect investors by requiring companies to provide adequate information about the quality of their stock.

The SEC requires three reports: a quarterly 10-Q report, which includes financial statements along with a discussion of overall operations and significant corporate events; an annual 10-K report, which contains a comprehensive update on most of the information in the original registration statement; and an 8-K report; which outlines significant events in the corporation's affairs, such as ownership or accountant changes, acquisitions, and other events significant to investors.

Filing Expenses. A public stock offering usually is an expensive way to generate funds for start-up or expansion. The largest cost is the underwriter's commission, which is typically 6 to 10 percent of the of-

---

[1]*Deciding to Go Public*, E&W No. 42323, Ernst & Whinney, 1984.
[2]Bruce G. Posner, "In Search of Equity," *Inc.*, April 1985, p. 55.

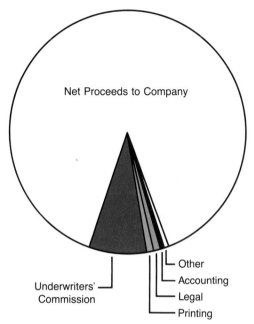

FIGURE 10–1 Typical distribution of gross proceeds from a public offering.

Source: Deciding to Go Public, E&W No. 42323, Ernst & Whinney, 1984, p. 77.

fering's proceeds. Legal and accounting fees, filing fees, and printing costs can add from $175,000 to $350,000 to a stock issue that is in the $5 to $10 million range. Figure 10–1 gives a breakdown of the costs involved in a typical $10 million public offering. Typically, these costs are not deductible as business expenses for income tax purposes. In addition, the increased reporting requirements of the SEC mean higher overhead expenses for the public company.

Accountability to Shareholders. The capital that the entrepreneur manages, and risks, is no longer just his own. The manager of a publicly held firm must be accountable to the shareholders. Indeed, the law requires that he recognize and abide by a relationship built on trust.

Venture Capital Companies

An entrepreneur also can obtain equity funding from venture capital firms, although most venture capitalists prefer not to invest in businesses that are only at the idea stage. Instead, they look for promising ventures that are already developed and have some operating history, even though they may not be profitable. Venture capital firms are private organizations that purchase equity positions in fledgling businesses with promising futures. More than 1,200 companies (up from approximately 600 in 1978) invest in excess of $4 billion each year (up from $39 million in 1977) in growing businesses (see figure 10–2). Despite slowing growth rates in the venture capital industry, these financiers still control the fortunes and the futures of many small companies hoping to follow in the footsteps of Lotus Development Corporation and Compaq Computer Corporation.*

Like all financiers, venture capitalists are interested in reviewing the small firm's financial history, but venture capital companies are more concerned with the future profit potential the business investment offers. As a result, they invest funds in return for a share of the ownership (instead of loaning funds as a bank or other credit would) and try to develop long-term capital gains. Venture capital companies are *not* charitable organizations; they gamble that an investment in a risky business will return three to five times the original capital in five to seven years.[3]

A number of different types of venture capital firms have developed in recent years, including:

■ *Traditional partnerships*, usually created by wealthy families seeking high profitability through aggressive investments.

■ *Professionally managed pools*, composed of

---

[3]U.S. Small Business Administration, *A Venture Capital Primer for Small Business*, Management Aid No. 235, Washington, 1980, p. 2.

*Launched with the help of venture capital, Lotus Development Corporation earned a record $14.3 million profit on sales of $53 million in its first year of operation, while Compaq Computer Corporation set a record for first-year sales of $111 million.

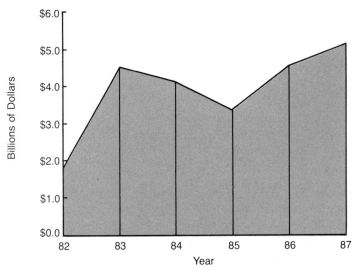

FIGURE 10–2   Venture capital funding.

Source: U.S. News and World Report, May 18, 1987, p. 92.

banks and other financial institutions operating as a partnership in a joint venture.

■ *Investment banking companies,* which usually look for more established, less risky firms in which to invest.

■ *Manufacturing companies,* which invest in small firms that perform much of the required research and development and keep abreast of technological advances.

■ *Small Business Investment Companies (SBICs),* privately and publicly owned businesses licensed by the SBA that provide equity and debt financing to small firms. (SBICs will be discussed more fully under Debt Financing, although some SBICs prefer equity positions in firms.)[4]

■ *State sponsored venture capitalists,* whose investment objectives stress job creation more than return on investment. Twenty states (seven more have legislation pending) have created three different types of venture capital programs:[5]

—Corporations for Innovation Development (CIDs) offer a combination of debt and equity financing to start-ups with prototypes, and typically take less than 10 percent equity in a company.
—State pension funds can invest up to 5 percent of their portfolios in new ventures. Most funds are passive limited partners in private venture funds although some make direct investments.
—Private state venture capital funds are managed by professional venture capitalists.

Policies and Investment Strategies. Venture capital firms usually establish stringent policies to implement their overall investment strategies.

Investment Size and Screening. Depending on the size of the venture capital corporation and its cost structure, minimum investments range from $10,000 to $500,000. Investment ceilings, in effect, do not exist. Most firms seek investments in a range from $250,000 to $1,500,000 to justify the cost of investigating the large number of proposals received. For example, the average venture capital firm screens in

[4]Ibid. pp. 6–7.
[5]Lori Ioannou, "States Move to Stake Entrepreneurs," *Venture,* July 1985, pp. 60–69.

excess of 1,000 proposals a year, but over 90 percent will be rejected because they do not meet the firm's standards. The remaining 10 percent are investigated more thoroughly at a cost ranging from $2,000 to $3,000 per proposal. At this time, approximately 10 to 15 proposals will have passed the screening process, and these are subjected to comprehensive review. Of the three to five proposals finally remaining, the venture capital firm will invest in one or two.[6]

Ownership. Most venture capitalists prefer to purchase ownership in a small business through common stock or convertible preferred stock. The share of ownership a venture capital company purchases may be as low as 1 percent for a profitable company to possibly 100 percent for a financially unstable firm. Although there is no limit on the amount of stock it can buy, a typical venture capital company seeks to purchase 30 to 40 percent of the business.[7] Anything more incurs the risk of draining the entrepreneur's dedication and enthusiasm for managing the firm. Still, the entrepreneur must weigh the positive aspects of receiving the invested funds against the negative features of owning a smaller share of the business.

Control. Although the entrepreneur must sacrifice a portion of the business to the venture capitalist, he usually can maintain a majority interest and control its operations. Most venture capital firms do not assume an active role in managing the business since they lack the expertise and the personnel to run it properly. Instead, they allow the founding team of managers to employ its skills and managers to operate the venture.

However, many venture capitalists will become outside directors to the companies they invest in. The role they assume varies. Some are merely financial and managerial advisors, while others take an active role in the managing of the company—recruiting employees, providing sales leads, choosing attorneys and advertising agencies, and making daily decisions. At a minimum, the venture capitalist tracks the progress of the company and participates in making key strategic decisions and changes affecting the business.

Some entrepreneurs avoid venture capital financing because they fear losing control of their businesses. Rich Martin, founder of a small computer company, learned the hard way. He raised $5 million from a venture capital company, who then replaced him as president, forced a company reorganization, and claimed over half ownership in the firm.[8]

Investment Preferences. The venture capital industry has undergone important changes in the last decade. The pool of available capital is greater than ever before. In 1980, the average venture capital fund was $15 million and the largest firm had assets of $40 million. Today, more than a dozen megafunds—those of $100 million or more—have emerged.

The composition of the industry is changing, too. Large pension funds, corporations, and institutional investors have joined in, and the business is developing into a large-scale, institutionalized industry. As the industry grows, more venture capital firms are finding niches in which to specialize. Many of them invest only in specific industries. For example, Medical Technology Advisors invests only in medical technology businesses. Explains one venture capitalist, "It makes a lot of sense not to be all over the board, since many investors want their money going into funds with a focus. In addition, a venture capitalist just can't keep up with all the different technologies that are appearing."[9]

Many new regional firms, especially those cropping up in the Southeast, Southwest, and Mid-Atlantic states, prefer to invest their funds locally. Some venture capitalists specialize in different types of financing—seed, expansion, turnaround, or lever-

---

[6]*A Venture Capital Primer for Small Business*, pp. 2–3.
[7]Ibid. p. 5.

[8]Lynn Asinof, "Begging for Money: Young Firms Find Venture Capital Harder to Get," *The Wall Street Journal*, April 1, 1985, p. 25.
[9]Mary-Margaret Wantuck, "The Venture Specialists," *Nation's Business*, June 1984, p. 40.

aged buyout. For example, Narragansett First Fund finances only leveraged buyouts in the $20 million to $100 million range.[10] Although most venture capitalists prefer to invest in going concerns, the number of firms involved in start-up financing is growing. The director of the National Venture Capital Association sees "a more concentrated move on the part of venture capitalists toward start-ups. Other phases are much more expensive."[11]

Key Features.   The small business owner must realize that it is *very* difficult for any small business, especially fledgling or struggling firms, to pass the intense screening process of a venture capital company and qualify for an investment. The typical venture capitalist looks for the presence of the following features.

Competent Management.   The most important ingredient in the success of any business is the ability of the manager or the management team, and venture capitalists recognize this. Normally, a company is required to have a complete management team in the major functional areas of production, marketing, and finance to qualify for investment funds. Since management ability ultimately determines the success or failure of a business, this factor weighs heavily with venture capitalists. A common description of a likely candidate is "someone who knows exactly where he or she is going and exactly how to get there."[12]

Getting a proper introduction into the venture capital network is a crucial step in getting funded. The "insider's network" is comprised of venture capitalists, attorneys, accountants, and successful entrepreneurs. "You have to gain access through an intermediary whom the venture capitalist . . . knows and

respects," advises one financial officer.[13] Small Business Report 10–2 describes one way venture capitalists and entrepreneurs are getting together.

Competitive Edge.   Investors are searching for some factor that will enable the small business to set itself apart from the competition. This distinctive competence may range from an innovative product or service to a unique marketing or R&D approach. It must be something with the potential to make the business a leader in its field. Venture capitalists like to see unique business ideas that could at least double their investments in three years.

Growth Industry.   "Hot" industries attract profits—and venture capital. Most venture capital funds focus their searches for prospects in rapidly expanding fields because they believe the profit potential is greater in these areas. One venture capitalist admits, "If the business is not in one of the major trend areas, then I discard the business plan right away."[14] Favorable industries currently include information technology, laser and optical fiber transmission, artificial intelligence and "smart" robots, bionic medicine, hazardous waste management, housing rehabilitation, and consumer-related industries.

Intangible Factors.   Some other important factors considered in the screening process are not easily measured; they are the intuitive, intangible factors the venture capitalist detects by "gut feeling." This feeling might be the result of the small firm's solid sense of direction, its strategic planning process, the "chemistry" of its management team, or any number of other intangible factors. Successful venture capitalists rely on their instincts to judge entrepreneurs' proposals. Explains one, "The most exciting thing to the venture capitalist is talking to management one-on-one."[15]

---

[10]Ibid.

[11]Ibid. p. 41.

[12]Michael Gonnerman, "The Right Way to Raise Venture Capital," *S.A.M. Advanced Management Journal*, Spring 1984, p. 6.

[13]Susan Schoch, "The Rarefied Path of a Successful Business Plan," *Venture*, June 1985, p. 80.

[14]Ibid. p. 81.

[15]Ibid. p. 83.

The V-e-n-t-u-r-e Clubs

Entrepreneurs are flocking to venture capital clubs like children to a candy store. Designed to give entrepreneurs, private investors, venture capitalists, professional service providers (accountants, consultants, attorneys), and managers the opportunity to mingle, these clubs are beginning to proliferate across the nation. The atmosphere is relaxed. Participants don nametags—green for investors, red for entrepreneurs, blue for management applicants, and gold for professional service providers—and talk informally over breakfast or lunch. But, the highlight of each meeting is the "Five-Minute Forum," which actually a misnomer, since anyone can speak to the group for one minute about what he needs or has to offer. Entrepreneurs describe their products and services, investors announce the types of investments they seek, and managers seeking jobs publicize their skills and experience. "You have to sell the sizzle," says one club member.

Venture capitalists take an active interest in the clubs. Explains one, "The club allows us to broaden our contacts. The greatest benefit for us is associating with others who need a co-investor." Private investors, known as "angels," are frequent participants in the venture capital meetings. One club organizer states, "At club meetings, there are a lot of individual investors looking to make real commitments in start-ups, not just traditional venture deals." One study concluded that private investors provide as much money to small businesses as venture capitalists, but in smaller increments.

In addition to obtaining financing, entrepreneurs make valuable contacts. One new club member exclaims, "I have five leads I wouldn't have had if I hadn't come today."

Sources: Adapted from Lori Ioannou, "Venture Capital Clubs," *Venture*, September 1984, pp. 64–68, 89; Sanford L. Jacobs, "This Network Links Investors and Cash-Hungry Businesses," *The Wall Street Journal*, June 3, 1985, p. 25; "Clubs with Capital Ideas," *Changing Times*, January 1986, pp. 77–79.

III. TYPES AND SOURCES OF DEBT CAPITAL

Debt financing involves the funds that the small business owner has borrowed and must repay with interest. Very few entrepreneurs have adequate personal savings to finance the complete start-up costs of a small business, so virtually all of them engage in some form of debt financing.

Lenders of capital are more numerous than investors, although small business loans can be just as difficult (if not more difficult) to obtain. While borrowed capital allows the entrepreneur to maintain complete ownership of the business, it must be car- ried as a liability on the balance sheet as well as be repaid with interest at some point in the future. In addition, because small businesses are considered to be greater risks than bigger corporate customers, they must pay higher interest rates because of the "risk-return tradeoff"—the higher the risk, the greater the return demanded. Most small firms pay the prime rate—the interest rate banks charge their most creditworthy customers—*plus* a few percentage points.

The entrepreneur seeking debt capital is quickly confronted with an astounding range of credit options varying greatly in complexity, availability, and flexibility. Not all of these sources of debt capital are equally favorable to the small business owner. By understanding the various sources of capital—commercial and government lenders—and their characteristics, the entrepreneur will greatly increase the chances of obtaining a loan.

Commercial Banks

Commercial banks are the very heart of the financial market, providing the greatest number and variety of loans. A recent study by the National Federation of Independent Businesses found that 85 percent of loans to operating small businesses come from banks. In addition, bank loans are second only to entrepreneurs' personal savings as a source of capital for launching businesses.[16] However, banks tend to be conservative in their lending practices and prefer to make start-up loans that are supported by ample collateral or are guaranteed by the SBA. Banks are primarily short-term lenders of capital to small businesses, although they will make certain intermediate and long-term loans. They are concerned with a firm's operating past and will scrutinize its records to project its position in the immediate future. They are also concerned about the stability of the firm's sales and about the ability of the product or service to generate adequate cash flows to ensure repayment of the loan.

Short-Term Loans. Short-term loans, extended for less than one year, are the most common type of commercial loan granted to small firms. These funds typically are used to replenish the working capital account to finance the purchase of more inventory, to boost output, to finance credit sales to customers, or to take advantage of cash discounts. As a result, the loan is paid back when inventory and receivables are converted into cash. There are several types of short-term loans.

Commercial Loans (or "Traditional Bank Loans"). The basic short-term loan is the commercial bank's specialty. It is usually repaid as a lump sum within three to six months and is unsecured because secured loans are much more expensive to administer and maintain. In other words, the bank grants a loan to the small business owner without requiring him to pledge any specific collateral to support the loan in case of default. The owner is expected to repay the total amount of the loan at maturity. Sometimes the interest due on the loan is prepaid—deducted from the total amount borrowed. For example, if a business borrowed $5,000 for three months at 17 percent interest, the bank would deduct $209.59 and loan $4,790.41. Three months later the firm would repay the entire $5,000. Clearly, a commercial bank will grant unsecured credit only after the borrower has satisfactorily established creditworthiness. So, until a small business is able to prove its financial strength to the bank's satisfaction, it will probably not qualify for this kind of commercial loan.

If the commercial loan exceeds a particular amount, usually about $100,000, the bank may require the entrepreneur to maintain a compensating balance in a bank account as a form of security for the loan. The size of this reserve varies from bank to bank, but it often is 10 percent of the total line of credit granted plus 10 percent of the credit actually used. Some banks, however, will accept flat fees or higher interest rates in place of compensating balances.[17]

Lines of Credit. A line of credit is simply an agreement with a bank that allows a small business to borrow up to a predetermined amount at any time during the year. Banks usually limit the open line of credit to 40 to 50 percent of the firm's present working capital, although they will lend more for highly seasonal businesses. It is usually extended for one year and is secured by collateral.

---

[16]*Steps to Small Business Financing,* Joint project of the American Bankers Association and the National Federation of Independent Business, 1985, p. 1.

[17]"Financing Small Business," *Small Business Reporter,* 13, 1980, p. 9.

"My goodness, man, you don't need a loan granted, you need three wishes granted."

Source: From *The Wall Street Journal,* January 27, 1983, p. 27. Used with permission of *The Wall Street Journal* © Dow Jones & Company, Inc., 1983. All rights reserved.

In an effort to conserve time, energy, and money, the bank will approve a line of credit for a financially sound business. The business is then able to borrow, repay, and borrow again any part or all of the money up to the approved ceiling. Normally, a firm is required to pay a small "handling fee" (1 to 2 percent of the maximum amount of credit) plus interest on the amount borrowed. For example, Barney's Men's Shop negotiates a line of credit with the local bank for $50,000. As seasonal fluctuations deplete Barney's cash flow, he will borrow $15,000 against his line of credit to replenish his inventory. A few weeks later, as he sells the inventory, he will repay $10,000 plus interest. Then, to finance credit sales to customers, Barney may borrow another $5,000. Note that the outstanding balance of Barney's loan cannot exceed $50,000 at any time. So Barney

has the flexibility he needs to maintain adequate cash flows, and the bank is spared the necessity of evaluating and processing each of Barney's loan requests individually. This revolving loan arrangement is more efficient for both Barney and the local bank.

Once a year, the bank requires the business owner to pay up all unsecured borrowings for a short time (10 to 60 days). This annual "clean-up" is scheduled when the firm's cash balance is at its highest level, usually at the end of the busy season when inventories and receivables have been converted into cash. This standard repayment protects the bank against default by forcing the firm to prove its creditworthiness before continuing the line of credit for another year.

A credit arrangement similar to the line of credit is the revolving credit agreement. It operates the same way a line of credit does with one primary difference: a revolving credit agreement is legally binding and a line of credit is not. In other words, a revolving credit agreement legally commits the bank to lend the small business money as it is needed, up to the maximum amount.

Asset-Based Financing. Asset-based financing allows a small business to borrow money by pledging its assets as collateral. Even companies whose financial statements could not convince lending officers to make other types of loans can get asset-based loans. One banker offers a profile of the typical asset-based borrower:[18]

> Usually, he has a company which cannot borrow from a conventional bank source on an unsecured basis. He's growing too fast for his capital. The nature of his business is such that his receivables don't turn as quickly, so that he does need some sort of secured lending to support taking discounts from suppliers, getting into new products.

Asset-based borrowing enables a small company to put to work some of its most neglected resources—accounts receivable and inventory. The Ideal Toy

---

[18]Susan Schoch, "Access to Capital," *Venture,* June 1984, p. 106.

Company used asset-based borrowing to escape the jaws of bankruptcy. The firm owned the rights to Rubik's Cube, but it could not afford to market the toy. Pledging accounts receivable and inventory as collateral, Ideal borrowed enough working capital to bring Rubik's Cube to the market. The hot-selling toy turned the company's fortunes around.

Discounting Accounts Receivable.   The most common form of secured credit is accounts receivable financing. Under this arrangement, the small business pledges its accounts receivable as collateral; in return, the commercial bank advances the owner a loan against the value of approved accounts receivable. The amount of the loan tendered is not equal to the face value of the accounts receivable, however. Even though the bank screens the firm's accounts and accepts only "qualified" receivables, it makes an allowance for the risk involved since some will be written off as uncollectible. A small business usually can borrow an amount equal to 55 to 80 percent of its receivables, depending on their quality. Generally, banks hesitate to finance receivables that are past due, and no bank will accept accounts that are as much as 90 days past due. Some commercial finance companies also engage in accounts receivable financing.

As the firm receives payment from customers on its accounts receivable, it transfers them to the bank. The bank subtracts an agreed-upon percentage of the proceeds, applies it to the loan balance, and then deposits the remainder in the firm's account. If an unusual number of accounts are uncollectible, the firm must make up the deficit to satisfy the loan.

The interest rate the bank charges on accounts receivable financing is normally higher than that charged on unsecured loans. But when accounts receivable are pledged as collateral, no compensating balances (which raise the actual cost of borrowing) are required. The result is that while the cost differential between the two methods appears on the surface to be substantial, closer inspection shows it to be quite small. So, by pledging a security interest in its receivables to the bank, the firm is able to convert unpaid customer accounts into immediate cash, thus improving its liquidity and cash flow.

Inventory Financing.   Here the small business loan is secured by the firm's inventory—raw materials, work in process, and finished goods. If the owner defaults on the loan, the bank can claim the firm's inventory, sell it, and use the proceeds to satisfy the loan (assuming the bank's claim is superior to the claims of other creditors). Since inventory is not a highly liquid asset in most cases, banks are willing to lend only a portion of its worth—usually no more than 50 percent of the inventory's value.

The normal business cycle enables the small firm to combine effectively inventory financing and accounts receivable financing. For example, Barney's Men's Shop may get an inventory loan by pledging as collateral the inventory to be purchased. Then, as the inventory is sold, accounts receivable may be discounted to pay off the inventory loan. Finally, as accounts are collected, the cash generated may be used to repay the accounts receivable loan.

Asset-based financing is a powerful tool. A small business that could obtain a $1 million line of credit with a bank would be able to borrow as much as $3 million by using accounts receivable as collateral.[19] Asset-based loans also are an efficient method of borrowing money since the small business borrows only the money it needs.

But, asset-based loans are expensive because of the cost of originating and maintaining them and the higher risk involved. Rates usually run from two to seven percentage points above the prime rate. Because of this rate differential, small business owners should not use asset-based loans over the long term. The asset based borrower's "goal should be to actively seek moving to an open line of credit," explains one financial advisor.[20]

---

[19]Teri Agins, "Asset-Based Lending to Firms Has Found Favor with Banks," *The Wall Street Journal,* November 5, 1984, p. 35.
[20]Ibid.

Some small business owners convince their bankers to make loans on the basis of their companies' intangible assets. To make loans on the basis of intangibles, bankers consider the value of assets like patents, tradenames, key contracts, and customer lists that help a company succeed but do not appear on the balance sheet. One banker explains, "You look first at your hard assets. Then if there are any soft assets, you appraise them, too." The banker granted such a loan to a mud hauler on the basis of his highly valuable state license. The mud hauler's only assets were his trucks; but, when he proved that a license to haul fire-retardant mud is as valuable as a New York cab driver's permit, the bank granted the loan.[21]

Floor Planning. Floor planning is a form of financing frequently employed by retailers of "big ticket" items that are easily distinguishable from one another (usually by serial number), such as automobiles and major appliances. For example, the commercial bank finances Auto City's purchase of its automobiles, and maintains a security interest in each car in the order by holding its title as collateral. Auto City pays interest on the loan monthly, and repays the principal as the cars are sold. Banks often discourage retailers from using their money without authorization by performing spot checks to verify prompt repayment of the principal as items are sold.

Intermediate and Long-Term Loans Intermediate and long-term loans are extended for one year or longer and are normally used to increase fixed and growth capital balances. Commercial banks grant these loans for starting a business, constructing a plant, purchasing real estate and equipment, and other long-term investments. Loan repayments are normally made monthly or quarterly. Basically, three categories of intermediate and long-term loans exist: term loans; installment loans; and discounted installment contracts.

Unsecured Term Loans. Unsecured term loans are granted primarily to those businesses with past operating experience indicating a high probability of repayment. If an entrepreneur is successful in obtaining a term loan to begin a business, the bank will likely require him to provide roughly half of the start-up cost. Term loans normally involve very specific terms which may place restrictions and limitations on the firm's financial decisions. For example, a term loan agreement may set limits on owners' salaries or stipulate what percentage of profits will be used to repay the loan. So the owner must investigate and understand thoroughly the conditions of the loan agreement before accepting it.[22] Some banks will make only secured term loans.

Installment Loans. These loans are made to small firms for purchasing equipment, facilities, real estate, and other fixed assets. In financing equipment, a bank usually lends the small business from 60 to 80 percent of the equipment's value in return for a security interest in the equipment. The loan's amortization schedule typically coincides with the length of the equipment's usable life. In financing real estate (commercial mortgages), banks will lend up to 75 to 80 percent of the property's value and will allow a lengthier repayment schedule of 10 to 30 years.

Discounted Installment Contracts. Banks will also extend loans to small businesses when the owner pledges installment contracts as collateral. The process operates in the same manner as discounting accounts receivable. For example, Acme Equipment Company sells several pieces of heavy equipment to General Contractors Inc., on an installment basis. To obtain a loan, Acme pledges the installment contract as collateral and receives a percentage of the contract's value from the bank. As Acme receives installment payments from General Contractors, it transfers the proceeds to the bank to satisfy the loan. If the installment contract is negotiated with a reliable

---

[21]Tim Smart, "Banking on Goodwill," *Inc.,* May 1985, p. 164.

[22]"Financing Small Business", p. 9.

The H-Factor

Most bankers would jump at a technique that would allow them to determine a small company's financial health while being so simple that it would require no more than a set of financial statements, a calculator, and 5 minutes. Three professors have developed a multiple regression model to do just that. Based on the financial statements of 60 small companies, the model relies on nine ratios to perform the "one-minute" test. We will use the financial data from Sam's Appliance Shop (figures 6–13 and 6–14) to illustrate the test.

$$V_1 = \frac{\text{retained earnings}}{\text{total assets}} = \frac{\$40,000}{\$847,655} = 0.0472$$

Of the shop's $60,629 net profit, Sam used $40,000 as retained earnings. This ratio measures the company's profitability over time.

$$V_2 = \frac{\text{sales}}{\text{total assets}} = \frac{\$1,870,841}{\$847,655} = 2.2071$$

This ratio measures the speed at which the firm generates sales from its asset base.

$$V_3 = \frac{\text{earnings before taxes}}{\text{owners' equity}} = \frac{\$60,629}{\$267,655} = 0.2265$$

This measures the firm's profitability before the impact of taxes.

$$V_4 = \frac{\text{cash flow}}{\text{total liabilities}} = \frac{\$88,329}{\$580,000} = 0.1523$$
$$\text{(long- and short-term)}$$

where:

$$\text{cash flow} = \text{net earnings} + \text{depreciation}$$
$$= 60,629 + 27,700$$
$$= 88,329$$

$$V_5 = \frac{\text{total liabilities}}{\text{total assets}} = \frac{\$580,000}{\$847,655} = 0.6842$$

business, the bank may loan the small firm 100 percent of the contract's value.

Clearly, commercial banks offer a multitude of loans and financing arrangements. Before approaching a loan officer, the small firm must determine which of the credit arrangements best suit its particular financial needs.

Trade Credit

Because of its ready availability, trade credit is an extremely important source of financing to most small businesses. When banks refuse to lend money to a newly formed business because it is judged a bad credit risk, the owner is able to turn to trade credit as a viable credit source. So it is no surprise

This ratio measures the degree of the firm's leverage.

$$V_6 = \frac{\text{current liabilities}}{\text{total assets}} = \frac{\$367,850}{\$947,655} = 0.4340$$

This is another measure of leverage.

$$V_7 = \text{logarithm of tangible total assets}$$
$$= \log\,(\$847,655 - \$3,500)$$
$$= \log\,(\$844,155)$$
$$= 13.6461$$

This computation reflects the company's size.

$$V_8 = \frac{\text{working capital}}{\text{total liabilities}} = \frac{\$319,135}{\$580,000} = 0.5502$$

where: working capital = current assets − current liabilities
$$= \$686,985 - \$367,850 = \$319,135$$

$$V_9 = \text{logarithm}\left(\frac{\text{earnings before interest expense and taxes}}{\text{interest expense}}\right)$$
$$= \text{logarithm}\left(\frac{\$80,479}{\$19,850}\right)$$
$$= \text{logarithm}\,(4.0549)$$
$$= 1.3998$$

To compute the company's H-score, the banker simply plugs the nine variables into the following equation: $-6.075 + 5.528(V_1) + 0.212(V_2) + 0.073(V_3) + 1.270(V_4) - 0.120(V_5) + 2.335(V_6) + 0.575(V_7) + 1.083(V_8) + 0.894(V_9) = H$. Sam's Appliance Shop earns an H-score of 5.4889.

A positive H-score indicates a financially healthy firm, but a negative H-value is a sign that the company is headed for financial problems and is not a good credit risk.

Source: Adapted from Bruce G. Posner, "The One-Minute Lender," *Inc.,* December 1984, pp. 150–51, with permission of the publisher.

that businesses receive $3.00 of credit from suppliers for every $2.00 they receive from banks as loans.[23] Vendors and suppliers usually are willing to finance a small business owner's purchase of goods from 30 to 90 or more days, interest free.

For example, Buford's Hardware Store pur-chases a supply of garden tools from a nearby whole-saler on credit with payment due in 30 days. Buford's sells the inventory of garden tools, collects payment, and pays the wholesaler when the bill comes due. Some vendors offer their customers cash discounts, which Buford's may want to take advantage of. This process occurs on a continuous basis with many of the firm's vendors and suppliers, enabling Buford's

[23]Ibid.

to employ this cash productively for an additional 30 days or so without requesting a bank loan. To maintain its good credit rating with its suppliers, Buford's must keep them appraised of anything that might interfere with the firm's ability to pay its bills on time. Otherwise, Buford's may find that a very critical credit source has evaporated.

Equipment Suppliers

In an effort to encourage business owners to purchase their equipment, most equipment vendors offer to finance the purchase. This method of financing is similar to trade credit, but with slightly different terms. Usually, equipment vendors offer reasonable credit terms with only a modest down payment with the balance financed over the life of the equipment (usually several years). In some cases, the vendor will repurchase equipment for salvage value at the end of its useful life, and offer the business owner another credit agreement on new equipment.

This method of financing is frequently employed by beginning businesses to purchase equipment and fixtures—counters, display cases, refrigeration units, machinery, and the like. But the small business manager must be cautious not to overuse this type of credit, since debts must be repaid out of future profits.

Commercial Finance Companies

When denied a bank loan, a small business owner often is able to look to a commercial finance company for the same type of loan. Unlike their conservative counterparts, commercial finance companies are usually willing to tolerate more risk in their loan portfolios. Of course, their primary consideration also is collection of their loans, but they tend to rely more on obtaining a security interest in some type of collateral, although some commercial finance companies are beginning to extend unsecured loans based on a firm's projected profitability. Since com-

mercial finance companies depend on collateral to recover most of their losses, they do not require the complete financial projections of future operations as most banks do. However, this does *not* mean that they do not carefully evaluate a company's financial position.

Their most common methods of providing credit to small businesses are accounts receivable financing and inventory loans, and they operate exactly as commercial banks do. In addition to such short-term financing, commercial finance companies also extend intermediate and long-term loans. Some finance companies are willing to finance the purchase of real estate through commercial and industrial mortgages for up to 10 years.

Commercial finance companies usually offer many of the same credit options as commercial banks do. However, since their loans are subject to more risks, the finance companies charge a higher interest rate than commercial banks. In many cases, the entrepreneur whose loan requests were denied by the banks is able to obtain financing through a commercial finance company. With proper planning and stringent management, the owner can afford the higher finance charge without putting undue pressure on the financial health of the business.

Savings and Loan Associations

Savings and loan associations specialize in loans for real property. In addition to their traditional role of providing mortgages for personal residences, savings and loan associations offer financing on commercial and industrial property. In the typical commercial or industrial loan, the S&L will lend up to 75 percent of the property's value with a repayment schedule of up to 30 years.

Minimum loan amounts are typically $50,000, but most S&Ls hesitate to lend money for specially designed buildings for a particular customer's needs. S&Ls expect the mortgage to be repaid from the firm's future profits.

Stock Brokerage Houses

Stock brokers are getting into the lending business, too, and many of them offer loans to their customers at lower interest rates than banks. Broker loans carry lower rates because the collateral—stocks and bonds in the customer's portfolio—is of high quality and is highly liquid. Aspiring entrepreneurs can borrow up to 70 to 80 percent of the value of their portfolios. For example, a woman borrowed $60,000 to buy equipment for her New York health club. A St. Louis doctor borrowed $1 million against his brokerage account to help finance a medical clinic.[24] Brokers typically lend a maximum of 50 percent of the value of stocks and bonds in a portfolio, 70 percent for corporate bonds, and 85 to 90 percent for government securities.[25]

There is risk involved in using stocks and bonds as collateral on a loan. Brokers typically require a 30 percent cushion on the loan. If the value of the portfolio drops, the broker can make a margin call—that is, the broker can call the loan in and require the borrower to provide more cash and securities as collateral. If the account lacks adequate collateral, the broker can sell off the customer's portfolio to pay off the loan.

The interest rate the borrower pays depends on the "broker's call," the rate the broker pays to borrow the money. While there is no limit on the loan term, the interest rate changes from month to month. The longer the loan is outstanding, the greater is the chance that the rate will fluctuate. To avoid high risk levels from fluctuating rates, an entrepreneur should plan to repay the loan within a year.

Insurance Companies

For many small businesses, life insurance companies can be an important source of business capital. Insur-

ance companies offer two basic types of loans: policy loans and mortgage loans.

Policy loans are extended to the small business owner on the basis of the amount of money paid through premiums into the insurance policy. It usually takes about two years for an insurance policy to accumulate enough cash surrender value to justify a loan against it.

Once cash value is accumulated in the policy, the owner may borrow up to 95 percent of the value for any length of time. Interest is levied annually, but payment may be deferred indefinitely. However, the amount of insurance coverage is reduced by the amount of the loan.

Policy loans are secured by the best type of collateral—the cash the small business owner has already paid into the policy through premiums. Since the insurance company faces virtually no risk of default, these loans typically offer very favorable interest rates—often below 10 percent.

Mortgage loans are made on a long-term basis on real property worth a minimum of $500,000. They are based primarily on the value of the real property being purchased. The insurance company will extend a loan of up to 75 or 80 percent of the real estate's value, and will allow a lengthy repayment schedule over 25 or 30 years so that payments do not strain the firm's cash flows excessively. However, some companies require a "balloon payment," a large sum of money to satisfy the debt after 10 or 15 years, and this could overwhelm the small firm's financial resources. Because they involve more risk, mortgage loans carry a higher interest rate. Insurance companies are able to offer such long-term loans to businesses because they have very predictable cash flows. Typical examples of projects financed by mortgage loans from insurance companies are shopping malls, apartment complexes, office buildings, amusement parks, and land developments.

Insurance companies also make intermediate-term loans in addition to the long-term loans in which they specialize.

[24]Scott McMurray, "Personal Loans from Brokers Offer Low Rates," *The Wall Street Journal*, January 7, 1986, p. 31.

[25]"Want a Loan? See Your Broker," *Changing Times*, November 1985, p. 87.

Zero Coupon Bonds

Zero coupon bonds (nicknamed "junk bonds") are a popular debt instrument because they are attractive to both the investor and the issuing company. The investor earns a high yield for the duration of the bond. The issuing company gets the capital it needs, but does not have to make periodic interest payments as it would if it issued regular bonds. Instead, it sells the bond at a discount from its par value and then repays the investor the full par value at maturity. The difference between the bond's discounted price and the par value represents the missing interest. For instance, a small company might sell for $250 a series of bonds with a par value of $1,000 and a maturity of 10 years. The company would borrow the $250 now, make no interest payments over the 10-year span, and repay the full $1,000 at maturity.

To increase its zero coupon bonds' attractiveness, many companies include "equity kickers" as part of the issue. The bond might include warrants offering shares of stock at a discount or interest-bearing, non-voting stock or some other type of "sweetener."

Although primarily used by publicly held companies, zero coupon bonds can help small, private firms raise much-needed capital. One small airline company relies extensively on zero-coupons; approximately $19 million of its total funding of $54 million came from "junk bonds." The company first issued a five-year debenture with a par value of $4 million at a discount that netted $2.5 million. The bond also included a "kicker"—it could be converted into common stock. A company official explains, " . . . we sweetened it more. In this particular transaction, we gave them [the investors] some options at a very low price."[26]

Zero coupon bonds have certain disadvantages, however. Because they are unsecured—not backed by any specific collateral—they have above average risk for investors, especially if the company is a start-up. The issuing company must follow the same regulations that govern businesses selling stock to public investors. Even if the bond issue is private, the company must register the offering and file periodic reports with the SEC. Even though the law does not require a company to register with the SEC a private bond offering to fewer than 300 investors, most underwriters insist that the company release financial data and file 10-Ks. Explains one investment banker, "If there's no public information on a particular company, it's difficult to make a market."[27] However, the information required for a bond offering typically is not as detailed as that in a stock offering.

Issuing zero coupon bonds may not be practical for companies with small capital requirements. One investment banker suggests that the minimum issue is $12 million; anything less and investors lack confidence that the secondary market for the bonds will be large enough to justify buying them. To be able to service the debt on a $12 million issue, a company should have about $2 million in net after-tax earnings.[28] Small Business Report 10–4 describes how one small business used "junk bonds" to obtain needed capital.

IV. Small Business Investment Companies (SBICs)

SBICs, created in 1958 when Congress passed the Small Business Investment Act, are privately owned financial institutions that are licensed and regulated by the SBA. Their function is to provide long-term credit and capital to small businesses. Currently, approximately 360 SBICs provide financing for new and growing businesses.

In 1969, the SBA created Minority Enterprise Small Business Investment Companies [MESBICs or 301(d) licensees] to provide credit and capital to

---

[26]Robert A. Mamis, "A Deal for All Seasons," *Inc.*, January 1986, p. 107.

[27]Bruce G. Posner, "A Bond by Any Other Name," *Inc.*, November 1983, p. 78.
[28]Ibid. p. 74.

Growth Capital from the "Junk Pile"

Kevork Hovnanian's real estate development company had been borrowing $30 million each year from commercial banks. Loan terms were stringent since that was three times its equity investment. Hovnanian had to pledge specific property as collateral, sign personal guarantees, and repay the loans within two years. That was stifling the company's growth. Hovnanian explains, "We needed long-term money, but we had almost no security to offer a lender. Everything we owned was committed to the banks as collateral for current projects."

The company was straining to grow, but Hovnanian did not want to make a public stock offering to raise the capital. "I wasn't prepared to give away part of the company," he says. Instead, he took an unusual financing route; Hovnanian raised $25 million in growth capital by selling "junk bonds" in the public market. With a public debt issue, he could retain control over his business although he would have to report financial data to the public.

Hovnanian went on a six-city tour with his investment bankers to meet some of the leading institutional buyers of "junk bonds." "We showed off our numbers. And we talked about how we keep our inventory lower than most everybody in our industry," he remembers. Investors bought it—along with the company's bonds. Within days, the company had raised $25 million at an interest rate 4 percentage points *below* the rate on its short-term bank loans. Hovnanian even used some of the proceeds to pay off the bank loans. "It placed us in a much stronger financial position. It was a major milestone in the growth of the company," he claims.

Source: Adapted from Bruce G. Posner, "A Bond By Any Other Name," *Inc.,* November 1983, pp. 73–78, with permission of the publisher.

---

small businesses which are at least 51 percent owned by minorities and socially or economically disadvantaged people. MESBICs also are licensed and regulated by the SBA.

Over the past 30 years, SBICs have provided over $6.0 billion in financing to some 70,000 small businesses, adding many thousands of jobs to the American economy. In return for providing financial aid to small businesses, SBICs and MESBICs are eligible to receive long-term loans from the SBA. Both SBICs and MESBICs must be capitalized privately with a minimum of $500,000, at which point they qualify for three to four dollars in low-rate SBA loans for every dollar of private capital invested in small businesses. As a general rule, both SBICs and MESBICs may provide financial assistance only to small businesses with a net worth of under $6 million and average after-tax earnings of $2 million during its past two years. However, employment and total an-

nual sales standards vary from industry to industry. SBICs are limited to a maximum investment or loan amount of 20 percent of their *private* capital to a single client, while MESBICs may lend or invest up to 30 percent of their *private* capital in a single small business.

There are four primary classifications of SBICs and MESBICs:

1. *Private companies.* Some SBICs are small, privately owned corporations with only a few stockholders, and they are quite flexible in their mode of operation.
2. *Bank-related.* In large banks, the SBIC is an independent division and is able to coordinate its activities with the bank's loan department. In some cases, however, the SBIC may be controlled by the more conservative lending branch.
3. *Venture capital-related.* Some SBICs are associ-

219

ated with venture capital companies, allowing them to combine effective debt and equity packages.

4. *Specialty SBICs.* Some SBICs focus their financial assistance on particular industries such as construction, real estate, or mining.[29]

With the exception of 30 partnerships, all SBICs are corporations. About half are owned by banks and corporations and half are owned by individuals.

Although SBICs and MESBICs are regulated by the SBA, they are privately owned and make their own investment decisions. Because of their financial link with the government, SBICs and MESBICs can invest in small businesses that grow at a slower pace, unlike venture capitalists that prefer more "glamorous" industries. "SBICs are uniquely able to finance companies that are not explosive," says Walter Stults, head of the National Association of Small Business Investment Companies. The law requires SBIC investment terms to be at least five years, so their investments are for "patient money, not for traders," says Stults.[30] He claims, "It takes five to seven years for the companies in a typical SBIC portfolio to become profitable or for stock to be readily marketable." But, patience can pay off. For example, when an SBIC invested in Lifeline Systems, a manufacturer of home emergency response systems, the company had five employees and $100,000 in sales. Currently, Lifeline Systems employs 155 workers and has sales in excess of $8 million.[31]

In addition to the capital they invest, SBICs usually provide managerial advice and assistance to business owners.

Each SBIC will have its particular investment preferences in geographical area, industry, type of capital, and amount. For example, most SBICs make their loans and investments in the immediate geographical region surrounding their offices, although some of them operate on a regional or national basis. Many SBICs have particular industry preferences because the management team has skill and expertise in that area. And, because they differ in size and financial strength, SBICs create different investment strategies; some prefer to provide primarily debt financing while others focus on equity financing. A few have the financial capacity to provide financing up to several million dollars while others are able to offer only $100,000 or $200,000 in capital. In fact, most SBICs are small, and they rely on syndication to accumulate large amounts of capital. In other words, one SBIC acts as the financial leader in a group of SBICs who pool their funds to invest in a company.

Methods of Financing

SBICs can provide both debt and equity financing to small businesses. But, because of SBA regulations affecting the financing arrangements an SBIC can offer, most SBICs extend their investments as loans with an option to convert the debt instrument into an ownership interest later. In addition, SBICs are prohibited from obtaining a controlling interest in the companies in which they invest. Most SBICs are willing to negotiate with a small business to tailor the financial package to its particular needs. The most common forms of SBIC financing (in order of their frequency) follow.

Loan with Option to Buy Stock.   The loan maturity is eight years, with interest only paid during the first three years and both principal and interest paid in the last five years. An option to purchase 10 to 25 percent of the company's stock at below market prices is normally included. This type of financing is available mainly to well-established firms.

Convertible Debenture.   The maturity on the debenture (an unsecured bond) is 10 years with interest only paid during the first five years and both principal and interest paid during the last five. An option to convert the bond into a 25 to 30 percent equity

---

[29]"A Guide to SBC Money," *Inc,*. July 1981, p. 99.

[30]Wantuck, op. cit., pp. 40–41.

[31]"SBICs: They Get Investors in on the Ground Floor," *Changing Times,* February 1984, p. 60.

interest at a reasonable price is standard. This financing technique is primarily for growing companies.

Straight Loan. Loan maturities range from two and one-half years to seven years, and the loan is secured by specific assets. This financing technique is normally reserved for mature, profitable businesses.

Preferred Stock. The preferred stock pays a reasonable dividend and is redeemable after 10 years. It is normally used to provide equity capital to new firms.[32]

Most SBICs and MESBICs divest their interests in a small business within five to seven years, and they strive for at least an annually compounded 15 percent return on investment.[33] SBICs and MESBICs look for the same features in a firm that venture capital companies do—competent management, a growth industry, a competitive edge, and intangibles.

SBIC financing would be attractive to the capable entrepreneur whose primary concern is maintaining majority ownership in his business and who may not be in a "hot" industry.

V. SMALL BUSINESS LENDING COMPANIES (SBLCs)

Small Business Lending Companies (SBLCs) make only intermediate and long-term SBA-guaranteed loans. They specialize in loans that many banks would not consider and operate on a nationwide basis. "We make loans all over the U.S. I guess you'd call us a mail-order lending house," says an officer at a leading SBLC.[34] For instance, most SBLC loans have terms extending for at least 10 years. The maximum interest rate for loans of seven years or longer is 2.75 percent above the prime rate; for shorter term loans, the ceiling is 2.25 percent above prime. Another feature of SBLC loans is the expertise the SBLC offers borrowing companies in critical areas.

SBLCs also screen potential investors carefully, and most of them specialize in particular industries. The result is a low loan default rate at roughly 4 percent. Corporations own most of the nation's SBLCs, giving them a solid capital base. States one executive, "This is the only program I know of that attracts Wall Street money for small businesses."[35]

VI. FEDERALLY SPONSORED PROGRAMS

Federally sponsored lending programs have suffered from budget reductions in the past several years. Current trends indicate that the federal government is getting out of the lending business, although some programs still operate on a limited basis.

Economic Development Administration (EDA)

The Economic Development Administration, a branch of the Commerce Department, offers loan guarantees to create new business and to expand existing businesses in areas with below-average income and high unemployment. Loan requirements are strict and only a small number of loan guarantees are granted each year. In addition, the loan application process is lengthy and confusing. For example, guarantees for up to 85 percent of the loan value are permitted to purchase fixed assets only if the applicant supplies at least 14 percent of their cost in the form of equity capital. To qualify for a guaranteed loan for working capital, the borrower must supply 15 percent of the amount itself. Funds for direct loans from the EDA have dried up, and loan guarantee activity has dwindled significantly over the past five years.

EDA business loans are designed to help replenish economically distressed areas by creating or

---

[32]"SBA Revising Rules for SBICs," *Venture,* February 1982, p. 12.
[33]"Financing Small Business," p. 8.
[34]Phil Adamsak, "Why SBLCs Are Eager to Lend," *Venture,* June 1984, p. 158.

[35]Ibid.

expanding small businesses that provide employment opportunities in local communities. So, to qualify for a loan the business must be located in the disadvantaged area, and its presence must directly benefit local residents. Because the application process is lengthy and detailed, an entrepreneur should seek assistance from EDA personnel before filing an application.

Farmers Home Administration (FmHA)

The U.S. Department of Agriculture provides financial assistance to certain small businesses through the Farmers Home Administration. The FmHA loan program is open to all types of businesses and is designed to create nonfarm employment opportunities in rural areas—those with populations below 50,000 and not adjacent to a city where densities exceed 100 persons per square mile. Entrepreneurs in many small towns, especially those with populations below 25,000, are eligible to apply for loans through the FmHA program.

The FmHA does not make direct loans to small businesses, but it will guarantee up to 90 percent of a bank's loan to qualified applicants. Entrepreneurs apply for loans through private lenders. Unlike many other federal loan programs, the FmHA has no ceiling on the amount it will guarantee, and the borrower does not have to be turned down by a bank to be eligible. But the FmHA does require much of the same documentation as many of the other loan programs. Because of its emphasis on developing employment in rural areas, the FmHA requires an "environmental impact" statement describing the jobs created and the effect the business has on the area.

The FmHA guarantees loans to qualified business owners who, based on past performance, are judged to be good credit risks. In some cases, the owner can supply as little as 10 percent of the capital requirement, but usually the program requires a higher equity investment, especially for business start-ups. Interest rates and collateral terms are negotiated between the borrower and the participating bank. Loan maturities for real estate purchases are 30 years; but loans for acquiring fixed assets mature in 15 years, and working capital loans must be repaid in 7 years.

Department of Housing and Urban Development (HUD)

HUD sponsors several loan programs to assist a qualified entrepreneur in raising needed capital. The Urban Development Action Grants (UDAG) are extended to cities and towns that, in turn, lend or grant money to entrepreneurs to start small businesses that will strengthen the local economy. Grants are aimed at cities and towns which HUD considers "economically distressed." Funds are normally used to construct buildings and plants to be leased to entrepreneurs, sometimes with an option to buy. No ceilings or geographic limitations are placed on UDAG loans and grants.

UDAG loan and grant terms are negotiated individually between the town and the entrepreneur. An entrepreneur might negotiate a low-interest, long-term loan, while another might arrange for a grant in return for a promise to share a portion of the company's profits for several years with the town. For example, Barry Lebost, founder of Lebost Turbines, Inc., needed $3 million to build and equip a plant to manufacture a wind turbine to generate electricity and hot water more efficiently. Lebost raised $300,000 in equity capital from individuals and received a grant for $150,000 from the New York State Energy Research and Development Authority to build a prototype. Then he applied for a UDAG of $1 million, and the remaining $1.4 million of the capital was supplied by an Economic Development Administration loan. Lebost determined that he raised the necessary capital at a cost well below the existing prime rate.[36] But despite the many positive features

---

[36]"Places That Give Money Away," *Venture,* June 1980, pp. 22–23.

of the UDAG program, very few entrepreneurs have used it.

Prospective entrepreneurs should be aware that other smaller loan programs are offered by other federal agencies, including the Department of the Interior and the National Science Foundation.

Local Development Companies (LDCs)

The federal government encourages local town residents to organize and fund local development companies on either a profit or nonprofit basis. After raising initial capital by selling stock to at least 25 residents, the company seeks loans from banks and from the SBA. Each LDC can qualify for up to $1 million per year in loans and guarantees from the SBA to assist in starting small businesses in the community. LDCs enable towns to maintain a solid foundation of small businesses even when other attractive benefits such as trade zones and tax breaks are not available.

Three parties are involved in providing the typical LDC loan—the LDC, the SBA, and a participating bank. An LDC normally requires the small business owner to assist by supplying about 10 percent of a project's cost, and then arranges for the remaining capital through SBA loans and bank loans. LDCs finance only the fixed assets of a small business; they cannot provide funds for working capital to supply inventory, supplies, or equipment, but they can help arrange loans from banks for working capital. LDCs usually purchase real estate, refurbish or construct buildings and plants, equip them, and then lease the entire facility to the small business. The lessee's payments extend for 20 to 25 years to allow repayment of SBA, bank, and LDC loans. When the lease expires, the LDC normally gives the small business owners an option to purchase the facility, sometimes at prices well below market value. Most LDCs are nonprofit, and the interest rates they charge on their share of the funds are far below the prime rate. One major advantage of these loans to prospective entrepreneurs is that most LDCs are willing to supply capital

to high-risk ventures that other lenders would reject.

VII. SMALL BUSINESS ADMINISTRATION (SBA)

To be eligible for SBA funds, a business must be "small"; that is, it must be within the SBA's criteria for defining a small business (discussed in chapter 1). Also, some types of business are ineligible for SBA loans. The SBA will not make a loan under the following conditions:

■ The loan is to pay off a loan to a creditor (or creditors) of the applicant who are inadequately secured and in a position to sustain loss; provide funds for distribution or payment to the principals of the applicant; or replenish funds previously used for such purposes.

■ The loan allows speculation in any kind of property.

■ The applicant is a nonprofit enterprise.

■ The applicant is a newspaper, magazine, book publishing company or similar enterprise, excepting radio, cable, or TV broadcasting companies.

■ Any gross income of the applicant (or of any of its principal owners) is derived from gambling activities, except for small firms which obtain less than one-third of their income from the sale of state lottery tickets under a state license, or from gambling activities in those states where such activities are legal within the state.

■ The loan finances real property that is, or is to be, held for investment.[37]

In addition, the applicant must be declined by at least one bank (or two banks in cities with populations over 200,000) before the SBA will extend a loan. The reasoning is simple: Congress did not intend the SBA to compete for financing opportunities with private lenders.

---

[37]U.S. Small Business Administration, *SBA Business Loans*, pamphlet, Washington, 1980, pp. 7-8.

Types of Loans

The SBA offers three basic types of loans in administering its 19 different programs: direct, immediate participation, and guaranteed. *Direct loans* are made by the SBA directly to the small business with public funds and no bank participation. Generally, a direct loan cannot exceed $150,000. (A lower ceiling, $100,000, applies to a direct Economic Opportunity loan.) The interest rate charged on direct loans depends on the cost of money to the government, and it changes as general interest rates fluctuate.

Immediate participation loans are made from a pool of public funds and private loans. The SBA provides a portion of the total loan and a private lender supplies the remaining portion. The SBA's general policy is to fund no more than 75 percent of a participation loan, but there are exceptions. The SBA's portion of an immediate participation loan may not exceed $150,000 (except that Economic Opportunity loans are limited to $100,000). The interest rate the SBA charges on its share of the loan is usually the same as that charged on direct loans.

Guaranteed loans are extended to the small business owner by a private lender, but are guaranteed by the SBA for up to $500,000 or 90 percent of the bank loan, whichever is less. In other words, the SBA guarantees the bank this much repayment in case the borrower defaults. The participating bank determines the loan's terms and sets the interest rate within SBA limits. The SBA receives a one-time assessment from the bank of 1 percent of the loan amount for guaranteeing the loan and for "handling fees." Traditionally, about 90 percent of the SBA's financial assistance is in the form of loan guarantees.

The term of most guaranteed loans may be for as long as 10 years. Working capital loans are usually limited to 6 or 7 years, but loans for construction or real estate can be extended for up to 20 years.

Direct loans from the SBA are frozen, for all practical purposes. Only veterans and handicapped persons are eligible for SBA direct loans. SBA loan guarantee programs are still alive, but budget cuts are putting pressure on them, too. It is likely that, in the future, government-sponsored loans and guarantees will play a minimal role in small business financing.

State Loan and Development Programs

Just when federally funded programs are declining, state-sponsored loan and development programs are becoming more active in providing funds for business start-ups and expansions. Many states have decided that their funds are better spent encouraging small business growth rather than trying to entice large businesses to locate in their boundaries. These programs come in a wide variety of forms, but they all tend to focus on developing small businesses that create the greatest number of jobs and economic benefits. For example, South Carolina's Jobs Economic Development Authority (JEDA) is a direct lending arm of the state, offering low interest loans to manufacturing, industrial, and service businesses. JEDA also provides financial and technical assistance to small companies seeking to develop export markets.[38]

Clearly, the prospective entrepreneur has a large number of financial sources, both private and public, from which to solicit funding for start up and expansion. The government, however, plays the role of a lender of last resort for qualified entrepreneurs who cannot obtain financing through private financial institutions. In searching for capital, the entrepreneur should exhaust all possible sources before conceding defeat.

VIII. INTERNAL METHODS OF FINANCING

The small business owner does not have to rely solely on external financial institutions and govern-

---

[38]*South Carolina Business Formation and Expansion Manual,* South Carolina State Development Board, 1984, p. 67.

ment agencies for capital. Instead, the business itself has the capacity to generate capital. This type of financing, called "bootstrap" financing, is available to virtually every small business and encompasses factoring, leasing rather than purchasing equipment, and managing the business frugally.

Instead of carrying credit sales on its own books (some of which may never be collected), a small business can sell outright its accounts receivable to a factor. Once the factor purchases the business' accounts, the owner is relieved of the responsibility for collecting them. So by factoring, a small business receives cash for its accounts receivable, and customers get the credit they seek. Since the factoring company assumes the risk of collecting the accounts, it normally screens the firm's credit customers, accepts those judged to be creditworthy, and pays the small business owner the value of the accounts receivable. However, the factor will advance only 60 to 80 percent of the worth of the accounts at the time of the sale, remitting the balance when the customer pays. If some accounts are not collected, the factor bears the loss. For assuming this risk, the factor charges a fee of 1 or 2 percent on each account, plus interest on the advance. Usually, the effective interest rate is above that charged by banks and commercial finance companies. So, although factoring eliminates the need for performing the credit function, it tends to be an expensive method of financing.

By leasing expensive assets, the small business owner is able to use them without "locking in" valuable capital for an extended period of time. In other words, the manager can reduce the long-term capital requirements of the business by leasing equipment and facilities, and he is not investing his capital in depreciating assets. Also, because no down payment is required and because the cost of the asset is spread over a longer time (lowering monthly payments), the firm's cash flow improves. Buildings, furniture, display cases, and other items can be leased from suppliers, but the total cost of leasing is higher than that of purchasing.

A small business also can minimize its capital requirements by conserving on expenses whenever possible. The entrepreneur must consider cost-saving steps such as purchasing used or reconditioned equipment, converting personal assets to business use, and cutting business expenses wherever possible. For example, one entrepreneur who operated a part-time skeet range was able to start his business with minimal capital by purchasing used skeet-throwing equipment. Other owners have used family cars, home computers, and other personal assets in their businesses to lower their capital outlays.

IX. WHERE NOT TO SEEK BUSINESS FUNDS

Small business owners searching for cash infusions to expand the business, introduce new products, or maintain adequate working capital must be wary of the many fraudulent schemes perpetrated by con artists whose targets frequently include financially strapped small businesses. In the past, authorities rarely caught these scam artists; but recently, the federal crackdown on white collar crime has netted more of them.

The swindle usually begins when the con man scours an area for "DMs"—Desperate Men—in search of quick cash injections to keep their businesses going. Once he finds a desperate, unsuspecting small business owner who "takes the bait," the swindler begins the scam. Usually, the small business scheme follows one of two patterns (although a number of variations exist). Under one scheme, the small business owner is guaranteed a loan for whatever amount he needs from a nonexistent bank with false credentials. The con man tells the owner that loan processing will take time, and that in the meantime he must pay a percentage of the loan amount. Then the owner is given a bogus certificate of deposit on the loan he is to obtain. Of course, the loan never materializes and the small business owner loses his deposit, sometimes several thousand dollars.

SMALL
BUSINESS
REPORT
10–5

How Not to Borrow Money

The federal truth-in-lending law requires a lender to give a complete, clear explanation of the loan and all fees and charges involved. The borrowing cost must be stated as an annual percentage rate (APR). But, the law does *not* cover business loans. Carlton and Ada Poston learned this lesson the hard way when they got a loan for their trucking business from a lending company. Loan officers loaned the couple $25,000 and told them the interest rate was 12 percent per year. The couple pledged their home as collateral. At the closing, the couple signed several legal documents, one of which stated that the loan was for $28,750, discounted by $5,750, and payable in one year. The effective interest rate on the loan was 40 percent! Unable to repay the loan, the Postons refinanced it twice, and, at one point, they were paying an effective interest rate of 100 percent! Finally, a savings and loan association purchased their $58,400 note and worked out a payment plan with the couple.

The Postons' lesson was an expensive one.

Source: Adapted from "Five Ways to Lose When You Borrow," *Changing Times,* April 1985, pp. 72–74, with permission of the publisher.

Another common scam begins with a con artist who claims to be a representative of the Small Business Administration. He promises the cash-hungry small business owner an SBA loan if he pays a "small" processing fee. Again, the loan never appears, and the small business owner loses his deposit.

Because of the drastic problems the agricultural industry has endured in recent years, desperate farmers are frequent victims of con men. One farmer was facing foreclosure procedures when he heard about an Oklahoma businessman who offered help to troubled farmers. The farmer sent soil samples, financial information, and a check for $2,500. The help never materialized, and the farmer lost his money. Several months later, the farmer sought help from another stranger promising to bail out troubled farmers in a joint-venture scheme. He never saw the $3,500 he gave this con artist again, either.[39]

These con artists move fast and cover their trails well. The message to the small business owner is clear: Beware of "easy" loan offers and investigate financial institutions thoroughly before paying any

loan-related fees. Small Business Report 10–5 tells the story of an unfortunate couple who became victims in a loan scam.

X. SUMMARY

Depending on the nature of the firm's particular capital requirements, both the potential entrepreneur and the small business owner face a multitude of sources for funding the financial needs of a small business venture. To increase the chances of successfully obtaining capital, the entrepreneur must know what sources are available, and must understand the operations of the various financial institutions. Preparing a solid business and financial plan before beginning the capital search enables the entrepreneur to determine which sources would be most likely to assist in capitalizing the business. Many entrepreneurs in search of venture capital have succeeded in ferreting out the capital needed to start a small business and to keep it growing at a healthy pace.

Many would-be entrepreneurs never raise the capital required to start a business. Both new and existing businesses are confronted with the problem of obtaining "adventure" and venture capital.

Capital is any form of wealth employed to pro-

---

[39]Wendy L. Wall, "Desperate to Survive, Many Farmers Fall Prey to Wiley Con Men," *The Wall Street Journal,* August 13, 1985, p. 1.

duce more wealth. Three forms of capital are commonly identified: fixed capital, working capital, and growth capital.

Equity financing represents the personal investment of the owner (or owners), and it offers the advantage of not having to be repaid. The most common source of equity funding is the entrepreneur's personal savings. As a general rule, the entrepreneur should expect to supply at least one-half of the venture's initial capital requirement. Lacking sufficient capital, the owner may turn to "angels" (outside investors in search of tax shelters) or to partners for financial support. The owner may choose to attract capital by incorporating and "taking the company public."

Going public offers the advantages of raising large amounts of capital, improved access to future financing, improved corporate image, and gaining listing on a stock exchange. The disadvantages include dilution of the founder's ownership, loss of privacy, reporting to the SEC, filing expenses, and accountability to shareholders.

An entrepreneur might also convince a venture capital company to invest in the business. These are private companies that provide equity capital to fledgling businesses in return for a share of ownership. In screening prospects, venture capital firms look for competent management, a competitive edge, a growth industry, and important intangibles that will make a business successful.

As the number of venture capitalists grows, more firms are choosing to specialize in different industries and even different types of financing.

Debt financing encompasses the funds the entrepreneur/owner borrows and must repay at some time in the future. A great many debt financing options are open to the typical borrower.

Commercial banks offer the greatest variety of loans, although they are conservative lenders. Typical short-term bank loans include commercial loans, lines of credit, discounting accounts receivable, inventory financing, and floor planning. Intermediate and long-term loans typically include unsecured

term loans, installment loans, and discounting installment contracts.

Trade credit is used extensively by small businesses as a source of financing. Vendors and suppliers commonly finance sales to businesses for 30, 60, or even 90 days.

Equipment suppliers offer small businesses financing similar to trade credit, but with slightly different terms.

Commercial finance companies offer many of the same types of loans that banks do, but they are more risk oriented in their lending practices. They emphasize accounts receivable financing and inventory loans.

Savings and loan associations specialize in loans to purchase real property—commercial and industrial mortgages—for up to 30 years.

Stock-brokerage houses offer loans to prospective entrepreneurs at lower interest rates than banks because they have high quality, liquid collateral—stocks and bonds in the borrower's portfolio.

Insurance companies provide financing through policy loans and mortgage loans. Policy loans are extended to the owner against the cash surrender value of insurance policies. Mortgage loans are made for large amounts and are based on the value of the land being purchased.

Zero coupon bonds allow a company to borrow the funds it needs without having to make periodic loan payments. But, a public bond issue does require the company to make public certain financial information.

Small business investment companies are privately owned companies licensed and regulated by the SBA. Once they are privately capitalized, SBICs may qualify for SBA loans to be invested in or loaned to small firms. The most common methods of financing through SBICs include loans with options to buy stock and convertible debentures.

Small business lending companies make only intermediate and long-term loans that are guaranteed by the SBA.

The Economic Development Administration, a

branch of the Commerce Department, makes loan guarantees to create and expand small businesses in economically depressed areas.

The Farmers Home Administration's loan program is designed to create nonfarm employment opportunities in rural areas through loans and loan guarantees.

The Department of Housing and Urban Development extends loans to cities that, in turn, lend and grant money to small businesses in an attempt to strengthen the local economy.

Local development companies, financed privately, seek loans from banks and from the SBA. They lend this money to small businesses to develop a sound economic base in the local community.

The Small Business Administration has three types of loans: direct, immediate participation, and guaranteed. Direct and immediate participation loan programs are frozen, and even guaranteed loan programs are under pressure. State loan and development programs have taken up much of the "slack" left by dwindling federal programs. By offering direct loans and loan guarantees to small companies, these programs help to create jobs and strengthen the state's economic base.

Finally, the small business owner may look inside his firm for capital. By factoring accounts receivable, leasing equipment instead of buying it, and by minimizing costs, the owner's supply of capital can be stretched.

Many sources of capital are available to the small business manager who has "done his homework." If an entrepreneur prepares adequately to present his idea to the various financial institutions, his chances of obtaining needed capital are greatly enhanced.

STUDENT INVOLVEMENT PROJECTS

1. Visit a local small business owner and ask the following questions.
   a. How did you raise your starting capital? What percent did you supply on your own? What percent was debt capital and what percent was equity capital?
   b. Which of the sources of funds described in this chapter are used? Are they used to finance fixed, working, or growth capital needs?
2. After a personal visit, prepare a short report on a nearby factor's operation. How is the value of the accounts receivable purchased determined? Who bears the loss on uncollected accounts?
3. Interview the administrator of a financial institution program offering a method of financing with which you are unfamiliar, and prepare a short report on its method of operation.
4. Contact your state's business development board and prepare a report on the financial assistance programs it offers.

DISCUSSION QUESTIONS

1. Why is it so difficult for most small business owners to raise the capital needed to start, operate, or expand their ventures?
2. What is capital? List and describe the three types of capital a small business needs for its operations.
3. Define equity financing. What advantage does it offer over debt financing?

4. What is the most common source of equity funds in a typical small business? If an owner lacks sufficient equity capital to invest in the firm, what options are available for raising it?

5. How do venture capital firms operate? Describe their procedure for screening proposals for equity capital. What factors does a venture capitalist look for before investing in a business venture?

6. Define debt financing. What role do commercial banks play in providing debt financing to small businesses?

7. Outline and briefly describe the major types of short-term, intermediate, and long-term loans offered by commercial banks.

8. What is trade credit? How important is it as a source of debt financing to small firms?

9. What types of loans do savings and loan associations specialize in? Describe the two types of loans extended by insurance companies.

10. How do zero-coupon bonds differ from "standard" bonds?

11. What function do SBICs serve? How does an SBIC operate? What methods of financing do SBICs rely on most heavily?

12. Briefly describe the loan programs offered by:
    a. the Economic Development Administration
    b. the Farmers Home Administration
    c. the Department of Housing and Urban Development
    d. Local Development Companies

13. How can a firm employ "bootstrap" financing to stretch its current capital supply?

14. How does a factor operate?

SECTION FOUR

LOCATION AND LAYOUT: KEY CRITERIA

Location, Layout, and Physical Facilities

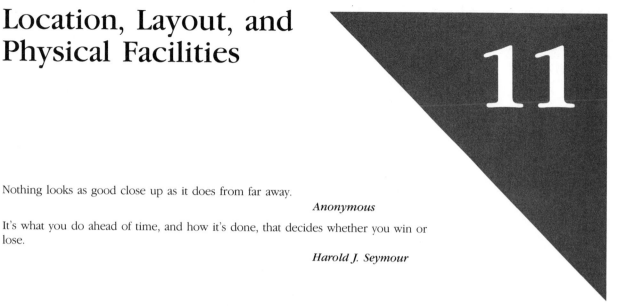

11

Nothing looks as good close up as it does from far away.

Anonymous

It's what you do ahead of time, and how it's done, that decides whether you win or lose.

Harold J. Seymour

Upon completion of this chapter, you will be able to:

- Appreciate the importance of the location decision to most businesses.

- Recognize that the location decision should include a wide geographic search.

- Understand that the location decision requires a screening of a wide variety of criteria at the regional, state, city, and neighborhood levels.

- Recognize the diverse set of factors that affect the final site selection.

- Describe the location factors that are common to both retailers and service businesses.

- Appreciate the importance of physical facilities and layout.

- Evaluate the advantages and disadvantages of building, buying, or leasing.

- Recognize the fundamentals of facilities consideration.

- Understand how layout principles differ for retailers and manufacturers.

- Discuss the various types of layouts used in manufacturing.

For most businesses, choosing a location is a permanent decision. The larger the investment in land, buildings, fixtures, and other immovable assets, the more likely it is that the location will be permanent. Consequently, location becomes a critical decision, because once the choice is made the owner usually does not alter it. Many businesses are costly to move, and moving, therefore, becomes impractical.

Each type of business has its own criteria for what constitutes a "good" location. What may be ideal for a lumber mill or warehouse may be totally unacceptable for a shoe store or ice cream parlor. A region of the country perfect for one business may be totally inappropriate for another. Location can be divided into a series of decisions. Each decision helps the owner focus more closely on finding the best location for his business. This process of loca-

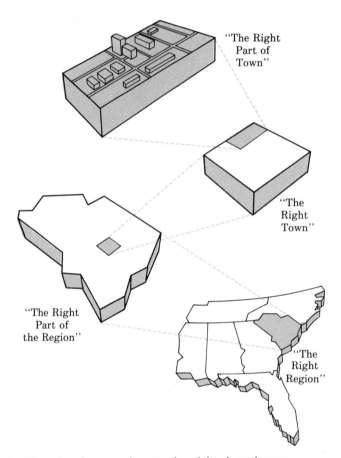

FIGURE 11–1   The identification of regional and local market areas.

Source: From Dale M. Lewison and M. Wayne DeLozier, *Retailing: Principles and Practices* (Columbus, Ohio: Merrill Publishing Company, 1982), p. 197. Used with permission.

tion selection is illustrated in figure 11–1. The owner begins with a very broad focus, and narrows it down by asking the following questions.

1. Which region of the country?
2. Which state within that region?
3. Which city within that state?
4. Which specific site?

Location decisions are often biased by the owner's short-sightedness when the owner considers locating the business only in a familiar area. This type of decision short-circuits the location process since the owner ignores the first three steps of the location analysis. Personal preference for a given location within the city could cause the owner to be blind to superior opportunities elsewhere.

Most people who fail in business say they chose their business locations by chance when they noticed a vacant building that suited their needs. They should have considered why it was vacant. A vacant building is unlikely to be a top location. If the location has a history of being vacant, it likely has a history of business failures. Many locations that look "right" on the surface later turn out to be unsuitable. This chapter will explore the criteria for selecting the "right" location.

I. THE LOCATION FOCUS

Selecting the Region

Entrepreneurs assume that their businesses will continue forever. Therefore, you should find out which areas within the country are experiencing substantial growth. Studying shifts in population and industry should provide a general overview of this. For each area, consider questions such as: What is the average income of the population? What is the construction rate for industry, business, and housing? Where is the "action"? Then consider the reverse. You do not want to open a business in a dying region.

Your customers will be people, businesses, and industry, and if you are to be successful you must locate in a place that is convenient to them. In recent years, the urban East and the central states have experienced a decline in the population growth rate and, in some cases, have actually experienced a net decline. The "sun belt" region of the United States has grown more rapidly than the nation as a whole. As business and industry move, people will follow closely behind. The *Statistical Abstract of the United States* and other census publications can help the owner collect the facts about what regions of the country are growing most rapidly. Contact the national trade association which represents your product or service for more specific growth trends related to your potential business.

Unfortunately, most businesses will be located without adequate research, and this will increase their chances of failure. There are many publications to aid you in your search for the best location. The Census Bureau has produced two that are based on the most recent nationwide census: *Census '80: Introduction to Products and Services* and *1980 Census Basics*. The Small Business Administration has a number of valuable aids to help you throughout your location search. Some of these include *Practical Use of Government Statistics, Using Census Data to Select a Store Site,* and *Using Census Data in Small Plant Marketing. American Demographics* magazine has two valuable booklets also: *The 1980 Census: The Counting of America* and *A Researcher's Guide to the 1980 Census.*

Selecting the State

Every state has a business development office to recruit new businesses to that state. Even though the publications produced by these offices will be biased in favor of locating in that state, they still are an excellent source of facts. You will want to assess the business climate in each state. Become familiar with state business laws, regulations, and taxes. Find out if the state encourages new business formation through tax incentives or investment credits.

Some key criteria for screening state locations are discussed next.

Proximity to Markets. Locating close to markets they plan to serve is extremely critical to manufacturers when the cost of transportation of finished goods is high relative to their value. Locating near customers is necessary to remaining competitive. Service firms often find that proximity to their clients is essential. If your business is involved in repairing equipment used in a specific industry, it should be located where that industry is concentrated. For instance, if you repair and service oil well drilling equipment, you would need to locate in areas of the country where oil fields are found. The more specialized the business, or the greater the relative cost of transporting the product to the customer, the more likely it is that proximity to the market will be of critical importance in the location decision.

Proximity to Needed Raw Materials. If your business requires raw materials that are difficult or expensive to transport, you may need to locate near the source of those raw materials. In other situations

Locating in the Land of the Rising Sun

No matter what country a business chooses to conduct business in, location analysis is an important element of the location decision. Kentucky Fried Chicken's method of choosing its store locations in Japan is a prime example. To qualify as a potential site, a district must have at least 50,000 people per day using its train station. Then, management evaluates the number of people within 15 minutes' walking and driving time of the site to get an estimate of the trading area. Next, analysts determine the number of passersby by a traffic count and multiply this by the amount of store frontage to arrive at a "location factor." Finally, this number is plugged into a formula to determine what portion of fast food sales the store could expect.

Photo courtesy of Kentucky Fried Chicken Corporation.

Based on these results, management selects a specific site and begins construction. But the store is not an exact replica of its American counterpart. The shops are much smaller than U.S. shops because KFC recognized the importance of adapting them to Japanese cities, which are much more crowded than the typical U.S. city. One Japanese manager compares a full-size store in Japan to driving a Cadillac down the narrow, crowded streets of Tokyo. The stores are only one-third the size of a regular U.S. store, and the equipment is streamlined to fit them. Space is at a premium, and rental rates reflect this reality. One KFC location goes for $85,000 per month.

Source: Adapted from Eric Sevareid and John Case, *Enterprise: The Making of Business in America* (New York: McGraw-Hill, 1983), pp. 129–37.

---

where bulk or weight is not a factor, locating in close proximity to the supplier can facilitate quick deliveries and reduce holding costs for inventories. The value of products and materials, their cost of transportation, and unique function all interact in deciding how close the business needs to be to its source of supplies. Fish canneries locate on the coast to reduce transportation and to retain the freshness of the catch. Small electronic appliance manufacturers locate close to the major sources of electronic components. In the latter case, neither transportation cost nor spoilage is a problem, but access to many suppliers may result in lower cost and prompt deliveries.

Labor Supply Needs. There are two distinct factors in an analysis of labor supply needs: the number of workers available in the area, and their level of education, training, and experience. The potential business owner wants to know how many qualified people are available in the area to do the work required in the business. Unemployment and labor cost statistics can be misleading if you need people with specific qualifications. Some states have attempted to attract industry with the promise of cheap labor. Unfortunately, these businesses found exactly what the term implied—unskilled, low-wage labor. Unskilled laborers can be difficult to train and may have poor work habits.

Know the exact nature of the labor you need. Have job descriptions and job specifications worked out in advance to facilitate determining if there is a good match with the people who are available for work. States will generally have their labor supplies broken down by region. Check with trade schools about curriculum and the number of persons presently enrolled in the programs which are applicable to your needs. Such planning may result in choosing an area where you can identify a constant source of high-quality labor.

Business Climate. You will need to investigate the state's overall attitude toward your kind of business. Does the state have laws which will work a hardship on your business? For example, some states have a weight limit for trucks below that set by federal laws. This type of legislation may indicate a business climate unfavorable for trucking companies. You should investigate the existence of any laws that restrict entry or require payment of unusually high taxes. Does the state have a corporate income tax? If you are a retailer, find out if the state has laws which severely limit business activity on Sunday. There are many laws, regulations, and taxes which the owner should compare on a state-by-state basis to determine which state is most favorable to his business.

Wage Rates. The existing wage rates will provide another measure for comparison among states. Be sure you are measuring wage rates for jobs that relate to your business. In addition to government sources, local newspapers will give you some idea of wages paid by competitors. Study the trend in wage rates. How does the rate of increase in wage rates compare among states? The Houston and Dallas areas once had low wage rates in comparison with areas of like size, but today their wage rates are some of the highest in the nation.

Selecting a City

Population Trends. A new business owner should know more about a city and its various neighborhoods than the people do who live there. Through analyzing population and other demographic data, an entrepreneur can examine a city in detail, and the decision on where to locate becomes more than "a shot in the dark." You should study characteristics of a city and its citizens, including population size and density, growth trends, family size, age breakdowns, education, income level, sex, religion, race, and nationality. A location should match the market for your product. If you wish to open a fine china shop, you would likely want specific information on family income, size, age, and education. Such a shop will need to be in an area where people appreciate the product and have the discretionary income to purchase it.

Trends or shifts in population components may have more meaning than total population trends. For example, if the population of a city is aging, its disposable income may be increasing or decreasing. If its disposable income is declining, the city may be gradually dying.

Table 11–1 shows the national average of a city's inhabitants per store. By comparing the average number of people required to support a type of business to the population in the proposed trading area, the entrepreneur can judge the suitability of a location.

A business involved in furniture sales may wish to turn to the *Census of Housing* and the *Annual Housing Survey* to determine housing trends in an area. Data on owner characteristics, occupants' characteristics, household composition, number of rooms per house, number of bedrooms, and housing quality can help determine if an area could support the business.

The amount of available data on the population of any city or town is staggering. These statistics will allow the potential owner to compare a wide variety of cities or towns and to narrow the choices to those few which warrant further personal investigation. The mass of data may make it possible to screen out undesirable locations, but it does not make a decision for you. The owner needs to see the locations firsthand. Only by personal investigation will he be able to add that intangible factor of intuition into the decision-making process.

Local Laws and Regulations. Before selecting a particular site within a city, the small business owner must explore the local zoning laws to determine if there are any ordinances that would place restrictions on business activity or that would prohibit establishing a business altogether. Zoning is a system that divides a city or county into small "cells" or districts to control the use of land, buildings, and sites. Its purpose is to contain similar activities in suitable locations. For example, one section of town composed of several subdivisions might be zoned residential, while the primary business district is zoned commercial. These ordinances protect the homeowners from having, for example, a large smoke-belching, foul-smelling chemical plant locate next door, ruining the neighborhood's quality of life.

Make sure *before* you locate that your proposed location conforms to local zoning ordinances. A county map and an interview with the local zoning board before you settle on a particular location could save you a great deal of trouble later. One entrepreneur planned to open a bar catering primarily to college students near a housing development in a small town. Many businesses operated in the immediate area and the entrepreneur never considered zoning regulations. Two weeks before the grand opening, the owner applied for a liquor license, but the local residents raised such a furor that the zoning board rejected all requests to sell alcoholic beverages at the site. The entrepreneur proceeded with the grand opening, but was forced to change drasti-

TABLE 11-1   Number of inhabitants per store by selected kind of business (national average).

Kind of Business	Number of Inhabitants per Store	Kind of Business	Number of Inhabitants per Store
Food Stores		**Automotive Dealers**	
Grocery stores	1,534	Motor vehicle dealers—new and	
Meat and fish (seafood) markets	17,876	used cars	6,000
Candy, nut, and confectionery stores	31,409	Motor vehicle dealers—used cars only	17,160
Retail bakeries	12,563	Tire, battery, and accessory dealers	8,764
Dairy products stores	41,587	Boat dealers	61,526
		Household trailer dealers	44,746
		Gasoline service stations	1,195
Eating, Drinking Places		**Miscellaneous**	
Restaurants, lunchrooms, caterers	1,583	Antique and secondhand stores	17,169
Cafeterias	19,341	Book and stationery stores	28,584
Refreshment places	3,622	Drug stores	4,268
Drinking places (alcoholic beverages)	2,414	Florists	13,531
		Fuel oil dealers	25,425
		Garden supply stores	65,118
General Merchandise		Gift, novelty, and souvenir shops	26,313
Variety stores	10,373	Hay, grain, and feed stores	16,978
General merchandise stores	9,837	Hobby, toy, and game shops	61,340
		Jewelry stores	13,495
		Liquified petroleum gas (bottled gas)	
Apparel and Accessory Stores		dealers	32,803
Women's ready-to-wear stores	7,102	Liquor stores	6,359
Women's accessory and specialty stores	25,824	Mail order houses	44,554
Men's and boys' clothing & furnishing		Merchandising machine operators	44,067
stores	11,832	Optical goods stores	62,878
Family clothing stores	16,890	Sporting goods stores	27,063
Shoe stores	9,350		
		Furniture, Home Furnishings and Equipment	
Building Material, Hardware, and Farm Equipment Dealers		Furniture stores	7,210
		Floor covering stores	29,543
Lumber and other building materials		Drapery, curtain, and upholstery stores	62,460
dealers	8,124	Household appliance stores	12,585
Paint, glass, and wallpaper stores	22,454	Radio and television stores	20,346
Hardware stores	10,206	Record shops	112,144
Farm equipment dealers	14,793	Musical instruments stores	46,332

Source: U.S. Small Business Administration, "Starting and Managing a Small Business of Your Own," Washington, 1981, p. 27.

cally the club's image. The "bar" was billed as a non-alcoholic attraction for high school students. The new image was not successful, and the club closed its doors in less than a year. In another case, a young woman wanted to open a small beauty shop and, to save money on rent expense, planned to operate from a small room in her house. When applying for a license, she discovered that the neighborhood was zoned residential, and businesses were not allowed to locate there.

In some cases, the entrepreneur may convince the zoning board to rezone a site or to grant a "variance" (a special exception to a zoning ordinance), but this is risky and could be disastrous if the variance is not allowed.

Competition. If you are a retailer, there may be reason to believe that locating near competitors is a good strategy, since similar businesses located near one another may serve to increase traffic flow to both. Of course, this strategy has limits. Overcrowding of businesses of the same type in an area can create an undesirable impact on the profitability of all firms. Consider the specific nature of the businesses in the area. Do they offer the same quality merchandise or comparable services? The products or services of your business may be superior to those presently being offered. Studying the size of the market for your products or services and the number of existing competitors will help you determine if you can capture a sufficiently large enough market share.

Compatibility with the Community. One of the intangibles which can only be determined by a visit to the community is the degree of compatibility your business has with the community. Consider the costs associated with opening a business in a high-income community. Your business would need to match the flavor of the surrounding businesses. Rents, along with fixtures and other decor items, would likely be expensive. Is there an adequate markup in your merchandise to justify such cost? A reverse situation can

also occur—your business may not be compatible with an area of town where image is not important.

Transportation. Manufacturers and wholesalers will need to investigate the quality of local transportation systems. If you need to locate on a railroad spur, is such a location available in the city you are considering? How regular is truck service? Are the transportation rates reasonable? In some situations, double or triple handling of merchandise or inventories causes transportation costs to skyrocket.

Police and Fire Protection. Does the community in which you plan to locate offer adequate police and fire protection? If these services are not adequate, it will be reflected in the cost of your business insurance.

Public Services. The location should be served by some governmental unit that provides water and sewer services, trash and garbage collection, and other necessary utilities. The streets should be in good repair with adequate drainage. If the location is not within the jurisdiction of a municipality that provides these services, they will become a continuing cost to the business.

The Reputation of the Location. Can a location have a bad reputation? In some cases, the reputation of the previous business will lower the value of the location. Some locations have changed hands numerous times in past years and local patrons may view them negatively. The customer may view your business as another that will soon be gone.

II. SELECTING THE FINAL SITE

The final step in the location selection process is choosing the actual site for the business. Each type of business will evaluate criteria differently. A manufacturer's prime consideration may be access to raw materials, supplies, labor, transportation, and customers. Service firms need access to customers, but can generally survive in lower rent properties. A retailer's prime consideration is customers. The one element common to all three is the need to locate where customers wish to do business.

Site location draws on the most precise information available on the makeup of the area. Through the use of published statistics, the owner can develop valuable insights regarding the characteristics of people in the immediate community.

Retail Site Selection Analysis

Every retail business should determine the extent of its trading area—the region from which a business can expect to draw customers over a reasonable time span. The variables which influence the scope of a trading area are the type and size of the operation. If the retailer is a specialist with a wide assortment of products, he may draw customers from a great distance. In contrast, a convenience store with a general line of merchandise may have a small trading area, since it is unlikely that anyone would drive across town to purchase what is available within blocks of his home or business. As a rule, the larger the store and the greater the selection, the broader the trading area.

The following environmental factors will influence the retail trading area size:

1. The number, size, and type of other stores presently located in or planned for the area.
2. The nature of competing businesses.
3. The character of the transportation network.

These three factors are considered environmental because they are outside the range of the owner's influence.

Knowing the number, size, and type of stores located or planned for the area will provide you with some idea of how customers are presently drawn to stores. Look over the area for the presence or absence of a dominant cluster of stores. If a store is in a shopping mall that has a low vacancy rate due to a composite of successful stores, and there are no rival clusters of stores in the trading area, it might be wise to pay the high rent and locate there where other stores are already drawing in customers. Of course, it may also be possible to choose an "isolated" location and do well. By isolated we do not mean that the business site can't be found; on the contrary, the site might be located on a major highway or road, but not as part of a shopping center. In other words, the building would be "freestanding."

The size, location, and activity of competing businesses also influence the size of the trading area. If your business will be the first of its kind, the trading area might be quite extensive. However, if the area already has eight or ten stores which directly compete with your business, the trading area might be very small. How does the size of your planned operation compare with those which presently exist? Your business may be significantly larger and so have a stronger drawing power. When size and character of the stores are relatively comparable, you may wish to locate directly next to a competitor to encourage comparison shopping.

The transportation networks are the highways, roads, and public service routes which presently exist or are planned in the future. If it is inconvenient to get to an area, the trading area size is reduced. Check to see if the transportation system works smoothly and is free of barriers that might prevent customers from reaching your business. Is it easy to cross traffic if the customer is traveling in the opposite direction? Are there turn signals or well-planned traffic patterns?

Trading area shape and size are influenced by the transportation network, location of competitors, and any physical, racial, or political barriers that may exist. Physical barriers may be parks, rivers, lakes, or any other natural or man-made obstruction that hinders customer access to the area. Being located on one side of a large park may reduce the number of customers that will drive around this obstruction to get to your store. If high crime areas exist in any

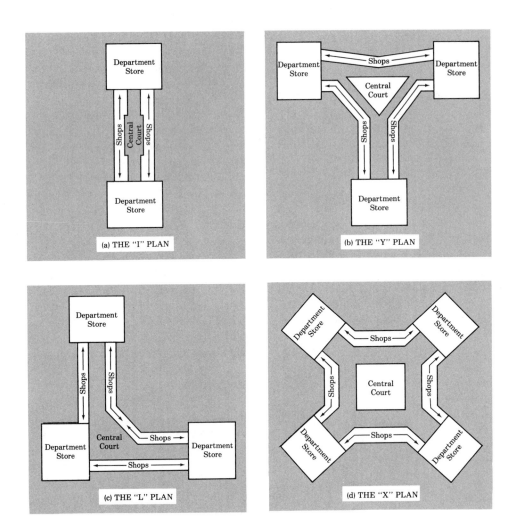

FIGURE 11–2   Shopping center configurations.

Source: From Lewison and DeLozier, *Retailing,* p. 234. Used with permission.

direction from the site, most of your potential customers will not be traveling through those neighborhoods to reach your business. Some ethnic groups will patronize only the businesses in their neighborhoods. The "Little Havana" section of Miami or Chinatown sections of San Francisco, New York, and Los Angeles are examples. Political barriers are creations of law. County, city, or state boundaries are examples. Consider the value of locating a liquor store on a major highway just across the line from a county that does not allow the sale of liquor. Thirsty customers from the "dry" county will likely patronize the first convenient location. State tax laws also create conditions where customers cross over to the next state to save money. North Carolina has a very low cigarette tax, and businesses located on its borders do a brisk business in the product.

Another factor important to selecting a site is the volume of traffic past the site. A traffic count should include both automobiles and pedestrians. Foot traffic is most important for shopping centers or mall locations. The shape of the shopping center or mall is a prime consideration. The most common shapes are illustrated in figure 11–2. The foot traffic that passes the store will vary considerably based on the layout of the shopping center and the other stores which act as magnets, drawing people into the center. Quite often one side of the center will have more traffic than the other. Count the number of shoppers that pass the location you are considering. Check the shopping pattern at different times of day and on different days of the week. Compare this traffic pattern with similar data from other sections of the shopping center at similar times and days. Your traffic count should be tailored to the persons who would be potential customers for your store. If you plan to open a specialty women's apparel store catering to women who wear petite sizes, you would include only the women in that category.

Automobile traffic counts can be made by sitting in your car and counting the passing traffic. As with the foot traffic count, you should include only those persons who would be potential customers. This is, of course, more difficult to determine when the people are in cars moving quickly down the highway. Many cities have already collected traffic data. Check with the city highway engineering department to determine what, if any, data are available to the public. Compare your current data with their studies. Another critical bit of information you may wish to collect concerns cars backed up at stop lights. Cars may spend time stopped in front of the store of the potential business. If the driver and passengers have to spend 15 to 30 seconds at the traffic light, they will likely spend the time glancing about the area. Find out if the city traffic engineer plans to erect a traffic light near your site in the future.

Criteria for Locating a Service Business

Many service companies do not need to have customers come to the place of business, so an expensive location is not necessary. Customers typically contact plumbers or exterminators by telephone, and the work is performed in the customers' homes. Location for such businesses should be functional, but certainly not fancy. Other service businesses,

---

Street Location

When an entrepreneur chooses a specific street site for a small business, he should locate on the side of the street that has the following

- the highest pedestrian traffic count where major department stores and other "business attractors" are located
- nearest the town's primary area of population growth
- shielding customers from extreme weather conditions
- with the afternoon shade
- with the fewest "interrupters" of pedestrian traffic (e.g., alleys, loading zones)

SMALL
BUSINESS
REPORT
11–2

such as travel agencies or barber shops, need to locate in high traffic areas since visibility is critical to
success. Some service businesses even pay for exclusive locations. A beauty shop or barber may pay high
rent to be in a famous hotel, and they will prosper
because of a captive market. The type of service offered and the customers the business is attempting to
attract will determine where it must locate.

Most small service firms are located in the
immediate area they serve and their clients are
drawn mostly by convenience. A laundry/cleaner is
an example. It is unlikely that anyone would go
across town for this service when it is competitively
priced in his own neighborhood. So, convenient location is an integral part of the service the service
business provides.

Location Criteria for Retail and Service Businesses

Two location criteria common to both retailers and
service businesses include the following.

Adequate Parking. If customers cannot find convenient and safe parking, they are not likely to shop in
the area. Many downtown areas have lost customers
because of inadequate parking. Customers generally
will not pay to park if parking is free at shopping
centers or in front of competitive stores. Even when
free parking is provided, some potential customers
may not feel safe on the streets, especially after dark.
Many large city downtown business districts become
virtual ghost towns at the end of the business day. A
location where traffic vanishes after 6 P.M. may not be
as valuable as those at malls and shopping centers
where 6 P.M. marks the beginning of prime sales
time.

Room for Expansion. The location should be flexible enough to provide for expansion if success warrants it. Failure to consider this factor can result in a
successful business being forced to open a second

store when it would have been better to expand in its
original location. Manufacturers also should consider expansion in their location decisions.

Location Criteria for a Small Manufacturer

Local zoning ordinances will limit a manufacturer's
choice of location. If the manufacturing process
creates offensive odors or noise, the business may be
even further restricted in its choices. City and county
planners will be able to show potential manufacturers the areas of the city or county set aside for industrial development. Some cities have developed industrial parks in cooperation with private industry.
These industrial parks typically are equipped with
sewage and electrical power sufficient for manufacturing. Many locations are not so equipped, and it
can be extremely expensive for a small manufacturer
to have such utilities brought to an existing site.

Location of the plant can, in some cases, be dic-
tated by the type of transportation facilities needed.
Some manufacturers may need to locate on a railroad siding, while others may only need reliable
trucking service. If raw materials are purchased by
the carload for economies of scale, the location must
be convenient to a railroad siding. Bulk materials are
sometimes shipped by barge and consequently require a facility convenient to a navigable river or
lake. The added cost of using multiple shipping (i.e.,
rail-to-truck or barge-to-truck) can significantly increase the cost of shipping and make a location un-
feasible for a manufacturer.

In some cases, the perishability of the product
dictates location. Vegetables and fruits are canned in
close proximity to the field in which they are har-
vested. Fish are processed and canned at the water's
edge. Location is determined by quick and easy access to the perishable products.

Needed utilities, zoning, transportation, and
special requirements all work together to limit the
number of locations which are suitable for the manu-

Where Not To Locate

Choosing a location is a major decision for the small business manager because it has lasting effect on the company. Poor site selection *can* lead directly to failure. Consequently, the wise entrepreneur will avoid the following types of locations:

- Districts with vacant or abandoned buildings or with unattractive vacant lots. These give the image of a dying area.
- Sites that are inaccessible (e.g., on narrow back streets or alleys).
- Sites where many businesses have failed.
- Areas suffering from intense traffic congestion (e.g., most downtown areas).
- Areas with poor lighting or low levels of night or weekend activity.
- Near businesses where parking times are lengthy (e.g., movie theaters).
- Locations surrounded by incompatible businesses (e.g., a stylish men's shop in a shopping center with a supermarket, a drugstore, a hardware store, and several factory outlets).
- Sites that have not been studied and evaluated.

---

facturer. Table 11–2 provides a rating system to determine the suitability of various locations.

III. USING CENSUS DATA IN SCREENING ALTERNATIVE SITES

Would you like to know how many people or families are living in your trading area, what type of jobs they have, how much money they make, their ages, the value of their homes, their education level, as well as a variety of other useful information? Sometimes businesses and individuals pay large fees to firms for this market research information. However, this information is available free from your public library and the various publications of the Bureau of the Census. The Bureau of the Census has divided the United States into Standard Metropolitan Statistical Areas (SMSAs). These SMSAs are then subdivided into census tracts. The average census tract contains 4,000 to 5,000 people. These census tracts are subdivided into block statistics and are available only for urban areas.

As an illustration, the Bureau of the Census recognizes two census tracts less than one-half mile apart in Charleston, South Carolina. Census tract

0002 comprises part of the beautiful refurbished historical Charleston district. This section includes a portion of the Battery and all of Rainbow Row. Census tract 0007 is not in the restored area. Tables 11–3 through 11–7 present selected statistics on the people who live in these two small areas of Charleston, South Carolina.

From table 11–2, we see that very little significant difference exists between the number of people in each neighborhood: census tract 0002 has 2,053 people compared with 2,163 in census tract 0007. From that point on significant differences seem to exist. Census tract 0002 has a significantly larger percentage of married-couple families than 0007, and, correspondingly, 0007 has over twice as many female households with no husband present. Table 11–4 reveals the great differences in income by household. What type of businesses would be viable in the neighborhood defined by census tract 0007? What type of business would you expect the families in census tract 0002 to frequent? Almost 50 percent of the families in census tract 0002 have incomes above $25,000 and the mean income is $36,716, indicating that those families whose income was listed over $50,000 were likely to be substantially over $50,000. In comparison, census tract 0007 is comprised of

TABLE 11–2 Rating the suitability of sites for a business.

Common Factors	Factor Importance (10 high–1 low)	Actual Scores for Alternative Sites (10 high–1 low)				Total Scores for Alternative Sites (Factor Importance × Actual Score)			
		Site A	Site B	Site C	Site D	Site A	Site B	Site C	Site D
Located to serve the customer (demographic trends)									
Cost of the location (rent or purchase price)									
Quantity and quality of the labor supply									
Zoning restrictions									
General business climate									
Transportation									
—For customer (highways, public transportation)									
—For raw material or inventories (rail, barge, air freight)									
Proximity to raw material or inventory									
Quality of public services (fire and police protection)									
Taxes (if owning)									
Adequacy for future expansion									
Value of the site in future years									
Labor cost and anticipated productivity									

TABLE 11–3 General characteristics of the population.

Characteristic	0002	0007
Age		
Total persons	2,053	2,163
Under 5 years	52	98
5– 9 years	113	87
10–14 years	106	149
15–19 years	115	331
20–24 years	146	271
25–34 years	351	240
35–44 years	236	142
45–54 years	222	195
55–64 years	266	247
65–74 years	252	222
75 years and older	194	181
Household Type and Relationship		
In household	2,053	2,163
Householder	988	1,908
Family householder	541	401
Nonfamily householder	447	384
Living alone	384	339
Spouse	455	186
Other relatives	527	845
Nonrelatives	83	92
Inmate of institution	0	0
Others in group quarters	0	255
Persons per household	2.08	2.43
Persons per family	2.82	3.57
Family Type by Presence of Own Children		
Families	541	401
with own children under 18 yrs.	190	207
Number of own children under 18 yrs.	339	425
Married-Couple Families	455	186
with own children under 18 yrs.	160	64
Number of own children under 18 yrs.	292	136
Female Household—No Husband Present	80	190
with children under 18 yrs.	29	80
Number of own children under 18 yrs.	46	167
Marital Status		
Male, 15 yrs. and older	770	666
Single	233	309
Now married, except separated	464	203
Separated	20	44
Widowed	22	33
Divorced	31	26
Female, 15 yrs. and older	1,012	1,163
Single	272	535
Now married, except separated	469	210
Separated	21	99
Widowed	192	265
Divorced	58	54

247

TABLE 11–4 Household income (1979 data).

	0002	0007
Households	1,014	763
Less than $ 5,000	71	242
$ 5,000–$ 7,499	46	120
$ 7,500–$ 9,999	51	106
$10,000–$14,999	135	90
$15,000–$19,999	136	84
$20,000–$24,999	90	54
$25,000–$34,000	135	36
$35,000–$49,999	160	31
$50,000 or more	190	0
Median	$24,113	$ 7,960
Mean	$36,716	$11,155
Families		
Median income	$37,042	$12,330
Mean income	$54,008	$14,506

households with very low incomes. In this neighborhood, 61 percent of the households have incomes of less than $10,000 per year. The business which might be properly located in census tract 0002 would be inappropriate in census tract 0007.

Table 11–5 shows similarity in the size of the labor force in both census tracts; however, tract 0002 residents are predominantly managerial and professional (45 percent). Census tract 0007 is dominated by technical, sales, and administrative support people (35 percent), as well as operators, fabricators and laborers (19 percent). These differences in occupation may play a key role in the types of businesses that will be most effectively located in each area.

People 25 years of age and up in census tract 0002 who have completed four years of college total an amazing 66 percent, in comparison with 13 percent in tract 0007 (see table 11–6). This higher level of formal education may indicate that businesses such as bookstores could be successful.

Table 11–7 presents a vivid illustration of the difference in the value of housing units in the two census tracts. Remember that tract 0002 is part of the restored historic district Seventy-four percent of the

homes in tract 0002 were valued at over $100,000; consequently, businesses such as remodeling and repairs, landscaping, and various other home services are needed. People with such beautifully restored homes are likely to take pride in projects that keep their homes in "top-flight" condition. With their incomes, they tend to furnish their homes with beautiful antiques, and such businesses are likely to flourish. These homes also will need modern-day services. The census data reveal that 983 of the homes in tract 0002 have air-conditioning—495 of these with central air-conditioning. Such statistics reveal a need for service industries to care for and maintain these homes. Owners of retail stores, such as bed-and-bath specialty stores, would be interested to find that of the individually owned homes in tract 0002, 39 percent have four or more bedrooms, and 84 percent have two or more bathrooms.

A potential automotive repair shop owner would find it helpful to know that 49 percent of the households in tract 0007 have *no* automobiles, but 41 percent of the persons in tract 0002 have two or more automobiles.

Businesses that cater to young people, such as

TABLE 11-5   Labor force statistics.

	0002	0007
Persons 16 yrs. and over	1,716	1,800
Labor force	1,430	989
Percentage of persons 16 yrs. and over	57.5%	54.9%
Civilian labor force	1,390	979
Employed	1,312	888
Unemployed	78	91
Occupation		
Managerial and professional	633	123
Technical, sales, and administrative		
support occupations	265	341
Service occupations	74	157
Farming, forestry, and fishing	0	0
Precision production, craft,		
and repair occupations	10	79
Operators, fabricators and laborers	0	188
Workers in Family in 1979		
No. workers	69	76
Mean family income	$47,848	$ 7,844
One worker	194	177
Mean family income	$54,414	$ 9,344
Two workers	230	121
Mean family income	$54,762	$17,526
Three workers	33	57
Mean family income	$59,244	$33,007

TABLE 11-6   Education statistics.

		0002	0007
Persons 25 yrs. old and older		1,515	1,302
Elementary:	0–4 years	0	191
	5–7 years	6	262
	8 years	10	127
High School:	1–3 years	57	231
	4 years	137	229
College:	1–3 years	299	88
	4 years	1,006	174
Percentage of high school graduates		95.2%	37.7%

TABLE 11–7 Value of housing units.

	0002	0007
Less than $10,000	1	2
$ 10,000–$ 14,999	0	6
$ 15,000–$ 19,999	0	11
$ 20,000–$ 24,999	1	9
$ 25,000–$ 29,999	0	9
$ 30,000–$ 34,999	1	4
$ 35,000–$ 39,999	1	6
$ 40,000–$ 49,999	2	8
$ 50,000–$ 59,999	16	7
$ 60,000–$ 79,999	35	9
$ 80,000–$ 99,999	55	2
$100,000–$149,000	146	1
$150,000–$199,999	78	0
$200,000 or more	93	0
Median	$134,000	$30,000
% Owning Homes	57.7%	21.9%

record stores, movie theaters, and ice cream stores would need to be aware (from table 11–3) that 602 people in tract 0007 were between ages 15 and 24 (compared to only 261 in tract 0002).

Most prospective small business owners will be shocked to find that this amount of detailed information is available about the locations they are considering. They need to find the information and study it carefully. A little research can be an excellent guide to locating the business in the "best" place.

Now that you have chosen a location for your business, you must decide what type of building is optimal for your business, and which layout is appropriate for it. Just as with location analysis, the entrepreneur must study carefully the physical arrangement of the building. The physical facilities and layout of your business can influence your ability to attract customers and aid in achieving the needed volume of sales, the efficiency of day-to-day operations, and the bottom line—profitability.

IV. BUILD, BUY, OR LEASE?

Your ability to obtain the best possible physical facilities in relation to available capital may depend largely on whether you decide to build, buy, or lease your building.

The Decision to Build

If a business had unlimited funds, the owner could design and build a perfect facility. However, many new business owners do not have this luxury. Therefore, it is valuable to construct a plan which outlines the most essential features of the firm's layout. Even if you are not going to have the financial resources to build the ideal facility, this outline can be useful in comparing other facilities you may buy or lease.

Constructing a new facility can project a positive image to potential customers. The business *looks* new, and consequently creates an image of being modern, efficient, and top quality. A new building can incorporate the most modern features during construction, and these might significantly lower operating costs. When such costs are critical to remaining competitive, it may be reasonable to build. You should consider the long-term lower cost for utilities and materials handling in total cost considerations.

In some growth locations, there are no existing buildings to buy that match your requirement or facilities to lease. In these situations, the business owner must consider the cost of constructing a building as a significant factor in his initial estimates of capital needs and break-even point. Constructing your own building has high initial fixed expenses that must be weighed against the facility's capability to both attract additional sales revenue and to reduce operating costs.

The Decision to Buy

In many cases, there may be an ideal building in the area where you wish to locate. If you buy the facility, you can remodel without seeking prior permission from anyone else. As with building, buying can put a drain on the financial resources of the business, but you will know exactly what your monthly payments will be. When you lease, the rent can increase over time. If you believe that the property will actually appreciate in value, a decision to purchase may be a wise investment. In this case, the down payment, which is typically 30 percent for commercial property, must be viewed as an investment. The owner can depreciate the building each year, and both depreciation and interest are tax-deductible expenses.

When considering purchasing a building, the owner should use the same outline of facilities requirements developed for the building option to ensure that this property will not be excessively expensive to modify for his use. Remodeling can add a significant initial expense. The location of the building may be ideal in many ways, but it may not be suitable for your business. Even if yours is the same

kind of business as the one moving out, the building layout may be completely unsuitable for the way you plan to operate.

If you build or buy a building, your mobility is greatly limited. Some business owners prefer to stay out of the real estate business to retain maximum flexibility and mobility. All real estate does not appreciate in value. Surrounding property can become run down and consequently lower your property's value despite your efforts to keep it in excellent condition. Many downtown locations have gone this route.

The Decision to Lease

The major advantage of leasing is that it requires no large initial cash outlay, so the business' funds are available for purchasing inventory or for current operations. Firms that are short on cash will inevitably be forced to lease facilities. All lease expenses are tax deductible, and the costs of insuring the building are not incurred by the lessor.

One major disadvantage of leasing is that the owner of the property may not choose to renew your lease. A successful business might be forced to move to a new location, and such relocation can be extremely costly and could result in a significant loss of established customers. In many cases, it is almost like starting the business again! Also, if a business is successful, the owner of the building will likely ask for a significant increase in rent when the renewal of the lease is negotiated. The owner is well aware of the costs associated with moving and has the upper hand in the negotiations. In some lease arrangements, the owner is compensated, in addition to a monthly rental fee, by a percentage of gross sales. This is common in shopping centers.

Still another disadvantage to leasing is the many limitations on remodeling. If the owner believes that your modifications will reduce the future rental value of the property, he will likely require a long-term lease at increased rent or will not allow you to make the needed changes. In addition, all per-

Leasing offers many advantages, but it can be dangerous. (Photo by Jill R. Johnson.)

manent modifications of the structure become the property of the owner.

Whatever choice you make, it is important that the selection matches the plan you have for your business. Throughout this chapter you will be presented with material that presents questions to guide you in evaluating the options.

V. FUNDAMENTAL CONSIDERATIONS IN CHOOSING FACILITIES

Size

The building you choose must be large enough to accommodate the daily operations of your business. If it is too small at the outset of operations, efficiency will suffer. There must be room enough for custom-

ers' movement, inventory, displays, storage, work areas, offices, and restrooms. Most small businesses wait too long before moving into larger facilities. For instance, when Enhansys, a computer software company, started in 1982, it had four employees in 750 square feet of space. As the company grew to 35 workers, it was forced to find more space. The only spot available was 2,200 square feet located across a courtyard. Enhansys' president recalls, "We had people running back and forth between three locations, and only one office had a copying machine. It was crazy."[1]

If you plan to expand in any way, will the building accommodate it? Will growth require a new location? Lack of adequate room in the building may become a limitation to the growth of the business. Too

---

[1]Cathy Hedgecock, "Planning Ahead," *Venture,* March 1984, p. 42.

The store front should project the proper image. (Photo by Jill R. Johnson.)

many small business owners start their operations in locations that are already crowded and lack the ability to be expanded. The result is that the owner is forced to make a costly move to a new location within the first few years of operation. The owner of one small sporting goods store realized this when he started his business in a very small building since it was "all he could afford." Not only did the moving expenses consume valuable working capital, but sales also suffered when customers had difficulty finding the new location. To avoid such problems, one design expert recommends that new businesses plan their space requirements one to two years ahead and update the estimates every two months. When preparing the plan, managers should include the expected growth in the number of employees, manufacturing, selling, or storage space requirements, and the number and location of "branches" to be opened.[2]

---

[2]Ibid.

Construction and External Appearance

Is the construction of the building sound? Have an expert look it over before you buy or lease the property. Beyond the soundness of construction, does the building have attractive external and internal appearances? The physical appearance of the building provides customers with their first impression of a business. This is especially true in retail businesses. Many retailers provide the customer with identical building appearance as they expand (e.g., fast food restaurants and motels). Is the appearance of the building consistent with the image of your business? How many people would go to a retailer who had her office in a mobile home?

The small retailer must recognize the importance of creating the proper image for the store and how the shop's layout and physical facilities influence this image. The store's external appearance contributes significantly to identifying its personality in the consumer's mind. Should the building project an exclusive image or an economical one? Is the atmosphere informal and relaxed or formal and businesslike? Physical facilities send these messages to customers.

Be careful to ensure that the exterior and interior colors are both pleasing and effectively coordinated with each other and surrounding buildings. Most businesses do not wish to have a building so unusual that it draws negative attention. Individuality and good taste can harmonize to develop a good reputation for the business. Businesses whose appearance draws undue attention are more than likely eyesores which cause city building officials and nearby businesses and residents to complain. The reputation of the business can hardly be enhanced by such an image. The trend in recent years has been toward more function-oriented buildings due to the high construction costs.

A storefront should look fresh and clean. There are three basic storefront designs available to the small retailer (see figure 11–3): the straight front; the angled front; and the arcade front.[3] As the name implies, the straight front runs parallel to the street or walkway. Although this design maximizes interior selling space, it is not an especially attractive configuration because of its monotony. An angled front breaks the monotony of the straight front and funnels customers into the store. This design makes window shopping easier by providing the customer with a better view of display merchandise. It does, however, reduce interior selling space. The arcade front uses a variety of window and door designs. It provides more display window space and offers window shoppers protection from the elements. It also contributes to a unique image for the store. Its primary disadvantages include increased construction costs and reduced space available for selling activities.

For retail establishments, a glass front en-

hances the display of merchandise. Potential customers can look in and see either the window display or, in many cases, the overall nature of the business. Window shoppers should be drawn into the store by the ability to see a sample of the merchandise offered. All displays of merchandise should be neat and attractive and should avoid a cluttered and unorganized appearance. The merchandise should be at eye level to waist level to avoid the need for customers to stoop or bend.

All entrances to retail stores should invite entry. Large doors and attractive displays that are set back from the doorway can lure customers into a business. Retailers with heavy traffic flows—supermarkets or drugstores—often install automatic doors to ensure a smooth traffic flow into and out of the store. A retailer should remove any barriers that interfere with easy access to the store. Broken sidewalks, sagging steps, mud puddles, sticking or heavy doors, and other negative factors create obstacles that might discourage potential customers. Entrances should be lighted to create a friendly atmosphere that encourages entry.

Entrances should be convenient for handicapped persons. For years, businesses seemed to have overlooked the needs of the handicapped. Today's business managers are modifying existing structures to accommodate handicapped people. Besides being socially responsible, it is good business to provide such facilities. Handicapped customers may trade exclusively with those businesses that remove barriers to their mobility.

An owner must pay close attention to his business sign. Most communities have sign regulations, so businesses must check on the limitations local regulations impose. For instance, one resort community limits the size, location, and composition of business signs to avoid a sloppy, cluttered appearance. As a communications media, signs should be visible, simple, and clear. They help customers find your business, tell them what you sell, and create an image for your business. The most common problems associated with ineffective signs are that they

---

[3]Dale M. Lewison and M. Wayne DeLozier, *Retailing: Principles and Practices* (Columbus, Ohio: Merrill Publishing Company, 1982), pp. 161–62.

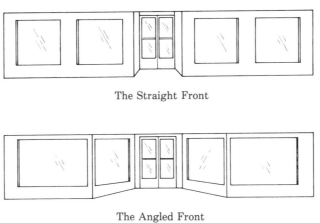

The Straight Front

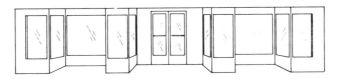

The Angled Front

The Arcade Front

FIGURE 11–3 Storefront configurations.

Source: From Lewison and DeLozier, *Retailing,* p. 162. Used with permission.

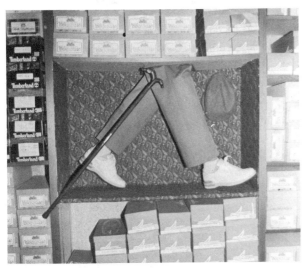 

Displays should be neat and attractive, not clustered and disorganized. (Photo by Jill R. Johnson.)

Unique signs can make a small business stand out. (Photo by Jill R. Johnson.)

are illegible, poorly designed, improperly located, in poor condition, and have color schemes which are either unattractive or are difficult to read.

The small business owner should not adopt a "second class" attitude toward store design just because his shop is small. Effective store design can give a business a competitive edge.

Building Interiors

Like exterior considerations, the functional aspects of building interiors are very important and require careful evaluation. Designing a functional, efficient interior is not easy. Technology has changed drastically the way employees, customers, and the environment interact with one another. Piecing together an effective layout is *not* a haphazard process. Ergonomics, the science of adapting work and working conditions to complement employees and to suit customers, is an integral part of a successful design. For example, chairs, desks, and table heights that allow people to work comfortably can help employees perform their jobs faster and more easily.[4] Design experts claim that improved lighting, better acoustics, and proper climate control benefit the company as well as employees. Paying attention to such details "can pay off in more productivity and higher efficiency," claims one designer.[5]

Are the floors sufficiently strong to hold the business' equipment, inventories, and personnel? Strength is an especially critical factor for manufacturing firms that use heavy equipment. When multiple floors exist, are the upper floors anchored as solidly as the primary floor? Can inventory be moved safely and easily from one area of the plant to another? Is the floor space adequate for safe and efficient movement of goods and people? Consider the cost of maintaining the floors. Hardwood floors may be extremely attractive, but require expensive and time-consuming maintenance. Carpeted floors may be extremely attractive in a retail business but may be totally impractical for a manufacturing firm. The small business manager must consider both the utility and attractiveness of flooring for his business. Factors to consider are initial cost; durability and maintenance requirements; attractiveness; and, if important, effectiveness in reducing noise.

---

[4]Sanford L. Jacobs, "Industrial Hygienists Increase Firm's Output and Efficiency," *The Wall Street Journal,* March 5, 1985, p. 33.
[5]Ibid.

The Business Sign

One of the most efficient and effective methods of communicating with customers is the business sign. Signs tell potential customers who you are and what you are selling. The American public is very mobile, and signs are the most direct method of reaching potential customers. An effective business sign reaches the group of customers most likely to make actual purchases.

Signs offer a number of advantages to the small business manager:

- Signs are always on the job; they repeat a message 24 hours a day, seven days a week.
- Signs are commonly read. Many people read business signs without realizing it.
- Signs are inexpensive communication devices. The cost-per-thousand persons reached for a sign is lower than that of many other media.
- Signs are easy to use and easy to change.

What makes a good sign? After a time, a sign becomes a part of the surrounding scenery, and the owner should consider changing some of its features to retain its effectiveness. Animated parts and unusual designs can attract interest. A sign must be large enough to read, given the location and speed of surrounding traffic arteries. The message should be short, clear, and simple to be most effective. The sign must be legible both in daylight and at night. Proper illumination is a must. Before constructing a sign, the owner must consider its energy consumption.

A sign is exposed to the elements throughout the year and must be maintained properly to retain its effectiveness. Depending on the material used, the life of the average sign ranges from five to eleven years.

Generally, an effective sign will complement the environment, create a favorable business image, and reach potential customers.

Signs should be accurate. Otherwise, potential customers might get the wrong "massage." (Photo by Mark King.)

Source: Adapted from Karen E. and R.J. Claus, U.S. Small Business Administration, *Signs and Your Business,* Small Marketers Aid No. 161, Washington, 1979, pp. 2–8.

Like floors, walls and ceilings must be both functional and attractive. On the functional side, walls and ceilings should be fireproof and soundproof. Are the colors of walls and ceilings compatible, and do they create an attractive atmosphere? Retail stores should have a light and bright appearance. Ceilings should therefore be done in light colors to reflect the store's lighting.

Walls may range from purely functional unpainted cement block in a factory to wallpapered showpieces in expensive restaurants and exclusive shops. Wall coverings are traditionally expensive, and should be considered only when the additional cost will enhance the sale of goods or services.

Lights and Fixtures

Good lighting allows employees to work at maximum efficiency. Proper lighting is measured by what is ideal for the job being done. Proper lighting in a factory may be quite different from that required in an office or retail shop. Retailers often use creative lighting to attract customers to a specific display. Jewelry stores provide excellent examples of how lighting can be used to display merchandise.

Lighting is often an inexpensive investment when considering its impact on the overall appearance of the business. Few people seek out businesses that are dimly lit because they convey an image of distrust. The use of natural and artificial light in combination can give a business an open and cheerful look. Many restaurant chains have added "greenhouse glass" additions to accomplish this.

Color Coordination and Interior Design of Retail Shops

Color not only can brighten the appearance of a retail store, but it also can create desired illusions. In general, "cool" colors tend to be relaxing while "warm" colors tend to be stimulating. Bright colors and bold contrasts produce more stimulating environments than do pastel shades with little or no contrast. Table 11–8 describes typical consumer perceptions of colors.

A store which lacks size can use darker colors on the rear walls to create the illusion of a wider shop. Mirrors on one wall can produce the illusion of a wider or longer shop.

The age of the building also influences the owner's choice of colors. Older buildings are not suited to deep, intense colors; these shades conflict with the classic architectural styles of these traditional structures. Deep colors are more appropriate

TABLE 11–8 Perceptions of colors.

Cool Colors		
Blue	*Green*	*Violet*
Coolness	Coolness	Coolness
Aloofness	Restful	Retiring
Fidelity	Peace	Dignity
Calmness	Freshness	Rich
Piety	Growth	
Masculine	Softness	
Assurance	Richness	
Sadness	Go	
Warm Colors		
Red	*Yellow*	*Orange*
Love	Sunlight	Sunlight
Romance	Warmth	Warmth
Sex	Cowardice	Openness
Courage	Openness	Friendliness
Danger	Friendliness	Gaiety
Fire	Gaiety	Glory
Sinful	Glory	
Warmth	Brightness	
Excitement	Caution	
Vigor		
Cheerfulness		
Enthusiasm		
Stop		

Source: Dale M. Lewison and M. Wayne De Lozier, *Retailing: Principles and Practices* (Columbus, Ohio: Merrill Publishing Company, 1982), p. 154.

Efficient Lighting

One very important aspect of interior store design is the light source the small business owner chooses. Selecting the most efficient light source can greatly reduce the cost of operating the business. There are a number of types of light that the manager can select to get the job done.

Incandescent light is most commonly used in homes. The lamp is small and can focus its beam to cover a specific area. But incandescent lamps are the least efficient and most expensive method of lighting. As a result, most stores use them only to highlight specific areas or displays.

Fluorescent light is very efficient and economical. Also, because it can illuminate large areas, this lighting source is practical for use throughout the store. These lamps are versatile since they can be purchased in a variety of colors.

Metal halide light (tungsten, halogen) is very efficient, producing the greatest amount of light for the cost of power used. Traditionally, these lights have been used for exterior purposes, but recent advances have made them practical for interior use.

The following table compares the life spans of various light sources.

Light Source	Life Span
Incandescent	750 hours
Fluorescent	18,000 hours
Metal halide	3,000 hours

Light intensity is measured in footcandles. The following offers guidelines for lighting specific items.

Item	Footcandles
Furniture	30–60
Clothing	40–50
Self-service	75–100
Displays	100–200
China, silver, etc.	100–300
Show windows	200–400

Generally, merchandise should receive three times as much light as circulation areas in the store. Displays should have roughly five times as much illumination as merchandise.

Placement of light fixtures is also important. Generally, the space between ceiling light fixtures should be less than the floor-to-ceiling height. Track lighting, an electrical track into which a number of light fixtures can be added, offers maximum flexibility. Track lights are normally incandescent and can be added or removed to fit the store's budget.

Source: Adapted from Herbert Berman, U.S. Small Business Administration, *Efficient Lighting in Small Stores,* Small Marketers Aid No. 157, Washington, 1979, pp. 3–8.

Store layout should invite customers to enter. (Photos by Susan Baynes.)

for newer buildings with lower ceilings and modern architectural features.

Expensive merchandise sells better when the color schemes are in grays, blues, greens, and black. Lower priced merchandise should be accented by combining yellows, oranges, and reds with white. In most cases, the retailer should avoid color shades that are too bright because they overpower and detract from the merchandise. However, some firms' merchandise and clientele are suited for louder colors. For example, shops specializing in blue jeans often cater to teenagers who appreciate bright, vibrant colors in a shopping environment. Steak houses frequently employ a great deal of red in their interiors because they rely on a high customer turnover to generate sufficient profits and red does not create a soothing atmosphere and so discourages customers from lingering after dining. Similarly, many fast food restaurants use bright colors and somewhat uncomfortable furnishings to assure high turnover.

More expensive restaurants rely on soft, soothing colors to encourage customers to linger after dining. Generally, pastel colors are best suited for overall store decor, and they add an attractive, cheerful touch to the store's interior. Darker colors can be used with pastels to highlight or accent a specific area.

VI. LAYOUT

Layout is the logical arrangement of physical facilities that provides for efficient operations. The principles of layout vary greatly depending on the type of business. In this section we will investigate how layout influences the appearance and efficiency of both retail and manufacturing businesses. Although the re-

TABLE 11–9   Classification and arrangement of merchandise in small retail stores.

Merchandise Type	How or Why Bought	Placement in Store
Impulse Goods	As result of attractive visual merchandising displays	Small store—near entrance Larger store—on main aisle
Convenience Goods	With frequency in small quantities	Easily accessible feature locations along main aisle
Necessities or Staple Goods	Because of need	Rear of one-level stores, upper floor(s) of multi-level stores (not a hard-and-fast rule)
Utility Goods	For home use—brooms, dustpans, similar items	As impulse items, up front or along main aisle
Luxury and Major Expense Items	After careful planning and considerable "shopping around"	Some distance from entrance

Source: U.S. Small Business Administration, "Small Business Location and Layout," *Administrative Management Course Program, Topic 13,* Washington, 1980, p. 6.

quirements differ dramatically, the process of analysis is similar.

Layout for Retailing

For retailers, layout is the arrangement of merchandise and its method of display. A retailer's success depends, in part, on a well-designed floor display. It should "pull" customers into the store and make it easy for them to locate merchandise, compare price, quality, and features, and ultimately make a purchase. In addition, the floor plan should take customers past displays of other items that they may buy on impulse. Retailers have always recognized that some locations within a store are superior to others. Customer traffic patterns give the owner a clue to the best location for the highest gross margin items. One retailer says, "People gravitate along certain lines, and that leads to spots where sales increase."[6] Mer-

chandise purchased on impulse and convenience goods should be located near the front of the store. Items people shop around for before buying and specialty goods will attract their own customers and should not be placed in prime space. Prime selling space should be restricted to products that carry the highest markups. Table 11–9 offers suggestions for locating merchandise in a small retail store.

Layout in a retail store evolves from a clear understanding of customers' buying habits. If customers come into the store for specific products and have a tendency to walk directly to those items, it will behoove the retailer to place complementary products in their path. Observing customer behavior can help the owner identify the "hot spots"—where items sell briskly—and the "cold spots"—where merchandise may sit indefinitely—in the store. By experimenting with factors such as traffic flow, lighting, aisle size, noise levels, signs, and colors, an owner can discover the most productive layout for his store. One appliance retailer discovered a hot spot near the cash register; he says, "We make sea-

[6]"Floor Display: Selling Appliances #2," *The Retail Appliance Management Series, Handbooks on the Business of Running Your Dealership,* November 1983, p. 5.

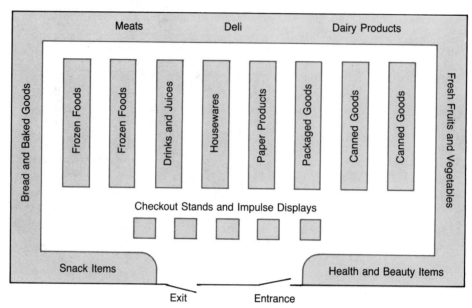

FIGURE 11-4   The grid layout.

sonal changes there. Near Christmas we put microwaves there, and in the summer, air conditioners."[7] Another appliance retailer converted a "cold spot" into an effective selling device—he changed store space into a working kitchen filled with microwaves where microwave cooking classes are conducted. "It's really a good close on the sale when we can say that we offer microwave cooking classes," he claims.[8]

Retailers have three basic layout patterns to choose from: the grid; the free-form; and the boutique. The grid layout arranges displays in rectangular fashion so that aisles are parallel. It is a formal layout that controls the traffic flow through the store. Most supermarkets and many discount stores use the grid layout because it is well suited to self-service stores. This layout uses the available selling space most efficiently, creates a neat, organized environment, and facilitates shopping by standardizing the

location of items. Figure 11-4 shows a typical grid layout.

Unlike the grid layout, the free-form layout is informal, using displays of various shapes and sizes. Its primary advantage is the relaxed, friendly shopping atmosphere it creates, which encourages customers to shop longer and increases the number of impulse purchases they make. Still, the free-form layout is not as efficient as the grid layout in using selling space, and it can create security problems if not properly planned. Figure 11-5 illustrates a free-form layout.

The boutique layout divides the store into a series of individual shopping areas, each with its own theme. It is like building a series of specialty shops into a single store. The boutique layout is more informal and can create a unique shopping environment for the customer. Department stores sometimes use this layout to develop a distinctive image for their businesses. Figure 11-6 shows a boutique layout for a small department store.

[7]Ibid. p. 7.
[8]Ibid. p. 5.

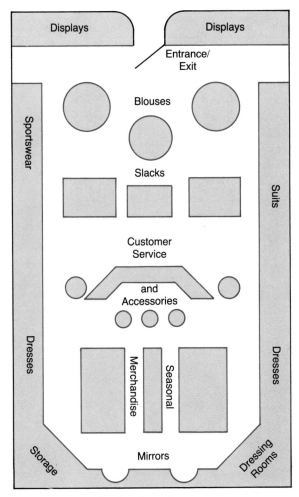

FIGURE 11–5 The free-form layout.

nique. For example, dress shirts and ties or shoes and socks can be displayed near one another.

Spacious displays provide shoppers an open view of merchandise and reduce the likelihood of shoplifting. A spacious image is preferable to a cluttered appearance.

You should separate the selling and nonselling areas of the store. Never waste valuable selling space with nonselling functions. While nonselling activities are necessary for a successful retail operation, they should not take precedence and occupy valuable selling space. Storage and office space should be located in the rear of the building. Always recognize the value of each foot of space within a retail store and locate high mark-up items in the best selling areas.

Clearly, not every portion of a small store's interior space is of equal value in generating sales revenue. Certain areas contribute more to revenue than others. The value of store space depends on floor location in a multi-story building, location with respect to aisles and walkways, and proximity to entrances. Space values decrease as their distance from the main entry-level floor increases. Selling areas on the main level contribute a greater portion to sales than those on other floors in the building because they offer greater exposure to customers than either basement or higher-level locations. Therefore, main level locations should be charged more "rent." Figure 11–7 offers one example of how rent and sales could be allocated by floors.

The layout of aisles in the store also has a major impact on the customer exposure merchandise receives. Items located on primary walkways should be assigned a higher share of rental costs and should contribute a greater portion to sales revenue than those displayed along secondary aisles. Figure 11–8 shows that high value areas are exposed to two primary aisles, medium value areas are exposed to one primary and one secondary aisle, and low value areas are exposed to two secondary aisles.

Space values also depend on their relative position to the store entrance. The farther away an area is

You should display merchandise as attractively as your budget will allow. Customer's eyes focus on displays, which tell them the type of merchandise you have to sell. It is easier for customers to relate to one display than to a rack or shelf of merchandise. Open displays of merchandise can surround the focus display, creating an attractive selling area.

Display items which complement each other together. You can make multiple sales with this tech-

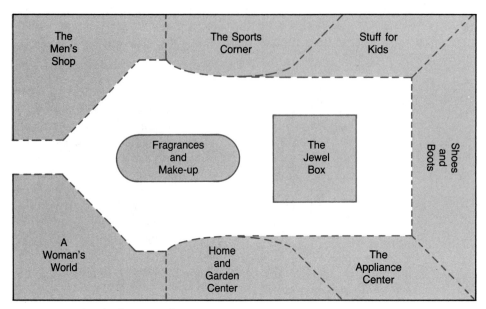

FIGURE 11–6   The boutique layout.

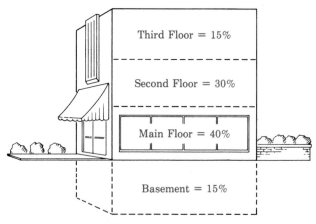

FIGURE 11–7   Rent allocation by floors.

Source: From Lewison and DeLozier, *Retailing*, p. 164. Used with permission.

Romancing the Veggies

In response to stiffer competition, grocers are taking a different tact in marketing their products. Store design and layout are the central features of the new approach. For instance, planners locate bakeries near the front door to entice customers by the smell.

Most grocers focus on specialty departments like the bakery, deli, produce, and meat counters because they produce the highest profit margins. Store designers speak about layouts in terms reminiscent of a major Hollywood production. Theatrical lighting in an otherwise dark atmosphere should "romance" shoppers through the produce department. In fact, proper lighting is a critical part of a store's ambiance. The harsh supermarket lights popular in the 1950s and '60s are no longer acceptable. Instead, soft, subdued lighting is supposed to put shoppers in a more cheerful, free-spending mood. Many states outlaw the use of colored lights to artificially brighten food colors, but a new incandescent white light that naturally brings out red colors is very popular. One planner claims the lights make produce look brighter and fresher and shoppers look ruddier and happier. But on aisles with "dry goods"—canned goods, cereal, and laundry detergent, for instance—stores turn the lights up and use warehouse shelving to create the impression that price is the store's top priority.

A&P is experimenting with all black-&-white store interiors. In that environment, "the products really start to talk," says an A&P official. The surroundings are simpler and more peaceful. "And if our customers feel at ease, they'll come back," he claims.

Many grocers put the same products in several places so shoppers will have to resist them more than once. They also put high-profit general merchandise—hardware, toys, household items—on different aisles. If they were put together on the same aisle, "the customer would never go down it," says one food store executive. Most grocers also spread the most popular items around the store so shoppers will have to pass many attractive displays of other products. That is the reason for placing staples such as milk and sugar near the rear of the store.

Grocers are not stopping here, however. They are exploring electronic voices that remind shoppers of daily specials, shopping from home by computer, and a store that is one long aisle. The major problem with the linear store, of course, is getting the shopper with his groceries from the exit back to his car, which would be parked at the entrance.

Source: Adapted from Betsy Morris, "Romanced by the Produce: How Design Sells Groceries," *The Wall Street Journal,* August 26, 1985, p. 19. Used with permission of *The Wall Street Journal,* © Dow Jones and Company. All rights reserved.

from the entrance, the lower its value. In other words, space in the front of the store has more customer traffic than the areas at the rear of the store; therefore, front space is more valuable. Another consideration is that most shoppers turn to the right upon entering a store and move around it counterclockwise. Finally, only about one-fourth of a store's customers will go more than halfway into the store. Using these characteristics, figure 11–9 illustrates space values for a typical small store layout.

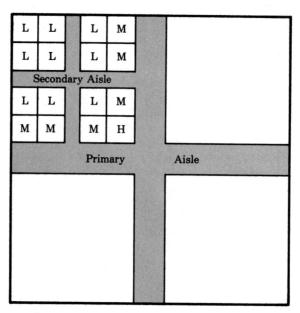

FIGURE 11–8 Rent allocation based on traffic aisles.

Source: From Lewison and DeLozier, *Retailing,* p. 165. Used with permission.

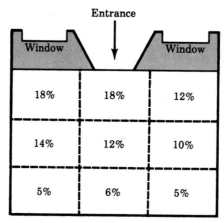

FIGURE 11–9 Space values for a small store.

Source: From Lewison and DeLozier, *Retailing,* p. 164. Used with permission.

The 4-3-2-1 Rule

The decline in value of store space from front to back of the shop is expressed in the 4-3-2-1 rule. This rule assigns 40 percent of a store's rental cost to the front quarter of the shop, 30 percent to the second quarter, 20 percent to the third quarter, and 10 percent to the final quarter. Similarly, each quarter of the store should contribute the same percentage of sales revenue.

For example, suppose that a small department store anticipates $120,000 in sales this year. Each quarter of the store should generate the following sales volume:

Front quarter	$120,000 \times 0.40 =$	$ 48,000
Second quarter	$120,000 \times 0.30 =$	36,000
Third quarter	$120,000 \times 0.20 =$	24,000
Fourth quarter	$120,000 \times 0.10 =$	12,000
Total		$120,000

Understanding the value of store space ensures proper placement of merchandise. The items placed in the "high rent" areas of the store should generate adequate sales and contribute enough to profit to justify their high value locations. Another guideline, the "front-to-back" layout, is illustrated in Small Business Report 11–7.

Facility Layout for Manufacturing

Manufacturing layout decisions take into consideration the arrangement of departments, work stations, machines, and stock-holding points within a productive facility. The general objective is to arrange these elements to assure a smooth work flow (in a production facility) or a particular traffic pattern (in a service facility or organization).

Manufacturing facilities have come under increasing scrutiny as firms attempt to improve quality, decrease inventories, and increase productivity through facilities which are integrated, flexible, and controlled. Facilities layout has a dramatic effect on product mix, product processing, and materials handling, storage, and control, as well as production volume and quality.

Factors in Manufacturing Layout Design. The way a productive facility should be arranged depends on a number of factors, including the following.

■ *Type of product,* which concerns the product design and quality standards, whether the product is produced for inventory or for order, and the physical properties such as the size of materials and products, special handling requirements, susceptibility to damage, and perishability.

■ *Type of production process,* which relates to technology used, types of materials handled, means of providing a service, and processing requirements in terms of number of operations involved and amount of interaction between departments and work centers.

■ *Economic considerations,* such as volume of production; costs of materials, machines, work stations, and labor; pattern and variability of demand; and length of permissible delays. *Space availability* within the facility itself.

Types of Layout. The basic layout types may be viewed either in terms of work flow or the function of the productive system. Looking first at work flow layouts, there are three basic types that may be used separately or in combination. These three—product, process, and fixed position—are differentiated according to their applicability to different conditions of volume and demand.

Product Layouts. In a product (or line) layout, workers and equipment are arranged according to

267

the sequence of operations performed with the product or customer (see figure 11–10). Conceptually, the flow is an unbroken line from raw material input or customer arrival to finished goods or customer's departure. This type of layout is applicable to rigid-flow, high-volume, continuous- or mass-production operations, or when the service or product is highly standard. Automobile assembly plants, paper mills, and oil refineries are examples of product layouts.

Product layouts offer the advantages of lower material handling costs; simplified tasks that can be done with low-cost, unskilled labor; reduced amounts of work-in-process inventory; and relatively simplified production control activities. All units are routed along the same fixed path, and scheduling consists primarily of setting a production rate.

Disadvantages of product layouts are their inflexibility, monotony of job tasks, high fixed investment in specialized equipment, and heavy interdependence of all operations. A breakdown in one machine or at one work station can idle the entire line. Such a layout also requires the owner to duplicate many pieces of equipment in the manufacturing facility, and for a small firm the cost can be prohibitive.

Process Layouts.   In a process or functional layout workers or equipment are grouped according to the general function they perform, without regard to any particular product or customer (see figure 11–11). Process layouts are applicable when production runs are short; when demand shows considerable variation and the costs of holding finished goods inventory are high; or when the service or product is customized.

Process layouts have the advantages of being flexible to do custom work and promoting job satisfaction by offering employees diverse and challenging tasks. Its disadvantages are the higher costs of materials handling, more skilled labor, lower productivity, and more complex production control. Because the work flow is intermittent, each job must be individually routed through the system, scheduled at the various work centers, and its status monitored.

Fixed Position Layouts.   In fixed position layouts labor and materials are brought to the location where the work is done. The product, by virtue of its bulk or weight, remains at one location. Aircraft assembly shops and shipyards typify this kind of layout.

Function Layouts.   Many layouts are designed with more than one objective or function in mind, and therefore combinations of the various layouts are common. For example, a supermarket, though primarily arranged on the basis of marketing, is partly a

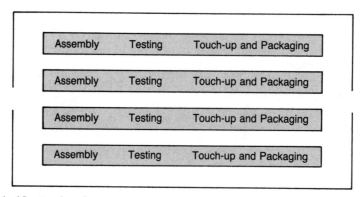

FIGURE 11–10   Product layout.

Layout and Productivity

Can plant and office layout have an impact on employee productivity? Research answers with a resounding "Yes." For example, one study conducted by the Buffalo Organization for Social and Technical Innovation concludes that good office design can improve managerial productivity by over $1,000 per person per year. The study also finds that proper lighting and adequate privacy are more important to employees than room temperature.

Source: Adapted from "Business Bulletin," *The Wall Street Journal,* October 19, 1982, p. 1, with permission of *The Wall Street Journal,* © Dow Jones & Company, Inc., 1982. All rights reserved.

SMALL BUSINESS REPORT 11–8

storage layout; a cafeteria represents not only a layout by marketing function but also by work flow (a food assembly line); and a factory may arrange its machinery in a process-oriented layout and perform assembly operations on a product-line basis.

Designing Layouts. The starting point in layout design is determining how and in what sequence product parts or service tasks flow together. This can be accomplished by developing assembly charts and process flow charts. Given the tasks and their sequence, plus knowledge of the volume of products to be produced or of customers to be served, the owner can analyze space and equipment needs to get an idea of the demands of the facility. When a product or line layout is used, these demands have precedence, and equipment and work stations are arranged to fit the production tasks and their sequence. With a process or functional layout, different products or customers with different needs place demands on the facility. Rather than a single best flow, there may be one flow for each product or cus-

tomer, and compromises are necessary. As a result, any one product or customer may not get the "ideal" layout.

Analysis of Production Layouts. Although there is no general procedure for analyzing the numerous interdependent factors that enter into layout design, specific layout problems lend themselves to detailed analysis. Two important criteria for selecting and designing a layout are worker effectiveness and materials handling costs.

The layout should be designed to improve job satisfaction and to use workers at the highest skill level for which they are being paid. This applies just as much to an office layout, where an engineer may spend half of a working day delivering blueprints, as it does to a plant layout, where a machinist travels a long distance for tools.

Materials handling cost can be lowered by using layouts that are designed so that product flow is automated whenever possible, and flow distances and times are minimized. The extent of automation

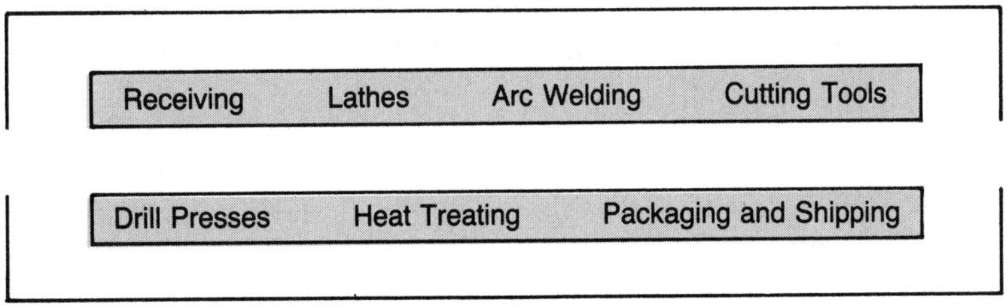

FIGURE 11–11   Process layout.

269

depends on the level of technology and amount of capital available, as well as behavioral considerations of employees. Flow distances and times are usually minimized by locating sequential processing activities or interrelated departments in adjacent areas. The following features are important to a good manufacturing layout.

1. Planned materials flow pattern
2. Straight-line layout where possible
3. Straight, clear-marked aisles
4. Backtracking kept to a minimum
5. Related operations close together
6. Minimum of in-process inventory
7. Easy adjustment to changing conditions
8. Minimum materials handling distances
9. Minimum of manual handling
10. No unnecessary rehandling of materials
11. Minimum handling between operations
12. Materials delivered to production employees
13. Materials efficiently removed from the work area
14. Materials handling being done by indirect labor
15. Orderly materials handling and storage
16. Good housekeeping

Product Layout Design. Arranging a product flow layout requires fitting the equipment and work stations needed into the available facilities in the proper sequence, giving due consideration to any special requirements such as environmental control, materials handling capability, safety, or interfaces with other product or service lines. Several design rules have evolved to help the planner lay out a product flow line. The most basic rule states that direct paths should be used whenever possible. Such paths eliminate backtracking and crosshauling. Other design rules suggest minimizing walking, using mechanical handling devices, and placing closely related activities near one another.

Process Layout Design. In process layouts, different products do not require the same operations in the same environment. In an auto repair shop, for example, a car may need a tune-up, oil change, wheel bal-

ancing, brake work, or some combination of these. With such varied requirements resulting in varied paths, and different amounts of time needed in various work stations or departments, process layouts are usually designed with the aim of minimizing the material handling costs, transportation costs, or time. A number of quantitative techniques and computer programs have been developed to help planners design such layouts.

Detailed Layout Design. Once the type of layout is decided and space relationships established, detailed layout analysis is required. This includes sizing work stations; placing machines and equipment; determining space requirements for inventory at various work stations; determining the space of product lines and the distances between stations or machines; and locating support facilities, such as equipment and toolrooms, stockrooms, rest rooms, and waiting areas. Scale models with moveable parts or templates on scale drawings are useful in finalizing layouts.

VII. SUMMARY

For a small business the location decision is critical because of its lasting effects. Criteria for a good location depend on the nature of the business. A good approach to choosing a location follows this pattern:

1. Select the region
2. Select the state
3. Select the city
4. Select the specific site

Too many owners select a location by chance; the most common reason for selecting a location is a noticed vacancy. Planning and location analysis seldom enter the process.

To choose the proper region, you must evaluate the general demographic characteristics of the population. Government publications and a number of the U.S. Commerce Department's statistics can provide a wealth of valuable resource data.

In selecting the state and community within the

specific region, you should consider proximity to markets, proximity to raw materials, labor supply needs, business climate, wage rates, population trends, local regulations, competition, compatibility, transportation, and public services.

The final step in the location decision is choosing the specific site. For a retailer, it involves determining the trading area—the geographic region from which the business will draw its clientele. He must consider how far people will travel to purchase the firm's products. Of course, the retailer must also consider the degree of competition in the local area and the convenience of the area's transportation networks. Psychological and social barriers, as well as physical barriers, can limit the size of a trading area also.

Traffic studies can be very beneficial in evaluating a specific site. Traffic studies must consider the characteristics and number of the passersby. The other important consideration is the number of failures occurring at that specific site.

For a service firm that makes calls on its customers, location selection is usually not a crucial element for success. Other businesses whose clients call on them must be concerned with finding a convenient and attractive location.

A manufacturer's location decision is strongly affected by local zoning ordinances. Some regions offer industrial parks specifically designed to attract manufacturers. Two critical factors for a manufacturer in choosing a location are the reliability and the cost of transportation for raw materials.

Census data, available free of charge to the small business owner, can be of tremendous value in evaluating a particular site. Most entrepreneurs are amazed at the quantity and detail of the information found in census publications. Using this data can help an entrepreneur pinpoint the best location for a new business.

A small firm's physical facilities and layout can enhance or restrict its ability to serve customer needs and generate a profit. One way to achieve a layout that is tailored to the small company's specific

needs is to build a new facility. While building is usually the most expensive option, it may offer the advantage of reducing operating costs over time. A new building also creates a positive image in the customer's mind. Another option is to buy an existing building and make necessary modifications. This method can also be expensive, but purchasing commercial property can be an investment. A primary disadvantage of building or buying real property is the limited mobility that results. Leasing does not require a large initial cash outlay, which puts less strain on limited start-up funds. The primary disadvantages of leasing include the possibility of less termination, rising lease payments, and limited freedom to remodel the facility.

The building must be large enough to accommodate normal business operations. Selecting a facility that is too small and cannot be expanded may force the owner to make several expensive moves as the business grows.

The building should be structurally sound and attractive. Often, this determines the customer's impression of the business, and the building's appearance must be consistent with the firm's image. The store front should be fresh and clean; it should offer customers a clear view of the merchandise for sale, inviting them to enter. There should be no barriers which discourage customers from entering the store. The building should provide easy access for handicapped customers.

Signs are an important part of a business' exterior environment. Signs tell customers who you are, where you are, and what you sell. They should be attractive and properly maintained.

Evaluating the building's interior involves many of the same considerations as analyzing its exterior. Floors should be sturdy, durable, and easy to maintain. The owner should check to see if walls and ceilings are soundproof and fireproof. Lighting should be bright enough to get the job done but not so bright that it glares or detracts from the merchandise being displayed.

Color can brighten the store's overall appearance and can create certain images and impressions in the consumer's mind. The manager can use certain colors to complement the merchandise displayed. Generally, the retailer should avoid bright colors that overpower the merchandise.

Layout for a retail store depends on the owner's understanding of customers' buying habits. Retailers have three basic layout principles to follow—the grid, the free-form, and the boutique.

Certain areas of the store represent a greater value than others. Main-level selling areas contribute more to sales than sites on other levels. Locations at the intersection of main shopping corridors provide greater customer exposure and are more valuable. The farther a selling area is from the store's entrance, the less valuable it is.

Complementary goods should be displayed together. Nonselling areas should be kept separate from selling activities and should not infringe on valuable selling space. Impulse and convenience items should be placed at the front, while specialty and shopping goods belong at the rear or upstairs of the store.

The goal of manufacturing layout is to create a smooth, efficient work flow. In planning work flow, three layout types exist—product layout, process layout, and fixed position.

Two key factors to consider in planning layouts are worker effectiveness and materials handling costs. Models, diagrams, and templates are useful in planning layout.

STUDENT INVOLVEMENT PROJECTS

1. Select a specific type of business you would like to go into one day and use census data and Commerce Department reports from the local library to choose a specific site for the business in the local region. What location factors are critical to the success of this business? Would it be likely to succeed in your hometown?

2. Interview a sample of local small business owners. How did they decide on their particular locations? What are the positive and negative features of the locations?

3. If you are located in a city which has a traffic engineer, request data about automobile traffic on the major business sectors of your city and discuss how each road or highway brings potential customers in contact with certain stores.

4. Select a manufacturing operation, a wholesale business, and a retail store, and evaluate their layouts using the guidelines presented in this chapter. What changes would you recommend? Why? Does the layout contribute to a more effective operation?

DISCUSSION QUESTIONS

1. How do most small business owners choose a location? Is this wise?

2. What factors should a manager consider when evaluating a region in which to locate? Where is such data available?

3. Outline the factors important to the selection of a state in which to locate.

4. What factors should a seafood processing plant, a beauty shop, and an exclusive jewelry store consider in choosing a location? List factors for each type of business.

5. What intangible factors might enter into the en-

trepreneur's location decision?

6. What are zoning laws? How do they affect the location decision?

7. What is a trade area? What determines a small retailer's trading area?

8. Why is it important to discover more than just the number of passersby in a traffic count?

9. How is the location decision for a manufacturer different from that of a retailer?

10. What type of information can the entrepreneur collect from census data?

11. Why may a cheap location not be the best location?

12. Summarize the advantages and disadvantages of building, buying, and leasing a building.

13. Why is it costly for a small firm to choose a location that is too small?

14. Describe the three basic storefront designs available to the small retailer.

15. What function does a small firm's sign serve? What are the characteristics of an effective business sign?

16. Why is good lighting not necessarily bright lighting?

17. Explain the statement: "Not every portion of a small store's interior space is of equal value in generating sales revenue." What areas are most valuable?

18. How can a small retailer use a knowledge of store space value to increase sales?

19. Explain the characteristics of the grid layout, the free-form layout, and the boutique layout.

20. What are the primary considerations for the manufacturing layout?

21. Describe the differences among product, process, and fixed position layouts.

SECTION FIVE

CONTROLLING THE SMALL BUSINESS: TECHNIQUES FOR ENHANCING PROFITABILITY

Purchasing and Inventory Control

12

Goods well bought are goods half sold.

Anonymous

You never know what is enough until you know what is more than enough.
William Blake

Great American Axiom: Some is good, more is better. Too much is just right.
Anonymous

Upon completion of this chapter, you will be able to:

- Define purchasing and its primary objectives.

- Identify and explain the five key elements of the small firm's purchasing plan.

- Explain the Economic Order Quantity (EOQ) analysis as a technique to help determine the proper level of stock.

- Differentiate among the three types of purchase discounts many vendors offer.

- Illustrate why it pays to take advantage of purchase discounts.

- Explain the concept of the firm's reorder point and show how it is computed.

- Identify various sources for locating suppliers.

- Explain the development of a vendor rating scale using key supply factors.

- Describe the importance of inventory control to the small company's profits.

- Explain the "80/20 rule" and its application to inventory management.

- Define a perpetual inventory system and explain four common variations of such a system.

- Identify the advantages and disadvantages of the visual inventory control system.

- Explain the value of partial inventory control systems.

- Describe the operation of an ABC inventory control system.

- Highlight popular "Just-in-Time" inventory control techniques.

- Explain the importance of taking a physical inventory count.

- Outline several techniques for minimizing inventory costs.

Purchasing is an important function in many businesses because it determines the firm's ability to sell a quality product or service at a reasonable price. Depending on the type of business involved, the amounts spent by the purchasing department range from $0.25 to $0.85 for every $1.00 of sales revenue. Naturally, service companies spend a smaller portion

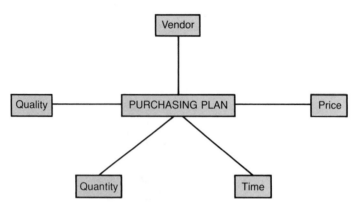

FIGURE 12–1   The elements of a purchasing plan.

of each sales dollar on purchases than manufacturers, wholesalers, or retailers. Whatever the business, purchasing is a vital management function. Careful purchasing can minimize not only the cost of goods sold but also the costs of supplies and fixed assets. One study suggests that a 1 percent savings in purchasing can generate as much profit as a 10 percent increase in sales.

I. WHAT IS PURCHASING?

Purchasing involves the acquisition of needed materials, supplies, services, and equipment of the right quality, in the proper quantities, for reasonable prices, at the appropriate time, from the right vendor or supplier. A major objective of purchasing is to acquire enough stock to ensure smooth, uninterrupted production or sales and to see that the merchandise is delivered on time. Clearly the purchasing plan must address the trade-off between the quality of merchandise and its price. Finally, the purchasing plan must establish the criteria for determining the "best" supplier, considering such factors as reliability, service, and cooperation.

The purchasing program is closely related to the other functional areas of the small business operation—production, marketing, engineering, accounting. A purchasing plan should recognize this interaction and help integrate the purchasing function into the total organization. The small company's purchasing plan should focus on the five key elements of purchasing: quality; quantity; price; time; and vendor (see figure 12–1).

Quality

The small business manager must purchase items of quality high enough to meet customer or production requirements, but not so high that they exceed specifications and create excessive costs. Because of this quality/cost trade-off, a small business may not always require "high" quality merchandise and materials. Also, if customers are unable to discern the extra quality built into a product, they are not likely to pay a higher price for it. For example, a manufacturer of stereo equipment that purchases extra-quality speakers may find that customers cannot distinguish the difference in sound and are not willing to pay extra for an unidentifiable characteristic.

If quality is not synonymous with perfection, then what does it mean? For the typical business owner, a quality product or service is one that conforms to predetermined standards and specifications. So the primary objective in purchasing quality merchandise should be to obtain the product or service that most effectively serves the purpose for which it is purchased. A product or service that cannot meet its purpose is no bargain at any price! Similarly, purchasing goods or services that exceed specifications without justification is a waste of money. Clearly, the purchasing function can save the owner a great deal of money if it is managed properly.

Quantity

The typical small business has its largest investment in inventory. But an investment in inventory is not profitable because dollars return nothing until the inventory is sold. In a sense, the small firm's inventory is its largest noninterest-bearing "account." The owner must focus on controlling this investment and on maintaining proper inventory levels.

A primary objective of this portion of the purchasing plan is to generate an adequate turnover of merchandise by purchasing proper quantities. For example, maintaining extra inventory means that an excessive amount of the company's capital is tied up in inventory, which limits the firm's working capital and exerts pressure on its cash flows. Also, the firm risks the danger of being "stuck" with spoiled or obsolete merchandise, an extremely serious problem for many small businesses. Excess inventory also takes up valuable storage or selling space that could be used for items with higher turnover rates and more profit potential. On the other hand, maintaining too little inventory can be extremely costly. The owner will be forced to reorder merchandise frequently, escalating total inventory costs. Also, inventory "stockouts" will occur when customer demand exceeds the firm's supply of merchandise, causing customer ill will. Persistent stockouts are inconvenient for customers, and many eventually will choose to shop elsewhere.

The Economic Order Quantity (EOQ). Clearly, the small business must maintain enough inventory to meet customer orders, but not so much that storage costs and inventory investment are excessive. The analytical techniques used to determine economic order quantities (EOQ) will help the manager compute the amount of stock to purchase with each

order or to produce with each production run to minimize total inventory costs. To compute the proper amount of stock to order or to produce, the small business owner must first determine the three principal elements of total inventory costs: the cost of the units; the holding (or carrying) cost; and the setup (or ordering) cost.

Cost of Units. The cost of the units is simply the number of units demanded for a particular time period multiplied by the cost per unit. Suppose that a small manufacturer of lawnmowers forecasts demand for the upcoming year to be 100,000 mowers. He needs to order enough wheels at $1.55 each to supply the production department. So, he computes

$$\text{cost of units} = D \times C$$

where D = annual demand
C = cost of a single unit

In this example,

$$D = 100,000 \text{ mowers} \times 4 \text{ wheels}$$
$$= 400,000 \text{ wheels}$$
$$C = \$1.55/\text{wheel}$$
$$\text{cost of units} = D \times C$$
$$= 400,000 \text{ wheels} \times \$1.55$$
$$= \$620,000$$

Holding (Carrying) Costs. The typical costs of holding inventory include the costs of storage, insurance, taxes, interest, depreciation, spoilage, obsolescence, and pilferage. The expense involved in physically storing the items in inventory is usually substantial, especially if the inventories are large. The owner may have to rent or build additional warehousing facilities, pushing the cost of storing the inventory even higher. The firm may also incur expenses in transferring items into and out of inventory. The cost of storage also includes the expense of operating the facility (e.g., heating, lighting, refrigeration), as well as the depreciation, taxes, and interest on the building. Generally, the larger the firm's average inventory, the greater its storage cost.

Most small business owners purchase insurance on their inventories to shift the risk of fire, theft, flood, and other natural disasters to the insurer. The premiums paid for this coverage also are included in the cost of holding inventory.

Taxes on the value of stock held in inventory also represent a cost to the small business owner. Many retailers employ end-of-the-year inventory close-out sales to avoid paying taxes on a large stockpile of merchandise.

Many small business owners fail to recognize the interest expense associated with carrying large inventories. In many cases, the interest expense is evident when the firm borrows money to purchase inventory. But a less obvious, although important, interest expense is the opportunity cost associated with investing in inventory. In other words, the money invested in inventory (a noninterest-bearing investment) could have been used for some other purpose, such as plant expansion, research and development, or reducing debt. Thus, the cost of independent financing of inventory is the cost of forgoing the opportunity to use these funds elsewhere. A substantial inventory investment means that a large amount of money is tied up unproductively.

Depreciation costs represent the reduced value of inventory over time. Some businesses are strongly influenced by the depreciation of inventory. For example, a small auto dealer's inventory is subject to depreciation because models left over from one year must be sold at reduced prices.

Spoilage, obsolescence, and pilferage also add to the costs of holding inventory. Some small firms, especially those which deal in fad merchandise, assume an extremely high risk of obsolescence.

Setup (Ordering) Costs. The various expenses incurred in actually ordering materials and inventory, or in setting up the production line to manufacturer them, determine the level of setup or ordering costs of a product. The costs of obtaining materials and inventory typically include preparing purchase orders; analyzing and choosing vendors; processing, handling, and expediting orders; receiving and in-

specting items; and performing all the required accounting and clerical functions. Even if the small company produces its own supply of goods, it encounters most of these same expenses. Usually, ordering costs are relatively fixed, regardless of the quantity ordered.

Setup or ordering cost is found by multiplying the number of orders made per year (or the number of production runs per year) by the cost of placing a single order (or the cost of setting up a single production run). Using the earlier lawnmower manufacturing example, where the annual requirement is 400,000 wheels per year and the cost to place an order is $9.00, to illustrate ordering costs:

$$\text{setup (ordering) cost} = \frac{D}{Q} \times S$$

where D = annual demand
Q = quantity of inventory ordered (EOQ)
S = setup (ordering) cost for a single run (or order)

The greater the quantity ordered, the smaller the number of orders placed. This relationship is shown in table 12–1.

TABLE 12–1 Economic order quantity and ordering cost.

If Q is	Number of Orders Per Year, D/Q	Ordering (setup) Cost, D/Q × S
500	800	$7,200
1,000	400	3,600
2,000	200	1,800
3,000	134	1,206
4,000	100	900
5,000	80	720
6,000	67	603
7,000	58	522
8,000	50	450
9,000	45	405
10,000	40	360

Solving for EOQ. Clearly, if carrying costs were the only expense involved in obtaining inventory, the small business manager would purchase the smallest number of units possible in each order to minimize the cost of holding the inventory. For example, if the lawnmower manufacturer purchased one wheel per order, carrying cost would be minimized:

$$\text{carrying cost} = \frac{Q}{2} \times H$$

$$= \frac{1}{2} \times 1.25$$

$$= \$0.625$$

but his ordering cost would be outrageous:

$$\text{ordering cost} = \frac{D}{Q} \times S$$

$$= \frac{400,000}{1} \times 9$$

$$= \$3,600,000$$

Obviously, this is not the small manufacturer's ideal solution!

Similarly, if ordering costs were the only expense involved in procuring inventory, the small business manager would purchase the largest number of units possible in order to minimize the cost of ordering. In our example, if the lawnmower manufacturer purchased 400,000 wheels per order, ordering cost would be minimized:

$$\text{ordering cost} = \frac{D}{Q} \times S$$

$$= \frac{400,000}{400,000} \times 9$$

$$= \$9$$

but his carrying cost would be tremendously high:

$$\text{carrying cost} = \frac{Q}{2} \times H$$

$$= \frac{400,000}{2} \times 1.25$$

$$= \$250,000$$

A quick inspection shows that neither of these solutions minimizes the total cost of the manufacturer's inventory. As indicated in the last section, total cost is composed of the cost of the units, carrying costs, and ordering costs:

$$\text{total cost} = (D \times C) + \left(\frac{Q}{2} \times H\right) + \left(\frac{D}{Q} \times S\right)$$

These costs are graphed in figure 12–2. Notice that as the quantity ordered increases, the ordering costs decrease and the carrying costs increase.

The economic order quantity (EOQ) formula simply balances the ordering costs and the carrying costs of the small business owner's inventory so that total costs are minimized. Table 12–2 summarizes the total costs for various values of Q for our lawnmower manufacturer.

As table 12–2 and figure 12–2 illustrate, the EOQ formula locates the minimum point on the total cost curve, which occurs where the cost of carrying inventory $(Q/2 \times H)$ equals the cost of ordering inventory $(D/Q \times S)$. If the small business places the smallest number of orders possible per year, its ordering cost is minimized, but its carrying cost is maximized. Conversely, if the firm orders the smallest number of units possible per order, its carrying cost is minimized, but its ordering cost is maximized. Total inventory cost is minimized when carrying costs and ordering costs are balanced.

Let us return to our lawnmower manufacturer and compute its economic order quantity (EOQ):

$$D = 400,000 \text{ wheels}$$
$$H = \$1.25 \text{ per wheel per year}$$
$$S = \$9.00 \text{ per order}$$
$$C = \$1.55 \text{ per wheel}$$

$$\text{EOQ} = \sqrt{\frac{2 \times D \times S}{H}}$$

$$= \sqrt{\frac{2 \times 400,000 \times 9.00}{1.25}}$$

$$= 2,400 \text{ wheels}$$

To minimize total inventory cost, the lawnmower manufacturer should order 2,400 wheels at a time.

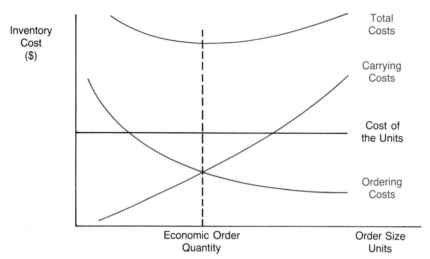

FIGURE 12–2   Inventory costs.

Further,

$$\text{number of orders per year} = \frac{D}{Q}$$
$$= \frac{400,000}{2,400}$$
$$= 166.67$$

This manufacturer will place approximately 167 orders this year at a total cost of $623,000, computed as follows:

$$\text{total cost} = (D \times C) + \left(\frac{Q}{2} \times H \right) + \left(\frac{D}{Q} \times S \right)$$
$$= (400,000 \times 1.55) + \left(\frac{2,400}{2} \times 1.25 \right) + \left(\frac{400,000}{2,400} \times 9.00 \right)$$
$$= \quad \$620,000 \quad + \quad \$1,500 \quad + \quad \$1,500$$
$$= \$623,000$$

Economic Order Quantity (EOQ) with Usage. The preceding EOQ model assumes that orders are filled instantaneously; that is, fresh inventory arrives all at once. This assumption does not hold true for many small manufacturers; therefore, it is necessary to consider a variation of the basic EOQ model which allows inventory to be added over a period of time rather than instantaneously. In addition, the manufacturer is likely to be taking items from inventory for use in the assembly process over the same time period. For example, the lawnmower manufacturer may be producing blades to replenish his supply, but, at the same time, assembly workers are reducing the supply of blades to make finished mowers. The key feature of this version of the EOQ model is that inventories are used while inventories are being added.

Using the lawnmower manufacturer as an example, we can compute the EOQ for the blades. To make the calculation, we need two additional pieces of information: the usage rate for the blades, U, and the plant's capacity to manufacture the blades, P. Suppose that the maximum number of lawnmower blades the company can manufacture is 480 per day. We know from the previous illustration that annual demand for mowers is 100,000 units (therefore, 100,000 blades). If the plant operates five days per week for 50 weeks, its usage rate is:

$$U = \frac{100,000}{50 \times 5} \approx 400 \text{ units per day}$$

It costs $325 to set up the blade manufacturing line

TABLE 12–2   Economic order quantity and total cost.

If Q is	D × C Cost of the Units	Q/2 × H Carrying Cost	D/Q × S Ordering Cost	Total Cost*
500	$620,000	$ 312.50	$7,200.00	$627,512.50
1,000	620,000	625.00	3,600.00	624,225.00
2,000	620,000	1,250.00	1,800.00	623,050.00
2,400	620,000	1,500.00	1,500.00	623,000.00
3,000	620,000	1,875.00	1,206.00	623,081.00
4,000	620,000	2,500.00	900.00	623,400.00
5,000	620,000	3,125.00	720.00	623,845.00
6,000	620,000	3,750.00	603.00	624,353.00
7,000	620,000	4,375.00	522.00	624,897.00
8,000	620,000	5,000.00	450.00	625,450.00
9,000	620,000	5,625.00	405.00	626,030.00
10,000	620,000	6,250.00	360.00	626,610.00

*Notice that the total cost curve is saucer-shaped and that total cost is relatively insensitive to errors in selecting the ideal quantity.

and $8.71 to store one blade for one year. The cost of producing a blade is $4.85.

To compute EOQ, we modify the basic formula:

$$EOQ = \sqrt{\frac{2 \times D \times S}{H \times \left(1 - \dfrac{U}{P}\right)}}$$

For the lawnmower manufacturer:

$D = 100,000$ blades
$S = \$325$ per production run
$H = \$8.71$ per blade per year
$U = 400$ blades per year
$P = 480$ blades per day

$$EOQ = \sqrt{\frac{2 \times 100,000 \times 325}{8.71 \times \left(1 - \dfrac{400}{480}\right)}}$$

$$= 6,691.50 \text{ blades}$$
$$\approx 6,692 \text{ blades}$$

Therefore, to minimize total inventory cost, the lawnmower manufacturer should produce 6,692 blades

per production run. Also,

$$\text{Number of production runs per year} = \frac{D}{Q}$$
$$= \frac{100,000}{6,692}$$
$$= 14.9$$
$$\cong 15$$

The manufacturer will make 15 production runs during the year at a total cost of:

$$\text{total cost} = (D \times C) + \left(\frac{\left(1 - \dfrac{U}{P}\right) \times Q}{2} \times H\right) + \left(\frac{D}{Q} \times S\right)$$

$$= (100,000 \times \$4.85) + \left(\frac{\left(1 - \dfrac{400}{480}\right) \times 6,692 \times \$8.71}{2}\right)$$

$$+ \left(\frac{100,000}{6,692} \times \$325\right)$$

$$= \$485,000 + \$4,857 + \$4,857$$
$$= \$494,714$$

The small business manager must remember that the EOQ analysis is based on estimations of costs and demand. The final result is only as accurate as the input used. Thus this analytical tool serves only as a guideline for decision making. The "answer" may not be the "ideal" solution for a particular small business owner's situation due to any number of other intervening factors, such as opportunity costs or seasonal fluctuations. The knowledgeable entrepreneur will employ EOQ analysis as a starting point in making a decision and then will use managerial judgment to produce a final ruling.

Price

For the typical small business owner, price is always a substantial factor in purchasing inventory and supplies. In many cases, the entrepreneur can negotiate price with potential suppliers on large orders of frequently purchased items. In other instances, perhaps when small quantities of items are purchased infrequently, the small business owner must pay list price. Small Business Report 12–1 describes the growing popularity of wholesale warehouses among price-conscious small business owners.

Generally, the small firm shops around at several different vendors and then orders from the supplier offering the best price. Still, this does *not* mean the small business manager should always purchase inventory and supplies at the lowest price available. The best purchase price is the lowest price at which the owner can obtain goods and services of *acceptable quality*. This guideline usually yields the best value more often than simply purchasing the lowest priced goods. John Ruskin describes the pricing component of a small business purchasing plan in the following passage:

> It's unwise to pay too much, but it's unwise to pay too little, too. When you pay too much, you lose a little money . . . that is all. When you pay too little, you sometimes lose everything because the thing you bought was incapable of doing the thing it was bought to do. The Common Law of

business prohibits paying a little and getting a lot . . . it can't be done.[1]

Small Business Report 12–2 offers several reasons a small business manager might not select the lowest selling price.

Small business owners should avoid speculative buying, where the firm purchases excessively large quantities of supplies and materials in anticipation of escalating prices. If prices rise, the firm earns a profit on its inventory. But, if prices fall, the firm may suffer a substantial loss which might threaten its survival. Speculative buying is nothing more than gambling with inventory, and is one risk the small business owner should avoid.

Purchase Discounts.   Many vendors offer their customers various types of purchase discounts that, in most cases, substantially lower the price of inventories and supplies to the small business. Many owners fail to take advantage of these discounts and pay full price for the merchandise. Surveys of purchasing departments show that most firms do not realize the value of capitalizing on discounts offered by vendors and suppliers. Vendors typically offer three types of discounts: trade discounts; quantity discounts; and cash discounts.

Trade Discounts.   Trade discounts are established on a graduated scale and depend on the small firm's position in the channel of distribution. In other words, trade discounts recognize the fact that manufacturers, wholesalers, and retailers perform a variety of vital functions at various stages in the channel of distribution and compensate them for providing these needed activities. Figure 12–3 illustrates a typical trade discount structure.

Quantity Discounts.   Quantity discounts are designed to encourage businesses to order large quantities of merchandise and supplies. Vendors are able to offer lower prices on bulk purchases because the

---

[1]*The Works of John Ruskin*, Vol. 17 (London: The Chesterfield Society), p. 129.

"Cash and Carry" Clubs Cut Costs

At Sam's Wholesale Club there are no amenities like charge accounts, shopping bags, or a delivery service. Instead, shoppers at the wholesale warehouse load their purchases onto flatbed dollies, pay with cash or check at the checkout, and then cart their items out to their cars or trucks, where they load them themselves. What the store lacks in convenience and panache, it makes up for with rock-bottom prices, which many shoppers find are "dramatically less" than other suppliers.

Sam's Wholesale Club is just one example of the latest breed of wholesaler cropping up across the nation. Their philosophy is to sell merchandise at wholesale prices to small businesses and to individuals who work for a "qualified" group, like a credit union or bank. Only 75 wholesale warehouses are in operation across the U.S. today, but the number is growing. Industry sales are expected to climb from $4 billion to $20 billion by 1990.

Small business owners can buy products ranging from food and tires to office supplies and janitorial equipment. In addition to their low prices, wholesale clubs also allow members to buy in smaller quantities than other wholesalers. This, says one club owner, gives the typical small business owner "the ability to effectively manage his inventory." For example, a restaurateur buying at a wholesale club does not have to worry about spoilage since he can buy just one ham if that is all he needs. One business owner states, "We started on a shoestring with $2,000 in capital. I could not buy through normal distribution channels because I would have to buy in full case lots."

Buying only the quantities needed can improve a small company's cash flow. One small business customer says, "I could build my stock without large capital outlay." The owner of one wholesale warehouse explains, "Some may bring in their morning receipts and buy their supplies for the afternoon, so they are borrowing no money."

One business owner who purchases all of his office supplies at a wholesale club suggests that before joining a club (most charge membership fees), an entrepreneur should make sure it carries the items and brand names he needs. He made a list of the items his company used most often, and when he toured the facility, he checked the prices on each one. "That is the way we realized how substantial the savings would be," he says.

Wholesale warehouses help small business owners gain control over the crucial purchasing function. One enterpreneur claims, "It means a great deal to a small business like ours if we can save $1,000 or $2,000 a year by going out and buying it ourselves and bringing it back ourselves."

Source: Adapted from Sharon Nelton, "They Really Can Get It for You Wholesale," *Nation's Business*, March 1985, pp. 74–76, with permission of the publisher.

SMALL
BUSINESS
REPORT
12–2

When the Lowest Price is not the Best Bargain

In some instances, buying at the lowest price does not yield the best bargain. The following reasons suggest when not to choose the lowest price.

- A higher bidder may provide better after-sale service.
- A higher bidder may have better plant facilities and be able to offer better quality products.
- The low bidder may not be reliable.
- Reciprocity may favor some company other than the low bidder.
- The low bidder may be located so far from the company that transportation costs more than offset the price advantage.
- Exceptional goodwill may exist between a higher bidder and the company because of credit terms, returns allowances, discounts, handling of rush orders, and other service.
- The procurement department may adhere to a policy of dealing with local suppliers, even though the local supplier's bid is sometimes higher than a distant supplier's bid.

Source: Adapted from Richard J. Hopeman, *Production and Operations Management*, 4th ed. (Columbus, Ohio: Merrill, 1986), p. 345.

---

cost per unit of producing and processing large orders is less than the cost per unit of handling small orders. Quantity discounts normally exist in two forms: noncumulative and cumulative. Noncumulative discounts are granted only if a large enough volume of merchandise is purchased in a single order. For example, a wholesaler may offer a small retailer a 3 percent discount only if he purchases 10 gross of Halloween masks in a single order. Table 12–3 shows a typical noncumulative quantity discount structure.

Cumulative quantity discounts are offered if a firm's purchases from a particular vendor exceed a specified quantity or dollar value over a predetermined time period. The time frame varies, but a yearly basis is most common. For example, a manufacturer of appliances may offer a small firm a 3 percent discount on subsequent orders if its purchases exceed $10,000 per year.

Cash Discounts. Cash discounts are offered to customers as an incentive to pay for merchandise

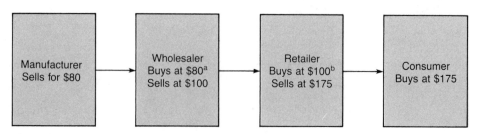

[a]Wholesale discount = 43% of suggested retail price.

[b]Retail discount = 54% of suggested retail price.

FIGURE 12–3 Trade discount structure.

TABLE 12–3 Noncumulative quantity discount structure.

Order Size	Price
1– 1,000	List price
1,001– 5,000	List price – 2%
5,001–10,000	List price – 4%
10,001 & above	List price – 6%

promptly. Many vendors grant cash discounts to avoid being used as an "interest-free bank" by customers who purchase merchandise and then neglect to pay within the invoice due date. To encourage prompt payment of invoices, many vendors allow customers to deduct a percentage of the purchase amount if payment is remitted within a specified time. Cash discount terms "2/10, net 30" are common in many industries. This notation means that the total amount of the invoice is due 30 days after its date; but, if the bill is paid within 10 days, the buyer may deduct 2 percent from the total. A discount offering "2/10, EOM" (EOM means end of month) indicates that the buyer may deduct 2 percent if the bill is paid by the tenth day of the month after purchase.

Generally, it is sound business practice to take advantage of cash discounts. The money saved by paying invoices promptly is free to be used elsewhere. Conversely, there is an implicit (opportunity) cost of forgoing a cash discount. By forgoing a cash discount, the small business owner is, in effect, paying an annual interest rate to retain the use of the discounted amount for the remainder of the credit period. For example, suppose that the Print Shop receives an invoice for $1,000 from a vendor offering a cash discount of 2/10, net 30. Figure 12–4 illustrates this situation and shows how to compute the cost of forgoing the cash discount.

Actually, it costs the Print Shop $20 to retain the use of its $980 for an extra 20 days. Translating this into an annual interest rate:

$$I = P \times R \times T$$

where I = Interest in $
P = Principal in $
R = Rate of interest in %
T = Time factor (number of days/360)

So, to compute R, the annual interest rate:

$$R = \frac{I}{P \times T}$$

In our example:

$$R = \frac{\$20}{980 \times \dfrac{20}{360}}$$

$$= 36.735\%$$

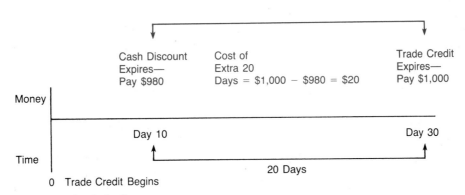

FIGURE 12–4 Cash discount.

The cost to the Print Shop of forgoing the cash discount is 36.735 percent per year. If there is $980 available on day 10 of the trade credit period, the owner should pay the invoice unless he is able to earn a return greater than 36.735 percent on it. If $980 is not available on day 10 but it can be borrowed at less than 36.735 percent, the loan should be made to take advantage of the cash discount. Table 12–4 summarizes the cost of forgoing cash discounts offering various terms.

Time

Timing the purchase of merchandise and supplies is also a critical element of the purchasing plan. The owner must schedule delivery dates so that the firm does not lose customer goodwill from stockouts. Also, the owner must concentrate on maintaining proper control over the firm's inventory investment without tying up an excessive amount of working capital. There is a trade-off between the cost of running out of stock and the cost of carrying additional inventory.

In planning delivery schedules for inventory and supplies, the owner must take into consideration the time gap between placing an order and receiving it. Generally, business owners cannot expect instantaneous delivery of merchandise. As a result, the manager must plan its reorder points for inventory items with lead times in mind.

To determine when to order merchandise for inventory, the small business manager must calculate the reorder point for key inventory items. Developing a reorder point model involves determining the

TABLE 12–4   Cost of forgoing cash discounts.

Cash Discount	Cost of Forgoing (Annually)
2/10, net 30	36.735%
2/30, net 60	24.490%
2/10, net 60	14.693%
3/10, net 30	55.670%
3/10, net 60	22.268%

lead time for an order, the usage rate for the item, the minimum level of stock allowable, and the economic order quantity (EOQ). The lead time for an order is the time gap between placing an order with a vendor and actually receiving the goods. It may take as little as a few hours or as long as several weeks to process purchase requisitions and orders, contact the supplier, receive the goods, and sort them into the inventory. Obviously, owners who purchase from local vendors encounter shorter lead times than those who rely on distant suppliers.

The usage rate for a particular product can be determined from past inventory and accounting records. The small business owner must estimate the speed at which the supply of merchandise will be depleted over a given time. The anticipated usage rate for a product determines how long the supply will last. For example, if the owner projects that 900 units will be used in the next six months, the usage rate is 5 units per day (900 units ÷ 180 days). The simplest reorder point model assumes that the firm experiences a linear usage rate; that is, depletion of the firm's stock continues at a constant rate over time.

The small business owner must determine the minimum level of stock allowable. If the firm runs out of a particular item (i.e., incurs stockouts), customers may lose faith in the business, and customer ill will may develop. To avoid stockouts, many firms establish a minimum level of inventory greater than zero. In other words, they build a "cushion," called safety stock, into their inventories in case demand runs ahead of the anticipated usage rate. In such cases, the owner can dip into the safety stock to fill customer orders until the stock is replenished.

To compute the reorder point for an item, the owner must combine this inventory information with the product's economic order quantity (EOQ). The following example will illustrate the reorder point technique:

L = lead time for an order = 5 days
U = usage rate = 18 units/day
S = safety stock (minimum level) = 75 units
EOQ = economic order quantity = 540

The formula for computing the reorder point is:

$$\text{reorder point} = (L \times U) + S$$

In this example:

$$\text{reorder point} = (5 \text{ days} \times 18 \text{ units/day}) + 75 \text{ units}$$
$$= 165 \text{ units}$$

Thus, 540 more units of inventory should be ordered when inventory drops to 165 units. Figure 12–5 illustrates the reorder point situation for this small business.

The simple reorder technique makes certain assumptions that may not be valid in particular situations. First, the model assumes that the firm's usage rate is constant, when in fact for most small businesses demand varies daily. Second, the model assumes that lead time for an order is constant, when in fact few vendors deliver precisely within lead time estimates. Third, in this sample model, safety stock is never used; however, late deliveries or accelerated demand may force the owner to dip into this inventory reserve. Although more advanced models moderate some of these assumptions, this simple model can be a useful inventory guideline for making inventory decisions in a small company.

For many small businesses, these assumptions are not realistic. More often, demand is *not* known and constant. Using the previous model under these conditions would lead to stockouts, lost sales, and customer ill will. Another popular reorder point model assumes that the demand for a product during its lead time is normally distributed (see figure 12–6). The area under the normal curve at any given point represents the probability of that particular demand level occurring.

Figure 12–7 illustrates the application of this normal distribution to the reorder point model. The model recognizes that three different demand patterns can occur during a product's lead time. Demand pattern 1 is an example of a below-average demand during lead time; demand pattern 2 is an example of average demand during lead time; and demand pattern 3 is an example of an above-average demand during lead time. If the reorder point for this item is $\overline{D}_L$, the average demand for the product during lead time, 50 percent of the time demand will be below average (note that 50 percent of the area under the normal curve lies "below average"). Similarly, 50 percent of the time demand during lead

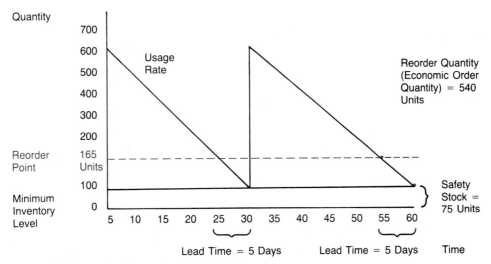

FIGURE 12–5 Simple reorder point model.

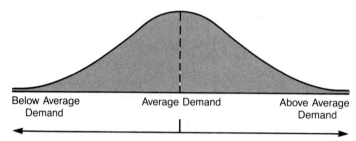

FIGURE 12–6   Demand during lead time.

time will exceed the average, and the firm will experience "stockouts" (note that 50 percent of the area under the normal curve lies "above average").

To reduce the probability of inventory shortages, the small business owner can *increase* the reorder point above $\overline{D}_L$ (average demand during lead time). But, how much should the owner increase the reorder point? Rather than attempt to define the actual costs of carrying extra inventory versus the costs

of stockouts (remember the trade-off described earlier), this model allows the small business owner to determine the appropriate reorder point by setting a desired customer service level. For example, the owner may wish to satisfy 95 percent of customer demand for a product during lead time. This service level determines the amount of increase in the reorder point. In effect, these additional items serve as a "safety stock."

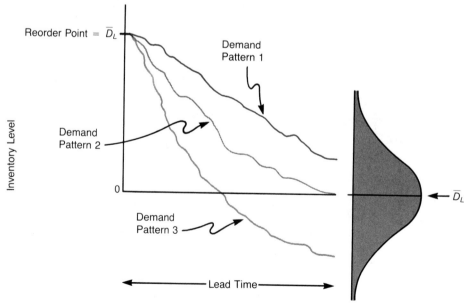

FIGURE 12–7   Reorder point without safety stock.

$$\text{safety stock} = SL \times S_{DL}$$

where SL = service level factor (the appropriate Z score)

S_{DL} = standard deviation of demand during lead time

Table 12–5 shows the appropriate Z score for some of the most popular target customer service levels.[*]

Figure 12–8 shows the shift to a normally distributed reorder point model with safety stock. In this case, the manager has set a 95 percent customer service level—that is, to meet 95 percent of the demand during lead time. The normal curve in the model without safety stock (from figure 12–8) is "shifted" up so that 95 percent of the area under the curve lies above the zero inventory level. The result is a reorder point that is higher than the original reorder point by the amount of the safety stock:

$$\text{reorder point} = \overline{D}_L + (SL \times S_{DL})$$

where $\overline{D}_L$ = average demand during lead time (original reorder point)

S_L = service level factor (the appropriate Z score)

S_{DL} = standard deviation of demand during lead time

To illustrate, suppose that the average demand for a product during its lead time (1 week) is 325 units with a standard deviation of 110 units. If the service level is 95 percent, the service level factor (from table 12–5) would be 1.645. The reorder point would be:

$$R = 325 + (1.645 \times 110) = 325 + 181$$
$$= 506 \text{ units}$$

Figure 12–9 illustrates the shift from a system without safety stock to one with safety stock for this example. With a reorder point of 325 units ($\overline{D}_L$), this small business owner will experience inventory shortages during lead time 50 percent of the time.

TABLE 12–5 Service level factors and Z scores.

Target Customer Service Level	Service Level Factor (Z Score)
99%	2.33
97.5%	1.96
95%	1.645
90%	1.275
80%	0.845
75%	0.675

With a reorder point of 506 units (i.e., a safety stock of 181 units), the business owner will experience inventory stockouts during lead time only 5 percent of the time!

Vendor

The experienced business manager will shop around to find the right vendor of merchandise and supplies. Although many items are standard no matter where they are purchased, others have greatly divergent price and quality characteristics depending on the supplier. The entrepreneur may realize substantial savings simply by investigating the variety of selling terms offered by different vendors. For example, when one small business owner was shopping for a popular software package, he found that he could purchase it at a retail computer store for $495 or through a mail-order software supplier for $299. Since the software was a "standard" package with complete documentation, the owner bought from the mail-order vendor. But, a few months later, the same business owner bought a more complex software package for $399 from a local retailer who offered instructional and support services rather than for $295 from a discount mail-order vendor which offered no support. Price is always an important consideration for a small business owner, but, in some cases, other considerations, such as reliability, sup-

[*]Any basic statistic book will provide a "table of areas under the normal curve," which will give the appropriate Z score for *any* service level factor.

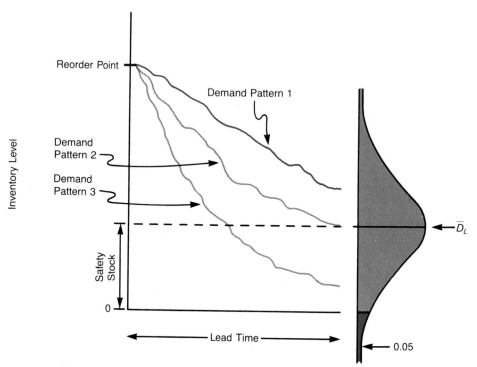

FIGURE 12–8   Reorder point with safety stock.

port services, proximity, and quality override the price component.

Finding Sources of Supply.   Many new entrepreneurs have difficulty locating supplies of inventory and materials to start their businesses. One obvious way to find vendors for your products is to approach established businesses selling similar lines and interview the managers. Clearly, local competitors are not likely to be very cooperative with new competition, but a beginning entrepreneur may get the necessary information from businesses outside the immediate trading area.

Another source for establishing vendor relationships is the industry trade association. These associations often have available to members lists of vendors and suppliers as well as other useful information. They also sponsor trade shows, where large numbers of vendors and suppliers promote their versions of the latest styles, product innovations, and technological advancements.

The local Chamber of Commerce may be able to provide vendor and supplier connections, especially if your company is located in a large city.

A number of publications offer the entrepreneur a great deal of assistance in locating vendors. A ready source of cheap information for any new owner is the telephone directory's Yellow Pages. Scouring the appropriate product category should yield a good list of prospective vendors. Vendor advertisements in trade publications also offer a great deal of information about needed merchandise and materials. Library reference books that list national distributors and their product lines are another information source. Publications such as *MacRae's Blue Book* and the *Thomas Register of American*

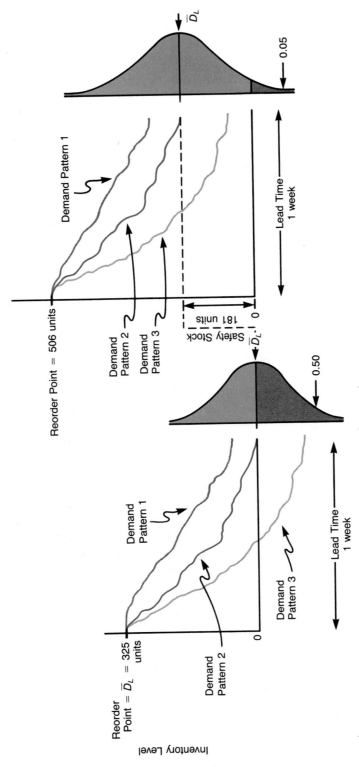

FIGURE 12–9 Shift from a no safety stock system to a safety stock system.

Manufacturers provide lists of products and services along with names, addresses, telephone numbers, and ratings of manufacturers. The *U.S. Industrial Directory* is similar to the *Thomas Register*, although its coverage is not as broad. The owner also should consult the U.S. Chamber of Commerce publication, *Sources of State Information and State Industrial Directories*, which lists state directories of manufacturers. Entrepreneurs whose product lines have an international flair may look to *Kelly's Manufacturers and Merchants Directory*, *Marconi's International Register*, or *Trade Directories of the World* for information on companies throughout the world dealing in practically every type of product or service.

The well-prepared entrepreneur who utilizes these resources should have little difficulty in locating vendors and suppliers and in establishing sound relationships with them.

Selecting a Vendor.   Once the small business owner identifies potential vendors and suppliers, he must decide with which one (or ones) to do business. A critical task in this process is specifying key factors in selecting a vendor and then employing them in analyzing the options. The following discusses some of the factors relevant to choosing the right supplier.

Number of Suppliers.   One of the first questions the small business owner faces is, "Should I buy from a single supplier or from several different sources?" By concentrating purchases at a single supplier, the owner gains several advantages. First, the small business receives a good deal of individual attention from the single supplier, especially if orders are substantial. Second, the firm may receive quantity discounts if its orders are large enough. Finally, the firm is able to cultivate a closer, more cooperative relationship with the supplier. Suppliers are more willing to assist companies they consider to be "their" customers.

However, using a single vendor also has disadvantages. The small firm may experience shortages of critical materials if its only supplier suffers a catastrophe, such as a fire, strike, or bankruptcy. In this case, the small business owner might have trouble establishing an alternate source of supply and be forced to shut down for a time.

If the firm diversifies its purchases among a number of vendors, it reduces the risk of losing its supply, but it sacrifices the opportunity to receive special attention and quantity discounts. To balance these outcomes, most firms purchase 70 to 80 percent of their materials and supplies from the one vendor who best meets their standards, and buy the remaining 20 to 30 percent from several vendors. If the small company's primary supplier suffers a catastrophe, it will be able to shift to other suppliers more easily. Also, the competition from other suppliers serves to keep the principal supplier "on the ball."

Reliability.   The business owner must evaluate the potential vendor's ability to deliver adequate quantities of quality merchandise when it is needed. Late deliveries or shortages cause lost sales and create customer ill will unnecessarily.

Proximity.   The small firm's physical proximity to the vendor is an important factor in choosing a supplier. Costs for transporting merchandise can substantially increase the cost of merchandise to the buyer. For example, one East Coast glass manufacturer found that to obtain proper quality sand for its production operation it had to make its purchases from a midwestern supplier. The company found that the cost of transporting the sand was greater than the cost of the sand itself! Also, some vendors offer better service to local small businesses because they know the owners. In addition, a small business owner is better able to solve coordination problems with nearby vendors than with distant vendors.

Services.   The small business owner must evaluate the range of services vendors offer. Do salespeople make regular calls on the firm and are they knowledgeable of their product line? Will the sales representatives assist in planning store layout and in creating attractive displays? Will the vendor make convenient deliveries on time? Is the supplier reasonable in making repairs on equipment after instal-

Getting the Most for Your Money

Purchasing equipment, materials, and supplies consumes a significant portion of the typical small business' cash. But, many business owners fail to get the most for their money. Just when the company has found what it is looking for and is ready to buy, the owner may let his emotions take over. He gets so anxious to have the new equipment in operation or to have use of the materials that he signs the vendor's standard contract—often without exploring its details. But that could be a major mistake. One purchasing manager claims, "You don't have to sign such a contract. And you'll invariably be better off if you don't."

The small business owner must recognize that he has leverage he can put to work in the negotiation process. The primary source of that leverage is money—the amount of the order and the vendor's profit. Other leverage tools include the method of payment (lump sum gives the owner more "power" than installments) and the potential for future orders. Once a small business owner makes the final payment, he loses practically all of his leverage; so he should "spend" it carefully. He should get everything he can from the vendor before tying up the deal.

The next step is to locate the equipment or material needed and then to choose an *alternate* vendor. The owner then should prepare to negotiate. It may be helpful to enlist the help of a technical expert, attorney, or financial specialist.

Before negotiating, the owner should verify that the vendor's contract covers all of the crucial points: a description of the goods; delivery terms; quality standards; preventive maintenance; service terms and fees; "lemon clauses"; liability limits; and warranties. These elements establish the duties and responsibilities of the seller and the buyer—which are not important until something goes wrong or a dispute arises.

The next phase is to compile a list of all of the elements the owner wants in the contract and then *prioritize* them. List first those that are absolutely essential, then those that are important but not mandatory, and then those that would be nice but are not necessary.

Next, the owner should prepare a contract. To minimize vendor objections, the buyer should start with the vendor's standard contract and then add and delete clauses. The owner should get his attorney to review the result.

Finally, the owner is ready to begin negotiations. Most often, initial negotiations will be with a sales representative. The wise business owner should present his version of the contract, explain his company's position, and try to win the sales representative as an ally. Remember, he (and his company) are eager to sell.

When negotiating, the owner must be firm. He may have to resort to tactical maneuvers. Ultimately, the owner must insist that all terms be in writing.

Following these steps may appear tedious when making purchases, but small business owners who rely on them will get the most for their money.

Source: Adapted from John F. Hamilton, "Buy It Your Way," *Industry Week*, September 30, 1985, pp. 67–68, with permission of the publisher.

"Scoring" Vendors

American Manufacturing, Inc., is faced with choosing from among several suppliers of a critical raw material. The company's owner has decided to employ a vendor rating scale to select the "best" vendor using the following procedure.

Step 1—Determine important criteria. The owner of American Manufacturing has selected the following criteria:

> Quality
> Price
> Prompt delivery
> Service
> Assistance

Step 2—Assign "weights" to each criterion to reflect its relative importance.

Criteria	Weight
Quality	35
Price	30
Prompt delivery	20
Service	10
Assistance	5
Total	100

Step 3—Develop a grading scale for each criterion.

Criteria	Grading Scale
Quality	$\dfrac{\text{number of acceptable lots from vendor}}{\text{total number of lots from vendor}}$
Price	$\dfrac{\text{lowest quoted price of all vendors}}{\text{price offered by vendor } X}$
Prompt delivery	$\dfrac{\text{number of on-time deliveries from vendor}}{\text{total number of deliveries from vendor}}$
Service	a subjective evaluation of the variety of services offered by each vendor
Assistance	a subjective evaluation of the advice and assistance provided by each vendor

Step 4—Compute a weighted score for each vendor.

lation and in handling returned merchandise? Are sales representatives able to offer useful advice on purchasing and other managerial functions? Before choosing a vendor, the small business owner should answer these and other relevant questions about suppliers.

Vendor Rating Scale. How can the small business owner objectively evaluate the various advantages and disadvantages of each vendor? One method is to develop a vendor rating scale to score each supplier on key purchasing variables. The first step in developing a scale is to determine which criteria are most

Vendor 1

Criteria	Weight	Grade	Weighted Score (Weight × Grade)
Quality	35	9/10	31.5
Price	30	$\frac{12.50}{12.50}$	30.0
Prompt delivery	20	10/10	20.0
Service	10	8/10	8.0
Assistance	5	5/5	5.0
Total weighted score			94.5

Vendor 2

Criteria	Weight	Grade	Weighted Score (Weight × Grade)
Quality	35	8/10	28.0
Price	30	$\frac{12.50}{12.50}$	27.8
Prompt delivery	20	8/10	16.0
Service	10	8/10	8.0
Assistance	5	4/5	4.0
Total weighted score			83.8

Vendor 3

Criteria	Weight	Grade	Weighted Score (Weight × Grade)
Quality	35	7/10	24.5
Price	30	$\frac{12.50}{12.50}$	30.0
Prompt delivery	20	6/10	12.0
Service	10	7/10	7.0
Assistance	5	1/5	1.0
Total weighted score			74.5

Based on this analysis of the three suppliers, American should purchase the majority of this raw material from Vendor 1.

important in selecting a vendor (e.g., price, quality, prompt delivery). The next step is to assign "weights" to each criterion to reflect its relative importance. The third step involves developing a grading scale for comparing vendors on the criteria. Developing a usable scale requires that the owner maintain proper records of past vendor performances. Finally, the owner must compute a weighted total score for each vendor and select the vendor scoring the highest on the set of criteria. Small Business Report 12–4 presents an example of a vendor rating scale for a small manufacturer.

II. RECEIVING MERCHANDISE

Once the merchandise is received, the buyer must verify its identity and condition. When the goods are delivered, the owner should check the number of cartons unloaded against the carrier's delivery receipt so that none is overlooked. It is also a good idea to examine the boxes for damage; if shipping cartons are damaged, the carrier should note this on the delivery receipt. The owner should open all cartons immediately after delivery and inspect the merchandise for quality and condition and also check it against the invoices to eliminate discrepancies. If merchandise is damaged or incorrect, the buyer should contact the supplier immediately and follow up with a written report. The owner must *never* destroy or dispose of tainted or unwanted merchandise unless the supplier specifically authorizes it. Proper control techniques in receiving merchandise prevent the small business owner from paying for suppliers' and shippers' mistakes.

III. INVENTORY CONTROL

For many small companies, especially wholesalers and retailers, the investment in inventory is the firm's largest outlay, and the owner must take active steps to protect this valuable asset. In addition to the direct costs of purchasing inventory, the small business incurs several other types of inventory expenses. Depending on the nature of the materials, the owner must protect them from the elements; secure them from theft and damage; categorize them for easy access; and maintain timely, accurate records of them. The business incurs an interest expense if it must borrow the funds to purchase inventory. Also, the owner must recognize the "opportunity costs" of tying up working capital in merchandise and materials. Virtually every small business faces the danger of stocking obsolescent merchandise—goods that are rendered useless because of changes in style, design, technology, or consumer tastes. Some items, such as fashion clothing and automobiles, clearly have lim-

ited lives due to obsolescence, but even goods such as bathroom fixtures and heavy machinery have become outmoded. Perishable items, such as fresh produce, meats, and seafood, obviously have short life spans and must be closely controlled.

The small business owner should carry insurance (primarily fire and theft policies) on inventory to protect against any losses that might occur. Finally, the store owner will incur the costs involved in handling the merchandise in stock. Handling costs typically include receiving, transporting, and shipping goods and materials, plus the expenses associated with damaged goods. Clearly, all of these costs can exert great pressure on the small firm's profits unless the owner implements a well-organized inventory management system to control them.

The small business owner's goal must be to balance the costs involved in holding and maintaining inventory with customer requirements for merchandise. In other words, the business should strive to keep a minimum level of inventory on hand to reduce costs while maintaining enough stock to meet customer demand. If the firm focuses solely on minimizing costs, it is likely to lose sales and generate customer ill will due to stockouts. If, on the other hand, the firm strives to meet every peak customer demand, inventory costs will be high. Thus, every small business needs an inventory control system.

IV. INVENTORY CONTROL SYSTEMS

Regardless of the type of inventory control system an owner chooses, he must recognize the importance of the "80/20 rule," which says that about 80 percent of the value of the firm's inventory comes from about 20 percent of the items kept in stock. Some of the firm's items are high dollar volume goods, while others account for only a small portion of sales volume. Because most sales are generated by a small percentage of items, the owner should focus the majority of inventory control efforts on this 20 percent. Observing this simple principle ensures that the entrepreneur will only spend time controlling the most productive—and, therefore, most valuable—inventory items. With this technique in mind, we will examine three basic types of inventory control systems: perpetual; visual; and partial.

Perpetual Inventory Systems

Perpetual inventory systems are designed to maintain a running count of the items in inventory. Though a number of perpetual inventory systems exist, they all have a common element—they all keep a continuous tally of each item added to or subtracted from the firm's stock of merchandise. The basic perpetual inventory system uses a perpetual inventory sheet that includes fundamental product information such as the item's name, stock number, description, economic order quantity, and reorder point (see figure 12–10).

The perpetual inventory sheet usually is placed next to the merchandise in the warehouse or storage facility. Whenever a shipment is received from a vendor, the quantity is entered in the receipts column and added to the total. When a delivery of the item is made, it is recorded in the disbursements column

and deducted from the total. As long as this procedure is followed consistently, the owner can glance at the inventory sheet and determine quickly the number of items on hand.

While consistent use of the system yields accurate inventory counts at any moment, sporadic use creates problems. If managers or employees take items out of stock or place them in inventory without recording them, the perpetual inventory sheet will yield incorrect totals and can foul up the entire inventory control system. Another disadvantage of this system is the cost of maintaining it. Keeping such records for a large number of items and ensuring the accuracy of the system can be excessively expensive. For example, it would be impractical for the owner of a small hardware store to use a perpetual inventory system on every item in stock. Therefore, these systems are used most frequently and most successfully in controlling high dollar volume items that require strict monitoring. Management must watch these items closely and ensure that inventory records are accurate.

Technical advances in computerized cash registers have overcome many of the disadvantages of using the basic perpetual inventory system. Small

Item Name _____						
Item Number _____ Item Description _____						
Location in Storage _____						
Receipts			Disbursements			
Date	Shipper	Quantity	Checked by	Quantity	Checked by	Balance

FIGURE 12–10   Typical perpetual inventory sheet.

businesses now are able to afford a computerized system which performs all of the functions of a traditional cash register and maintains an up-to-the-minute inventory count. The system relies on an inventory data bank, and as items are rung up on the register, product information is recorded and inventory balances are adjusted. Using the system, the owner can determine the amount of inventory on hand for any product listed in the data bank. The system can also be programmed to alert the owner when the supply of a particular item drops below a predetermined reorder point, or even to print automatically a purchase order for the EOQ indicated. Computerized systems such as these make it possible for the owner to employ a basic perpetual inventory system on a large number of items—a task that, if performed manually, would be virtually impossible.

Specific Perpetual Inventory Systems.   Perpetual inventory systems operate in a number of ways, but four basic variations are particularly common: the sales ticket method; the sales stub method; the punch card method; and the floor sample method.

The Sales Ticket Method.   Most small businesses use sales tickets like the one pictured in figure 12–11 to summarize individual customer transactions. These tickets serve two major purposes: they provide the customer with a sales receipt for the merchandise purchased, and they provide the owner with a daily record of the number of specific inventory items sold. One method of gathering input for a perpetual inventory system is to collect all the sales tickets at the end of each day and transcribe the data onto the appropriate perpetual inventory sheet. By posting inventory deductions to the perpetual inventory system from sales tickets, the small business manager can monitor sales patterns and keep close control on inventory. The primary disadvantages of using such a system is the time required to make it function properly. Most managers find it difficult to squeeze in the

time needed to post sales tickets to the perpetual inventory system.

The Sales Stub Method.   The principle behind the sales stub method of inventory control is the same as that underlying the sales ticket method, but its mechanics are slightly different. Retail stores often attach a ticket with two or more parts (see figure 12–12) containing relevant product information to each inventory item in stock. When an employee sells an item, he removes a portion of the stub and places it in a container. At the end of the day, the owner posts the inventory deductions recorded by the stubs to the proper perpetual inventory sheet.

The Punch Card Method.   Instead of attaching a sales stub to each inventory item, some business owners use punch cards to generate basic inventory data. Each card is prepunched to include basic product information, and when an employee sells an item, he removes the card and places it in a container. At the end of the work day, the owner collects the cards and feeds them through a card sorter or compiler to generate a complete inventory report for the day.

The Floor Sample Method.   The floor sample method of controlling inventory is commonly used by businesses selling "big ticket" items with high unit cost. In many cases, these items are somewhat bulky and are difficult to display in large numbers. For example, the owner of a small furniture store might receive a shipment of 15 roll-top desks in a particular style. A simple technique for maintaining control of these items is to attach a small pad to the display desk with sheets numbered in descending order from 15 to 1. Whenever an employee sells a roll-top desk, he removes a sheet from the pad. As long as the system is followed consistently, the owner is able to determine accurate inventory levels with a quick pass around the sales floor. When the supply of a particular item dwindles, the owner simply calls the vendor to replenish the inventory. The procedure is simple and serves its purpose.

101   Date _____ 198__

M_____

Address_____

Employee   Department   Code
_____

Item   Amount
_____

1._____

2._____

3._____

4._____

5._____

6._____

7._____

8._____

9._____

10._____

FIGURE 12–11   Sales ticket.

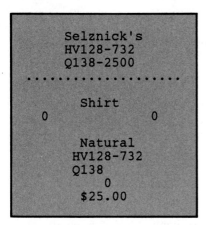

FIGURE 12–12   Sales stub.

Visual Inventory Control Systems

The most common method of controlling inventory in a small business is the visual control system, in which the manager simply conducts a periodic visual inspection to determine the quantity of various items he should order. As mentioned earlier, perpetual inventory systems, especially manual ones, can be excessively costly and time consuming. Such systems are impractical when the business stocks a large number of low-value items with low dollar volume. So many owners rely on the simplest, quickest inventory control method—the visual system. Unfortunately, this method is also the least effective for ensuring accuracy and reliability. Oversights of key items often lead to stockouts and resulting lost sales. The biggest disadvantage of the visual control system is its inability to detect and to foresee shortages of inventory items.

Generally, a visual inventory control system works best in firms where daily sales are relatively consistent, the owner is closely involved with the inventory, the variety of merchandise is small, and items can be obtained quickly from vendors. For example, small firms dealing in perishables use visual control systems very successfully, and rarely, if ever, rely on analytical inventory control tools. For these firms, shortages are less likely to occur under a visual system; when they do occur, they are less likely to create major problems. Still, the manager who uses a visual inventory control system should leave reminders to make regular inspections and be alert to shifts in customer buying patterns that alter required inventory levels.

Partial Inventory Control Systems

For the small business owner with limited time and money, the most viable option for inventory management is a partial inventory control system. Such a system relies on the validity of the 80/20 rule. For example, if a small business carries 5,000 different items in stock, roughly 1,000 of them account for about 80 percent of the firm's sales volume. Still, many managers seek to maintain tight control over the remaining 4,000 items which produce only 20 percent of annual sales. The cost of the time involved in maintaining intense control over these items is wasteful. The wise small business owner will design an inventory control system with this principle in mind.

The ABC Method of Inventory Control. Too many managers apply perpetual inventory control systems universally across every item maintained in stock when a partial control system would be much more practical. Partial inventory systems minimize the expense involved in analyzing, processing, and main-

taining records, a substantial cost of any inventory control system. The ABC method is one such approach, focusing control efforts on that small percentage of items that accounts for the majority of the firm's sales. The typical ABC system divides a firm's inventory into three major categories:

A items: those items that account for a large dollar usage volume

B items: those items that account for a moderate dollar usage volume

C items: those items that account for a low dollar usage volume

The dollar usage volume that an item accounts for measures the relative importance of that item in the firm's inventory. Note that value is *not* necessarily synonymous with high unit cost. In some instances, a high-cost item that generates only a small dollar volume can be classified as an A item. But, more frequently, A items are those that are low-cost and high-volume by nature.

The initial step in establishing an ABC classification system is to compute the annual dollar usage value for each product (or product category). Annual dollar usage value is simply the cost per unit of an item multiplied by annual quantity used. For instance, the owner of a stereo shop may find that he sold 190 pairs of a popular brand of speaker during the previous year. If the speakers cost him $75 per pair, their annual dollar usage value would be:

$$190 \times \$75 = \$14,250$$

The next step is to arrange the products in descending order based on the computed annual dollar usage value. Once so arranged, they can be divided into appropriate classes by applying the following rule:

A items: roughly the top 15 percent of the items listed

B items: roughly the next 35 percent

C items: roughly the remaining 50 percent

For example, Florentina's, a small retail shop, is interested in establishing an ABC inventory control system to lower losses from stockouts, theft, or other hazards. The manager has computed the annual dollar usage value for the store's merchandise inventory, as shown in table 12–6. (For simplicity, we will use only 12 inventory items.)

The ABC inventory control method divides the firm's inventory items into three classes depending on the items' value. Figure 12–13 graphically portrays the segmentation of the items listed in table 12–6.

The purpose of classifying items according to their value is to establish the proper degree of control over each item held in inventory. Clearly, it is wasteful and inefficient to exercise the same level of control over C items as A items. Items in the A classification should be controlled under a perpetual inventory system with as much detail as necessary. Analytical tools and frequent counts may be required to ensure accuracy, but the extra cost of tight control

for these valuable items usually is justified. The manager should not retain a large supply of reserve or safety stock since this ties up excessive amounts of money in inventory, but he must monitor the stock closely to avoid stockouts and lost sales. Weekly or even daily inspections may be required to control A items properly.

Control of B items should rely more on periodic control systems and basic analytical tools such as EOQ and reorder point analysis. The manager can maintain large levels of safety stock for these items to guard against shortages, and can afford monthly or even bimonthly merchandise inspections. Because B items are not as valuable to the business as A items, less rigorous control systems are required.

C items typically comprise a minor proportion of the small firm's inventory value and, as a result, require the least effort and expense to control. These items are usually large in number and small in total value. The most practical way to control them is to

TABLE 12–6   Calculation of annual dollar usage value, Florentina's.*

Item	Annual Dollar Usage	Percent of Annual Dollar Usage
Paragon	374,100	42.0
Excelsior	294,805	33.1
Avery	68,580	7.7
Bardeen	54,330	6.1
Berkeley	27,610	3.1
Tara	24,940	2.8
Cattell	11,578	1.3
Faraday	9,797	1.1
Humboldt	8,016	0.9
Mandel	7,125	0.8
Sabot	5,344	0.6
Wister	4,453	0.5
Total	890,678	100.0

*A items: $12 \times 0.15 = 1.8 \approx$ top 2 items
 B items: $12 \times 0.35 = 4.2 \approx$ next 4 items
 C items: $12 \times 0.50 = 6.0 \approx$ remaining 6 items

TABLE 12–6 (*continued*)   ABC analysis, Florentina's.

Classification	Item	Annual Dollar Usage	Percent of Total
A	Paragon, Excelsior	$668,905	75.1
B	Avery, Bardeen, Berkeley, Tara	175,460	19.7
C	Cattell, Faraday, Humboldt, Mandel, Sabot, Wister	46,313	5.2
Total		$890,678	100.0

use uncomplicated records and procedures. Large levels of safety stock for these items are acceptable since the cost of carrying them is usually minimal. Substantial order sizes often enable the business to take advantage of quantity discounts without having to place frequent orders. The costs involved in using detailed recordkeeping and inventory control procedures greatly outweigh the advantages gleaned from strict control of C items.

One practical technique for maintaining control of these "nuts and bolts" C items is the two-bin system. Using this process, the owner simply keeps two separate bins full of material. The first bin is used to fill customer orders while the second bin is filled with enough safety stock to meet customer demand during the lead time. When the first bin is empty, the owner places an order with the vendor large enough to refill *both* bins. During the lead time

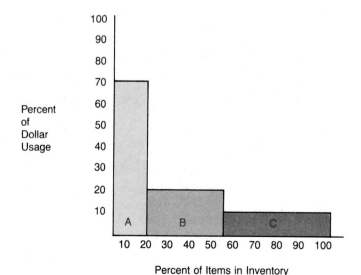

FIGURE 12–13   ABC method of inventory control.

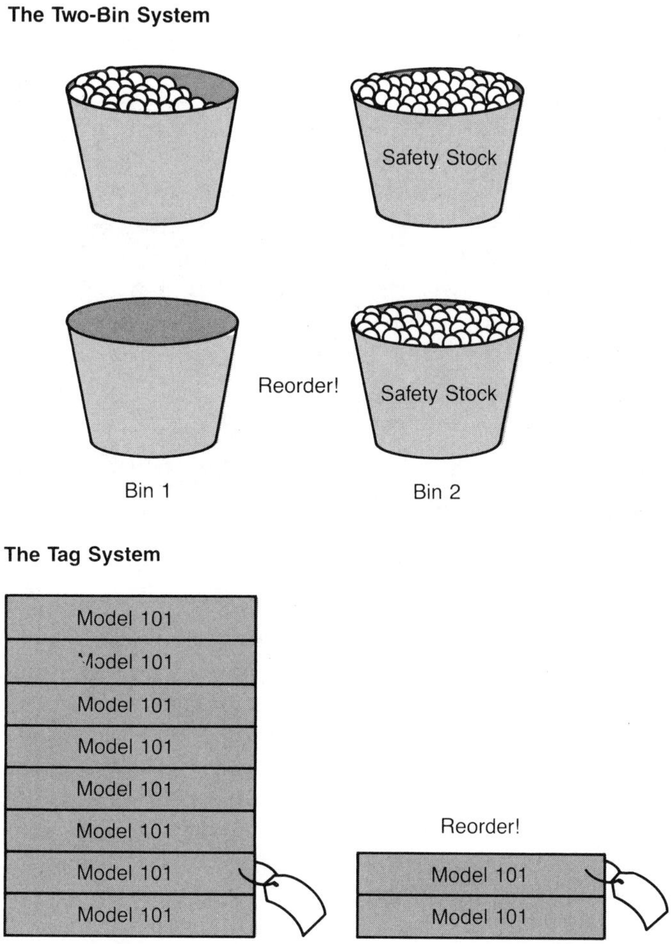

The Two-Bin System

The Tag System

FIGURE 12–14   The two-bin and tag systems of inventory control.

for the order, the manager uses the safety stock in the second bin to fill customer demand. A variation of this technique is the level control system. Here, the manager fills the bin with the usual amount of safety stock and marks the level with a brightly colored line. When the supply of material reaches the colored line, he orders enough stock to refill the bin.

When storage space or the type of item does not suit the two-bin system, the owner can use a tag system. Based on the same principle as the two-bin

system, which is suitable for many manufacturers, the tag system applies to most retail, wholesale, and service firms. Instead of placing enough inventory to meet customer demand during lead time into a separate bin, the owner marks this inventory level with a brightly-colored tag. When the supply is drawn down to the tagged level, the merchandise is reordered. Figure 12–14 illustrates the two-bin and tag systems of controlling C items.

In summary, total inventory costs are reduced

TABLE 12–7   ABC control features.

A Items	B Items	C Items
Monitor closely and maintain tight control	Maintain moderate control	Maintain loose control
Based on forecasted requirements	Based on EOQ calculations and past experience	When level gets low, reorder
Keep detailed records of receipts and disbursements	Use periodic inspections and control procedures	No records required
Low levels of safety stock	Moderate levels of safety stock	High levels of safety stock
Frequent monitoring of schedule changes	Periodic checks on changes in requirements	No checks on requirements

when the small business manager spends her time and effort controlling items that represent the greatest inventory value. Some inventory items require strict, detailed control techniques, while others cannot justify the cost of such systems. Because of its practicality, the ABC inventory system is commonly used in industry. In addition, the technique is easily computerized, speeding up the analysis and lowering its cost. Table 12–7 summarizes the use of the ABC control system.

Just-in-Time Techniques.   Many U.S. manufacturers have turned to a popular inventory control technique called "Just-in-Time" (JIT) to reduce costly inventories and turn around their fortunes. Until recently, these firms had accepted and practiced without question the following long-standing principles of manufacturing: long production runs of standard items are ideal; machines should be up and running as much as possible; machines must produce a large number of items to justify long setup times and high costs; similar processes should be consolidated into single departments; tasks should

be highly specialized; and inventories (raw material, work-in-process, and finished goods) should be large enough to avoid emergencies such as supply interruptions, strikes, and breakdowns. One manufacturing consultant summarizes the traditional approach: " . . . we've sold our soul to Murphy's law. We believe that there's some mystical force out there that's going to do us in—that's going to shut down a line—and so we protect ourselves with inventory."[2]

The Just-in-Time philosophy views excess inventory as a "blanket" that masks problems and as a source of unnecessary costs that inhibit a firm's competitive position. Under a JIT system, materials and inventory should flow smoothly through the production process without stopping. They arrive at the appropriate location "just in time" instead of becoming part of a costly inventory stockpile. JIT is a manufacturing philosophy that seeks to improve a company's efficiency. The key measure of manufacturing efficiency is the level of inventory maintained; the lower

---

[2]Craig R. Waters, "Why Everybody's Talking About Just-In-Time," *Inc.,* March 1984, p. 78.

the level of inventory, the more efficient the production system.

Almost any change that has this aim can be counted as part of the JIT philosophy. Companies adopting the JIT system look for ways to cut machine setup times, reduce the number of adjustments made during production, redesign plants so that machines involved in the same processes are closer together, and move parts to each manufacturing station only when they are needed. One manufacturer of plastic products implemented a simplified machine setup procedure as part of its JIT system and reduced setup time on a key machine by 50 percent. Another manufacturer reduced its finished goods inventory by 32 percent, eliminated costly warehouse space, and consolidated two plants into one.[3]

When Omark Industries instituted a JIT program called ZIPS (Zero Inventory Product System) in several of its plants, it eliminated $7 million in inventory carrying costs in one year. Managers at Omark set challenging three-year objectives for the program and conducted an extensive JIT training program for the workforce. One manager recalls, "One of the first things we did was arbitrarily eliminate a week's lead time. We told people, We're going to take a week's worth of parts out of the system and see what happens.'" When the managers did just that to the piles of items sitting throughout the plant, the system ran smoother. After just five months of ZIPS, the plant had already accomplished its three-year objectives—plus some! At another plant, ZIPS cut inventory by 92 percent, increased productivity by 30 percent, reduced scrap and rework by 20 percent, and shortened lead time (the time required to go from an order to a finished shipment) from 3 weeks to 3 days. The entire JIT system gave managers more time to question their traditional manufacturing methods. Explains one manager, "That (ZIPS) gave us an opportunity to take a closer look at what we were doing." The result was a change in the delivery sys-

tem, where Omark had been "staging" materials in an initial delivery area. Exclaims one executive, ". . . Suddenly, it seemed stupid to stage materials at all. Why not put them where they were going to be used? Now, as soon as it comes in the door, it goes to the area where it's needed."[4]

Indeed, giving managers more time to question accepted manufacturing principles is a key benefit of a JIT system. Explains one management consultant:

> Traditionally, American industries have considered shutting down a line the worst possible thing that could happen. The Japanese have taught us that that's the third worst. The worst thing that can happen is that bad products get made; the second worst is that inventory hides a plant's problems and inefficiencies; the third worst is interrupting the flow of production.[5]

Although the majority of companies currently employing JIT are large, the philosophy is spreading to small companies. There are limitations, however. JIT is most successful in repetitive manufacturing operations where there are significant inventory levels at the outset; where production requirements can be forecasted accurately; and where suppliers are local, produce quality materials, and are cooperative.

Difficulty in convincing suppliers to cooperate with a new JIT system can be a serious obstacle. Manufacturers, however, must learn to be selective, focusing on those suppliers that can be involved in JIT, even if it is just a few. For example, at one manufacturing company only 60 of 500 items (12 percent) are under JIT. Still, these 60 items represent a significant portion of the company's volume, and the JIT system reduced total inventories by more than 50%.[6]

Small Business Report 12–5 demonstrates how one manufacturing company used the JIT philosophy to pull itself from the red into the black.

---

[3]Ibid. p. 85.

[4]Ibid. pp. 83–86.

[5]Ibid. p. 87.

[6]"Letters," *Inc.,* July 1984, p. 10.

A New Manufacturing Philosophy "Just in Time"

Xaloy, Inc. (pronounced "Exaloy"), a small manufacturer of steel-and-alloy extrusion cylinders, was staggering from the blows of recession, foreign competition, and production inefficiencies. The company had laid off 100 employees, revenues were falling, and the business was operating at a loss. Xaloy managers knew that they had to make some drastic changes if the company was to survive. So, they turned to a production philosophy called Just-in-Time.

The idea began when a pair of production managers attended a JIT seminar presented by professor-turned-consultant Ed Heard. His message was simple: inventory is the best measure for judging the efficiency of a manufacturing operation. The greater the inventory level, the less efficient the process. Heard claims, "Inventory is simply the best indicator of manufacturing performance we have."

When Heard visited the Xaloy plant to judge the potential for JIT, he saw clutter, little organization, and a great deal of inventory—the results of uncontrolled growth. Heard knew that Xaloy could benefit greatly from JIT, but that progress would be one step at a time.

The cylinders the company produced looked rather simple and uncomplicated, but each one took, on average, 13 weeks to produce since error tolerances were as small as two mils. The result was that cylinders crept through the plant at a snail's pace. At one time, Xaloy was producing about 200 units per month, but there were more than 2,000 cylinders stacked around the plant!

The JIT team's first step was to get workers to cut raw steel only when it was needed and to group together machines by product size to minimize transporting work-in-process throughout the plant. The result was an immediate reduction in inventory. Nearly 25 percent of floor space was freed, the distance cylinders traveled during production was cut by 50 percent, and the time required to manufacture a cylinder fell from 13 weeks to just 6 1/2 weeks.

Another critical step came when the JIT team examined the long-established cylinder straightening process. At one stage of production, men with sledge hammers or automatic straightening machines would pound the bends and curves out of the cylinders. Heard queried, "The steel came in straight, and was machined precisely. Who the heck was bending it?" The team discovered that the steel became misshapen as it cooled on the production floor. So, they designed and built a new cooling system in which cylinders hung vertically. That change took 20 percent of the labor out of making the cylinders.

Although the team encountered many problems and obstacles in implementing the JIT system, the steps it has taken came just in time to save the company. In a little more than a year, sales went up 70 percent; work-in-process inventory was cut by 75 percent; total inventory was reduced by 35 percent; and inventory turnover had risen from four to eight times per year. The company regained its once declining market share, which now stands at about 60 percent. The total cost of implementing the JIT changes was about $75,000, while actual savings from the new system totaled "at least $500,000 and possibly as much as $750,000." That, according to Xaloy's chief executive officer, "is not a bad return on investment."

Source: Adapted from Craig R. Waters, "Profit & Loss," *Inc.*, April 1985, pp. 103–12, with permission of the publisher.

V. PHYSICAL INVENTORY COUNT

Regardless of the type of inventory control system used, the small business owner must always conduct a periodic physical inventory count. Even when the firm employs a perpetual inventory system, it must still count the actual number of items on hand because of the possibility of human error. A physical inventory count allows the manager to reconcile the actual amount of inventory in stock with the amount reported through the inventory control system. These counts give the manager a fresh start in determining the actual number of items on hand, and enable him to evaluate the effectiveness and the accuracy of his inventory control system.

The typical method of taking inventory involves two employees, one who calls out the relevant information for each inventory item and the other who records the count on a tally sheet. There are two basic methods of conducting a physical inventory count. One alternative is to take inventory at a regular interval. Many businesses take inventory at the end of the year. In an attempt to minimize counting, many managers run special year-end inventory reduction sales. This periodic physical count generates the most accurate measurement of inventory. The other method of taking inventory involves counting a number of items on a continuous basis. Instead of waiting until year-end to tally the entire inventory of items, the manager counts a few types of items each week and checks the numbers against the inventory control system. Such a system allows for continuous correction of mistakes in inventory control systems and detects inventory problems sooner.

VI. SUMMARY

Proper administration of the purchasing function is vital to the success of every small business because it influences the firm's ability to sell quality goods or services at a reasonable price. Purchasing is the requisition of needed materials, supplies, services, and equipment of the right quality, in the proper quantities, for reasonable prices, at the appropriate time, from the right supplier.

A quality product is one which conforms to predetermined standards. Perfect quality does not exist, but the owner should try to obtain goods that serve the purposes for which they are purchased.

Many small businesses encounter difficulty in controlling the inventory investment. A major goal is to generate adequate inventory turnover by purchasing proper quantities of merchandise. A useful analytical device for computing the proper quantity is economic order quantity (EOQ). The results of the EOQ analysis yield the ideal quantity, the amount which minimizes total inventory costs. Total inventory costs consist of three components: the cost of the units, holding (carrying) costs, and ordering (setup) costs. The EOQ balances the costs of ordering merchandise and the costs of carrying merchandise to yield minimum total inventory cost.

One variation of the basic EOQ model allows inventory to be added over a period of time rather than instantaneously. The minimum cost solution is found by modifying the basic formula.

Price is always an important variable in the small firm's purchasing plan. But the lowest price is not always the best price; rather, the best purchase price is the lowest price at which the owner can obtain goods and services of *acceptable quality*.

Purchase discounts can lower the price of goods and services substantially, and the small business owner should take advantage of them. Discounts come in three versions: trade discounts; quantity discounts; and cash discounts.

Timing of purchases is also a crucial element in administering a purchasing plan. The small business owner must recognize that there is a time gap between the placing of an order and actual receipt of the goods. The owner can use a formula to compute the firm's reorder point.

Another popular reorder point model assumes that the demand for a product during its lead time is

There's an Exception to Every Rule

The Simon Harris Company, the country's oldest family-owned sporting goods store, is an anathema in the industry. The shop is extremely successful, but not because proprietor Sam Harris is a marketing genius. There are no catchy slogans or jingles, no fancy displays, and not even an endorsement from a well-known athlete.

Instead, the 98-year-old store is a wreck. The long wooden counter in the store—complete with an antique cash register—is covered with dust and with boxes containing everything from turn-of-the-century golf clubs and barbells to hockey sticks and ancient T-shirts touting "Simon Harris, your old friend." Thousands of pairs of athletic shoes are stacked against the walls in no apparent order. One youngster earned an "A" on an English paper in which he offered this accurate description of the store: "It's like a bowling alley because wherever you go, you knock something over."

Sam Harris can't stand to throw anything away. When the basement flooded and ruined a boxer's bag, Sam hauled it into upstairs storage. He sold it a few days later for $2.00. "There ain't no fanciness here," says Sam as he makes his way into his tiny cubicle of an office, also cluttered with sports relics.

What keeps customers coming back to Simon Harris Company is the incredible bargains they find and the unique atmosphere they encounter. The company's low overhead allows it to keep its prices low and its sales volume high. On Saturdays, the store is so busy that a security guard at the door lets customers in one at a time. Fourteen sales representatives hustle around the store serving one customer after another. One supplier says, "People chuckle at the stuff crammed in there, but the store has to be respected. It's the only one left."

Mr. Harris never takes inventory, so no one knows for sure exactly how many items are crammed into the store. Explains one employee at a nearby competitor, "That place is so disorganized, I don't think I could ever work in there." One employee claims he was buried under an avalanche of clothing for several hours." It took a rescue crew to pull me out," he declares.

But more boxes arrive each day. Harris is always looking for other stores to buy out or for production overruns to buy at a bargain. Explains one employee, "It doesn't matter how many of a thing he already has. If it's a good deal, he'll buy it." There is a danger to the store's "inventory control" system (or lack of one). If anything were to happen to Sam, the business could fall apart. One employee claims, "All these boxes around here, and Sam's the only one who knows where anything is."

Source: Adapted from "Samuel Harris Flouts Rules of Retailing, Flaunts His Success," *The Wall Street Journal,* September 23, 1985, pp. 1, 24, with permission of *The Wall Street Journal,* © Dow Jones & Company, Inc. All rights reserved.

---

normally distributed. To compute the reorder point, the owner must identify a desired customer service level.

The small business owner must shop around to find the "right" supplier. There are many sources a small business owner can turn to for locating suppliers—similar businesses, the Chamber of Commerce, industry trade associations, trade shows, and a number of publications.

To select the best vendor, the small business

owner can employ an objective vendor rating scale. First, he must determine which criteria are most important in a vendor. Then he must assign weights to each criteria. Finally, he must develop a grading scale for each criterion and score each vendor.

For most small businesses, the greatest investment of available capital is in inventory. When managed properly, inventory can be the firm's most profitable asset. However, if inventory is poorly controlled or fails to sell, it can be a costly burden which drains the firm's profitability. With a bit of sound planning and a few simple inventory control techniques, the small business manager can make the inventory investment the firm's hardest working and most productive asset.

Inventory represents the largest investment for the typical small business. Unless properly managed, the cost of inventory will strain the firm's budget and cut into its profitability. The goal of inventory control is to balance the costs of holding and maintaining inventory with meeting customer demand.

Regardless of the inventory control system selected, the owner must recognize the relevance of the "80/20 rule," which states that roughly 80 percent of the value of the firm's inventory is in about 20 percent of the items in stock. Because only a small percentage of items account for the majority of the value of the firm's inventory, the manager must focus control on these items.

Three basic types of inventory control systems are available to the small business owner: perpetual, visual, and periodic. Specific perpetual inventory control systems include the sales ticket method, which uses daily sales tickets to post inventory deductions to the perpetual inventory sheet; the sales stub method, which uses a sales stub of two or more parts to accomplish the same purpose as the sales ticket method; the punch card method, which uses punched inventory cards and data processing equipment to control inventory; and the floor sample method, which involves attaching pads with numbered sheets to display items to keep track of the items in inventory.

The visual inventory system is the most common method of controlling merchandise in the small business. Although it is simple and easy to use, it cannot detect shortages. This system works best when shortages are less likely to cause major problems. Partial inventory control systems are most effective for small businesses with limited time and money. These systems operate on the basis of the 80/20 rule.

A perpetual inventory control system is too costly to implement across the entire inventory. The ABC system divides a firm's inventory into three categories depending on each item's dollar usage volume (cost per unit multiplied by quantity used per time period). The purpose of classifying items according to their value is to establish the proper degree of control over them. A items are most closely controlled by perpetual inventory control systems, while B items use basic analytical tools, and C items are controlled by very simple techniques like the two-bin system, the level control method, or the tag system.

The Just-in-Time system of inventory control sees excess inventory as a "blanket" that masks production problems and adds unnecessary costs to the production operation. Under a JIT philosophy, the level of inventory maintained is the measure of efficiency. Materials and parts should not build up as costly inventory. They should flow through the production process without stopping, arriving at the appropriate location "just in time."

Every small business manager must conduct a physical inventory count no matter what type of inventory control system is used. The owner can take inventory on either a periodic or a continuous basis.

STUDENT INVOLVEMENT PROJECTS

1. Interview the owner of a local small business about his purchasing plan. How does he locate and evaluate suppliers? How does he compute order quantities? Does he take advantage of purchase discounts? What factors are most important to him in selecting vendors? Are products sold on consignment?

2. Assume that you are about to open a small business. Describe how you would locate reliable suppliers for your products. Use some of the sources described in this chapter to prepare a list of vendors for your product line.

3. Contact a local small business owner and request the following information: (1) What type of inventory control system is used? How does it work? (2) Does the 80/20 rule apply to the inventory? (3) Does the owner's inventory control system reflect the 80/20 rule? (4) How does the owner liquidate slow-moving merchandise?

4. Prepare a brief report outlining some suggestions you would offer a small business to improve its inventory control system.

DISCUSSION QUESTIONS

1. What is purchasing? Why is it important for the small business owner to develop a purchasing plan?

2. List and briefly describe the three components of total inventory costs.

3. What is the economic order quantity? How does it minimize total inventory costs?

4. Should a small business owner always purchase the products with the lowest prices? Why or why not?

5. Briefly outline the three types of purchase discounts. Should the owner take advantage of them?

6. What is lead time? Outline the procedure for determining the reorder point for a product.

7. Explain how a small business entrepreneur could locate suppliers and vendors for a new business.

8. What factors are commonly used to evaluate suppliers? Explain the procedure for developing a vendor rating scale.

9. What should a small business owner do when merchandise is received?

10. Describe some of the incidental costs of carrying and maintaining inventory for the small business owner.

11. What is a perpetual inventory system? How does it operate? What are the advantages and disadvantages of using such a system?

12. List and describe briefly the four versions of a perpetual inventory system.

13. Give examples of small businesses which would find it practical to implement the four systems described in question 12.

14. What advantages and disadvantages does a visual inventory control system have over other methods?

15. For what type of business or product line is a visual control system most effective?

16. What is the 80/20 rule and why is it important in controlling inventory?

17. Outline the ABC inventory control procedure. What is the purpose of classifying inventory items using this procedure?

18. Briefly describe the types of control techniques that should be used for A items, B items, and C items.

19. What is the basis for the JIT philosophy? Under what conditions does a JIT system work best?

20. Outline the two methods of taking a physical inventory count. Why is it necessary for every small business manager to take inventory?

Computers and Small Business

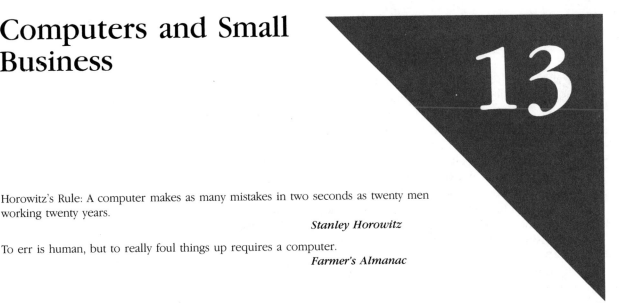

13

Horowitz's Rule: A computer makes as many mistakes in two seconds as twenty men working twenty years.

Stanley Horowitz

To err is human, but to really foul things up requires a computer.

Farmer's Almanac

Upon completion of this chapter, you will be able to:

- Illustrate the importance of avoiding "computer illiteracy" in the small business.

- Indicate the flexibility of modern computers and demonstrate their applicability to a number of business functions.

- Identify the advantages and disadvantages of computerization to the small business.

- Outline the basic options available to the owner in establishing a computer system.

- Understand a procedure for choosing a personal computer.

- List guidelines for choosing reliable computer software and outline the seven major software applications.

- Identify the most important criteria in choosing computer hardware and describe common hardware maintenance problems.

- Understand fully the issue of "where to buy a computer."

- Discuss the importance of computer security and suggest security options

Just a few years ago, only the largest corporations could justify the cost of buying a computer. Recently, however, technological advances have skyrocketed, boosting the capability of the computer beyond the predictions of even the most imaginative futurist. This increase in technological capacity has been accompanied by the dramatic decline in computer prices. These two forces have brought a spectacular amount of processing power into the grasp of the smallest businesses. According to one small business owner:

> Information—or the lack of it—is fast becoming the competitive edge by which the growing company wins or loses in the marketplace. The ability of small business management to use the new computer and communications technologies to access information will determine a company's future just as much as product design or marketing savvy has in the past.[1]

Those small companies that collect *and use* valuable information to manage their operations more effectively will have a competitive advantage. They

---

[1] Robert B. Forest and F. Douglas DeCarlo, "Computer Information Strategies for Smaller Corporations," *Inc.*, November 1984, p. 129.

will be able to boost productivity, control inventory and cash flow, collect accounts promptly, produce goods and services efficiently, identify customer needs and preferences, and anticipate problems and opportunities. Indeed, the small business owner who fails to educate herself in the practical applications of the computer in a variety of business situations risks becoming obsolete and endangers her company's existence. One small business owner claims, "No one who has a business has any business being in business without thinking of getting a computer."[2]

"Getting a computer" is no easy task, however. When shopping for a computer the small business owner quickly discovers the jungle of choices available. Literally thousands of computer hardware and software options are available. One frustrated shopper describes his experience:

> Naively, I assumed it was as simple as walking into a store, telling the salesperson what you wanted, paying, and walking out with the machine under your arm . . . . But each of my questions produced only lengthier and more confusing answers from the salesman . . . . Lacking fluency in "computerspeak," I found myself baffled by the salesman's rapid-fire discussion of CPU, RAM, bytes, and hard vs. floppy disks.[3]

Overcoming computer illiteracy is not a simple process.

When the small business owner decides to buy a computer, someone in the company will more than likely come up with "sound reasons" not to buy one. Some common reasons given for not investing in a computer and argument against them follow.

"*It won't save us money.*" By performing a large number of routine tasks in a very short time, a computer frees employees to concentrate on more valuable, productive work. One small business

owner claims, "I run a $4 million business with *five* people. If I didn't have the software I'm currently running, I would probably need at least 15 people for the large amount of paperwork we handle. My system saves a tremendous amount of money and time."[4]

"*We'll have to shut down if the computer breaks.*" One of the first procedures a computer owner should learn is how to make a backup copy of data. Backup copies protect against the loss of hours of work in case of an accident. The owner of a small consulting company claims, "All our files are secure in one place, and we can easily back them up (make copies) every day."[5]

A small business also should have a manual back-up system for the computerized one (probably "the old way" of performing a task). The owner of a bridge construction company says, "If the computer is ever out of commission, I can always process the bids, billing, payroll, and government reports the old way—by hand. It would take a lot longer, but I can do it."

"*We'll all have to become computer programmers.*" Given the large number and variety of business software packages available for almost every business application, it is highly unlikely that a computer user will require extensive programming skills. The small business owner needs to be *computing* literate—able to use a computer and software to solve business problems—rather than *computer* literate—able to write computer programs and to understand computer technology. To a small business manager, a computer is a means to an end and not an end itself.

The key issues facing the small business owner who decides to buy a computer are when to buy a computer; how much to spend; what functions to computerize first; which software to use; which hardware to buy; and where to buy the computer. Making

[2]Doni Fordyce, "The User Challenge," *Venture*, November 1985, p. 86.

[3]Johnathan Simonds, "Who Needs It?" *The Wall Street Journal*, January 28, 1985, p. 30.

[4]"The Big Five," *Venture*, March 1986, p. 80.

[5]Randy J. Goldfield, "The Software Boom," *Venture*, May 1985, p. 90.

The Components of a Computer System

The basic elements of a personal computer system include the following.

- *Central Processing Unit (CPU)*. This is the "brains" of the system. All of the data and calculations are processed here. The computer strings together the most basic data elements—bits (*binary digits*)—to form numerical codes for processing. An 8-bit CPU processes 8 bits (a byte) at a time. A 16-bit CPU processes data in 16-bit bytes, and is twice as fast as an 8-bit chip. Newer machines are built on a 32-bit CPU chip and handles bytes 4 times faster than its older cousin.
- *Floppy Disk Drive*. Disk drives frequently have 360k storage ability, although some have greater capacity. These drives read data from and write data to floppy disks, thin plastic platters with a coating similar to magnetic tape.
- *Hard Disk Drive*. A hard disk has a much greater storage capacity than a floppy disk. They usually contain 10 to 20 megabytes (10 to 20 million bytes) of data. They are more convenient than floppy disks since they can store several software programs and data files simultaneously.
- *Video Display Terminal (VDT)*. Similar to a TV screen, a VDT displays computer input and output. VDTs can be monochrome or color.
- *Keyboard*. The keyboard usually is separated from the console for greater flexibility. Separate function keys and a numeric keypad are convenient features.
- *Printer*. Dot-matrix printers are fast and relatively inexpensive, but the hard copy they produce is not "letter quality." Letter quality printers produce high-quality documents, but they are slower and much more expensive.
- *Disk Operating System (DOS)*. The computer's disk operating system is a set of software tools that governs program and data file management. It serves as a "middleman" between the computer hardware and the software, controlling basic tasks: reading information; storing it; updating it; maintaining it; and printing it out. There are several popular operating systems, including MS-DOS, PC-DOS, Apple-DOS, CP/M, and UNIX.

---

these decisions is not easy—especially for the novice. But, by following a rational, step-by-step approach, the small business owner can navigate "the computer jungle" and avoid common pitfalls along the way.

I. THE ADVANTAGES AND DISADVANTAGES OF GETTING A COMPUTER

Advantages of Computerization

Computers specialize in performing functions that can make a small business more productive. One writer states:

Computers, if used correctly, can become very potent business tools. They consolidate information, and then allow you to access it in a quick and easy fashion. They can eliminate the need of shuffling through large stacks of paper, only to find that what you were looking for is gone. Computers are organizers. The preparation of graphics, proposals, presentations, budgets, and analysis work can be done with greater ease. And the increase in productivity can be phenomenal.[6]

These are just some of the benefits a computer offers. Many of them are related to improved information processing and decisionmaking. In chapter 1, we saw how a substantial number of small business

---

[6]Fordyce, op. cit. p. 94.

failures result from problems that the owner might have detected if he had had the proper information. By improving data collection and information generation, computers can help many small business managers avoid failure.

Better Information.   Computers can provide the manager with better information for making business decisions. One fallacy many managers have about the advantages of computerizing is that more information will be available to them and this will improve their decisionmaking abilities. But, although a manager can retrieve volumes of information in just a few seconds with a computer, *more* information does *not* necessarily mean *better* information or better decisions. Most managers have an overabundance of information available to them. A properly designed computer system filters and condenses relevant information and presents it to the manager in a usable form.

More Timely Information.   Because computers can process data and instructions with lightning speed, computers offer a small business manager up-to-date information to use in decisionmaking. For example, the owner of an industrial chemical retail operation complains that before computerizing, his company was "way behind in getting reports and summaries to our sales representatives. The trouble was that they *needed* the information to make effective [sales] calls. [Since converting to a computerized system,] we cut the time required to get the information to the sales representatives from two weeks to two days. And, the reports are more reliable."

Accurate Information.   The computer improves the accuracy of the information used in decisionmaking. Using more accurate information yields higher quality business decisions and better solutions to problems. For instance, a partner in a supermarket began using a spreadsheet program to make a decision about adding another store to the chain. "I did all the projections on the computer and found the figures to

be a lot more accurate than those I did the old-fashioned way for my previous expansions," he says.[7]

Monotony Eliminated.   The computer can eliminate many of the dull, monotonous tasks of compiling and maintaining routine records. A significant proportion of paperwork involved in operating a small business deals with routine recordkeeping, a task that consumes an inordinate amount of the manager's and the employees' time. The computer is capable of completing these tasks in just a few seconds, freeing employees and the manager to focus on the major tasks of operating the business.

Improved Internal Control.   The computer can improve the degree of internal control over the small firm's basic operations. Cash management and inventory control are two of the most important functions performed in a small business; yet, in many firms, manual systems fail to provide the manager with the information needed. The availability of this data for making strategic decisions often spells the difference between the success and failure of the entire business. A properly designed computer system will generate this critical information early enough to improve the manager's ability to control inventory stocks and plan cash requirements.

Improved Customer Service.   The computer can improve customer service and customer relations. By increasing organizational efficiency, the computer contributes to the firm's ability to serve its customers promptly and accurately.

Electronic shopping services provide a good example of how computers offer customers maximum shopping convenience. Computer owners tap into an electronic service and, after paying an annual fee, can order everything from flowers to snow skis through their computers at home. One electronic shopper says, "I'm still a competitive shopper, and I'm using this as a tool to be more competitive." Although a survey found that 83 percent of electronic

---

[7]Goldfield, op. cit.

service users were satisfied, shopping by computer does not appeal to everyone. "You can't discuss the purchase with anybody, see it, handle it, or try it out," says one customer.[8]

Computerized checkout systems used by many supermarkets reduce the time that customers spend standing in checkout lines. These systems use an optical scanner to record each item's price, product number, and other data by "reading" the code of bars found on many packages. These bars, called the Universal Product Code (UPC), enable supermarkets to employ electronic checkout equipment to speed checkout time and automatically record inventory information. As the clerk passes the UPC on each item over the scanner, it reads this information, records it, and prints a receipt for the customer (see figure 13–1 and Small Business Report 13–2).

Early Problem Recognition. The computer can increase the manager's capacity to recognize problems early, before they threaten business survival, by making information readily available. Since small business managers get so involved in the operating details of the firm, they often overlook problems. Before a small business manager can resolve a problem, she must recognize that it exists. Computers can alert her to problems that might have gone undetected before.

Decisions Pretested. The computer allows the manager to test business decisions before actually implementing them. Because it takes just a few seconds for the computer to evaluate models under a variety of assumptions, it gives the small business manager the ability to foresee the effects of different solutions to problems. If the manager wanted to test the effects of different inventory levels on total inventory costs, he could feed the data into the computer and generate total cost estimates for each stock level. Henry Lee found this to be a major advantage in developing strategic plans for his pharmaceutical operation. Be-

FIGURE 13–1   Use of the Universal Product Code (Photo courtesy NCR Corporation).

fore using a microcomputer, Lee admits that corporate planning was ineffective: "Even when planning sessions were held, things were a bit informal. We really just eyeballed the numbers and made our best guesses." Then Lee purchased VisiCalc, a program that presents a financial "spreadsheet." With this new tool, Lee says, "Instead of having a blackboard session with everyone guessing what the numbers would be, we could run three different sets of assumptions through the computer almost instantly."[9] The computer quickly estimated the expected costs of implementing a richer sales mix and the impact such a move would have on profits. Small business managers can make better decisions when they have the capacity to "test" them before they implement them.

Improved Production Function. The computer can improve production scheduling and increase the efficiency of the production process. Because computers help the manager monitor inventory items

---

[8]Jeanne Saddler, "Computer Users Shop at Home over the Phone," *The Wall Street Journal*, February 20, 1985, p. 35.

[9]Steve Ditlea, "The New Software: A Powerful Ally," *Inc.*, November 1981, pp. 103–10.

What's Black and White and Read by a Computer?

In 1973, eight supermarkets introduced computers for automatic checkout systems using the Universal Product Code—the patch of lines and numbers now on practically every item in the store. Today, more than one-fourth of all supermarkets rely on such systems. A laser in the checkout counter "wraps around" each product as it passes by and reads the series of bars. One part of the bar code designates the manufacturer, while the other identifies the product itself.

Once it reads the UPC, the computer automatically deducts the item from the store's inventory, records the sale, and prints the item and its price on the cash register tape. Although the system is expensive to install (as much as $100,000), it lowers the food store's costs by streamlining and improving inventory control and recordkeeping. It also saves money by eliminating the need to stamp prices on every item in the store (prices are marked on shelves instead) and by speeding up checkouts. Grocers are not the only ones switching to UPC-based computer systems. John Hill, former president of the Materials Handling Institute, says, "Bar coding can go on any product, whether it's an automobile or a shipment of caviar." Nicholas Turkey Farms uses the system to keep track of its prime turkey stock. Each hen turkey has a bar code on its tail that can be scanned when the bird produces a healthy egg.

Even the U.S. Army uses the code on cars and gas pumps. "You drive up to a pump and scan the vehicle, and bill it directly to the correct department," says a Pentagon official.

Another benefit of the systems is their accuracy. A defense department study showed that one of every 300 manual entries is in error compared to one in every 3 million entries with a bar code system.

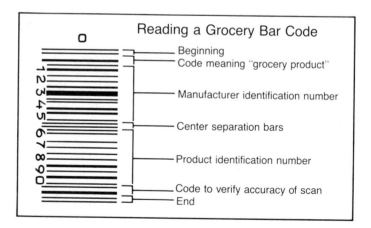

Reading a Grocery Bar Code

- Beginning
- Code meaning "grocery product"
- Manufacturer identification number
- Center separation bars
- Product identification number
- Code to verify accuracy of scan
- End

Sources: Randolph E. Schmid, "Computers Revolutionize the Grocery Business," *The Greenville News*, Food Section, February 1, 1984, p. 1; Linda M. Watkins, "Bar Codes Are Black-&-White Stripes and Soon They Will Be Read All Over," *The Wall Street Journal*, January 8, 1985, p. 39.

and maintain control over raw materials, they can be valuable tools in scheduling production. Timely records on stock levels allow managers to anticipate shortages and surpluses and to plan ahead for fluctuations in supply. Also, many analytical production scheduling models—Materials Requirements Planning (MRP), Program Evaluation and Review Technique (PERT), Critical Path Method (CPM), Gantt Charts, and others—are easily adapted to the computer. The speed with which computers can solve these models enables managers to determine the effects of changing one or more variables in the production process. Performing this "sensitivity analysis" on a computer helps management determine the optimum production schedule at minimum cost.

Computers now play active roles in the production process itself. In some industries, they control the operation of certain continuous process operations, such as oil refineries or power plants. One textile manufacturer uses a computer to control the production of oriental-style rugs. Once a production run is programmed into the machine, it can produce high-quality rugs in a multitude of colors and a variety of patterns for a fraction of the cost of an original rug, averaging one rug every 12 seconds!

Other manufacturers rely on computer-aided design and manufacturing (CAD/CAM) systems to improve the production process. Once available only on mainframe computers, CAD/CAM systems are becoming popular on personal computers.

Increased Productivity. Small business owners who implement effective computer systems frequently find that worker productivity rises. The computer frees employees to focus on their most important tasks. Workers are more efficient, and the quality of work is higher. The owner of a consulting and publishing firm claims, "when used effectively, computer programs can be extremely productive. The amount of work one person can do goes up by many hundreds of percent."[10] One small French

winemaker uses a computer to analyze the sugar levels of grapes to determine the ideal picking pattern for each day. The innovation is aimed at improving quality and boosting productivity because that "is the only way to stay viable," according to owner Bernadette Villars.[11]

Disadvantages of Computerization

For one reason or another, many small business owners have resisted the trend toward electronic data processing. A recent survey of chief executives found that 52 percent never use a computer (and only 19 percent use one often).[12] In addition, only 15 percent of all U.S. workers will be using a personal computer by the beginning of the next decade.[13] Many small businesses still operate without the help of a computer. While forgoing many of the benefits of using a small business computer, these firms also avoid the disadvantages of computerizing.

Expense. Computer systems can be expensive. Purchasing or leasing a computer, plus maintaining the system properly, can be costly to the small business. One shopper complains, " . . . you don't just buy a computer. You buy parts you hope will work together. It's like buying a car part-by-part."[14] In addition to the computer itself, the small business must purchase peripheral equipment, such as printers, modems, memory expansion boards, as well as software packages and supplies.

As technology advances, prices for computer systems are dropping and will continue to decline. Technological innovations have brought personal computer prices down so low that excessive cost is no longer a valid excuse for not purchasing one.

Obsolescence. The computer system purchased

---

[10]Goldfield, op. cit.

[11]Roger Ricklefs, "Many Wine-Makers in France Are Striving to Improve Quality," *The Wall Street Journal*, January 16, 1986, p. 1.
[12]"The Boss's Computer," *The Wall Street Journal*, May 2, 1986, p. 23.
[13]"Using Computers," *The Wall Street Journal*, April 26, 1985, p. 1.
[14]Simonds, op. cit.

today may become obsolete tomorrow. Some small business owners refuse to buy a small computer because they fear that it will become useless before the firm gets maximum value from it. Indeed, many small companies must change computers often because models become technologically obsolete as new models are introduced. But just because a computer is obsolete does not make it useless. Any piece of equipment, including a computer, will eventually become obsolete but may still retain its usefulness to the business for many years. In many cases the small business owner can still use a computer to perform another function even though it has become too outdated to handle its primary purposes. Obsolescence is not necessarily a problem for the small business owner who takes a long-term perspective and plans for computer utilization. One computer consultant suggests that "The real question for the user is what will happen to his business as the years go by, not what will happen to his computer. Will it . . . need a more complex computer in a few years, or will the current model still be functional in [the] operation down the road?"[15] A computer becomes obsolete only when it ceases to be useful and fails to meet any of the firm's data processing needs.

Costly Programming Errors. The computer can commit costly mistakes if it is programmed incorrectly. The information a computer generates for decisionmaking is only as accurate as the data fed into the system. The acronym GIGO—Garbage In, Garbage Out—means that if the basic data given the computer is faulty, the information it produces will be worthless. Small Business Report 13–3 describes several examples of incorrect data or instructions which create useless output and numerous business problems.

Management "Crutch." The computer can become a management "crutch" if relied on too heavily as a decisionmaking tool. When they purchase a com-

puter, some small business managers expect the machine to make managerial decisions for them. These managers are quite disappointed when they feed into the computer multitudes of data describing a difficult managerial decision, and the system fails to provide the answer. Computers are *not* substitutes for managers. They are simply tools that can assist small business managers in solving problems and making decisions. The manager must be the final judge.

A computer also will not solve poorly defined problems. In an effort to solve production problems, the manager of one small electronics firm purchased a microcomputer, just as a major competitor had done. The problems worsened after the firm purchased the computer, resulting in the loss of what little faith the manager had in computers as managerial tools. He did not recognize that the computer could not solve a problem he had not yet defined. Computers can be valuable management tools, but only when applied to specific problems. One expert advises, " . . . a personal computer tends to amplify whatever it is that you already are. To take something that you are doing poorly and begin doing it with a computer may only intensify the problem."[16]

Customer Alienation. Computers are just beginning to overcome their image as cold, insensitive machines that people cannot deal with. As Small Business Report 13–3 illustrates, computers can make mistakes that to customers are unreasonable. A thinking, reasoning human would understand the particular circumstances surrounding the issue, but a computer will not. It is no wonder that many customers see computers, and the companies that use them, as impersonal. One woman who was the victim of a computerized mistake lamented, "You can talk to people to get things like this straightened out, but you can't talk to computers."[17]

---

[15]James Robertson, "Living with Obsolescence," *Venture,* November 1982, p. 20.

[16]Richard B. Byrne, " 'Leveraging' Productivity," *Personal Computing,* June 1985, p. 43.

[17]"When Computers Goof—Consumers Air Their Frustrations," *U.S. News & World Report,* May 2, 1977, p. 61.

Snafu!!

A common myth is that computers never make mistakes. But computer systems can, and often do, commit errors when faulty circuits or improper instructions produce gremlin-like foul-ups in program execution. The majority of mistakes are the result of programmer errors—"bugs" in computer software that wreak havoc with output accuracy. Some examples follow.

- A woman ordered one book from a publisher. Her name was added to a computer list, and she began to receive a new book every month without placing an order.
- One magazine subscriber received 700 copies of the same issue as a result of a computer error.
- A credit card company sent a San Francisco woman two letters simultaneously. One commended her good credit rating and boosted her credit limit, but the other notified her that her account had been discontinued. All this because she exceeded her credit limit.
- A Chicago hotel sent out letters to past customers informing them of its remodeling plans, but a programming error caused a printer to send the letters to the wrong mailing list. Men deluged the hotel's management demanding that it explain to their wives, many of whom were threatening divorce.
- One woman received a credit card bill for $00.00 from a persistent computer. She ignored the bill, but the computer kept sending the bill. Finally, as a last resort, she sent the company a check for $00.00 and the bills ceased.
- When a computerized air defense system for North America was first brought online, it alerted officials of an approaching object so large and so fast that escape was virtually impossible. Officials quickly realized that programmers made a major mistake with the sky-scanning system—it was tracking the moon in its orbit around Earth!
- A chain of retail bookstores had problems with its computer that kept returning unsold books to the wrong publisher and then following them up with bills, past due notices, and threatening letters.

The small business manager who uses a computer system must recognize this feeling and be prepared to deal with it. He must also accept the responsibility and the costs of any errors caused when the computer fouls up. As technology continues to refine computer capabilities and improve flexibility, this "impersonal machinery" image should lessen. But for now this is a problem nearly every computer user faces.

Employee Anxiety. A common fear among employees of a company about computerizing is that they might be replaced by the computer. When computers burst into the business community over 20 years ago, many employees, especially middle managers, feared becoming one of the displaced unemployed—those whose jobs had been taken over by computers. While computerization displaced a number of jobholders, it created many more jobs than it eliminated, although many at different skill levels. A few companies have been able to reduce their work forces, especially clerical staff, by introducing a computer system, but in most cases the work force stays the same. The computer just creates different ways of solving problems and making decisions.

The wise small business manager will recognize that the decision to computerize will create anxiety among employees—either from fear of being replaced or from having to work with a machine they do not understand—and will take steps to alleviate this discomfort. A simple, yet effective, technique is to focus on communicating with employees about the change. Question-and-answer sessions, in which employees openly and honestly express fears, doubts, and reservations they have about the new computer, can reduce greatly the level of anxiety concerning the change. Also, a well-planned training program to familiarize employees with the computer and its applications can reduce the fear that arises in many workers simply because they do not understand the machine. One small company turned resistance into excitement by offering to sell computers to employees for their personal use at a steep discount. Such techniques reduce employee resistance to change and allow for a smooth transition to computerization.

Employers are becoming more concerned about the health risks to workers who spend long hours in front of computer video display terminals (VDTs). The most common complaints include eyestrain, fatigue, headaches, dizziness, and blurred or double vision. Twenty-five state legislatures are considering VDT bills aimed at protecting workers from these problems. One expert offers the following tips to avoid these problems:[18]

- Look away from the screen every few minutes; this gives the eyes lots of little breaks.
- Take a break every hour. Walk around for a minute or two.
- Get an eye examination every 6 months.

II. ALTERNATIVES TO CONSIDER WHEN CHOOSING A COMPUTER

The small business manager must evaluate the firm's needs and its specific situation before making a final decision about buying a computer. Some business

owners purchase computers hastily without proper preparation and for the wrong reasons. Says one small business owner, "I've seen businesses . . . just go out and buy an Apple or IBM PC and think that's all they need to do. An awful lot of money is spent and wasted that way—the computer just sits there gathering dust."[19]

The variety of computer options facing the small business owner is staggering. But, equipped with a sound plan, he can sort through them and choose the best alternative for his business. There are three basic options: service bureaus; time-sharing centers; and in-house computers.

Service Bureaus

The service bureau's name implies the nature of the functions it performs for the small business—it offers the services of a computer and relieves the small firm of the costs of purchasing, implementing, and maintaining a computer system. The services the bureau sells to its client firms include transforming the small firm's basic input data into computer-acceptable form; processing the data; and producing the appropriate output documents in the format the manager requests. The small business gives the service bureau input data, such as checks, sales tickets, journal entries, and deposit slips. The service bureau then supplies output in the form of check registers, various journals (sales, cash receipts, purchases), the general ledger, financial statements, tax reports, or other vital managerial information. The service company picks up the input documents, takes them to its computer center, processes them, and then returns the output.

Before choosing a service bureau, the small business manager must evaluate the quality of the service offered. Will the bureau accept the firm's source documents in their present form, or will they require major modifications? Will the bureau assist the firm and its employees in interpreting the output

---

[18]Jim Seymour, "VDT Precautions Pay Large Return for Small Expense," *PC Week*, April 16, 1985, p. 26.

[19]Fordyce, op. cit. p. 86.

"*Do you have one that can help me decide which is the one for me?*"

Source: From *The New Yorker* 56, no. 45, December 29, 1980, p. 61.
Drawing by Modell; © 1980 The New Yorker Magazine, Inc.

reports and in integrating them into the decision-making process? Will the service bureau generate the required output reports quickly enough to suit the firm's information needs? Other points the small firm should consider in choosing a service bureau include:

- What is the bureau's reputation? Are present clients satisfied with the service they receive from the bureau?
- Is the bureau reliable? Will it keep your data confidential? Are its employees competent and capable of handling the work load?
- Is the bureau financially sound? Will it be in business tomorrow?
- What type of backup procedures for processing data does the bureau have? If the system is "down," how quickly can you get your output reports?

- What rates does the service bureau charge? Are its fees competitive?
- Does the firm require a long-term contract? Are contract terms not in your favor?

Time-Sharing Centers

Under a time-sharing arrangement, a small business shares a computer owned by someone else. The main computer is housed at the time-share center's facility, and the small business purchases computer time through a terminal at the small business location. The small firm must lease or rent a computer terminal (usually $50 to $200 per month), but it does not have to install and maintain a complete computer system. The time-sharing operation works like a public utility—the small business pays only for the computer time it uses. Using the keyboard on the terminal, an employee enters the firm's source data, which is transmitted through telephone lines to the center's main computer. The computer processes the data and transmits the output back to the small business subscriber within seconds. The turnaround time for a time-sharing arrangement is much shorter than that for a service bureau since the small business is linked directly to the center's computer. Turnaround time for a time-sharing operation averages under two hours, compared to an average of just under two days for a service bureau.

Time-sharing arrangements handle the routine information requirements of the small business quite easily and are very efficient in producing special reports on short notice. In some cases, the small firm must retain a computer programmer on staff at least part time to create the software to generate needed reports. In other instances, the time-sharing center has computer consultants to assist the small firm in creating programs. These consultants interview the manager and his employees to determine the small company's information needs and develop the appropriate software to meet these needs.

In-House Computers

As technology forces computer prices down and escalates computer capability, a growing number of small business owners are choosing to purchase microcomputers (also called personal computers). Blinded by dreams of increasing their businesses' productivity, many business owners rush into the purchase without a working plan, resulting almost always in a system that fails to live up to the owner's expectations. The process of choosing a personal computer must begin with what the owner knows best—the business and its needs. The key to making a wise purchase is to translate what the owner knows about the company into the criteria a computer system must meet, following the steps described next.

Step 1. Develop a List of Current Activities. What is the nature of the business? Does it move merchandise, sell ideas, process information, serve people, or crunch numbers? After defining the general scope of

the business, the owner should break down current business activities into more detailed categories that can be computerized. Popular candidates for computerization include accounting, recordkeeping, inventory control, file management, graphics, time management, financial analysis, forecasting, word processing, training, and telecommunications. This is a process that requires the involvement of employees who will be using the system or be affected by it. Their input also might identify areas the owner would have overlooked.

At this stage, the owner should separate the most important activities of the business from the least important ones. Not every activity in the business is equally important. Focusing efforts on improving the performance of a "least important" activity produces little benefit to the company.

Step 2. Decide How Much and Which Areas of the Business to Computerize. The small business manager getting started with computing should *not* choose a problem area when he begins computerizing. If the source of trouble is in the manual system itself, computerizing it will generate the same faulty information, only faster. The owner who buys a computer to unravel an organizational mess will end up with a computerized mess.

A better approach is to start with a smooth, well-functioning system. The chances for success are much greater, and success in the early stages of computerization builds confidence in the new computer system. In addition, computerizing a company strength increases the owner's understanding of exactly what a computer can do for the company. As one expert claims, "Managers should always use the personal computer to leverage what they do best. They should *not* use it to try and fix that part of the business which is broken, at least not at first."[20]

This step also determines the amount of money the company will invest in the computer system. An attorney may want a relatively simple system aimed

---

[20]Byrne, op. cit. p. 41.

at improving word processing efficiency. But, the owner of a retail shop may want an integrated multi-user system to track inventory, process receivables and payables, produce financial reports, and forecast sales and cash flow. The budget must consider the proposed use of the system as well as "incidental costs" such as training, peripheral equipment, software, consultants (if necessary), and maintenance.

Step 3. Define the Informational Needs of the Function(s) to be Computerized First.

The firm's information needs manifest themselves in a number of ways. For example, if the manager plans to computerize the inventory control system, he should begin by studying the flow of information through the manual inventory recordkeeping system. How are purchase orders and invoices routed and recorded? What is the system for recording inventory receipts and distributors? Are employees needlessly recording the same information more than once? Which employees produce and receive what reports? Identifying these and other related issues will help the owner define the nature and form of the information the company needs.

Despite his best planning efforts, the owner's definition of the information needed and its users will change. Explains one small business manager who followed this approach, "The one thing you don't know until you have a system up and running is exactly what information you're going to be extracting."[21] Still, the owner must define the type, the quantity, the flow, and the users of the information needed. Describing the importance of this phase, a small business manager says, "You have to anticipate the answers you want to get out of a computer. The computer is only going to give you back what you decide to put in."[22]

Step 4. Shop for Software Packages That Will Perform the Required Functions.

A computer without software is like a car without an engine; both are utterly useless! Each year, computer users spend about $3 on software for every $1 they spend on hardware. Not all computers run all software programs; therefore, the best approach is to choose the appropriate software first and then select a computer that will run it. Unfortunately, most managers choose the opposite—and most treacherous—option; they buy the hardware first and then purchase the software. One owner bought a personal computer because "it was a real deal" only to find that it would not run the software he needed most, so his "deal" was not a good one after all.

The first phase of evaluating software packages is to collect information on those that perform the functions the owner is most interested in. Computer magazines such as *Info World, Personal Computing, Byte, PC, PC World*, and *List* contain detailed descriptions of popular programs, comparisons of similar packages, and reviews of software. Computer user groups are another valuable source of information. A user group is an informal "club" with members who use a similar type of computer. Most groups meet frequently (and are easy to find) to swap information on their computers as well as software and its applications.

Trade associations also may be able to offer advice on which programs companies in an industry rely on. In addition, directories such as the *Datapro Directory of Microcomputer Software* provides detailed listings of thousands of different packages. These sources can help the manager answer key questions about software: Is it easy to use (i.e., "user friendly")? How good is the documentation? Will the publisher or the vendor provide service and support? How long does it take to learn to use? Section III will explore software in detail.

Step 5. Choose the Hardware.

By selecting the software first, the owner narrows the field of hardware candidates from the "hardware jungle." The final

---

[21]Fordyce, op. cit.

[22]Jeffrey Tarter, "Confronting the Computer Age," The Retail Appliance Management Series, *Planning and Management #2*, General Electric Company, p. 5.

decision depends on many features, but the machine's processing power, expandability, compatibility, and serviceability are crucial. Hardware will be discussed in more detail in Section III of this chapter.

Step 6. Integrate the System into the Business. Converting a business from a manual system to a computerized one takes time and hard work. Employees who will be using the new system must have time to become familiar with it *before* it is put into action. In addition, the system must be tested thoroughly. The manager must be sure that the system is free of all "bugs" *before* converting existing procedures onto the computer.

The conversion process takes time, money, and a great deal of patience. One small business owner describes his company's conversion to a computer system, "The consultation period took several months. The hand-holding took close to six months. And it took a year and a half before we went on line completely . . . . It was a difficult transition."[23] Computer experts estimate that a user can expect to spend at least four hours learning to use the machine and up to forty hours learning the software.

Conversion also requires a financial investment. One expert states, "Business users will pay at least twice the cost of the hardware for the software to be up and running." In addition to the cost of getting the hardware and the software in place, there is the cost of training employees to use the system. Cutting corners here is dangerous since employees who are unskilled in running the computer system will render it useless. Adequate training is vital to the success of a new computer system. On-site sessions, training consultants, vendor representatives, and full-blown courses to improve employees' computing skills are well worth the price. One small business owner found that sharing the cost of computers for his employees' use at home drastically boosted their level of computer expertise on the job.

Most companies find that a gradual phasing in of the computer system works much better than an overnight change. This allows the company enough time to solve the nagging little problems that inevitably arise when introducing a computer system. One business owner says, "We first started working with the accounting system and installed it in sections—general ledger, accounts receivable, accounts payable, inventory, and sales orders. The last part was purchase orders."[24] Typically, with such a step-by-step process, each subsequent phase becomes easier due to the effects of the "learning curve."

Another advantage of a gradual phase-in is that the small business owner has the advantage of running the new system parallel to the old one before relying solely on the new one. Computer experts highly recommend parallel operations to ensure the reliability of the new computer system. The owner should compare the results of the two systems for at least a month or two. Doing the same work twice may appear to be a waste of time, but the confidence it builds in the new system is worth the extra work.

The small business owner can make the conversion process go much more smoothly by heeding the following suggestions:

- Do not be intimidated by computers. The manager must be determined to get control of the computer system.
- Become computing literate. The best way to avoid intimidation is to learn more about computers and how to use them.
- Set a good example. The owner must take the lead in showing how the computer can boost efficiency and productivity in the company.
- Reward employees for becoming computing literate. This can help overcome employees' misgivings and anxieties about the new system.
- Be sensitive to employees' feelings. Emphasize their skills that the computer cannot replace.
- Create an appropriate environment for learning. The *least* effective setting is in the midst of the

---

[23]Fordyce, op. cit. p. 92.   [24]Ibid.

workplace with its constant distractions and pressures.

- Set up a training center. A manager should offer instruction of the new computer system and its applications *on company time.*
- Offer incentives for improved performance. Reward teams of employees (if possible) for increased productivity. Recognition can be as effective as money.
- Set up controls. A system of controls ensures that the company will get the most from its computers.

III. CHOOSING SOFTWARE AND HARDWARE

Software Considerations

There are two broad categories of software: horizontal and vertical. Horizontal programs have broad appeal and are based on standard applications like spreadsheets, word processing, database management, graphics, and communications. Horizontal packages are available in three different formats: stand-alone programs; families of programs, each with a different application, but sharing a similar set of commands; and integrated programs, which combine two or more applications (like a spreadsheet, word processing, and graphics) into a single package.

Vertical programs are available in the same applications as horizontal programs, but they are aimed at a narrower group of users. A custom-designed program is an example of vertical software. These packages tend to be more expensive and are tailored to a company's particular situation. Unless a business is highly unique—like a highly specialized print shop—horizontal programs probably are more suitable.

Software Applications. The majority of small businesses rely on horizontal programs for seven primary applications: word processing; spreadsheets;

database management; accounting; graphics; communications; and integrated software.

Word Processing. The most popular business (and home) application for personal computers is word processing. Some experts estimate that word processing is the primary use for 75 percent of all computer systems.

Word processors come in two types, screen and format. The more popular screen version follows a "what you see is what you get" philosophy. The system will print out just what you see on the screen. A format program is more complex; the owner can see the text on the screen, but she must use a series of special commands to set up page specifications. She won't be able to see what a document looks like until she prints it out.

Popular features of word processing programs include: automatic wrap-around; automatic deletion and insertion of text; virtual memory; spell checking; automatic pagination; footnoting; indexing; and the ability to merge "form letters" with a mailing list. Some businesses may require special features such as superscripts and subscripts, foreign language characters, or mathematical and engineering symbols. Popular word processing programs include WordStar, Easywriter, Word Perfect, Word, PFS: Write, Displaywrite, Xywrite II, Volkswriter Deluxe, Samnat, Multimate, and Office Writer.

Spreadsheets. Electronic spreadsheets have remained a popular application since VisiCorp introduced VisiCalc in 1979. A spreadsheet is simply a grid of rows and columns, much like an accountant's pad. The owner can enter data, text, and formulas into the "cells" on the spreadsheet. Once the owner sets up the format of the spreadsheet, he can take advantage of its powerful "what if" capacity. He can evaluate the outcome of various scenarios and assumptions merely by changing the appropriate cell value and pushing a button. For example, the manager could determine the effects of various product prices on the company's bottom line in just a matter of seconds. The chief executive of one small firm says:

We started using spreadsheets about a year ago for analyzing our sales territories and our products in ways we'd never thought of before. We've got some twenty-seven product lines, and we actively deal with approximately 2,000 accounts. Our spreadsheet capability has had a tremendous effect on the way we handle our planning; it's meant important changes in our sales territories, and it's helped us create more salable products, too.[25]

Most spreadsheets allow the analyst to enter data; create formulas; format cells; copy and move entries; and make simple graphs. They also include routine arithmetic and statistical calculations and valuable financial functions (present value, future value, payments, etc.). Popular spreadsheet packages include Lotus 1-2-3, VisiCalc, SuperCalc, PFS: Plan, PC-Calc, Perfect Calc, Multiplan, Excel, Framework, and Enable.

Database Management.   These programs are the equivalent of electronic file folders and file cabinets. A computer file is merely a collection of individual records. Database management software includes two types of programs: file managers and database managers. Both types perform similar functions. However, file management programs process only one file at a time, while database management programs permit a manager to create and to work with numerous files simultaneously. Both types of programs record information into *fields*, which are accumulated into *records*, which, in turn, are compiled into *files*. They allow the owner to search through a large number of files to gather necessary information (although a database manager is usually quicker than a file manager). For example, an owner could search his entire list of accounts receivable to find those customers whose accounts have balances of $100 or more and are more than 30 days past due. Many programs also permit the owner to transfer data from a database file to other programs (like spreadsheets).

Database management programs are spreading quickly because of their flexibility, speed, ability, and ease of use. Popular packages include dBase III + , PFS:File, R:Base 4000, Reflex, PC File, Paradox, Knowledgeman, Dayflo, and Data Ease.

Accounting.   A growing number of small business owners are turning their accounting functions over to personal computers. Software packages can handle a company's general ledger, accounts payable and receivable, inventory control, purchasing, and financial statement preparation much faster and more accurately than manual systems. There are two types of accounting software: modular and integrated. A modular program is built around a specific accounting application (such as accounts receivable) and can be used alone or combined with other modules. A complete accounting system built from modules is more expensive than an integrated system, but it usually is more flexible. In addition, the owner can choose only those modules he needs in his accounting system.

An integrated package is a comprehensive accounting system that usually operates from the transactions entered through the general ledger. Once the owner enters transactions into the general ledger, the integrated accounting package automatically posts them to the appropriate subprogram.

A small business owner can spend as little as $50 for an accounting program that will perform the complete accounting function. Popular accounting programs include ACTG-1, DAC Easy Accounting, Rags to Riches, BPI Support Plus, Back to Basics, and Interconnect Software's modular package. One accounting software manufacturer says, "Our philosophy is to give the masses a product they cannot afford at a price they can."[26]

Graphics.   Businesses that need basic graphics capability (bar and line graphs or pie charts) may find that a spreadsheet program meets their needs. But,

---

[25]"The Big Five," p. 72.

[26]Tom Bodgett, "Getting a Handle on Your Business," *Personal Computing*, April 1986, p. 120.

for more sophisticated graphs, the business owner could turn to a specialized graphing program. Some packages can transform a personal computer into a professional slide presentation. Others create customized graphs that can be printed in a variety of sizes and colors. Popular graphics packages include Chart, PFS:Graph, Boardroom Graphics, Chart-Master, Graphease, Super Chartman, VisiPlot, Mac-Paint, MacDraw, Frame-Up, and Executive Briefing.

Communications. Communications programs enable a small business owner to use her computer to communicate with other computers. To do this she needs a modem, which links the computer to the telephone line. With this system, the owner can use computer linkups, remote computer terminals, and large databases like CompuServe and The Source. Still, only about one-fourth of the personal computers in use have communications capability.

Telecommunications packages enable an owner to exchange information with branch offices or sales representatives in the field. They also provide automatic telephone dialing and answering, electronic mailbox services, and access to an unbelievable amount of up-to-the-minute information on a wide variety of topics. Popular telecommunications programs include Smartcom II, Crosstalk, Datapath, Passport, PFS: Access, Starlink, Lync, PC-Dial, Mite/TS, and Softcall.

Integrated Software. Integrated packages, which combine what are normally separate programs into one, are becoming a dominant force in the software market. An integrated package might contain word processing, spreadsheet, graphics, communications, and even accounting applications. These programs can help managers perform more work in less time.

There are three types of integrated software programs: tightly integrated; integrated series; and systems integrator. Tightly integrated programs offer an important advantage: when the manager changes data in one application, the program automatically updates it in every other application. While these packages contain a variety of software applications in one, none of them is quite as complete as an individual software package. Popular tightly integrated programs include Symphony, Framework, Encore, Enable, and Open Access.

The integrated series of software is a related set of separate programs that allow the user to transport data easily from one program to another. There are several advantages to this approach. Once the owner learns one part of the series, he can learn the others very quickly. These programs require about half as much computer memory as tightly integrated packages since the computer runs only one program at a time. The key disadvantage of an integrated series is that moving data from one program to another is more difficult; in addition, revised data in one program is not carried over to other programs. Popular integrated series software includes Smart Software, the PFS: Family, the Profit Center Series, the Plan Family, the Perfect Family, the Assistant Series, and the VisiSeries.

The system integrator combines the advantages of the two previous types of packages. These packages allow the manager to store several individual applications programs in the computer's memory and to run them simultaneously. Their primary drawback is the huge amount of memory they require. Popular systems include DesQ, Concurrent PC-DOS, Top-View, and Microsoft Windows.

Hardware Considerations

The computer's processing power determines the amount of information it is capable of handling in its data processing duties as well as the type of software packages it can run. Most small business computers have a minimum of 256k of memory capacity. (Memory size is measured in kilobytes, k, which represent 1,024 bytes or characters.) The majority of serious business programs require a minimum of 256k, although some may take 512k or more. To avoid buying a system that cannot handle the job, the small business owner should try essential software packages out on every machine he considers.

Many computers come with a standard 256k memory board, which can be expanded with add-on boards (in multiples of 64k) or with integrated microchips. Expandability and its cost are crucial to choosing the right system for a small business. As a business grows, its computing needs will increase, and the computer system must be able to expand to meet those needs. In addition, by adding peripheral equipment, such as hard disk drives, printers, modems, graphics cards, and color monitors, the small business manager can expand the computer and its capability as the company grows. The ideal computer system serves the business needs today as well as several years down the line. The machine's expandability is a major determinant of its ability to meet the small firm's future needs.

Compatibility of machines is a crucial issue for many computer users. Compatible machines can run the same software packages and can access information stored on disks by other computers. Unlike telephones, many computer systems are incompatible. Computer manufacturers have used different methods and systems to accomplish the same end. Thus, a small business owner with two different machines has no guarantee that they can communicate with one another or even run the same software packages.

IBM set the standard in the computer industry when it introduced the IBM PC in 1981. Recognizing the giant company's "staying power" in the business, software manufacturers rushed to provide software for the IBM PC. Software for the PC quickly became the standard for hardware manufacturers to mesh with. Today, many computer manufacturers produce "compatible" machines that mimic IBM's products. But, *there are different degrees of compatibility*. A 100 percent compatible machine (there are several) will read from and write to any disk designed for a "big-name" computer. (There are thousands of programs written for the IBM PC). The owner who purchases a noncompatible machine runs the risk of buying the equivalent of a computer "Edsel."

Compatibility also is important when the small business adds new machines to its system. If new computers are not compatible with existing ones, the company's existing programs and data will be useless on the new machines.

As with the purchase of any technical piece of equipment, the small business owner must consider a computer's serviceability. Although computer reliability is increasing, computers occasionally break down. For some companies, a computer breakdown can interrupt the entire flow of business. Still, too many owners give little, if any, consideration to a computer's serviceability. Before purchasing a computer, the wise business manager will investigate the manufacturer's after-sale support. What happens when the computer breaks down? Will the vendor repair it, or must the owner return it to the manufacturer for repair? Does the computer come with a warranty? If so, what are its terms? Will the vendor offer a "loaner machine" until repairs are made? If not, how long can the business operate without the computer? What backup plan does the company have during a breakdown? Finally, the owner must remember that the lowest priced computer may not be the best deal when it comes to service and support. Small Business Report 13–4 offers suggestions on keeping a small computer healthy.

The owner also must consider the "staying power" of the computer manufacturer whose machine he is considering buying. If the company fails (not an uncommon occurrence), the purchaser may find it impossible to get service and replacement parts for these "orphaned computers." According to an attorney, once a company files for bankruptcy, "for all practical purposes, [customers] are out of luck."[27]

IV. WHERE TO BUY

Not only must the small business owner decide which software and what hardware to buy, he also must decide *where* to purchase them. The majority of shoppers turn to a computer retail store first because

27Abby Soloman, "Gone, but Not Forgotten," *Inc.*, June 1984, p. 168.

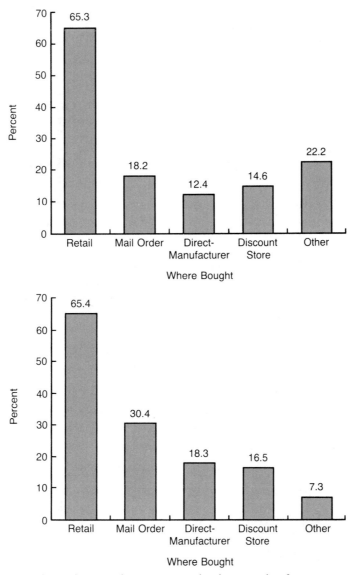

FIGURE 13–2   Where shoppers buy computer hardware and software.

Source: "The Man-Machine Interface," *Venture,* May 1985, p. 100.

they can see their choices firsthand and actually try them out. In the store, the owner should study the various software packages and ask lots of questions about each brand and type of computer and how they can perform the jobs he has defined. The man-

ager should take nothing for granted when purchasing a computer or software.

While the retail shop is the primary place of purchase for both hardware and software, there are other options. An owner can purchase virtually every

Thwarting Computer Gremlins

Most small business computers suffer from the effects of neglect when it comes to proper maintenance. The small business manager may use the computer daily, but often disregards its upkeep. Such a mistake can lead to a number of costly computer "glitches," brief malfunctions in computer circuitry, which have been known to destroy programs and information. If the temperature in the computer room rises 20 degrees or more above room temperature (68°F), miscues often occur. The ideal site for a computer is an office where the temperature is about 75 degrees and the humidity is about 50 percent. Locating the computer next to a heater or a window with direct sunlight can cause serious damage to its circuitry. A well-ventilated, air conditioned room or a portable fan will help keep the computer cool.

Static electricity is another potential source of damage to the computer. The touch of a finger to the computer can send a surge of static electricity through the system capable of destroying information, programs, and circuits. Since static electricity is conducted through dry air, humidifiers can help eliminate it. Anti-static mats, sprays, and towelettes may also be a deterrent.

Another common element creating computer problems is dust. Dirt and dust cause excessive wear on disk systems and foul computer circuitry. The best way to prevent such damage is to place the computer in a relatively clean area—not in a remote corner of some dusty warehouse. Also, a dust cover placed over the hardware when it is not in use could eliminate these difficulties. Be careful when choosing a dust cover. Vinyl covers tend to retain heat, so many experts recommend using a cover made of a cotton and polyester blend.

Cigarette smoke not only is dangerous to human health, but it also is a hazard to the computer's well-being. Tar and tiny particles from the smoke work their way into the computer. Avoid smoking, eating, and drinking while working with the machine.

To avoid "etching"—burning an image on the computer screen into the screen itself—it is wise to turn the brightness level all the way down when leaving the monitor for more than a minute or two. Etching cannot be removed once it happens.

Voltage fluctuations—dips, surges, spikes, brownouts—can damage the com-

computer and computer-related product through the mail. Software prices typically are 20 percent to 50 percent lower when purchased through the mail. But, shopping by mail has disadvantages. The owner is buying merchandise sight-unseen, and there is no support available in case questions or problems arise. The manager also should ensure that the mail order company's ads appear regularly since this suggests that the company is reputable. Figure 13–2 shows where shoppers buy their hardware and software.

Another alternative to buying retail is to pur-chase a used computer. Computers, made mostly of electronic circuits and chips, do not wear out rapidly. In fact, a slightly used computer is less likely to break down since it has been "burned in." On the other hand, mechanical parts, like printers, keyboards, and disk drives, wear out more frequently. There are only a handful of used computer stores across the country, so shoppers must turn to the classified ads, user groups, and publications such as *Computer Shopper*.

The primary advantage of buying a used computer is price. Many start-up companies have no puter's circuits or destroy programs and information. These glitches can be avoided by attaching a voltage regulator (which costs about $1,000) to smooth out irregular currents. A voltage suppressor/noise regulator is less expensive (about $60), but it protects the machine only from voltage increases.

Floppy disk drives have moving parts and are subject to potential problems. Most computer specialists recommend frequent cleaning (every 6 to 15 hours of "pure operation") to avoid losing valuable data. There are many types of cleaners, but most experts recommend the "wet/dry" drive cleaner. These cleaners rely on a white fiber disk sprayed with a cleaning solution, which is put into a disk jacket and spun for a few revolutions. Do *not* use cotton swabs dipped in alcohol to clean drive heads; the direct pressure can misalign or damage them.

Floppy disks, which store computer software and valuable information, often suffer from neglect and misuse. They are more sensitive than phonograph records, and fingerprints, bends, creases, scratches, and dents can render them useless. There are three "don'ts" for floppy disks: don't touch the surface of the disk itself; don't forget to keep a disk in its protective sleeve; and don't *ever* wipe it off as though it were a record. Extreme temperatures and markings from ballpoint pens often ruin disks, too. Magnetic fields from any source (radios, tape recorders, televisions) can destroy the data on a disk in seconds.

Damage frequently occurs when the computer is moved. Always use the cardboard disk head protectors when moving a computer, even a portable. Jostling and jarring the machine can cause the disk drive heads to become misaligned.

Experts also recommend the use of miniature vacuum cleaners and moist towelettes to remove dust, dirt, and paper bits from printers and computer keyboards. Putting a single drop of lubricating oil on a dot-matrix printer's carrier bar will improve its performance as well.

Of course, a computer is subject to normal wear and tear just like any other machine. But a little common sense and the investment of a little time and money in preventive maintenance can keep a small computer functioning well for years to come.

Source: Adapted from Matt Mihovich, "How to Keep a Small Computer Healthy," *Inc.* reprint, with permission of publisher; Sid Kane, "Upkeep Reminder," *Venture*, April 1984, pp. 35–36, with permission of the publishers.

---

choice but to buy used systems. Used computer prices can be 30 percent to 40 percent below the cheapest mail-order firm's price on similar new equipment. Used computer prices tend to be highest during tax season, back-to-school, and Christmas. Says one dealer, "The best bargains are in January."[28]

There are disadvantages to buying used computers, however. The biggest drawback is the lack of service and support. Therefore, used computers are

not the best buy for the computer novice. Used machines are not likely to be state-of-the-art equipment either, but for many owners, this is not a crucial point.

The buyer should look for dents, scratches, stains, and other signs of extraordinary wear and tear. He should look for sticking keys, listen for strange noises from disk drives and printers, and try several software packages to make sure they run. Disk drives are especially vulnerable; when moved improperly, the disk heads can be knocked out of alignment. In general, the manager should look for

[28]Bob Davis, "Used Computers Can Be a Bargain, But Pray They Don't Break Down," *The Wall Street Journal*, December 3, 1985, p. 33.

SMALL
BUSINESS
REPORT
13–5

A Checklist for Buying Used Computers

- Know the name of the computer vendor and the specific model number for each part in the system.
- Shop around for the best price. Use classified ads, trade periodicals, advertising lists, user groups, and other sources to locate sellers.
- Check the record of the broker or dealer you are thinking about buying from. Ask for the names of past customers and contact them.
- Make sure the dealer has the specific model you want. Sometimes a dealer will promise a computer and *then* find it, but at a higher price.
- Examine the computer carefully for signs of abnormal wear and tear. Find out who owned the machine before. Ask the dealer to perform minor repairs.
- Stay clear of equipment that is in poor shape. The "do-it-yourselfer's dream" can turn into the computer user's nightmare.
- Lock the dealer into a firm delivery date. Make sure you get all of the peripheral equipment and software that is included in the package.
- Do not pay for the system until it is completely installed and running to your satisfaction.

Source: Adapted from Ronald Rosenberg, "Should You Buy a Used Computer?" *Inc.*, September 1979, pp. 66–71 with permission of the publisher.

---

signs that indicate how well (or how poorly) the previous owner maintained the computer.

V. ENSURING COMPUTER SECURITY

For years, only large corporations had to be concerned about computer crime. But, because of the rapid proliferation of personal computers, small companies are becoming the favorite targets of electronic thieves. One security specialist claims, "Small companies are often pushovers. They're concerned with growth and cash flow. They don't understand computer security and don't have money to implement it. They become prime targets."[29] Their vulnerability is likely to increase in the future because the growing number of standardized software packages and companies using telecommunications programs to set up networks make theft by computer easier. A recent study by the American Bar Association found that half of the small companies surveyed reported some type of computer crime in their businesses within the past year. No one knows how much victims of computer-related crime lose each year. Authorities estimate that less than 20 percent of all computer crimes are even reported. Explains a computer consultant, "The bigger the theft, the greater the embarrassment to the company. Who the hell wants to display their managerial shortcomings to their constituents?"[30]

Computer criminals get plenty of rewards for their illicit efforts. One FBI official estimates that a computer thief nets $500,000 in the average "job." According to one computer security specialist, "If you want to steal money and get away with it, use a computer and steal a lot."[31]

Many small business owners who end up declaring bankruptcy never realize that computer theft was the culprit. The computer has become the bur-

[29]William Souder, "Computers Vulnerable in Small Companies," *Inc.*, October 1985, p. 22.

[30]Erik Larson, "Crook's Tool," *The Wall Street Journal*, January 14, 1985, p. 1.

[31]"When Thieves Sit Down at Computers," *U.S. News & World Report*, June 25, 1985, p. 8.

glary tool of the electronic age. Despite the prominent media attention given to "hackers" (outsiders who illegally invade a company's computer file), the greatest threat to computer security comes from *within*. Computer security specialists offer a profile of the potential "inside" computer criminal:

> He or she is a trusted employee of long tenure, but has recently become a gambler, a boozer, or a helpless victim of love. He or she has a sick spouse, hungry kids. He or she is overwhelmed, most commonly by debt, but occasionally by an unappeasable longing for the rich life. He or she is disappointed, disgruntled, torn apart by resentment and envy. He or she is not just anyone—clerk, manager, teller, salesperson, friend, relative, or anyone in the stockroom—but anyone, under certain circumstances could be he or she.[32]

Another security expert came up with a description of the most feared electronic crook: a "disgruntled employee who, until he was passed over for a promotion or raise or (his) family situation suddenly changed drastically for the worse, was a sterling middle-aged company man . . . ."[33]

Sabotage is another worry for the small business owner. Shortly after one company fired a data-processing employee, she returned to the computer room with a load of hard feelings and a powerful magnet. The value of the data she destroyed was estimated to be $10 million![34]

Computer security experts have defined three types of computer crimes:[35]

- *Input Scams.* These are the most common type and involve changing or creating data ("diddling," in computer slang) while entering it.
- *Output Scams.* The thief simply steals valuable

computer files and information, such as customer lists, bank account numbers, etc.

- *Thruput Scams.* These require the highest level of expertise. "Trojan horses" and "logic bombs" are examples of these scams.

Securing computer data against such scams requires a common-sense plan. First, the small business owner must determine the value of the data he wants to protect. If it leaks out, will it threaten the business (e.g., trade secrets) or create legal liability (credit records)? *He should secure only the data that needs to be secured.*

Next, he should determine how to secure the data. There are many physical measures on which the owner can rely. Long used by mainframe computer owners, encryption devices are now affordable by even the smallest business. These devices use a "password" key and a mathematical formula (an algorithm) to scramble and unscramble data. They also restrict entry to computerized files because only those persons who know the password can gain access to them. A key can be used on the computer itself to prevent unauthorized users from "booting up." Other simple security measures include locking office doors after hours, keeping floppy disks in a safe (and lockable) place, and making backup copies of disks to be stored off-site. Another effective security measure is to divide computer tasks among several employees to avoid having one employee with complete access to every computer file. Such concentration of "computer power" encourages some employees to tamper with information banks.

Most computer security experts agree that the key to computer security is *people*. One expert says, "The real bottom-line issue is the user, who has to be educated to the importance of security."[36] Another concurs, "Improperly trained people are the weakest link."[37] A common problem is that some employees

---

[32]Vin McClellan, "Of Trojan Horses, Data Diddling, & Logic Bombs," *Inc.*, June 1985, p. 106.

[33]Larson, op. cit.

[34]Winn L. Rosch, "The Law on Mischievous PC Tampering: Don't," *PC Week*, October 8, 1985, p. 30.

[35]McClellan, op. cit. p. 106.

[36]Dan Hall, "How to Protect Your Business Data," *Business Computing*, October 1984, p. 51.

[37]Erik Larson, "For Fun or Foul, Computer Hackers Can Crack Any Code," *The Wall Street Journal*, April 13, 1983, p. 1.

innocently give classified information to outsiders who claim to be systems analysts or consultants.

Encouraging employees to maintain security standards on a daily basis is crucial to the success of a security system. Another key is avoiding reliance on a single form of security. The ideal system uses two independent methods in tandem.

Generally, the type of security system a small business owner chooses depends on the cost of security devices, the impact of potential data losses on the company, and the way the system affects employee productivity. As one expert explains, "It's always a balancing act against the value and the productivity of the system that you're dealing with."[38] While no security system is foolproof, the small business manager who uses a balanced approach will protect data adequately without alienating honest employees.

VI. SUMMARY

Once cost effective for only large businesses, computers have become functional and cheap enough for small companies to employ. In the near future, the small business manager who is not computer literate will be obsolete. The benefits of computerization are:

1. Better information for use in making business decisions.
2. More timely information.
3. Increase in the accuracy of the information used in decisionmaking.
4. Elimination of many of the monotonous tasks of compiling and maintaining routine records.
5. Improvement of the degree of internal control exercised over the firm's basic operations.
6. Improvement of customer service and customer relations using existing facilities.
7. Improvement of production scheduling and increased efficiency of the production process.
8. Increased managerial capacity to recognize

problems early before they threaten business survival.
9. The manager can test business decisions before actually implementing them.
10. Allow workers to focus on their most important tasks, boosting the company's productivity.

Despite its many advantages, computerization still has certain drawbacks:

1. It can be expensive.
2. A system purchased today may become obsolete tomorrow.
3. It can commit costly mistakes if programmed incorrectly.
4. It can become a management crutch if the manager relies too heavily on it as a decisionmaking tool.
5. It can alienate customers.
6. It can create anxiety and distrust among employees.

In evaluating the decision to purchase a computer, the manager must first consider the firm's data processing needs. A basic cost/benefit analysis should point out the firm's need for a small business computer. Examining the firm's goals, its growth rate, the current flow of information through the organization, the desired flow of information, and other factors can help the manager decide whether the firm needs a computer.

If an analysis indicates that it does, the small business manager faces three basic options: a service bureau; a time-sharing center; and an on-site computer.

Technological advances have brought the microcomputer into the small firm's reach. Choosing a personal computer involves six basic steps:

1. Develop a current list of business activities.
2. Decide how much and which areas of the business to computerize.
3. Define the informational needs of the function(s) to be computerized first.
4. Shop for software packages that will perform the required functions.

---

[38]A. Richard Immel, "Data Security," *Popular Computing*, May 1984, p. 68.

5. Choose the hardware.
6. Integrate the system into the business. Most experts recommend running the new system parallel with the existing manual system before relying solely on the new one.

The small business owner must decide where to buy computer products. Retail shops frequently offer support and service, but charge higher prices than mail-order houses. Used computers offer 50 to 80 percent savings, but are best for experienced computer users.

Personal computers have brought with them the possibility of computer crime. In fact, small companies have become a favorite target of electronic thieves. The greatest threat to computer security comes from *within* the company. The owner must take steps to secure data, but only the data that needs to be secured. Encryption devices, duplicate records, and separated job functions are some of the techniques that help secure data, although no security system is foolproof. Experts agree that the *real* key to computer security is *people*.

STUDENT INVOLVEMENT PROJECTS

1. Locate a small business that does not use a small computer. Assist the owner in evaluating the firm's computer needs. What business functions, if any, could benefit from computerization? Would you recommend the purchase of a small computer? Why?
2. Contact a local small business that uses a small computer. How is it used in the firm? What functions does it perform? Can you suggest an expansion of the system into other functional areas? Did the manager follow the procedure for purchasing a small computer outlined in this chapter? Is the computer well-suited to the firm's needs?

DISCUSSION QUESTIONS

1. Why are computers becoming more feasible for use in small businesses?
2. Outline and briefly explain the advantages of computerization.
3. Explain the statement, *"More* information does not necessarily mean *better* information."
4. Will the introduction of a computer normally eliminate employees? Why or why not?
5. How can the computer help the small business manager solve problems and make decisions?
6. Outline and briefly explain the disadvantages of computerization.
7. Is obsolescence a problem for most small business computers?
8. What does "garbage in, garbage out" mean?
9. What factors should the manager consider in the decision to computerize?
10. Explain the advantages and disadvantages of each of the three computer options available to a small company: service bureaus; time-sharing centers; and on-site computers.
11. What is software? How should the small business manager select software? What is a "friendly" program?
12. What is hardware? What factors should the small business manager consider in evaluating hardware?
13. Outline the steps involved in choosing a personal computer. Why should an owner choose software before selecting hardware?
14. Why is computer security a problem? What can the small business manager do to improve computer security?

SECTION SIX

MANAGING PEOPLE:
THE MOST VALUABLE
RESOURCE

Human Resources Management

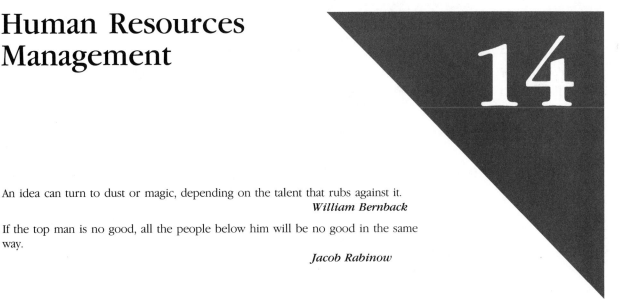

An idea can turn to dust or magic, depending on the talent that rubs against it.

William Bernback

If the top man is no good, all the people below him will be no good in the same way.

Jacob Rabinow

Upon completion of this chapter, you will be able to:

- Recognize that acquisition and management of the firm's human resources is a critical factor in the organization's long-term success.

- Recognize the negative impact to a small business of the loss of key employees and the value of personnel planning.

- Perform a job analysis, which includes the creation of job descriptions and job specifications.

- Evaluate techniques available for recruiting new employees.

- Evaluate the advantages and disadvantages of the various sources of potential employees.

- Evaluate the methods used in selecting the best qualified person.

- Develop the skills of interviewing potential employees.

- Recognize the value of employee orientation and what should be included during the orientation.

- Appreciate the contribution training can make to the productivity of employees.

- Explain both the theoretical and critical aspects of determining employee compensation.

- Explain employee stock ownership plans as a method of financially involving employees in their business.

- Recognize the need for performance appraisals and how they impact the output of employees.

The productive and creative power of people can never fully be appreciated. In a small business, each employee has a dramatic impact on the firm's overall performance. The growth and development of the business is inevitably tied to the ability of the owner and founder to surround herself with the proper combination of employees. This chapter will explore human resources management, a series of interrelated activities designed to help the small business owner determine how many and what kind of employees the business will need; predict when these

┌───┐

| SMALL | The Emergence of Expressivism
| BUSINESS
| REPORT | The term "the emergence of expressivism" was coined by Yonkelovich and Immer-
| 14–1 | wahr to describe what they predicted to be the attitudes of employees in the future.
| | In the future, employees will see themselves as primarily working to fulfill their ex-

The term "the emergence of expressivism" was coined by Yonkelovich and Immerwahr to describe what they predicted to be the attitudes of employees in the future. In the future, employees will see themselves as primarily working to fulfill their expressive needs, rather than their needs for survival or material success. Increasingly, employers must find ways of structuring work so that it appeals to jobholders' expressivist needs for autonomy, creativity, community, and entrepreneurship. Managers will need to reevaluate the rigid hierarchies and sharp status differences that characterized the low discretion [traditional] workplace.

A recent book by Levering, Moskowitz and Katz, *The 100 Best Companies to Work for in America*, brings together many themes that are important to keep good employees. The firms listed in the book have good workplace climates and low turnover. The authors cite characteristics beyond good pay and benefits, including the following:

1. Encourage open communication.
2. Promote from within.
3. Stress quality, fostering a sense of employee pride in output.
4. Allow employees to share in the profits.
5. Reduce distinctions among ranks.
6. Create as pleasant a workplace environment as possible.
7. Encourage employees to be active in community services.
8. Help employees by matching funds they save.
9. Make people feel part of a team.

The payoff to firms with these characteristics are significantly higher productivity, lower employee turnover, and higher profits.

Source: Adapted from Henry Eason, "Keeping Good People," *Nation's Business,* July 1984, pp. 37–39, with permission of the publisher.

additional people will be needed; develop descriptions and specifications for each job; recruit and select the "best" people to fill the jobs; orient new employees as well as train both new and experienced employees; and decide on the proper compensation for each employee.

I. HUMAN RESOURCES PLANNING

For a large organization, the untimely loss of a good employee or manager can be frustrating, but for a small business it can be devastating. Key people in small businesses are likely to shoulder a larger share of responsibility than they would in larger organizations because small businesses can rarely afford to be overstaffed.

Expansion of the business requires the proper timing in hiring new personnel. Planning, therefore, is critical. If you fail to hire new employees as the work load grows, you are likely to lose good employees who find themselves constantly overworked. Routinely working overtime and weekends can lead to fatigue and a decline in employee productivity. As you plan for growth, you need to develop a corresponding plan for adding new people to accomplish the added tasks. Further, you need to make sure new employees have the skills they will need to fulfill these tasks. Being caught short of skilled personnel

FIGURE 14-1 Job analysis questionnaire.

Name _____   Department _____

Payroll title _____

Name, immediate supervisor _____

Instructions: Please read the entire form before making any entries. Answer each question as accurately and carefully as possible. When you complete it, return this form to your supervisor. If you have any questions, ask your supervisor.

Your duties

What duties and tasks do you personally perform daily?

What duties do you perform only at stated intervals such as semi-weekly, weekly, or monthly? Indicate which period applies to each duty.

What duties do you perform only at irregular intervals?

Supervision of others

How many employees are directly under your supervision? (List job titles and number of people assigned to each job.)

Do you have full discretionary authority to assign work; correct and discipline; recommend pay increases, transfers, promotions and discharge; and to answer grievances?

Do you assign work, instruct, and coordinate the activities of your subordinates?

Materials, tools, and equipment

What are the principal materials and products that you handle?

List the names of the machines and equipment used in your work.

List the names of the principal hand tools and instruments used in your work.

What is the source of your instructions? (e.g., oral, written, blueprints, specifications, other.)

What contacts are you required to make with persons other than your immediate supervisor and departmental associates?

Give the job titles and the department or organization of those with whom you deal and describe the nature of these contacts.

Decisions

What decisions do you have to make without consulting your supervisor?

Responsibility

Describe the nature of your responsibility for money, machinery, equipment, and reports.

What monetary loss can occur through an honest error?

may greatly damage the firm's ability to meet its commitments. When there is a shortage of these key high-skilled people, a company must train lower-skilled employees to assume these expanded responsibilities. So, a human resources plan must take into account the time and effort associated with teaching the necessary skills. In today's competitive market a cross-trained staff is no longer a luxury, but a means of both improving overall performance and insuring against the calamity that would result from losing key highly-skilled people.

Job Analyses, Descriptions, and Specifications

It takes very little effort to thoroughly analyze each job in a firm, but this analysis creates a foundation for future job performance evaluations. A job analysis is an orderly and systematic evaluation of all the facts about a job. When a small business is expanding, established job boundaries often become fuzzy. When this occurs, the owner must ask the following questions: Are the job duties rigid, or can they be reassigned to other employees as needed? Does the employee need special training to perform the job, or can she learn the job by doing it? In small firms, management conducts job analyses somewhat informally and often in conjunction with the employees who are presently doing the jobs. A job analysis questionnaire such as that in figure 14–1 will aid the small business owner in asking the right questions to help collect all the facts about a job.

Information gathered through job analysis helps the owner develop job descriptions and job specifications. A job description describes the duties and responsibilities associated with a job, along with the working conditions involved. Sometimes a statement as to where the job is performed and how the duties are carried out is included. A job specification describes the type of person best suited to fill the position in terms of skills, education, experience, and other personal job-related characteristics. The

job description sets forth duties; the job specificat[] translates these duties into qualifications necess[] to perform the duties. Figure 14–2 shows a sam[] job description form.

Developing job specifications is never e[] because it requires a series of decisions ab[] thetype of people the firm wants to hire. For [] stance, if the firm anticipates rapid growth in [] near future which will require more sophistica[] employee or supervisor talent, the job specificati[] will likely call for a person whose talents exceed [] initial job for which she is being hired. If you wish[] cross-train your staff, then everyone being hi[] needs to have the potential to master each job. []

However, it is critical that job specifications [] flect the company's real needs. The firm must av[] hiring overqualified workers as a result of job spe[] fications written to require skills beyond the[] needed to do the job. Overqualified employees [] likely to become bored and dissatisfied with []] work and quit. In addition, while they are employ[] the firm is paying wages beyond what are needed [] the job, and the higher turnover rate produces c[] stant human resources problems.

II. RECRUITING THE BEST EMPLOYEES

When a small business owner needs to replace[] employee because of expansion or a vacancy, he [] explore four general areas: within the business; [] side competitor's businesses; outside sources; a[] within the schools.

Recruiting from Within

Promotion from within can be a powerful policy [] motivate and retain quality employees. Someo[] who knows the operations of the business can beg[] to contribute quickly to the new job. If cross-traini[] has taken place on a regular basis, only a minimu[] amount of additional skill training may be require[]

FIGURE 14–1 *Continued*

Records and reports

What records and reports do you personally prepare?

What is the source of the data?

Checking of your work

How is your work inspected, checked or verified?

Who does this?

Physical requirements

What percentage of the time do you spend in the following working positions?
  Standing _____% Sitting _____% Walking about _____%

What weight in pounds must you personally lift and carry? _____ pounds

What percentage of the working day do you actually spend lifting and carrying this weight?
_____%

Are any special physical skills, eye-hand coordination, and manual dexterity skills required of your job?

Working conditions

Describe any conditions present in the location and nature of your work, such as noise, heat, dust, or fumes, which you consider unfavorable or disagreeable.

Hazards

Describe the dangers or accident hazards present in your job.

THIS PORTION IS TO BE FILLED OUT BY YOUR SUPERVISOR.

Education requirements

What is the lowest grade of grammar school, high school, or college required of a person starting in this job?

Previous experience

What kind of previous work experience is necessary for minimum satisfactory performance for a new employee on this job?

Give the length of experience required.

Teaching

Assuming that a new employee on this job has the necessary education and experience to qualify for the work, what training is necessary after the employee is on the job to achieve an acceptable performance level? (Specify training needed and period of time to acquire it.)

_____   _____
  Date   Signature of Supervisor

FIGURE 14–2 Sample job description form.

Form 1   **Identification Facts**

Job title _____   Location _____

Other titles used _____   Number employed: M _____   F _____

Brief summary of nature or function of job[a]

Code number[b] _____

Salary range: Minimum _____   Maximum _____
  Average bonus or incentive payment _____

Working hours: Shift: _____   from _____ to _____
  Overtime hours: _____ never   _____ seldom   _____ frequent
  Average hours per week _____

Misc:

[a]A one-sentence description, to give a general idea of job.
[b]Job definition (from the *Dictionary of Occupational Titles;* your local State Employment Service Office can be helpful.)

Form 2   **Skill Requirements**

Educational requirements (general education—grade or years)
Grammar   High   Business
School _____   School _____   School _____   College _____

Specific education for the job:

Job experience

Previous experience required:
  Acceptable type and length:
Length of time with organization:
Previous jobs held:
Next job in line of promotion:

FIGURE 14–2 *Continued*

Contacts made regularly as part of the job

Within the company

Outside the company

Exercises supervision over

Position of individual

Subject of supervision

Is supervised by   (position and type of supervision)

Job duties

  Regular:
    Before open for business

    During business hours

    After business hours

  Periodic (weekly or monthly):
    Performed on regular time

    Performed after hours

  Occasional:
    Performed on regular time

    Performed after hours

Job knowledge
  General

  Special and departmental

Procedures and methods required
  Technical information

  Related information

Use of equipment

  Type of equipment used

  Special operations

FIGURE 14–2 *Continued*

Form 3   **Effort Demand**

<u>Physical Activities</u>

_____ Standing	_____ Turning	_____ Reaching	_____ Pushing	_____ Smelling
_____ Walking	_____ Running	_____ Throwing	_____ Pulling	_____ Tasting
_____ Balancing	_____ Stooping	_____ Lifting	_____ Fingering	_____ Hearing
_____ Climbing	_____ Sitting	_____ Carrying	_____ Feeling	_____ Seeing

<u>Work Characteristics</u>

_____ Planning	_____ Showing initiative
_____ Directing others	_____ Getting along with people
_____ Writing	_____ Working at various tempos
_____ Showing enthusiasm	_____ Concentrating amid distractions
_____ Being well groomed	_____ Remembering names and faces
_____ Controlling emotions	_____ Examining and observing details
_____ Using arithmetic	_____ Remembering details
_____ Working accurately	_____ Attending to many items
_____ Discriminating colors	_____ Making decisions
_____ Talking	_____ Working rapidly

Form 4   **Working Conditions**

_____ Inside	_____ Hot	_____ Dirty	_____ Inadequate light
_____ Outside	_____ Cold	_____ Dusty	_____ Inadequate ventilation
_____ Humid	_____ Dry	_____ Odors	_____ Working with others
_____ Hazards	_____ Wet	_____ Noisy	_____ Working around others
_____ High places			_____ Working alone
_____ Change of temperature			_____ Working under pressure

Details of working conditions (summary based on working conditions):

Details of hazards:

Permissible handicaps: Limb _____   Hearing _____   Sight _____

Source: U.S. Small Business Administration, "How to Write a Job Description," Management Aid No. 171, Washington, Rev. September 1976, p. 2.

The following are some well-established advantages to promoting existing employees to fill job vacancies.

1. As their manager, you know employees' work habits. You will not have the same opportunity to assess the work behavior of outside applicants.
2. The cost of recruiting internally is very low.
3. The transition into the new job is generally accomplished with the least amount of disruption to ongoing operations.
4. Promoting from within can motivate others to work harder to prepare for future opportunities.

However, there are some drawbacks to filling vacancies from within. First, the new employee must be qualified. To simply promote on the basis of seniority creates hostility among those persons who believe they are better qualified. Secondly, inbreeding through a promote-from-within policy can stifle new and fresh ideas. Whether or not a business chooses to develop a promote-from-within policy, the small business owner should at least allow existing employees to apply before looking outside the business.

Recruiting from Competitors

By hiring competitors' employees, not only does the owner gain an employee who already has the skills to do the job, but also who can provide knowledge of competitors' operations. New employees are likely to give you information about the operations of the firm they just left, which can be very valuable.

The repercussions of "raiding" or "pirating" competitors is normally reciprocal behavior on their part. This trend can result in a costly upward spiral of labor cost as each business hires away the competitors' key people at ever-rising rates. In some cases, local businesses agree that they will not directly contact competitors' employees.

Recruiting from Outside Sources

Recommendations of Current Employees. If current employees enjoy working in the business, they may be willing to recommend a friend or relative who is both qualified and a good worker. Employees generally do not recommend someone who will reflect poorly on them.

Former Employees. In many cases former employees who for one reason or another dropped out of the work force may be encouraged to return. This has been especially true for people who chose to care for young children at home. As the children reach school age, many of these former employees seek work again. They know the "ropes" and can make a rapid transition back to their old jobs. Some businesses have filled vacancies through job sharing. This technique divides one full-time job into two or more part-time jobs. Some people find that these part-time jobs fit the lifestyles they have chosen.

Walk-Ins. During the regular operations of the business, job applicants walk in seeking employment. By retaining the applications of those who seem qualified, a firm can create a pool of potential candidates. From the pool of applicants, the firm can extend selected invitations to reapply. In effect, some initial screening has already taken place. Through the selective use of this pool of applicants, the company can recruit without announcing the vacancy to the entire business community.

State Employment Agencies. Most larger cities or towns have branch offices of the state employment agency. These state agencies are affiliated with the U.S. Employment Service and offer their services free of charge. For lower-level entry positions, these agencies can be quite effective in providing lists of job candidates.

Private Employment Agencies. Private employment agencies can be effective in locating employees with specialized skills or experience, but can be very expensive. The agencies conduct the initial screening and recommend only the candidates who fit your job specifications.

Newspapers and Trade Magazines. Advertising a vacancy in the local newspaper is the most popular recruiting method. A large number of applicants usually respond to these advertisements, although many will not be qualified for the job. Thus, hours must be spent screening applications to find those with the potential for the job. Further, response to these ads can be unpredictable. For example, one small company advertising for a manufacturing position got no responses, while another had over 2,000 responses for just four positions. Advertising in trade magazines is most effective because their readers likely have at least an interest in the type of position advertised.

Recruiting from Schools

The schools are an often overlooked source of entry-level employees. Building a working relationship with high schools, community colleges, and technical education centers can reap real benefits. By volunteering time as an instructor, the small business owner can come face-to-face with potential candidates. This investment of time may result in a continuous flow of the best qualified students directly into the business.

III. SELECTING THE BEST QUALIFIED PERSON

Applications

When recruiting efforts produce a number of qualified applicants, the emphasis shifts to selecting the *best-qualified* person for the job. To ensure that she has appropriate information about each candidate, a manager should use an application that gives the needed information. The application should seek only job-related information. In creating an application, a manager should concentrate on obtaining information that will assist her in evaluating the applicant's potential for success on the job. An application should emphasize a candidate's educational background, work experience, skills applicable to the job,

work history, special job training, military experience, and managerial or supervisory experience. Most applications ask the candidate to supply both work and personal references. The manager should *always* check work references to ensure that the applicant has had the work experience claimed and to detect, if possible, previous positive or negative work habits.

Tests

In some instances, small business managers employ a variety of tests to aid them in the selection process. Tests can be very useful in providing information; however, tests alone do *not* select people. Tests only provide additional information, which can be blended with other inputs in making a decision.

There are a few basic types of employment tests that can be used for screening. Measurement and performance tests have the greatest reliability. As the name implies, performance tests ask the candidate to demonstrate the ability to perform the tasks associated with the job. For example, a person who applies for a secretarial position may be asked to take a typing and shorthand test. It is reasonable to expect a candidate to have the skills necessary to do the job being applied for and to be able to demonstrate them. The focus should always be on giving the applicant a fair chance to demonstrate skills at doing work directly associated with the job.

General intelligence tests measure the ability to do well on traditional school topics. Aptitude tests indicate an applicant's ability in specialized skills. They can measure manual dexterity, or verbal, numerical, or psychomotor skills. These specialized tests can give the manager a measure of the applicant's potential to do a job that demands these skills.

Personality tests attempt to determine how applicants will relate to co-workers and how they will respond under stressful conditions. Closely related to personality tests are interest inventories, which attempt to measure the applicant's interest in a specific type of work. However, personality and in-

Fighting the War Against Drugs

American society is confronting a drug crisis that poses many dangers. Every day, thousands of people destroy themselves a little bit at a time by taking drugs. In addition to the obvious toll on human lives, there are other costs, and businesses shoulder a substantial burden of them. The annual economic cost of drug and alcohol abuse in America now exceeds $140 billion. As many as 10 million workers are regular drug users. A recent study lists the characteristics of the typical drug user in the workforce:

- Is born between 1948 and 1965.
- Asks for early dismissal or time off 2.2 times as often as fellow employees.
- Is late 3 times as often.
- Has 2.5 times as many absences of 8 or more days.
- Is 5 times more likely to file a workers' compensation claim.
- Is involved in accidents 3.6 times more often than other workers.

Businesses are a major force in the battle against drugs. One anti-drug consultant claims, "Businesses are doing more than any other sector to combat the use of illegal drugs in society. One reason is the impact of losing a job on the drug user." One manager says, " . . . the threat of losing a job seems to be the most effective means of getting a person to face the problem."

Small business owners must realize that the starting point in avoiding drug-related problems is hiring drug-free employees. It is much easier not to hire a drug abuser than to fire an employee who has become one. However, even the best screening device won't catch every drug-user.

The technique of testing employees for drug use causes controversy: Should employers test job applicants and current employees for evidence of drugs? Do such tests violate laws against unlawful search and seizure, or do they enhance the safety and welfare of other employees? Most courts and arbitrators agree that drug testing is acceptable for new job applicants. However, opinions of drug tests for current employees whose job agreements never mentioned them are more varied. Companies with clearly defined anti-drug policies and employee assistance programs are likely to run into the least resistance. One manager whose company has instituted an employee assistance program claims, "We stress that the supervisor's job is to document, not diagnose." First, a manager should establish a record of an employees declining job performance, increased absenteeism and tardiness, or faltering productivity. Then, he must show that drugs are causing the problems before giving the employee the ultimatum—get help through the employee assistance program (or some other source) or lose his job. In most cases, the employee chooses to get help.

To protect itself from lawsuits, a small business should develop a drug policy that is effective, consistent, and respects individual rights. The policy must apply to *everyone*, and the company must communicate it to all employees.

Source: Adapted from William Hoffer, "Business' War on Drugs," *Nation's Business*, October 1986, pp. 18–26 with permission of the publisher.

terest tests have been criticized because applicants can fake them.

Interviews

The final selection among candidates is usually made following personal interviews with each person. The interview process is of utmost importance because it brings the manager face-to-face with potential employees. The manager must plan for an effective interview. She should use the information collected from previous sources to prepare interview questions. She should always write down the questions and build an outline for the interview. A specific time should be set for the interview which should take place in a setting free from interruptions. The manager should first make the applicant as comfortable as possible by asking a couple of general questions about background or interests. Since the applicant likely will be nervous, she should try to put the candidate at ease before beginning to ask the more important questions. Some managers find it useful to use job descriptions and specifications in conjunction with the application form to discuss the job and the applicant's qualifications. Managers adopt individual interview styles with which they feel most comfortable. The interviewer can then develop follow-up questions that require thoughtful answers. The interview should help uncover the candidate's real knowledge of the job and attitude about work.

After interviewing all candidates, the owner must make a final decision. She must consider the skills and the temperament of each applicant, keeping in mind that while she can teach an applicant skills, it is unlikely she can modify his personality.

IV. ORIENTATION AND TRAINING

Orientation

The person selected and hired should be brought quickly and effectively into the business' work environment. Most small business managers overlook the orientation of new employees. A manager cannot assume that employees will already know what it has taken others months or years to learn. He should be sure that the new employee has an opportunity to meet each co-worker. The owner must invest time early on to ensure that the employee is comfortable with the new responsibility. New questions arise each day, so he should be available to answer them. He should be sure that the new employee is familiar with the business' products or services. He should emphasize how important the new employee is to the success of the business, and explain again the employee's role in the business. If the employee has to report to someone other than the owner, he should be sure the employee understands the chain of command.

A new employee is as close to the "ideal worker" as any business can get. An effective orientation program can help keep her that way. It should focus on showing the new employee how the company is different from competitors; what its strengths and weaknesses are; what its purpose, goals, and objectives are; and how it plans to accomplish the goals. The owner must cultivate the new employee's enthusiasm for her job and get her started in the right direction. Typical orientation programs, which cover all of the routine details of the job the first day, don't work. While these "housekeeping" issues are important, the owner should not bore the employee with them on the first day at work. *These* are the issues the owner can help the new employee pick up as she grows into the job. Showing the employee how her work contributes to the total organization is much more valuable.

Training

Employee training goes beyond the initial training period. The key to continued employee growth is training and providing the opportunity to use what is learned. Employees generally recognize that in this time of rapid technological change, learning new skills is the only protection against obsolescence.

Avoiding Invasion of Privacy Lawsuits

SMALL BUSINESS REPORT 14–3

Each of us expects our right to personal privacy to be respected in the workplace. But, where do public good and employee privacy collide? The following are the 10 Commandments to follow in reducing your risk of being sued over violation of employees' privacy.

1. *Adopt a sensible policy* that is the least intrusive into an employee's legitimate privacy rights yet reasonably protects the company's interest.
2. *Publish* the policy so that employees clearly know the rules of the game.
3. *Distribute* the rules so that managers and employees know what to expect.
4. *Train managers* in the proper ways to implement policy daily.
5. *Monitor* disciplinary records relating to privacy for adherence to company policy.
6. *Collect* confidential information *only* when necessary. Protect confidential information. Allow disclosure of data only with the written consent of the employee involved.
7. *Establish* complaint procedures to ensure adherence to policy.
8. *Segment personnel files* so that only the relevant data are available to those who have signed in to review files.
9. *Avoid* inquiries and observations regarding employee's outside relationships unless they are absolutely necessary to protect trade secrets, keep information confidential, or guard against a serious conflict of interest. In such cases, an employee should be counseled and given reasonable options.
10. *Leave* suspected criminal activities for authorities to deal with.

Source: Adapted from John S. McClenahen, "The Privacy Invasion in a Job Setting, How Personal is 'Too Personal'?" *Industry Week*, November 11, 1985, pp. 50–53, with permission of the publisher.

Training is an investment in the firm's human resources as well as in the business. Effective training works to increase productivity and to improve employee morale; helps to develop participants' personal confidence; and, in the long run, lowers the cost of doing business.

Training methods can be divided into two broad categories: on-the-job and off-the-job. Most training in small businesses is on-the-job, which has the greatest impact on workers since it is performance related. People generally want to do a good job and enjoy being able to improve their job performance.

New employees may be trained directly on the job or through vestibule training. In both cases, the training is directly job related. Vestibule training usually is associated with manufacturing. In vestibule training, new employees are trained on the same equipment they will be using on the line, but in an area away from the production line. After achieving an acceptable level of performance, the new employee joins the line.

Apprenticeship is the most traditional type of on-the-job training. Employees in an apprenticeship program work alongside experienced workers and are taught by example. In many highly skilled disciplines, the apprentice may spend years learning the trade. Formal tests are given before a person is allowed to practice the trade as a journeyman. To a large extent, these traditions still thrive in small business. Although it may not be called apprenticeship training, owners hand down the skills of the trade to employees. Employees learn mostly by watching, asking questions, being asked questions, and most important, doing the job.

Off-the-job training involves attending schools

or seminars, or doing work away from the job. Trade or technical schools are a good source of training for employees who wish to advance in the business. For the most part, these institutions have low tuition and conduct both daytime and evening classes. Cooperation with these schools can be very rewarding. Community colleges also are an excellent choice for learning about supervision. In addition to regularly scheduled classes, many organizations such as Small Business Development Centers offer seminars tailored to the needs of small business. Equipment vendors also provide employees with specialized training.

The most influential factor in the development of employees is the owner's commitment to training. If the small business manager demonstrates through personal involvement that continued learning is important, others will follow suit. A firm's competitive edge is sharpened by having a team of highly quali-fied employees who find that continuing education is closely correlated with increased organizational performance.

V. COMPENSATION

Compensation consists of wages and fringe benefits. Very often businesses never explain to employees either in absolute terms or in after-tax dollar terms the cost the companies assume for the fringe benefits. When an employer purchases a fringe benefit for an employee, the employee no longer has to obtain it from wages earned. Consequently, the employee receives a benefit at a substantial bargain. For example, assume that the business provides an employee with life, medical, and disability insurance at no cost. If required to purchase this insurance personally, the employee would need to earn the money; pay federal, state, and possibly local income taxes on it; and

---

SMALL BUSINESS REPORT 14–4

Is a Flexible Benefits Program Suitable for Your Business?

Flexible benefit programs don't fit everybody; however, you may want to consider them if you can answer "yes" to the following five questions.

1. Does your company have a high percentage of younger employees, women, or professionals?
2. Do you sense a lack of appreciation among employees for the high value of benefits in relation to salaries?
3. Is your company trying to attract and retain a higher caliber of employees than in the past, as competition increases or your industry changes rapidly?
4. Is there a need to get better control over future benefits costs or to find immediate cost savings?
5. Have you recently made or are you contemplating a merger or acquisition requiring the integration of different benefits programs?

An affirmative response to these questions indicates that you may wish to take a hard look at a flexible benefits program.

Source: Adapted from Lance D. Tane and Michael E. Treacy, "Benefits that Bend with Employees' Needs," *Nation's Business,* April 1984, pp. 80–82, with permission of the publisher.

then purchase the insurance. Studies have revealed that most employees do not know the value of fringe benefits received, so it would benefit the company to provide employees with this information.

Wages are determined by a variety of interrelated factors: the supply of and demand for the type of people you employ; federal and state minimum wage legislation; the cost of living in the geographic region; the firm's ability to pay; and the wage rate set by organized labor.

Supply and demand are forces that no business can control. When there is a shortage of people with the skills your business needs and there is a great demand for this type of person, the price of this labor increases. Skilled labor is greatly influenced by supply and demand forces. In recent years, there has been a glut of unskilled workers accompanied by a falling demand for this labor. The opposite is true of many highly skilled workers. Although the forces of supply and demand work very slowly, their impact is powerful.

Federal and state laws regulate compensation for some workers. Laws set the minimum wage rate and overtime wage rates. The original federal legislation established in 1938 by the Fair Labor Standards Act created minimum wages. The minimum wage rates have since been amended many times by congressional actions. The Wage and Hour Division of the Department of Labor can provide the latest minimum wage and overtime rates. The passage of the Equal Pay Act in 1963 requires employers to pay all employees the same wage rates for doing the same work.

The local cost of living has an impact on wage rates. Some parts of the country have a lower cost of living, which is reflected in the level of wages paid. In some businesses, owners increase wages as a reaction to increases in the cost of living. Such adjustments in wages are designed to protect employee buying power.

Ability to pay is a factor that can work against a new small business. Wage increases and the level of compensation, of course, depend on the profitability of the business. Established businesses may enjoy profit levels that make it possible for the owners to pay higher than average wages, as well as provide workers with attractive fringe benefit packages.

If the firm's employees are members of a union, wages and fringe benefits paid are a result of a negotiated contract. In most instances, small business owners feel threatened by organized labor because they believe their size puts them at a disadvantage in any negotiations. Even when employees are not union members, the compensation package negotiations by unions in the area of industry becomes a standard against which other nonunion compensation packages are compared. Most nonunion businesses meet or exceed the union compensation package to reduce the likelihood of unionization.

Wages or salary can be based on a variety of systems. The most common wage system is based on time. Wages are defined in terms of dollars and cents per hour (e.g., $7.85/hr). A second method ties compensation to productivity. Under a "piece rate" system, which applies mostly to production, employees are paid according to how much they produce. In some complex production operations, a group is compensated based on the total output of the group (e.g., an assembly line). In nonmanufacturing businesses, this compensation is referred to as pure commission compensation. Sales representatives are compensated based on how much they sell. There are, of course, many combinations of these two basic methods of compensation. Incentive systems typically pay a salary or wage rate up to a specified level of performance (units produced or dollar volume of sales), and then incremental incentive compensation is provided for those persons or groups who exceed the standard. For such a system of compensation to be effective, it must be easy for the employees to understand and calculate, and be perceived as fair and attainable. The standard of performance should be neither too low nor too high. If the standard is set too low, labor costs rise above those of competitors. If the standard is too high, workers believe there is no opportunity to earn the incentive pay and that the compensation system is a "rip-off." People want to have confidence in their compensation system. They want to understand how it operates and to know that it is fair and equitable to them.

Businesses sometimes elect to pay employees an annual bonus. The bonus depends on the firm's profits for the year. This is a generous gesture, but to be effective, the bonus must be clearly tied to individual or group performance. If it is not, employees begin to expect a bonus no matter how they perform. Small businesses have an opportunity to focus their rewards on those individuals who really contribute to the firms' profits. Determining who those major contributors are requires an accurate performance appraisal system.

An interesting fringe benefit some firms are using is the sabbatical leave. About one out of every 10 major companies have some form of sabbatical. Typically, sabbaticals are provided to attract and keep workers, deal with stress and burnout on the job, broaden professional skills, or simply provide veteran employees with an opportunity for personal growth. Employees return with new perspective, renewed energy, and eager to use what they have learned. A few of the companies which advocate the use of sabbatical leaves are IBM, McDonald's, Tandem Computers, and Rolm Corporation.

VI. THE USE OF EMPLOYEE STOCK OWNERSHIP PLANS IN SMALL BUSINESSES

Employee Stock Ownership Plans (ESOPs) are sweeping across the nation as a growing number of business owners embrace the idea of employees as owners. The National Center for Employee Ownership estimates that more than 8,000 companies offer ESOPs. These involve over 11.5 million workers—a drastic increase from fewer than 500,000 employees a decade ago. Because of more favorable tax treatment from the 1984 Deficit Reduction Act, companies are adding ESOPs at a rate of 10 percent each

year (see figure 14–3). If that pace continues, 25 percent of all U.S. workers will be owners in their companies by the year 2000. Small companies, which may benefit most from ESOPs, have been a major force behind this impressive growth rate. One attorney specializing in ESOPs estimates that 80 percent of the companies implementing ESOPs have between 50 and 150 employees. A recent survey of *Inc.*, magazine's 100 fastest growing small firms found that 43 of them had ESOPs.

The concept of making employees owners in their companies is not new. In fact, Karl Marx and Friedrich Engels proposed the idea in their 1848 work, *Communist Manifesto*, but it was not well received. Still, one German economist, Von Thuenen, picked up on the idea and applied an early version of an ESOP in his own business in the late 1800s. As a result, he reported lower absenteeism and increased productivity.

Although primitive by today's standards, Von Thuenen's ESOP had many of the same objectives as modern plans. Essentially, an Employee Stock Ownership Plan is a stock bonus/retirement plan designed to invest primarily in the sponsoring company's stock. Although an ESOP is functionally a part of the founding company, the Securities and Exchange Commission and the Internal Revenue Service have ruled that technically it is a "third party" in all stock transactions. Therefore, an ESOP is a special form of "qualified employee benefit plan" (i.e., one governed by the Employee Retirement Income Security Act of 1974) that allows a company to deduct contributions to it as a business expense. The ESOP can accept either cash or stock contributions from the sponsoring company.

Three types of ESOPs have emerged over the past decade: ordinary plans; leveraged plans; and transfer of ownership plans.

Ordinary Plans

In an ordinary plan, the employer makes annual cash or stock contributions (which are discretionary) of

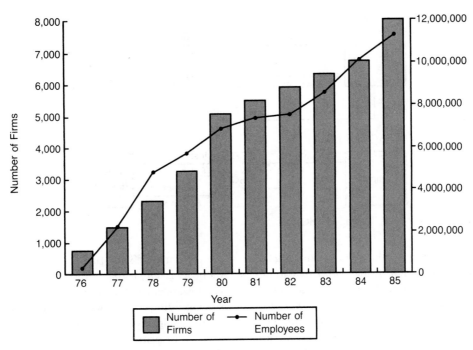

FIGURE 14–3   The growth of ESOPs.

Source: From John Hoerr, "ESOPs: Revolution or Ripoff?" *Business Week*, April 15, 1985, p. 102.

up to 15 percent of its payroll into a trust. If the contribution is in cash, the trust (ESOT) buys company stock with the same fair market value as the cash contribution from the employer. The ESOT, controlled by a company-appointed board, administers individual accounts for each employee (see figure 14–4). The employee gets a share of the ownership in the company from his company's contribution to the ESOT. And, he gets the benefit of a company-sponsored retirement fund. The employer can avoid a direct cash outlay for the deferred compensation (by contributing stock), but the company still is entitled to a tax deduction for the contribution.

Leveraged Plans

In a leveraged plan, the employer sets up an ESOT, which borrows money from a financial institution and then uses it to buy stock from the company. The company guarantees that, in subsequent years, it will make contributions to the ESOT to cover the principal and interest on the trust's loan. The company pledges stock as collateral for the loan (see figure 14–5).

The money the company pays into the ESOT is *not* treated as a loan repayment; instead, it is counted as a contribution to a qualified employee benefit

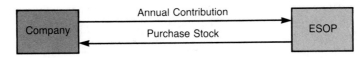

FIGURE 14–4   An ordinary ESOP.

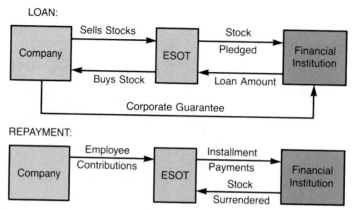

FIGURE 14–5 A leveraged ESOP.

plan and, therefore, is tax deductible. By running the transaction through the ESOT, the company can deduct both the interest and the principal amounts. (The principal amount cannot exceed 25 percent of the payroll, but the interest deduction is unlimited.) An ESOP, therefore, can be an effective tool for improving a small company's cash flow.

Transfer of Ownership Plans

Transfer of ownership plans are the most commonly used ESOPs. Employers frequently rely on transfer of ownership plans for raising capital, restructuring debt, financing acquisitions, planning for management succession, and implementing employee buyouts. The company typically makes a cash contribution into the ESOT to purchase outstanding shares from existing stockholders or from the company itself in the case of a complete divestiture (see figure 14–6). A transfer of ownership plan allows the company to maintain control over the timing and size of stock transfers and to retain voting control in the hands of selected trustees.

No matter what plan a company uses to implement its ESOP, it must abide by certain restrictions. For instance, when the company allocates the ESOP's stock holdings to employee accounts, it must not discriminate in favor of more highly paid employees, officers, or principal shareholders. Specifically, these three groups, together, cannot own more than one-third of the allocations. In most cases, employers choose a salary/seniority-based formula to allocate shares to employee accounts. It is acceptable to exclude part-time, short-term, and temporary employees, as well as those covered by collective bargaining agreements, from the ESOP. The plan also may be limited to one class of employees (within these restrictions).

Legislation governing ESOPs imposes other restrictions. The stock allocated to the employees must have voting rights although many plans retain these rights in a company-controlled trustee-rather than passing them through to the employee shareholders. In addition, employees cannot sell their stock allocations until they retire or leave the com-

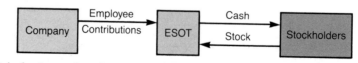

FIGURE 14–6 A transfer of ownership ESOP.

pany (although there are some exceptions). The plan must meet minimum vesting standards. As employees gain seniority, they acquire an increasing right to the stock held in their accounts. There are three common vesting options.

1. The "rule of 45" where an employee with at least five years of service has the service years added to his age for a total of 45 or more. The employee must be 30 percent vested and must reach 100 percent vesting at 10 years of service if the com-

bined age and service total 55. The minimum vesting schedule is 50 percent at 10 years of service with 10 percent increments for each subsequent year of service.

2. At least 25 percent vesting after 5 years of service with the requirement of reaching 100 percent vesting after 15 years in increments of 5 percent per year.

3. Complete vesting after 10 years of service with increments the employer chooses. The most com-

---

New Sick Leave Policy—Effective Immediately

SMALL
BUSINESS
REPORT
14–5

The attendance record of this office is a disgrace to our gracious benefactor who, at your request, has given you your job. Due to your lack of consideration for your job with so fine an institution, as shown by your frequent absenteeism, it has become necessary for us to revise some of our policies. The following changes are in effect as of today.

Sickness (no excuse): We will no longer accept your doctor's statement as proof. We believe that if you are able to go to the doctor, you are able to come to work.

Death (other than your own): This is no excuse—there is nothing you can do for them and we are sure that someone less important than you can attend to the arrangements. However, if the funeral is held in the late afternoon, we will be glad to let you off one hour early, provided that your work is all completed for the day.

Leave of absence (for an operation): We are no longer allowing this practice. We wish to discourage any thought that you may need an operation, as we believe as long as you are in our employment, you need all of whatever you have, and you should not consider having anything removed. We hired you as you are and to have anything removed would certainly make you less than we bargained for.

Death (your own): This will be accepted as an excuse, but we shall require two weeks' notice as we feel it is your duty to teach someone else to fill your position.

Pregnancy: In the event of an extreme pregnancy, you will be allowed to go to the first-aid room when the pains are five minutes apart. If it is a false alarm, you will be docked an hour's pay.

Also, entirely too much time is being spent in the restrooms. In the future, we will follow the practice of going in alphabetical order. For instance, those whose names begin with "A" will go from 8:00 to 8:15, "B" will go from 8:15 to 8:30, and so on. If you are unable to go at your time, it will be necessary to wait until the next day when your turn comes again.

FIGURE 14-7 Performance appraisal review (hourly employees).

Employee's name _____ Date _____

Employee's title _____ Supervisor _____

Instructions: Please review the performance of the employee whose name is listed above on each of the following items. In order to guide you in your rating, the five determinants of performance have been defined.

Rating Points

5   OUTSTANDING

A truly outstanding employee whose achievements are far above acceptable. Has consistently performed far beyond established objectives and has made significant contributions beyond current position. Requires minimal direction and supervision. (Relatively few employees would be expected to achieve at this level.)

4   SUPERIOR

An above-average employee whose performance is clearly above acceptable. Has usually performed beyond established objectives and, at times, has made contributions beyond responsibilities of present position. Requires less than normally expected degree of direction and supervision.

3   AVERAGE

A fully acceptable employee who consistently meets all requirements of position. Has consistently met established objectives in a satisfactory and adequate manner. Performance requires normal degree of supervision and direction. (The majority of employees should be at this level.)

2   BELOW AVERAGE

A somewhat below-average employee whose performance, while not unsatisfactory, cannot be considered fully acceptable. Generally meets established objectives and expectations, but definite areas exist where achievement is substandard. Performance requires somewhat more than normal degree of direction and supervision.

1   UNACCEPTABLE

A far-below-average employee whose performance is barely adequate to meet the requirements of the position. Generally performs at a level below established objectives with the result that overall contribution is marginal. Performance requires an unusually high degree of supervision. (This level is considered acceptable only for employees new to the job.)

JOB CRITERIA   POINTS

1. Amount of work.   Consider here only the *quantity* of the employee's output.   _____
    Supervisor's comments:

2. Quality of work.   Consider how well the employee does each job assigned. Include your appraisal
    of such items as accuracy, thoroughness, and orderliness.   _____
    Supervisor's comments:

FIGURE 14–7 *Continued*

3. Cooperation.   How well does this employee work and interact with you and co-workers for the accomplishment of organization goals? _____
    Supervisor's comments:

4. Judgment.   Consider this employee's ability to reach sound and logical conclusions. _____
    Supervisor's comments:

5. Initiative.   The energy or aptitude to originate action toward organization goals. _____
    Supervisor's comments:

6. Job knowledge.   How well does the employee demonstrate an understanding of the basic fundamentals, techniques, and procedures on the job? _____
    Supervisor's comments:

7. Interest in job.   Does the employee demonstrate a real interest in the job and the organization? _____
    Supervisor's comments:

8. Ability to communicate.   How well does this employee exchange needed information with others in the work group and with supervisors? _____
    Supervisor's comments:

9. Dependability.   Consider the employee's absences, tardiness, punctuality, timeliness in completing job assignments, and the amount of supervision required. _____
    Supervisor's comments:

10. Adaptability.   Consider the degree to which this employee demonstrates adjustment to the varying requirements of the job. _____
    Supervisor's comments:

                                                              TOTAL POINTS _____

    Supervisor's general comments:

Instructions: After you have rated the employee and made whatever comments you feel are pertinent to each criterion and the overall evaluation, schedule a meeting to review each item with the employee. An employee wishing to make comments about the evaluation should be asked to do so in the following space.

Employee's comment:

Date _____

Supervisor present (Name) _____

Employee's signature _____   Date _____

Notice to employee: Signing the form does not imply that you either agree or disagree with the evaluation.

mon vesting schedule is based on the following plan:

0% for the first three years
30% after the third year
40% after the fourth year
100% after the tenth year

VII. PERFORMANCE APPRAISAL

Evaluating employee performance is a necessary function of management. Performance appraisal consists of both an annual performance review and an ongoing evaluation process. Performance evaluation provides the manager with an opportunity to pat employees on the back for a job well done or, if necessary, help them correct nonproductive behavior. No one should sit back and watch someone do a job incorrectly for a year and then tell the worker he or she is wrong and should change.

An annual evaluation can help determine wage or salary increases, promotion, needed training, and overall job progress. Figure 14–7 is a sample performance appraisal document for an hourly employee.

Appraisals are important to people because they tell workers how well they have done the jobs assigned them. Table 14–1 reviews some important points about performance appraisals.

The people who work for you may be the most important element in the success of a business. Performance appraisal is the control functions for the firm's human resources. Therefore, the manager should always use it with a positive approach. By doing so, she will increase employee productivity and with it, company profitability.

VIII. SUMMARY

Human resources management practices influence the quality of employees a firm will be able to attract and retain. Good human resources management directly impact on the firm's bottom line. This compre-

hensive function involves a variety of separate, yet highly interrelated, activities.

Human resources planning involves determining how many and what kind of employees the business will need in the near future. Costs are reduced through avoiding overstaffing and loss of skilled key personnel is prevented by avoiding the negative consequences of understaffing.

Each job should be analyzed for content so that job descriptions and job specifications can be developed. A job description lists the duties, responsibilities, and working conditions of a job, while a job specification lists the characteristics of the individual best suited for the job. To avoid numerous costly problems, the job specifications must be kept realistic.

Recruiting deals with locating employees to fill vacant jobs. A promotion-from-within policy can be an effective motivation device. Small firms can also recruit employees from competitors. Outside sources of employees include referrals from current employees, walk-ins, government or private employment agencies, and advertisements in trade papers. Schools offer another prime source of job candidates.

Selection of the best applicant is facilitated by the use of application blanks and employment tests that provide needed information. Care must be taken to seek only information that is job related, or the manager may risk job discrimination lawsuits.

A well-planned interview can give the manager maximum insight into a candidate's qualifications. Again, the manager must avoid asking illegal questions in the interview.

The orientation program should be designed to bring the new employee into the work environment smoothly and effectively. This stage, which is often overlooked, can be critical to the success or the failure of a new employee.

One key to continued growth for both the business and its employees is effective training. A sound training program can avoid employee obsolescence and boost productivity and morale. The most com-

TABLE 14–1   Manager's guide to employee performance appraisal.

1. Recognize that performance appraisal takes place whether you conduct it or not. People tend to compare. An employee will automatically compare his or her work with that of others. If the process of evaluation or comparison is natural, then it is necessary that the supervisor formalize the process whereby the greatest value can be obtained for both the individual and the organization.
2. Recognize that not all employees want a good evaluation system. Employees who know that their performance is below standard *do not* want the supervisor to do accurate evaluations. These employees will resist the use of an accurate evaluation system.
3. Beware of any bias you may have. Prejudice that is personal in nature does not belong in supervision or evaluation. Every employee has a right to a fair evaluation of performance.
4. Review the employee's performance for the whole period. Don't just look at or remember the last few months. Consider improvement made by the employee.
5. Be as complete as possible. Have all the facts. Be prepared for the evaluation interview. Have all your notes and records.
6. Supervisors have found the following procedure effective in good performance evaluation meetings.

Meeting Time Allocated (%)	Nature of Discussion
5	Get the employee to relax and describe how the evaluation works.
20	Review with the employee the positive features of the evaluation and specific areas where performance was outstanding.
20	Review with the employee the negative features of the evaluation and specific areas where improvement is needed.
50	Mutually discuss what the employee should do for the next evaluation period. Supervisor and employee agree upon specific targets of performance. Agree upon how the supervisor can help the employee reach goals.
5	Schedule another meeting where the employee can report on progress in reaching those goals.

Spend half the time planning for the future. You cannot change the past, so put your efforts into improving performance in the future.

Show Employees What They Earn

Most small business managers never show their employees their *total* compensation. Employees take it for granted that they have some types of insurance. In fact, some workers have never had to pay for medical, life, disability, or even dental insurance. Consequently, an annual reminder of what their total compensation really is can be both an eye-opener and a powerful incentive. The following is a simple way of communicating the total compensation concept to each employee.

Based on your W-2 Form for the year, the company paid these amounts:

Wage or salary	$
Incentive or bonus compensation	$

The firm also paid the following amounts on your behalf for a comprehensive program of benefits:

1. Medical and dental insurance	$
2. Life insurance	$
3. Additional accidental death and dismemberment	$
4. Long-term disability	$
5. FICA (Social Security)	$
6. Worker's Compensation	$
7. Unemployment insurance	$
Total benefits paid	$

Also, we instituted a pension and profit-sharing program and contributed $_____ to your account.

The total annual compensation paid you during the following year amounts to:

Salary or wages	$
Incentive or bonus	$
Benefits	$
Profit-sharing/pension	$
Total compensation	

A story untold is a story unheard and unappreciated.

Source: Adapted from Thomas N. Richman, "This Isn't a Raise. It's an Insult," *Compensation and Benefits: A Report from Your Partner, Inc.*, pp. 9–12, with permission of the publisher.

mon method is on-the-job training, although off-the-job techniques can be quite productive.

Compensation management is another critical function because pay is important to employees, not only for financial reasons but also for psychological reasons. Compensation is affected by numerous factors, including labor market conditions, prevailing wages, federal and state regulations, union contracts, and the firm's ability to pay.

Evaluating an employee's performance on the job through performance evaluation is an important aspect of the personnel function. The evaluation should not center around criticism, but instead, should be a positive, confidence-building exercise.

STUDENT INVOLVEMENT PROJECTS

1. Interview the owner of a local small business about its personnel program. Does the firm have written job descriptions and job specifications? When a job vacancy arises, how does the owner recruit candidates? What sources of employment does the manager rely on most? What selection tools does the owner employ? How are they used? Is there an orientation program? Is it formal or informal? What training methods does the owner use? How is employee compensation determined? Does the manager use a performance appraisal program to evaluate employees? Is it successful?

2. Prepare a list of suggestions to improve the personnel policies of the small business you studied in project 1.

DISCUSSION QUESTIONS

1. What are job descriptions and job specifications? Why are they important?
2. Outline the various sources of recruiting employees for a small firm.
3. What selection tools are available to help a manager choose the best-qualified applicant?
4. Describe an effective interview.
5. What role does employee orientation play?
6. List and briefly describe the various methods of training employees. Which method is most common?
7. What factors influence the level of employee compensation in a small business?
8. What is the purpose of performance appraisal? How should it be handled? What mistakes do managers commonly make in evaluating employees?

SECTION SEVEN

MARKETING FOR THE SMALL BUSINESS: BUILDING A COMPETITIVE EDGE

Successful Marketing Fundamentals

15

Customers want 1/4″ holes—not 1/4″ drills.

Anonymous

In the factory we make cosmetics, and in the drugstores we sell hope.

Charles Revson

Upon completion of this chapter, you will be able to:

■ Recognize that the customer or client is the foundation of any business and that profits result only from customer satisfaction.

■ Understand that marketing is the process of delivering to customers the goods and services they desire.

■ Describe the components of a marketing plan and the benefits of preparing one.

■ Emphasize the value of market research and outline the market research process.

■ Describe and give illustrations of how a business identifies its target market.

■ Define the concept of "competitive edge."

■ Examine the factors that are key to building a marketing strategy.

■ Discuss the process of choosing a marketing strategy and the various types of strategies available to the small business owner.

■ Describe how the elements of the marketing mix work together to enhance a small business' success in marketing its goods or services.

■ Demonstrate the stages of the product life cycle and the various channels of distribution.

■ Discuss the two types of consumer credit.

■ Recognize the opportunities associated with exporting as well as the steps that should be taken in assessing export opportunities and how a small business can implement an export program.

The marketing function is awash with changes. Shifting social and demographic trends—an aging population, a growing number of dual-career couples, more single adults, and a more educated society—mean that even the most sophisticated marketers must adjust their strategies constantly. New techniques, such as telemarketing and marketing with video and computers, are growing in popularity. A 1977 Supreme Court decision struck down restrictions on advertising by professional groups such as dentists, lawyers, and physicians. Now, these professionals are free to advertise their services. Even the scope of the marketing function is expanding; it affects every aspect of the small company—from finance to personnel. Small businesses are recognizing the importance of developing marketing strategies; they are no longer reserved only for megacorporations competing in international markets.

Marketing is the process of delivering desired goods and services to customers and involves all of the activities associated with winning and retaining customers. Marketing success depends on the creation of a well-designed plan. For example, when three entrepreneurs together developed the idea to make videodiscs that profile colleges and universities for high school students, they began with a marketing plan. Before launching their business, the three spent months studying the recruiting needs of colleges, locating high schools with a high proportion of college-bound students, and interviewing high school students. They assembled a written marketing plan to focus their business concept, and it helped them build their business successfully.[1]

A marketing plan provides the small business with several important benefits.

- It analyzes the firm's competitive situation.
- It gives a realistic appraisal of a market's potential and uncovers new opportunities.
- It suggests alternative marketing strategies.
- It coordinates the firm's marketing weapons.
- It provides a framework for establishing a budget.
- It sets objectives and the responsibility for achieving them.
- It improves individual and corporate performance reviews.
- It focuses on maintaining profitability.

A marketing plan should accomplish four objectives:

1. It should determine customer needs and wants through market research.
2. It should pinpoint the specific target markets the small company will serve.
3. It should analyze the firm's competitive advantages and build a marketing strategy around them.
4. It should help create a marketing mix that meets customer needs and wants.

The plan focuses the company's attention on the "marketing concept." The marketing concept recognizes that satisfying the customer's needs and wants is the foundation of every business. Any business, large or small, can survive and prosper only as long as it can provide its customers with the goods and services they want at a price they are willing to pay and at a price that produces a profit for the business. The marketing concept encourages the small business owner to evaluate her business *from the customer's point of view*. Indeed, the customer *is* the central player in the cast of every business venture. Every area of the business must practice the marketing concept of putting the customer first in planning and actions. This chapter will focus on building this orientation into the four objectives of the small company's marketing plan.

I. THE VALUE OF MARKET RESEARCH

Every business can benefit from a better understanding of its market, customers, and competitors. Market research is the vehicle for gathering the information that serves as the foundation for the marketing plan. It involves systematically collecting, analyzing, and interpreting data pertaining to the small company's market, customers, and competitors. It answers questions such as: Who are my customers and potential customers? What kind of people are they? Where do they live? How often do they buy these products or services? What models, styles, colors, or flavors do they prefer? Why do or don't they buy from my store?

---

[1]"How to Find Your Own Market," *Changing Times*, September 1985, p. 33.

Letting Your Customers Do The Talking

When John and Robert Grubb wanted to gain a competitive edge over other San Francisco construction companies, they relied on market research. They felt that the people best qualified to answer questions about the market and the competition were those who buy their services. They asked their customers about the competition's worst habits. The answers: impolite personnel, workers who track dirt across carpets, and dilapidated crew trucks and equipment which clashed with their wealthy clientele's preferences.

These seeming insignificant facts gave the brothers the idea to move their company into an upscale market position. They bought a new truck and kept it spotless, trained workers in proper etiquette, and dressed them in jackets and ties. Work crews began using protective runners over clients' carpets to avoid soiling them. "We are looking at the competition by focusing on the customer," explains Robert.

Their market research and subsequent repositioning in the market paid off handsomely for the brothers. In less than two years, the company's annual sales shot up to $1 million from $200,000!

Source: Adapted from Steven P. Galante, "More Firms Quiz Customers for Clues about Competition," *The Wall Street Journal*, March 3, 1986, p. 21, with permission of *The Wall Street Journal*, © Dow Jones & Company, Inc., 1986. All rights reserved.

What hours do they prefer to shop? How do they perceive my business? Which advertising media are most likely to reach them? Information like this is an integral part of developing a productive marketing plan. In marketing its goods and services, a small company must avoid marketing mistakes since there is no margin for error when funds are scarce and budgets are tight. Market research often uncovers unmet needs in the market that the owner can take advantage of.

Small companies have a definite advantage over their large counterparts in market research. While they lack the large budgets and teams of research specialists, small business owners are close to their customers and know what they like and don't like. However, these owners still can benefit from market research. Sometimes the owner's knowledge of the market is either outdated or vague, and in some cases, is simply inaccurate. Many business owners who use market research are surprised when they learn something new about their markets or see their customers from a new angle. Small Business

Report 15–1 demonstrates how one business used market research to gain a competitive edge.

Despite the many benefits of market research, an alarming number of small businesses fail each year because their owners neglected to do research to identify the features and the needs of the markets they are trying to reach. The result is poor locations, improper product lines, inappropriate prices, and misaligned strategies which lead ultimately to failure. Common reasons for failure to use market research include lack of time to perform research, insufficient knowledge about conducting research, excessive cost of the research, and impracticality of its results.

However, market research does *not* have to be time consuming, complex, or expensive to be useful. Small Business Report 15–1 demonstrates how much valuable information an owner can get simply by asking customers about their needs, wants, likes, and dislikes. One retailer discovered the most common traffic pattern and most popular displays and items with a very simple, inexpensive, and creative form of market research. He offered shoppers free roasted peanuts, and by the end of the promotion, he had "peanut hull trails" showing the most heavily traveled areas. Mounds of hulls piled up in front of the most popular items. This store owner learned a great deal about his customers' behavior literally "for peanuts."[2] Thus, market research for the small business can be informal—it does *not* have to be highly sophisticated nor expensive to be valuable. In many cases, the process of searching for information is itself valuable.

The goal of market research is to reduce the risks associated with making business decisions. It can replace misinformation and assumptions with facts. Opinion and hearsay are not viable foundations upon which to build a solid marketing strategy. Successful market research consists of four steps.

1. Define the specific nature of the problem to be investigated.
2. Collect data from available sources.
3. Analyze the data and interpret the results.
4. Draw conclusions.

Define the Problem

The first, and most crucial, step in market research is defining the research problem clearly and concisely. A common flaw at this stage is to confuse a symptom with the true problem. For example, dwindling sales is *not* a problem, but rather a symptom. To get to the heart of the issue, the owner must list all the possible factors that could have caused it. Is there new competition? Are the firm's sales representatives impolite or unknowledgeable? Have customer tastes changed? Is the product line too narrow? Do customers have trouble finding what they want? The research question may be more general. What are my competitors up to and how do customers perceive my business in comparison to the competition? On the other hand, the owner may be interested in researching a specific type of question. What are the characteristics of

my customers? What are their income levels? What radio stations do they listen to? Why do they shop here?

Market research is not restricted solely to business problems. Business owners can use it to uncover potential opportunities as well. For example, when the owner of a fitness center surveyed his customers, he discovered that many had an interest in aerobic exercises. He added an aerobics program, and within a year his revenues had grown by 25 percent.

Collect the Data

The business owner has two sources of data: internal and external.

Internal Data. The first place the existing business owner should look for marketing information is in her own business records. Sales records, mailing lists, complaint files, and other records can provide the owner with valuable information to use to improve her business. For example, one business owner discovered that he could define his firm's trading area and pinpoint his customers from the addresses on checks and sales receipts. Owners wanting to develop productive mailing lists have long recognized the value of checks and sales receipts.

External Data. If internal information is unavailable or inadequate, the small business owner must turn to external data, which comes from two sources: secondary and primary. Secondary data have already been assembled; the owner simply has to "dig it up." Sources of secondary data include census reports, magazines, trade publications, advertising media, local colleges, trade associations, and subscription services. Subscription services, such the "Survey of Buying Power" published by *Sales & Marketing Magazine* and the Market Research Corporation of America consumer problems data, are popular secondary data sources. Secondary data usually are very inexpensive, but it is not always up-to-date.

---

[2]J. Ford Laumer, James R. Harris, and Hugh J. Guffey, *Learning about Your Market*, Management Aid #4.019, U.S. Small Business Administration, Washington, D.C., 1982, p. 2.

Primary data are "first-hand" data; the owner collects the information she needs most often by using personal interviews, telephone interviews, mail surveys, or focus groups. Personal interviews, where an interviewer asks respondents questions face-to-face, are the most versatile and flexible method. They are ideal for collecting complex information and can be longer than telephone or mail questionnaires. They are the most expensive method, however, and interviewers sometimes influence (unintentionally) results.

Telephone interviews are the primary method for conducting survey research. Their speed, moderate cost, and wide reach make them popular for collecting data. Because they are less personal than face-to-face interviews, respondents often will answer more confidential questions. Of course, telephone surveys do not permit the use of visual aids, and they cannot be lengthy. A telephone interview should not be more than 10 minutes long.

Mail surveys are relatively low cost compared to the other methods, and they are convenient for the respondents, who can answer at their convenience. However, the owner has no control over who actually answers the questionnaire. Response time for mail surveys is slow—typically two to three weeks. In addition, the owner has no guarantee that respondents will interpret the written questions in the same manner. The biggest disadvantage, however, is low response rates. Poorly designed or administered surveys commonly produce response rates of 15 percent or lower.

A focus group consists of 8 to 10 respondents who meet for an unstructured, free-flowing conversation with a moderator. The moderator "guides" the group's discussion, but individuals are free to express their true likes, dislikes, and anxieties. Researchers (usually observing through a two-way mirror) watch respondents' "body language" for additional clues during the conversation. They are commonly used in the development stages of new products. One business owner used a focus group to judge the reaction to a new line of clothing he was considering adding. Focus group interviews are relatively easy to conduct, fast, and inexpensive.

Analyze and Interpret the Data

The results of market research alone do not provide a solution to the problem; the owner must attach some meaning to them. What do the facts mean? Is there a common thread running through the responses? Do the results suggest any changes needed in the way the business is run? Are there new opportunities the owner can take advantage of? There are no "hard-and-fast" rules for interpreting market research results; the owner must use judgment and common sense to determine "what the numbers mean."

Small Business Report 15–2 offers some interesting practice at interpreting research results.

Draw Conclusions

In many cases, the conclusion is obvious once the small business owner interprets the results of the market research. Based on her understanding of what the facts really mean, the owner must then decide how to use the information in the business. For example, the owner of a retail shop discovered from a survey that her customers preferred evening shopping hours over early morning hours. She made the schedule adjustment, and sales began to climb.

The market research process is not complete until the business owner acts upon the information collected. Research is fruitless if the owner fails to incorporate the results into the operation of the business.

II. PINPOINTING THE TARGET MARKET

One of the primary objectives of market research is to identify the small business' target market—the specific group of customers at whom the company aims its goods or services. An effective marketing program depends on a clear, concise definition of

You Decide What It Means . . .

Assume the role of a small business manager. How would you interpret the following market research results, and what implications might they have for your business?

- Business travelers' biggest complaints about hotel service are: poor attitude among employees (22%); rooms not being ready (14%); poor maintenance and worn facilities (13%); no record of reservations (10%); and check-in/out problems (9%).
- When choosing a supermarket, consumers say the most important features are: low prices (43%); location (42%); wide selection (35%); courteous employees (25%); and store cleanliness (23%).
- Seventy-nine percent of U.S. households clip coupons. The heaviest users are in the $10,000 to $35,000 income range.
- Sixty-four percent of U.S. households have one or more person on a diet. The most common regimens are: reducing calories (57%); reducing sugar (37%); reducing salt (37%); and reducing cholesterol (21%).
- Americans buy about 7 billion greeting cards annually. The most popular holidays (in descending order) are: Christmas, Valentine's Day, Easter, and Mother's Day.
- Diners prefer going to a restaurant offering: low prices and a casual setting (30%); large portions served quickly (21%); unusual atmosphere and menu (29%); and special and expensive meals (20%).
- Even if the food was good and prices were reasonable, diners would not return to a restaurant if: service was poor (83%); music was too loud (64%); service was too slow (61%); too dark to see food (57%); and tables too close together (46%).
- The most popular dinner entrees among the dining public are: steak (19%); prime rib/roast beef (12%); fish (12%); shrimp (11%); chicken (11%); and seafood combination (10%).
- Women accompany men shopping for clothes 50% of the time and exert: a major influence on the purchase (61%); some influence on the purchase (20%); and no influence on the purchase (19%).
- Eighty-three percent of U.S. households have their cars serviced rather than doing it themselves. The main reasons for choosing a service station are: better service (34%); good reputation (32%); like/know personnel (26%); good location (14%); and less expensive (14%).
- By 1995, women will represent more than 47% of the work force (up from 32% in 1960); 27% of U.S. households will consist of single individuals; more than 50% of U.S. households will have "dual-career" couples (up from 12% in 1959); and more than 33 million Americans will be 65 or older (up from 17 million in 1960).

Source: The Wall Street Journal; Nation's Restaurant News; U.S. News & World Report; and Nation's Business.

---

the firm's targeted customers. The most successful businesses have well-defined portraits of the customers they are seeking to attract. From market research, they know their customers' income levels, lifestyles, buying patterns, likes and dislikes, and even psychological profiles. The target customer should permeate the *entire* business—from the merchandise purchased to the layout and decor of the store. The "image" the owner creates for his business must appeal to the target customer if the venture is to prosper. Without a clear image of its target market, the small business tries to reach almost everyone and usually ends up appealing to almost no one.

Clothing designers, manufacturers, and retailers provide a classic example of the importance of clearly defining the target market. Their survival depends on knowing who their primary customers are, what their preferences are, and how they change over time. For instance, when Heather Evans launched her fashion house, she had a specific customer in mind: career women who want fashionable and practical dresses and jackets appropriate for both office and evening wear. "Our market is the woman who makes $25,000 a year but is expected to dress the same as a woman making $300,000," says Evans. Her casual-yet-formal designs are suitable for both work and play. For maximum flexibility, Evans uses soft fabrics like silk, cotton, wool, gabardine, and rayon and features removable parts—for instance a formal white collar that can be removed for a casual evening. Her designs retail for $125 to $270.[3]

Identifying a target market is just as important in men's clothing. Marketers have identified four brand customer types: Advanced, Updated, Traditional, and Mainstream. About 50 percent of the men's clothing market is the Mainstream man, who buys to replace old clothing rather than to expand his wardrobe. He does not enjoy shopping and does it infrequently. The Traditional man, who comprises 30 percent of the market, is the best educated and the highest paid. His taste is "classic-conservative," and he is inclined toward pin-striped suits, button-down pinpoint shirts, rep ties, and wingtips. Some Traditional men may switch categories away from work—becoming Updated or even Advanced. The Updated man accounts for about 10 percent of the market. He tends to be younger and less affluent, but he is very fashion-conscious and tends to be impulsive. He adopts new fashions that are not too outlandish rather quickly. The Advanced man, who makes up about 8 percent of the market, is a fashion innovator. He is the first to experiment with new styles and usually does not shy away from unusual clothing. The more outlandish the fashion, the better

he likes it.[4] Clearly, to prosper in such a diverse market, a men's clothing business must have a concise definition of its target market. Small Business Report 15–3 demonstrates the opportunities and the threats of appealing to a specific target market in the fashion business.

III. PLOTTING A MARKETING STRATEGY: HOW TO BUILD A COMPETITIVE EDGE

A competitive edge is crucial for business success. A small company has a competitive edge when customers perceive that its products or services are superior to those of its competitors. A business owner can create this perception in a variety of ways. Small companies sometimes try to create a competitive edge by offering the lowest prices. This approach may work for many products and services—especially those that customers see as being "commodities"—but price can be a dangerous criterion upon which to build a competitive edge. Independent book stores have discovered that large chains can use their buying power to get volume discounts and undercut the independents' prices. Individual shopowners are finding new ways, such as special ordering, adult reading groups, children's story hours, newsletters, and autograph parties, to differentiate themselves and to retain customer loyalty.

In fact, small businesses have special advantages over their larger competitors that allow them to create competitive advantages using factors other than price. Their close contact with the customer, personal attention, focus on service, and organizational and managerial flexibility provide a solid foundation from which to build a towering competitive edge in the market. Many small businesses rely on four important sources to develop a competitive edge: a focus on the customer; devotion to quality; concentration on innovation; and dedication to service.

---

[3]Verne Gay, "A Retailer Targets Career Women," *Venture*, February 1984, p. 18.

[4]Joan Kron, "A Few Daring Dressers Risk Sneers to Push Menswear into the Future," *The Wall Street Journal*, March 11, 1986, p. 33.

The Ups . . .

Tired of dressing in "bulletproof polyester" designed for "camouflage," Marcia Stafford and a friend formed Oink, Inc. to make clothing for larger girls and women. Full-figured females have long been in marketer's sights, but in a different light. Until recently, the focus has been on the "get-thin" trend. Diet books, exercise records, pills, plastic surgery, and "fat camps" were aimed at unleashing the large ladies' petite potential. But, social trends have changed the fashion industry's attitude toward the 40 million American women who were a size 16 or larger. The editor of *Big Beautiful Woman* magazine explains, "Companies sterotyped the large woman as over 50, under 5 feet, with hundreds of children, who sat in front of the TV and ate bonbons."

Now, specialty shops and department stores are recognizing the potential of this $6 billion market. One ad touts, "Who says large women can't look good in stylish clothes?" Even *Vogue* magazine, which has devoted special sections to large women, admits, "It's really been an explosion."

Mrs. Stafford's vision has paid off. She is selling her clothing to many major retailers, and others are eager to handle Oink's product line.

. . . And Downs of Fashion

Clement Soffer is in a dangerous line of work. He is not a high-steel man nor a shark-tamer. He owns Jon Jon Designs, Inc., which markets clothing to teen-age girls. "You may get wiped out in this business if you aren't careful," he says. Then, he adds, "You may anyway."

Teenage girls comprise a major market segment—12.8 million of them spend roughly $30 billion each year—but they are extremely dangerous as customers because of their fickle nature. They can send the sales of a product soaring or plummeting in a flash. "Teenage girls have more discretionary income than you can believe. Most have jobs, a lot have big allowances, and none of them have to pay the mortgage or the gas bill," says one marketing manager. But, comments another, "It's a hazardous market."

Fads—from hoola hoops to miniskirts—always have been a part of growing up. But, teen-age girls often take fads to the limits. One designer claims, "When one of the young ladies has to have something, they all do. It's like mass hysteria."

One clothing retailer claims that selling to teen-age girls "requires a corporate culture that's comfortable with constant change." To keep up with the fast-paced market, the company employs 25 fashion consultants, who travel from store-to-store interviewing teen-agers about their tastes and preferences. The company uses this information to keep its product lines up-to-date. Constant monitoring may be the only way to avoid being burned in this market.

Sources: Jolie Solomon, "Fashion Industry Courting Large Women, Offering Stylish Clothes in Big Sizes," *The Wall Street Journal*, September 27, 1985, p. 31; John Koten, "Teen-Age Girls, Alas, Are Big Consumers But Poor Customers," *The Wall Street Journal*, November 9, 1984, p. 1.

Focus on the Customer

For a time, many companies, small and large, lost sight of the most important aspect of every business: the customer. Lew Young, editor of *Business Week*, claims, "In too many companies, the customer has become a bloody nuisance whose unpredictable behavior damages carefully made strategic plans, whose activities mess up computer operations, and who stubbornly insists that purchased products should work."[5] Businesses have come to realize that *everything* in the business—even the business itself—depends on the satisfied customer. A manager at a very successful (and very customer-oriented) grocery store keeps a small notebook with him at all times for recording customers' requests and comments. Everyone in the store is obsessed with pampering customers. When a woman approached a manager and asked, "Will you tell me where the mustard is?" he replied, "No ma'am I won't . . . . I'm going to take you there."[6] Special treatment like this wins customers and keeps them coming back. Small Business Report 15–4 demonstrates how one small company created a competitive advantage by cultivating a close relationship with its "family" of customers.

A customer orientation can be as simple as practicing the Golden Rule of Business: Treat your customers the way you would like to be treated. For example, one mail-order customer was delighted when she received a $0.01 refund on merchandise she had ordered from L.L. Bean. The customer couldn't believe it, but such policies are part of Bean's customer orientation.

Devotion to Quality

Quality has become the "buzz word" of the decade. Customers have come to expect and demand quality goods and services, and those businesses that provide them consistently have a distinct competitive advantage. The owner of a very successful pest-control company offered his customers a unique unconditional guarantee—if the company fails to eliminate all roach and rodent breeding and nesting areas on the client's premises, it will refund the customer's last 12 monthly payments and will pay for one full year's service by another exterminator. The company has had to honor its guarantee only once in 17 years.

At Spectrum Control Inc., managers were desperately searching for ways to reduce the rejection rate on capacitors (32 percent) and bushings (50 percent). Spectrum, with four plants and customers such as IBM and Hewlett Packard, was afraid of losing customers to Japanese companies. Managers turned to the philosophies of Philip Crosby (author of *Quality Is Free*) and W. Edwards Deming, the father of statistical quality control, for help. Slowly and painfully, Spectrum developed a quality perspective: Why not do things right the first time? The company began to search for permanent solutions (not temporary fixes) to its quality problems; track the "cost of quality" as a control device; invest in updated equipment; and encourage suggestions for boosting quality from line employees. One manager claims, "One of their suggestions actually increased our productivity by something like 50 percent." The effort paid off. After its first year under the new program, Spectrum's quality was up, its rejection rate was down, and savings amounted to more than $767,000.[7]

Concentration on Innovation

Innovation is the key to future success. Markets change too quickly and competitors move too fast for a small company to stay still and remain competitive. Because of their organizational and managerial flexibility, small businesses often can detect and act on new opportunities faster than large companies. Innovation is one of the greatest strengths of the entrepreneur, and it shows up in the new products,

---

[5]Thomas J. Peters and Robert H. Waterman, Jr., *In Search of Excellence*, New York: Harper & Row, Publishers, 1982, p. 156.

[6]Tom Richman, " *Super* Market," *Inc.*, October 1985, pp. 116–18.

[7]Craig R. Waters, "Quality Begins at Home," *Inc.*, August 1985, pp. 68–71.

We Are Family

Vermont Castings, a privately-owned manufacturer of cast-iron wood- and coal-burning stoves, knows how to throw a great party. To celebrate its 10th anniversary, the company sponsored an old-fashioned New England picnic, complete with quilting parties; pie-baking, corn-shucking, and watermelon seed-spitting contests; musicians; plant tours; and a fireworks show. The company spent $50,000 on the wing-ding.

What, one may wonder, is so unusual about a small company putting on a special celebration for its employees? What is unusual is that the special guests at the company picnic were not employees; they were *customers*. Eleven thousand customers came to Clayton, Vermont, from as far away as California to join in the reunion! The annual bash is the highlight of Vermont Castings' approach to maintaining a personal relationship with its customers. Another key element is the lifetime subscription to *Vermont Castings' Owners' News*, a newsletter offering stove operating advice, dealer profiles, and other information, that each customer receives. One customer says, "In America today, a manufacturer produces a product, you purchase it, and that's the end of your association with that manufacturer in most cases. Not so with Vermont Castings. Once you have bought their product, you become a member of their family."

The company recognizes the value of a good reputation. The heart of its business is customers sitting in front of their hearths enjoying the warmth of their stoves. Vermont Castings' marketing director says, "People develop a very emotional tie to their hearth. You wouldn't develop that same attachment to a refrigerator."

Vermont Casting's old-fashioned New England picnic. (Photo courtesy of Vermont Castings, Inc.)

Source: Adapted from Nancy L. Croft, "Casting Stoves Upon The Waters," *Nation's Business*, February 1986, pp. 44R-45R, with permission of the publisher.

unique techniques, and unusual approaches they introduce. Despite financial constraints, small businesses frequently are leaders in innovation. For example, Elizabeth Arden, the cosmetic company, has developed a computer system called "Elizabeth" that gives the company a definite marketing edge. A video camera transfers a customer's image to a computer screen where she can watch a professional makeup artist transform four images of her face. Using a graphics tablet, the artist can apply different colors and patterns of foundation, blush, eye shadow, and lipstick. The system helps the customer learn how to apply makeup properly, allows an artist to show four different images in the time it usually takes to show one, and eliminates the need for customers to have a variety of makeup smeared all over their faces. The result is "a much more satisfied customer spreading the word and expanding our market," explains the system's designer.

Dedication to Service

Small businesses are learning that one of the best ways to maintain an existing customer base and to attract new customers is to provide incomparable service. No matter how innovative or quality-conscious a business is, success boils down to a sales clerk selling to a customer. Businesses have lost countless numbers of sales from "transactions" such as the following.

- Sales clerk stubbornly remains behind the counter as customer approaches. Customer: "Do you have this in a size 6?" Sales clerk: "If it's not on that rack, we don't have it."
- Customer: "Could you tell me about how this item works?" Sales clerk: "I'm really not sure, I'm just terrible with gadgets."

To provide adequate customer service, a sales representative should:[8]

- learn to acknowledge the waiting customer.
- know how to handle all computer-register transactions.

- review rack and shelf stocks for proper placement of sizes and colors.
- be able to talk about product content and usage.
- give customers proper directions pleasantly.
- alert their superiors—pronto—to out-of-stocks, especially on advertised items.
- follow-up on stock replacements as promised.
- point out alternative sales possibilities.

For instance, Nordstrom, Inc., the specialty retailer, has built its competitive edge on customer service. Sales clerks always respond to shoppers within 2 minutes. After shopping in a competitor's store, one customer complained, "I unwrapped, unpinned, and unfolded shirts and waved them like red flags in front of bulls. The salesgirl remained in her original position behind the counter." At Nordstrom, courteous salespeople escort customers to spotless dressing rooms and return often to offer additional items. At a competitor's, customers find the unkept dressing rooms on their own, where a dressing room "cop" checks their apparel.[9] Nordstrom recognizes the importance of customer service in closing a sale and invests money and time hiring and training quality personnel to do the job properly. Small Business Report 15–5 takes a humorous look at customer service.

Every business must make a conscious strategic decision about how it hopes to create its competitive edge. The entire organization must be committed to producing products or providing services consistent with the competitive edge target. Successful businesses do not accidentally fall into competitive niches; they create them.

IV. CHOOSING A MARKETING STRATEGY

A marketing strategy results when the small business owner blends together results from the four market research steps to develop a successful marketing mix. There is a great deal of truth to Wallace's Two-

---

[8]Ralph Shaffer, "High-Tech Gadgetry Can't Replace the Human Touch," *The Wall Street Journal*, January 27, 1986, p. 24.

[9]Tom Peters, "The Store Is Where the Action Is," *U.S. News & World Report*, May 12, 1986, p. 58.

OFFICE HOURS

Open Most Days About 9 or 10

Occasionally as Early as 7, But SOME DAYS

As Late As 12 or 1.

WE CLOSE About 5:30 or 6

Occasionally About 4 or 5, But

Sometimes as Late as 11 or 12.

SOME DAYS OR Afternoons, We

Aren't Here At All, and Lately

I've Been Here Just About All The Time,

Except When I'm Someplace Else,

But I Should Be Here Then, Too.

Out-of-Three Theory:

Speed.
Quality.
Price.
Pick any Two.

There are several marketing strategies the small business can use to establish a competitive edge. A *market penetration* strategy seeks to increase sales of existing products in current markets (or in current locations) through greater selling and advertising efforts, and is quite feasible for many small businesses. On the other hand, a *market development* strategy attempts to increase sales by introducing existing products or services into new markets. For example, a small accounting firm may boost sales by opening a "satellite" office in a nearby town. Introducing its services to this new market increases the firm's sales. A *product development* strategy tries to increase sales by adding new goods or services in existing markets. These new products may be modifications of existing items or entirely new ones. For instance, a small fast-food restaurant whose menu is built primarily around hamburgers might increase sales by adding ham, fish, and chicken dishes.

Market segmentation is another popular marketing strategy. Here, the small business manager segments the mass market—that is, carves it up into smaller, more homogenous segments. This provides the opportunity to attack each segment with a spe-

cific marketing strategy designed to maximize the effectiveness of the marketing effort. Usually, such a "rifle" approach to marketing is more successful than the "shotgun" approach used to appeal to the general market. Successful restaurants most often appeal to a specific clientele; very few eating establishments succeed by trying to be "everything to everyone." The specific approach comes down to knowing who the firm's customers are.

To segment a market successfully, the small business owner must do the following.

- Identify the characteristics of two or more segments. Effective segmentation requires that the firm differentiate among its customers on the basis of their traits, personalities, buying patterns, or some other characteristic.
- Verify that the segments are large enough and have enough purchasing power to generate a profit for the firm. Segmentation is useless if the firm cannot profit from serving its segments.
- Reach the market. To be profitable, the firm's market segment must be accessible.

Closely tied to market segmentation is "*niche-picking*"—when a small business concentrates its marketing efforts on a single or a limited number of market segments. Rather than compete head-to-head, most small businesses choose their niches carefully and defend them fiercely. A niche strategy allows a

Going "Bananas" Over Mail Order

Catalogs have undergone some interesting changes in the last several decades. Several mail-order houses have closed in an industry "shakeout," and companies have become more focused in their marketing approaches, aiming their products at precise segments. In fact, Montgomery Ward shut down its 113-year-old general merchandise catalog. Says one mail-order manager, "The day of the generalist is probably gone. Now you've got to have a mission, find a niche, and stay in it." Since only about 2 percent of the catalogs mailed produce orders, a company must focus on the right customers.

Many small catalog companies are leading the charge into narrow market segments. Banana Republic Travel and Safari Clothing Company, founded in 1978 by Mel and Patricia Ziegler, have found a way to stand out from the crowd of catalogs. It offers classic, durable, and comfortable safari-style clothing from around the world. The catalog is more like a "travelogue," chronicling the Ziegler's worldwide trips in search of authentic safari styles. Customers who call the toll free, 24-hour order line have a unique experience when put on hold; instead of the traditional "elevator music," they hear jungle sounds—monkey screeches and bird calls.

Banana Republic has created the same unique atmosphere in its retail stores. The stores are decorated like African safari lodges or jungles. Some shops come complete with land rovers and bush planes suspended from the ceiling. *Out of Africa*, the 1986 academy award winning film with its safari styles from the 1920s, helped popularize Banana Republic's products.

Sources: Adapted from Joan O'C. Hamilton, "A Shakeout Has Mail-Order Houses Aiming at Smaller Targets," *Business Week*, September 9, 1985, pp. 98–100; "Cash in on Your Bright Idea," *Changing Times*, September 1985, pp. 31–37.

---

small company to maximize the advantages of its smallness and to compete effectively even in industries dominated by giants. For instance, Joan Venturino's business, Bears to Go, is aimed at an extremely narrow niche—she sells only teddy bears. Her latest innovation was a teddy bear reunion (with Lauren Bearcall, Kareem Abdul Jabear and Humphrey Beargart). Two-hundred-fifty customers from across the country brought their bears "back home."[10]

Pursuing a niche strategy does involve risks, however. There is always the danger that the niche market is not large enough to be profitable, that it will attract larger companies that will erode the niche, or that the market may "dry up." L.L. Sams & Sons Inc. discovered the dangers of serving a niche market. For 88 years, the company supplied churches with stained-glass windows and furniture. As the number of churches being built dropped, so did Sams & Sons' sales. According to a business consultant, "It's a fate that befalls many companies. They may thrive for years on a single product or narrow market, but when that business languishes, what's a company to do?" What L.L. Sams & Sons did was diversify. The company has become a full-line distributor of church goods, and its catalog now lists more than 600 items—from collection plates to steeples.[11]

Developing a marketing strategy to gain a competitive edge is never easy; but, to survive and prosper in the market, the small business must set itself apart from its competitors. Small Business Report 15–6 describes how one mail-order house has created a unique image in a crowded industry.

---

[10]Susan Buschbaum, "A Nation of Shopkeepers," *Inc.*, November 1985, pp. 66–76.

[11]Steven P. Galante, "Counting On a Narrow Market Can Cloud Company's Future," *The Wall Street Journal*, January 20, 1986, p. 19.

V. THE MARKETING MIX

The major elements of a marketing strategy are the four "*Ps*" of marketing—product, place, pricing, and promotion. These four elements are self-reinforcing, and when coordinated, increase the salability of a product or service. Small business managers must attempt to integrate these elements to maximize the impact of their product or service on the consumer. For example, if a business sells its product in retail outlets that cater to lower-income families, it should not advertise in a magazine read primarily by the rich, nor should it attempt to sell the product at a price substantially above competitors' prices. However, if a company directs its product at a very rich market, it normally will price the product higher than competitors' products to take advantage of the "snob appeal" of owning an expensive product. For example, Countess Mara offers a $5,000 necktie for its exclusive customers. The company says that no two $5,000 ties are alike although all include some design of 14-karat gold and diamonds.[12]

All of the marketing elements must reinforce the image of the product or service the company presents to the potential customer.

Product

The product itself is an essential element in marketing. A product is any item or service that satisfies the need of a consumer. Products can have form and shape, or they can be services with no physical form. For example, an attorney's products are knowledge of law and time devoted to a client. Someone interested in beginning a business may need to purchase the services (product) of an attorney before going into business. The advice "bought" satisfies the needs of the new business person for information about business laws.

An important part of marketing is creating new products. In many industries, survival depends on a constant process of product innovation. In the toy industry, for example, manufacturers are constantly challenged to create new toys for children. The 37-year-old classic toy, Mr. Potato Head (a plastic potato with interchangeable body parts) now has a "son" called Potato Chip. Even companies producing relatively stable products must innovate. For instance, food companies have introduced a variety of new products recently, including brand-name fresh produce, buffalo stew, Texas-shaped noodles ("they hold sauce real well") and Cointreau souffle in a jar.[13] Other businesses rely on a constant flow of new products for a distinctive image in the market. For example, Advanced Genetic, a biotechnology firm, has developed Snomax, a product designed to relieve the greatest fear of ski resort owners: no snow. It actually is a strain of bacteria ("snow germs") that is as harmless and common as dust, but produces more and better snow when mixed in water and sprayed from snow-making machines.[14]

Packaging is an important aspect for most products. A well-designed, attractive package can help catch the consumer's eye and so boost sales. Indeed, many firms rely on packaging and logos to help create a visual company identity. Claims one business owner, "It is most important to have something immediately identifiable so that it cannot be mistaken for someone else's product."[15]

Product packaging appears to be important to consumers. One survey found that 46 percent of the respondents had discarded or returned a product because of defective packaging; 19 percent refused to buy the same brand again; and 24 percent would buy a different type of package. Packaging also has

---

[12]Joan Kron, "Some Salesmen Can Make Buying A $5,000 Tie Extremely Difficult," *The Wall Street Journal*, May 10, 1984, p. 37.

[13]Trish Hall, "Brand-Name Produce Hits Stores—But Will It Really Taste Better?" *The Wall Street Journal*, September 23, 1985, p. 33; Robert Johnson, "Texas-Shaped Noodles (and Other Things That You Never Realized You Needed)," *The Wall Street Journal*, May 5, 1986, p. 31; and Wendy E. Lane, "Buffalo Stew, Souffle in a Jar—and a Lot More," *The Wall Street Journal*, July 29, 1985, p. 17.

[14]Patricia Bellew Gray, "Ski Resorts Try Snow Germs As a Remedy for Bare Slopes," *The Wall Street Journal*, January 3, 1986, p. 15.

[15]Pam Ellis-Simons, "Picking An Image," *Venture*, February 1986, p. 30.

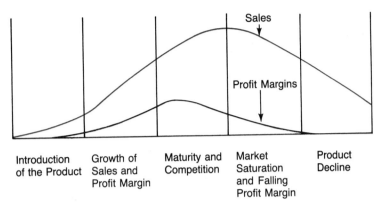

Sales

Profit Margins

| Introduction of the Product | Growth of Sales and Profit Margin | Maturity and Competition | Market Saturation and Falling Profit Margin | Product Decline |

FIGURE 15–1   Product life cycle.

Source: From *Changing Times,* May 1984. Used with permission.

become a safety issue. An alarming number of product tampering cases have plagued companies in recent years, including cases where over-the-counter drugs have been laced with cyanide. Thus, tamperproof packaging has become a high priority item. Even though researchers know they cannot make a truly tamperproof package, they continue their work. Some manufacturers are experimenting with hologram packages, which would be difficult and expensive for tamperers to copy.

Products travel through various stages of development. The product life cycle (see figure 15–1) measures these stages of growth, and these measurements enable the company's management to make decisions about whether to continue selling the product.

In the *introductory stage,* the marketers must present their product to the potential consumers. Initial high levels of acceptance are rare. Generally, new products must "break in" to existing markets and compete with established products. Advertising and promotion help the new product be more quickly recognized. The potential consumers must get information about the product and the needs it can satisfy. For competitive products, consumers must be convinced that the new product is superior to what they currently purchase. The cost of market-

ing a product at this level of the life cycle is usually high. Sales resistance must be met and overcome. Thus, profits are generally low, or even negative at the introductory stage.

After the introductory stage, the product enters the *growth or acceptance stage.* In the growth stage, consumers begin to compare the product in large enough numbers for sales to rise and profits to increase. Products that reach this stage, however, do not necessarily become successful. If in the introductory or the growth stage the product fails to meet

From *Changing Times,* May 1984. © 1984 M. Twohy.

consumer needs, it does not sell and eventually disappears from the marketplace. For successful products, sales and profit margins continue to rise through the growth stage.

In the *maturity and competition stage*, sales volume continues to rise, but profit margins peak and then begin to fall as competitors enter the market. Normally, this causes reduction in the product's selling price to meet competition and to hold its share of the market.

Sales peak in the *market saturation stage* of the product life cycle and give the marketer fair warning that it is time to begin product innovation.

The final stage of the product life cycle is the *product decline stage*. Sales continue to drop, and profit margins fall drastically. However, when a product reaches this stage of the cycle, it does not mean that it is doomed to failure. Products that have remained popular are always being revised. No firm or product can maintain its sales position without product innovation and change. In effect, innovation results in the creation and reintroduction of a new product that will continue to satisfy consumers' needs.

The time span of the stages in the product life cycle depends on the type of products involved. High-fashion and fad clothing have a short product life cycle, lasting for only four to six weeks. Products that are more stable may take years to complete a life cycle. For example, the standard household refrigerator went through a long product life cycle. Profit margins and sales began to decline, but the cycle began again with the introduction of product variations, such as the addition of a freezer, frost-free operation, automatic ice-makers, water, juice and ice dispensers, and a variety of door locations. The latest models include motors that drastically reduce energy consumption. The introduction of such models sent the sales and profit margins of less sophisticated models into severe decline.

Products may be classified in terms of who purchases them and what their intended use is. Consumer products are goods or services purchased for final consumption by people. Most of us purchase these frequently, and include clothing, appliances, and cars bought for personal use. Industrial goods are purchased by businesses for use directly in the production of other goods. For example, a manufacturing company might purchase steel to use in the production of another product. Raw materials, machinery, and equipment also are examples of industrial goods. Commercial goods are products not used directly in the production of other goods, but assist in that production. For example, typewriters, filing cabinets, and office supplies are commercial goods because they are indirectly consumed in the production of other goods.

Consumer products are often classified according to consumers' buying habits. Such products usually fall into three categories: convenience; shopping; and specialty goods.

Convenience goods are those that consumers can readily purchase at a variety of locations. They usually are low priced and do not rely on strong brand-name recognition. It is possible to further classify convenience goods as staple goods, impulse goods, and emergency goods.

Staple goods are those bought and used frequently, and are found in virtually every home. Examples of staple goods include potatoes, coffee, and meat. Services that can be considered staples include dry-cleaning, automobile servicing, and garbage collection.

Impulse goods, as the term implies, are those that consumers buy on impulse. They are sold by placing them at places in the store where customers are most likely to pick them up and buy them. The unit price of impulse goods is usually low, again to encourage an impulsive buy decision. Impulse goods are often placed at the checkout counter of supermarket or discount stores. They include candy, gum, razor blades, tobacco products, magazines, and a wide variety of similar products. A shoe shine might classify as an impulse service.

Emergency goods are purchased as a result of an urgent need. Examples of emergency goods

Rejuvenating Obsolete Products

SMALL
BUSINESS
REPORT
15–7

Very few new products succeed in the market. Says one advertising specialist, "Marketers spend an unbelievable amount of money on new products with very low success ratio." So his firm has compiled a vitality test for older products designed to help businesses decide whether a product is worth an attempt at rejuvenation. The 10-point "Life Signs" quiz follows.

1. Does the product have new or extended uses? The classic example is Arm & Hammer baking soda, which can be used to absorb odors in refrigerators and drains, to deodorize carpets, to brush teeth, and to bake.

2. Is the product a generic item that can be branded? Sunkist successfully branded a generic agricultural product—oranges.

3. Is the product category unadvertised? Many women's products went unadvertised for years before International Playtex and Johnson & Johnson took an aggressive advertising approach.

4. Is there a broader target market? Johnson & Johnson found that babies weren't the only consumers of its baby shampoo.

5. Can you turn disadvantages into advantages? Orville Redenbacher created a memorable image for his product based on his unusual name.

6. Can you cut price and build volume and profit? This may be a key to success, especially for highly competitive products.

7. Can you market unused by-products? Many lumber companies sell sawdust to kitty litter companies.

8. Can you sell it in a more compelling way? Pampers did not sell well until Proctor & Gamble put more emphasis on the diaper's ability to keep babies dry and comfortable than on its convenience for parents.

9. Is there a marketplace or social trend to exploit? What makes people pay $1 per bottle for spring water?

10. Can you expand distribution channels? Hanes has been tremendously successful expanding the availability of its L'eggs pantyhose beyond traditional outlets.

Source: Adapted from Bill Abrams and Janey Guyon, "Ten Ways to Restore Vitality to Old, Worn-out Products," *The Wall Street Journal*, February 18, 1982, p. 28, with permission of *The Wall Street Journal*, © Dow Jones & Company, Inc. 1982. All rights reserved.

might include medication, bandages, sandbags for flood protection, and plywood for hurricane or tornado protection. Emergency services include those provided by a telephone booth late at night, or by an ambulance service company.

Shopping goods are purchased only after customers make comparisons among a variety of similar and competitive products. They are generally compared by price, style, quality, or service provided by the seller. Shopping goods generally have higher unit prices than do convenience goods, thus making the purchase decision more important. Examples of shopping goods are furniture, television sets, appliances, automobiles, clothing, and housing. Shopping services include such things as auto body repair or house painting and repair.

Specialty goods are identified by strong brand names. A specialty product has a particular feature that distinguishes it from its competitors and justifies a special purchase. People at all levels of marketing go to great expense and effort to make these distinctions and to develop brand-name recognition for their products.

The distinctions made among convenience,

TABLE 15–1   Classification of consumer products.

Convenience Goods	Staple	Food, nonprescription drugs
	Impulse	Candy bar, gum, magazine
	Emergency	Doctor's visit, ambulance service
Shopping Goods	Lesser expenditure	Suit, shirt and tie, dress
	Greater expenditure	Automobile, vacation, household appliances
Specialty Goods	Lesser expenditure	Gant shirt, Bobbie Brooks blouse, Coco-Cola
	Greater expenditure	G.E. dishwasher, Porsche automobile

shopping, and specialty goods (and the many subsections of each) are frequently blurred and overlapping. This is inevitable because of the changing habits of consumers in the marketplace; the many different uses to which various products and services can be put; and the innumerable places where such goods and services can be purchased. Consumer product categories are reviewed in table 15–1.

Place

Place (or method of distribution) has grown in importance as customers expect greater service and more convenience from businesses. Because of this trend, mail-order houses offering the ultimate in convenience—"shop at home"—have experienced booming sales in the last decade. In addition, many traditionally stationary businesses have added wheels, becoming mobile animal clinics, computer shops, and dentist offices.

Any activity involving movement of goods to the point of consumer purchase provides place utility. Place utility is directly affected by the marketing channels of distribution. A channel of distribution is the path that goods or services and their titles take in moving from producer to consumer. Channels typically involve a number of middlemen who perform specialized functions that add valuable utility to the goods or service. Specifically, these middlemen provide time utility (making the product available when customers want to buy it) and place utility (making the product available where customers want to buy it).

Although middlemen are frequently the subjects of advertisements offering bargain prices (one jeweler claims, "We cut the cost of the middleman and pass the savings on to you.") they perform services that add value to the product and make it easier to purchase. Without middlemen the consumer's task of making everyday purchases would be complicated substantially. This concept, illustrated in figure 15–2 by the principle of minimum transactions, says that the most efficient channel of distribution is the one involving the fewest number of transactions. Transaction A in figure 15–2 shows a simplified market with four producers and four consumers and no middlemen. Sixteen transactions are required, and customers are inconvenienced because they must exert more effort to purchase the goods and services. Transaction B in figure 15–2 shows the same market but with middlemen added. Now only eight transactions are required, and the channel of distribution is more efficient because the middlemen perform marketing functions like storage, transportation, risk-bearing, and financing.

For consumer goods, there are four common channels of distribution (see figure 15–3).

■ *Manufacturer to Consumer.* In some markets, producers sell their goods or services directly to

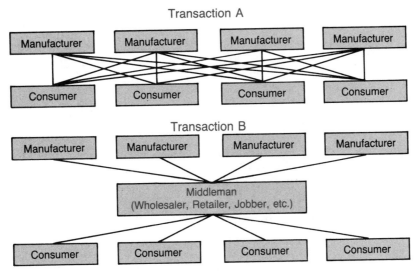

FIGURE 15–2 The principle of minimum transactions.

consumers. Services, by nature, follow this channel of distribution. Dental care and haircuts, for example, go directly from creator to consumer.

- *Manufacturer to Retailer to Consumer.* Another common channel involves a retailer as a middleman. Many clothing items, books, shoes, and other consumer products are distributed in this manner.
- *Manufacturer to Wholesaler to Retailer to Consumer.* This is the most common channel of distribution. Prepackaged food products, hardware, toys, and other items are commonly distributed through this channel.

- *Manufacturer to Wholesaler to Wholesaler to Retailer to Consumer.* A few consumer goods (e.g., agricultural goods and electrical components) follow this pattern of distribution.

Two channels of distribution are common for industrial goods (see figure 15–4).

- *Manufacturer to Industrial User.* The majority of industrial goods are distributed directly from manufacturers to users. In some cases, the goods or services are designed to meet the user's specifications.

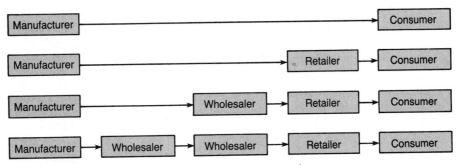

FIGURE 15–3 Channels of distribution—consumer goods.

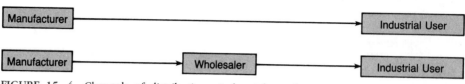

FIGURE 15–4   Channels of distribution—industrial goods.

- *Manufacturer to Wholesaler to Industrial User*. Most "expense" items (paper clips, paper, rubber bands, cleaning fluids) that firms commonly use are distributed through wholesalers.

For most small manufacturers, distributing goods through established wholesalers and agents is often the most effective route.

The type of transportation used by a business depends on its needs. Small, expensive, and perishable goods are often transported by air. While air is usually the most expensive form of transportation, its speed often makes it cost effective. Roses from Washington State or orchids from Florida cannot reach the florists of New York, Chicago, or Cleveland without air transport. The opposite is true of barge transport. Barges travel the waterways, moving nonperishable bulk commodities such as coal, iron ore, and cement; heavy construction equipment and materials; and goods that do not have to be rushed to market. Some automobile firms have employed water transportation to move their products to market. The National Aeronautics and Space Administration (NASA) moved the big rockets of the space program by water transportation.

However, the major movement of goods in our country is done by railroads and trucks. On long hauls, railroads and trucking companies cooperate through "piggybacking" truck trailers on flatbed rail cars to lower transportation costs. Each transportation system provides the nation's businesses and consumers with products at prices that reflect the optimal combination of all the systems. Some transportation systems are built to move high volumes of products to consumers at low cost. Refined oil and natural gas are examples of products transported through pipelines. Pipelines are expensive to build, but they provide lower-cost transportation in the long run by providing fast, uninterrupted delivery of the product to consumers.

The *storage function* of marketing is another phase of physical distribution. Storage involves holding goods from the time they are produced until they are purchased. Storage or warehousing is done by manufacturers, wholesalers, and retailers, depending on the length of the channel of distribution. If a consumer goes directly to the manufacturer to purchase goods, the manufacturer is the storage point. Some goods may be transported from warehouse to warehouse en route to the market. Food is an example of a well-traveled product. When a breakfast cereal is packaged by the manufacturer, it is stored until it is shipped to a wholesaler, who stores it until it is distributed to retailers. The retailers then store the product until the consumer purchases it.

The entire marketing function depends on the goods and services reaching the consumer where and when they are demanded. For this reason, transportation and storage become critical segments of the marketing function. Thus, the channels of distribution, transportation, and storage are all part of the place variable of the marketing mix.

Price

Almost everyone agrees that the price of the product or service is a key factor in the decision to buy. Price affects both sales volume and profits. Marketers must decide how much influence price fluctuations have on the consumer. If an increase in product price causes consumers to reduce their purchases more than proportionally, the product is said to be price

This truck is carrying wine to a seaport from Bordeaux, France. (Photo courtesy of CTI, Inc.)

elastic. For example, at $1.00 your company is able to sell 100,000 units per month. Management decides to increase the price 10 percent to $1.10, and the result is a decrease in sales from 100,000 to 80,000 units. This price action demonstrates that in the market the product is price elastic because the total revenue fell.

Price increase from $1.00 to $1.10 results in 20 percent sales decrease from 100,000 to 80,000 units as in the following:

price × quantity sold = total revenue
$1.00 × 100,000 units = $100,000   Total revenue
$1.10 × 80,000 units = $ 80,000   Total revenue
                        $ 12,000   Revenue loss

Piggybacking involves loading truck trailers on barges to lower transportation costs while maintaining flexibility. (Photo courtesy of CTI, Inc.)

If the increase in price had resulted in an increase in total revenue, we could state that the product was price inelastic. In this case although demand fell, total revenue increased. For example, a price increase from $1.00 to $1.10 results in 5 percent sales decrease from 100,000 to 95,000 units as in the following:

price × quantity sold = total revenue
$1.00 × 100,000 units = $100,000   Total revenue
$1.10 × 95,000 units = $104,500   Total revenue
$ 4,500   Revenue gain

For many small businesses, nonprice competition—focusing on factors other than price—is a more effective strategy than trying to beat larger competitors in a price war. Nonprice competition, such as free trial offers, free delivery, lengthy warranties, and "money back" guarantees, intend to play down the product's price and stress its durability, quality, reputation, or special features. Because of the special features and service they offer, some small companies follow a "premium price" strategy. One firm markets a $300 talking scale that offers congratulations for weight losses and catty comments like "Would one of you get off me?" for weight gain.[16]

Promotion

Promotion aims to inform and persuade consumers. Promotion involves both advertising and personal selling. Advertising communicates to potential customers through some mass medium the benefits of a good or service. Personal selling involves the art of persuasive sales on a one-to-one basis.

Although advertising cannot create demand for a product, it certainly can awaken the demand for a good. Its purposes are to create a brand image, to persuade customers to buy, and to develop brand loyalty. Federal Express developed a series of ads that performed these functions quite well ("When it

absolutely, positively has to be there overnight"). Customers noticed the ads and identified with the situations they portrayed. Advertising can take many forms and is put before the public through a variety of media. Chapter 17 is devoted to creating an effective advertising campaign for a small company.

Personal selling may be more art than science. It is especially important to small businesses because of their limited (and sometimes deficient) advertising budgets. Therefore, it is critical that the small business owner hire qualified, competent sales representatives and invest enough money to train them adequately. To customers, sales representatives *are* the company. Impolite, impatient, or incompetent sales personnel reflect negatively on the business. The wise small business owner will maintain close contact with the firm's customers to get constant feedback on sales representatives' effectiveness.

Consumer Credit

To gain a competitive edge, many small businesses are compelled to offer credit to their customers. There are two basic types of consumer credit: installment credit and charge account credit.

Installment Credit. Small companies that sell big-ticket consumer durables—major appliances, cars, and boats—frequently rely on installment credit. Very few customers can purchase such items in a single lump-sum payment; therefore, small businesses finance them over an extended time. The time horizon may range from just a few months up to 30 or more years. Most companies require the customer to make an initial down payment for the merchandise and then finance the balance for the life of the loan. The customer repays the loan principal plus interest on the loan. One advantage of installment loans for a small business is that the owner retains a security interest as collateral on the loan. If the customer defaults on the loan, the owner still holds the title to the merchandise. Because installment credit absorbs a small company's cash, many rely on financial institu-

---

[16]Lynn Asinoff, "Business Bulletin," *The Wall Street Journal*, May 8, 1986, p. 1.

Most small businesses offer some type of credit card.
(Photo by Jill R. Johnson.)

tions such as banks and credit unions to provide installment credit.

Charge Account Credit. Companies that sell small-ticket items frequently offer their customers trade credit—that is, they create customer charge accounts. The typical small business invoices credit customers each month. To speed collections, some offer cash discounts if customers pay their balances early; others impose penalties for late payers. Before deciding to use trade credit as a competitive weapon, the small business owner must be sure that the firm's cash position is strong enough to support the additional pressure.

Some small businesses issue their own credit cards for customer convenience and to build customer loyalty. There usually is a credit limit on each

customer's account, and most card issuers compute interest charges based on the customer's average daily balance during the billing cycle. State usury laws set the maximum interest rate the company can charge on credit cards.

Almost every financial institution issues credit cards—Visa, MasterCard, Diner's Club, American Express, or Discover. These cards allow small companies to offer credit without putting a burden on their cash flows since they receive almost immediate credit for credit card purchases. Credit card companies usually bear the risk of bad debts (except on invalid or unauthorized cards). The small business, however, must pay a fee—typically 2 to 6 percent of total credit card charges—to use the system. Figure 15–5 shows that a significant proportion of consumers prefer using credit cards to make purchases.

VI. ADVANTAGES OF EXPORTING

Exporting is an excellent method of increasing sales and boosting profits for the small business. Indeed, as the world economy becomes more interdependent, small firms must assume a global marketing posture if they are to survive. Yet very few small businesses take advantage of this prime marketing opportunity, with only 100 companies accounting for 50 percent of all U.S. export sales. Despite the encumbrances involved in selling goods and services abroad, export marketing offers even small businesses an opportunity to broaden their customer bases and to improve their profits.

In establishing an export business the initial steps are the most difficult ones for an entrepreneur. Lack of experience and confidence are common psychological barriers he must overcome. A successful exporting program requires that the owner do the following:

■ *Assess export potential.* The first step in assessing export potential is to evaluate the small firm's own potential. Many small business owners are surprised to learn that the products they manufacture

Export markets can boost sales and profits for small businesses. (Photo courtesy of CTI, Inc.)

can be marketed "as is" or with only minor modifications in foreign countries. Before proceeding, the owner should ask: What characteristics make the product attractive to foreign markets? Do some countries have negative attitudes toward the product? Are there any trade restrictions or import barriers?

■ *Target export markets.* In a typical small business, the owner will discover that export potential exists. Should the manager decide to capitalize on

this opportunity, he must target the markets to penetrate. In most cases, it is best to begin exporting a few of the firm's best products to one or two prime markets. The only way to determine what markets are ideal for exporting is to research them using foreign market information available from a variety of sources, including Commerce Department reports such as Foreign Trade Reports, Foreign Economic Trends, Overseas Business Reports, and Global Market Surveys.

■ *Develop and implement an export marketing strategy.* One of the keys to a successful export program is developing an export strategy to guide the small firm in the international market.

The process outlined in this chapter applies to foreign as well as to domestic markets. There are two basic approaches to exporting: (1) indirect selling, where the firm sells goods through intermediary companies that assume responsibility for transporting the merchandise overseas; and (2) direct selling, where the exporter locates foreign distributors and sells directly to them. Direct sales require more time and work and are best suited for experienced exporters. Table 15–2 outlines the four levels of exporting.

VII. SUMMARY

Marketing involves delivering customers the goods and services they desire; therefore, the customer is the foundation of any business, and the modern marketing concept recognizes this. A written marketing plan is an integral part of a successful business venture. It should determine customer needs and wants through market research; pinpoint the specific target markets the company will serve; analyze the firm's competitive advantages and build a marketing strategy around them; and create a marketing mix that meets customer needs and wants.

Market research is the vehicle for gathering the information that serves as the foundation of the marketing plan. Sound market research helps the owner

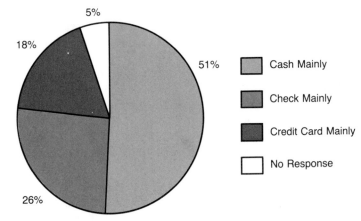

FIGURE 15–5   Cash, check, or credit card?

TABLE 15–2   Four levels of exporting.

Level 1: Export of surplus	The firm is interested only in overseas sales of surplus products, or is without resources to fill overseas orders for most products on an ongoing basis. *An observation:* If you have some available resources to devote to exporting, there is much to gain by selling in an area similar to your domestic market.
Level 2: Export marketing	The firm actively solicits overseas sales of existing products and is willing to make limited modifications in its products and marketing procedures to accommodate the requirements of overseas buyers. *Recommendation for management action:* If you can see overseas sales as a regular part of your future, move to this level as quickly as possible.
Level 3: Overseas market development	The firm makes major modifications in products for export and in marketing practices to be better able to reach buyers in other countries. *An observation:* One-half of exported products require little modification; about one out of three requires moderate modification; only a few require major changes.
Level 4: Technology development	The firm develops new products for existing or new overseas markets.

Source: U.S. Small Business Administration, *Export Marketing for Small Firms,* 4th ed., Washington, 1978, p. 8.

pinpoint his target market. The most successful businesses have well-defined portraits of the customers they are seeking to attract. Even small business managers who are close to their customers can get a new perspective of the market with research. Good research does *not* have to be complex and expensive to be useful.

When plotting a marketing strategy, the owner must strive to achieve a competitive advantage—some way to make her company different from and better than the competition. Few firms succeed by attempting to appeal to the mass market. Instead, it is usually more profitable for the small business owner to target a particular segment of the market and to seek a niche in it. The small business must be able to identify two or more segments with different characteristics, prove that the segments are capable of producing a profit, and reach the market.

The marketing mix is composed of the "four *P*s": product, price, place, and promotion. Every small firm must develop its marketing strategy on the basis of these four elements. Products take many forms; the important characteristic is their ability to satisfy consumer needs and wants.

Products progress through several stages of development in the product life cycle. In the introductory stage, new products must "break in" to a market dominated by other goods. Costs are high and sales are low at this point. In the growth stage, consumers begin to accept the product, and sales increase. Profits begin to appear. In the maturity stage, sales volume continues to rise but profit margins begin to fall as competition becomes more intense. Sales peak in the saturation stage and then taper off; profits continue to decline. In the decline stage, sales continue their decline, and profits disappear.

Consumer products can be classified according to consumers' buying habits. Convenience goods have low unit prices and are purchased frequently without much thought or effort. Impulse goods, as the name implies, are brought on impulse and rely on strategic placement in the store. Shopping goods are bought infrequently and have substantial unit prices. Consumers shop and compare before buying them. Specialty goods have some strong characteristic that distinguishes them from those of competitors.

The "place" variable of the marketing mix deals with distributing the firm's product or service. In providing customers with place utility, the small business owner has several options for channels of distribution. Another consideration is the mode of transportation. Generally, the faster the method, the greater its cost.

A product's price has substantial impact on a firm's sales volume and profits. While every business owner must be concerned with the product's price elasticity (or inelasticity), many firms focus more heavily on nonprice competitive factors such as delivery, service, or credit.

Promotion gives customers information about goods or services and influences them to buy. Advertising attempts to improve a firm's image in the community or to directly influence consumer behavior.

Many small businesses sell on credit. There are two basic types of consumer credit: installment credit and charge account credit. Bank-issued credit card programs are relatively low cost, and they allow the company to sell on credit without straining cash flow.

Exporting represents a prime marketing opportunity that few small businesses use. The hardest part of exporting is getting started. After making an assessment of the firm's export potential, the small business owner must target the export markets to focus on. Next, the owner must create an export strategy to guide the marketing effort. When implementing the export program, the owner can choose either indirect or direct selling. The small exporter must consider the product's features, packaging, and pricing in adapting it to foreign markets. The exporter must also be sure to obtain all required licenses and permits before shipping any merchandise.

STUDENT INVOLVEMENT PROJECTS

1. Interview the owner of a local restaurant about its marketing strategy. From how large a geographic region does the restaurant draw its clientele? What is the firm's target market? What are its characteristics? Does the restaurant have a "competitive edge"?

2. Select a local small manufacturing operation and evaluate its primary product. What stage of the product life cycle is it in? What channels of distribution does the product follow after leaving the manufacturer?

3. Obtain a copy of Management Aid #4.012, *Marketing Checklist for Small Retailers*, from the SBA. Interview a local business owner, using the checklist as a guide. What sources for developing a competitive edge did you find? What weaknesses do you see? How do you recommend overcoming them?

DISCUSSION QUESTIONS

1. Define the marketing concept. What lies at its center?

2. What is a competitive edge? How might a small company gain a competitive edge?

3. Define market segmentation. Why is it an effective marketing strategy? What requirements must be met to segment a market?

4. How can market research benefit the small business owner? List some possible sources of market research information.

5. Briefly describe the steps involved in starting an ineffective export program.

6. Explain the concept of the marketing mix. What are the four *P*s?

7. List and explain the stages in the product life cycle. How can a small firm extend its product's life?

8. Explain the categories of products according to consumers' buying habits.

9. Outline the common channels of distribution for consumers for industrial goods.

Pricing for Profit

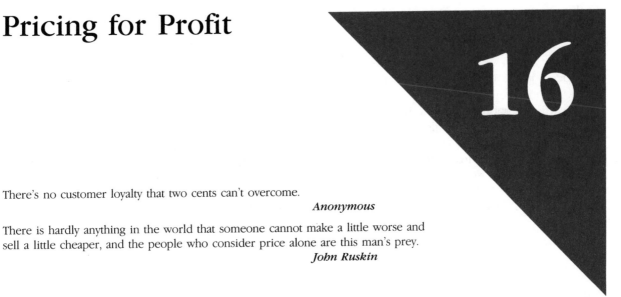

16

There's no customer loyalty that two cents can't overcome.

Anonymous

There is hardly anything in the world that someone cannot make a little worse and sell a little cheaper, and the people who consider price alone are this man's prey.

John Ruskin

Upon completion of this chapter, you will be able to:

- Outline the factors that determine the "best" price for a good or service.

- Define price from the customer's viewpoint.

- Describe how price conveys image and identify the different types of outlets, their images, and their usual clientele.

- Discuss the effect of competition on pricing policies.

- Explain effective pricing techniques to use when introducing a new good or service.

- Identify pricing strategies including odd pricing and price lining.

- Discuss the use of discounts and suggested retail prices.

- Explain the pricing methods and strategies for retailers, manufacturers, service firms, and wholesalers.

Most business managers do not understand the intricacies of the pricing function. Thus, many set prices by vague, poorly defined techniques or by "hunches." Such haphazard pricing policies can threaten a business' ability to make a profit. Therefore, it is essential that the small business manager understand pricing and its effects.

Price is the monetary value of a product or service in the marketplace. It is a measurement of what the customer must exchange to obtain various goods and services. Price is also a signal of a product or service's value to an individual, and different customers assign different values to the same goods and services. From the manager's viewpoint, price should be compatible with the customer's definition of value. In other words, the product or service the consumer purchases must be worth the price charged. If customers consider an item's price excessively high relative to its value, the firm's sales will suffer. Therefore, setting prices with a customer orientation is perhaps more important than trying to choose the ideal price for a product. In fact, for most products there is an acceptable price range, not a single ideal price. The price range is the area between the price ceiling defined by the market and the price floor established by the firm's cost structure. The manager's goal should be to position the firm's prices within this acceptable price range.

Determining the final price for a product or service is not easy. Most business owners consider a variety of relevant factors and then make a "best guess." Some of these factors are:

- product/service costs
- market factors
- sales volume
- competitors' prices
- economic conditions
- business location
- seasonal fluctuations
- psychological factors

Although the owner probably cannot isolate the ideal price for a product, she should set the price high enough to cover costs and earn a reasonable profit but low enough to attract customers and generate an adequate sales volume. Furthermore, the right price today may be completely inappropriate tomorrow because of changing market conditions.

SERVICE EXTRA

The following sign in a small service station illustrates the "gut feeling" approach most small business managers take in establishing prices: "Prompt, courteous service $2.00 extra."

I. THE EFFECTS OF PRICING

Price Conveys Image

The small company's pricing policies generate important information about its overall image. For example, the prices charged by a posh men's clothing store reflect a completely different image from those charged by a factory outlet. Customers look at prices to determine what type of store they are dealing with. High prices frequently convey the idea of quality, prestige, and uniqueness to the customer. When developing a marketing approach to pricing, the small business manager must establish prices that are compatible with what customers expect and are willing to pay.

The marketing approach to pricing is based on defining the firm's target market, the customer groups at which the small company aims its goods or services. Target market and business image are closely related. There are five different types of stores that create certain images and normally attract particular types of customers: exclusive outlets; specialty outlets; regular outlets; discount outlets; and combined outlets.

Exclusive Outlets. An exclusive outlet establishes higher-than-normal prices to create an exclusive image of its goods or services and to differentiate itself from competitors. Frequently, an exclusive outlet has special distribution rights for a prestige product in a given territory. This combination of prestige pricing and exclusive distribution induce a psychological effect which links high quality with high prices. To compensate for higher prices, customers expect the exclusive outlet to provide more services, better quality products, and more "extras." For example, customers might expect the firm to offer additional services like special showings of products, free delivery and installation, and special sales or credit terms. One small New York retailer of luxury clothing offers luncheons and private showings of the upcoming season's merchandise for its preferred customers. This firm's customers expect such extras in return for the higher prices they pay. By using its pricing policies to complement these additional services, this retailer has created an image of exclusiveness. Many small companies have created such an image quite successfully through prestige pricing policies.

Specialty Outlets. A specialty outlet is a shop that sells only one type of merchandise. Because of its

Pricing: Art, Science, or Both?

The law of demand states that the quantity of a product demanded will decrease when the price of that product increases, other things being equal. So when the Fleischman Division of Nabisco, Inc., raised the price of a fifth of gin from $4.50 to $5.50 over a two-year period, sales should have dropped off. Right? Not exactly. "The strategy helped incredibly," exclaims the company's manager. "Sales were deteriorating; now they're coming up. Sales are considerably above last year."

Although much has been written on the science of pricing products, the fact is that pricing, in many cases, remains an art. Of course, production costs and factory overhead figure into a product's price, but many other less tangible, less measurable factors also influence a pricing decision. Lower prices are preferred for most products, but there are exceptions. According to Gerald Katz, vice-president of a pricing consulting firm, "The higher you price certain products like a Mercedes Benz, the more desirable they become."

Pricing is a function subject to much criticism. One consumer advocate claims, " . . . everybody thinks people go about pricing scientifically. But, very often the process is incredibly arbitrary." Companies consider costs, competitors' prices on similar items, or image, "and then take a good guess," as one apparel manufacturer says.

Psychology also plays a role in pricing. Cowden Manufacturing sells jeans at $9.86 in its outlet stores. According to sales manager James McAskill, "When people see $9.99 they say, 'That's $10.' But $9.86 isn't $10. It's just psychological."

Another psychological factor is the link between price and quality. Most consumers tend to associate high quality with high prices. But the link is questionable. One researcher attempted to relate the prices of a broad range of packaged foods with their quality ratings and found that "the correlation . . . is near zero." Still, image plays an important role in setting prices. For example, the ingredients of a bottle of perfume retailing for $100 may cost only $20, but the $100 creates an air of mystique and sophistication. "Women are buying atmosphere, and hope, and the feeling they are something special," says a major perfume manufacturer.

Clearly, consumers purchase more than a tangible product when they buy an item. As Ronald Glatz, Proctor-Silex marketing manager, explains, "There is a segment of the market that wants to buy the best despite the cost."

Source: Adapted from "Pricing of Products Is Still an Art, Often Having Little Link to Costs," *The Wall Street Journal*, 25 November 1981, p. 49, with permission of *The Wall Street Journal*, © Dow Jones & Company, Inc. 1981. All rights reserved.

---

specialization, the outlet becomes an "expert" in its particular product. For example, a customer may patronize the local gun shop rather than the sporting goods section of a department store because the specialty shop offers a great deal of knowledge and expert advice about guns. Also, the gun shop provides a larger selection of merchandise, and special services like gun repair or a shooting range, all of which can be powerful factors in attracting customers. Jewelry stores, shoe stores, video shops, and blue jeans shops are examples of specialty outlets which sell specific types of merchandise and offer a variety of extra services. Naturally, the prices specialty shops charge reflect the extra costs and the extra value of these special services, although they are not nearly as high as the prices charged by exclusive outlets.

Regular Outlets. The majority of stores in the marketplace are regular outlets, selling a relatively broad line of merchandise at normal prices. Most department stores, restaurants, and hardware stores are examples of regular outlets. These firms offer fewer special services and other extras than either exclusive outlets or specialty outlets, and their pricing policies reflect this. In many regular outlets, prices are based on the manufacturer's suggested retail prices. Of course, the managers of these firms must establish their prices with an eye toward their competition, since their customers normally do a substantial amount of comparison shopping. Regular outlets do not have exclusive distribution rights and must rely on building a sizable clientele to be successful. Effective pricing policies are prerequisite to the survival of a regular outlet.

Discount Outlets. Discount outlets target the bargain hunting segment of the market. Like department stores (regular outlets), discount outlets usually carry a broad spectrum of products. But, unlike department stores, they offer no sales assistance; shopping is strictly self-service. The discount outlet eliminates all of the "luxuries" of other outlets in favor of discount prices. The basic idea is that the low prices will generate greater volume to compensate for the lower profit margins on each unit. K mart has built a profitable business on the basis of discount prices, and many small companies have followed the national retailer's lead.

Combined Outlets. To some degree, virtually every small business is a *combined outlet*, taking on some of the characteristics of each type of outlet. A small store could be a regular outlet in some products, a discount outlet in others, and an exclusive outlet in still others. But maintaining a desired image can be difficult if the store attempts to distribute products in the form of too many different outlets. Reduced sales may result if the firm's pricing policies create contradictory images in the consumer's eyes.

Competition

Two factors are vitally important in studying the effects of competition on the small firm's pricing policies: the location of the competitors and the nature of the competing goods. In most cases, the small business owner must match the prices charged by nearby competitors on identical items, unless the firm's customers perceive a difference in the quality and the quantity of "extras" provided. If the firm cannot justify an unfavorable price differential through a positive image, sales will suffer. For example, if a self-service station charged a nickel more per gallon for gasoline than another self-service station across the street, customers would simply go across the street to buy. Without the advantage of a unique business image—quality of goods sold, number of services provided, convenient location, favorable credit terms—the small company must match local competitors' prices or lose sales. While the prices that distant competitors charge are not nearly as critical to the small business as those of local competitors, it can be helpful to know them and to use them as reference points.

The nature of the goods competitors sell also influences the small firm's pricing policies. The manager must recognize which products are substitutes for those he sells and then strive to keep his prices in line with them. For example, the local sandwich shop should consider the hamburger restaurant, the taco shop, and the roast beef shop as competitors since they all serve fast foods. Although none of them offers the identical menu of the sandwich shop, they all compete for the same quick meal dollar. Of course, if the small firm can differentiate its product by creating a distinctive image in the consumer's mind, it can afford its own line of prices.

Generally, the small business manager should avoid head-on competition with other firms that can more easily achieve lower prices through a more favorable cost structure, quantity discounts, and other factors. Most locally owned drugstores cannot compete with the prices of large national drug chains.

The Price of Convenience

SMALL
BUSINESS
REPORT
16–2

In her first year of marriage, Gail Becker tried, unsuccessfully, to cook everything for her family "from scratch" and to run her own business. Now, she cooks just two nights a week, depending on restaurants and gourmet frozen foods on the remaining nights. "I won't give them run-of-the-mill old frozen Salisbury steak. I pay more to give them something closer to restaurant fare so I'll feel less guilty," she says.

Customers like Gail will pay a premium "for anything that will help them get control of their lives," says one marketing consultant. In response to the trend, food companies are finding new ways to "add value" to their products, which is reflected in their prices. Food companies are making their products more convenient, easier to prepare, or just more "gourmet."

Customers don't seem to mind paying the extra price either. The Food Marketing Institute estimates that only four of ten shoppers look for advertised specials, and only 27 percent compare prices from store to store. The result is impressive prices—and profit margins—on many items. A customer might pay six times more for frozen breaded chicken breast fillets than for a whole fryer or seven times more for au gratin potato mix than for a five-pound bag of potatoes. One manager explains, "Sometimes consumers like food to look posh so they can one-up on somebody else."

Source: Betsy Morris, "How Much Will People Pay to Save A Few Minutes of Cooking? Plenty," *The Wall Street Journal,* July 25, 1983, p. 23, with permission of *The Wall Street Journal,* © Dow Jones & Company, 1983. All rights reserved.

However, many local drugstores operate successfully by using nonprice competition; these stores offer more personal service, free delivery, credit sales, and other "extras" the chains eliminated. Nonprice competition can be an effective strategy for a small business in the face of larger, more powerful enterprises, especially since there are many dangers in experimenting with price changes. For instance, shifts cause fluctuations in sales volume that the small firm may not be able to tolerate. Also, price changes may damage the company's image and its customer relations.

II. EFFECTIVE PRICING TECHNIQUES

The small business manager can use a number of pricing strategies and techniques when facing a variety of business situations. The pricing strategies used in one situation, however, may be totally inappropriate in another. For example, the pricing techniques employed when introducing a new product are different from those used to rebuild the firm's market share. By implementing the appropriate pricing strategy, a manager can position a product in the desired market sector.

Introducing a New Product

Most small business managers approach setting the price of a new product with a great deal of apprehension because they have no precedent on which to base a decision. If the new product's price is excessively high, it is in danger of failing because of low sales volume. However, if its price is too low, the product's sales revenue might not cover costs. In pricing any new product, the owner should strive to satisfy three primary objectives:

1. *Getting the product accepted.* No matter how unique a product is, its price must be acceptable to the firm's potential customers.
2. *Maintaining market share as competition grows.*

401

If a new product is successful, competitors will enter the market, and the small company must work to expand or at least maintain its market share. Making continuous reappraisals of the product's price in conjunction with special advertising and promotion techniques helps the firm acquire and retain a satisfactory market share.

3. *Earning a profit*. Obviously, the small firm must establish a price for the new product higher than its cost. The manager should *not* introduce a new product at a price below cost; it is much easier to lower the price than to increase it once the product is on the market.

The small business manager has three basic strategies to choose from in establishing the new product's price: a penetration pricing strategy; a skimming pricing strategy; and a sliding-down-the-demand-curve strategy.

Penetration.   If a small business introduces a product into a highly competitive market where a large number of similar products compete for acceptance, the product must penetrate the market to be successful. To gain quick acceptance and extensive distribution in the mass market, the firm introduces the product with a low price. In other words, it sets the price just above total unit cost to develop a "wedge" in the market and to quickly achieve a high volume of sales. The resulting low profit margins discourage other competitors from entering the market with similar products.

In most cases, a penetration pricing strategy is used to introduce relatively low-priced goods into a market where no "elite" segment exists. The introduction is usually accompanied by heavy advertising and promotional techniques, special sales, and discounts. The small firm must recognize that penetration pricing is a long-range strategy; until the firm achieves customer acceptance for the product, profits are likely to be small. But if the strategy works and the product achieves mass market penetration, sales volume increases and the company earns adequate profits. The basic objective of the penetration strat-

egy is to achieve quick access to the market to realize high sales volume as soon as possible. Many consumer products, such as soap, shampoo, and light bulbs, are introduced through penetration pricing strategies.

Skimming.   A skimming pricing strategy often is used when a company introduces a new product into a market with little or no competition. Sometimes the firm employs this tactic when introducing a product into a competitive market where there is a "prestige" segment that is able to pay a higher price. Here the firm uses a higher-than-normal price in an effort to quickly recover the initial developmental and promotional costs of the product. Start-up costs are usually substantial due to intensive promotional expenses and high initial production costs. The idea is to set a price well above total unit cost and to promote the product heavily to appeal to the segment of the market that is not sensitive to price. Such a pricing tactic often reinforces the unique, prestigious image of a store and projects a quality picture of the product. Another advantage of this technique is that the manager can correct pricing mistakes quickly and easily. If the firm sets a price that is too low under a penetration strategy, raising the price can be very difficult. But if a firm using a skimming strategy sets a price too high to generate sufficient volume, it can always lower the price.

Sliding-Down-the-Demand-Curve.   One variation of the skimming price strategy is called "sliding-down-the-demand-curve." Using this tactic, the small company introduces a product at a high price. Then, technological advancements enable the firm to lower its costs quickly and to reduce the product's price sooner than its competition. By beating other businesses in a price decline, the small company discourages competitors and gradually becomes a high-volume producer over time. Computers and calculators are prime examples of products introduced at a high price that quickly cascaded downward as companies forged important technological advances.

An example of odd pricing. (Photo by Larry Hamill/ Merrill.)

Early five-function calculators cost nearly $200; today, the same calculator sells for under $10!

"Sliding" is a short-term pricing strategy which assumes that competition *will* eventually emerge. Even if no competition arises, the small business almost always lowers the product's price to attract a larger segment of the market. Yet, the initial high price contributes to a quick return of start-up costs and generates a pool of funds to finance expansion plans and technological advances.

Other Pricing Techniques

Odd Pricing. Although studies of consumer reactions to prices are mixed and generally inconclusive, many small business managers use the technique known as odd pricing. These managers prefer to establish prices that end in odd numbers (5, 7, 9) because they believe that merchandise selling for

$12.95 appears to be much cheaper than the item priced at $13.00. Psychological techniques such as odd pricing are designed to appeal to certain customer interests, but their effectiveness remains to be proven.

Price Lining. Price lining is a technique that greatly simplifies the pricing function. Under this system, the manager stocks merchandise in several different price ranges, or price "lines." Each category of merchandise contains items that are similar in appearance, quality, cost, performance, or other features. For example, most record and tape stores use price lines for their merchandise to make it easier for customers to select items and to simplify stock planning. Most lined products appear in sets of three—good, better, and best—at prices designed to satisfy different market segment needs and incomes. For example, many small garages use a lining technique to price services like tune-ups. The basic tune-up might cost $29.95, while the middle-of-the-road and the top-of-the-line tune-ups cost $49.95 and $69.95, respectively. Shops that sell a greater variety of merchandise often carry six or seven different price lines, but the idea is still the same: to simplify the buying, pricing, and stocking procedures for the busy small business manager.

Price lining. (Photo by Cindy Scarborough.)

Leader Pricing.   Leader pricing is a technique in which the small retailer marks down the customary price (i.e., the price consumers are accustomed to paying) of a popular item in an attempt to attract more customers. The company earns a much smaller profit on each unit since the markup is lower, but purchases of other merchandise by customers seeking the "leader" item often boost sales and profits. In other words, incidental purchases consumers make when shopping for the "leader" item boost sales revenues enough to offset a lower profit margin on the leader. One baker explains his use of leader pricing: "Strudel coffee cakes are labor intensive, and I can only get $2.89. But appearance means a lot, so what I lose there I make up on butter cinnamon pullaparts. It's just dough, but it looks like a coffee cake, so people will pay $2.99. On fruit pies (about $3), I hardly make any money at all, but you've gotta have them for customers. I get it back on angel food for $2.63."[1]

One version of leader pricing, called loss-leader pricing, is outlawed in many states that have laws dealing with unfair competition. The practice is outlawed because the business lowers the price of a popular leader item so drastically that it sells below cost. A small business usually employs loss-leader pricing to reduce supplies of overstocked items while increasing traffic flow in the store.

Geographical Pricing.   Small businesses whose pricing decisions are greatly affected by the costs of shipping merchandise to customers across a wide range of geographical regions frequently employ one of the geographical pricing techniques. For these companies, freight expenses comprise a substantial portion of the cost of doing business and may cut deeply into already narrow profit margins. One type of geographical pricing is zone pricing, where a small company sells its merchandise at different prices to customers located in different territories. For example, a manufacturer might sell at one price to customers east of the Mississippi and at another to those west of the Mississippi. The United States Postal Service's varying parcel post charges offer a good example of zoning pricing. The small business must be able to show a legitimate basis (e.g., differences in selling or transporting costs) for the price discrimination or risk violating Section 2 of the Clayton Act.

Another variation of geographic pricing is uniform delivered pricing, a technique in which the firm charges all of its customers the same price regardless of their location, even though the cost of selling or transporting merchandise varies. The firm calculates the proper freight charges for each region and combines them into a uniform fee. The result is that local customers subsidize the charges the firm incurs in shipping merchandise to distant customers.

A final variation of geographical pricing is FOB-Factory, where the small company sells its merchandise to a customer under terms that the customer pays all shipping costs. In this way, the company can set a uniform price for its product and let each individual customer cover freight costs.

Discounts.   Many small business managers use markdowns—reductions from normal list prices—to move stale, outdated, damaged, or slow-moving merchandise. A seasonal discount is a price reduction designed to encourage shoppers to purchase merchandise prior to an upcoming season. For instance, many retail clothiers offer special sales on winter coats in midsummer. Some firms grant purchase discounts to special groups of customers, such as senior citizens or students, to establish a faithful clientele and to generate repeat business. For example, one small drugstore located near a state university offered a 10 percent student discount on all purchases and was quite successful in developing a large volume of student business. The manager should consult a lawyer or the local Federal Trade Commission office for specific advice concerning "rain checks" on special sale merchandise because some statutes require businesses to offer rain checks on certain merchandise in particular situations.

Multiple pricing is a promotional technique

---

[1]Tom Richman, "*Super* Market," *Inc.*, October 1985, p. 120.

Source: From *The New Yorker, 57,* November 16, 1981, p. 52. Drawing by R. Chast; © 1981 *The New Yorker Magazine.* Used with permission.

which encourages customers to make quantity purchases by offering some savings. Many products, especially those with relatively low unit value, are sold using multiple pricing. For example, instead of selling an item for 50¢ a small company might offer 5 for $2.

Some businesses offer their customers trade-in allowances, which are deductions from normal selling prices granted when a customer trades in a used item of the same type. For instance, some auto parts stores offer price breaks to customers who trade in old batteries. Other businesses use trade-in allowances as promotional gimmicks. One new car dealer offered a discount of $800 for any used car, no matter how old, in any condition, on the purchase of a new automobile.

Suggested Retail Prices. Many manufacturers print suggested retail prices on their products or include them on invoices or in wholesale catalogs. Small business owners frequently follow these suggested retail prices because this eliminates the need to make a pricing decision. Yet, following prices established by a distant manufacturer may create problems for the small firm. For example, a haberdasher may try to create a high-quality, exclusive image through a prestige pricing policy, but manufacturers may suggest discount outlet prices that are incompatible with the small firm's image. Another danger of accepting the manufacturer's suggested price is that it does not take into consideration the small firm's cost structure or competitive situation. Usually, blind acceptance of suggested prices restricts the manager's pricing options. A manufacturer cannot force a business to accept a suggested retail price, nor require a business to agree not to resell merchandise below a stated price because such practices violate the Sherman Antitrust Act and other legislation.

III. MAJOR PRICING CONSIDERATIONS

Pricing by the Retailer

When developing an integrated pricing strategy a small retailer must first consider the customer. The retailer must prove that the price charged for a product or service is consistent with the utility gained from it. Further, the small business must prove to the customer that the value received relative to the price paid is greater than the value/price ratio of its competitors' merchandise. Unless the retailer creates this image of value in the customer's mind, adequate volume to sustain the business cannot be achieved. Every retailer knows that one key factor to success is moving merchandise, and competitive pricing policies must accomplish this. And without an efficient operation the retailer cannot offer competitive prices and quality goods and services—in short, *value*!

Practical Retail Pricing Concepts

Markup. The basic premise of a successful business operation is selling a good or service for more than it costs to produce it. The difference between the cost of a product or service and its selling price is called markup (or markon). Markup can be expressed in dollars as a percentage of either cost or selling price:

$$\text{dollar markup} = \text{retail price} - \text{cost of the merchandise}$$

$$\text{percentage (of retail price) markup} = \frac{\text{dollar markup}}{\text{retail price}}$$

$$\text{percentage (of cost) markup} = \frac{\text{dollar markup}}{\text{cost of unit}}$$

For example, if a man's shirt costs $15, and the manager plans to sell it for $25, markup would be:

$$\text{dollar markup} = \$25 - \$15$$
$$= \$10$$

$$\text{percentage (of retail price) markup} = \frac{\$10}{\$25}$$
$$= 0.40$$
$$= 40\%$$

$$\text{percentage (of cost) markup} = \frac{\$10}{\$15}$$
$$= 0.6667$$
$$= 66.67\%$$

Figures 16–1 and 16–2 illustrate the markup for this shirt. Notice that the cost of merchandise used in computing markup includes not only the wholesale price of the merchandise but also any incidental costs (e.g., selling or transportation charges) the retailer incurs and a profit minus any discounts (quantity, cash) the wholesaler offers.

Most retailers compute markup as a percentage of the retail price of their merchandise because most of the operating records the business owner prepares are expressed as a percentage of sales. All operating expenses, cost of goods sold, and profits are expressed as a percentage of total sales, not of the cost of the merchandise being sold.

Once the owner develops a financial plan, including sales estimates and anticipated expenses, she can compute the firm's initial markup. The initial markup is the *average* markup required on all merchandise to cover the cost of the items, all incidental expenses, and a reasonable profit:[2]

$$\frac{\text{initial}}{\text{dollar}} = \frac{\text{operating expenses} + \text{reductions} + \text{profits}}{\text{net sales} + \text{reductions}}$$

where operating expenses are the cost of doing business, such as rent, utilities, and depreciation; and reductions include employee and customer discounts, markdowns, special sales, and the cost of stockouts.

If, for example, a small retailer forecasts sales of $380,000, expenses of $140,000, and $24,000 in reductions, and she expects a profit of $38,000, the initial markup percentage would be:

$$\text{initial markup percentage} = \frac{140,000 + 24,000 + 38,000}{380,000 + 24,000}$$
$$= 50\%$$

[2]Bruce J. Walker, U.S. Small Business Administration, "A Pricing Checklist for Small Retailers," Small Marketers Aid No. 158, Washington, 1981, p. 23.

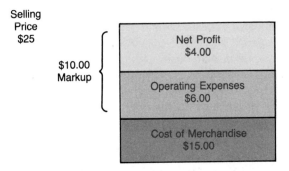

FIGURE 16–1   Dollar markup.

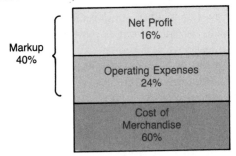

FIGURE 16–2   Percentage (of retail price) markup.

So, this retailer knows that a markup of 50 percent is required *on the average* to cover costs and generate an adequate profit.

Some businesses employ a standard markup on all of their merchandise. This technique, which is usually used in retail stores carrying related products, applies a standard percentage markup to all merchandise. Although it is somewhat inflexible in its applications, a standard markup is practical for specialty outlets. For example, some jewelry stores commonly use a standard markup of 50 percent, doubling the cost of the merchandise.

Most stores find it much more practical to employ a flexible markup. A flexible markup uses various markup percentages for a number of different types of products. Because of the wide variety of prices and types of merchandise they sell, department stores frequently rely on a flexible markup. It would be impractical for them to use a standard markup on all items because they have such a divergent cost and volume range. For instance, the markup percentage for socks is not likely to be suitable as a markup for washing machines.

Generally, highly speculative merchandise and slow-moving goods carry a higher markup than the initial markup percentages discussed in the last section. For example, shoes, furniture, and large appliances tend to have low turnover rates and typically have higher markups than the average item. Other factors contributing to above-average markups include popular "faddish" items at their peaks; bulky items with high selling and transportation costs; items requiring large reductions because of spoilage or obsolescence; and items requiring the extra expense of delivery, alteration, or installation.

Conversely, fast-moving merchandise with low carrying costs normally employ a lower markup than the average product. For instance, shirts, ties, and many grocery items carry low markup percentages since their turnover rates tend to be relatively high. In addition, those products on which the small company faces intense competition, or those which consumers are most likely to shop around for, should have relatively low markups.

Once the owner determines desired markup percentage, she is able to compute the appropriate retail price. Knowing that the markup of a particular item represents 40 percent of the retail price

$$\text{cost} = \text{retail price} - \text{markup}$$
$$= 100\% - 40\%$$
$$= 60\% \text{ of retail price}$$

and assuming that the cost of the item is $18.00, the retailer can rearrange the percentage (of retail price) markup formula:

$$\text{retail price} = \frac{\text{dollar cost}}{\text{percentage cost}}$$

Solving for retail price, the retailer computes a price of:

$$\text{retail price} = \frac{\$18.00}{0.60} = \$30.00$$

Thus, the owner would establish a retail price of $30.00 for the item using a 40 percent markup.

Finally, the retailer must verify that the computed retail price is consistent with his planned initial markup percentage. Will it cover costs and generate the desired profit? Is it congruent with the firm's overall price image? Is the final price in line with other store policies? Is it within an acceptable price range? How does it compare to the prices charged by competitors? And, perhaps most important, are customers willing and able to pay this price?

Follow-the-Leader Pricing.   Some small companies make no effort to be price leaders in their immediate geographic areas and simply follow the prices that competitors establish. Managers wisely monitor their competitors' pricing policies and individual prices by reviewing their advertisements or by hiring part-time or full-time comparison shoppers. But the retailers use this information to establish a "me too" pricing policy, which eradicates any opportunity to create a special price image for their businesses. Although many retailers must match competitors' prices on identical items, maintaining a follow-the-leader pricing policy may not be healthy for a small business since it automatically robs the company of the opportunity to create a distinctive image in its customers' eyes.

In addition, follow-the-leader pricing may lead to violations of antitrust legislation such as the Sherman Antitrust Act, which forbids businesses from engaging in price collusion or in any joint price determination that may tend to limit competition.

Below-Market Pricing.   Some small businesses choose to create a discount image in the market by offering goods at below-market prices. By setting prices below those of their competitors, these firms hope to attract a sufficient level of volume to offset lower profit margins. Many retailers using a below-market pricing strategy eliminate most of the extra services that their above-market pricing competitors offer. For instance, these businesses trim operating costs by cutting out services like delivery, installa-

tion, credit granting, and sales assistance. K mart is probably the best example of a business that has developed a successful image as a discount retailer.

Some small businesses fall victim to the "I-can-do-it-cheaper" mistake in pursuing a below-market pricing strategy. When competing with larger companies, especially chains with volume purchasing power, small retailers find that they can rarely undercut their prices. In many cases, it is possible in the short run to offer prices lower than those of larger competitors. But over the long run, most small companies discover that large firms have a greater pool of resources and more favorable cost structures. The result is that larger companies often undercut the prices of small discount retailers, dissolving any strategic advantage below-market pricing may afford. Unless a small company truly is a low-cost producer, it would be better off building its competitive edge on the basis of something other than price—quality, technology, performance, or delivery time.

Pricing by the Manufacturer

For the manufacturer, a pricing decision requires the support of accurate, timely accounting records. The most commonly used pricing technique for manufacturers is cost-plus pricing. Using this method, the manufacturer establishes a price composed of direct materials, direct labor, factory overhead, selling and administrative costs, plus a desired profit margin. Figure 16–3 illustrates the cost-plus pricing components.

The primary advantage of the cost-plus pricing method is its simplicity. Given the proper cost accounting data, computing a product's final selling price is relatively easy. Also, because he adds a profit onto the top of the firm's costs, the manufacturer is guaranteed a desired profit margin. This process, however, does not encourage the manufacturer to use his resources efficiently. Even if the company fails to employ its resources in the most effective manner, it still earns a reasonable profit. Thus, there is no motivation to conserve resources in the manu-

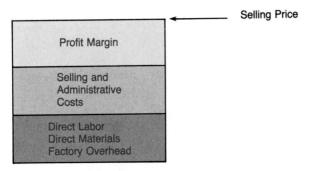

FIGURE 16-3   Cost-plus pricing components.

facturing process. Finally, because manufacturers' cost structures vary so greatly, cost-plus pricing fails to consider competition appropriately. Despite its drawbacks, the cost-plus method of establishing prices remains prominent in many industries such as construction and printing.

Direct Costing and Price Formulation   A manufacturing operation's cost structure and required profit margin establish a minimum floor for its prices, while its market creates a maximum price ceiling for them. Within this range, the manufacturer must determine a reasonable price for his product. One requisite for a successful pricing policy in manufacturing is a reliable cost accounting system that can generate timely reports to determine the costs involved in processing raw materials into finished goods. The traditional method of product costing is called *absorption costing*, since all manufacturing and overhead costs are "absorbed" into the finished product.[3] Absorption costing includes direct materials, direct labor, plus a portion of fixed and variable factory overhead in each unit manufactured. Full-absorption financial statements are used in published annual reports and in tax reports and are very useful in performing financial analysis. But full-absorption statements are of little help to the manu-

facturer when determining prices or the impact of price changes.

A more useful technique for managerial decisionmaking is *variable (or direct) costing*, where the cost of the products manufactured includes *only* those costs that vary directly with the volume produced. In other words, variable costing assigns direct materials, direct labor, and factory overhead costs that vary with the level of the firm's output of finished goods. Those factory overhead costs that are fixed (rent, depreciation, insurance) and are not included in the costs of finished items. Instead, they are considered to be expenses of the period.

The manufacturer's goal in establishing prices is to discover the cost combination of selling price and sales volume that will cover the variable costs of producing a product and contribute toward covering fixed costs and earning a profit. The problem with using full-absorption costing for this is that it clouds the true relationships among price, volume, and costs by including fixed expenses in unit cost. Using a direct costing basis yields constant unit cost for the product no matter what volume of production occurs. The result is a clearer picture of the price-volume-costs relationship.

The starting point for establishing product prices is the direct cost income statement. As table 16-1 indicates, the direct cost statement yields the same net profit as the full-absorption income statement. The only difference between the two statements is the format. The full-absorption statement allocates costs such as advertising, rent, and utilities according to the activity that caused them, but the direct cost income statement separates expenses into fixed and variable categories. Fixed expenses remain constant regardless of the production level, but variable expenses fluctuate according to production volume.

When variable costs are subtracted from total revenues, the result is the manufacturer's contribution margin—the amount remaining which contributes to covering fixed expenses and earning a profit. Expressing this contribution margin as a percentage

[3]Philip E. Fess and C. Rollin Niswonger, *Accounting Principles*, (Cincinnati, Ohio: South-Western Publishing Company, 1981), p. 625.

TABLE 16–1 A full-absorption vs. direct cost income statement.

FULL-ABSORPTION INCOME STATEMENT

Revenues		$790,000
Cost of goods sold:		
Materials	250,500	
Direct labor	190,200	
Factory overhead	120,200	560,900
Gross Profit		229,100
Operating expenses:		
General & administrative	66,100	
Selling	112,000	
Other	11,000	
Total Expenses		189,100
Net Profit (before taxes)		$ 40,000

DIRECT COST INCOME STATEMENT

Revenues (100%)		790,000
Variable costs:		
Materials	250,500	
Direct labor	190,200	
Variable factory overhead	13,200	
Variable selling expenses	48,100	
Total Variable Costs (63.54%)		502,000
Contribution Margin (36.46%)		288,000
Fixed Costs		
Fixed factory overhead	107,000	
Fixed selling expenses	63,900	
General & administrative	66,100	
Other	11,000	
Total Fixed Costs		248,000
Net Profit (before taxes)		$ 40,000

of total revenue yields the firm's contribution percentage. Computing the contribution percentage is a critical step in establishing prices through the direct costing method. This manufacturer's contribution percentage is 36.5 percent.

Computing Break-Even Selling Price. The manufacturer's contribution percentage tells what portion of total revenues remains after covering variable costs to contribute toward meeting fixed expenses and earning a profit. Our manufacturer's contribu-

We *Thought* We Were Making A Profit . . .

The owners of Contextural Design Inc., a small manufacturer of oak and pine furniture in Raleigh, N.C., knew how to build fine furniture to sell to retail stores. What they didn't know, however, was how to establish prices for their 70-item product line. When the founders (all in their twenties) established the company in 1977, they decided they could control quality better if they manufactured their own parts rather than if they bought them. So, they set up a complete production line that started with rough lumber at one end and spit out finished furniture at the other.

The obvious question was: How do we calculate prices, given the large number of operations each item goes through? The partners decided that a 50 percent gross profit "felt like it would work," covering overhead and a modest net profit. So, they added the costs of direct labor and raw material and multiplied by two. The resulting price appeared to be reasonable, and, for a time, business went well.

Then, something happened.

When the partners finally got around to preparing their June 30 year-end financial statements in November, they discovered that the company's net worth was dropping fast. "But, we feel we have things under control," one cofounder assured a nervous creditor. "Well, we don't think you do," came the reply.

Only after it was too late to save the company did the founders discover the sources of the company's problems. One cause of the firm's failure was the seat-of-the-pants accounting system the company used. Financial miscalculations here led to fatal errors in pricing. One cofounder remembers, "It was always a very small margin we ended up with." Another problem was that at first, the accounting system worked. But, it crumbled under the pressure of rapidly growing sales.

At one point, the owners began to suspect that product costs might be exceeding their prices. Time confirmed their suspicions; they had miscalculated direct labor costs in their pricing formula and they had ignored factory overhead, which proved to be a major expense. With the help of a new computer system, one of the owners calculated that overhead amounted to $1.50 for every $1.00 of direct labor. Recognizing how rapidly the company's sales were growing, he admitted, "Well, if overhead on those workers is one-and-a-half times labor, we *are* losing money—and we're about to lose a lot more."

The company's basic problem was improper pricing. One partner who pushed for a price increase (which might have saved the company) but was voted down by the others, says, "Their attitude was, everything has to be fine. They were too busy getting the stuff out the door to bother with details." He continues, "There never was a market analysis of price, never any consideration of what the market would bear. That's what was so crazy."

Source: Adapted from Robert A. Mamis, "The Price Is Wrong," *Inc.*, May 1986, pp. 159–63, with permission of the publisher.

tion percentage is 36.5 percent, which means that variable costs absorb 63.5 percent of total revenues. In other words, variable costs should be 63.5 percent $(1.00 - 0.365 = 0.635)$ of the product's selling price. Suppose that this manufacturer's variable costs include:

Material	$2.08/unit
Direct labor	$4.12/unit
Variable factory overhead	$0.78/unit
Variable cost	$6.98/unit

The minimum price our manufacturer would sell the item for is $6.98. Any price below this would not cover variable costs. To compute the *break-even* selling price for this product, we must solve for selling price using the following equation:

$$\text{profit} = \frac{\left(\begin{array}{c}\text{selling} \\ \text{price}\end{array} \times \begin{array}{c}\text{quantity} \\ \text{produced}\end{array}\right) + \left(\begin{array}{c}\text{variable cost} \\ \text{per unit}\end{array} \times \begin{array}{c}\text{quantity} \\ \text{produced}\end{array}\right) + \begin{array}{c}\text{total} \\ \text{fixed cost}\end{array}}{\text{quantity produced}}$$

which becomes:

$$\begin{array}{c}\text{break-even} \\ \text{selling price}\end{array} = \frac{\text{profit} + \left(\begin{array}{c}\text{variable cost} \\ \text{per unit}\end{array} \times \begin{array}{c}\text{quantity} \\ \text{produced}\end{array}\right) + \begin{array}{c}\text{total} \\ \text{fixed cost}\end{array}}{\text{quantity produced}}$$

To break even, the manufacturer assumes $0 profit. Suppose that plans are to produce 50,000 units of the product and that $110,000 of fixed cost will be incurred. Break-even selling price would be:

$$\begin{array}{c}\text{break-even} \\ \text{selling price}\end{array} = \frac{\$0 + (\$6.98 \times 50,000 \text{ units}) + \$110,000}{50,000 \text{ units}}$$

$$= \frac{\$459,000}{50,000 \text{ units}}$$

$$= \$9.18/\text{unit}$$

Thus, $2.20 ($9.18/unit − $6.98/unit) of the $9.18 break-even price contributes to meeting fixed production costs. But suppose the manufacturer wants to earn a $50,000 profit. The selling price would be:

$$\begin{array}{c}\text{selling} \\ \text{price}\end{array} = \frac{\$50,000 + (\$6.98/\text{unit} \times 50,000 \text{ units}) + \$110,000}{50,000 \text{ units}}$$

$$= \frac{\$509,000}{50,000 \text{ units}}$$

$$= \$10.18/\text{unit}$$

Now the manufacturer must decide whether the market will purchase 50,000 units at $10.18. If not, he must make a decision to either produce a different, more profitable product or reduce the selling price. Any price above $9.18 will generate some profit, although less than the desired profit. In the short run, the manufacturer could sell the product for less than $9.18 if competitive factors so dictated, but not below $6.98 since this would not cover the variable cost of production.

Because the manufacturer's capacity in the short run is fixed, pricing decisions should be aimed at employing these resources most efficiently. Fixed costs of operating the plant cannot be avoided, but variable costs can be eliminated only if the firm ceases production of the product. Therefore, selling price must be at least equal to the variable costs (per unit) of producing the product. Any price above this amount contributes toward covering fixed costs and providing a reasonable profit.

Of course, over the long run, the manufacturer cannot sell beneath total costs and continue to survive. So, selling prices must cover total product cost—both fixed and variable—and generate a reasonable profit.

Pricing by Service Firms

The typical service firm can benefit from effective pricing techniques. Too often, small service firms simply charge the "going rate," or they set a price they deem appropriate for the specific set of circumstances. Prices for identical services often vary substantially, even in the same geographical region. Service firms relying on such volatile pricing policies run the risk of alienating customers.

A service firm must establish a price based on the materials used to provide the service, the labor employed, an allowance for overhead, and a profit. As in the manufacturing operation, a service firm must have a reliable, accurate accounting system to keep a tally of the total costs of providing the service. Most of these firms charge customers for their ser-

TABLE 16–2   Direct-costing income statement, Ned's T.V. Repair Shop.

Sales Revenue			$ 199,000
Variable Expenses:			
Labor		52,000	
Materials		40,500	
Variable factor overhead		11,500	
Total		104,000	
Fixed Expenses:			
Rent		2,500	
Salaries		38,500	
Fixed overhead		27,000	
Total		68,000	
Total Costs			$ 172,000
Net Income			27,000

vices on an hourly basis, usually the actual number of hours required to perform the service. Some companies, however, base their fees on a standard number of hours, determined by the average number of hours needed to perform the service. For most firms, labor and materials comprise the largest portion of the cost of the service. To establish a reasonable, profitable price for service, the small business owner must identify the cost of materials, direct labor, and overhead involved in each unit of service. Using these basic cost data and a desired profit margin, the owner of the small service firm can determine an appropriate price for the service.

Consider a simple example for pricing a common service—television repair. Ned's T.V. Repair Shop uses the direct costing method to prepare an income statement for exercising managerial control (see table 16–2). Ned estimates that he and his employees spent about 12,800 hours in the actual production of television service. So total cost per productive hour for Ned's T.V. Repair Shop comes to:

$$\frac{\$172,000}{12,800 \text{ hours}} = \$13.44/\text{hour}$$

Now Ned must add in an amount for his desired

profit. Ned expects a net operating profit of 18 percent on sales. To compute the final price:

$$\frac{\text{price}}{\text{per hour}} = \frac{\text{total cost per}}{\text{productive hour}} \times \frac{1.00}{1.00 - \text{net profit as \% of sales}}$$
$$= 13.44 \times 1.219$$
$$= \$16.38/\text{hour}$$

A price of $16.38 per hour would cover Ned's costs and generate the desired profit. The wise service shopowner will compute his cost per production hour at regular intervals throughout the year. Rapidly rising labor costs and material prices dictate that the service firm's price per hour be computed even more frequently. As in the case of the retailer and the manufacturer, Ned must evaluate the pricing policies of competitors, and decide whether his price is consistent with the firm's image.

Of course, the price of $16.38 per hour assumes that each job requires the same amount of materials. If this is not a valid assumption, Ned must recompute the price per hour *without* including the cost of materials:

$$\text{cost per productive hour} = \frac{\$172,000 - 40,500}{12,800 \text{ hours}}$$
$$= \$10.27/\text{hour}$$

Adding in the desired 18 percent net operating profit on sales:

$$\text{price per hour} = \$10.27/\text{hour} \times \frac{1.00}{1.00 - 0.18}$$
$$= \$10.27/\text{hour} \times 1.219$$
$$= \$12.52/\text{hour}$$

So under these conditions Ned would charge $12.52 per hour plus the actual cost of material used and any markup on the cost of material. A repair job which takes four hours to complete would have a price of:

Cost of service (4 × 12.52/hour)	$50.08
Cost of materials	21.00
Markup on material (10%)	2.10
Total price	$73.18

Pricing by Wholesalers

The pricing considerations for a wholesaler are much the same as for those of retailers and manufacturers. A wholesaler bases price on the cost of goods sold (including transportation and handling expenses) plus a markup for profit. Many wholesalers rely on catalogs to disseminate information—including prices—about their products. Catalogs, however, cause problems for wholesalers, especially during periods of inflation. Many wholesalers distribute catalogs to their customers only to discover that prices which generated a profit at the year's beginning fail to cover even operating costs later in the year. One way to avoid this difficulty is to advise customers that "prices are subject to change" and to follow up annual catalogs with more frequent price revisions. Some wholesalers prefer to issue smaller, shorter-term catalogs. One appliance wholesaler, for example, mails attractive new catalogs to its customers every quarter, advertising a different special for each season. Using this strategy, the wholesaler keeps prices up-to-date and boosts the advertising effort.

IV. SUMMARY

Pricing is one of the most important, yet least understood, of all the managerial duties. Many small business managers establish prices without formal pricing policies, basing them on what competitors charge or on what manufacturers suggest. Relying on such procedures, a small business manager incurs the problem that plagues the majority of small companies—underpricing goods and services. The result is lower revenues, diminished profits, and pressure on cash flows. The seasonal small business owner knows that costs establish a minimum price floor and the market defines a price ceiling. Within this range, the owner must determine a reasonable price—one that generates a profit—that customers are willing and able to pay. In addition, the manager must consider whether the established price matches the firm's desired image. Basing prices on reliable cost data and using established pricing techniques instead of intuition often spells the difference between business success and failure.

A "reasonable price" is one that covers the cost of providing the product or service, earns a profit, and generates adequate sales volume. Of course, prices must change as market conditions change.

Price is what the customer must exchange in order to obtain various goods and services in the marketplace. Price is also a signal of the value of a product or service to an individual. So, for the customer, the goods or service must be worth the price charged. The price will fall between the price floor established by the firm's cost structure and the price ceiling defined by the market.

Pricing policies inform customers about the small company's image. In pursuing a marketing approach, therefore, the manager must set prices that are consistent with those customers expect to pay. Five types of shops attract specific customer groups: exclusive outlets; specialty outlets; regular outlets; discount outlets; and combined outlets.

Ignoring competitors' pricing practices can be

dangerous for the small business manager. Unless the firm can create a unique quality or service image among its customers, it must meet competitors' prices on identical goods. The manager must also recognize which products are substitutes for the goods usually sold and keep prices in line with competition. Generally, head-on price competition with larger firms better equipped to reduce prices is unwise for the small company. Nonprice competition is safer and often more successful for small businesses.

Pricing a brand-new product is often difficult for the small business manager. Pricing a new product should accomplish three objectives: getting the product accepted; maintaining market share as competition grows; and earning a profit. Generally, there are three major pricing strategies used to introduce new products into the market: penetration, skimming, and sliding-down-the-demand-curve.

Odd pricing is a form of psychological pricing. Although studies are inconclusive, some small business managers believe that prices like $1.39 or $12.95 encourage customers to buy.

Price lining simplifies pricing for the manager. Each category of merchandise—or "price line"—the firm sells carries a single price. Many stores carry three lines—good, better, and best.

Leader pricing is a tactic in which the small firm marks down the price of a popular product or service in an attempt to attract greater customer volume. The hope is that customers will come into the store to purchase the leader and will purchase other, more profitable items while there. Loss leader pricing, where the firm sells a popular item below its cost, is outlawed in some states.

Firms affected by shipping costs often rely on geographical pricing techniques. One version is zone pricing, where the company sells its product to customers in different territories at different prices. Uniform delivered pricing establishes the same product price for all regions although shipping costs vary. A uniform fee for shipping means that some

customers subsidize transportation costs of other customers.

Discounts help small firms move stale, outdated merchandise. Seasonal discounts encourage customers to purchase merchandise in advance of the upcoming season. Multiple pricing encourages customers to make quantity purchases and save money.

Small business owners frequently use the manufacturer's suggested retail price because this avoids the necessity of making a pricing decision. This price, however, may not contribute to the firm's desired image and may not reflect its competitive situation.

Pricing for the retailer means pricing to move merchandise. Markup is the difference between the cost of a product or service and its selling price. Most retailers compute markup as a percentage of retail price. Some retailers employ a standard markup on all their merchandise; more frequently, they use a flexible markup.

Some small retailers utilize follow-the-leader pricing, where they set prices according to their competitors. This "me-too" pricing eliminates the opportunity to create a special price image for the firm. Also, price collusion among competitors is a violation of the Sherman Antitrust Act.

Some small businesses seek a discount image in the market by selling goods and services at below-average price. A few, however, fall victim to the "I can do it cheaper" mistake when trying to compete with larger companies. Over the long run, the small firm finds that many larger competitors have more favorable cost structures.

The manufacturer's pricing decision depends upon the support of accurate cost accounting records. The most common technique is cost-plus pricing, where the manufacturer charges a price to cover the cost of producing a product plus a reasonable profit. The cost-plus method is simple, but it does not encourage the efficient use of resources.

A direct costing accounting system is very useful in making pricing and other managerial decisions. The system includes only variable costs in the cost of goods manufactured. Fixed costs are expenses of the period. The minimum price the owner would be willing to sell a product for is its variable cost of production.

Service firms often suffer from the effects of vague, unfounded pricing procedures. They frequently charge "the going rate" without any idea of their costs. A service firm must set a price based on cost of materials used, labor involved, overhead, and a profit. The proper price reflects the total cost of providing a unit of service.

Pricing considerations for small wholesalers are much the same as for other small businesses. Catalogs used to generate customer orders pose a particular problem for wholesalers, especially in inflationary times. Some firms use catalog revision sheets while others prefer to issue shorter, more frequent catalogs.

STUDENT INVOLVEMENT PROJECTS

1. Interview small business owners in each of the industrial categories—retailer, wholesaler, manufacturer, and service firm—about their pricing policies. Do they seek a specific image through their prices? What type of outlet would you consider the retailer to be? What role do competitors play in pricing? Do they employ specific pricing techniques such as odd pricing, price lining, leader pricing, geographical pricing? How are discounts used? What markup percentage does the firm employ? How are prices derived? What are their cost structures?

2. Select an industry that has several competing small firms in your area. Contact these firms and compare their approaches to determining prices. Do prices on identical or similar items differ? Why?

3. Obtain a copy of Management Aid (MA) number 4.013, *A Pricing Checklist for Small Retailers*, from the SBA. Use the checklist to interview a local small retailer about her pricing policies. What suggestions can you make to improve her pricing system?

DISCUSSION QUESTIONS

1. What does a price represent to the customer? Why is a customer orientation to pricing important?
2. How does pricing affect a small firm's image?
3. Outline and briefly describe the characteristics of the five types of outlets.
4. What competitive factors must the small firm consider in establishing prices?
5. Describe the strategies a small business could employ in setting the price of a new product. What objectives should the strategy seek to achieve?
6. Define the following pricing techniques: odd pricing; price lining; leader pricing; geographical pricing; and discounts.
7. Why do many small businesses use the manufacturer's suggested retail price? What are the disadvantages of this technique?
8. What is markup? How is it used to determine individual price?
9. What is a standard markup? A flexible markup?
10. What is follow-the-leader pricing? Why is it risky?
11. What is cost-plus pricing? Why do so many man-

ufacturers use it? What are the disadvantages of using this technique?

12. Explain the difference between full-absorption costing and direct costing. How does absorption costing help a manufacturer determine a reasonable price?

13. Explain the techniques involved in setting an hourly price for a small service firm.

14. How do catalogs pose pricing problems for small wholesalers? How can a wholesaler deal with them?

15. What is the relevant price range for a product or service?

Creative Use of Advertising and Promotion

17

It's not the steak; it's the sizzle.

Anonymous

Public Relations Truism: There's nothing neither good nor bad that can't be made more so.

Earle Ferris

Upon completion of this chapter, you will be able to:

- Describe the importance of a unified advertising program to successful business operation.

- Define advertising and distinguish it from publicity, sales promotion, and personal selling.

- Identify the purposes of advertising for the small business.

- Understand the reasons manufacturers, retailers, and service firms use promotional advertising.

- Explain the value of institutional advertising to the small business owner.

- Point out key questions to consider before choosing advertising media.

- Illustrate the advantages and disadvantages of the various advertising media.

- Present the steps in the development of a business advertising plan.

- Introduce valuable principles to guide the development of an advertising message.

- Identify four basic methods for preparing an advertising budget.

- Identify practical methods of stretching the small business owner's advertising budget.

Too many small business owners believe that because of limited budgets they cannot afford the "luxury" of advertising. In their view, advertising is an expense to be undertaken only when the budget permits; in other words, it is a "leftover" expense, something to be incurred if anything remains after paying the other bills. However, failure to advertise will threaten the small firm's survival and will reduce substantially its chances of success.

The small business manager must recognize that large size and market power are *not* prerequisites for a successful advertising program. Indeed, most advertising is done by local small businesses rather than large national companies (see figure 17–1). Advertising on a regular basis is a critical element in sustaining a healthy, growing, vibrant small business. Since the lifeblood of every business entity is

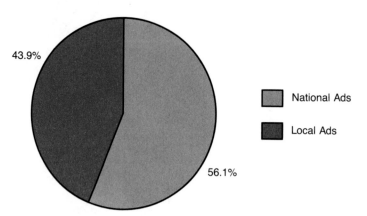

FIGURE 17–1   Percent spent on local and national advertisements.

Source: Statistical Abstract of the United States, 1985, U.S. Department of
Commerce, Bureau of the Census, 105th Edition, p. 539.

sales, the typical small business cannot prosper without a unified advertising program designed to boost
sales. Advertising can be an effective means of increasing sales by informing customers of the business and its goods or services; by improving the
image of the firm and its products; or by persuading
customers to purchase the firm's goods or services.

But advertising does not cast some mystical
spell over consumers, forcing them into a small shop
to purchase its products. By advertising, a business
owner is trying to remind potential customers of a
need or want and tell them how and why her products or services are the best way to satisfy it. Most ads
attempt to convince the customer—with practical or
psychological means—that the advertiser's products
or services are the best way to meet his needs. It will
not guarantee business success. It will not force consumers to buy goods or services they do not need or
want. In fact, if a small firm is poorly managed, its
goods or services inferior, or its employees rude, its
advertising efforts are largely a waste of time and
money.

The terms *advertising* and *promotion* are often
confused. *Promotion* is a broad term meaning any
form of persuasive communication designed to inform consumers about a product or service and in-

fluence them to purchase these goods or services. It
includes publicity, sales promotion, personal selling,
and advertising.

Publicity is any commercial news covered by
the media that boosts sales but for which the small
business does not pay. Small firms can make contributions of goods, services, or money to nonprofit
organizations and can sponsor public and community service events to generate valuable publicity. Not
only does the firm serve the public interest, but it
also reaches a segment of the public that normal advertising cannot reach. For example, the owner of a
new travel agency saw an opportunity for a great deal
of "free publicity" in a local golf tournament sponsored by a popular radio station to raise money for
the city's zoo. She offered an all-expense-paid Carib-
bean cruise to the winner of a certain hole. Her
fledgling business got more public exposure from
this one event than from all the ads she could have
bought with her limited budget.

Sales promotion entails any special promotion
techniques designed to influence customer demand.
Small firms often sponsor special promotions to attract attention to their businesses and to encourage
customers to come into their shops. For example,
bookstores sometimes feature autograph sessions

with famous authors to increase customer traffic and boost sales. When one bank introduced new automated teller machines, it placed a few bills of large denomination (20s and 100s) at random among the regular money packages as a bonus to encourage customers to use the machines.

Personal selling is the personal contact between sales personnel and potential customers resulting from sales efforts. Effective personal selling can give the small company a definite advantage over its larger competitors by creating a feeling of personal attention. Personal selling deals with the salesperson's effort to match customer needs to the firm's goods and services. Successful personal selling requires five key factors:

1. The salesperson must want to succeed.
2. The salesperson must identify with people.
3. The salesperson must exercise self-discipline.
4. The salesperson must develop selling skills.
5. The salesperson must have product knowledge.[1]

Advertising is any sales presentation that is non-personal in nature and is paid for by an identified sponsor. The remainder of this chapter will focus on the purposes of advertising, selecting media, and creating an advertising budget.

I. THE PURPOSES OF ADVERTISING

Consumers have different opinions about advertising. Some people find advertising to be intrusive, annoying, and insulting. Indeed, anyone who has attempted to read a newspaper or magazine article only to find the pages cluttered with distracting ads, or who has watched an exciting movie on television only to have the most suspenseful scenes interrupted by commercials may agree that advertising is bothersome. Some advertising is offensive simply because

it is so insulting. Everyone can identify an advertisement that grates on the nerves so much that one cringes when exposed to it.

On the other hand, advertising can be informative and, at times, even entertaining. How often do you catch yourself whistling or humming the jingle from a commercial that you thought you never paid attention to? Businesses spend a great amount of time and money trying to create memorable, effective advertisements to present to the public. In fact, the advertising industry presents an annual award, the Clio, that recognizes the highest quality, most effective advertisements on television.

In general, advertising can perform the following functions:

- *It can inform.* Advertising disseminates one of the most valuable commodities in any economy: information. By informing consumers of the products offered for sale, as well as their prices and features (and other relevant facts), firms enable customers to comparison shop conveniently and maximize the use of their budgets. Businesses also benefit from advertising since some sales are generated simply by telling customers who they are and what they sell.
- *It can persuade.* From the small business owner's perspective, the most important function of advertising is persuading customers to buy his company's product or service. An ad's primary objective is to *sell*, and the more persuasive it is, the more effective it is.
- *It can remind.* Advertising also keeps the small company's products and services fresh in the potential customer's mind.

Obviously, these three functions are closely interrelated, and virtually every ad incorporates elements of all three. Still, ads that do these things will not *make* a sale, but they will *help* the small business owner make a sale. One advertising expert explains:

Businesses use advertising, hope it works, but rely as little as possible on its persuasive powers. They want ads to inform people about new products,

[1]John C. Gfeller, "Five Keys to Better Salesmanship," *Nation's Business*, reprint.

but they really don't believe that this will turn anyone's head around who already knows about some product category. So they tend to put their advertising behind products that are already doing well. And they put their advertising most heavily in front of audiences . . . already inclined toward the product.

. . . Businesses indicate that they think ads are going to work most of all by reminding people who already know what they want rather than by persuading people of something new.[2]

Promotional Advertising

Promotional Advertising for Retailers and Service Firms. The small retail or service firm may use promotional advertising for several specific reasons. One of the most common purposes of advertising is to produce immediate sales by encouraging customers to purchase goods or service promptly. Specific tactics include ads that encourage potential customers to visit the store, offer special promotions, or create deadlines for sale merchandise. For example, television ads for record albums often encourage the viewer to "order before midnight tonight." Other small businesses employ different media to get their messages across. A hotel located on a long stretch of highway posts billboards in strategic places that announce, "Wanted: Sleepy People!" The signs also specify the hotel's rates and special discounts. By advertising in this manner the hotel hopes to generate direct sales by attracting weary highway travelers.

Another frequent purpose of advertising is to make potential customers aware of the firm's goods or services and to create consumer interest by providing information about them. While this type of advertising is important for existing small businesses, it is especially critical for newly formed firms that have not yet established their reputations in the market. Existing firms also use this tactic to develop a new image for their businesses in the public eye.

Small businesses can create consumer interest by advertising how their goods and services can be used, the benefits gained from using them, their prices and special promotions, and where they can be purchased.

No small retailer or service firm can succeed by relying solely on the volume of customer traffic passing the store; therefore, advertising is used to attract customers into the shop. The owner can then use layout, displays, and personal selling to close sales. Encouraging present customers to patronize the store more frequently is beneficial, but attracting new customers is critical since products, services, and markets are constantly changing—competitors are likely to enter the trading areas and introduce new goods and services, and old customers will leave the market and new ones will enter. The small firm's advertising program must address these changing conditions and produce increased sales from both existing and new customers. One small drugstore mails out weekly fliers advertising well-known name brand products and uses leaders and special promotions such as coupons or two-for-one sales. Using this technique, the drugstore hopes to sell large quantities of the advertised goods, generate impulse sales of other items, and establish a pattern among customers of shopping at the drugstore. Other small stores use sales promotion techniques to accomplish the same results. In-store demonstrations, contests, and promotions are often successful in increasing store traffic and sales.

Once the small business establishes a solid reputation in the business community, the owner must use advertising to maintain an adequate level of sales volume. Competitors are constantly improving old products and services, introducing new ones, and creating new ways to gain market leadership. All of these events threaten the survival of any small business that fails to keep up with changes in the market. Small firms must continue to advertise their goods or services and their advantages if they are to remain competitive.

In addition, the small business owner must rec-

---

[2]"Advertising Says, 'Let Us Feel Good about Ourselves,'" *U.S. News & World Report*, January 28, 1985, p. 62.

ognize that the store's clientele changes drastically over time. Stores constantly gain and lose customers as population and migration patterns change, and advertising can be an important tool in maintaining current sales volume. According to the National Retail Merchants Association, the small business that stops advertising will be forced to close in three or four years because its clientele will have turned over almost completely in that time. (The typical store loses 20 to 25 percent of its customers annually.)

Many small businesses advertise to introduce new goods and services or encourage increased use of existing products. Well-designed ads create interest in the product and encourage customers to try it. Consumers develop fierce brand loyalties for some products, and advertising is one of the most effective techniques to overcome this loyalty. In fact, several studies have concluded that consumers of products with high levels of advertising are much less brand loyal than those that are advertised little.

Advertising also can enlighten customers about alternative uses for a firm's product, a tactic that often leads to increased sales. This tactic has been very successful for the manufacturer of Arm & Hammer baking soda. Through a comprehensive advertising campaign, the company has been successful in getting customers to use its product as a carpet cleaner, deodorizer, and dentifrice, in addition to baking.

Promotional Advertising for Manufacturers. Retail and service firms are not the only businesses that can benefit from promotional advertising; manufacturers can also use it to their advantage.

Manufacturers frequently use advertising to stimulate primary demand for a generic product. These ads do not promote a specific brand name; instead, they attempt to stimulate demand for a broad category of goods. This type of advertising is commonly used for homogeneous products for which consumers cannot distinguish one brand from another, such as agricultural goods. For example, the orange growers of California use advertising to encourage the public to consume more oranges, and the prune growers promote the increased use of prunes while stressing their nutritional value.

Some manufacturers, like most retailers and service firms, use advertising in an attempt to stimulate selective demand—to differentiate their products from those of their competitors. These ads are aimed at creating a unique image for the manufacturer's goods and stimulating demand for them. For example, a small manufacturer of golf balls might focus its advertising efforts on the quality and unique features of its product, showing consumers why its golf balls are superior.

Depending on their target markets, manufacturers aim their ads at either "middlemen (wholesalers and retailers) or at the final consumer. The advertising campaign should be directed at the group that actually makes the purchasing decision. For instance, publishers of college textbooks do not advertise to the students who purchase their books; instead, they advertise to the professors who make the actual purchase decisions. On the other hand, manufacturers of frozen pizzas spend the bulk of their advertising budgets attempting to stimulate selective demand for their products among consumers.

Advertising also can facilitate sales representatives in making customer calls. Manufacturers can make their sales representatives' jobs much easier by advertising in various media to potential customers on whom the sales personnel will call. It is terribly difficult, and usually ineffective, for sales representatives to make calls on potential customers who are unfamiliar with their products. Even the best salesperson will have difficulty overcoming the customer attitude, "I've never heard of your company or your product. Now, what is it you want to sell me?"

Manufacturers frequently use ads in trade journals and papers or direct mail campaigns to sell the company name and product line. They aim to create a positive image for themselves and familiarize customers with their products *before* sales representatives make personal calls to close deals. A well-designed ad campaign can assist sales representatives to become a more effective marketing tool.

Institutional Advertising

Small businesses often find it beneficial to engage in a certain amount of institutional advertising, designed to provide the public with information about the company. Also called attitude advertising, its purposes are to ensure the public's awareness of the small company's name as well as its products or services; to create goodwill and customer confidence; and to improve the company's overall image in the community. In other words, institutional advertising seeks to build a favorable public image for the small firm. These ads typically are more subtle than promotional ads since the company actually is trying to sell itself.

Institutional advertising differs from promotional advertising in the time required to produce results. While promotional advertising is designed to stimulate immediate customer response, institutional advertising takes much longer to produce results. Sales are usually delayed until long after the ad has run. Most attitude ads attempt to "plant the seed" of a purchase decision in the customer's mind.

In summary, institutional advertising helps remind the public that the small company is a good business citizen. In addition, it reinforces the positive image of the firm's goods and services in the marketplace. Accounting for only a fraction of advertising expenditures a decade ago, institutional advertising now is the fastest growing segment in the ad industry.

II. SELECTING ADVERTISING MEDIA

One of the most important decisions the small business manager must make is which media to use in disseminating his promotional message. The medium used to transmit the message influences the consumer's perception of it and determines how broad its coverage is. By choosing the proper advertising means, the small business owner can reach his target audience effectively at minimum cost. While no single formula exists for determining the ideal medium to use, there are several important characteristics that make some media better suited than others. Understanding the qualities of the various media available can simplify the company's decision. Before selecting the vehicle for the message, the owner should consider several questions.

How large is my firm's trading area? How big is the geographical region from which the firm will draw its customers? The size of this area clearly influences the choice of media.

Who are my customers and what are their characteristics? Determining a customer profile often points to the appropriate medium to use to get the message across most effectively.

What budget limitations do I face? Every business owner must direct the firm's advertising program within the restrictions of its operating budget. Certain advertising media cost more than others.

What media do my competitors use? It is helpful for the small business manager to know the media his competitors use, although he should not automatically assume that they are the best. An approach that differs from the traditional one may produce better results.

How important is repetition and continuity of the advertising message? Generally, an ad becomes effective only after it is repeated several times, and many ads must be continued for some time before they produce results. Some experts suggest that an ad must be run at least six times in most mass media before it becomes effective.

What does the advertising medium cost? There are two types of advertising costs the small business manager must consider: the absolute cost and the relative cost.

Media Options

This section will outline the characteristics of various advertising media available to the small business owner. Figure 17–2 gives a breakdown of the allocation of advertising expenditures on each medium,

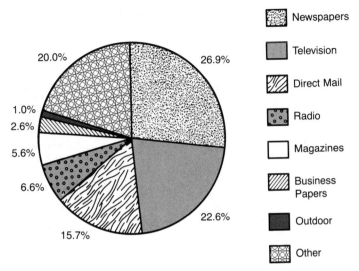

Newspapers

Television

Direct Mail

Radio

Magazines

Business Papers

Outdoor

Other

FIGURE 17–2 Advertising expenditures by medium.

Source: The 1986 Information Please Almanac, 39th Edition. (Boston: Houghton Mifflin Company, 1986), p. 61.

and table 17–1 illustrates how advertising is practiced by selected small businesses.

Newspapers. Traditionally, the local newspaper has been the medium that most advertisers rely on to get their messages across to customers. Although the number of newspapers in the U.S. has declined 19 percent since 1960, this medium attracts nearly 27 percent of all advertising dollars nationwide, establishing it as the leader among all media.[3] Newspapers provide several advantages to the small business advertiser:

- *Selected geographical coverage.* Newspapers are geared to a specific geographic region, and they reach potential customers across all demographic classes. Generally, they provide broad coverage in the firm's trading area.
- *Flexibility.* Newspaper advertisements can be changed readily on very short notice. The owner can select the size of the ad and its location in the paper. For example, garages often advertise their tune-up specials in the sports section, while party shops display their ads in the entertainment pages. (There may be an additional fee for placing an ad in a particular location.)
- *Timeliness.* Papers almost always have very short closing times, which is the publication deadline prior to which the advertising copy must be submitted. For instance, the local paper may permit an ad to be submitted as late as 24 hours before its publication.
- *Communication potential.* Newspaper ads can convey a great deal of information by employing attractive graphics and copy. Ads can be very effective in attracting attention and persuading consumers to buy.
- *Low costs.* Newspapers normally offer advertising space at low absolute cost and, because of their blanket coverage of a geographic area, at low relative cost. Absolute cost is the actual dollar outlay required to run an ad, while relative cost compares the dollar cost of the ad with the number of

---

[3]"Reading Matter," *The Wall Street Journal,* May 24, 1985, p. 27.

TABLE 17–1   Advertising as practiced by selected small businesses.

Type of Business	Average Ad Budget (% of Sales)	Favorite Media	Other Media	Special Considerations	Promotional Opportunities
Apparel Stores	2.5–3.0%	Weekly or suburban newspapers; direct mail.	Radio; Yellow Pages; exterior signs.	Cooperative advertising available from manufacturers.	Fashion shows for community organizations or charities.
Auto Supply	0.5–2.0%	Local newspapers; Yellow Pages.	Point-of-purchase displays; exterior signs.	Cooperative advertising available from manufacturers.	For specialty stores, direct mail is a popular medium.
Bars and Cocktail Lounges	1.0–2.0%	Yellow Pages; local newspapers (entertainment section).	Tourist publications; radio; specialties; exterior signs.	Manufacturers do all product advertising.	Unusual drinks at "happy hour" rates; hosting postevent parties.
Bookstores	1.5–1.7%	Newspapers; shoppers; Yellow Pages; local magazines.	Radio; exterior signs.	Cooperative advertising available from publisher.	Autograph parties.
Coin-Op Laundries	0.6–2.0%	Yellow Pages; handbills distributed in area; local newspapers.	Direct mail; exterior signs.		Coupons in newspaper ads for "free trial."
General Job Printing	0.4–1.0%	Yellow Pages; trade journals.	Local newspapers; direct mail; exterior signs.		Samples of work can be used as promotional tools.
Gift Stores	1.5–2.5%	Weekly newspapers; Yellow Pages	Radio; direct mail; consumer magazines; exterior signs.		Open houses; instore demonstrations of products such as cookware.
Hairgrooming/ Beauty Salons	2.5–3.0%	Yellow Pages.	Newspapers; name credits for styles in feature articles; exterior signs.	Word-of-mouth advertising is very important to a salon's success.	Styling for community fashion shows; conducting free beauty clinics and demonstrations.
Health Food Stores	1.1–2.8%	Local newspapers; shoppers; college newspapers.	Direct mail; point-of-purchase displays; exterior signs.		Educational displays and services.
Restaurants	0.8–3.0%	Newspapers; radio; Yellow Pages; transit; outdoor.	Local entertainment guides or tourist publications; theater programs; TV for chain or franchise restaurants; exterior signs.	Word-of-mouth advertising is relied upon heavily by independently owned restaurants.	"Free" advertising in critics' columns; specialties; birthday cakes or parties for customers.

Source: Reprinted with permission from Bank of America, NT&SA, "Advertising Small Business," *Small Business Reporter,* Vol. 15 No. 2, Copyright 1976, 1978, 1981, 1982.

The Costs of an Advertisement

SMALL
BUSINESS
REPORT
17–1

While every small business manager realizes the importance of staying within his advertising budget constraints, only a few consider the importance of an ad's relative cost. Suppose a manager decides to advertise his product in one of two newspapers in town. The *Sentinel* has a circulation of 21,000 and charges $1,200 for a quarter-page ad. The *Democrat* has a circulation of 18,000 and charges $1,300 for the same space. The manager estimates that 25 percent of *Sentinel* readers and 37 percent of the *Democrat* readers are potential customers.

Using this information, the manager computes the following relative costs:

	Sentinel	*Democrat*
Circulation	21,000	18,000
Percent of readers that are potential customers	× 25%	× 37%
Potential customers reached	5,250	6,660
Absolute cost of ad	$1,200	$1,300
Relative cost of ad (per potential customer reached)	$\dfrac{\$1,200}{5,250} = 22.86¢$	$\dfrac{\$1,300}{6,660} = 19.52¢$

So, although the *Sentinel* has a larger circulation and a lower absolute cost for running the ad, the *Democrat* will serve the small business owner better because it offers a lower cost per potential customer reached.

It is important to note that this technique does *not* give a reliable comparison across media; it is a meaningful comparison only within a single medium. Differences among the format, presentation, and coverage of ads in different media are so vast that such comparisons are not meaningful.

---

customers it reaches. Small Business Report 17–1 gives an illustration of these two costs.

- *Prompt responses.* Newspaper ads typically produce relatively quick customer responses. A newspaper ad is likely to generate sales the very next day.

Of course, newspaper advertisements also have disadvantages:

- *Wasted readership.* Since newspapers reach such a variety of people, at least a portion of an ad's coverage will be wasted on those who are not potential customers. Such nonselective coverage makes it difficult for a newspaper advertisement to reach a specific target market. In larger cities, the newspaper ad is likely to reach people outside the small firm's trading area who are not likely to be customers.

- *Reproduction limitations.* The quality of reproduction in newspapers is limited, especially when it is compared to that of magazines and direct mail. Recent technological advances, however, are rapidly improving the quality of reproduction in newspaper ads.

- *Lack of prominence.* One frequently cited drawback of newspapers is that they carry so many ads the small firm's message might be lost in the crowd. One way to overcome this disadvantage, of course, is to increase the size of the ad or to add color to it. Large advertisements are appropriate when the small store features special sales and other bargain offers. Bold headlines, illustrations,

and photographs also increase an ad's prominence.

- *Short ad life.* The typical newspaper is soon discarded and, as a result, an ad's life is extremely
  short.

Most business owners can increase the effectiveness of their newspaper ads by giving them
greater continuity. Spot ads will produce results, but
maintaining a steady flow of business requires some
degree of continuity in the advertising program.

Buying Newspaper Space.   Newspapers typically
sell ad space by lines and columns or inches and
columns. For instance, a 4-column × 100-line ad oc-
cupies four columns and 100 lines of space (14 lines
are equal to 1 column inch). For this ad, the small
business owner would pay the rate for 400 lines.
Most papers offer discounts for bulk, long-term, and
frequency contracts and for full-page ads. Advertising
rates vary from one paper to another, depending on
such factors as circulation and focus. The small business owner would do well to investigate the circulation statements, advertising rates, and reader profiles
of the various newspapers available before selecting
one.

Radio.   Although newspapers offer blanket coverage
of a region, radio permits the advertiser to appeal to
a specific audience over a broader region. By choosing the appropriate station, program, and time for
the radio ad, the small firm can reach virtually any
market it targets. Today radio accounts for a growing
volume of local advertising, especially by retailers, as
broadcast media assume an ever-increasing role in
the customer's life. Small Business Report 17–2 describes some facts about radio that help explain its
increasing popularity as an advertising medium for
small businesses.

Radio advertising has several advantages:

- *Universal infiltration.* The radio's nearly universal presence gives advertisements in this medium
  a major advantage. As noted in Small Business Re-

port 17–2, virtually every home and car in the
United States is equipped with a radio, which
means that these advertising messages receive a
tremendous amount of exposure in the target
market.

- *Market segmentation.* Radio advertising is flexible
  and efficient because it can be directed toward a
  specific market within a broad geographic region.
  Radio stations design their programming to appeal
  to specific types of audiences. Easy listening, country and western, top 40, and rhythm and blues stations all appeal to particular customer groups, and
  most radio stations have "listener profiles" to help
  the small business manager pinpoint the advertising target.

- *Flexibility and timeliness.* Radio commercials
  have short closing times and can be changed
  quickly. Small firms dealing in seasonal merchandise or advertising special sales have the ability to
  change their radio ads on short notice to match
  variable market conditions. For example, if the
  weatherman is predicting a major snowstorm, the
  owner of a small tire store could get radio spots
  advertising snow tires almost immediately.

- *Friendliness.* Radio ads are more "active" than ads
  in printed media since they use the spoken word
  to influence customers. Vocal subtleties used in
  radio ads are impossible to convey through
  printed media. Spoken ads can suggest emotions
  and urgency, and they lend a personalized atmosphere to the message.

Radio advertisements also have a number of
disadvantages:

- *Poor listening.* Radio's intrusiveness into the public life almost guarantees that customers will hear
  ads, but they may not *listen* to them. Listeners
  often are engaged in other activities while the
  radio is on and may ignore the message.

- *Need for repetition.* A listener usually will not respond to the radio message after a single exposure
  to it. Radio ads must be broadcast repeatedly to be
  effective.

Radio's Reach

SMALL
BUSINESS
REPORT
17–2

Radios outnumber people in the United States by more than two to one. There are 478.7 million radios in use, and consumers purchase about 70 million new ones each year. Listeners receive signals from 9,824 radio stations—4,718 AM, 3,875 FM, and 1,231 noncommercial stations (mostly on the FM dial). Ninety-nine percent of homes in the United States have at least one radio; the average household has 5.5. Radio reaches 88 percent of Americans at home each week. Radios are in 95 percent of the cars in the U.S., and they will reach three out of four adults within the course of a week. In a week's time, radio's cumulative adult (18 or older) audience reach is 95 percent, while television and newspapers reach 90 percent and 84 percent, respectively. Adults spend an average of 3 hours and 34 minutes per day with radio, an amount exceeded only by television with an average of 4 hours and 2 minutes.

Given these impressive facts, radio can be one of the most effective forms of advertising for the small business manager who identifies his advertising target and plans his advertising program.

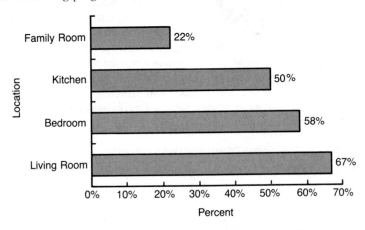

Source: Adapted from *Radio Facts*, Radio Advertising Bureau, Inc., 1986–87.

■ *Limited message.* Since radio ads are limited to one minute or less, the message must be brief. Therefore, the small business owner must include in an ad only one or two points. Also, radio does not permit benefits of the goods or service to be demonstrated; spoken messages can only describe the product.

Buying Radio Time. The small business owner can zero in on a specific advertising target by using the appropriate radio station. Radio advertising time usually sells in 10-second, 20-second, 30-second, and 60-second increments, with the latter being the most common. Fixed spots are guaranteed to be broadcasted at the times specified in the owner's contract with the station. Preemptible spots are less costly than fixed spots, but the advertiser risks being preempted by an advertiser willing to pay the fixed rate for a time slot. Thus, preemptible spots are semifixed. Floating spots are least expensive, but the advertiser has no control over broadcast times. The station uses them as "fillers" and decides on the broadcast time. Many radio stations offer package plans, using flexible combinations of fixed, preemptible, and floating spots. Figure 17–3 shows a sample "tear sheet" used to prepare radio spots.

ANA/RAB FORM FOR SCRIPT (IF TAPE IS USED, PREPARE SCRIPT FROM TAPE)

ANA/RAB RADIO "TEAR-SHEET"

W___ ___ ___

FORM AT BOTTOM OF SCRIPT PERMITS KNOWING HOW MANY TIMES THIS SCRIPT RAN, AT WHAT COST.

Client:				For:	
		Begin:	End:		Date:

HERE'S NEWS FOR YOU HANDY HOMEOWNERS. IF YOU'D LIKE TO LEARN HOW TO PUT UP A BEAUTIFUL NEW ARMSTRONG CEILING IN YOUR HOME, COME TO ACE LUMBER THIS SATURDAY AT 10 A.M. ACE LUMBE_ _ _LDING A HOME IMPROVE-MENT. IT WILL TEACH YOU EVE_ _ _ _ED TO KNOW. YOU'LL LEARN HOW EASY IT IS TO INST^_ _ _LING TILE IN BASEMENTS, ATTICS, OR ANY ROOM '_ _ _U'LL SEE HOW TO CUT AND FIT BORDER TILES AND HO_ _ _AT JOB AROUND LIGHTING FIXTURES. YOU'LL ACTUALLY INSTAL_ _ACTICE CEILING TILES YOURSELF. ACE LUMBER IS HEADQUARTERS FOR ALL THE NEW AND EXCLUSIVE ARMSTRONG CEILING DESIGNS, SO IF YOU'RE PLANNING TO REMODEL OR REDECORATE YOUR HOME, IT WILL PAY YOU TO ATTEND THIS CEILING CLINIC. AND THERE'S NO OBLIGA-TION TO BUY A SINGLE THING. WRITE IT DOWN. THE PLACE IS ACE LUMBER. THE TIME IS THIS SATURDAY AT 10 A.M.

SAMPLE

▼ **(STAMP OR PRINT THIS FORM ON THE BOTTOM OF YOUR SCRIPT PAPER)**

Hand Billing Form

STATION DOCUMENTATION STATEMENT APPROVED BY THE CO-OPERATIVE ADVERTISING COMMITTEE OF THE ASSOCIATION OF NATIONAL ADVERTISERS

This announcement was broadcast _____ times, as entered in the station's program log. The times this announcement was broadcast were billed to this station's client on our invoice(s) number/dated _____ at his earned rate of:

$_____ each for _____ announcements, for a total of $_____
$_____ each for _____ announcements, for a total of $_____
$_____ each for _____ announcements, for a total of $_____

_____
(Notarize above)

_____
Signature of station official

_____
Typed name and title

_____
Station

▼ **(STAMP OR PRINT THIS FORM ON THE BOTTOM OF YOUR SCRIPT PAPER)**

Computer Billing Form

This announcement was broadcast a total of _____ times at the dates and times coded _____ on our at-tached invoice(s) numbered/dated _____ , as entered in the station's program log. This announce-ment was billed to this station's client at a total cost of $ _____ .

Sworn to and subscribed before me and in my presence on this _____ day of _____ , 19 _____ .

_____
Signature of station official

_____
(Notarized above)

_____
Typed name and title

_____
Station call letters

FIGURE 17-3 Radio tear sheet.

Grid Card No. 4
Effective March 1, 1986

		WFBC FM					WFBC AM/FM					WFBC AM				
		I	II	III	IV	V	I	II	III	IV	V					
AAAA (*Mon. - Sat. 5AM - 10AM)	:60	140	130	120	110	100	150	140	130	120	110	55	50	45	40	35
	:30	120	110	100	90	80	130	120	110	100	90	45	40	35	30	25
AAA (Mon. - Sat. 10AM - 8PM / **Sat. 8PM - Midnight)	:60	110	100	90	80	70	120	110	100	90	80	40	35	30	25	20
	:30	100	90	80	70	60	110	100	90	80	70	35	30	25	20	15
AA (Mon. - Fri. 8 PM - Midnight / Sun. 5AM - Midnight)	:60	55	50	45	40	35	80	70	60	50	40	30	25	20	15	10
	:30	50	45	40	35	30	70	60	50	40	30	25	20	15	10	5

*Live Ad-Lib Spots are $130
**Solid Gold Saturday Night

*Live Ad-Lib Spots are $45

FIGURE 17–4   Radio rate sheet.

Radio rates vary depending on the time of day they are broadcast, and, like television, has prime time slots known as "drive-time spots." While exact hours may differ from station to station, the following classifications are common:

Class AA: Morning drive time—6 A.M. to 10 A.M.
Class A: Evening drive time—4 P.M. to 7 P.M.
Class B: Home worker time—10 A.M. to 4 P.M.
Class C: Evening time—7 P.M. to Midnight
Class D: Nighttime—Midnight to 6 A.M.

Some stations may also have different rates for weekend time slots. Figure 17–4 shows a typical rate sheet for a radio station.

Television. In advertising dollars spent, television ranks second in popularity of all media. While the cost of national TV ads precludes their use by most small businesses, local spots can be an extremely effective means of broadcasting the small advertiser's message. A 30-second commercial on network television may cost over $500,000, but a 30-second spot on a local station may go for $200 or less.

Television offers a number of distinct advantages:

■ *Broad coverage.* Television ads provide extensive coverage of a sizable region, and they reach a significant portion of the population. About 97 per-

Snappy Radio Copy

Effective radio copy should:

Stress Benefit to the Listener: Don't say "Bryson's has new fall fashions"—say "Bryson's fall fashions make you look fabulous."

Use Attention Getters: Radio has a whole battery—music, sound effects, unusual voices. Crack the barrier with sound.

Zero in on Your Audience: Know who you're selling. Radio's selectivity attracts the right audience. It's up to the writer to communicate in the right language.

Keep the Copy Simple and to the Point: Don't impress listeners with vocabulary. "To be or not to be" may be the best-known phrase in the language . . . and the longest word has three letters.

Sell Early and Often: Don't back into the selling message. At most, you've got sixty seconds. Use them all for your client's benefit.

Write for the Ear: Write conversationally.

Prepare Your Copy: Underline words for emphasis. Triple space. Type copy clean. Make the announcer rehearse.

Use Positive Action Words: Use words like "now" and "today," particularly when you're writing copy for a sale. Radio has qualities of urgency and immediacy. Take advantage of them.

Put the Listener in the Picture: Radio's "theater of the mind" means you don't have to talk about a new car. With sounds and music you put the listener behind the wheel.

Mention the Client Often: This is the single most important and inflexible rule in radio advertising. Also make sure listeners know the advertiser's location. If the address is complicated, use landmarks.

Source: Radio Basics, Radio Advertising Bureau.

cent of the homes in any area will have a television, and those sets are switched on an average of 7 hours and 2 minutes each day. As cable networks increase the variety of programming aired, television exposure time is likely to increase. Television ads are more likely to reach people with lower educational levels since there is an inverse relationship between time spent in viewing and educational level.

■ *Visual advantage.* The primary benefit of television is its capacity to present the advertiser's product or service in a graphic, vivid manner. With TV ads the manager is not restricted to a description of her product or service. Instead, she can demonstrate its use and illustrate its advantages. For instance, the specialty shop selling a hydraulic log splitter can design a TV commercial to show how easily the machine operates by giving a live demonstration. Advertising executives frequently extol TV ads as "an unbeatable combination of sight, sound, and motion."[4]

■ *Flexibility.* Television ads can be modified quickly to meet the rapidly changing conditions in the marketplace. Advertising on TV is the closest substitute for personal selling. Like a sales representative's call, ads can follow a number of approaches to influence consumers. Television commercials

[4]Bill Abrams, "Advertisers Grow Restless over Rising Costs of TV Time," *The Wall Street Journal*, January 27, 1983, p. 29.

can use "hard sell" techniques, attempt to convince through logic, appeal to sentiment, persuade through subtle influence, or use any number of strategies. In addition, the small advertiser can choose the length of the spot, the time slot, and the program for his message. On television, 30-second spots are the most common, and these ads offer plenty of opportunity for frequent repetition.

■ *Design assistance.* Few small business owners have the skills to prepare an effective television commercial. While professional production firms might easily charge $50,000 for a commercial production, the television station from which the manager purchases the air time may be willing to offer design assistance very inexpensively.

Television advertising also has several disadvantages:

■ *Brief exposure.* Most television ads are on the screen for only a short time and require substantial repetition to achieve the desired effect. Many viewers perform other activities during commercials and so miss them. One recent study of viewer behavior concludes that 43 percent of the audience misses one or more commercials during a half-hour program. One of advertisers' most popular targets—mothers with school-age children—are most likely to miss commercials. Specific reasons cited for not watching ads included talking to someone else, performing household duties, eating, reading and other leisure activities, and talking on the telephone.

■ *Costs.* TV commercials can be expensive to create. A 30-second ad can cost several thousand dollars to develop, even before the owner purchases air time. Advertising agencies and design firms can provide professional assistance in preparing commercials. Table 17–2 offers some suggestions for developing creative television commercials.

Magazines. Another advertising medium available to the small business owner is the magazine. Some

TABLE 17–2 Guidelines for creative TV ads.

1. *Keep it simple.* Avoid confusing the viewer by sticking to a simple concept.
2. *Have one basic idea.* The message should focus on a single, important benefit to the customer. Why should people buy from your business?
3. *Make your point clear.* The benefit should be obvious and easy to understand.
4. *Make it unique . . . different.* To be effective, an ad must reach out and grab the customer's attention. Take advantage of television's visual experience.
5. *Get viewer attention.* Unless the customer watches the ad, its effect is lost.
6. *Involve the viewer.* To be most effective, an ad should portray a situation to which the viewer can relate. Common, everyday experiences are easy to identify with.
7. *Use emotion.* The most effective ads evoke an emotion from the viewer—a laugh, tear, or pleasant memory.
8. *Consider production values.* Television offers vivid sights, colors, motions, and sounds. Use them!
9. *Prove the benefit.* Television allows the advertiser to prove the customer benefit by actually demonstrating it.
10. *Identify yourself well.* Make the store name, location, and product line stand out. The ad should portray the company's image.

Source: Adapted from "How to Make a Creative Television Commercial," Television Bureau of Advertising, Inc.

1,800 non-trade magazines are in circulation across the U.S. Magazines have a wide reach; today, nearly 9 out of 10 adults read an average of seven different magazines per month. The average magazine attracts 6 hours and 3 minutes of total adult reading time, and studies show that the reader is exposed to 89 percent of the ads in the average copy.[5]

Magazine circulation growth has outstripped the growth rate of the U.S. adult population. From 1950, the adult population grew 53 percent while magazine circulations grew by 95 percent. Most of the magazines printed today are special interest publications. Very few general interest, mass circulation periodicals remain on the market. Currently, there are special interest magazines covering photography, fashion, yachting, cooking, hunting, fishing, gardening, and many other topics. Such special interest publications permit the small advertiser to pinpoint his advertising target and to appeal to a specific need in the market. Magazines offer several advantages for advertising.

- *Long life spans.* Magazines have a long reading life because readers tend to keep them longer than other printed media. Few people read an entire magazine at one sitting. Instead, most pick it up, read it at intervals, and come back to it later. The result is that each magazine ad has a good chance of being seen several times. In fact, research suggests that the average reader sees each magazine ad page twice.
- *Multiple readership.* The average magazine has a readership of 3.9 adult readers, and each reader spends about one hour and 33 minutes with each copy. Many magazines have a high "pass-along" rate—they are handed down from reader to reader. For example, travel magazines like the "inhouse" publications given to passengers on airlines may reach many readers in their lifetimes.
- *Target marketing.* By selecting the appropriate special interest periodical, the small business

owner can reach those customers with a high degree of interest in the goods or service. These customers are likely to be more receptive to advertising messages. Once the target market is defined, the owner can choose a magazine whose readers match the firm's customer profile. In addition, many magazines offer geographic editions so advertisers do not have to waste scarce advertising dollars on readers outside the firm's target area, but instead can purchase only a portion of the magazine's total coverage. This limited coverage permits advertising in national magazines whose rates would otherwise be beyond a small firm's budget. Regional and city magazines also offer advertisers the opportunity to reach local customers.

- *Ad quality.* Magazine ads usually are of high quality. Photographs and drawings can be reproduced very effectively, and color ads are readily available. The advertiser can choose the location of the ad in the magazine and can design an outstanding ad to attract the reader's attention.

Magazines also have several disadvantages:

- *Costs.* Magazines can be either local or national in their coverage, but national magazines are not practical advertising vehicles for the typical small business. Many national publications have circulations of up to several million, and their rates are usually too high to suit the small company's advertising budget.

Magazine advertising rates vary according to their circulation rates; the higher the circulation, the higher the rate. Thus, local magazines, whose rates are often comparable to newspaper rates, may be the best bargain for the small advertiser. Also, magazines offer special ad formats and positioning that sell at premium prices.

- *Long closing times.* Another disadvantage of magazines is the relatively long closing times they require. For a weekly periodical, the closing date for an ad may be several weeks before the actual pub-

---

[5]*The Dynamics of Change in Markets and Media,* from a Magazine Publishers Association seminar, New York.

lication date. A monthly magazine may require an ad to be in a few months before the front-cover date. Long lead times and the need to plan and design magazine ads reduce the timeliness of this medium.

■ *Lack of prominence*. Another disadvantage of magazine ads arises from their popularity as an advertising vehicle. Because advertisers frequently employ them to disseminate information, the effectiveness of a single ad may be reduced because of a lack of prominence. The number of magazine ad pages has grown steadily over the years, but the ratio of ad pages to editorial pages has remained relatively constant. Currently this ratio is exactly 50:50.

Direct Mail. Direct mail has always been a popular method of advertising for both large and small businesses. This medium includes tools such as letters, postcards, catalogs, discount coupons, brochures, and many other printed advertisements mailed to homes or businesses. Direct mail offers a number of distinct advantages:

■ *Selectivity*. The greatest strength of direct mail advertising is the extent to which it permits the small business to select the specific audience to receive the message. The manager advertises only to those people who are interested in the firm's goods or service. Depending on mailing list quality, the owner can select an audience with virtually any set of characteristics. The knowledgeable small business manager can develop, rent, or purchase a mailing list of prospective residential, commercial, or industrial customers. One baby-product retailer develops its own mailing list through free subscriptions to its *American Baby* magazine. Each year it compiles about 1.5 million names.[6]

---

[6]Bob Davis, "Baby-Goods Firms See Direct Mail as the Perfect Pitch for New Moms," *The Wall Street Journal*, January 29, 1986, p. 33.

■ *Flexibility*. Another advantage of direct mail is its capacity to tailor the message to the target. The advertiser's presentation to the customer can be as simple or as elaborate as necessary. For instance, one small men's shop achieved a great deal of success with a flier that included a swatch of material from the new season's suits. The tone of the message can be more personal, creating a positive psychological effect. In addition, the advertiser controls the timing of the campaign. There are no closing times or deadlines to meet, and the manager can distribute the ad when it is most appropriate.

■ *Reader attention*. With direct mail, the advertiser's message does not have to compete with other ads for the reader's attention. People enjoy getting mail, and a study by the U.S. Postal Service shows that 78 percent of all direct mail promotional material is opened and read. So, for at least a moment, direct mail gets the recipient's undivided attention. If the message is well prepared and is received by the right person, direct mail ads can be an effective advertising technique.

■ *Rapid feedback*. Direct mail advertisements produce quick results. In most cases the ad will generate sales within three to four days after it is received. So within two weeks of the advertisement the small business manager should know whether the direct mailing is a success.

Direct mail campaigns also have several disadvantages:

■ *Inaccurate mailing lists*. The key to the success of the entire mailing is the accuracy of the customer list. If the mailing list is inaccurate or incomplete, the advertiser will be addressing the wrong audience and alienating customers with misspelled names. The result is that the advertiser is throwing his advertising dollars away!

■ *High relative costs*. Direct mail has a higher cost per thousand than any other advertising medium. Relative to the size of the audience reached, the cost of designing, producing, and mailing an advertisement via direct mail is high. But if the mailing is well planned and properly executed it can produce a high percentage of returns, making direct mail one of the least expensive advertising methods in terms of results. The most representative measurement of a direct mailing is its "cost per result"—the cost per sale or the cost per inquiry resulting from the ad.

■ *High throwaway rate.* Direct mail advertisements often are called "junk mail," and many recipients give them only a cursory glance before throwing them away; but they become junk mail primarily because the advertiser selected the wrong audience or broadcast the wrong message.

How to Use Direct Mail. The key to a direct mailing's success is the mailing list. To get maximum benefit from a mailing, the small business owner should pinpoint his advertising target and then compile or obtain a mailing list to reach the desired customer base. The owner can develop the list herself, using customer accounts, telephone books, city and trade directories, and other sources. For instance, the owner of a small wine shop boosted his sales by 50 percent using a powerful direct mail management program designed to run on a personal computer. The $1,500 program allowed him to build an extensive database of potential customers and to tailor mailings to suit the needs and tastes of individual recipients.[7]

Developing an accurate mailing list and keeping it current requires time and hard work. As a result, many managers use alternate sources for mailing lists. Potential sources include:

■ Companies selling complementary, but not competing goods.
■ Services and professional organizations' membership lists.
■ Business and professional publications' subscription lists.

[7]Jeffrey L. Seglin, "The Direct Approach," *Inc.*, September 1984, pp. 149–54.

■ Mailing list companies whose business is compiling lists for advertisers.
■ Mailing lists brokers who do not compile their own lists, but serve as agents for owners of lists.

Whatever the source of the mailing list, the small advertiser must make sure it is correct and up-to-date.

Another less expensive mailing option is a "resident" mailing. Instead of addressing the ad to specific customers, the firm blankets a geographic area with a mailing addressed to "resident." The major disadvantage of these mailings, however, is the negative psychological effect of such a nonpersonal appeal.

Outdoor Advertising. National advertisers have long used outdoor ads, and small firms (especially retailers) are now using this medium. Very few small businesses rely solely on outdoor advertising; instead, they supplement other advertising media with billboards. Currently, an estimated 500,000 billboards line interstate highways and primary roads—14 signs for every 10 miles of pavement. Outdoor advertising offers certain advantages to the small business:

■ *High exposure.* Outdoor advertising offers a high frequency exposure; studies suggest that the typical billboard reaches an adult 29 to 31 times each month. Most people tend to follow the same routes in their daily traveling, and billboards are there waiting for them when they pass. These traits make outdoor ads particularly effective for goods and services related to travel and outdoor living. Also, when located near the advertising store, billboards can be effective as last-minute reminders.
■ *Broad reach.* The nature of outdoor ads makes them effective devices for reaching a large number of potential customers within a specific area. Clearly, those people who drive the most are the ones most often reached by outdoor ads. For instance, the people targeted by outdoor ads tend to be younger, wealthier, and better educated than

Appearance Is Everything

Direct mail advertisers are constantly searching for their "Holy Grail"—the perfect envelope. The right envelope can double or triple the response from a direct mail ad. Customers scan their mail for clues to its contents. Any indication of "junk mail" could mean that the advertiser's message—and his money—ends up in the trash can. Says one direct mail expert, " . . . most people don't read (a direct mail ad) carefully. They just give it a quick glance and throw it away. We only have a few seconds . . . . "

Given that the typical direct mailing draws a response rate of only 5 percent, getting people to open an ad is critical. One ad writer claims, "Once you get people to open the envelope, you're almost 90 percent home." The result has been a proliferation of attention-grabbing envelopes. Some popular tactics include:

- for male recipients, a handwritten envelope with a smudge of lipstick on the back. (Computers that duplicate a person's handwriting "address" the envelopes.)
- envelopes that mimic those used by overnight express mail companies.
- "blind" envelopes with only the recipient's address and a regular postage stamp. The suggestion is that there might be something important inside.
- simulated parchment and linen envelopes that resemble personal stationery.
- envelopes that allow the recipient to see "action devices"—removable tabs, tokens, and stickers that are supposed to bring out "the child in us."
- envelopes that simulate official government mail.

Still, because of federal law, the "perfect" envelope is off limits to direct mail advertisers. As one designer puts it, "The envelope that gets opened the quickest is the envelope that bears the IRS eagle."

Source: Adapted from Erik Larson, "In Direct Mail Biz, Envelopes Are What Are Run Up Flagpole," *The Wall Street Journal*, May 5, 1986, pp. 1, 20, with permission of *The Wall Street Journal*, © Dow Jones & Company, 1986. All rights reserved.

---

the average person. While an effective outdoor ad reaches an average of 86 percent of all adults, it also reaches nearly 91 percent of all adults in professional or managerial occupations.[8]

- *Flexibility*. Outdoor advertising units can be bought separately or in a number of "packages." Through its variety of graphics, design, and unique features, outdoor advertising enables the small advertiser to match his message to the particular audience. Cleverly designed billboards like those pictured in this chapter can attract customers' attention and produce desired results.
- *Cost efficiency*. Outdoor advertising offers one of

the lowest costs per thousand customers reached of all the advertising media. There are no national and local rates in outdoor advertising. All buyers are charged one price, regardless of size.

- Outdoor ads also permit small advertisers to take advantage of cooperative advertising programs that many manufacturers offer. Retailers selling brand name products can share the cost of billboard space and paper with the manufacturer. These arrangements reduce the total cost of billboards to the small firm, easing pressure on the advertising budget.

Outdoor ads also have several disadvantages:

- *Brief exposure*. Because billboards are immobile, the reader is exposed to the advertiser's message

[8]*The Big Outdoor* (New York: Institute of Outdoor Advertising), p. 15.

for only a short time. As a result, the message must be short and to the point. The advertising copy cannot be as detailed or informative as in other media ads, and customers cannot keep billboard messages and refer to them at a later date.

■ *Legal restrictions.* Outdoor billboards are subject to strict regulations and to a high degree of standardization. At the federal level, the Highway Beautification Act of 1965[*] requires signs and billboards to be a standard size and to be attractive. At the local level, many cities place limitations on the signs and billboards allowed along the roadside. These laws attempt to control the amount of "eye pollution" to which the public is subjected.

■ *Lack of prominence.* A clutter of billboards and signs along a heavily traveled route tends to reduce the effectiveness of a single ad which loses its prominence among the crowd of billboards.

Using Outdoor Ads.   There are two basic types of billboard advertisements: poster panel and painted bulletin. Poster panels come in various sizes. Large posters are referred to by "sheet size," a standard unit in the outdoor industry. A 24-sheet poster has a printed area of $19'6'' \times 8'8''$ and white border; 30-sheet posters have a printed area of $21'7'' \times 9'7''$ and offer 25 percent more design space than the 24-sheet poster. Posters also are available in smaller sizes, called junior posters ($6' \times 12'$), and 3-sheet posters that vary in dimension.

Poster panels are sold on a monthly basis by "showings." A #100 showing provides enough panels to produce daily exposure opportunities equal to 100 percent of the market in which it appears. A #50 showing offers half coverage, and so on. In a very large city, a #100 showing may be 20 posters, while in a small town it might be one poster. The number

of exposure opportunities is based on traffic patterns at the poster site.

Professional printers lithograph or silk-screen posters with the desired design and then the outdoor company applies the sheets to the panel(s) the small business rents. Posters typically are sold on a 30-day basis at an average cost of $200 to $400 per month (a c.p.m. of 60¢ to 90¢).

Painted bulletins are created individually by outdoor advertising artists to meet design requirements the advertiser provides. Advertisers typically contract for painted bulletins for one year and can purchase them either individually or in a package. Painted bulletins are often very artistically created, using attractive designs and visual effects that extend beyond the borders of the standard frame. The average cost for a painted bulletin ranges from $1,000 to $3,000 per month (a c.p.m. of $1 to $2). Because they are more costly than posters, painted bulletins are less common.

Because the outdoor ad is stationary and the viewer is in motion, the small business owner must pay special attention to its design. An outdoor ad should:[9]

■ Identify the product and the company clearly and quickly.

■ Use a simple background. The background should not compete with the message.

■ Rely on large illustrations that jump out at the viewer.

■ Include clear, legible type. All lower case or a combination of upper and lower case letters are best. Very bold or very thin type faces become illegible at a distance.

■ Use bold, brash colors. The best color combinations contrast both in hue and brightness. Black-on-yellow and black-on-white are two of the best combinations.

■ Include short copy and short words.

---

[*]The Highway Beautification Act bans billboards outside commercially and industrially zoned areas but is so weakened from loopholes that it has ended up protecting billboards. Since its passage, 600,000 billboards have been removed, but 320,000 have been erected. The Act also allowed outdoor signs to grow to a much larger size (2,500 square feet).

[9]*Outdoor Advertising* (New York: Institute of Outdoor Advertising).

Creative use of an outdoor ad. A "bite" was removed from the board each week for 13 weeks. (Photo courtesy of the Institute for Outdoor Advertising.)

In designing an effective outdoor ad, the small advertiser also should consider the following questions:

1. Are the key lettering and visual effects big enough?
2. Could the message contain fewer or simpler words?
3. Does the design hold together as a single unit?
4. Will it register quickly from a distance?[10]

[10]*The Big Outdoor*, p. 25.

Transit Advertising. Transit advertising traces its history back to the pre-Civil War era, when companies hung handbills from the ceilings of public transportation vehicles to advertise their goods and services. Today, transit advertising includes advertising signs inside and outside some 70,000 public transportation vehicles throughout the country's urban areas. The medium is likely to grow as more cities look to public transit systems to relieve transportation problems.

Known as the "home-town medium," transit

Outdoor painted bulletin. (Photo courtesy of Foster and Kleiser.)

advertising combines two media into one: Inside ads reach transit riders, while outside ads reach a substantial portion of the population along the transit route. Transit ads offer a number of advantages:

- *Wide coverage.* Transit advertising offers the small business advertiser mass exposure to a variety of customers. The message literally moves to where the people are. This medium also reaches people with a wide variety of demographic characteristics. Its inside messages reach a large number of the to-and-from-work segment plus a substantial portion of shoppers on their way to downtown and suburban centers.
- *Repeat exposure.* Transit ads provide repeated exposure to a message. The typical transit rider averages 24 rides per month and spends 61 minutes per day riding.[11] This gives an advertiser ample opportunity to present a continuous message to the mass transit public.
- *Low cost.* Even the small business owner with a limited budget can afford transit advertising. One study shows that transit advertising costs average

only $0.30 per thousand.[12] Fees are usually based on monthly showings, and transit systems offer discounts for multi-month contracts.
- *Flexibility.* Transit ads come in a wide range of sizes, numbers, and durations. With transit ads the owner can select an individual market or any combination of markets across the country. Within this market, the advertiser can choose the specific transit routes that will benefit his firm most.

Transit ads also have several disadvantages:

- *Generality.* Even though the small business can choose the specific transit routes on which to advertise, it cannot target a particular segment of the market through transit advertising. The effectiveness of transit ads depends on the routes that public vehicles travel and on the people they reach, which, unfortunately, the advertiser cannot control.
- *Limited appeal.* Unlike many of the media, transit ads are not beamed into the potential customer's residence or business. The result is that customers cannot keep them for future reference. Also, these

---

[11]*TAA Rate Directory of Transit Advertising* (New York: Transit Advertising Association), p. 3.

[12]Ibid. p. 2.

ads do not reach with great frequency the upper income, highly educated portion of the market.

- *Brief message.* Transit ads do not permit the small advertiser to present a detailed description or a demonstration of the product or service for sale. Although inside ads have a relatively long exposure (the average ride lasts 22.5 minutes), outside ads must be brief and to the point.

Directories. Directories are an important advertising medium for reaching those customers who have already made purchase decisions. The directory simply helps these customers locate the specific product or service they have decided to buy. Directories include telephone books, industrial or trade guides, buyer guides, annuals, catalog files, and yearbooks that list various businesses and the products they sell.

The most common directory is the Yellow Pages listing found in the telephone book. While primarily a consumer advertising tool, these listings also reach industrial buyers. For years, there was only one telephone directory that reached every household in a city. Now, the problem facing many small business owners is choosing in which directory to advertise. Since the 1984 breakup of AT&T, telephone directories have proliferated, especially in major metropolitan areas.

Many organizations publish more specific trade directories that are organized on the basis of the industrial category or that provide listings by product groups or geographic location. In many cases, a simple listing of names and addresses is free, but many small firms elect to purchase a bold listing—a listing printed in heavy black type—to make themselves more prominent. Some directories offer paid display advertisements that permit businesses to elaborate on their operations and on the products or services sold.

Directories offer several advantages to the small advertiser.

- *Prime prospects.* Directory listings reach customers who are prime prospects, since they have al-

ready decided to purchase an item. The directory just helps them find what they are looking for.

- *Long life.* Directory listings usually have long lives. A typical directory may be published annually.

However, there are certain disadvantages to using directories:

- *Lack of flexibility.* Listings and ads in many directories offer only a limited variety of design features. The small business owner may not be as free to create unique ads as in other printed media.
- *Obsolescence.* Because directories are commonly updated only annually, some of their listings become obsolete. This is a problem for the small firm that changes its name, location, or phone number.

In choosing a directory, the small business owner should evaluate several criteria:

- *Completeness.* Does the directory include enough listings that customers will use it?
- *Convenience.* Are the listings well organized and convenient? Are they cross-referenced?
- *Evidence of use.* To what extent do customers actually use the directory? What evidence of use does the publisher offer?
- *Age.* Is the directory well established and does it have a good reputation?
- *Circulation.* Do users pay for the directory or do they receive complimentary copies? Is there an audited circulation statement?[13]

Trade Shows. Trade shows provide manufacturers and distributors with a unique opportunity to advertise to a preselected audience of potential customers. Literally thousands of trade shows are sponsored each year, and careful evaluation and selection of a few shows can produce profitable results for the

---

[13]U.S. Small Business Administration, *Selecting Advertising Media: A Guide for Small Business*, 2nd ed. Small Business Management Series No. 34, Washington, 1977, p. 56.

small business owner. Trade shows offer the following advantages:

- *A natural market*. Trade shows bring together buyers and sellers in a setting where products can be explained, demonstrated, and handled. Comparative shopping is easy and the buying process can be shortened.
- *Preselected audience*. Trade exhibits attract potential customers with a specific interest in the goods or services being displayed. There is a high probability that these prospects will make a purchase.
- *New customer market*. Trade shows offer exhibitors a prime opportunity to reach new customers and to contact people who are not accessible to sales representatives.
- *Cost advantage*. As the cost of making a field sales call continues to escalate, more companies are realizing that trade shows are an economical method for making sales contacts and presentations.

There are, however, certain disadvantages associated with trade shows:

- *Increasing costs*. The cost of exhibiting at trade shows is rising quickly. Registration fees, travel and set-up costs, sales salaries, and other expenditures may be a barrier to some small firms.
- *Wasted effort*. A poorly planned exhibit ultimately costs the small business more than its benefits are worth. Too many firms enter exhibits in trade shows without proper preparation, and they end up wasting their time, energy, and money on unproductive activities.

To avoid these disadvantages, the manager should establish several clearly defined objectives, which might include a specific number of contacts, new customers, or orders.

Specialty Advertising. Specialty advertising includes all customer gift items imprinted with the company's name, address, telephone number, and slogan. These items are best used as reminder advertising to supplement other ads. Specialty ads create goodwill among present customers by thanking them for their patronage. They are more effective in maintaining current customers than in attracting new business. Common specialty advertising items include matches, calendars, pens, pencils, key chains, and other commonly used items. When choosing advertising specialties, the small business owner should consider using items that are unusual and related to the nature of the business. For instance, many hardware stores offer yardsticks to their customers.

Special Events and Promotions. A growing number of small companies are finding that special events and promotions attract a great deal of interest and provide a lasting impression of the company. For instance, almost everyone knows that Macy's sponsors the annual Thanksgiving Day parade. Sponsoring such special events can be an effective method of advertising for virtually any small business. For example, the owner of For Paws, a California pet boutique, sponsors free "doggy brunches" each week, complete with "kibble quiche" and "wheat-germ woofies." The shop also caters birthday parties, beach parties (picture a dog with a whistle around his neck, a muscle T shirt, and a dab of Noxema on his nose), and other gala events.[14] A small art-importing company uses a Carmen Miranda hot air balloon—complete with fruit coiffure—as a key part of its advertising campaign. "It's one of the most exciting ways to spend advertising dollars because it generates interest in the community," says the balloon's creator.[15]

Point-of-Purchase Ads. In the last several years, in-store advertising has become more popular as a way of reaching the customer at a crucial moment—the point-of-purchase. Research suggests that consumers make two-thirds of all buying decisions at the point

---

[14]Carrie Dolan, "Putting on the Dog Just Comes Naturally in Fey Marin County," *The Wall Street Journal*, September 20, 1985, p. 1.
[15]John F. Persinos, "Advertising that Really Takes off," *Inc.*, April 1984, p. 37.

of sale. Supermarkets are especially well suited for in-store ads as they remind people of the products as they walk the aisles. These in-store ads are not just blasé signs or glossy photographs of the product in use. Some stores are testing electronic shopping cart handles that flash messages and "Star Trek" technology, where laser images of celebrities "beam down" from store ceilings to give their sales pitches.[16] Other companies use in-store music interspersed with household hints and, of course, ads. Another ploy involves tiny devices that sense when a customer passes by and trigger a pre-recorded sales message. Other machines emit scents—chocolate chip cookies or pina coladas—to appeal to passing customers' sense of smell.[17]

There is an endless array of advertising techniques available to the small business owner. Even postage stamps and parking meters offer advertising space! Table 17–3 summarizes the different advertising media and their suitability for various kinds of businesses aiming at particular customer groups.

III. DEVELOPING AN ADVERTISING PLAN

Every small business needs an advertising plan to assure that the money spent on ads is not wasted. A well-developed plan does not guarantee advertising success, but it does increase the likelihood of good results.

The first step in creating an advertising plan is establishing specific, measurable objectives. In general, the small firm can employ advertising to inform the public about the goods and services it sells, to persuade potential customers to purchase its products or services, and to remind present customers of the firm's existence.

In establishing objectives the owner must decide, "What do I expect to accomplish with this ad-

vertising? Some ads are designed to stimulate immediate responses by encouraging customers to purchase a particular product in the immediate future. The hope here is to trigger a purchase decision. An example would be ads promoting a special sale or product offering. Other ads seek to build the firm's image among its customers and the general public. These ads try to create goodwill by keeping the firm's name in the public's memory so that customers will recall the small firm's name when they decide to purchase a product or service.

The next step in developing an advertising plan is to analyze the firm and its customers. The small business owner should address the following questions:

- What business am I in?
- What image do I want to project?
- Who are my customers and what are their characteristics?
- Where can they best be reached?
- What do my customers really purchase from me?
- What advertising approach do my competitors take?

Answering these questions should help the owner define the business and profile its customers, which will help her focus the advertising message on a specific target and get more for the advertising dollar.

Once the small business owner has defined her target audience, she can begin to design an advertising message and choose the media for transmitting it. At this stage, the owner decides what to say and how to say it.

While there are no hard-and-fast rules to follow when developing an advertising message, the small business owner can increase an ad's impact by observing certain principles.

- An ad should be easily recognizable. The owner should design her message with a unique style which reflects the firm's image.
- The owner should advertise products and services that customers perceive as valuable. Popular

---

[16]Ronald Alsop, "Companies Cram Ads in Stores to Sway Shopping Decisions," *The Wall Street Journal*, August 22, 1985, p. 25.

[17]Ronald Alsop, "To Snare Shoppers, Companies Test Talking, Scented Displays," *The Wall Street Journal*, June 12, 1986, p. 31.

TABLE 17−3 Advertising media chart.

Medium	Market Coverage	Type of Audience	Sample Time/Space Costs
Daily Newspaper	Single community or entire metro area; zoned editions sometimes available.	General; tends more toward men, older age group, slightly higher income and education.	Per agate line, weekday; open rate. Circ: 7,800: $ .25 16,500: $ .35 21,300: $ .60 219,200: $ 2.10
Weekly Newspaper	Single community usually; sometimes a metro area.	General; usually residents of a smaller community.	Per agate line; open rate: Circ: 5,400: $ .35 20,900: $ .55 40,000: $ 1.20
Shopper	Most households in a single community; chain shoppers can cover a metro area.	Consumer households.	Per one-quarter page, black and white; open rate: Circ: 13,000: $ 45.00 22,500: $ 185.00 183,400: $ 760.00
Telephone Directories	Geographic area or occupational field served by the directory.	Active shoppers for goods or services.	Yellow Pages, per double half column; per month: Pop: 10–49,000: $ 35.00 100–249,000: $ 63.00 500–999,000: $ 152.00
Direct Mail	Controlled by the advertiser.	Controlled by the advertiser through use of demographic lists.	Production and mailing cost of an 8½″ × 11″ 4-color brochure; 4-page, 2-color letter; order card and reply envelope; label addressed, third-class mail: $.35 each in quantities of 50,000.
Radio	Definable market area surrounding the station's location.	Selected audiences provided by stations with distinct programming formats.	Per 60-second morning drive-time spot; one time: Pop: 400,000: $ 45.00 1,100,000: $ 115.00 3,500,000: $ 200.00 13,000,000: $ 385.00
Television	Definable market area surrounding the station's location.	Varies with the time of day; tends toward younger age group, less print-oriented.	Per 30-second daytime spot; one time; nonpreemptible status: Pop: 400,000: $ 125.00 1,100,000: $ 370.00 3,500,000: $ 615.00 13,000,000: $ 740.00
Transit	Urban or metro community served by transit system; may be limited to a few transmit routes.	Transit riders, especially wage earners and shoppers; pedestrians.	Inside 11″ × 28″ cards; per month: 1 bus: $ 5.00 500 buses: $ 2,500.00 Outside 30″ × 144″ posters; per month: 1 bus: $ 85.00 170 buses: $ 14,110.00
Outdoor	Entire metro area or single neighborhood.	General; especially auto drivers.	12′ × 25′ posters; 100 GRP per month: Pop: 17,900: $ 650.00 (5 posters) 484,900: $ 9,770.00 (54 posters) 10,529,300: $ 162,400.00 (500 posters)
Local Magazine	Entire metro area or region; toned editions sometimes available.	General; tends toward better educated, more affluent.	Per one-sixth page, black and white; open rate: Circ: 30,000: $ 285.00 43,750: $ 435.00 161,460: $ 770.00

444

TABLE 17–3 *Continued*

Particular Suitability	Major Advantage	Major Disadvantage
All general retailers.	Wide circulation.	Nonselective audience.
Retailers who service a strictly local market.	Local identification.	Limited readership.
Neighborhood retailers and service businesses.	Consumer orientation.	A giveaway and not always read.
Services, retailers of brand-name items, highly specialized retailers.	Users are in the market for goods or services.	Limited to active shoppers.
New and expanding businesses; those using coupon returns or catalogs.	Personalized approach to an audience of good prospects.	High CPM.
Business catering to identifiable groups; teens, commuters, housewives	Market selectivity, wide market coverage.	Must be bought consistently to be of value.
Sellers of products or services with wide appeal.	Dramatic impact, market selectivity, wide market coverage.	High cost of time and production.
Businesses along transit routes, especially those appealing to wage earners.	Repetition and length of exposure.	Limited audience.
Amusements, tourist businesses, brand-name retailers.	Dominant size, frequency of exposure.	Clutter of many signs reduces effectiveness of each one.
Restaurants, entertainments, specialty shops, mail-order businesses.	Delivery of a loyal, special-interest audience.	Limited audience.

Source: Reprinted with permission from Bank of America, NT&SA. *Advertising Small Business, Small Business Reporter,* Vol. 15 No. 2, Copyright 1976, 1978, 1981, 1982.

brand names make ads more attractive. Too many firms advertise only those items that are difficult to sell.

■ The ad should translate the product's or service's attributes into a specific consumer benefit—saving money, performing a distasteful task, or whatever. Consumers do not buy products as such; they buy what the product will do for them.

■ The ad's layout should be simple. The design should not detract from the message. Usually, simple layouts permit the reader to focus on the message's content.

■ The message should be easy to understand. Advertising copy should be short and direct. The message should be built around a single idea.

■ The manager should treat the message seriously. Generally, the advertiser should avoid injecting humor into the message because it may be misunderstood and considered offensive. Disseminating facts about the firm and its products is safer.

■ The manager should build the ad around a central theme. The owner should not try to communicate too many ideas in a single ad; and every ad should contribute to the firm's overall advertising theme.

■ The ad should use illustrations that complement the product or service. Photographs or drawings of the product or service often attract more attention than simple script.

■ The ad should identify the store clearly. Its name and logo should appear in the ad often enough to identify the firm, but not enough to distract attention from the message. The store's address, telephone number, and hours of operation are important parts of the ad.

Ten "Don'ts" in Advertising

When developing an effective advertising program, the small business manager should not make the following mistakes.

1. *Plan only one advertisement at a time*. An advertising campaign is likely to be more effective if it is developed from a comprehensive plan for a specific time period. A "piecemeal" approach produces ads that lack continuity and a unified theme.
2. *Never set any long-run advertising objectives*. One cause of inadequate planning is the failure to establish specific objectives for the advertising program. Without defining what is expected from advertising, the program lacks a sense of direction.
3. *Use only those advertisements, themes, and vehicles that have a personal appeal to you*. Although personal judgment influences every business decision, the manager cannot afford to let bias interfere with advertising decisions. For example, the manager should not use a particular radio station just because he likes it.
4. *View advertising expenditures as expenses*. In an accounting sense, advertising is a business expense, but money spent on ads tends to produce sales and profits over time that might not be possible without advertising. An effective advertising program generates more sales than it costs. The owner must ask, "Can I afford *not* to advertise?"
5. *Never deviate substantially from the type of advertising done by your competitors*. Some managers tend to "follow the advertising crowd" because they fear being different from their competitors. "Me-too" advertising frequently is ineffective because it fails to create a unique image for the firm. Don't be afraid to be different!

- The ad should include the product's (or service's) price or price range. The small business manager should not be afraid to state prices in an ad since this is one of the most important considerations for many customers.
- The ad should be truthful, believable, and in good taste.

Generally, a good advertisement should follow the acronym, AIDCA. It should attract *attention*, develop *interest, describe* the product or service, *convince* the reader, and get *action*.[18]

When the ad is broadcast to the target audience, the small business manager must evaluate its effectiveness. Advertising should produce enough sales and profits to justify its cost. Immediate response ads can be evaluated in a number of ways. For instance, the manager can include coupons that customers redeem to get price reductions on products and services. Dated coupons identify customer responses over certain time periods. Some firms use "hidden offers"—statements hidden somewhere in an ad that offer customers special deals if they make a special request. For example, one small firm offered a price reduction to any customer who mentioned that he heard the advertisement for the product on the radio.

The manager can also gauge an ad's effectiveness by measuring the volume of store traffic generated. Effective advertising should increase store traffic, which boosts sales of advertised and nonadvertised items. Of course, if an advertisement promotes a particular bargain item, the manager can judge its effectiveness by comparing sales of the items to preadvertising sales levels.

---

[18]Ovid Riso, U.S. Small Business Administration, "Advertising Guidelines for Small Retail Firms," Small Marketers Aid No. 160, Washington, 1980, p. 7.

6. *Always go with the media vehicle that claims to be number one.* It is not uncommon for several media within the same geographic region to claim to be "number one." As pointed out in this chapter, different media offer certain advantages and disadvantages. The manager should evaluate each according to its ability to reach his target audience effectively.

7. *Always be the spokesperson on your TV and radio commercials.* While this may lend a personal touch to your ads, the commercial may be seen as being non-professional or "homemade." The ad may detract from the firm's image rather than improve it.

8. *Cram as much as possible into every ad.* Some small business managers think that to get the most for their advertising dollar, they must pack their ads full of facts and illustrations. But overcrowded ads confuse customers and are often ignored. Simple, well-designed ads are more effective.

9. *Assume your ad is good if two or three customers mention it to you.* Measuring the effectiveness of advertising is an elusive art at best. But the opinions of a small sample of customers whose opinions may be biased is not a reliable gauge of an ad's effectiveness. The techniques described earlier offer a more objective measurement of an ad's ability to produce results.

10. *If something does not happen immediately, stop the ad.* Some ads are designed to produce immediate results, but many ads require more time because of the lag effect they experience. The manager must be patient, giving the advertising campaign a reasonable time to produce results.

Source: Adapted from Danny R. Arnold and Robert H. Solomon, "Ten 'Don'ts' in Bank Advertising," *Burroughs Clearing House* 16, No. 12, September 1980, pp. 20–24, 42–43.

Ad tests can help determine the most effective methods of reaching potential customers. The owner can design two different ads (or use two different media or broadcast times) that are coded for identification and see which one produces more responses. For example, the manager can use a "split run" of two different ads in a local newspaper. That is, he can place one ad in part of the paper's press run and another ad in the remainder of the run. Then he can measure the response level to each ad. Small Business Report 17–5 offers 10 "don'ts" in creating an advertising program.

IV. PREPARING AN ADVERTISING BUDGET

One of the most challenging decisions confronting the small business owner is how much money to invest in advertising. Usually the amount the owner wants to spend and the amount the firm can afford to spend on advertising usually differ significantly. There are four methods of determining an advertising budget: what is affordable; matching competitors; percentage of sales; and objective-and-task.

Under the what-is-affordable method, the owner sees advertising as a luxury. She views advertising completely as an expense, not as an investment that produces sales and profits in the future. Therefore, as the name implies, management spends whatever it can afford on advertising. Too often, the advertising budget is allocated funds after all other budget items have been financed. The result is an inadequate advertising budget. This method also fails to relate the advertising budget to the advertising objective.

Another approach is to match the advertising expenditures of the firm's competitors, either in a flat dollar amount or as a percentage of sales. The manager assumes that her firm's advertising needs and strategies are the same as those of her competitors. While competitors' actions can be helpful in establishing a floor for advertising expenditures, reliance on this technique can lead to blind imitation instead of a budget suited to the small firm's circumstances.

The most commonly used method of establishing an advertising budget is the simple percentage-of-sales approach. This method relates advertising expenditures to actual sales results. Tying advertising expenditures to sales is generally preferred to relating them to profits because sales tend to fluctuate less than profits.

But which sales should the manager base her budget on—past or forecasted? Using past sales assumes that advertising is the result of sales instead of sales being the result of advertising. A past sales basis is not future-oriented; it does not consider potential sales increases or the rising costs of advertising. Basing advertising expenditures on forecasted sales means that advertising is considered a method of boosting future sales. This technique avoids many of the problems associated with using past sales, but there is also the danger of pegging the advertising budget to an overly optimistic sales forecast. Another problem comes in choosing the proper percentage to apply to sales. Too many managers rely almost religiously on the advertising percentages published in industrial and government manuals. Although these figures are useful guidelines, the manager must recognize that they are averages of the advertising budgets for competitors of all sizes. They may not be representative of the firm's advertising needs.

The objective-and-task method is the most difficult and least used technique for establishing an advertising budget. It also is the method most often recommended by advertising experts. With this method, the owner must first decide what the advertising program should accomplish by defining specific objectives. While the previous methods break down the total amount of funds allocated to advertising, the task method builds up the advertising funds by analyzing what it will cost to accomplish these objectives. For example, suppose that a manager wants to boost sales of a particular product 10 percent by attracting local college students. He may determine that a nearby rock radio station would be the best medium to use. Then he must decide on the number and frequency of the ads and estimate their costs. He must remember that advertising costs include charges for preparing ads as well as for buying media space or time. The manager follows this same process for each advertising objective.

A common problem with the method is the tendency for the manager to be overly ambitious in setting advertising objectives, which leads to unrealistically high advertising expenditures. The manager may be forced to alter objectives, or the plans to reach them, to bring the advertising budget back to a reasonable level. However, the plan can still be effective.

Once the owner establishes a reasonable advertising budget, she must decide how to allocate it. The most common method of allocation is by department or by product; the department or product that accounts for the greatest portion of sales receives the largest share of the advertising budget. Most small businesses also allocate their advertising budgets on either a monthly or weekly basis. Once again, the percentage-of-sales technique is helpful. If March accounts for 8 percent of the firm's annual sales, the owner would allocate 8 percent of the ad's budget for that month. Most small companies find it useful to plan their advertising expenditures on a weekly basis. This short-term planning ensures a more consistent advertising effort throughout the year. A calendar like the one pictured in figure 17–5 can be one of the most valuable tools in planning a small company's advertising program. The calendar enables the owner to prepare for holidays and special events, to monitor actual and budgeted expenditures, and to ensure that ads are scheduled on the appropriate media at the proper times.

How to Advertise "Big" on a "Small" Budget

The typical small business does not have the luxury of an unlimited advertising budget. This does not

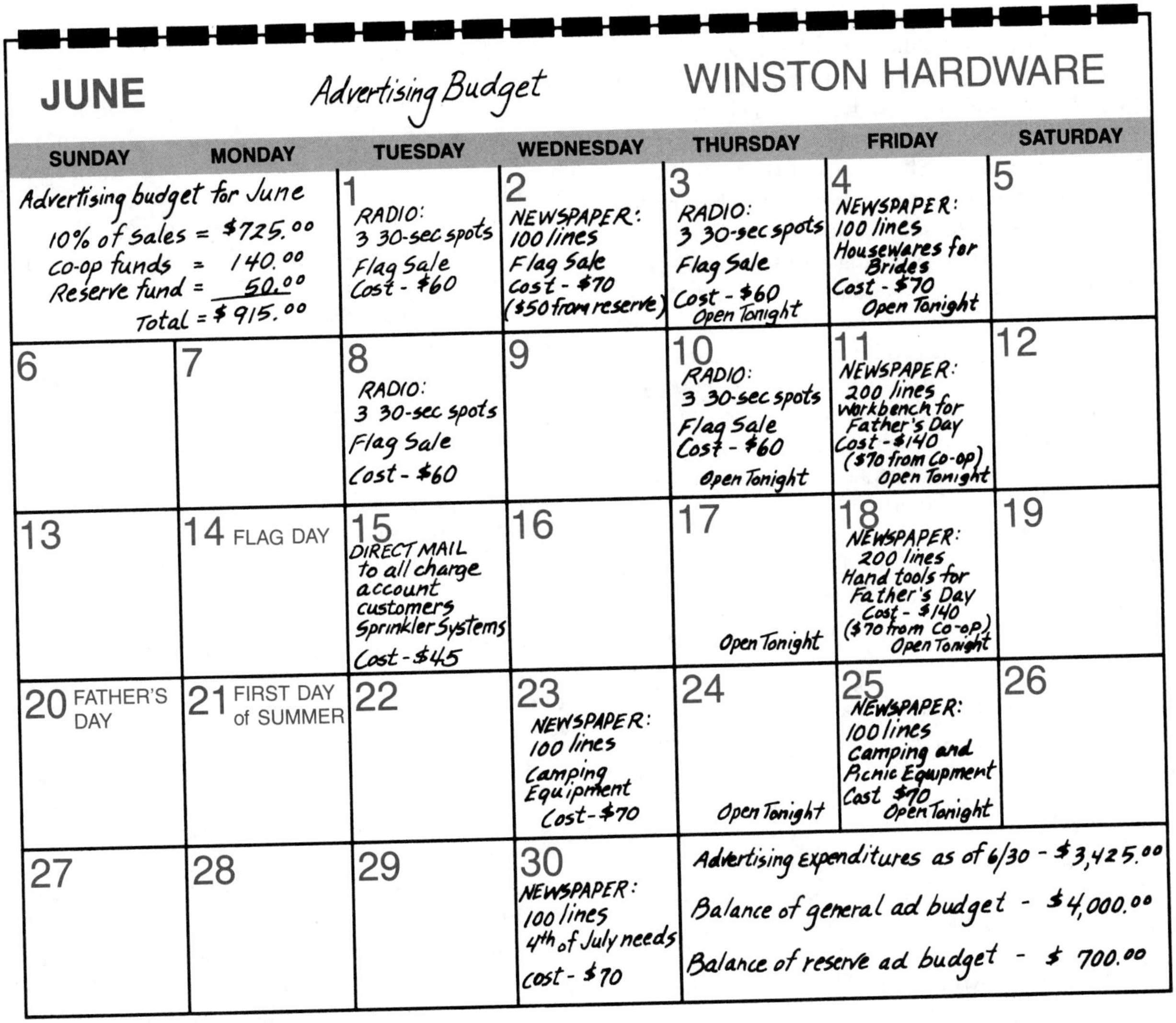

JUNE — Advertising Budget — WINSTON HARDWARE

SUNDAY	MONDAY	TUESDAY	WEDNESDAY	THURSDAY	FRIDAY	SATURDAY
Advertising budget for June 10% of sales = $725.00 Co-op funds = 140.00 Reserve fund = 50.00 Total = $915.00		**1** RADIO: 3 30-sec spots Flag Sale Cost - $60	**2** NEWSPAPER: 100 lines Flag Sale Cost - $70 ($50 from reserve)	**3** RADIO: 3 30-sec spots Flag Sale Cost - $60 Open Tonight	**4** NEWSPAPER: 100 lines Housewares for Brides Cost - $70 Open Tonight	**5**
6	**7**	**8** RADIO: 3 30-sec spots Flag Sale Cost - $60	**9**	**10** RADIO: 3 30-sec spots Flag Sale Cost - $60 Open Tonight	**11** NEWSPAPER: 200 lines Workbench for Father's Day Cost - $140 ($70 from Co-op) Open Tonight	**12**
13	**14** FLAG DAY	**15** DIRECT MAIL to all charge account customers Sprinkler Systems Cost - $45	**16**	**17** Open Tonight	**18** NEWSPAPER: 200 lines Hand tools for Father's Day Cost - $140 ($70 from Co-op) Open Tonight	**19**
20 FATHER'S DAY	**21** FIRST DAY of SUMMER	**22**	**23** NEWSPAPER: 100 lines Camping Equipment Cost - $70	**24** Open Tonight	**25** NEWSPAPER: 100 lines Camping and Picnic Equipment Cost $70 Open Tonight	**26**
27	**28**	**29**	**30** NEWSPAPER: 100 lines 4th of July needs Cost - $70	Advertising expenditures as of 6/30 - $3,425.00 Balance of general ad budget - $4,000.00 Balance of reserve ad budget - $700.00		

FIGURE 17–5   Advertising planning calendar.

mean, however, that the small company should assume a "second-class" advertising posture. With a little creativity and a dose of ingenuity, most small business owners can stretch their advertising dollars and make the most of what they spend. Three useful techniques to do this are cooperative advertising; shared advertising; and publicity.

Cooperative Advertising. In a cooperative arrangement, a manufacturing company shares the cost of advertising with a small retailer if the retailer features its product. Both the manufacturer and the retailer get more advertising per dollar by sharing expenses. Manufacturers offer cooperative advertising programs in almost every medium. For example, when a steep sales decline hit Bromby's Sport & Ski, Inc., owner Susan Fabbiano was forced to cut her advertising budget. Recognizing the importance of advertising to her business, Fabbiano was determined to maintain quality advertising despite a reduced budget. So, she began to pursue co-op ads with the manufacturers of her product line. One company split the costs of radio and outdoor ads with Fabbiano 50–50! She claims, "Co-op advertising has allowed the store to keep its name before the public without increasing expenditures.[19]

Another source of savings is the free advertising package that many manufacturers supply to retailers. These packages usually include photographs and illustrations of the product as well as professionally prepared ads to use in different media. Once, when Fabbiano was preparing an outdoor ad featuring Solomon products, she requested "a good photograph" from a sales representative. The supplier sent her, free of charge, the artwork for a billboard that would have cost $700 to produce. On another occasion, Fabbiano found and used two 30-second radio spots that had been "professionally written by the manufacturer's agency." Her cost: only the air time.[20]

Shared Advertising. In a shared advertising program, a group of similar businesses forms a "syndicate" to produce "generic" ads that allow the individual businesses to dub in local information. The technique is especially useful for small businesses that sell relatively standardized products or services such as legal assistance, autos, and furniture. Because the small firms in the syndicate pool their funds, the result usually is higher quality ads and significantly lower production costs.

The cost of syndicated ads varies substantially, and not all programs emphasize quality. The owner should avoid syndicators who do not understand his business' and his customers' needs. In addition, he should negotiate a contract specifying that the syndication will not sell the same campaign to other companies in his trading area.[21]

Other cost-saving suggestions for advertising expenditures include:

- *Repeating ads that have been successful.* In addition to reducing the cost of ad preparation, this may create a consistent image in the small firm's advertising program.
- *Using identical ads in different media.* If a billboard has been an effective advertising tool, consider converting it to a newspaper or magazine ad or a direct mail flier.
- *Hiring the services of independent copywriters, graphic designers, photographers, and other media specialists.* Many small businesses that cannot afford a full-time advertising staff buy their advertising services a la carte. They work directly with independent specialists and usually receive high-quality work that compares favorably to that of advertising agencies without paying a fee for overhead.

Publicity. The press can be either a valuable friend or a fearsome foe to a small business, depending on how well the owner handles her firm's public relations. Too often, entrepreneurs take the attitude, "My business is too small to be concerned about public relations." However, the wise small business manager recognizes that investing time and money in public relations benefits both the community and the company. The community gains the support of a good business citizen, and the company earns a positive image in the marketplace.

Many small businesses rely on media attention to get noticed. While such publicity may not be free, it definitely can lower the firm's advertising expenditures *without* suffering a lack of customer recognition. The manager of one charitable organization says, "Most small companies can't afford to give for the sheer fact of giving. But by donating time, goods, or services, they can often reach a population through the media that they couldn't get to otherwise."[22] For example, during the Muscular Dystro-

[19]Carol Rose Carey, "Cut Ad Costs without Cutting Quality," *Inc.*, April 1982, pp. 108–10.

[20]Ibid. p. 108.

[21]Richard Kneisman, "Shared Benefits," *Inc.*, October 1985, p. 134.

[22]Sara Delano, "Give and You Shall Receive," *Inc.*, February 1983, p. 128.

phy Association's annual telethon, a local shop, Cookies Cook'n donated over 100 pounds of cookies and brownies to feed telephone volunteers. Several giant cookies were auctioned off during the telethon, and the small cookie shop's name was mentioned frequently.[23] Cookies Cook'n got more television exposure for donating these cookies than it could have gotten spending its entire advertising budget on TV commercials. The owner of a quick-oil-change chain donates 50¢ from every oil change during a certain time period to the March of Dimes. When a new store opens, the company gives away free oil changes for one day. "It gets real jammed up, and we always get an article in the local paper about it," says the owner.[24]

The owner must be careful to avoid overextending herself financially with donations. After all, she is in business to earn a profit, not to support every worthy cause in the community. The manager should pick one or two "special causes" and focus the majority of her public relations efforts there. According to one public relations expert, "Ideally, the public service campaign you choose to work on should be related to who you are and what you do."[25]

V. SUMMARY

Advertising can mean the difference between success and failure for a small business. Still, some small firms see it as a "leftover expense" to be increased only after all other costs are paid. Advertising, however, can boost sales and profits for the small firm.

Advertising is often criticized for being intrusive and insulting, but it also serves a very important function in the marketplace: disseminating information. The small retail or service firm advertises for several purposes:

1. To produce immediate sales
2. To create interest in the firm's goods or services
3. To attract customers into the store

4. To maintain adequate business volume
5. To promote special sales
6. To introduce new goods and services or encourage increased use of existing products

Small manufacturers advertise for these basic reasons:

1. To stimulate primary demand
2. To stimulate selective demand
3. To assist sales representatives in making customer calls

Some firms advertise to provide the public with information about their businesses. Such institutional advertising is designed to create goodwill for the company and improve its image in the community.

One of the most important questions facing the small business manager is choosing the media through which to transmit the advertising message. There are several media options, including: newspapers; radio; television; magazines; direct mail; transit advertising; directories; trade shows; specialty advertisements; special events and promotions; and point-of-purchase ads.

An advertising plan increases the probability that the small firm's advertising program will be more effective. The first step is to establish specific, measurable advertising objectives. Then the manager must analyze the firm and its customers. When the definition of his target audience is clear, the manager can begin to design an advertising message and to choose media. Finally, the manager must evaluate the ads' effectiveness. Sales increases, coupons, "hidden offers," and ad tests can be indicative of how successful an ad campaign is.

Establishing an advertising budget presents a real challenge to the small business owner. There are four basic methods: what is affordable; matching competitors; percentage of sales; objective-and-task.

Practically every small business owner can stretch his advertising dollars by taking advantage of cooperative advertising, shared advertising, and publicity.

[23]Ibid.
[24]Ibid. p. 24.
[25]Delano, op.cit p. 129.

STUDENT INVOLVEMENT PROJECTS

1. Contact a small retailer, manufacturer, and wholesaler and interview each one about his advertising program.
   a. Are there specific advertising objectives?
   b. What media does the manager employ? Why?
   c. How does the manager evaluate an ad's effectiveness?
   d. What assistance does the manager receive in designing ads?

2. Contact several small business owners and determine how they establish their advertising budgets. Why do they use the method they do?
3. Interview local representatives from several of the media mentioned in this chapter. What advantages and disadvantages does each one's particular vehicle offer the small business owner?

DISCUSSION QUESTIONS

1. What are the four elements of promotion?
2. Outline and briefly describe the purposes of advertising for a small retailer or service firm.
3. Explain the basic reasons for a manufacturer to advertise.
4. What is institutional advertising? How does it differ from immediate response advertising?
5. What factors should a small business manager consider when selecting advertising media?
6. Create a table to summarize the advantages and disadvantages of the following advertising media:

   Newspapers   Direct mail
   Radio   Outdoor advertising
   Television   Transit advertising
   Magazines   Directories
   Specialty advertising Trade shows

7. What are fixed spots, preemptible spots, and floating spots in radio advertising?
8. Describe the characteristics of an effective outdoor advertisement.
9. Briefly outline the steps in creating an advertising plan. What principles should the small business owner follow when creating an effective advertisement?
10. Describe the common methods of establishing an advertising budget. Which method is most often used? Which technique is most often recommended? Why?

APPENDICES

A Sample Loan and Investment Package

Summary of Loan Application

Applicants:	Mr. James K. Quadrant 978 Lakeside Drive Hamilton, New York 13346 (315) 824–5431
	Mr. Isiah M. Gradient 113 Broughton Rd. Hamilton, New York 13346 (315) 824–6871
Business:	Plumb-Bob Surveying & Equipment Company 600 Madison Drive Hamilton, New York 13346
Business size:	$330,000 in latest fiscal year. Qualify under SBA definition of a "small business."
Form of ownership:	S Corporation
Loan purpose:	To purchase 1 Zeiss total stage with data storage and transfer capabilities to improve the quantity and the quality of the surveying jobs performed for clients.
Amount requested:	$25,000

Mr. James K. Quadrant
987 Lakeside Drive
Hamilton, New York 13346
(315) 824–5431

Work experience:

1974–present **Plumb-Bob Surveying & Engineering Company**, Hamilton, New York. Manager-Partner. Created business and continues to actively manage technical aspects of field operations. Supervises project managers of six field crews.

1970–1974 **Boise-Cascade Timber Co.**, Freeport, Maine. Survey project manager. Supervised field activities of a six-man survey crew. Planned weekly work schedules and monitored work quality.

1965–1970 **Hi-Tech Survey Co.**, Albany, New York. Technician. Performed various surveying tasks as a part-time member of a field crew while attending college. Earned 80% of college expenses.

Education:

1969–1970 **Rensselaer Polytechnical Institute**, Troy, New York. Master of Science in Engineering Management. Grades in top 10% of class, GPR of 3.7/4.0.

1965–1969 **Rensselaer Polytechnical Institute**, Troy, New York. Bachelor of Science degree in Civil Engineering. Graduated with honors.

References:

Mr. Frank Boland
President, Hi-Tech Survey Co.
Troy, New York 12180
(315) 623–1890

Ms. Sally LeGrand
Account Executive
Merrill, Lynch, Pierce, Fenner, and Smith
Portland, Maine 04111
(207) 563–1218

Mr. Jeff Anderson
President, Sound Investment Company
Hamilton, New York 13346
(315) 824–3671

Personal Financial Statement

Assets		Disbursements	
Cash–Savings account	$12,000	Notes payable	$10,000
Checking account	3,000	Mortgage	41,000
Stocks	22,000	Miscellaneous	6,000
Keogh contributions	31,000	Total liabilities	$57,000
Home	96,000		
Autos	20,000	Net worth	$135,000
Miscellaneous assets	8,000		
Total assets	$192,000	Total liabilities & net worth	$192,000

Mr. Isiah M. Gradient
113 Broughton Road
Hamilton, New York 13346
(315) 824–6871

Work experience:

1976–present   Plumb-Bob Surveying & Engineering Co., Hamilton, New York. Managing partner. Supervises internal managerial operations, including financial, accounting, personnel, and planning duties.

1971–1975   New York Department of Health & Sanitation, Albany, New York. District Maintenance Engineer. Designed water and sewage projects for cities. Supervised staff of twelve.

1966–1970   Hi-Tech Survey Co., Albany, New York. Technician. Worked part-time as field crew member performing various surveying duties.

Education:

1975–1976   University of Virginia, Charlottesville, Virginia. Master of Business Administration. GPR of 4.0/4.0.

1966–1970   Clemson University, Clemson, South Carolina. Bachelor of Science degree in Civil Engineering.

References:

Mr. Lowell Mooney
Assistant Vice President
Con-Edison
New York, New York 10014
(212) 666–2268

Dr. Foard Tarbert
Professor of Engineering
Rensselaer Polytechnical Institute
Troy, New York 12181
(518) 527–3196

Mr. Sam Howell
Certified Public Accountant
Charlottesville, Virginia 22201
(804) 786–3241

Personal Financial Statement

Assets		Disbursements	
Cash–Savings account	$ 6,000	Mortgages	$59,000
–Checking account	4,000	Notes payable	14,000
Mutual funds	27,000		6,000
Stocks	18,000	Total liabilities	$79,000
Keogh contributions	24,000		
Home	94,000	Net worth	138,000
Real estate	17,000	Total liabilities	
Autos	19,000	& net worth	$217,000
Miscellaneous assets	8,000		
Total assets	$217,000		

APPENDIX A

Business Summary

Company History

James K. Quadrant created Plumb-Bob Surveying Engineering Company in 1974 as a part-time business venture designed to serve the surveying needs of the local community. Mr. Quadrant began full-time operation of the business in 1975, and Mr. Gradient joined the firm in 1976 to manage the internal operations of the business while Mr. Quadrant's major responsibilities remained in the area of surveying operations. The two principals' skills, abilities, and areas of concentration are complementary. Annual sales have increased steadily to a record high of $330,000 in the latest fiscal year, and profits peaked at $40,920.

Industry Trends and the State of the Art

Demand for surveying and engineering services should continue to climb during the next decade for three important reasons. First, the unpaid escalation of property values during the late 1970s and early 1980s has increased the need for these services by several customer groups. Second, greater mobility among the general public has increased the number of land transfers. Third, the trend of larger financial institutions to buy and sell residential and commercial mortgages translates into more work for surveyors, who must provide closing plats showing property boundaries, location of permanent fixtures, encroachments, and easements.

The development of the "state of the art" in the surveying engineering industry has paralleled the expansion in the service's demand. The surveyor's tools have undergone a major transformation in the last ten years; they are more sophisticated, more accurate, and more refined than ever before. Technological advances have manifested themselves in two important forms: (1) the development of speedy, accurate computational equipment (e.g., microcomputers, programmable calculators, etc.) that allows the surveyor to perform complex calculations on field data, and (2) the introduction of electronic distance meters (EDMs), which yield more accurate survey measurements faster and facilitate data processing.

Competition

Plumb-Bob Surveying & Engineering Company faces no direct competition in its home town, Hamilton, New York. But there are three primary competitors conducting similar operations in towns within a 50-mile diameter of Hamilton.

Geodetic Survey, Inc. A small corporation (three principals) whose primary focus is surveying large land tracts for timber companies. Serves 28% of local markets.

Photogrammetry Engineers, Ltd. A small partnership which performs all types of surveying jobs and specializes in surveying by aerial photography. Controls 22% of local market.

Land Surveyors, Inc. A relatively new, aggressive company which also performs all types of surveying jobs and specializes in surveying for local architectural firms. Controls 18% of the local market.

Goals, Objectives, and Strategies

The principals of Plumb-Bob recognize the importance of quality management in successfully meeting competitors. To focus the firm's activities, the principals define its mission: "To meet the spectrum of surveying and engineering needs of private landowners, large tract owners, financial institutions, attorneys, realtors, and timber companies with high-quality service, rapid turnaround, and unparalleled professionalism, at a profit."

The overall mission of Plumb-Bob is more clearly defined by dissecting it into the following objectives:

- to boost annual sales to $400,000.
- to increase market share from 31% to 36% of the local market.
- to expand into a larger geographic trading area, encompassing twelve counties.
- to increase by 10% the number of engineering jobs performed for local towns and districts (e.g., water and sewage systems design).
- to improve profit margin from 12% to 17.5%.

To obtain these objectives, Plumb-Bob will employ a business strategy designed to exploit the four key factors for success in the surveying business—to maintain: (1) a prompt turnaround time on jobs; (2) a professional image with the clientele; (3) a continuous relationship with "return customers;" and (4) a healthy customer mix to ensure a steady flow of work. The following key points illustrate this strategy:

- to utilize equipment offering the latest technological advances.
- to train employees in implementing advanced survey techniques into their work.
- to provide the opportunity for clients to consult with project managers (or principals, if desired) on all projects.
- to keep the customer informed of the job's progress on a timely basis.
- to "crack the engineering market" by obtaining small jobs with cities, districts, and subdivisions.
- to increase the number of government contracts bid on.
- to acquire and to develop "regional accounts"—clients with large land holdings (e.g., large timber companies).

Marketing and Pricing Strategies

The principals of Plumb-Bob have identified their primary target market (in descending order of importance) as: (1) timber companies; (2) realtors; (3) attorneys; (4) financial institutions; and (5) private landowners. The firm's marketing strategy is designed to attain the return customer by providing *quality* surveying and engineering service with prompt turnaround. The firm has built its reputation by focusing on quality, and its pricing policy reflects this professional image. General strategy is to tailor pricing to the "cream of the crop."

Plan of Operation

Plumb-Bob employs the S Corporation form of ownership primarily for tax reasons. The organizational chart is attached on a separate form.

Financial Data

The following audited financial statements summarize Plumb-Bob's latest operations:

Plumb-Bob Surveying and Engineering Company
Balance Sheet

Assets		Liabilities	
Current assets:		Current liabilities:	
Cash	$ 5,000	Accounts payable	$ 2,500
Accounts receivables	4,700	Long-term liabilities:	
Total current assets	$ 9,700	Notes payable	11,500
Fixed assets:		Mortgage on real property	43,000
20 vehicles	40,500	Total L-T liabilities	$54,500
3 computers	30,000	Total liabilities	57,000
6 sets EDM equipment	48,000	Owners' equity	127,500
4 transits	6,000		
4 levels	4,800	Total liabilities & owners' equity	$184,500
Misc. field equipment	20,000		
Office fixtures & equip.	18,000		
Leasehold improvements	7,500		
Total fixed assets	$174,800		
Total assets	$184,500		

Plumb-Bob Surveying & Engineering Company
Break-Even Analysis

$$\text{Break-even sales} = 1.00 - \frac{\text{total fixed expenses}}{\text{variable expenses expressed as percentage of sales}}$$

Total expenses	$320,100
Fixed	88,122
Variable	231,978

$$\text{variable expenses as a percentage of sales} = \frac{231,978}{400,000} = 0.58$$

$$\text{break-even sales} = \frac{88,122}{1.00 - 0.58} = \$209,814$$

Income Statement

Net sales		$330,000
Operating expenses:		
Labor expense	$184,800	
Gas expense	21,600	
Telephone expense	6,270	
Equipment repair expense	5,600	
Insurance expense	9,025	
Rent expense	5,400	
Depreciation expense	9,200	
License expense	1,500	
Payroll taxes	11,050	
Office supplies expense	7,200	
Field supplies expense	10,900	
Miscellaneous expenses	4,700	
Total operating expenses		$277,245
Net operating profit		52,755
Income taxes		9,047
Net profit		$ 43,708

Pro Forma Income Statement*
(*Assuming loan is granted)

Net sales		$400,000
Operating expenses:		
Labor expense	$222,000	
Gas expense	16,000	
Telephone expense	10,650	
Equipment repair expense	6,500	
Insurance expense	11,000	
Rent expense	6,000	
Depreciation expense	10,000	
License expense	1,500	
Payroll expense	12,750	
Office supplies expense	7,400	
Field supplies expense	11,200	
Miscellaneous expenses	5,100	
Total operating expenses		$320,100
Net operating profit		79,900
Income taxes		17,520
Net profit		$ 62,380

Pro Forma Income Statement**
(**Without loan)

Net sales		$350,000
Operating expenses:		
Labor expense	$196,000	
Gas expense	23,000	
Telephone expense	7,100	
Equipment repair expense	5,600	
Insurance expense	11,000	
Rent expense	6,000	
Depreciation expense	9,200	
License expense	1,500	
Payroll taxes	13,500	
Office supplies expense	7,400	
Field supplies expense	11,200	
Miscellaneous expenses	5,100	
Total operating expenses		$296,600
Net operating profit		53,400
Income taxes		9,200
Net profit		$ 44,200

Loan Proposal

Loan purpose: To purchase a Zeiss total station with data storage and transfer capabilities that will facilitate taking angular and distance measurements in the field and performing survey computations.

Amount requested: $25,000 (see attached vendor's estimate)

Terms: One year and no prepayment penalty.

Interest rate: Prime

Collateral: Personal guarantees of principals' title to Zeiss total station.

Repayment: Plumb-Bob's ability to repay is illustrated on the accompanying pro-forma financial statements. The cash budget projected for the upcoming year shows the company will be able to repay the loan within one year. Benefits accruing from the purchase of this EDM equipment include the ability to:

- reduce the number of field personnel by one-third through the elimination of the chairman.
- reduce office personnel by the immediate transferring field data to the home office via telephone.
- minimize the number of return trips to the job site, a significant cost of doing business.
- improve productivity by performing more jobs in less time.

- improve the firm's "professional image" with its clientele by employing the latest, most advanced equipment.

- obtain government contracts which require a level accuracy attainable only with EDM devices.

Cash Budget

CASH RECEIPTS	JAN	FEB	MAR	APR	MAY	JUNE	JULY	AUG
SALES COLLECTIONS:	20,000	25,000	28,000	33,000	47,000	54,000	58,000	55,000
20% same month			5,600	6,600	9,400	10,800	11,600	11,000
60% first month after sale			15,000	16,800	19,800	28,200	32,400	34,800
18% second month after sale			3,600	4,500	5,040	5,940	8,460	9,720
Other cash receipts			250	50	380	160	400	100
TOTAL CASH RECEIPTS			24,450	27,950	34,620	45,100	52,860	55,620
CASH DISBURSEMENTS:								
Wages			15,680	18,480	26,320	30,240	32,480	31,147
Taxes								
Payroll			532	628	987	1,011	1,375	1,163
Property			0	0	400	0	0	0
Transportation			790	840	1,380	1,525	1,780	1,645
Repairs & maintenance			375	450	575	625	700	675
Field supplies			650	800	1,050	1,240	1,500	1,375
Rent			500	500	500	500	500	500
Utilities			100	110	130	140	150	140
Telephone (including yellow pages ad)			450	575	800	950	1,075	990
Entertainment			200	200	200	200	200	200
Insurance								
Malpractice			0	9,000	0	0	0	0
Tenant's			0	0	1,500	0	0	0
Auto			0	0	0	500	0	0
Licenses			0	0	0	1,500	0	0
Miscellaneous			210	340	425	490	510	500
TOTAL CASH DISBURSEMENTS			19,487	31,923	34,267	38,921	40,270	38,335
END OF MONTH BALANCE								
Beginning cash balance			5,000	9,963	5,990	6,343	12,522	25,112
+ cash receipts			24,450	27,950	34,620	45,100	52,860	55,620
− cash disbursements			19,487	31,923	34,267	38,921	40,270	38,335
CASH END OF THE MONTH (REPAYMENT)			9,963	5,990	6,343	12,522	25,112	42,397
			0	0	0	0	0	0
or								
(BORROWING)			0	0	0	0	0	0
CASH END OF THE MONTH			$ 9,963	$ 5,990	$ 6,343	$12,522	$25,112	$42,397

Minimum Cash Balance = $5,000

The Small Business Management Audit

A financial audit is a thorough analysis of a firm's past and current financial position and is designed to verify and evaluate the effectiveness of its financial operations. It can help management detect circumstances that could lead to financial problems in the future.

Similarly, a management audit, although much broader in scope than a financial audit, aims at detecting potential managerial problems in the small company which threaten its existence. Frequently a small business manager is so closely involved in the firm's operation that he never recognizes its primary problem areas. The typical owner, working with the firm's problems daily, finds it difficult to view them objectively. As a result, he has difficulty assessing the need for changes in policies and procedures to meet fast-changing business conditions.

The following series of questions is designed to assist the small business manager in candidly and honestly evaluating strengths and weaknesses and in defining opportunities and potential difficulties. It is a beginning point for the owner to create a plan for improving the performance of the company. The material serves as a quick-glance checklist. (For more information, obtain a copy of the SBA booklets from which it was drawn.[1])

Students of small business management will find this audit useful in performing consulting services for small businesses. When properly used, the management audit should offer pertinent suggestions for improving managerial and business performance.

Yourself

1. Are you well qualified to manage a small business successfully? Are you energetic? enthusiastic? willing to learn? willing to assume responsibility and make decisions? Do you get along well with other people? Can you motivate subordinates?
2. Do you listen well? A manager can learn a great deal by listening to employees, customers, suppliers, competitors—anyone exposed to the firm's operations.
3. Do you monitor changes in the market that affect your business operation? Do you read relevant

463

business and trade newspapers and periodicals? These publications offer valuable information to the typical small business owner.

4. Do you belong to a trade association or other business organization? An owner can learn quite a bit by fraternizing with other business owners who encounter similar problems and opportunities.

5. Do you attend seminars or classes designed for small business owners sponsored by local trade associations, colleges, or chambers of commerce? These classes often provide suggestions for improved managerial techniques and are usually quite inexpensive.

6. Are you active in local clubs and organizations? Assuming an active role in the local community can be an effective way to create a positive business image and to boost sales.

7. Do you draw a reasonable salary as owner and manager of the business? Are you earning at least as much as you could earn working for someone else?

8. Does the business generate a reasonable return on your investment? Do you earn as much from the business (over and above your salary) as you could earn by investing an equal amount in an investment of similar risk?

9. Do you use any of the services the Small Business Administration and other government agencies offer? Publications, seminars, and consulting services can be valuable managerial aids.

Strategic Planning

1. Do you know what business you are in? In other words, have you developed a written statement of your firm's basic mission? Without a guiding mission statement, a business is bound to fail.

2. Do you have a written description of your firm's target market? Knowing where your product or service is aimed facilitates the creation of a unified "theme" for your business.

3. Do you know what your customers' characteristics are? Where are your customers? In addition to a tangible product or service, what are they purchasing when they buy from you?

4. Do you have a master strategy designed to keep your firm ahead of the competition? Have you identified your firm's distinctive competence— the quality that sets it apart from the competition? Every small firm should define its competitive advantage and then seek to maintain it through planning.

5. Do you have written objectives to guide your company's performance in critical areas? Are they specific and measurable? Do they include a time frame and an index for measuring progress?

6. Have you created written policies to guide action and decisionmaking in the organization and to ensure consistency? Do employees know what these policies are? Are they followed?

7. Have you identified potential opportunities for increased sales and profits for your firm? New products, new markets, or new locations could generate more business for the small firm if management has the capacity to reach them.

8. Do you attempt to foresee future conditions and changes that have a significant impact on your business? Do you predict future economic trends and their effect on your business? Although no forecast is ever completely accurate, managers should attempt to peer into the future to avoid being surprised by unforeseen changes.

9. Do you make an assessment of your competitors' actions so that you can plot a strategy to meet them? How do customers perceive your firm in comparison to your competitors?

Organizational Structure

1. Have you developed a current organizational chart? Does the organization chart illustrate the proper relationship between individuals and functions?

2. Does the organizational chart clearly indicate who has the authority, responsibility, and accountability for each function.

3. Does each person in the organization have a clearly written current job description? Does the job description define accurately all work responsibilities as well as the superior-subordinate relationship?

4. When delegation occurs, it is the agreement put in writing to ensure mutual understanding of responsibilities?

Human Resources Management

1. Are you presently in compliance with all federal and state laws and regulations involving employees?
   a. Employment (recruiting and selection)
   b. Training
   c. Job safety and health
   d. Performance appraisal
   e. Wages, hours, and working conditions

2. Are all personnel records kept in accordance with federal, state, and local governmental reporting requirements?

3. Have you developed and do you use validated job specifications in hiring employees?

4. Is there a well-developed program for job orientation provided to each new employee?

5. Does each employee who is either new to the company or transferred to a new job receive adequate training on all facets of that job?

6. Are the wages, salaries, and fringe benefits comparable with other firms in the industry or geographic area?

7. Do you have a formal performance evaluation or appraisal system? Is it tied to employees' pay?

8. Is there a training program that is primarily for self-improvement for employees who would like to move up in the organization?

9. Do all employees have a copy of the company's policies and procedures? Are these reviewed regularly?

Accounting System

1. Do you have an accounting system that is sufficient in providing a full range of data needed to make management decisions?

2. Does your accounting system provide you with monthly statements?

3. Do you understand every element of the accounting statements you receive?

4. Are your books audited yearly by an independent public accountant?

5. Do you consistently apply break-even analysis and opportunity cost analysis to your business activities?

6. Are accounts receivable aged regularly?

7. Does your accounting system provide for the funds and statements needed for payroll taxes and deposits, income tax deposits, and deposits and payments of unemployment compensation taxes and workmen's compensation liabilities?

8. Is your accounting system adequate for present business and immediately foreseeable growth?

9. Do you reconcile your bank statements monthly?

10. Do you keep wage and salary records on hourly employees?

11. Are you adequately managing cash through a cash budget?

Budgeting and Expense Control

1. Are the expenditures of your firm based on allocations established by a budgeting system?

2. Are your budgets tied to set time periods, performance standards, and incentives?

3. Do you require a budget proposal with any proposal for future business operations?

4. Are budgets used to control the amount and rate of expenditures?

5. Do your budgets provide a record for improved performance?

6. When you set your budgets, do you discuss them with key employees?

7. Have you analyzed the costs of your business that are fixed for a period, such as rent and salaries of clerical and supervisory personnel?
8. Have you attempted to construct a break-even model for your business?
9. Have you compared your cost, revenue, and profit figures against industry data from your trade association?
10. At the end of each accounting period, do you review your actual operations and your forecast together?

Cash Management

1. Are all cash receipts deposited to the firm's bank account?
2. Are cash receipts records processed by two or more people working independently?
3. Are all withdrawals of cash controlled by numbered checks?
4. Do you continuously monitor and reconcile all cash disbursements against the original authorization?
5. Are all checks and purchase orders prenumbered and accounted for?
6. Do you invest seasonal excess cash productively?
7. Can you use lines of credit to decrease the demands for cash?
8. Do you calculate your cash flow regularly?

Taxes and Legal Obligations

1. Do you maintain a tax calendar showing when the various requested federal, state, and local reports are to be filed or payments made?
2. Is someone specifically responsible for all tax reports and payments?
3. Do you keep adequate individual payroll records to ensure that quarterly payroll returns for state and federal tax authorities may be completed without undue difficulty?
4. Is the person who prepares your payroll kept up-to-date on maximum wages for payroll tax purposes?

5. If your payable withholding is above the minimum amount, are you making timely deposits with a federal depository?
6. If some of your sales are subject to state or local taxes, do your records adequately differentiate between taxable and nontaxable sales?
7. Do you have adequate equipment records, giving the date purchased, basis of the asset (cost or otherwise), estimated useful life, method of depreciation, accumulated depreciation, and location of the asset?
8. If you have a pension plan or a profit-sharing plan, have you conferred with your attorney regarding reporting requirements to the government and to the employees?
9. Are all necessary business licenses up-to-date?

Risk and Insurance

1. Have you analyzed the risks your business and employees are exposed to under normal operations?
2. Are you assuming unnecessary risk?
3. Has a professional insurance broker inspected your business to help you identify areas where risk can be reduced?
4. Do you have insurance on key personnel in the business?
5. Have you taken advantage of all premium cost-cutting possibilities?
6. Do you periodically review your insurance program?

Purchasing

1. Do you regularly review the quality of products purchased, their timely delivery, and the quality of other services provided by your suppliers?
2. Do you solicit bids on purchases when you are not sure what the price ought to be?
3. Do you have more than one source of supply for any critical item?
4. Are most of your purchases made at the "right" price?

5. Do you buy largely by specification, rather than by brand name or simply by accepting what the vendor offers?
6. Do you have specific policies and procedures regarding who is authorized to purchase goods and services? receive salesmen's calls? place requisitions? process records?
7. Have you reviewed existing purchasing procedures to see if they meet your needs?
8. Does the volume of purchasing for any particular item warrant your dealing directly with its manufacturer?

Marketing and Sales Promotion

1. Do you know the specific segment of the market your business is attempting to serve?
2. Are you able to determine why your products or services sell against those of your competitors?
3. Is the service you provide with your products superior to that of your competition?
4. Does your firm and its products or services have a good reputation in the minds of customers?
5. Do you attempt to meet competitors head-on or sell differentiated products that carry a different price/value relationship?
6. Are your marketing and promotion efforts honest and straightforward?
7. Are all aspects of marketing and promotion coordinated with production planning and scheduling?
8. Are your marketing and promotion efforts controlled by budgets which are changed only for compelling reasons.

Location

1. Is your operation convenient and easily accessible to your target market?
2. Are transportation facilities such as access, parking, loading and unloading, public transportation, and lighting well developed at your location?

Pricing

1. Are your prices competitively based on the quality and services that go with each product sold?
2. Do you use break-even analysis in computing cost for price setting?
3. Are there economies of scale in your operation which enable you to sell at a lower price than competitors?
4. Have you developed a pricing strategy that allows you to adjust prices to meet competitive situations as they develop?

Planning for Growth

1. Do day-to-day activities involve you so much that you find no opportunity for advance planning?
2. Do you find that recurring crises force you to make most of your changes before you have been able to give them thoughtful analysis?
3. Are you grooming someone to succeed you?

Source: U.S. Small Business Administration, *Management Audit for Small Service Firms,* Small Business Management Series No. 38, Washington, 1979; John B. Kline, U.S. Small Business Administration, *Management Audit for Small Manufacturers,* Small Business Management Series No. 29, Washington, 1979; U.S. Small Business Administration, *Management for Small Retailers,* Small Business Management Series No. 31, Washington, 1979.

Small Business Administration Management Aids

Part 1—Free Publications

Accounting, Financial Management and Analysis

New	Old	Title
_*_ MA 1.001	MA 170	The ABC's of Borrowing
_*_ MA 1.002	MA 193	What Is the Best Selling Price?
_*_ MA 1.003	MA 206	Keep Pointed Toward Profit
___ MA 1.004	MA 220	Basic Budgets for Profit Planning
___ MA 1.005	MA 226	Pricing for Small Manufacturers
_*_ MA 1.006	MA 229	Cash Flow in a Small Plant
_*_ MA 1.007	MA 232	Credit and Collections
_*_ MA 1.008	MA 234	Attacking Business Decision Problems with Breakeven Analysis
___ MA 1.009	MA 235	A Venture Capital Primer For Small Business
_*_ MA 1.010	SMA 126	Accounting Services For Small Service Firms
___ MA 1.011	SMA 130	Analyze Your Records to Reduce Costs
_*_ MA 1.012	SMA 140	Profit By Your Wholesalers' Services
_*_ MA 1.013	SMA 142	Steps in Meeting Your Tax Obligations
_*_ MA 2.003	MA 207	Pointers on Scheduling Production
_*_ MA 2.004	MA 208	Problems in Managing a Family-Owned Business
___ MA 2.005	MA 212	The Equipment Replacement Decision
_*_ MA 2.006	MA 216	Finding a New Product for Your Company
___ MA 2.007	MA 218	Business Plan for Small Manufacturers
_*_ MA 2.008	MA 221	Business Plan for Small Construction Firms
___ MA 2.009	MA 222	Business Life Insurance
_*_ MA 2.010	MA 233	Planning and Goal Setting for Small Business

468

New	Old	Title
___ MA 2.011	MA 242	Fixing Production Mistakes
_*_ MA 2.012	MA 243	Setting Up a Quality Control System
___ MA 2.013	MA 248	Can You Make Money With Your Idea or Invention
_*_ MA 2.014	MA 249	Can You Lease or Buy Equipment
_*_ MA 2.015	MA 250	Can You Use a Minicomputer
___ MA 2.016	SMA 71	Check List for Going Into Business
___ MA 2.017	SMA 143	Factors in Considering a Shopping Center Location
_*_ MA 2.018	SMA 148	Insurance Checklist for Small Business
_*_ MA 2.019	SMA 149	Computers for Small Business—Service Bureau or Time Sharing
_*_ MA 2.020	SMA 150	Business Plan for Retailers
_*_ MA 2.021	SMA 152	Using a Traffic Study to Select a Retail Site
_*_ MA 2.022	SMA 153	Business Plan for Small Service Firms
___ MA 2.023	SMA 154	Using Census Data to Select a Store Site
___ MA 2.024	SMA 168	Store Location "Little Things" Mean a Lot
_*_ MA 2.025	SMA 170	Thinking About Going Into Business?
_*_ MA 1.014	SMA 144	Getting the Facts for Income Tax Reporting
_*_ MA 1.015	SMA 146	Budgeting in a Small Business Firm
_*_ MA 1.016	SMA 147	Sound Cash Management and Borrowing
_*_ MA 1.017	SMA 155	Keeping Records in Small Business
_*_ MA 1.018	SMA 165	Check List for Profit Watching
___ MA 1.019	SMA 166	Simple Breakeven Analysis for Small Stores
___ MA 1.020	—	Profit Pricing and Costing for Services

Planning

New	Old	Title
_*_ MA 2.001	MA 189	Should You Make or Buy Components
_*_ MA 2.002	MA 201	Locating or Relocating Your Business
_*_ MA 4.008	MA 236	Tips on Getting More for Your Marketing Dollar
___ MA 4.009	MA 245	Exhibiting at Trade Shows
_*_ MA 4.010	MA 246	Developing New Accounts
___ MA 4.011	MA 178	Effective Industrial Advertising for Small Plants
_*_ MA 4.012	SMA 156	Marketing Checklist for Small Retailers
_*_ MA 4.013	SMA 158	A Pricing Checklist for Small Retailers
_*_ MA 4.014	SMA 159	Improving Personal Selling in Small Retail Stores
_*_ MA 4.015	SMA 160	Advertising Guidelines for Small Retail Firms
___ MA 4.016	SMA 161	Signs in Your Business
___ MA 4.017	SMA 163	Public Relations for Small Business
_*_ MA 4.018	SMA 164	Plan Your Advertising Budget
_*_ MA 4.019	SMA 167	Learning About Your Market
_*_ MA 4.020	SMA 169	Do You Know the Results of Your Advertising

Organization and Personnel

New	Old	Title
___ MA 5.001	MA 186	Checklist for Developing a Training Program
_*_ MA 5.002	MA 195	Setting Pay for Your Management Jobs
___ MA 5.003	MA 197	Pointers on Preparing an Employee Handbook
_*_ MA 5.004	MA 205	Pointers on Using Temporary-Help Services

New	*Old*	*Title*
___ MA 5.005	MA 209	Preventing Employee Pilferage
_*_ MA 5.006	MA 241	Setting Up a Pay System
_*_ MA 5.007	SMA 162	Staffing Your Store
_*_ MA 5.008	—	Managing Employee Benefits

General Management and Administration

___ MA 3.001	MA 191	Delegating Work and Responsibility
_*_ MA 3.002	MA 225	Management Checklist for a Family Business
___ MA 3.003	MA 239	Techniques of Time Management
_*_ MA 3.004	SMA 119	Preventing Retail Theft
_*_ MA 3.005	SMA 123	Stock Control for Small Stores
_*_ MA 3.006	SMA 129	Reducing Shoplifting Losses
_*_ MA 3.007	SMA 134	Preventing Burglary and Robbery Loss
_*_ MA 3.008	SMA 137	Outwitting Bad-Check Passers
_*_ MA 3.009	SMA 151	Preventing Embezzlement

Marketing

___ MA 4.001	MA 178	Effective Industrial Advertising for Small Plants
___ MA 4.002	MA 187	Using Census Data in Small Plant Marketing
___ MA 4.003	MA 190	Measuring Sales Force Performance
___ MA 4.004	MA 192	Profile Your Customers to Expand Industrial Sales
_*_ MA 4.005	MA 200	Is the Independent Sales Agent for You?
___ MA 4.006	MA 203	Are Your Products and Channels Producing Sales?
_*_ MA 4.007	MA 230	Selling Products on Consignment

Legal and Governmental Affairs

_*_ MA 6.001	MA 217	Reducing Air Pollution in Industry
_*_ MA 6.002	MA 219	Solid Waste Management in Industry
_*_ MA 6.003	MA 223	Incorporating a Small Business
_*_ MA 6.004	MA 231	Selecting the Legal Structure for Your Business
___ MA 6.005	MA 240	Introduction to Patents
___ MA 6.006	MA 244	Product Safety Checklist

Miscellaneous

___ MA 7.001	MA 214	The Metric System and Small Business
_*_ MA 7.002	MA 224	Association Services for Small Business
___ MA 7.003	MA 237	Marketing Overseas with U.S. Government Help
___ MA 7.004	MA 247	Negotiating International Sales Contracts
___ MA 7.005	SMA 135	Arbitration: Peace-Maker in Small Business
_*_ MA 7.006	SMA 157	Efficient Lighting for Small Stores

*Aids converted to a new number

For reference, the following conversion list shows old numbers to new numbers.

Management Aid (MA)

Old	New	Old	New
170	1.001	223	6.003
178	4.001	224	7.002
186	5.001	225	3.002
187	4.002	226	1.005
189	2.001	229	1.006
190	4.003	230	4.007
191	3.001	231	6.004
192	4.004	232	1.007
193	1.002	233	2.010
195	5.002	234	1.008
197	5.003	235	1.009
200	4.005	236	4.008
201	2.002	237	7.003
203	4.006	239	3.003
205	5.004	240	6.005
206	1.003	241	5.006
207	2.003	242	2.011
208	2.004	243	2.012
209	5.005	244	6.006
212	2.005	245	4.009
214	7.001	246	4.010
216	2.006	247	7.004
217	6.001	248	2.013
218	2.007	249	2.014
219	6.002	250	2.015
220	1.004		5.008
221	2.008		
222	2.009		

Small Manager Aids (SMA)

Old	New	Old	New
71	2.016	161	4.016
119	3.004	162	5.007
123	3.005	163	4.017
126	1.010	164	4.018
129	3.006	165	1.018
130	1.011	166	1.019
134	3.007	167	4.019
135	7.005	168	2.024
137	3.008	169	4.020
140	1.012	170	2.025
142	1.013		
143	2.017		
144	1.014		
146	1.015		
147	1.016		
148	2.018		
149	2.019		
150	2.020		
151	3.009		
152	2.021		
153	2.022		
154	2.023		
155	1.017		
156	4.012		
157	7.006		
158	4.013		
159	4.014		
160	4.015		

Small Business Bibliographies (SBBs) list key reference sources for many business management topics. (The SBBs numbering is the same as before and is unaffected by the MA conversion.)

SBBs

___ 1. Handicrafts
___ 2. Home Businesses
___ 3. Selling By Mail Order
___ 9. Marketing Research Procedures
___10. Retailing
___12. Statistics and Maps for National Market Analysis

___ 13. National Directory for Use in Marketing
___ 15. Record Keeping Systems—Small Store and Service Trade
___ 18. Basic Library Reference Sources
___ 20. Advertising—Retail Store
___ 29. National Mailing-List Houses
___ 31. Retail Credit and Collection
___ 37. Buying for Retail Stores
___ 55. Wholesaling
___ 72. Personnel Management
___ 75. Inventory Management
___ 79. Small Store Planning and Design
___ 80. Data Processing for Small Businesses
___ 85. Purchasing for Owners of Small Plants
___ 86. Training for Small Business
___ 87. Financial Management
___ 88. Manufacturing Management
___ 89. Marketing for Small Business
___ 90. New Product Development
___ 91. Ideas Into Dollars

Part 2—For-Sale Publications

Small Business Management Series

The booklets in this series provide discussions of special management problems in small companies.

No.	Stock No.	Pages	Price
1. An Employee Suggestion System for Small Companies Explains the basic principles for starting and operating a suggestion system.	045-000-00020-6	18	$1.10
9. Cost Accounting for Small Manufacturers Assists managers of small manufacturing firms establish accounting procedures that help control production and business costs.	045-000-00162-8	180	4.25
15. Handbook of Small Business Finance Indicates the major areas of financial management and describes a few techniques that can help the small business owner.	045-000-00139-3	63	3.00
20. Ratio Analysis for Small Business The purpose of the booklet is to help the owner-manager in detecting favorable or unfavorable trends in the business.	045-000-00150-4	65	2.20

22. Practical Business Use of Government Statistics
Illustrates some practical uses of Federal Government statistics. — 045-000-00131-8 — 28 — 1.40

25. Guides for Profit Planning
Guides for computing and using the breakeven point, the level of gross profit, and the rate of return on investment. — 045-000-00137-7 — 59 — 2.50

27. Profitable Community Relations for Small Business
Practical information on how to build and maintain sound community relations by participation in community affairs. — 045-000-00033-8 — 36 — 1.50

28. Small Business and Government Research and Development
Includes a discussion of the procedures necessary to locate and interest Government markets. — 045-000-00130-0 — 41 — 1.25

29. Management Audit for Small Manufacturers
A series of questions about small manufacturing plant planning, organizing, directing, and coordinating efficiency. — 045-000-00151-2 — 44 — 1.60

30. Insurance and Risk Management for Small Business
A discussion of what insurance is, the necessity of obtaining professional advice on buying insurance, and the main types of insurance a small business may need. — 045-000-00037-1 — 72 — 3.00

31. Management Audit for Small Retailers
149 questions guide the owner-manager in a self examination and a review of the business operation. — 045-000-00149-1 — 61 — 1.80

32. Financial Record Keeping for Small Stores
Written primarily for the small store owner or prospective owner whose business doesn't justify hiring a full-time bookkeeper. — 045-000-00142-3 — 135 — 4.00

33. Small Store Planning for Growth
Included is a consideration of merchandising, advertising and display, and checklists for increase in transactions and gross margins. — 045-000-00152-1 — 102 — 2.40

35. Franchise Index/Profile
Presents an evaluation process that may
be used to investigate franchise
opportunities.

045-000-00125-3   56   2.00

36. Training Salesmen to Serve Industrial
Markets
Discusses role of sales in marketing
program of small manufacturer and
offers suggestions for sales force to use
in serving customers.

045-000-00133-4   85   2.20

37. Financial Control by Time-Absorption
Analysis
A profit control technique that can be
used by all types of businesses.

045-000-00134-2   138   2.75

38. Management Audit for Small Service
Firms
A do-it-yourself guide for owner-
managers of small service firms to help
them evaluate and improve their
operations.

045-000-00203-9   67   3.75

39. Decision Points in Developing New
Products
Provides a path from idea to marketing
plan for the small manufacturing or
R & D firm that wants to expand or
develop a business around a new
product, process, or invention.

045-000-00146-6   64   1.50

40. Management Audit for Small
Construction Firms
Helps top executives of small
construction firms to make a self-
appraisal of their management practices.

045-000-00161-0   53   2.50

41. Purchasing Management and Inventory
Control for Small Business
Explains how to manage purchasing and
inventory dollars.

045-000-00167-9   66   3.25

42. Managing the Small Service Firm for
Growth and Profit
This booklet aids you in developing a
marketing strategy to improve services
to assure growth as customer needs change.

045-000-00165-2   58   3.50

43. Credit and Collection for Small Stores
Discusses credit plans to help owner-
managers pick and run credit systems.
Includes information on legal
restrictions, record keeping, and trade
credit.

045-000-00169-5   66   3.50

Starting and Managing Series

This series is designed to help the small entrepreneur "to look before leaping" into a business. The first volume in the series—Starting and Managing a Small Business of Your Own—deals with the subject in general terms. Each of the other volumes deals with one type of business in detail. Available titles:

No.	Stock No.	Pages	Price
1. Starting and Managing a Small Business of Your Own	045-000-00123-7	95	3.75

Nonseries Publications

	Stock No.	Pages	Price
Export Marketing for Smaller Firms A manual for owner-managers of smaller firms who seek sales in foreign markets.	045-000-00158-0	84	2.20
U.S. Government Purchasing and Sales Directory A directory for businesses that are interested in selling to the U.S. Government. Lists the purchasing needs of various Agencies.	045-000-00153-9	204	5.50
Managing for Profits Ten chapters on various aspects of small business management, for example, marketing, production, and credit.	045-000-00004-2	155	2.75
Buying and Selling a Small Business Deals with the problems that confront buyers and sellers of small businesses.	045-000-00164-4	122	3.50
Strengthening Small Business Management Twenty-one chapters on small business management.	045-000-00144-8	155	4.00
Small Business Goes to College This booklet traces the development of small business management as a college subject and provides samples of courses offered at 200 colleges and universities.	045-000-00159-8	82	3.25
The Best of the SBI Review—1973–1979 Management ideas for the small business owner-manager.	045-000-00172-5	145	4.50

Business Basics

Each of the 23 self-study booklets in this series contains text, questions, and exercises that teach a specific aspect of small business management.

No.		Stock No.	Pages	Price
1001	The Profit Plan	045-000-00192-0	33	$2.25
1002	Capital Planning	045-000-00193-8	42	2.50
1003	Understanding Money Sources	045-000-00194-6	50	3.50
1004	Evaluating Money Sources	045-000-00174-1	64	3.75
1005	Asset Management	045-000-00175-0	20	1.50
1006	Managing Fixed Assets	045-000-00176-8	48	2.50
1007	Understanding Costs	045-000-00195-4	48	2.75
1008	Cost Control	045-000-00187-3	48	2.75

No.		Stock No.	Pages	Price
1009	Marketing Strategy	045-000-00188-1	52	3.50
1010	Retail Buying Function	045-000-00177-6	40	2.25
1011	Inventory Management—Wholesale/Retail	045-000-00190-3	40	2.50
1012	Retail Merchandise Management	045-000-00178-4	52	3.25
1013	Consumer Credit	045-000-00179-2	40	2.25
1014	Credit and Collections: Policy and Procedures	045-000-00180-6	48	2.50
1015	Purchasing for Manufacturing Firms	045-000-00181-4	52	3.25
1016	Inventory Management—Manufacturing/Service	045-000-00182-2	52	3.25
1017	Inventory and Scheduling Techniques	045-000-00183-1	60	3.50
1018	Risk Management and Insurance	045-000-00184-9	44	2.25
1019	Managing Retail Salespeople	045-000-00189-0	60	3.75
1020	Job Analysis, Job Specifications, and Job Descriptions	045-000-00185-7	40	2.25
1021	Recruiting and Selecting Employees	045-000-00186-5	40	2.25
1022	Training and Developing Employees	045-000-00191-1	40	2.50
1023	Employee Relations and Personnel Policies	045-000-00196-2	36	2.25

Trade Associations and Professional Publications

Trade Associations

American Advertising Federation
1225 Connecticut Avenue, NW
Washington, DC 20036

American Federation of Small Business
407 South Dearborn Street
Chicago, IL 60605

American Fur Merchants Association
101 West 30th Street
New York, NY 10011

American Mail-Order Merchant Associations
2409 South Monroe Street
Tallahassee, Florida 32301

American Management Association
135 West 50th Street
New York, NY 10020

American Marketing Association
222 South Riverside Plaza
Chicago, IL 60606

American Retail Federation
1616 H Street, NW
Washington, DC 20006

American Society of Interior Designers
730 Fifth Avenue
New York, NY 10010

American Society of Travel Agents
711 Fifth Avenue
New York, NY 10022

Association of General Merchandise Chains
1625 Eye Street, NW
Washington, DC 20006

China, Glass and Giftware Association
245 Fifth Avenue
New York, NY 10016

Independent Fabric Retailers Association
112 West Lexington Avenue
Elkhart, IN 46514

International Florist Association
2117 Centre Avenue
Pittsburgh, PA 15219

International Society of Gourmet and Specialty Retailers
Davies Publishing Company
Hinsdale, IL 60521

Jewelry Industry Council
608 Fifth Avenue
New York, NY 10020

Marine Retailers Association of America
3003 West Alabama Street
Houston, TX 77098

Men's Fashion Association of America
1290 Avenue of the Americas
New York, NY 10019

Menswear Retailers of America
390 National Press Building
Washington, DC 20045

National Association of Catalog Showroom
Merchandisers
50 West 23rd Street
New York, NY 10010

National Association of College Stores
528 East Lorain Street
Oberlin, OH 44074

National Association of Convenience Stores
5205 Leesburg Pike
Falls Church, VA 22401

National Association of Independent Food Retailers
125 West Right Mile Road
Detroit, MI 48203

National Association of Men's and Boys' Apparel
185 Madison Avenue
New York, NY 10016

National Association of Retail Druggists
One East Wacker Drive
Chicago, IL 60601

National Association of Retail Grocers of United States
P. O. Box 17208
Washington, DC 20041

National Association of Variety Stores
7646 West Devon Avenue
Chicago, IL 60631

National Automatic Merchandising Association
Seven South Dearborn Street
Chicago, IL 60603

National Bicycle Dealers Association
29023 Euclid Avenue
Wickliffe, OH 44092

National Consumer Finance Association
1000 Sixteenth Street, NW
Washington, DC 20036

National Handbag Association
350 Fifth Avenue
New York, NY 10001

National Home Sewing Association
350 Fifth Avenue
New York, NY 10001

National Knitted Outerwear Association
51 Madison Avenue
New York, NY 10010

National Mass Retailing Institute
570 Seventh Avenue
New York, NY 10018

National Office Products Association
301 North Fairfax Street
Alexandria, VA 22314

National Retail Hardware Association
100 West 31 Street
New York, NY 10001

National Shoe Retailers Association
200 Madison Avenue
New York, NY 10016

National Sporting Goods Association
717 North Michigan Avenue
Chicago, IL 60611

Recreation Vehicle Dealers Association
3251 Old Lee Highway
Fairfax, VA 22030

Retail Advertising Conference
Post Office Box 2456
Gainesville, GA 30501

Retail Candy Store Institute
1701 Lake Avenue
Glenview, IL 60025

Retail Jewelers of America
1271 Avenue of the Americas
New York, NY 10020

Retail Rack Service Association
1225 Duncan Drive
Dresher, PA 19025

Retail Tobacco Dealers of America
Statler Hilton Hotel
Seventh Avenue and 33rd Street
New York, NY 10001

Ski Retailers Council
445 Park Avenue
New York, NY 10022

Toiletry Merchandisers Association
230 Park Avenue
New York, NY 10017

Volume Footwear Retailers of America
51 East 42nd Street
New York, NY 10017

Wool Bureau
360 Lexington Avenue
New York, NY 10017

Professional Publications and Directories

Advance News for Supermarkets
488 Madison Avenue
New York, NY 10022

Advertising Techniques
19 West 44th Street
New York, NY 10036

American Baby
575 Lexington Avenue
New York, NY 10022

American Bicyclist and Motorcyclist
461 Eighth Avenue
New York, NY 10001

American Druggist
224 West 57th Street
New York, NY 10019

American Fabrics and Fashions
24 East 38th Street
New York, NY 10016

American Hairdresser and Salon Owner
100 Park Avenue
New York, NY 10017

Antiques Dealer
1115 Clifton Avenue
Clifton, NJ 07013

Audio and Electronic Digest
P.O. Box 552
Beverly Hills, CA 90213

Army-Navy Store and Outdoor Merchandiser
225 West 34th Street
New York, NY 10016

Beauty Trade
1780 Broadway
New York, NY 10019

Black Enterprise
295 Madison Avenue
New York, NY 10019

Boating Industry
850 Third Avenue
New York, NY 10022

Campground Merchandising
401 North Broad
Suite 904
Philadelphia, PA 19108

Candy Marketer
747 Third Avenue
New York, NY 10017

Catalog Showroom Business
1515 Broadway
New York, NY 10036

Chain Store Age
425 Park Avenue
New York, NY 10022

China, Glass and Tableware
1115 Clifton Avenue
Clifton, NJ 07013

Consumer Reports
256 Washington Street
Mount Vernon, NY 10552

Convenience Store News
254 West 31st Street
New York, NY 10001

Cosmetic World
48 East 43rd Street
New York, NY 10017

Craft, Model and Hobby Industry
225 West 34th Street
New York, NY 10001

Curtain, Drapery and Bedspread Magazine
370 Lexington Avenue
New York, NY 10016

Daily News Record
7 East 12th Street
New York, NY 10010

Department Store Economist
48 East 43rd Street
New York, NY 10017

Direct Marketing
224 Seventh Street
Garden City, NY 11530

Discount Merchandiser
641 Lexington Avenue
New York, NY 10022

Discount Store News
425 Park Avenue
New York, NY 10022

Drug and Cosmetic Industry
757 Third Avenue
New York, NY 10017

Earnshaw's Infants
393 Seventh Avenue
New York, NY 10001

Electronic News
7 East 12th Street
New York, NY 10003

Fashion Accessories Magazine
22 S. Smith Street
Norwalk, CT 06855

Fashion Merchandising
3839 White Plains Road
Bronx, NY 10467

Floor and Wall Covering News
45 Crosby Street
New York, NY 10012

Footwear News
7 East 12th Street
New York, NY 10003

Foundation News
888 Seventh Avenue
New York, NY 10019

Frozen Food Age
230 Park Avenue
New York, NY 10017

Furniture World, Furniture Buyer and Decorator
127 East 31st Street
New York, NY 10016

Gas Appliance Merchandising
757 Third Avenue
New York, NY 10017

Gifts and Decorative Accessories
51 Madison Avenue
New York, NY 10010

Gifts and Tableware
1515 Broadway
New York, NY 10036

Glass Industry
747 Third Avenue
New York, NY 10017

Golf Magazine
380 Madison Avenue
New York, NY 10017

Grocers Journal of California
1636 West 8th Street
Los Angeles, CA 90017

Health Foods Business
567 Morris Avenue
Elizabeth, NJ 07208

Home and Auto
757 Third Avenue
New York, NY 10017

Home Lighting and Accessories
1115 Clifton Avenue
Clifton, NJ 07013

Home Furnishing
7 East 12th Street
New York, NY 10003

Home Sewing Trade News
129 Broadway
Lynbrook, NY 11563

Hosiery and Underwear
757 Third Avenue
New York, NY 10017

Housewares
757 Third Avenue
New York, NY 10017

Interior Design
850 Third Avenue
New York, NY 10022

Intimate Fashion News
95 Madison Avenue
New York, NY 10016

Journal of Business
Seton Hall University
South Orange, NJ 07079

Journal of Marketing
212 South Riverside Plaza
Chicago, IL 60606

Journal of Retailing
202 Tisch Building
New York, NY 10003

Juvenile Merchandising
370 Lexington Avenue
New York, NY 10017

Kitchen Business
1515 Broadway
New York, NY 10036

Knitting Industry
630 Third Avenue
New York, NY 10017

Linens, Domestics and Bath Products
370 Lexington Avenue
New York, NY 10017

Madison Avenue
750 Third Avenue
New York, NY 10017

Marine Business
48 East 43rd Street
New York, NY 10017

Marketing News
222 S. Riverside Plaza
Suite 606
Chicago, IL 60606

Men's Wear
7 East 12th Street
New York, NY 10003

Merchandising
1515 Broadway
New York, NY 10036

Modern Bride
One Park Avenue
New York, NY 10016

Modern Salon
300 West Adams Street
Chicago, IL 60606

Motor Boating and Sailing
224 West 57th Street
New York, NY 10019

MSU Business Topics
Michigan Avenue
Berkey Hall
East Lansing, MI 48824

Musical Merchandise Review
370 Lexington Avenue
New York, NY 10017

Narda News
2 North Riverside Plaza
Suite 222
Chicago, IL 60606

National Jeweler
1515 Broadway
New York, NY 10036

Non-Foods Merchandising
124 East 40th Street
New York, NY 10016

Office Product News
646 Stewart News
Garden City, NY 11530

Oklahoma Business Bulletin
307 West Brooks, Room 4
Norman, OK 73019

Outdoor Life
380 Madison Avenue
New York, NY 10017

Perspectives in Business
110 Commerce Building
1155 Observatory Drive
Madison, WI 53706

Pet News
44 Court Street
Brooklyn, NY 11201

Teens and Boys
210 Boylston
Chestnut Hills, MA 02167

Tennis Trade
122 East 42nd Street
New York, NY 10016

481

Texas Business Review
University of Texas
P.O. Box 7459
University Station
Austin, TX 78712

Tobacco Reporter
9800 D Avenue
Cleveland, OH 44102

Travel and Leisure
1350 Avenue of the Americas
New York, NY 10019

Upholstering Industry
192 Lexington Avenue
New York, NY 10016

Women's Wear Daily
7 East 12th Street
New York, NY 10003

Directories

Knit Goods Trade, Davison's
P.O. Drawer 477
Ridgewood, NJ 07451

Men's & Boys' Wear Buyers, Nationwide Directory
1140 Broadway
New York, NY 10001

Teens' & Boys' Outfitter Directory
71 West 35th Street
New York, NY 10001

Women's & Children's Wear & Accessories Buyers,
Nationwide Directory
1140 Broadway
New York, NY 10001

National Buyer's Guide 1980
115 Second Avenue
Waltham, MA 02154

American Art and Antique Dealers, Mastai's Classified
Directory
21 E. 57th Street
New York, NY 10022

NAMA Directory of Members
7 S. Dearborn Street
Chicago, IL 60603

Automotive Affiliated Representatives, Membership
Roster
625 S. Michigan Avenue
Chicago, IL 60611

Automotive Warehouse Distributors Association
Membership Directory
1719 W. 91st Place
Kansas City, MO 64114

Direct Selling Directory
307 N. Michigan Avenue
Chicago, IL 60601

Who's Who in Direct Selling
1730 M Street, NW
Washington, DC 20036

Chain Shoe Stores Directory
1800 Oakton Street
Des Plaines, IL 60018

Shopping Centers in the United States and Canada,
Directory
424 North Third Street
Burlington, Iowa 52601

Women's Specialty Stores, Phelon's
32 Union Square
New York, NY 10003

Sporting Goods Buyers, Nationwide Directory
1140 Broadway
New York, NY 10001

The Sporting Goods Register
1212 N. Lindbergh Boulevard
St. Louis, MO 63132

The Sporting Goods Dealer's Directory
1212 N. Lindberg Boulevard
St. Louis, MO 63132

Campground Directory, Woodall's North American/
Canadian Edition
500 Hyacinth Place
Highland Park, IL 60035

Trinc's Blue Book of the Trucking Industry and Trinc's
Five Year Red Book
P.O. Box 23091
Washington, DC 20024

General Merchandise, Variety and Junior Department
Stores
425 Park Avenue
New York, NY 10022

Distribution Services, Guide
Chilton Way
Radnor, PA 19089

Public Refrigerated Warehouses Directory
7312 Wisconsin Avenue, NW
Washington, DC 20014

Wholesale Stationers' Association Membership Roster
3166 Des Plaines Avenue
Des Plaines, IL 60018

Textile Blue Book, Davison's
P.O. Drawer 477
Ridgewood, NJ 07451

Toys, Hobbies & Crafts Directory
1 East First Street
Duluth, MN 55802

Wholesalers and Manufacturers Directory
1514 Elmwood Avenue
Evanston, IL 60201

Adhesives Age
461 Eighth Avenue
New York, NY 10011

Aerosol Age
200 Commerce Road
Cedar Grove, NJ 07009

Air Conditioning, Heating and Refrigeration News
P.O. Box 6000
Birmingham, MI 48102

American Druggist
224 W. 57th Street
New York, NY 10019

American Machinist
1221 Avenue of the Americas
New York, NY 10020

American Transportation Builder
625 School Street, SW
Washington, DC 20024

The Appraisal Journal
430 N. Michigan Street
Chicago, IL 60611

Bedding Magazine
1150 17th Street, NW
Washington, DC 20036

Buildings: The Construction and Building Management Journal
427 Sixth Avenue, SE
Cedar Rapids, IA 52401

C.L.U. Journal
P.O. Box 59
Bryn Mawr, PA 19010

Chain Store Age: Executives Edition
425 Park Avenue
New York, NY 10016

Mass Retailing Merchandisers Buyers' Directory
222 West Adams
Chicago, IL 60606

Metalworking Directory, Dun & Bradstreet
99 Church Street
New York, NY 10007

Buyers' Guide
475 School Street, SW
Washington, DC 20024

Non-Food Buyers, National Directory
1372 Peachtree Street, NE
Atlanta, GA 30309

Sources of Supply Buyers' Guide
P.O. Drawer 795
Park Ridge, IL 60068

Manufacturers' Representatives, Directory
135 Addison Avenue
Elmhurst, IL 60126

Premium and Incentive Buyers, Directory
1140 Broadway
New York, NY 10001

Incentive Marketing/Incorporating Incentive Travel:
Supply Sources Directory
633 Third Avenue
New York, NY 10017

U. S. Government Purchasing and Sales Directory
U. S. Government Printing Office
Washington, DC 20402

Air Conditioning, Heating & Refrigeration News
P.O. Box 2600
Troy, MI 48084

Air Conditioning & Refrigeration Wholesalers Directory
22371 Newman Avenue
Dearborn, MI 48124

Restaurant Operators
425 Park Avenue
New York, NY 10022

RSI Trade Directory
1 East First Street
Duluth, MN 55802

Direct Selling Companies/A Supplier's Guide
1730 M Street, NW
Washington, DC 20036

Interior Decorator's Handbook
370 Lexington Avenue
New York, NY 10017

Hotel-Motel Guide and Travel Atlas, Leahy's
2775 Shermer Road
Northbook, IL 60062

Hotel Red Book
888 Seventh Avenue
New York, NY 10019

Hotel Systems, Directory
888 Seventh Avenue
New York, NY 10019

Housewares Reps Registry
1 East First Street
Duluth, MN 55802

The Jewelers Board of Trade Confidential Reference
Book
70 Catamore Boulevard
East Providence, RI 02914

Wine and Spirits Wholesalers Blue Book
2033 M Street, NW, Suite 400
Washington, DC 20036

Mailing List Houses, Directory
P.O. Box 8503
Coral Springs, FL 33065

National Mailing-List Houses
Box 15434
Ft. Worth, TX 76119

Mail Order Business Directory
Box 8503
Coral Springs, FL 33065

MacRae's Blue Book
100 Shore Drive
Hinsdale, IL 60521

Manufacturers, Thomas' Register of American
One Penn Plaza
New York, NY 10001

Manufacturers & Agents National Association Directory
of Members
Box 16878
Irvine, CA 92713

Major Mass Market Merchandisers
1140 Broadway
New York, NY 10001

Fresh Fruit and Vegetable Dealers, The Blue Book
315 W. Wesley Street
Wheaton, IL 60187

Frozen Food Fact Book and Directory
Box 398
Hershey, PA 17033

Grocery Register, Thomas'
One Penn Plaza
New York, NY 10001

Quick Frozen Foods Directory of Wholesale Distributors
Box 612
Duluth, MN 55806

Supermarket, Grocery & Convenience Store Chains
425 Park Avenue
New York, NY 10022

Tea and Coffee Buyers' Guide, Ukers' International
Francis Lewis Boulevard
Whitestone, NY 11357

LP/Gas
1 East First Street
Duluth, MN 55802

Gift and Decorative Accessory Buyers' Directory
51 Madison Avenue
New York, NY 10010

Gift and Housewares Buyers, Nationwide Directory
1140 Broadway
New York, NY 10001

Gift and Tableware Reporter Directory Issue
1 Astor Place
New York, NY 10036

Gift Shop Directory
Box 642, RFD Station
New York, NY 10022

Hardware Wholesalers Guide, National
1760 Peachtree Road, NW
Atlanta, GA 30357

Hardware Wholesalers, Verified List
Chilton Way
Radnor, PA 19089

The Antiques Dealer
1115 Chilton Avenue
Clifton, NJ 07013

Home Lighting & Accessories Suppliers
1115 Chilton Avenue
Clifton, NJ 07013

Drug Topics Buyers' Guide
Medical Economics Company
Oradell, NJ 07649

National Wholesale Druggists' Association Membership
and Executive Directory
670 White Plains Road
Scarsdale, NY 10583

Electronic Industry Telephone Directory
2057-2 Aurora Road
Twinsburg, OH 44087

Electrical Wholesale Distributors
1221 Avenue of the Americas
New York, NY 10020

Who's Who in Electronics, including Electronic
Representatives
2057-2 Aurora Road
Twinsburg, OH 44087

Electrical Utilities, Electrical World Directory
1221 Avenue of the Americas
New York, NY 10020

Embroidery Directory
512 23rd Street
Union City, NJ 07080

American Register of Exporters and Importers
15 Park Row
New York, NY 10038

Canadian Trade Directory, Fraser's
481 University Avenue
Toronto, Ontario
Canada M5W1A4

Flooring Directory
1 East First Street
Duluth, MN 55802

Co-ops, Voluntary Chains and Wholesale Grocers
425 Park Avenue
New York, NY 10022

Food Brokers' Association, National Directory of
Members
1916 M Street, NW
Washington, DC 20036

Food Service Distributors
425 Park Avenue
New York, NY 10022

Municipal Year Book
1140 Connecticut Avenue, NW
Washington, DC 20036

College Stores, Directory of 1980
P.O. Box 8503
Coral Springs, FL 33065

Candy Buyers' Directory
175 Rock Road
Glen Rock, NJ 07452

Construction Equipment Buyer's Guide, AED Edition
615 West 22nd Street
Oak Brook, IL 60521

Director of Conventions
633 Third Avenue
New York, NY 10017

Exhibits Schedule
633 Third Avenue
New York, NY 10017

Dental Supply Houses, Hayes Directory
4229 Birch Street
Newport Beach, CA 92660

Department Stores
425 Park Avenue
New York, NY 10022

Sheldon's Retail
32 Union Square
New York, NY 10003

Discount Department Stores, Phelon's
32 Union Square
New York, NY 10003

Discount Department Stores
425 Park Avenue
New York, NY 10022

Drug Stores, Chain
425 Park Avenue
New York, NY 10022

Druggists-Wholesale
4229 Birch Street
Newport Beach, CA 92660

Druggist Directory, Hayes
4229 Birch Street
Newport Beach, CA 92660

Auto Trim Resource Directory
1623 Grand Avenue
Baldwin, NY 11510

Credit and Sales Reference Directory
222 Cedar Lane
Teaneck, NJ 07666

Home Center, Hardware, Auto Supply Chains
425 Park Avenue
New York, NY 10022

Jobber Topics Automotive Aftermarket Directory
7300 N. Cicero Avenue
Chicago, IL 60646

World Aviation Directory
1156 15th Street, NW
Washington, DC 20005

Book Trade Directory, American
1180 Avenue of the Americas
New York, NY 10036

Multiple Book Store Owners, Directory
560 Northern Boulevard
Great Neck, NY 11021

Building Supply News Buyers' Guide
5 S. Wabash Avenue
Chicago, IL 60603

Dun & Bradstreet Middle Market Directory
99 Church Street
New York, NY 10007

Dun & Bradstreet Million Dollar Directory
99 Church Street
New York, NY 10007

Buying Offices and Accounts, Directory
1140 Broadway
New York, NY 10001

American Glass Review
1115 Clifton Avenue
Clifton, NJ 07013

China, Glass & Tableware Red Book Directory Issue
1115 Clifton Avenue
Clifton, NJ 07013

Construction Contracting
1221 Avenue of the Americas
New York, NY 10020

Constructioneer
1 Bond Street
Chatham, NJ 07928

Cosmetics and Toiletries
Box 318
Wheaton, IL 60187

Distribution Worldwide
Chilton Way
Radnor, PA 19089

Drug and Cosmetic Industry
757 Third Avenue
New York, NY 10017

Factory
205 B 42nd Street
New York, NY 10017

Footwear News
7 E. 12th Street
New York, NY 10003

Forest Industries
500 Howard Street
San Francisco, CA 94105

Fuel Oil and Oil Heat
200 Commerce Road
Cedar Grove, NJ 07009

Hardware Retailing
964 N. Pennsylvania Street
Indianapolis, IN 46204

Heating, Piping & Air Conditioning
600 Summer Street
Stamford, CN 06904

Hotel & Motel Management
845 Chicago Avenue
Evanston, IL 60202

Industrial Distributor News
1 W. Olney
Philadelphia, PA 19120

Industrial Maintenance and Plant Operation
1 W. Olney
Philadelphia, PA 19120

Modern Plastics
1221 Avenue of the Americas
New York, NY 10020

Modern Textiles, Magazine
303 Fifth Avenue
New York, NY 10016

Nation's Restaurant News
425 Park Avenue
New York, NY 10022

Office Products
Hitchcock Building
Wheaton, IL 60187

Packaging Digest
1120 Chester Avenue
Cleveland, OH 44144

Printing and Publishing
U.S. Government Printing Office
Washington, DC 20402

Progressive Grocer: The Magazine of Supermarketing
708 Third Avenue
New York, NY 10017

Quick Frozen Foods International
757 Third Avenue
New York, NY 10017

Review of the Graphic Arts
Box 1030
Kissimmee, FL 32741

Service World International
5 S. Wabash Avenue
Chicago, IL 60603

Ski Area Management
Box 242
North Salem, NY 10560

Soap/Cosmetics/Chemical Specialties
101 W. 31st Street
New York, NY 10001

Stores
100 W. 31st Street
New York, NY 10001

Traffic Management
205 E. 42nd Street
New York, NY 10017

INDEX